LAW OF
MARINE
INSURANCE

Susan Hodges, LLB, LLM, PhD
Lecturer in the Department of Maritime Studies
and International Transport
University of Wales

D0241331

Cavendish
Publishing
Limited

First published in Great Britain 1996 by Cavendish Publishing Limited, The Glass House, Wharton Street, London WC1X 9PX, United Kingdom

Telephone: +44 (0)20 7278 8000   Facsimile: +44 (0)20 7278 8080

Email: info@cavendishpublishing.com

Website: www.cavendishpublishing.com

British Library Cataloguing-in-Publication Data

Hodges, S
Marine Insurance Law
1. Insurance, Marine - Law and Legislation - England
I Title
344.2'06862

ISBN 1 85941 227 0

Printed and bound in Great Britain

DEDICATION

In memory of Professor FJJ Cadwallader

PREFACE

This book is designed primarily for postgraduate students following a taught course of study in the law of marine insurance. It will prove useful not only to postgraduate students in law and maritime studies, but also to persons involved in the field of marine insurance such as arbitrators, adjusters of claims, brokers, in-house lawyers, legal practitioners, marine claims officers and P&I Clubs.

The approach of the works of *Arnould, Ivamy, Templeman* and *O'May* are professionally orientated and, therefore, are not ideally suited to student use. Moreover, they are all outside the range of the average student pocket. With the exception of the recent work by *O'May*, none of these discuss the cases of the last decade, some of which have introduced significant changes to the law. The need for such a book has become obvious over the years, and this work is designed to fill this gap by offering a reasonably priced, medium sized reference work aimed at the postgraduate and profession alike.

The aim of this book is to state the law as clearly as possible and to show the relationships between the Marine Insurance Act 1906, case law, and the standard terms of the Institute Clauses. As it is not possible to refer to all the Institute Clauses, this work will focus mainly on the Clauses for hulls and cargo. Emphasis is give to areas of the law which have been found by students to be particularly problematic. Special attention is awarded to recent leading judicial rulings. The intention has been to state the law as it stands at October 1995. Although the introduction of the new Institute Time Clauses, Hulls, on 1 November 1995 delayed the completion of this work, it has nevertheless enabled the changes made to the 1983 version of the Clauses to be discussed. As it is anticipated that the 1983 Institute Clauses will eventually be replaced by the new Clauses, the 1995 Clauses are used as the basis of the text.

It is a great pleasure to record my indebtedness to my friends who have helped me in the preparation of this book. I wish to express my thanks to Ms J Reddy, Ms K Nicol and the staff of Cavendish Publishing Ltd for their assistance, patience and understanding throughout the production of this work, Mr P Clinch, Mr D Montgomery and the staff of the law library for their help in locating materials, and Professor J King for his support and encouragement. I am also greatly indebted to Mr J Moloney, Secretary of Lloyd's Underwriters' Association, for his invaluable assistance and the many interesting and stimulating discussions which have helped to clarify my thoughts on some of the issues involved. Finally, I owe a particular debt of gratitude to P Wylie, and my colleague, Professor E D Brown for without their assistance and intervention the writing of this book would not have been possible.

Dr Susan Hodges

March 1996

ACKNOWLEDGMENTS

All Institute Clauses are reproduced by kind permission of The Institute of London Underwriters and Witherby & Co Ltd. The authors and publishers also thank Lloyd's of London for permission to reproduce Lloyd's Standard Form of Salvage Agreement, and Comité Maritime International for permission to reproduce The York-Antwerp Rules 1994.

CONTENTS

Contents

Contents

TABLE OF CASES

P

Table of Cases

TABLE OF STATUTES

Marine Insurance Act 1906 (contd)—

Marine Insurance Act 1906 (contd)—

Marine Insurance Act 1906 (contd)—

CHAPTER 1

CONTRACT OF INDEMNITY

A CONTRACT OF INDEMNITY

The basis of a contract of marine insurance is contained in the opening section of the Marine Insurance Act 1906,[1] which reads as follows:

> 'A contract of marine insurance is a contract whereby the insurer undertakes to indemnify the assured, in manner and to the extent thereby agreed, against marine losses, that is to say, the losses incident to marine adventure.'

The operative word here is 'indemnify'. A contract of marine insurance is essentially a contract of indemnity. This is the cardinal principle upon which the whole contract is founded, and from which the rules relating to the right of claim under a policy emanate. The rights and liabilities of the parties are dictated by this basic concept, and the amount recoverable by the assured, which is measured by the extent of his pecuniary loss, is also governed by it. This should not come as a surprise, for the very purpose of effecting a policy of insurance, marine or non-marine, is for indemnity for loss.

The most incisive comment on the subject of indemnity can be found in Lord Wright's judgment of the House of Lords in *Rickards v Forestal Land, Timber and Railways Co*,[2] where he said:

> 'The object both of the legislature and of the courts have been to give effect to the idea of indemnity, which is the basic principle of insurance, and to apply in the diverse complications of fact and law in respect of which it has to operate. In this way, the law merchant has solved, or sought to solve, the manifold problems which have been presented by insurances of maritime adventures.'

In *Castellain v Preston*,[3] Mr Justice Brett remarked:

> 'The contract of insurance contained in a marine or fire policy is a contract of indemnity, and of indemnity only, and this contract means that the assured, in case of a loss against which the policy has been made, shall be fully indemnified, but shall never be more than fully indemnified.'

As will be seen, the incidents and legal consequences of the contract all stem from this 'great principle'.[4] Many of the main legal principles, for example, the rules relating to insurable interest; gaming and wagering policies; excessive over-valuation; double insurance, contribution, and return of premium; abandonment and right of subrogation; and the merger of losses, all spring from this concept.

---

1 Hereinafter referred to simply as 'the Act'. See Appendix 1.

2 [1941] 3 All ER 62 at p 76, HL.

3 (1883) 11 QBD 380 at p 386.

4 *Per* Lord Ellenborough in *Brotherston v Barber* (1816), 5 M & S 418 at p 425, 'The great principle of the law of insurance is that it is a contract for indemnity. The underwriter does not stipulate, under any circumstances, to become the purchaser of the subject-matter insured; it is not supposed to be in his contemplation: he is to indemnify only'.

Not a perfect contract of indemnity

Lord Justice Bowen in *Castellain v Preston*[5] was confident that the principle of indemnity will solve all problems. His words were:

> 'In all these difficult problems, I go back with confidence to the broad principle of indemnity. Apply that and an answer to the difficulty will be found ... But can it be any exception to the infallible rule that a man can only be indemnified to the extent of his loss?'

Admittedly, most of the problems can be resolved by applying the principle. But this, as will be seen, is a somewhat optimistic point of view. A contract of marine insurance, though a contract of indemnity, is by no means a perfect contract of indemnity. As in all walks of life, there is always a margin of error: in some instances, the theory may more than indemnify the assured for his loss, and in others, he may be under-indemnified. That the principle is not infallible was noted by Lord Sumner in *British and Foreign Insurance Co Ltd v Wilson Shipping Co Ltd*[6] where he said: 'In practice contracts of insurance by no means always result in a complete indemnity, but indemnity is always the basis of the contract'. In similar terms, Mr Justice Patteson in *Irving v Manning*,[7] who, also resigned to the fact that perfection may be difficult, if not impossible, to achieve, openly declared that: 'A policy of assurance is not a perfect contract of indemnity.' He acknowledged the fact that it has to be taken with qualifications, one of which is the effects of a valued policy, the problem he was asked to resolve.[8]

Ideally, an assured should be compensated only to the extent of his loss. In practice, however, this is not always easy to attain. But having said that, the principle is always at hand and may be invoked whenever judges feel that justice may be better served by its application rather than by a strict and literal adherence to rules. It is fair to say that judges have in the past employed the principle of indemnity as a fall-back whenever the main ground of their decisions needed further support or reinforcement.

GAMING AND WAGERING CONTRACTS

There are essentially two broad types of gaming or wagering contracts identified by the Act. The first relates to contracts where the assured has no insurable interest or expectation of acquiring such an interest, and the second to policies which declare that the policy itself is proof of interest, commonly referred to as 'honour' or 'ppi' policies.

---

5   (1883) 11 QBD 380 at p 401, CA.

6   [1921] 1 AC 188 at p 214, HL.

7   (1847) 1 HLC 287 at p 307.

8   In a valued policy, the agreed total value is conclusive; the parties have conclusively admitted that this fixed sum shall be that which the assured is entitled to receive in event of a loss: see s 27(3).

No insurable interest or expectation of acquiring such an interest

As was seen, the very essence of a contract of marine insurance is that of indemnity. This necessarily means that an assured who has no insurable interest in the subject-matter insured, in the sense as defined in s 5(2), would not be able to show that he has suffered a loss. In the words of s 5(2), he is not 'prejudiced by its loss or by damage thereto, or by the detention thereof'. Such a contract, where the assured has not an insurable interest as defined by the Act, is deemed to be a gaming or wagering contract and, therefore, void by s 4(1). Where the policy is void, the general rule is that the assured is, by s 84(3)(a), entitled to a return of premium. But as such a contract is forbidden by the Marine Insurance (Gambling Policies) Act 1909, the premium is not refundable by reason of illegality – a defence specifically laid down in the said section.

There are two parts to s 4(2)(a): the first refers to the case discussed above, where the assured has not an insurable interest, and the second to 'where the contract is entered into with no expectation of acquiring such an interest'. The corollary of the latter is that if the assured has a genuine expectation of acquiring an interest, then the policy is not a wager policy. Naturally, this has to be read with s 6(1) where it is laid down that the crucial moment when the assured must have an insurable interest in the subject-matter insured is at the time of the loss; 'he need not be interested when the insurance is effected'.

'Honour' or ppi policy

Section 4(2)(b) states:

> 'A contract of marine insurance is deemed to be a gaming or wagering contract:
>
> Where the policy is made "interest or no interest" or "without further proof of interest than the policy itself," or "without benefit of salvage to the insurer", or subject to any other like term:
>
> Provided that, where there is no possibility of salvage, a policy may be effected without benefit of salvage to the insurer.'

It is to be noted that such a policy does not automatically rule out the possibility of the assured having, in fact, an insurable interest. The fact that the wording of the policy dispenses with proof of interest does not necessarily mean that the assured does not or cannot have an interest in the subject-matter insured.

Cheshire & Co v Vaughan Bros & Co[9] has ruled that such a policy is still void even though the assured may, in fact, have an interest. In an action brought by the assured against their brokers, the defendants, for negligence in failing to make full disclosure to the insurers, the defendants pleaded that the suit was not maintainable because the policy was void. This contention was upheld by both the trial judge and the Court of Appeal. The wording of s 4 clearly covers not only contracts of insurance where there is no insurable interest, but also

---

9   (1919) 25 Com Cas 242; [1920] 3 KB 240, CA.

those which use words that might well suggest that no insurable interest exists.[10]

But whether an action arising from such a contract may be adjudicated upon by a court of law is questionable. It is submitted that a court should not lend its hand to the parties by trying a case where the contract is void in law, and all the more so if the contract is illegal by reason of the assured not having in fact an insurable interest.[11]

The fact that the ppi clause may have been detached by the assured at the time of claim makes no difference to the validity of the contract. In *Re London County Commercial Reinsurance Office Ltd*,[12] it was held that the crucial moment for consideration is at the time when the policy was issued.

Though void in law, such policies are not illegal.[13] Thus, the assured is entitled to a return of premium, if he is able to prove that he has in fact an insurable interest in the subject-matter insured.[14]

Lord Robson, in *Thames and Mersey Marine Insurance Co Ltd v 'Gunford' Ship Co*,[15] observed that, 'The sums insured under such policies are, under ordinary circumstances, paid with the same regularity as if they were legally due'. By reason of this fact, ppi policies have earned the 'much-abused' name of 'honour' policies.

'Without benefit of salvage'

A policy 'without benefit of salvage' is a gaming or wagering policy and, therefore, void. But if the nature of the subject-mater insured is such that there is no possibility of salvage (eg, commission, unsecured loan or anticipated profit to be earned from the sale of cargo on its arrival at the port of destination), the policy, though 'without benefit of salvage', is valid.

---

10 It was argued that, as the plaintiffs had an insurable interest the section did not apply. Bankes LJ (at p 248) said: '... the language of the section does not permit that construction ... it makes void a contract where the instrument contains one of those objectionable clauses.'

11 In *Buchanan v Faber* (1899) 4 Com Cas 223; 15 TLR 383, the court acceded to the request made by the parties to try the case as though the contract did not contain the provision that the policy was to be deemed sufficient proof of interest. *Cf Gedge & Others v Royal Exchange Assurance Corpn* [1900] QB 214; 5 Com Cas 239; 16 TLR 344, where the court held that, though not pleaded by the insurers, the action could not be heard because of the ppi clause.

12 [1922] 2 Ch 67, Ch D.

13 Ppi policies were illegal under the Marine Insurance Act 1745, but with the repeal of this Act they are now no longer illegal, but merely void under the 1906 Act.

14 See s 84(3)(a) and s 1(1)(a) of the Marine Insurance (Gambling Policies) Act (1909) where it is only an offence if an assured effects a contract of insurance 'without having any *bona fide* interest ...'.

15 [1911] AC 529 at p 550, HL, hereinafter referred to as *The Gunford Case*.

DOUBLE INSURANCE, CONTRIBUTION AND RETURN OF PREMIUM

The legal rules on double insurance and the return of premium therefor, and contribution all emanate from the principle of indemnity that the assured is entitled only to indemnity and not profit. Just as the assured is not allowed to profit from a marine policy, the same applies to the insurer, who is not allowed to retain the premium for a policy where he runs no risk or where the subject-matter insured is not exposed to maritime perils.

Double insurance

Over-insurance by double insurance occurs when 'two or more policies are effected by or on behalf of the assured on the same adventure and interest or any part thereof, and the sums insured exceed the indemnity allowed by ... [the] Act'. The same assured is insuring the same subject-matter, for the same adventure, for the same interest, and for the same perils. There is no double insurance where one or more of these subjects are different, or where one of the policies is, for whatever reason, unenforceable.

The common law definition provided by Lord Justice Mellish in *North British and Mercantile Insurance Co v London, Liverpool and Globe Insurance Co*,[16] albeit a fire policy, clearly explains the basis of the rule. He said:

'The rule is perfectly established in the case of a marine policy that contribution only applies where it is an insurance by the same person having the same rights, and does not apply where different persons insure in respect of different rights.'

As two or more policies with different insurers are in operation, the assured is permitted by s 32(2)(a) to 'claim payment from the insurers in such order as he may think fit, provided that he is not entitled to receive any sum in excess of the indemnity allowed by ... [the] Act'. Should he receive more than full indemnity under either policy, valued or unvalued, he must give credit for the sum in excess of the indemnity and is deemed to hold such sum in trust for the insurers, according to their right of contribution among themselves.[17]

Double insurance on a ship is said to be extremely rare, but occasionally arises, inadvertently rather than intentionally, in practice in respect of insurance of cargo. In this regard, it has to be said that 'Increased Value Policies', common in cargo insurance, do not give rise to double insurance. This is because the subject-matter under such a policy is not on the goods themselves but the increased value thereof.

Over-insurance by ppi policies

An assured may over-insure by taking up a ppi policy in addition to the standard hull, cargo or freight policy. This occurred in *The Gunford Case*, where, in addition to the hull and freight policies, additional valued policies on

---

16   (1877) 5 Ch D 569 at p 583.
17   See s 32(2)(b)–(d).

disbursements, and on hull and disbursements, were also taken out by the assured.[18] The House of Lords held that even though the insurances on disbursements were ppi polices, nonetheless there was a double insurance, as much that was covered in the hull and freight polices were also covered by the polices on disbursements. To quote from the judgment of Lord Shaw of Dunfermline:[19]

> '... the disbursements were the very things which had been already accounted for in the freight, and when the ship became a wreck the payment on these policies was not to be a payment of indemnity, but a present to the assured of this sum of money ...'

There was clearly an over-insurance by double insurance. Though the disbursements policies may be void in law, nevertheless the assured could still be indemnified under them should the insurer chooses to honour them. He could not, however, 'legally avail [himself] of it to enforce recovery of any sum in excess of the indemnity allowed by law'. The House held that the hull and freight insurers were entitled to avoid their policy on the ground of non-disclosure of a material fact: the existence and the amounts of the wager policies were circumstances material to be disclosed.[20]

Contribution

In the event of over-insurance by double insurance, fairness has also to be observed amongst the insurers. Each insurer should not have to contribute more than his proportion of the loss. Section 80 spells out the rules as to how the matter is to be resolved amongst the insurers *inter se*. The fundamental rule is that he should not incur more than 'the amount which he is liable under his contract'.

Return of premium

An insurer is not liable for more than his share of the risk. The corollary of this is that an assured who has over-insured by double insurance would be able to recover a proportionate part of the several premiums which he has paid to the various insurers. The right to demand a return of premium in such a case is, however, subject to the proviso in s 84(3)(f) that a premium is not returnable if:

'(a) the polices are effected at different times, and an earlier policy has at any time borne the entire risk; or

(b) a claim has been paid on one policy in respect of the full sum insured thereby, or

---

18   The only source from which these disbursements could be repaid was the freight earned by the ship, which freight was itself insured Lord Robson observed (at p 549): 'So far as these payments consisted of current working expenses necessary to earn freight they were covered by the insurance on the gross freight, and so far as they consisted of repairs, outfit, and insurance premium on hull they would ordinarily be included in the policy on ship and materials.'

19   [1911] AC 529 at p 542, HL.

20   The over-insurance was a matter which 'might well make a prudent underwriter hesitate both as to undertaking the risk and consider the premium which he should require before doing so': *per* Lord Alverstone CJ, *ibid*, at p 538 in *The Gunford Case*.

(c) the double insurance is effected knowingly by the assured.'[21]

SUBROGATION

There is no doubt that the right of subrogation is a 'necessary incident of a contract of indemnity'.[22] In the words of Lord Justice Brett in *Castellian v Preston*, subrogation is '... a corollary of the great principle law of indemnity', and it is from this principle that an assured is not permitted to recover more than his actual loss. In the Act, the law relating to subrogation is contained in s 79 which is divided into two subsections. Subsection 79(1) refers to subrogation in the event of a total loss and sub-s 79(2), a partial loss.

Definition of 'subrogation'

According to Lord Blackburn in *Burnand v Rodocanachi*,[23] the doctrine of subrogation is a rule of law and of equity:

'The general rule of law (and it is obvious justice) is that where there is a contract of indemnity ... and a loss happens, anything which reduces or diminishes that loss reduces or diminishes the amount which the indemnifer is bound to pay; and if the indemnifier has already paid it, then, if anything which diminishes the loss comes into the hands of the person to whom he has paid it, it becomes an equity that the person who has already paid the full indemnity is entitled to be recouped by having that amount back.'

In the earlier case of *Simpson v Thomson*,[24] Lord Cairns described the principle in the following terms:

'I know of no foundation for the right of underwriters, except the well-known principle of law, that where one person has agreed to indemnify another he will, on making good the indemnity, be entitled to succeed to all the ways and means by which the person indemnified might have protected himself against or reimbursed himself for the loss.'

On settlement of a loss, the indemnifier, the insurer, is, by the rule of subrogation, entitled to step into the shoes of the assured.[25] Having paid the assured for the loss, he is 'subrogated to all the rights and remedies of the assured in and in respect of that subject-matter as from the time of the casualty causing the loss'. The objective of this process is to prevent the assured from taking with both hands: once indemnified, he would not be allowed to be compensated twice over for the same loss.

---

21 An assured who deliberately over-insures by double insurance may well be found guilty of a breach of the duty of utmost good faith (s 17) and of disclosure (s 18).

22 *Chalmers' Marine Insurance Act* (1906, 10th edn), p 131; hereinafter referred to simply as 'Chalmers'.

23 (1882) 7 App Cas 333 at p 339.

24 (1877) 3 App Cas 279 at p 284, HL.

25 By way of subrogation, the insurer has to sue in the name of the assured, whereas in the case of an assignment, he may sue in his own name.

It is to be noted that there is no right of subrogation in respect of a ppi policy. Void in law, the policy is not only unenforceable, but no rights can be derived from it.[26]

Settlement of total loss

In the event of a settlement of a total loss, the insurer is, by s 79(1):

- 'entitled to take over the interest of the assured in whatever may remain of the subject-matter so paid for'; and

- 'subrogated to all the rights and remedies of the assured in and in respect of that subject-matter as from the time of the casualty causing the loss'.

There are two separate aspects to this rule: the right to take over the interest in the remains of the subject-matter insured (involving abandonment and proprietary rights) and the right to subrogation. Though distinct, both rights are kindred to the principle of indemnity. In *Attorney-General v Glen Line Ltd and Liverpool & London War Risks Association Ltd*,[27] Lord Atkin, drawing the distinction between the rights of abandonment and the rights of subrogation, said that 'in respect of abandonment the rights exist on a valid abandonment, whereas in respect of subrogation they only arise on payment ...'. Later, Mr Justice Diplock in *Yorkshire Insurance Co v Nisbet Shipping Co Ltd*[28] warned that:

'It is to be noted that the subsection [referring to s 79(1)] which comes into operation only upon payment for the total loss by the insurer, deals with two distinct matters: (1) the interest of the assured in the subject-matter insured, and (2) the rights and remedies of the assured in and in respect of that subject-matter.'

A failure to recognise that they are distinct has caused some confusion in the law.

Abandonment and proprietary rights

The word 'entitled' appearing in s 79(1) clarifies that the insurer is not compelled to take over whatever may remain of the subject-matter insured. The effect of this rule has raised interesting questions relating to proprietary rights over the abandoned property. This provision has to be read with s 63 (on the effects of abandonment) stating that:

'Where there is a valid abandonment, the insurer is entitled to take over the interest of the assured in whatever may remain of the subject-matter insured, and all proprietary rights incidental thereto.'

The connection between a constructive total loss and the notice of abandonment was highlighted by Lord Justice Brett in *Castellain v Preston*[29] as follows:

---

26 See *Edwards & Co Ltd v Motor Union Insurance Co Ltd* [1922] 2 KB 249; 11 Ll L Rep 170; 27 Com Cas 367 where McCardie J remarked: 'Legal proceedings to enforce subrogative rights cannot be based on a document which is stricken with sterility by an Act of Parliament.'

27 (1930) 37 Ll L Rep 55 at p 61; (1930) 36 Com Cas 1 at p 13.

28 [1961] 1 Lloyd's Rep 479.

29 (1883) 11 QBD 380 at p 387, CA.

'The doctrine of constructive total loss and the doctrine of notice of abandonment engrafted upon it were invented or promulgated for the purpose of making a policy of marine insurance a contract of indemnity in the fullest sense of the term.'

Section 63(1), using the same expression – 'entitled to take over', emphasises the fact that the insurer has on abandonment the option to take over 'all proprietary rights incidental thereto'.

Acceptance of abandonment

In practice, insurers rarely accept the abandonment, for this carries with it not only rights but also liabilities in respect of the abandoned property.[30] However, should they agree, whether expressly or impliedly, to assume ownership over the remains of the subject-matter insured, they would be able to retain any profit made on its sale. This rule was first established in *Attorney General v Glen Line Ltd*,[31] where the insurer was allowed to retain the whole of the proceeds of the sale even though he profited as a result. Justice Diplock in *Yorkshire Insurance Co v Nisbet Shipping Co Ltd*[32] observed that in the case of abandonment, 'the insurer is entitled although not bound to take over; if he does, the whole interest of the assured in the subject-matter insured is transferred to him'.

In this regard, some may say that the principle of indemnity has failed to realise its full potential, that the contract is not one of perfect indemnity. In accepting the abandonment, the insurer takes over not only rights but also liabilities in relation to the remains of the subject-matter insured. Thus, it could be validly argued that as he had assumed all responsibility in respect of the subject-matter insured, he should be allowed to keep any reward arising therefrom, which may be regarded as the consideration (or 'price') for accepting the good with the bad with the transfer of ownership.[33]

The insurer is also, by reason of s 63(2), entitled to any freight earned after his acceptance of the abandonment.[34] According to Lord Blackburn in *Simpson v Thomson*,[35] 'the right to receive payment of freight accruing due but not earned at the time of the disaster is one of those rights so incident to the property in the ship, and it therefore passes to the underwriters because the ship has become their property ...'.[36]

---

30 Obvious liabilities are expenses incurred for the removal of the wreck and damage caused by oil pollution See *River Wear Comrs v Adamson* (1877) 2 App Cas 743; *The Mostyn* [1928] AC 57; and *Arrow Shipping Co v Tyne Improvement Comrs* [1894] AC 508.

31 [1930] 36 Com Cas 1; [1930] 37 Ll L Rep 55.

32 [1961] 1 Lloyd's Rep 479.

33 The same rule applies to the case of a missing ship: the insurer, on paying out, is entitled to keep the vessel should she later reappear: see s 58 and *Houstman v Thornton* (1816) Holt N P 242.

34 See *Stewart v Greenock Marine Insurance Co* (1848) 2 HL Cas 159. To negate the operation of s 63(2), the 'Freight Waiver' clause (cl 20 ITCH(95) and cl 18 IVCH(95)) states: 'In the event of total or constructive total loss no claim to be made by the Underwriters for freight whether notice of abandonment has been given or not.'

35 (1877) 3 App Cas 279 at p 292, HL.

36 How the ship has become the property of the underwriter is another separate question altogether which will be discussed later. Suffice it is here to say that Lord Blackburn was of the view that it automatically passes over to the insurer on settlement of the loss.

No acceptance of abandonment

Problematic issues, however, arise where the insurer does not exercise the right to 'take over the interest of the assured in whatever may remain of the subject-matter insured so paid for ...'. It is now necessary to consider the particular circumstance where the insurer who has paid the assured for the loss has declined to accept, expressly or impliedly, the abandoned property. The pertinent question is: Who is the owner of the abandoned property?

There are three possibilities as regards the subject of ownership on abandonment pursuant to a total loss: ownership could be automatically transferred to the insurer on settlement of the loss; the abandoned property could be *res nullius* – belongs to no one; or all proprietary rights remain with the shipowner.

Automatic transfer of ownership to insurer

In *Simpson v Thomson*, decided before the Act, Lord Blackburn of the House of Lords advocated the notion of automatic transfer. He had no doubt at all that:

> '... where the owners of an insured ship have claimed or been paid as for a total loss, the property in what remains of the ship, and all rights incident to the property, are transferred to the underwriters as from the time of the disaster ...'

He argued that the validity of the rule as regards the insurer's right to freight (now contained in s 63(2)) can only be supported if this was the case.[37] His comments on this subject have already been cited. It is to be noted that Chief Justice Cockburn in *North of England Steamship Insurance Association v Armstrong* also supported this rule.'[38]

Res nullius

Mr Justice Bailhache in *Mayor & Corpn of Boston v France, Fenwick & Co Ltd*[39] expressed the view that the wreck must be *res nullius*, meaning, in lay terms, that it belongs to nobody, but to the world at large. His remarks were: 'I will only say that there is a good deal to be said ... in favour of the wreck in such circumstances becoming a *res nullius*'. There does not appear to be overwhelming support for this view.

Both the above rule of automatic transfer of ownership and of *res nullius* are regarded by many as difficult to support, not only on the ground of the wording of both ss 63 and 79 but also of s 61 where an assured may, in the event of a constructive total loss, treat the loss as a partial loss. If the assured was held

---

37 The wording of s 63(2) does not say anything about transfer of ownership. It is capable of two interpretations, namely, that the insurer is entitled to the said freight only if he accepts the abandonment, or, regardless of whether or not he accepts the abandonment. Unless the insurer has exercised the right to take over the interest or the notion of automatic transfer of ownership applies, it is difficult to see how he could be entitled to the freight earned subsequent to the casualty causing the loss. Lord Blackburn obviously prefers the latter construction.

38 (1870) LR 5 QB 244 at p 248. He said: 'Now, I take it to be clearly established, in the case of a total loss, that whatever remains of the vessel in the shape of salvage, or whatever rights accrue to the owner of the thing insured and lost, they pass to the underwriter the moment he is called upon to satisfy the exigency of the policy ...'.

39 (1923) 15 Ll L Rep 85; 28 Com Cas 367 at p 373.

to have been divested of ownership of the remains, it would be impossible for him to treat the loss as a partial loss.

Ownership remains with the assured

The third view, held by Lord Justice Greer in *Oceanic Steam Navigation Co v Evans*,[40] is that if the abandonment is not accepted by the insurer, the owner (assured) is not divested of ownership of the wreck. In other words, there is no automatic transfer of ownership and the property is not *res nullius*, but remains in the ownership of the assured until such time as the insurer exercises his right to take over control or ownership over the abandoned property. This appears to be the preponderant view.[41]

Rights of subrogation

The second part of s 79(1) confers upon the insurer 'all the rights and remedies of the assured in and in respect of that subject-matter'. In this regard, the extent of the subrogative rights has to be considered in relation to recovery of damages from a wrong-doer; gifts and voluntary payments received by the assured; and the right to salvage in the case of under-insurance.

Recovery of damages from a wrong-doer

In the event of a collision for which a third party is liable, an assured may well receive by way of damages an amount in excess of what he is entitled to claim under the policy. It is also possible that the insurer himself may, after having indemnified the assured for his loss, by exercising his right of subrogation recover from the wrong-doer a sum in excess of what he has paid to the assured. The crux of the matter is: Which party, the assured or insurer, is entitled to keep the excess? It should not make any difference to the question of entitlement to the sum already paid by the insurer to the assured, and to the excess, whether the assured or the insurer has recovered the damages from the third party.

Recovery of the amount paid by the insurer

In the early case of *North of England Steamship Insurance Association v Armstrong*,[42] the insurer paid the assured the sum of £6,000 (the full sum insured) as for a total loss, when the insured vessel was run down and sunk by another ship. Subsequently, a sum of £5,000 was recovered against the owners of the other vessel. The real value of the insured vessel was £9,000. The insurers asserted that they were entitled to the whole of £5,000. Chief Justice Cockburn awarded judgment in favour of the insurers on two grounds: first, by reason of the conclusive nature of a valued policy,[43] and, secondly, on the point of law

---

40 (1934) 50 Ll L Rep 1 at p 3, CA.

41 See also *Blane Steamship Ltd v Minister of Transport* [1951] 2 KB 965 at p 990 where Cohen LJ agreed with Greer LJ's opinion; *Pesquerias y Secaderos de Bacalao de Espana SA v Beer* (1946) 79 Ll L Rep 417 at p 433; *Dee Conservancy Board v McConnell* [1928] 2 KB 159 at p 163; and *Allegemeine Versicherungs-Gesellschaft Helvetia v Administrator of German Property* [1930] 1 KB 672 at p 688.

42 (1870) LR 5 QB 244; 39 LJ QB 81.

43 This issue which need not concern us here will be examined later.

relating to the right to salvage pursuant to payment for a total loss.[44] Using the right to salvage as analogy, Chief Justice Cockburn has implied that the insurer would be entitled to the whole sum (including the excess) in the event of a settlement with the assured. He was only able to arrive at this decision on the ground of automatic transfer of ownership.[45] It has to be said, and with due respect, that he has failed to appreciate the distinction between the right of the insurer to take over the interest of the assured in whatever may remain of the subject-matter insured with all proprietary rights incidental thereto, and the right of subrogation. In so far as the sum recovered from the wrong-doer did not exceed the amount which the insurer had paid to the assured, the decision of the court is correct. But real problems, however, would arise if the recovery was to exceed the amount paid out by the insurer.[46]

In *Thames and Mersey Marine Insurance Co v British and Chilian Steamship Co*,[47] the Court of Appeal, on similar facts, also held that the insurer was entitled to the whole sum recovered by the assured from the wrong-doer. But again, as the amount so recovered was not in excess of the sum paid out by the insurer, the decision cannot be faulted. However, in so far as the amount of damages recovered was calculated on the basis of a figure (the real value of the ship) higher than the agreed value stated in the policy, the decision is open to criticism.

Recovery of the excess

As was seen, there was no excess in either of the above two cases. Thus, they cannot be cited as authority for having laid down the rule that an insurer is entitled to any excess which may be recovered from a wrong-doer. The case which is directly on point as regards such a claim is *Yorkshire Insurance Co Ltd v Nisbet Shipping Co Ltd*,[48] where the insurer had, in accordance with the terms of the policy, paid the assured £72,000 for a total loss. Subsequently, the assured, because of a devaluation of the pound, received from the third party liable for the collision a sum in excess of what they had received from the insurer. The

---

44 He said at p 248: 'It is admitted that if this ship had been recovered from the bottom of the sea ... the body of the vessel would have passed to the underwriters. If moreover, the value had proved to be more than the estimated value in the policy, the underwriters would still have been entitled to the vessel so recovered. And I think it is clear also, where we have, instead of the ship, the supposed value of the ship, or so much of it as the delinquent vessel could be called upon to contribute for the loss, that what is recovered must be taken to represent the lost ship; and then, just as the underwriters would be entitled to the ship if it could have been bodily got back, so they are entitled to what which is the representative of the ship in the shape of damage to be paid by the owners of the vessel which caused the collision.'

45 In *Goole & Hull Steam Towing Co Ltd v Ocean Marine Insurance Co Ltd* [1928] 1 KB 589 at p 598, Mackinnon J (as he then was) suggests that Cockburn CJ's reasoning can only be supported if it is based on 'cession of property to the underwriter upon payment for a total loss'.

46 Mellor J's views on the question of indemnity appears be more acceptable. Using the agreed valuation as the ceiling, he said, at p 250, that: '... as a matter of course ... all those rights, which spring out of the payment by an underwriter for a total loss, must be governed by the agreed value.'

47 [1916] 1 KB 30, CA.

48 [1961] 1 Lloyd's Rep 479.

insurers then proceeded against the assured claiming not only what they paid out, but the whole sum which the assured had received from the third party. There was no doubt whatsoever that the insurer was entitled to recover the sum which he had paid out to the assured under the policy. By the doctrine of subrogation, they were clearly entitled to at least £72,000. But whether this right to subrogation extends to recovery of the excess was the main ground of contention. The court held that the insurers were entitled to be paid only the amount which they had paid under the policy. The excess windfall belonged to the assured. According to Mr Justice Diplock, the law has never 'suggested that the insurer can recover from the assured the amount of the excess'. More pointedly, his interpretation of the second part of s 79(1) was that it was 'limited to recovering any sum which he has overpaid; he cannot recover more than he has in fact paid'.[49]

The rule that the insurer is entitled only to what he has in fact paid out under the policy is derived from the principle of indemnity as spelt out in s 1 of the Act; in this context, the words 'in the manner and to the extent thereby agreed' are particularly relevant. For the same reason, if the assured were allowed to retain both sums, he would be paid twice over for the same loss: He would be more than indemnified for the loss. Summing up, '[t]he simple principle ... is that the insurer cannot recover under the doctrine of subrogation now embodied in s 79 of the Marine Insurance Act 1906, anything more than he has paid'.[50] In the words of Lord Atkin, subrogation only arises on payment, and 'will only give the insurer rights up to 20s in the £ on what he has paid ...'.[51]

Gifts and voluntary payments

Whether an insurer who has paid the assured and has thereby been subrogated to the rights of the assured is entitled to claim any benefit which has been conferred on the assured by third parties is a question which has to be considered. The real issue here is: How far does the principle of subrogation extend? An assured may receive gifts and voluntary payments made by third parties for the purpose of compensating him for his loss. This precise point arose in *Burnand v Rodocanachi*,[52] where a compensation was paid to the assured in respect of the difference between the real value of the cargo and the sum which the assured received from their insurers. The insurers claimed from the assured, as salvage, this sum which the assured had received from the compensation fund. The House of Lords held that the insurers were not entitled to this sum because it was a gift made not for the purpose of reducing the loss against which the insurers had to indemnify the assured, but to compensate the assured personally for the loss actually sustained by him. In each case, the purpose of the gift or voluntary payment has to be ascertained. An insurer

---

49   The principle was applied in *Goole & Hull Steam Towing Co Ltd v Ocean Marine Ins Co Ltd* [1928] 1 KB 589 in relation to a partial loss.

50   [1961] 1 Lloyds Rep 479 at p 487, *per* Diplock J.

51   *Attorney General v Glen Line Ltd* [1930] 36 Com Cas 1 at p 13.

52   (1882) 7 App Cas 333.

cannot claim a gift or payment the purpose of which is to indemnify the assured for that portion of the loss which the insurance had not covered.

Under-insurance

An assured may insure 'for an amount less than the insurable value, or, in the case of a valued policy, for an amount less than the policy valuation'. In such an event, he is under-insured and is deemed by s 81 to be his own insurer in respect of the uninsured balance. An assured who is under-insured may find himself out of pocket even though he may have been fully indemnified by the insurer under the policy. As he is his own insurer for a proportion of the loss, he is entitled consequent to abandonment to a proportionate share of the salvage. The doctrine of subrogation, which originates from the principle of indemnity, will not permit an insurer from recovering more than he has paid out for his share of the risk. This principle was applied in *The Commonwealth*,[53] where the Court of Appeal held that '... the underwriters are to take all that is recovered, provided it does not exceed the amount they have paid ...'.

Settlement of partial loss

As there is no question of abandonment of the insured property in the case of an indemnity for a partial loss, the insurer has no proprietary right to the subject-matter (or the remains of it) insured. By s 79(2), he is subrogated only to the rights and remedies of the assured, but only in so far as the assured has been indemnified. On the other side of the coin, the assured would not be allowed to retain any recovery from a third party when he has already been indemnified by his insurers.

---

53 [1907] P 216, CA; affirming *The Welsh Girl* (1906) 22 TLR 475, the assured who were their own insurers for a 350/1,350th share were entitled to recover from their insurers that proportion of the sum which the insurer had obtained from the ship at fault.

CHAPTER 2

INSURABLE INTEREST

INTRODUCTION

An assured has to have an insurable interest in the subject-matter insured before he would be allowed to claim under a policy. Aside from defining insurable interest, s 5 does not explain its relevance to the scheme of things. Thus, for a proper understanding of the subject, it is necessary to refer to the basis or foundation of the notion; and only by reading s 5 with ss 1 and 4 of the Act does the picture become clearer.

A contract of indemnity

The requirement of insurable interest emanates from the cardinal principle of insurance law that a contract of insurance is a contract of indemnity: s 1 defines a contract of marine insurance as a contract whereby the insurer undertakes to indemnify the assured against marine losses. Thus, before an assured can seek for indemnity under any policy, it has first to be shown that he has in fact suffered a loss. To prove this, he has to show that he is 'interested in a marine adventure' as defined by s 5(1). Without going into a detailed study at this stage as to what constitutes 'insurable interest', it is sufficient to say, in simple terms, it signifies the relationship, if any, which the assured has with the subject-matter insured against.

If the assured has no interest whatsoever in the marine adventure, the contract which he has entered into will be deemed to be by way of gaming or wagering. Section 4(2)(a) states:[1]

'A contract of marine insurance is deemed to be a gaming or wagering contract –

Where the assured has not an insurable interest as defined by this Act, and the contract is entered into with no expectation of acquiring such an interest ...'

It would appear from the above that the assured, in not having an insurable interest in the subject-matter insured at the time of loss, would be caught not only by the fundamental principle of marine insurance, that of indemnity, but also by s 4, that every contract of marine insurance by way of gaming or wagering is void. Thus, his claim is not indemnifiable on both of these grounds.

DEFINITION OF INSURABLE INTEREST

Section 5 first defines insurable interest in general terms, and then proceeds to amplify its nature in more specific terms. It states: 'Subject to the provisions of this Act, every person has an insurable interest who is interested in a marine adventure'. Subsection 5(2) then goes on to elaborate that:[2]

'In particular a person is interested in a marine adventure where he stands in any

---

1   Section 4(2)(b) relates to an 'honour' policy, eg, a ppi policy.

2   This is derived from the words of Lawrence J in *Lucena v Craufurd* (1806) 2 Bos & PNR 269 at p 302.

legal or equitable relation to the adventure or to any insurable property at risk therein, in consequence of which he may benefit by the safety or due arrival of insurable property, or may be prejudiced by its loss, or by damage thereto, or by the detention thereof, or may incur liability in respect thereof.'

The persons who may stand in 'any legal or equitable relationship to the adventure or to any insurable property at risk therein' may be broadly divided into three main categories, the most obvious of which is the owner of the insurable property, whether it be ship, goods or freight. The second class covers persons who have lent money, in any emergency or otherwise, on the security of the ship and/or on her cargo; and, lastly, an insurer whose position clearly falls within the wording of the section. Besides these three categories, there are also other parties who, though they are not specifically mentioned in the Act, are generally recognised in the law of marine insurance to have an insurable interest: agents,[3] carriers, lien holders, pawnors and pawnees; trustees and executors;[4] captors; and, basically, any person who is to profit from a marine adventure. As the underlying principle is the same in all cases, it is unnecessary to examine the position of each and every one of these persons.

The simplest form of insurable interest is ownership of the subject-matter insured.[5] The position of the owner is laid down in s 14(3) which states that:

'The owner of insurable property has an insurable interest in respect of the full value thereof, notwithstanding that some third person may have agreed, or be liable, to indemnify him in case of loss.'

The interest of a part owner is by s 8 also insurable.

OWNER OF SHIP

The second limb of s 14(3) was enacted to take care of the situation, for example, where a charterer has agreed to indemnify the owner in case of loss. The fact that a third party may have agreed to indemnify the owner in case of a loss would not disentitle him of the right to claim that he still has an insurable interest in his ship. Needless to say, it would be highly dangerous for any owner to rely solely on such an undertaking to protect his interest.

OWNER OF GOODS

In the majority of cases, proof of ownership should not pose any problems. But having said that, it is not always easy to discern, especially in relation to cargo which has been the subject of a sale, whether the buyer or seller has the insurable interest at the time of loss. Most of the disputes which have arisen in

---

3 See s 14(2).

4 See *Stirling v Vaughan* (1809) 11 East 619.

5 See *Piper v Royal Exchange Assurance* (1932) 44 LlL Rep 103, KBD, where the dispute was in relation to the ownership of a vessel which was bought 'as she lies' by the plaintiff who, in the case, was the assured. Under the contract of sale, she was at the risk of the seller until she arrived in London. During the voyage to London, the vessel sustained some damage for which the plaintiffs claimed against their insurers. The claim for this loss was not recoverable under the policy, because at the time of the loss the property in the vessel had not passed to the plaintiffs.

this area of law relate to circumstances in which there is a change of ownership at some stage of the policy. The crucial question in each case is: which party (buyer or seller) is the owner of the subject-matter insured at the time of loss? The answer to this is dependent upon the answer to a further question: at what point in time is the property in the goods to pass from buyer to seller? This, naturally, depends upon the terms of the sale.[6] As the matter is purely a question of fact, no useful purpose could be served by going into the details of the cases.[7] The subject of contingent and defeasible interest, however, requires some comment.

Contingent and defeasible interests

Section 7 was especially framed to accommodate the concepts of contingent and defeasible interests which are peculiar to the law of sale of goods. These concepts are not defined by the Act. Looking at the subject from the point of view of the buyer, s 7(2) offers two examples of contingencies which could cause the reversion of the interest from him to the seller:

'In particular, where the buyer of the goods has insured them, he has an insurable interest, notwithstanding that he might, at his election, have rejected the goods, or have treated them as at the seller's risk, by reason of the latter's delay in making delivery or otherwise.'

A buyer of goods has always the right to reject the goods if they are found on arrival not to comply with the terms of the sale, for example, that they are not of merchantable quality. Thus, even though the interest in the goods may already have passed to the buyer, nonetheless, it could still revert to the seller should the buyer exercise his right of election to reject the goods. It is in this sense that the buyer's interest in the goods is contingent:[8] his interest is dependent upon certain contingencies.

The buyer's interest, as it is contingent, is also defeasible. Until the transit is completed, the seller may wish to exercise his right of stoppage in transit should he be unpaid. The buyer's interest could be defeated or forfeited by the action of the seller. Even though his interest may be defeasible, at the option of the unpaid seller, this does not prevent him from insuring his interest.

The seller is more concerned with the reversion of his interest than with the loss of his interest. In one sense, his interest is the mirror image of that of the buyer. Should he exercise the right of stoppage in transit, or the buyer the right of rejection, there would be a resumption of his interest in the goods.

In each case, the major difficulty is not whether there is an interest but where the interest lies (in the buyer or the seller) at the time of the loss.

---

6   See *Re National Benefit Assurance Co Ltd, Application of H L Sthyr* (1933) 45 Ll L Rep 147, Ch D, where it was held that the seller had the insurable interest in the goods since the sale was not an outright sale, but conditional on the arrival of the goods.

7   Moreover, it could well take us into the realms of the law on contract of sale of goods which is clearly outside the scope of this work.

8   A simple but clear definition of 'contingent' is, 'That which awaits or depends on the happening of an event': see *A Concise Law Dictionary*, P G Osborn.

OWNER OF FREIGHT

There is no specific provision in the Act on the subject of insurable interest as regards freight. The earning or acquisition of freight, however, falls within s 3(2)(b) in which it is declared that it is capable of being made the subject-matter of a contract of marine insurance. Read with s 14(3), the owner of freight clearly has an insurable interest in freight, if it is endangered by exposure to maritime perils.

There are basically three types of freight: ordinary freight or bill of lading freight; chartered freight; and owner's trading freight. Ordinary freight and chartered freight may be payable in advance, in which case it is called 'advance freight'.

The moment a ship commences her voyage with cargo on board, not only both ship and cargo but also ordinary freight and chartered freight are at risk. If ship and/or cargo are prevented by any peril from arriving at the agreed port of destination, a loss of cargo and freight would occur. The earning of ordinary bill of lading freight (but not advance freight) is dependent upon the performance of the adventure and the arrival of the cargo, albeit in a damaged state, at its proper destination.[9] Thus, should the cargo, by reason of a peril insured against, fail to arrive at its proper destination, a loss of ordinary freight would accrue.

The subject of advance freight is relatively straightforward. Section 12 states that:

'In the case of advance freight, the person advancing the freight has an insurable interest, in so far as such freight is not repayable in the case of loss.'[10]

Obviously the recipient of advance freight cannot claim that he has suffered a loss, for regardless of whether or not the cargo arrives at its proper destination, he has already been rewarded for the carriage. He will not be indemnified because he has not suffered a loss: the insurable interest lies with the party who has advanced the freight.

MORTGAGOR AND MORTGAGEE

Section 14(1) states that:

'Where the subject-matter insured is mortgaged, the mortgagor has an insurable interest in the full value thereof, and the mortgagee has an insurable interest in respect of any sum due or to become due under the mortgage.'

The mortgagor has an insurable interest in the mortgaged property in the capacity as owner of the ship. The case of *Samuel v Dumas*[11] has settled the principle that even if the mortgage is unregistered, the mortgagee would still

---

9 Under the law of contract of affreightment, if goods are landed at some port other than the agreed port of destination, freight is not payable. But it has to be emphasised that as a general rule, freight is payable even if the goods arrive in a damaged state at its proper port of destination.

10 See *Allison v Bristol Marine Insurance Co* (1876) 1 App Cas 209 at p 235.

11 [1924] AC 431.

have an insurable interest in the ship.[12] As he had an 'equitable' right in the mortgaged property, his case fell within the description of a person who is 'interested in a marine adventure'. Though not standing in any legal relation to the adventure or to any insurable property at risk therein, he clearly had an 'equitable relation' thereto.

A mortgagee may protect his interest in the security of the ship or a share in her in one or more of three ways. He may either:

- take out, as an original assured, his own standard hull policy incorporating the ITCH(83) or the ITCH(95);[13]
- take out his own mortgagee's interest policy – incorporating the Institute Mortgagee's Interest Clauses, Hulls [IMIC];[14] and/or
- obtain an assignment of the shipowner's hull policy.[15]

In the first two cases, as an original assured, the mortgagee would have no difficulty in showing that he has an insurable interest in the subject-matter insured. In the third, his position is critically dependent on the position of his assignor, the shipowner, of the policy.[16] It is to be remembered that his position is no better than that of the assignor. Following from this, it is significant to note the terms of s 51. A shipowner who does not have an insurable interest in the ship at the time of the assignment obviously cannot pass on to the mortgagee, the assignee, an interest which he does not possess. An assignment would therefore be inoperative, if the shipowner were to sell his ship before entering into an agreement to assign the policy to the mortgagee; for once he parts with his interest in the ship he would have nothing left to assign.[17]

Lender of money on bottomry and *respondentia*

Section 10 states that, 'The lender of money on bottomry and *respondentia* has an insurable interest in respect of the loan'. A lender on 'bottomry' is, as its name suggests, a person who advances money to a shipowner on the security of (the bottom) the ship. Unlike a mortgage, the loan has to be made in a time of urgent necessity at a port of distress. As the loan is secured, the lender, like a mortgagee, has an insurable interest to the extent of the loan. The term 'respondentia' refers to an advance obtained on the security or pledging of only the cargo.

INSURER

The position of an insurer is governed by s 9 of the Act, which states that: 'The insurer under a contract of insurance has an insurable interest in his risk, and may reinsure in respect of it.' He is not bound to state that he is reinsuring. As a

---

12 An unregistered mortgage is void by Greek law.
13 See Appendices 6 and 7.
14 See Appendix 23.
15 A marine policy is as a general rule assignable: see s 50(1).
16 See s 50(2) on the legal effects of an assignment.
17 See *Alston v Campbell* (1799) 4 Bro Parl Cases 476.

contract of re-insurance is a also contract of indemnity, the insurer, who is now an assured in the re-insurance, would not be indemnified for more than his share of loss under the original policy.[18]

WHEN INTEREST MUST ATTACH

Section 6(2) states that:

'Where the assured has no interest at the time of the loss, he cannot acquire interest by any act or election after he is aware of the loss.'

The above must be read with ss 4(2)(a) and 5, for they all relate to the time as to when an assured must be interested in the subject-matter insured.

An assured must be interested in the subject-matter insured at the time of the loss, though he is not required to have an insurable interest at the time when the insurance was effected. The concluding words of s 4(2)(a)[19] have, in a somewhat obscure manner, indicated that though the assured does not have to have an insurable interest at the time of the loss, nevertheless, if he had entered into the contract with an expectation of acquiring an interest, that would suffice.

In *Buchanan and Co v Faber*,[20] a policy was effected by the insurance brokers and the managing owners of the ship for the purpose of insuring the brokerage fee and the commission which they had hoped and expected to continue to earn from the ship. One of the issues was whether the interests of the brokers and managing owners were insurable at law. The court did not have to answer this question because the ship was unseaworthy at the commencement of the voyage; this ground alone was sufficient for the court to dismiss the plaintiffs' claim. However, Mr Justice Bingham chose to answer the question in the following terms:

'... I think they had none. They had nothing more than a hope that, if the vessel lived, they might continue to earn their commissions and brokerage. No contract ... was produced to show that they had a permanent right to be employed as managing owners. Every ship's husband and insurance broker has a right to entertain a similar hope, perhaps not so likely to be realised, but in its character the same.'

It is to be stressed that at the time of the loss, all that the plaintiffs had was a mere hope or expectation of earning a commission or brokerage fee. This 'hope' did not materialise into a contract. A hope is not in itself sufficient to establish that they had an insurable interest at the time of loss.

The insurable interest clause

To emphasise the importance of the requirement of insurable interest, the ICC has inserted its own provision, known as the 'insurable interest clause', echoing

---

18   See *British Dominions General Insurance Co Ltd v Duder and Others* [1915] 2 KB 394; *Uzielli v Boston Marine Insurance Co* (1884) 15 QBD 11; and *Western Ass v Poole* [1903] 1 KB 376.

19   'A contract of marine insurance is deemed to be a gaming or wagering contract – where the assured has not an insurable interest as defined by this Act, and the contract is entered into with no expectation of acquiring such an interest.'

20   (1899) 4 Com Cas 223.

the terms of s 6. The nature of a sale of goods, particularly an international sale, as was seen earlier, is such that the property in the goods may well 'move' from seller to buyer, and *vice versa*,[21] from time to time. Clause 11.1 was drafted to drive home the point that the crucial moment at which the assured must have an insurable interest is at the time of the loss; in simple but clear terms it states:

'In order to recover under this insurance the Assured must have an insurable interest in the subject-matter insured at the time of the loss.'

Exceptions

There are, however, two exceptions to the general rule that the assured must have an interest in the subject-matter at the time of loss. The first relates to a 'lost or not lost' policy and the other to the position of an assignee.

'Lost or not lost'

A loss, whether of ship or goods, may well occur before the contract of insurance was concluded, or before an assured acquires his interest in the subject-matter insured. In the days when communication technology was undeveloped, it was not always possible, at any given time, for any person on shore to obtain information as regards the whereabouts or safety of his property at sea. A buyer, for example, may have purchased goods which, unbeknown to both him and the seller, had already been lost at sea. In such an event, the buyer would have acquired his interest only after the loss of the goods. And if he were to take out a standard policy on goods, he would not be able to claim for the loss by reason of s 6(1). To overcome this difficulty, a 'lost or not lost' policy, which is recognised by the proviso to the said section, could be effected:

'Provided that where the subject-matter is insured, "lost or not lost", the assured may recover although he may not have acquired his interest until after the loss unless at the time of effecting the contract of insurance the assured was aware of the loss, and the insurer was not.'

An assured of a 'lost or not lost' policy is allowed to recover for a loss even though he may not have acquired his interest in the subject-matter insured until after the loss. The only condition which would bar him from recovery is if, at the time of effecting the contract of insurance, he was aware of the loss and the insurer was not.

Needless to say, if only the assured was aware of the loss, and the insurer was not, the assured would have committed not only a breach of the duty to observe utmost good faith, but also the duty to disclose all material facts. On either ground, the insurer is entitled to avoid the contract.[22]

An assured of goods, as was seen, is particularly susceptible to these problems. This perhaps explains why the ICC have found it necessary to repeat the statutory rules on the subject. Clause 11.2, even though it does not use the

---

21 See *Anderson v Morice* (1876) 3 Asp MLC 290.

22 If the insurer was aware that the subject-matter insured had arrived safely, and the assured was not, then the assured is entitled to a return of premium: the subject-matter insured was never at risk – s 84(3)(b) read with s 82.

expression 'lost or not lost', is, in effect, a reiteration of the rule contained in the proviso to s 6. It states:

> 'Subject to 11.1 above, the Assured shall be entitled to recover for insured loss occurring during the period covered by this insurance, notwithstanding that the loss occurred before the contract of insurance was concluded, unless the Assured were aware of the loss and the Underwriters were not.'

The above is in fact a clearer exposition of the law, for the words 'that the loss occurred before the contract of insurance was concluded' are helpful as they clarify the time of loss.

Assignee

A policy of insurance may be assigned before and even after a loss. It is to be remembered that by s 51:

> '...an assured who has parted with or lost his interest in the subject-matter insured, and has not, before or at the time of so doing, expressly or impliedly agreed to assign the policy, any subsequent assignment of the policy is inoperative.'

It is significant to note that an assignee can acquire no better right than the assignor. Thus, the policy is of benefit to the assignee only if the assignor has an insurable interest in the subject-matter insured at the time of loss. The policy may be assigned after a loss, but the assignor must have an insurable interest at the time of loss.[23]

---

23 See ss 15, 50 and 51.

CHAPTER 3

SUBJECT-MATTER INSURED

INTRODUCTION

All the provisions in the Act as to what may be made the subject-matter of a marine policy of insurance are derived from s 3 of the Act. It commences with the general statement that 'every lawful marine adventure may be the subject of a contract of marine insurance', and then lists three broad categories of matters which may be subjected to a marine adventure. The most obvious, namely, 'ship, goods and other moveables' are set out in s 3(2)(a); intangible property in s 3(2)(b); and liability to a third party in s 3(2)(c).

It is to be noted that by s 26(1), 'The subject-matter insured must be designated in a marine policy with reasonable certainty'. In some policies, the subject-matter is briefly described simply as 'ship', 'goods' or 'freight'; if the nature of the goods is such that, if it was not properly designated, it could mislead the insurer, then, the assured is bound to disclose the precise character of the subject-matter insured.[1] But this does not mean that the nature or extent of the assured's interest has to be specified in the policy. Thus, a re-insurer does not have to state that he is effecting a re-insurance.[2]

SHIP

Rule 15 of the Rules for Construction of Policy[3] states:

> 'The term "ship" includes the hull, materials and outfit, stores and provisions for the officers and crew, and, in the case of vessels engaged in a special trade, the ordinary fittings requisite for the trade, and also, in the case of a steamship, the machinery, boilers, and coals and engine stores, if owned by the assured.'

As can be seen, a policy on 'ship' is comprehensive covering more than just the hull. Thus, if a shipowner does not wish to insure the stores and provisions for the officers and crew, he would have to be more specific in his description of the subject-matter insured; a policy simply on 'hull and machinery' would not include these items.[4] Stores and provisions intended for passengers are not covered in a policy of insurance on 'ship', and should therefore be specifically insured. What constitutes the 'ordinary fittings requisite for the trade' is, of course, a question of fact.[5]

---

1   Failing which the assured could also be in breach of non-disclosure of a material circumstance, s 18; see Chapter 6.

2   See *Mackenzie v Whitworth* (1875) 1 Ex D 36.

3   The 'Rules for Construction of Policy' is part of the Marine Insurance Act 1906: see First Schedule. Hereinafter referred to simply as 'the Rules for Construction'.

4   See *Roddick v Indemnity Mutual Marine Insurance Co* [1895] 2 QB 380, CA

5   In *Hogarth v Walker* [1900] 2 QB 283, dunnage mats and separating cloths on board a vessel engaged in a grain trade, though not actually in use at the time of loss, was held covered.

The policy (MAR 91 Form) and the Clauses

At present, there are four standard sets of Clauses for hulls in use, namely, the Institute Time Clauses Hulls, 1/10/83 (the ITCH(83));[6] the Institute Time Clauses Hulls, 1/11/95 (the ITCH(95);[7] and the Institute Voyage Clauses Hulls, 1/10/83 (the IVCH(83)) and the Institute Voyage Clauses Hulls 1/11/95 (the IVCH(95)).[8] As will be seen, compared to the ITCH(83), the ITCH(95) are less favourable to the assured. All the Clauses are subject to English law and practice, and may be used only with the current Lloyd's Marine Policy, (MAR 91)[9] and the Institute of London Underwriters Companies Marine Policy Form (MAR 91),[10] both of which are expressly declared to be subject to the 'exclusive jurisdiction of the English Courts, except as may be expressly provided herein to the contrary'. As can be seen, attached to each of the MAR 91 Form is a schedule in which the details relating to the insurance are to be inserted.

The Institute Time Clauses – Hulls – Restricted Perils, 1/11/95 [11] were also introduced, and, as the name suggests, they restrict the cover for loss of or damage arising as a result of some of the perils insured under cl 6 of the ITCH(95). They provide a less comprehensive cover than the standard ITCH(95) and the IVCH(95).

GOODS

The first part of the statutory definition for 'goods' in r 17 states:

> 'The term "goods" means goods in the nature of merchandise and does not include the personal effects or provision and stores for use on board.'

'Goods' refer to goods which are merchantable, that is, merchandise put on board for the purpose of trade or commerce. Hence, it cannot include personal effects or the ship's provisions.[12]

Deck cargo and living animals

The second part of r 17 states that:

> 'In the absence of any usage to the contrary, deck cargo and living animals must be insured specifically, and not under the general denomination of goods.'

---

6   See Appendix 6.

7   See Appendix 7. At the moment both sets of the 1983 and 1995 Clauses are in use, but it is envisaged that the ITCH(95) to be used only with the current MAR 91 Policy Form, will eventually replace the ITCH(83).

8   See Appendix 9.

9   See Appendix 4.

10 See Appendix 5.

11 See Appendix 8.

12 *Duff v Mackenzie* (1857) 3 CBNS 16 is the authority for the principle that the personal effects of the master are not covered under the general denomination of 'goods'; they have to be specifically insured.

The nature of deck cargo and living animals is such that they are exposed to greater risks than goods carried in the normal way. Living animals, whether carried on or under deck, are vulnerable and susceptible to the stresses and strains of any form of transportation, not to mention a turbulent sea voyage. The general rule that they must be specifically insured also stems from the principle of disclosure. By insuring them specifically, and not just as 'goods', the insurer cannot later complain that he was unaware of the nature of the subject-matter insured or the extent of the risk which he has agreed to underwrite.

'Usage to the contrary'

The next question which arises is the meaning of the word 'usage'. Does it refer to the usage to carry the cargo on deck and/or the usage of the insurance market to insure it under the general denomination of 'goods'? The matter was resolved by the House of Lords in *British and Foreign Marine Insurance Co v Gaunt*[13] where wool, which was not specifically insured, was in accordance with the local usage of the wool trade carried on deck. This fact was, however, unknown in the insurance market. The House held the insurer liable for the damage caused by sea water. The word 'usage' was construed to mean a usage in the wool trade, and not of the business of insurance. Cargo insurers, according to this interpretation of the phrase, would have to familiarise themselves with the custom and usages of trade relating to the cargo which they have agreed to insure. Ignorance of the usage of a particular trade is clearly not a defence available to him.

It is of particular importance in cargo insurance that the goods be described with reasonable clarity.[14] This principle ties up neatly with the duty of disclosure of material facts.[15] If an insurer is required to underwrite any risk which is in excess of the ordinary, he ought to be informed of it. And one way of fulfilling this is to require that the assured specify the particular or special nature of the cargo which he has been asked to insure. Second-hand machinery, for example, has to be specifically insured.

Containers and packing materials

The statutory definition of 'goods' has failed to indicate whether containers and packing materials are covered by a policy on goods. No hard and fast rule can be extracted from the cases which have dealt with this problem.

One test is to ask the question: who provided the container? In other words, is the container owned or hired by the carrier or, is it owned by the persons interested in the cargo? It is possible, in the case of the latter, that it could be covered by the policy on the goods. The general rule appears to be that, if the container is virtually part and parcel of the goods, it is probably covered.

---

13   [1921] 2 AC 41, HL; hereinafter referred to as *The Gaunt Case*.

14   See s 26(1).

15   See Chapter 6.

Loss of voyage or of the adventure

When an assured effects a marine policy on goods at and from the port of loading to the port of destination, he probably has in mind that the only risk he is insured for is the risk against physical losses. But, in fact, his policy is much wider, for it extends to an indemnity to be paid in case the goods do not reach their destination. This additional coverage is commonly referred to as 'an insurance of the venture, or an insurance of the voyage, or an insurance of the market, as distinguished from an insurance of the goods simply and solely'.[16] However described, it stems from the doctrine of the loss of voyage.

The doctrine of loss of the voyage was in existence for a great many years before the Act; but doubts as to its validity and applicability crept in soon after the passing of the Act. The fact that the Act had omitted to cast the rule in statutory form has led some to believe that it no longer has a place in law after the promulgation of the Act.

The inveterate doctrine, which is by far one of the most important of rules in the law of marine insurance relating to a policy on goods, was firmly re-established in the case *British and Foreign Marine Insurance Co Ltd v Samuel Sanday and Co*[17] decided not long after the passing of the Act. As the facts of the case will vividly illustrate the principle, it would be helpful to state them: a cargo of linseed belonging to British merchants was shipped on a voyage from the Argentine to Hamburg for sale in Germany. The cargo owners had them insured for the voyage, and the perils insured against included restraint of princes. When war broke out, further prosecution of the voyage became illegal, and the vessel on which the goods were carried was ordered to proceed to British ports, which she did. The goods were then returned to the owners who had them warehoused. They then issued notice of abandonment claiming for a constructive total loss.

The issue in the case was framed with admirable clarity and precision by Earl Loreburn as thus:[18]

'The first question is whether the old rule still prevails, that upon an insurance on goods ... the frustration of the adventure by an insured peril is a loss recoverable against underwriters, though the goods themselves are safe and sound.'

The House held that as there was nothing to be found in the Act which was inconsistent with the law as was settled by authorities,[19] it must be still good

---

16 *Per* Lord Wrenbury in *British & Foreign Marine Insurance Co Ltd v Samuel Sanday & Co* [1916] 1 AC 650 at p 672, HL.

17 [1915] 2 KB 781; [1916] 1 AC 650, HL. For convenience, this case shall henceforth be referred to as *The Sanday Case* and the principle of law propounded therein as 'The *Sanday* Principle' discussed further in Chapter 15.

18 [1916] 1 AC 650, at p 656, HL.

19 The authorities, which had laid down the doctrine of loss of the voyage, before the passing of the Act are: *Anderson v Wallis* (1813) 2 M & S 240; *Barker v Blakes* (1808) 9 East 283, 293-294; and the well-known case, *Rodoconachi v Elliot* (1874) LR 9 CP 518 where the insured goods were detained in Paris by the German army when it became impossible to send them on to their proper destination. The assured was entitled to abandon the goods to the insurers and recover for a constructive total loss.

law. In support of this stand, the law lords relied on ss 26(4) and 91(2) of the Act. Lord Parmoor, who gave a most comprehensive summary of the law, said:[20]

> 'When the Act was passed the common form Lloyd policy of marine insurance on goods in transit from one port to another designated by usage that the contemplated adventure was part of the subject-matter, so that if the contemplated adventure was frustrated by a peril insured against, the insurer became liable to pay the insured the amount due under the policy. This position is not altered but preserved by subsection 4 [referring to s 26(4)].'

The House held that the cargo owners were entitled to recover for a constructive total loss of the goods by a peril insured against, even though the goods did not suffer any bodily damage. It is thus important to bear in mind that an insurance on goods is 'not merely an insurance of the actual merchandise from injury, but also an insurance of its safe arrival'.[21]

The doctrine of loss of voyage applies to goods, freight and profits, but has no application to a ship.[22]

The Frustration Clause

Following the decision of *The Sanday Case*, which allowed recovery for a claim which was in effect based upon loss of, or frustration of, the insured adventure resulting from 'restraint of princes', the frustration clause (clause 3.7) was introduced in the Institute War Clauses (Cargo) [IWC(C)] which declares that, 'any claim based upon loss of or frustration of the adventure' is not covered.[23]

The Institute Cargo Clauses (A), (B) and (C)

Cargo may be insured under either the Institute Cargo Clauses (A), (B) or (C), 1/1/82, (the ICC).[24] The ICC (A) is for all risks policy, whereas (B) and (C) are for enumerated risks; as in the case of the clauses for Hulls, they may be used only with the 'MAR Form'. Naturally, the ICC(A) is the most comprehensive cover available, and also has the advantage of the matter relating to the burden of proof.[25]

MOVEABLES

Section 90 defines 'moveables' to mean 'any moveable tangible property, other than the ship, and includes money, valuable securities, and other documents'.

---

20 [1916] 1 AC 650 at p 668, HL.

21 *Per* Earl Loreburn, [1916] 1 AC 650 at p 656, HL.

22 A long list of authorities supporting this statement can be found in a footnote (no 2) in Arnould, *Law of Marine Insurance and Average* (1981, 16th edn) para 1186. Hereinafter referred to simply as 'Arnould'.

23 This clause will be discussed more fully under insurance for war and strikes risks; see Chapter 14.

24 See Appendices 10, 11 and 12.

25 See Chapter 11.

Section 3(2)(a) states that if they are exposed to maritime perils, they may be made the subject-matter of a contract of marine insurance.

FREIGHT

The subject of freight can be daunting to the timid and the uninitiated; this is because it is abstract and intangible in nature and cannot, as in the case of ship or goods, itself suffer physical damage or loss. It is incapable of being exposed directly to maritime peril. Steeped in history and bounded by the rules of the common law, it is a difficult subject to grasp because there are so many different types of freight. Moreover, it is essentially a concept borrowed from the law of carriage of goods by sea, and when applied to marine insurance, the matter is aggravated by the fact that, 'The references to freight insurance in the Marine Insurance Act 1906 are particularly sparse'.[26]

Definition of 'freight'

Section 90 (and r 16 of the Rules for Construction) defines 'freight' as follows:

> '"Freight" includes the profit derivable by a shipowner from the employment of his ship to carry his own goods or moveables, as well as freight payable by a third party, but does not include passage money.'[27]

'Freight' is profit earned from the employment of the ship. The 'earning or acquisition of freight' and 'profit' are both specifically mentioned in s 3(2)(b). Provided that the 'insurable property' from which the freight is to be earned is endangered by exposure to 'maritime perils', they may be made the subject of a contract of marine insurance.[28]

Freight payable by a third party

This part of the definition is intentionally worded in general terms in order to embrace all the various types of freight known in the law of carriage of goods by sea. Also, the use of the word 'includes' implies that the definition is not exhaustive. Though incomplete, it is, nevertheless, comprehensive, covering any 'benefit derived by the shipowner from the employment of his ship'.[29] According to this judicial definition, freight may be divided into two broad categories: It covers freight earned from the carriage of goods and freight earned from the hire of the ship. There are basically two types of freight falling under this part of the statutory definition, namely:

---

26 See Ivamy, *Marine Insurance* (1985, 4th edn), p 10; hereinafter referred to simply as 'Ivamy'. Apart from ss 16(2), 70 and 90, and r 3(c), there does not appear to be any other provision in the Act dealing directly with freight.

27 'Goods' is defined in r 17 and 'moveables' in s 90. As regards passage money, see *Denoon v The Home and Colonial Assurance Co* (1872) LR 7 CP 341, where the passage money to be earned for the conveyance of coolies was held not recoverable under a policy on freight. Passage money has to be specifically insured: see s 3(2)(b).

28 Both 'insurable property' and 'maritime perils' are defined in s 3.

29 *Per* Lord Tenterden in *Flint v Flemyng* (1830) 1 B & Ad 45 at p 48.

- ordinary freight, also known as bill of lading freight; and
- chartered freight, sometimes referred to as charterparty freight.

It is to be noted that no distinction is made in the Act of the different types of freight; they are all referred to generally as 'freight'. Past cases have revealed that freight may be insured simply as 'freight' or comprehensively as 'freight and/or chartered freight and/or anticipated freight'.[30] The wide spectrum was not found unacceptable. The courts have not found the wide interpretation as infringing the rule contained in s 26(1) that the subject-matter insured must be designated with reasonable certainty. It has also to be said that there are two sets of Institute Clauses, namely, the Institute Time Clauses, Freight 1/11/95, (ITCF) and the Institute Voyage Clauses, Freight 1/11/95 (IVCF) (whose main clauses are identical) applicable to the insurance of freight covering marine perils.[31]

Ordinary freight

Mr Justice Hamilton in *Scottish Shire Line Ltd v London and Provincial Marine and General Insurance Co Ltd*,[32] when comparing chartered freight with ordinary freight, observed that:

> '... bill of lading freight is prima facie the shipowner's own contracted remuneration for the carriage of goods in his own ship by his own servants.'

It is evident from this comment that he obviously had in mind the circumstance where a shipowner, employing his ship as a general ship, himself enters into contracts with various third parties for the carriage of their goods to agreed destinations. A charterer may, of course, charter a ship in order that he himself can use her as a general ship to earn ordinary freight. But from the shipowner's standpoint, 'it is the same thing ... whether he receives the benefit of the use of his ship by a money payment from one person who charters the whole ship; or from various persons who put specific quantities of goods on board'.[33] However, any profit to be made by the charterer has to be insured as 'profit'.[34]

It is contended that the term 'bill of lading' freight is a better and more vivid description than ordinary freight. It is the reward paid to a 'carrier' for the service of the carriage of goods from one port to another. The word 'carrier' is specially chosen here to denote both shipowner and charterer. In summary, ordinary freight is, in effect, the remuneration earned by a carrier (whether

---

30 As in *Carras v London and Scottish Assurance Co Ltd* [1936] 1 KB 291, CA. In *Rankin v Potter* (1873) LR 6 HL 83, freight was insured as 'homeward chartered freight'; *Inman Steamship Co v Bischoff* (1882) 7 App Cas 670, HL, as 'on freight outstanding'; *Kulukundis v Norwich Union Fire Insurance Society* [1937] 1 KB 1, CA simply as on 'cargo and freight'; and *Robertson v Petros Nomikos Ltd* [1939] AC 371, HL as 'freight, chartered or otherwise ...' .

31 See Appendices 13 and 14. For war and strikes, see the Institute War and Strikes Clauses, Freight, Time, and the Institute War and Strikes Clauses, Freight, Voyage.

32 [1912] 3 KB 51 at p 65.

33 *Per* Lord Tenterden in *Flint v Flemyn* (1830) 1 B & Ad 45 at p 48.

34 Which presumably would be the difference between the ordinary freight payable to him by shippers and the chartered freight payable by him to the shipowner.

shipowner or charterer) who employs the ship as a 'general ship' carrying cargo for all and sundry. As such a contract of carriage is evidenced by a bill of lading, the freight so earned has come to be known as 'bill of lading' freight. The prefix, 'bill of lading', distinguishes it from chartered freight earned pursuant to a time or voyage charterparty. It also serves as a notification to the insurer the existence of a charterparty.

The acquisition of such freight is clearly dependent on the delivery of the goods at the agreed destination. The payment of ordinary freight and the delivery of the goods are thus concurrent conditions. Under the law of contract of carriage, freight is payable even if the cargo is delivered in a damaged condition at the agreed port of destination. An observation which is by far the most lucid on the subject can be found in an old case, *Weir & Co v Girvin & Co*[35] It states:

> '... freight is a payment to be made to the ship for the carriage and delivery, and until there has been carriage and delivery, the shipowner is not under ordinary circumstances entitled to demand freight at all.'

Freight, however, is not payable if the goods are so damaged as to lose its identity and can no longer be described as the same goods as that shipped.[36]

It has to be stressed that an assured of freight, which is to be derived from the carriage of cargo, would not be allowed to recover for a loss of freight unless the ship was, at the time of the loss, ready to receive the cargo, and the cargo ready to be shipped. This principle was established in *Forbes v Aspinall* where Lord Ellenborough declared that:[37]

> 'In every action upon such a policy, evidence is given either that the goods were put on board from the carriage of which the freight would result, or that there was some contract under which the shipowner, if the voyage were not stopped by the perils insured against, would have been entitled to demand freight.'

The same principle applies to chartered freight. An imaginary cargo or contract of affreightment would not suffice.

Chartered freight

The term 'chartered freight', though it appears in r 3(c) of the Rules for Construction in relation to commencement of risk, has not been defined by the Act. Its name, however, suggests the existence of a charterparty from which the 'chartered' freight is to be earned. A chartered freight policy is not unusual, but is not so common as a policy on freight in general terms. For the purpose of this discussion, chartered freight will be divided into voyage chartered freight and time charter hire.

Voyage chartered freight

A shipowner could, instead of employing his ship as a general ship, charter her to one person, the charterer, for the carriage of cargo to be provided by the charterer for a specified voyage. To insure the ability of the ship to earn the

---

35 [1899] 1 QB 193 at p 196.

36 The leading authority on the subject is *Asfar v Blundell* [1896] 1 QB 123, CA.

37 (1811) 13 East 323 at p 325. See also *Williamson v Innes* (1831), cited in 8 Bing 81; and *Barber v Fleming* (1869) LR 5 QB 59.

freight contemplated by the charterparty upon the cargo to be loaded for carriage between the agreed ports, the shipowner would take out a policy on 'chartered freight'.

As in the case of ordinary freight, the freight at risk is on goods which had been shipped. If the goods are not delivered at the proper destination, freight is not payable. This necessarily means that should the ship be unable to commence,[38] or continue with,[39] the chartered voyage with the cargo on board, a loss of voyage chartered freight would accrue. The whole matter is intertwined with the performance of the charterparty. Thus, should the voyage charterparty be cancelled or the chartered voyage discontinued, a loss of chartered freight would befall on the shipowner, for which he would wish to be indemnified under the policy on chartered freight. In each case, the loss of the freight, which has resulted from the non-performance of charterparty, is only recoverable if it was caused by a peril insured against.

It would appear from the following statement made by Arnould that there could be another species of voyage chartered freight.[40] He states:

'... a fixed sum stipulated to be paid to the shipowner by the terms of a charterparty for the use of his ship, or part of it, on an entire voyage therein described. Under such a contract the ship may earn freight though no goods may ever be put on board, and the question whether, at the time of loss, she had taken any goods on board for the voyage insured, or whether any were contracted to be shipped, does not arise.'

According to this explanation, it is possible for a shipowner to earn chartered freight independently of the carriage and delivery of goods. As soon as the ship commences her chartered voyage, chartered freight is at risk regardless of whether or not she has cargo on board at the time of loss. There is no principle in law saying that the payment of freight has to be made dependent upon the carriage and delivery of cargo. A shipowner could enter into any agreement with a charterer as regards the terms of payment of freight.[41] The expression 'chartered freight' is wide enough to accommodate any freight payable under a charterparty including a time charter.

---

38 See, eg, *Rankin v Potter* (1873) LR 6 HL 83, where cargo was not loaded because the ship, which was damaged from perils of the seas, was a constructive total loss; and *Jackson v The Union Marine Insurance Co Ltd* (1874) LR 10 CP 125. In *Re An Arbitration between Jamieson and The New Castle Steamship Freight Insurance Association* [1895] 2 QB 90 and *Carras v London and Scottish Assurance Co Ltd* [1936] 1 KB 291, CA, freight was lost when as a result of a peril of the seas, the ship was delayed, and the charter was cancelled.

39 See, eg, *Guthrie v North China Insurance Co Ltd* (1902) 7 Com Cas 130, CA, where chartered freight was not earned because of the ship on which the cargo was carried went ashore and was lost, and the chartered voyage was not completed; *Robertson v Petros Nomikos Ltd* [1939] AC 371, HL, where during the course of the chartered voyage, an explosion followed by fire caused the (constructive) total loss of the chartered vessel; and *Kulukundis v Norwich Union Fire Insurance Society* [1937] 1 KB 1, CA where shortly after the commencement of the chartered voyage, the ship went ashore and was abandoned to salvors when it was found that the cost of temporary repairs would exceed the repaired value of the vessel.

40 Arnould, para 356.

41 See, eg, *Griffiths v Bramley-Moore and Others* (1878) 4 QBD 70, where the charterparty provided for payment for freight at a specified rate. The shipowners, however, effected an insurance for only part (one third) of the chartered freight with the insurers. The clause in question read as: 'To cover only the one-third loss of freight in consequence of sea-damage as per charterparty.'

Time charter hire or time freight

There is no provision in the Act referring specifically to the payment of 'hire', sometimes referred to as 'time freight'[42] which is the name given to the reward payable by a time charterer to a shipowner for the hire of his ship for a specified period of time. But as it is a 'benefit derived by the shipowner from the employment of his ship' it falls within the common law definition of freight. It is, however, necessary to mention that hire is payable for the right to use the vessel irrespective of the extent to which it is employed by the charterer for the carriage of goods. Unlike ordinary freight, it does not depend on the delivery of the goods for its reward. It is, however, reliant on the physical well-being of the ship,[43] for should the ship be not made available to the charterer for their use, a loss of hire would ensue. In this regard, it is significant to note the effect of the off-hire clause invariably found in standard time charters and, in particular, the 'loss of time' clause, cll 15 and 11 of the ITCF and IVCF respectively.[44] It is also to be recalled that the shipowner would only be able to claim under his freight policy if the loss is caused by a peril insured against.[45]

Mr Justice Hamilton in *Scottish Shire Line Ltd v London and Provincial Marine and General Insurance Co Ltd* intimated that he had:[46]

'... no difficulty in understanding what is meant by chartered freight ... Chartered freight is remuneration paid to the shipowner by another who hires his ship or part of it, generally with an added contract that the shipowner's captain shall sign bills of lading for the charterer's benefit.'

Arnould has no doubt whatsoever that time charter hire, though not freight strictly so called, is included within the definition of 'chartered freight':[47]

'... in policies of insurance it also denotes that which is less properly called freight, *viz* the price agreed to be paid by the charterer to the shipowner for the hire of his ship, or a part of it, under a charterparty or other contract of affreightment.'

---

42 Note Lord Denning's warning in *The Nanfri* [1978] 2 Lloyd's Rep 132 at p 139 on the use of this term: 'So different are the two concepts that I do not think the law as to "freight" can be applied indiscriminately to "hire"'.

43 See cll 16.1 and 12.1 of the ITCF and IVCF: 'In the event of the total loss (actual or constructive) of the Vessel named herein the amount insured shall be paid in full, whether the Vessel be fully or party loaded or in ballast, chartered or unchartered.'

44 Clauses 15 and 11 state: 'This insurance does not cover any claim consequent on loss of time whether arising from a peril of the sea or otherwise.' *Jackson v Union Marine Insurance Co* (1874) LR 10 CP 125; *Inman Steamship Co Ltd v Bischoff* (1882) 7 App Cas 670; *The Alps* [1893] P 109; and *The Bedouin* [1894] P 1, CA, state the legal position before the introduction of the 'Loss of Time' Clause. See *Bensaude v Thames & Mersey Marine Insurance Co Ltd* [1897] AC 609, HL; *Turnbull, Martin & Co v Hull Underwriters' Association* [1900] 2 QB 402; *Russian Bank for Foreign Trade v Excess Insurance Co Ltd* [1918] 2 KB 123; and *The Playa de Las Nieves* (1978) AC 857, HL where the said clause was applied.

45 See *Court Line Ltd v R*, The Lavington Court [1945] 2 All ER 357, CA.

46 [1912] 3 KB 51 at p 65.

47 Arnould, para 311.

Advance freight

Ordinary freight and chartered (voyage and time) freight may be payable in advance, either before the delivery of the cargo or the commencement of the charterparty. Provided that it is 'not repayable in case of loss', it qualifies as advance freight. It is not the shipowner but the party who has paid the freight in advance who would insure the advance freight.[48]

The problem which is likely to arise here is with regard to payments made by the charterer to the shipowner: whether a payment is a mere loan (an advance) or advance freight is a question of fact. A mere unsecured loan which is repayable in any event and is not dependent on any property at risk is therefore not insurable.[49]

Owner's trading freight

Owner's trading freight, though not referred to specifically as such, is covered by the first part of the statutory definition of 'freight'. It refers to the circumstance where the shipowner carries his own goods in his own ship. In practical terms, he would not, of course, be paying himself for the carriage of his own cargo. It would perhaps be easier to grasp this principle if we were to pretend that the cargo (owned by the shipowner) belonged to a third party, for which freight would be payable by that third party to the shipowner on its arrival at the agreed destination. For all intents and purposes, the shipowner's cargo (carried in his own ship) is to be treated as if it belonged to someone else. In the words of Mr Justice Bayley in *Flint v Flemyng*:[50]

'Whether the shipowner carry his own goods or the goods of another person, is immaterial to him ... he may insure that profit under the name of freight, whether it accrue from the price paid for the carriage of the goods of others, or from the additional value conferred on his own goods by their carriage.'

Needless to say, as in the case of ordinary freight, there must actually be a cargo to be shipped, and the ship must be ready to carry that cargo.

PROFIT

That profit to be earned from a maritime adventure may be made the subject-matter of a marine policy of insurance was established as early as 1802 in *Barclays v Cousins*,[51] where the policy was on profits to be derived from a cargo which was liable to be affected by the perils insured against. Mr Justice Lawrence said:

---

48   See s 12 and *Allison v Bristol Marine Insurance Co* (1876) 1 App Cas 209 at p 235.

49   As this problem has not arisen in recent years and the question is one of fact, it would serve no useful purpose to spend time on it. The differences between the two forms of payment were discussed in *Manfield v Maitland* (1821) 4 B & Ad 582 at p 585; *Winter v Haldimand* (1831) 2 B & Ad 649; and *Hicks v Shield* (1857) 26 LJ QB 205. A secured loan whether upon ship, goods or moveables is insurable: see s 3(2)(b).

50   (1830) 1 B & Ad 45 at p 49.

51   (1802) 2 East 545 at p 546.

'As insurance is a contract of indemnity it cannot be said to be extended beyond what the design of such species of contract will embrace, if it be applied to protect men from those losses and disadvantages, which but for the perils insured against the assured would not suffer: and in every maritime adventure the adventurer is liable to be deprived not only of the thing immediately subjected to the perils insured against, but also of the advantages to arise from the arrival of those things at their destined port.'

Like freight and the other pecuniary benefits listed in s 3(2)(b), profit, even though it does not have a physical existence, may be made the subject-matter of a marine contract of insurance. The only *caveat* is that the ship, goods or moveables, from which the profit is to be derived, has to be endangered by exposure to maritime perils. If the insurable property does not arrive, 'his loss in such case is not merely that of his goods or other things exposed to the perils of navigation, but of the benefits which, were his money employed in an undertaking not subject to the perils, he might obtain without more risk than the capital itself would be liable to ...'.[52]

Profit on goods

First, it has to be mentioned that an insurance simply on 'goods' does not cover profits, which have to be specifically insured.[53] An assured of an insurance on profits upon goods has to show that the goods were at one time or another actually exposed to 'maritime perils' as defined by s 3. The policy attaches only to the goods which are actually on board.[54]

Profit on charter

The benefits which a charterer expects to earn from the use of the chartered vessel may also be insured. To make a profit, a charterer can either sub-charter the ship or enter into contracts with various shippers for the carriage of their goods. The expected profit to be earned from the sub-charter is generally insured either as 'profit on charter', 'difference of freight', or 'anticipated earnings'.[55]

Unless he has entered into a binding contract for freight, it is generally recognised that a 'carrier'[56] cannot insure his expected earnings under the denomination of 'freight'. Following from this, the question which then arises is whether it could be insured generally as 'profit'. There is no direct authority on the subject. However, in *Manchester Lines v British Foreign Marine Insurance Co*,[57]

---

52 (1830) 1 B & Ad 45 at p 49.
53 See *Anderson v Morice* (1875) LR 10 CP at p 621.
54 See *M'Swiney v Royal Exchange Assurance Corpn* (1849) 14 QB 634 at p 646.
55 See *Asfar v Blundell* [1896] 1 QB 123, CA; *US Shipping Co v Empress Assurance Corpn* [1908] 1 KB 259; *Scottish Shire Line Ltd v London & Prov Mar & General Insurance Co* [1912] 3 KB 51 at p 65; *Papadimitriou v Henderson* [1939] 3 All ER 908; and *Continental Grain Co v Twitchell* (1945) 61 TLR 291, CA.
56 Who could be a shipowner or charterer.
57 [1901] 7 Com Cas 26 at p 33. He said: 'It seems to me clear that a shipowner has an interest in the use of his ship, and that he may insure himself against the loss which he may undoubtedly suffer from being deprived of its use by perils of the sea or other causes.'

Mr Justice Walton seemed to be receptive to the suggestion that a shipowner could insure his interest in the use of his ship, entirely independently of any particular contract for the payment of freight or hire. He did not, however, as it was unnecessary for him so to do, indicate how the subject-matter insured is to be described. Thus, his comments, made by way of *obiter*, must still been given further thought.

COMMISSION

The earning of any commission is specifically named in s 3(2)(b) as a subject-matter which may be insured. In any sale or trade, a commission is likely to be made by an agent or any third party who is involved in the transaction. If the merchandise sold is prevented from arriving at its proper destination by a maritime peril, the person expecting the commission would suffer a loss. Though the commission may be dependent upon the goods, it is not covered by a policy on goods and has, therefore, to be specifically insured.

DISBURSEMENTS

There is no provision in the Act defining the word 'disbursements'. In lay terms, it refers to any expenditure of money, but in relation to marine insurance, it has to represent money spent on insurable property, 'the benefit of which will be lost or the object of which will be frustrated by marine perils ...'.[58]

For the purpose of earning freight, a shipowner may incur expenses before and during the course of a voyage in equipping, refitting, and supplying the ship. Expenditure on coal, engine-room stores, provisions, port charges;[59] dry dock and painting expenses;[60] and necessaries[61] have all been held insurable under the denomination of 'disbursements'.

In *Buchanan and Co v Faber*,[62] Mr Justice Bingham thought that 'disbursements' was well understood at Lloyd's to be a compendious term used to describe any interest which was outside the ordinary and well-known interests of 'hull,' 'machinery,' 'cargo,' and 'freight'. Later, Mr Justice Walton in *Moran, Galloway & Co v Uzielli and Others* remarked that:[63] 'disbursements represent expenditure by the shipowner either on his ship or for the purpose of earning his freight, and such policies are in the nature of insurance of the shipowner ...'. However defined, it has to be expended either upon his ship or upon his freight, because the money spent cannot itself be at risk.

---

58 See Arnould, para 325.
59 *Roddick v Indemnity Mutual Marine Insurance Co* [1895] 1 QB 836; 2 QB 380.
60 *Lawther v Black* (1900) 6 Com Cas 5.
61 See *Moran v Uzielli* [1905] 2 KB 555.
62 (1899) 4 Com Cas 223 at pp 226–227.
63 [1905] 2 KB 555 at p 558.

Double insurance

The major difficulty in this area of law lies with the principle against double insurance. Any outlay incurred by a shipowner before the commencement of the risk, whether for repairs of permanent fixtures or fittings, or for the purchase of stores and provisions, or for port charges, is either represented by some part of the value of the ship or is defrayed out of freight. Thus, the same item may be insured twice over, first, in the policy on ship, and then on disbursements or freight and disbursements, as the case may be. This problem of duplicity arose in *The Gunford Case*[64] where the owners, in addition to a policy on ship, effected a valued honour policy on disbursements. The House of Lords held that, as some of the payments consisting of current working expenses were also covered by the insurance on gross freight, and some of the expenses consisting of repair costs, outfit, and insurance premium on hull were also covered by their policy on ship and materials, there was over-insurance by double insurance. In the circumstances, the owners were not allowed recovery for any sum in excess of the indemnity allowed by law.

In determining whether there is duplicity of coverage, it is suggested that s 16 (on insurable value) should be borne in mind. In an unvalued policy, the insurable value of the subject-matter insured is taken as that at the commencement of the risk. Outlay incurred before the commencement of the risk would probably offend the principle of double insurance, for any expense incurred in enhancing the value of the ship would have been included in the insurable value of the subject-matter insured. It is difficult to say the same of outlay expended after the commencement of the risk.

Disbursements Warranty Clause

The decision of *The Gunford Case* has led to the introduction of the 'Disbursements Warranty' clause under which an assured is allowed to take out, *inter alia*, additional insurance on disbursements. The amount of such ancillary insurances is limited to the percentages specified in the clause.[65]

Institute Time Clauses – Hulls Disbursements and Increased Value Clauses (total loss only, including excess liabilities)

The above Institute Clauses are the facility for effecting an insurance on disbursements (or increased value). It is to be noted that this insurance is ancillary to the hull insurance, and recovery under it is dependent on a total loss of the ship.

Whether the words 'Total loss only' refer to a total loss of the ship or the subject-matter insured is unclear. Historically, however, policies on disbursements were almost invariably expressed to be 'free from average'

---

64 [1911] AC 529, HL.

65 See cl 22 of the ITCH(95) and cl 20 of IVCH(95) which also limit the amount that may be insured on freight.

which means that it is against total loss only. Further, indemnity under disbursements policies has always been in the past made payable only in the event of the vessel being settled under the hull policy as for a total (actual or constructive) loss of the ship.

SEAMEN'S WAGES

Historically, the law of most maritime countries had debarred seamen from insuring their wages. It was thought that if they were allowed such a privilege, they might be tempted not to exert themselves to the utmost for the preservation of the voyage. The old adage 'freight is the mother of wages' was obviously framed to promote this principle. If no freight was earned, there would not be a fund from which wages could be paid out.

With the abandonment of this harsh rule in 1854, upon which freight ceased to be the mother of wages, seamen became entitled to claim wages even in the event of the loss of ship. The employer became statutorily bound to pay wages up until the time of the loss. But even then, a seaman could still suffer a pecuniary loss, for he would have earned wages for the remainder of the voyage, or the period of time for which he was engaged, had the ship not been lost.

Seamen's wages fall within the category of 'pecuniary benefit' of s 3(2)(b). The earning of their wages is dependent on the well-being of 'insurable property', that is, the ship, which is endangered by the exposure to maritime perils. Further, s 11 expressly acknowledges that, 'the master or any member of the crew of a ship has an insurable interest in respect of his wages'.

SHAREHOLDER

Whether a shareholder of, for example, a shipping company may take out a marine policy to insure his interest in a particular adventure undertaken by a ship or ships of the company in which he holds shares, upon which profit is to be earned, and on which the value of his share is dependent, is a question which needs to be explored.

Though this may not be a matter of daily or frequent occurrence, it is nonetheless a legal issue not just of academic interest, as it could well arise in the case of a single-ship company or in the particular instance when the value of the shares in a company is critically dependent on the success or failure of an important enterprise or adventure involving great risks and uncertainty. If the stakes are high, a prudent shareholder would surely wish to protect his interest by taking out a policy of insurance. The crucial question is whether, legally, it is possible to do so by a marine policy of insurance.

First, it has to be emphasised that a non-marine case, *Macaura v Northern Assurance Co Ltd*,[66] has firmly established that a shareholder does not own or possess any propriety rights in the assets belonging to the company in which he holds shares. Thus, as a shareholder of a shipping company does not have an

---

66   [1925] AC 619.

insurable interest in the ship(s) owned by the company, he cannot take out a policy upon them. This authority, however, does not answer the above question. Some light on the subject is shed in a pair of old cases both arising out of the laying of the Atlantic telegraph cable in 1857–58. Though conflicting, they provide some insight as to how the matter may be argued, if not resolved.

In *Wilson v Jones*,[67] it was held that such an interest as described above is insurable, provided that the subject-matter insured is described with clarity. In a methodical fashion, the first question raised by Mr Justice Willes was, 'what was the subject-matter insured?' He observed that, as drafted, the policy was not an insurance on the cable, 'but on the interest which the plaintiff had in the success of the adventure'. As shareholder, he had an interest in the profits to be made by the company, for the value of his share was dependent upon the amount of profit the company was to make.

Mr Justice Blackburn, on the other hand, applying the well-known test framed by Mr Justice Lawrence in *Barclays v Cousins*,[68] which was later amplified in *Lucena v Craufurd*,[69] came to the conclusion that:[70]

> 'He was interested in a company which was about to lay down a cable across the Atlantic. If that event happened, there can be no doubt the owner of shares in the company would be better off; if it did not happen, there can be no doubt his position would be worse off. It follows, then, equally without a doubt, that if by proper words the parties have entered into a contract of insurance for that interest, the policy is good.'

Such a policy, according to Mr Justice Blackburn, resembles an insurance on profit, which is always insurable, with the proviso that it has to be 'endangered by the exposure of insurable property to maritime perils'. One of the arguments raised, but which was rejected, was that in the case of insurance on profits upon goods, the goods from which the profits were to be earned must actually be on board, and subject to the risks insured against. The profits here, it was said, must arise from the shares, which, not being on board, cannot be physically at risk. The line of this argument, it is submitted, could be taken one step further: the value of the shares is in turn dependent on the safety of the adventure. Is this one step too remote?

If the subject-matter insured is considered as 'profit', it falls squarely within the wording of s 3(2)(b) under 'profit' and 'pecuniary benefit'. The next query which then arises is: Is the profit 'endangered by the exposure of insurable property to maritime perils'? By s 3(2)(a) 'insurable property' refers to any ship, goods or other moveables which are exposed to maritime perils. A cable would fall within the term 'moveable' which is defined as any 'moveable tangible property ...'. In relation to the specific question raised, the insurable property which is at risk to maritime perils would be the ship.

---

67   (1867) LR 2 Exch 139.

68   (1802) 2 East 544.

69   (1806) 2 B & PNR 269 at p 301, HL.

70   (1867) LR 2 Exch 139 at p 151.

It could be said that what the shareholder is insuring in such a case is not the ship, goods or moveables belonging to the company, but the success of the adventure. In this sense, it is no different from an insurance on freight the earning of which is likewise dependent on (the delivery of) goods and/or the well-being of the ship. In terms of the fact that it is the safety of the adventure which is insured, it is analogous to the concept propounded by *The Sanday Case* discussed earlier.[71]

It is submitted that there is no principle in law preventing the subscription of such an insurance. Provided that the policy is clearly drafted, there is no reason why a shareholder should not be allowed to protect his interest by taking out such a policy. The only authority which could be used against this argument is the case of *Paterson v Harris*,[72] which has to be distinguished on the ground that the policy in question was not drafted with such clarity and precision as in the case of *Wilson v Jones*. In *Paterson v Harris*, the court held that:[73] '... on a true construction of this policy, the underwriters contract to indemnify the owner of that share against any loss arising to his interest in the cable ...'. The policy was, in effect, an insurance on 'moveables', property belonging to a third party, the Atlantic Telegraph Co. Thus, it would neither be fair nor proper to cite *Paterson v Harris* as the authority for laying down the rule that a shareholder can never insure his interest in the shares of a company, the value of which is reliant on the success of a particular marine adventure undertaken by that company.

LIABILITY TO A THIRD PARTY

A shipowner may incur liability to a third party arising from his interest in or responsibility for insurable property. He could be made liable to pay large sums of money to a third party in consequence of loss of life, injury to persons, or damage to property caused by the improper use of the vessel. If he wishes to be indemnified for third party liabilities, he must effect insurance specifically covering such risks. The validity of such a form of insurance is recognised not only by s 3(2)(c) of the Act but also by s 506 Merchant Shipping Act 1894.

The most glaring example of a third party liability that springs to mind is that arising from a collision. This is specifically covered by the Institute Hulls Clauses in a clause known as the '3/4ths collision liability', sometimes referred to as the 'running down clause'.[74]

If further illustration be required reference should be made to the case of *Oceanic Steam Navigation Co v Evans*,[75] where the owner of a wrecked vessel and a salvage company had jointly effected a policy to protect them from claims that the Harbour Commissioners might chose to levy against them. The salvors did not complete the work of removing the wreck to the satisfaction of the commissioners, who then charged the owners with the cost of buoying and lighting the wreck, and

---

71 See above.

72 (1861) 1 B & S 336; 30 LJQB 354.

73 *Ibid*, at p 355.

74 See Chapter 13.

75 (1934) 50 Ll L Rep 1, CA.

of certain removal costs. The owners succeeded in recovering the charges which they had to pay to the commissioners.

Third party liability which is outside the scope of the standard hulls Clauses is usually covered by mutual P & I Associations.

CHAPTER 4

TIME AND VOYAGE POLICIES

A contract of insurance may be for a period of time, for a voyage, or for both time and voyage. Where the subject-matter is insured for a fixed period of time, the policy is called a 'time policy,' and where it is insured 'at and from' or 'from' one place to another or others, it is called a 'voyage policy'.[1] The purpose of this chapter is to examine the rules, and in particular, the provisions in the Act and clauses in the ITCH(95), the IVCH(95) and the ICC pertaining to the duration and scope of those policies. The terms of a time policy will be discussed in Part A and a voyage policy in Part B.

A – TIME POLICY

A DEFINITE PERIOD OF TIME

A time policy is, according to s 25, a policy which insures the subject-matter for a 'definite' period of time. A specific date for the commencement and termination of the risk must be stated in the policy. To avoid uncertainty, the hour for the commencement and termination of the insurance policy should also be specified, but if there is no such provision, it is generally understood that a day starts from 0000 and ends at 2400.

A time policy may simply specify two days as the time the period is to begin and end, for example, from 20 September to 20 February. In *Scottish Metropolitan Assurance Co Ltd v Stewart*,[2] Mr Justice Rowlatt was asked to decide whether those two days were included in the period. He was clear that there was no technical rule of construction to be applied and the words must be construed in accordance with the intention of the parties as it could be gathered from the circumstances of the case. In his view, when two days are nominated, both days are included in the period. Thus, an insurance expressed to run from 20 September included the whole day of 20 September.

If the policy is made in Great Britain, it is generally accepted that, unless the policy otherwise provides, Greenwich Mean Time[3] (not the time where the ship may be at the time of loss) applies, subject to the Summer Time Act 1972.[4]

There is now no statutory limit on the period of time which may be insured under a time policy; in practice, time policies on hull are generally issued for 12 months.[5]

---

1   Section 25(1).
2   (1923) 39 TLR 497, KBD.
3   Now known as the 'UTC' (Universal Time Co-ordinated).
4   Sections 9 and 23(3) Interpretation Act 1978.
5   Section 25(2) which laid down the rule that a time policy for more than 12 months was invalid was repealed by the Finance Act 1959.

Time policy with an extension or cancellation clause

The most recent case which has queried whether a policy with specified dates for the commencement and termination of the risk, but incorporating an extension or cancellation clause, was still to be regarded as a policy for time is *Compania Maritime San Basilio SA v Oceanus Mutual Underwriting Association (Bermuda) Ltd, The Eurysthenes*.[6] In this case, the club's rule stated that the policy was for a year, but with the entry that the policy was 'to remain in force until expiry or cancellation'. It was argued by the shipowner that as it continued indefinitely until determined by one side or the other, the insurance was not for a 'definite period of time' within the meaning of s 25 of the Act. Lord Denning MR had no doubt whatsoever that it was sufficiently specified, '... even though that period is determinable on notice, and even though the assurance will be renewed or continued automatically at the end of the period, unless determined; or will continue under a continuation clause'. In similar tone, Lord Justice Roskill's comments were:[7]

> '... a policy for a period of time ... does not cease to be a time policy as defined merely because that period of time may thereafter be extended or abridged pursuant to one of the policy's contractual provisions ... In my view the word "definite" was added to emphasise the difference between a period of time measured by time and a period of time measured by the duration of a voyage.'

Time policy with a geographical limit

A policy for a definite period of time but with a clause specifying that the policy will only remain in force whilst traversing within a certain geographical limit is nonetheless a time policy. This was the ruling in the Australian case of *Wilson v Boag*,[8] where the policy under consideration was for a period of four months, but with a clause that it will only remain in force 'within a radius of fifty miles'. During a voyage when the vessel was taken outside the 50-mile perimeter, she became disabled, and salvage charges were incurred which the plaintiff now sought to recover from their insurers. The Supreme Court of New South Wales held that the policy was not a voyage but 'a time policy in which is contained a limitation of the liability of the insurer to loss sustained while the launch is within a defined geographical area'. In each case, it is essentially a question of the interpretation of the terms of the policy.

Such a policy being for time is unaffected by the rules relating to a change of voyage, deviation, or delay. Thus, the fact that the insured vessel may have commenced on a voyage to a destination outside the limits is irrelevant: provided that the loss occurs within the prescribed geographical limit, it is recoverable.[9]

---

6 [1977] 1 QB 49 at p 65, CA.

7 *Ibid*, at p 73.

8 [1956] 2 Lloyd's Rep, 564.

9 But the position would be different if such a cl was considered as a warranty: for a fuller discussion on warranties relating to geographical limits, see Chapter 7.

THE NAVIGATION CLAUSE

The aim of cll 1.1, 1.2 and 1.3 of the above clause of the ITCH(95) is to clarify that the insurance shall remain in force in spite of the occurrence of any of the listed contingencies.[10] Clause 1.2 and 1.3 to the ITCH(95) are new: the former qualifies cl 1.1 in relation to contracts for towage and pilotage services, whilst the latter relates to the use of helicopters for the transportation of personnel supplies and equipment to and/or from the Vessel. Clauses 1.1 to 1.4, which are relevant to the question of the duration of cover, will be discussed here, whereas cl 1.5, concerning scrapping voyages and the valuation of the vessel which is to be scrapped, will be discussed elsewhere.[11]

'At all times'

The purpose of cl 1.1 of the ITCH(95) (and of the IVCH(95)) is to confirm that the insured vessel is, subject to the provisions of the insurance, covered 'at all times'. It then proceeds to point out that the vessel is covered even whilst she is sailing or navigating:

- with or without pilots;
- to go on trial trips; and
- to assist and tow vessels or craft in distress.

Towage and salvage warranty

Having clarified that the policy shall remain in force during such events, cl 1 then proceeds to provide exceptions, in terms of a warranty, to the rule in respect to matters relating to towage: it is warranted that the vessel shall not:

- be towed, except as is customary or to the first safe port or place when in need of assistance, or
- undertake towage or salvage services under a contract previously arranged by the assured and/or owners and/or managers and/or charterers.

The clause also states that it 'shall not exclude customary towage in connection with loading and discharging'.

Except for customary towage, or towage to the first *safe* port or place[12] when the vessel is in need of assistance, it is a breach of a warranty for the insured vessel to be towed. It is also a breach of warranty for the insured vessel to undertake towage or salvage service under a previously arranged contract. Customary towage in connection with loading or discharging operations is specifically excluded from cl 1.1. This means that even though such operations may involve towage, nevertheless, the policy continues to remain in force.

---

10 Clause 1.1 of the ITCH(95) and cl 1.1 of IVCH(95); and cl 1.4 of the ITCH(95) and cl 1.2 of the IVCH(95), are identical.

11 Clauses 1.4 and 1.5 of the ITCH(95) were previously numbered as cll 1.2 and 1.3 of the ITCH(83).

12 It is not the first port, but the first safe port which may not necessarily be the nearest port in terms of mileage.

It is to be noted that the new cl 1.2 of the ITCH(95) has added another exception to the general rule regarding contracts for towage and pilotage services. It is envisaged by cl 1.2 that an assured may be obliged to enter into contracts for towage or pilotage services by reason of established local law or practice. Such contracts shall not prejudice the insurance even though their terms may not be favourable to the assured, who may have entered into a contract in which he has agreed to limit or except the liability of the pilots and/or tugs and/or towboats and/or their owners.

Couched in terms of a warranty, reference has to made to s 33(3) which spells out the legal effects of a breach. Though the insured vessel is covered 'at all times' the cover is stated to be 'subject to the provisions of this insurance'. As the warranty is a provision of the insurance, it becomes clear that the insured vessel will not be covered by the policy in the event of its breach. According to s 33(3), which has now to be read in the light of the case of *The Good Luck*,[13] the insurer would be 'discharged [now automatically discharged] from liability as from the date of the breach of the warranty'.

The use of helicopters

The use of helicopters for certain limited purposes – for the transportation of personnel, supplies and equipment – is covered by the new cl 1.3. The expression 'personnel' is likely to cause problems; whether it includes (besides crew members) the transportation of surveyors, engineers, and doctors to and/or from the vessel is unclear. The word 'supplies' is general enough to include medical supplies, food, provisions and stores.

Loading and discharging operations at sea

The loading and discharging of cargo at sea from or into another vessel are dangerous operations. Transhipment of cargo into smaller vessels has become increasingly common, and underwriters are not prepared to take the additional risks involved in such operations without making the assured pay an additional premium. Clause 1.4 of the ITCH(95) (cl 1.2 of the ITCH(83)) provides that:[14]

'In the event of the Vessel being employed in trading operations which entail cargo loading or discharging at sea from or into another vessel ... no claim shall be recoverable under this insurance for loss of or damage to the Vessel or liability to any other vessel arising from such loading or discharging operations, including whilst approaching, lying alongside and leaving, unless previous notice that the Vessel is to be employed in such operations has been given to the Underwriters and any amended terms of cover and any additional premium required by them have been agreed.'

The use of the word 'trading' connotes a sense of routine or regularity: it implies that if loading or discharging at sea from or into another vessel is a one-off operation, or is carried out in an emergency, cl 1.4 will not apply.

13 [1991] 2 Lloyd's Rep 191, HL.
14 In the 1969 version of the ITCH, it was unofficially known as the 'mothership clause'.

Loss of or damage to the insured vessel

Clause 1.4 is concerned not only with the loss of or damage to the insured vessel but also with 'liability to any other vessel arising from such loading or discharging operations'. First, it is to be noted that any physical damage suffered by the insured vessel resulting from such an operation is clearly not recoverable. No provision, however, has been made for general average contribution and salvage which the assured may have to incur as a result of such an operation. As these claims are generally preferred as a part of the claim for the loss of or damage to the insured vessel, they are likely also to be excluded.

Liability to any other vessel

Not only is the damage sustained by the insured vessel not recoverable, but the liability of the assured to 'any other vessel' is also not covered. It is submitted that the word 'liability', referring to third party liability in this context, is wide enough to exclude cover for liability in respect of:

- damage sustained by any other vessel;
- loss of or damage to the property on board any other vessel;[15] and
- loss of life of persons on board any other vessel, arising from such loading or discharging operations.

The word 'liability' is general enough to include claims for loss of hire, general average, and salvage. However, should the damage suffered by the insured vessel and the 'liability' incurred to any other vessel arise as result of a *collision* with any other vessel, then the application of the 3/4ths Collision Liability clause has to be considered. As a general rule, the owner of the insured vessel has a right to recover from his insurers under the said clause, 3/4ths of his liability to the third party.[16] However, it would appear that, in spite of the applicability of the 3/4ths Collision Liability clause, cl 1.4 would not, unless notice has been given and the payment of an additional premium has been agreed, allow recovery for such a loss. As there is no paramount clause, it is unclear which provision, cl 1.4 or the 3/4ths Collision Liability clause, is to prevail. It could be argued that the matter may be resolved by applying the rule of proximate cause.[17] However, the term 'arising from' (and not proximately caused by) used in cl 1.4 may be construed as an indication that it is wide enough to cover the circumstance even when a collision is involved. If it were not for cl 1.4, such a loss would have been covered by the 3/4ths Collision Liability clause.

---

15 But see K Goodacre, *Institute Time Clauses Hulls* (1983, 1st edn), p 2, where it is pointed out that, '... the exclusion does not embrace loss of or damage to property on the other vessel, which can, of course, be cargo intended for transfer to the vessel insured'. But the wording of cl 1.4 of the ITCH(95) (cl 1.2 of the ITCH(83)) has made it clear that cargo loading or discharging at sea both 'from or into another vessel' are covered.

16 Whether cargo damaged in the process of being transferred from the other vessel onto the insured vessel can still be described as property 'on' the other vessel for the purpose of the 3/4ths Collision Liability cl is, of course, another question altogether.

17 Section 55.

THE CONTINUATION CLAUSE

The fact that a policy may contain a continuation clause will not, provided that a definite period is specified in the policy, prevent it from being a time policy. This was made clear by Lord Denning MR in *Compania Maritima San Basilo SA v Oceanus Mutual Underwriting Association (Bermuda) Ltd, The Eurysthenes*[18] who remarked that '... in any ordinary time policy, the Institute Time Clauses (Hulls) include a continuation provision in cl 4 [now cl 2] but that does not prevent the policy being a time policy'. The new cl 2 of the ITCH(95) states:

'Should the Vessel at the expiration of this insurance be at sea and in distress or missing, she shall, provided previous notice be given to the Underwriters prior to the expiration of this insurance, be held covered until arrival at the next port in good safety, or if in port and in distress until the Vessel is made safe, at a *pro rata* monthly premium.'

Under the new clause, the vessel is only held covered if, at the expiry of the policy, the vessel is:

- at sea *and* in distress or missing; or
- in port *and* in distress.

Simply being at sea, in distress, or at a port of refuge is no longer sufficient to attract the new held covered clause. Whether at sea or in port at the expiry of the policy, the vessel must now also be in distress before she would be held covered. In any event, she is held covered until her arrival at the *next* port in good safety or, if in port, until made safe. Under the ITCH(83), she would be been held covered 'to her port of destination'. By the new cl 2, to be held covered, the assured has to give notice to the underwriters 'prior to the expiration' of the insurance.

AUTOMATIC TERMINATION

A policy may either expire naturally at the specified time, or terminate prematurely as a consequence of an event spelt out in cl 5, the termination clause of the ITCH(95). Clause 5.1. states that, 'Unless the Underwriters agree to the contrary in writing', the insurance will terminate automatically at the time of:

- change of the Classification Society of the vessel; or
- change, suspension, discontinuance, withdrawal or expiry of her class therein; or
- any of the Classification Society's periodic surveys becoming overdue, unless an extension of time for such survey be agreed by the Classification Society.[19]

The importance of cl 5 cannot be over-stated: in bold type, it commences with a paramount clause that: 'This clause shall prevail notwithstanding any provision whether written typed or printed in this insurance inconsistent therewith'.

---

18   [1977] 1 QB 49 at p 65, CA.

19   This part of the cl is new.

Clause 5.1 of the ITCH(95), which has widened the scope of the old cl 4 of the ITCH(83), has, however, to be read with cl 4.1.1 (the Classification Clause) which is another new addition to the ITCH(95). As cl 4.1.1 is related to cl 5.1, it is necessary to examine this cl here.

Change of Classification Society

The status of a Classification Society (and of a vessel's class) is, of course, a matter of great importance to underwriters, for the safety and seaworthiness of ships is to a very large degree dependent not only upon the vessel's class, but also upon the standing and reputation of the Classification Society with which she is classed. The new cl 4.1.1 and cl 5.1 of the ITCH(95), both concerned with matters relating to Classification Society, may, on first reading, appear to cover the same ground, but, in fact, they impose different responsibilities.

It would be appropriate to begin this part of the discussion with a few comments on the new cl 4.1.1 of the ITCH(95). Before the introduction of this clause, the assured, owners and managers virtually had a free hand to class the vessel with any Classification Society of their choice, and unilaterally to change Classification Society during the currency of the insurance if they so wish. The purpose of cl 4.1.1 is to impose a duty on the assured, owners and managers to ensure that the vessel is classed with a Classification Society agreed by the underwriters at the inception of, and throughout the period of, the insurance. The words 'throughout the period' clarify that once an agreement has been reached, any subsequent change of Classification Society would also require the approval of the underwriters.

Effect of an unauthorised change of Classification Society

Clause 5.1, which simply refers to a 'change of Classification Society', has now to be read with cl 4.1.1. Though the word 'change' is unqualified, obviously it has to be construed in the light of the new cl 4.1.1. This necessarily means that cl 5.1 must refer to a change, in breach of cl 4.1.1, occurring without the agreement of the underwriters.

Should the assured, owners or managers at any time, without the consent of the underwriters, change Classification Society, they would be in breach not only of cl 4.1.1, but also of cl 5.1. However, the effects of a breach of these clauses are different: whereas a breach of cl 4.1.1. would 'discharge' the underwriters from liability as from the date of breach, a breach of cl 5.1 would automatically terminate the insurance. Thus, one could validly ask which cl is to take precedence. In this regard, the paramount cl to cl 5, which has made it patently clear that cl 5 is to prevail in the event of a conflict, would have to be invoked.

The effect of an automatic termination of the insurance may be seen to be more serious than that of a discharge from liability. And even if one is to construe cl 4.1.1 as a warranty, and confer upon it the right of automatic discharge in accordance with Lord Goff's interpretation of the effect of a breach of a warranty in *The Good Luck*,[20] it would appear that the effect of an automatic termination is still much more serious: unlike a discharge from liability, a termination – *a fortiori*, an automatic termination – brings the contract to an end.[21] The word 'automatic' is used, presumably, to stress the fact that the termination is not dependent upon any decision or action to be taken by the insurer to treat the contract or the insurance as at an end: it is automatically brought to an end by the repudiatory breach committed by the assured.

It is perhaps necessary to point out that, although a breach of a warranty does not bring the contract to an end, nevertheless, as perceived by Lord Goff,[22] for all practical purposes the effect is the same as if it was brought to an end. Thus, whether the effect of the breach be a discharge under cl 4.1.1, an automatic discharge under Lord's Goff's interpretation of a breach of warranty, or an automatic termination of the contract under cl 5, the net result is the same: the underwriter is freed from liability as from the date of breach. The contract is neither void nor voidable *ab initio*; all rights and liabilities accrued before the breach will continue to be enforceable.[23]

Clauses 4.1.1 and 5.1 are similar in two respects: both clauses are prepared to defer the discharge of liability in the case of cl 4.1.1, and the automatic termination in cl 5.1, until the vessel arrives at her next port. Further, both clauses state that the breach may be waived by the underwriters in writing.

Change, suspension, discontinuance, withdrawal or expiry of her class

It is significant to note that here we are not concerned with a change of Classification Society, but a change of class within 'that Society', meaning, when read with cl 4.1.1, the Classification Society which the underwriters have agreed that the vessel be classed.

A change, suspension, discontinuance, withdrawal or expiry of class could, according to cl 5.1, result from a loss or damage which is:

1 covered by cl 6 of the insurance[24] or which would be covered by an insurance of the vessel subject to current Institute War and Strikes Clauses Hulls – Time; or

2 not covered by cl 6 or which would not be covered by an insurance of the vessel subject to the current Institute War and Strikes Clauses Hull – Time.

In the case of the former, the assured could prevent the automatic termination by obtaining the prior approval of the Classification Society before she sails from her next port. But in the case of the latter, there does not appear to

---

20 [1991] 2 Lloyd's Rep 191, HL.

21 A distinction which was strenuously emphasised by Lord Goff in *The Good Luck* [1991] 2 Lloyd's Rep 191, HL.

22 *Ibid*, at p 202.

23 Though this point is not made perfectly clear in cl 5.1, nonetheless, the fact that the termination of the contract may be deferred until the vessel's arrival at her next port implies that the termination takes effect either from the date of breach or the later date.

24 Clause 6 of the ITCH(95) states the insured perils.

be any reprieve: the insurance terminates automatically, with or without the prior approval of the Classification Society, when the vessel arrives at her next port of call. This type of change is voluntary and, in a sense, inexcusable, because it was not caused or brought about by an insured peril. This, perhaps, explains why there is no provision for the obtaining of prior approval for a change, suspension, discontinuance, withdrawal or expiry of class, as is available in the first case.

A change of class is also covered by cl 4.1.1. A failure, for whatever reason, to maintain the vessel's class with the agreed particular Classification Society would constitute a breach of cl 4.1.1. The question which now arises is: which clause, 4.1.1 or 5.1, regulates the effect of such a breach? Unlike cl 5.1, clause 4.1.1 does not give any regard to the cause of the failure of the vessel to maintain her class. A failure to maintain the vessel's class with the agreed Society would discharge the underwriters from liability. But if cl 5.1 is to prevail, then it is necessary to inquire whether the change, suspension, discontinuance or withdrawal of her class has resulted from loss or damage covered by cl 6 of the ITCH(95) or by the IWSC(H). If it has resulted from such a cause, the automatic termination shall only operate if the vessel sails from her next port without the prior approval of the Classification Society. But if the change was for a reason other than the one stated above, then the policy would terminate automatically.

In the recent case of *Prudent Tankers Ltd SA v The Dominion Insurance Co Ltd, The 'Caribbean Sea'*,[25] the rules of a classification society on a matter relating to the ship's class were placed under scrutiny. The vessel was insured under the American Institute hulls clauses which provided that the policy would automatically terminate 'if the Classification Society of the Vessel or her class therein be changed, cancelled or withdrawn', a clause not dissimilar to cl 5.1. By the rules of the Classification Society in question, it was laid down that: 'in the event of grounding or damage to hull … the classification certificate loses its validity'. During the course of a voyage, the master formed the opinion that the vessel had touched the bottom, but made no inquiries as to the possibility of any damage. As the incident appeared trivial to him, he did not inform the Society of the incident but merely entered a protest when the vessel arrived at the next port. Subsequently, she sank as a result of the entry of sea water into her engine room.

The court found that the vessel did in fact take the ground, but the grounding did not have any causative effect on the casualty. The insurers argued that by reason of the said clause, the policy had automatically terminated at the time of the grounding. To this, Mr Justice Goff, as he then was, drew the distinction between a loss of the validity of the certificate and a loss of class. The loss of the validity of the classification certificate did not amount to a 'withdrawal of class'. As there was neither a change, cancellation nor withdrawal of class – matters which require a positive action from the Society – the defence failed.

---

25   [1980] 1 Lloyd's Rep 338.

Overdue periodic survey

It is also to be noted that by the new addition to cl 5.1, the cover would also terminate automatically if the Classification Society periodic survey was to become overdue. Unless an extension of time for such a survey can be agreed by the Classification Society, the insurance terminates automatically.

Change of ownership, flag, transfer to new management, or charter on a bareboat basis, or requisition for title or use of the vessel

Clause 5.2 of the ITCH(95) refers to ownership and matters relating to the use of the ship:

- change, voluntary or otherwise, in the ownership or flag;
- transfer to new management;
- charter on a bareboat basis;
- requisition for the title or use of the vessel.

Its primary objective is to protect the insurer from material changes in the risk on significant and fundamental matters such as ownership, class, flag, management and the use of the vessel.

The occurrence of any one of the above events, voluntary or otherwise, would automatically terminate the insurance at the time of change. The automatic termination, however, may be deferred if:

- the vessel has cargo on board and has already sailed from her port of loading or is at sea in ballast; and
- a request for its deferment is made.

The automatic termination is deferred 'whilst the Vessel continues on her planned voyage, until arrival at final port of discharge if with cargo, or at a port of destination if in ballast'.

Clause 5.2 also provides that in the event of a requisition for title or use of the vessel 'without the prior execution of a written agreement by the Assured', the automatic termination of the policy will be deferred, whether the vessel is at sea or in port, until 15 days after the requisition. The corollary of this is that, if the vessel is requisitioned with the prior execution of a written agreement by the assured, the policy would terminate automatically without any period of grace, whether the vessel is at sea or in port. As the above general ground for deferment is also applicable to requisition for title or use of the vessel, it could be argued that, if its terms are complied with, the automatic termination could be deferred.

Return of premium

Clause 5 of the ITCH(95) has incorporated a new cl relating to a return of premium in the event of an automatic termination. It states that:

'A *pro rata* daily net return of premium shall be made provided that a total loss of the Vessel, whether by insured perils or otherwise, has not occurred during the period covered by this insurance or any extension thereof.'

The 'period covered by this insurance' could mean either the period intended to be covered by the insurance or the period from the commencement of the risk right up to the time of the automatic termination or any extension thereof. It is submitted that the words 'extension thereof' refer to the extensions mentioned in cl 5, where the automatic termination is deferred:

- until the vessel arrives at the next port in the event of a breach of cl 5.1; or
- until the vessel arrives at the final port of discharge if with cargo, or port of destination if in ballast, in the case of cl 5.2; or
- for 15 days after such requisition whether the vessel is at sea or in port in the event of requisition for title or use.

It is submitted that, read as a whole, it must refer to the period covered by the insurance from the inception to the time when the automatic or the deferred automatic termination takes place. The provision could for clarity have been better worded.

B – VOYAGE POLICY

A voyage policy is defined by s 25 as one where the subject-matter is insured 'at and from' or 'from' one place to another, or others. It is to be noted that s 25 is of general application, and, therefore, a voyage policy may be effected upon ship, goods or freight.

A policy on ship is nowadays almost invariably insured for a period of time, but there is nothing in law to prevent an assured from taking out a voyage or a mixed policy on ship. Time polices are more straightforward in the sense that there can be little doubt as to when a policy commences and terminates: as time and date are specifically set out, there can be no uncertainty or confusion as to the precise moment when the policy begins and ends. Furthermore, problems associated with the implied condition as to commencement of risk, change of voyage, delay, and deviation cannot arise in a time policy.

To avoid confusion, this study on voyage policies will be divided into two parts: the first will deal exclusively with a voyage policy on ship, and the second with goods which are nearly always insured for a voyage. Topics such as when a voyage policy attaches and terminates, and events which can cause a voyage policy to come to a premature end, will be discussed.

VOYAGE POLICY ON SHIP

As can be seen from the above definition, any subject-matter may be insured for a voyage 'from' or 'at and from' a particular place. This has to be set out in the Policy Schedule under the heading, 'Voyage or Period of Insurance'. Unless the policy otherwise provides, the words 'from' and 'at and from' will have the meaning given to them by rr 2 and 3 of the Rules for Construction. A voyage policy on hull may be effected in the form of the IVCH(83) or the IVCH(95).

'From'

When a ship is insured 'from' a particular place, 'the risk does not attach until the ship starts on the voyage insured' from that particular place. Whether a ship has or has not commenced on a particular voyage is in each case a question of fact. The act of quitting her moorings or breaking ground is generally recognised as an act signifying the commencement of a voyage.

This alone, however, is not sufficient to trigger the attachment of the policy. For r 2 to operate, she must start on the 'voyage insured'. This necessarily means that moving the ship from one part of the port to another will not count as starting on the voyage insured, nor does the moving out of port for a purpose other than for starting on the 'voyage insured'.[26] For the risk to attach, the physical act must be accompanied with the intention to start on the voyage insured.

Alteration of port of departure

Needless to say, if a ship is to sail from a port other than the named port, the risk does not attach.[27] This is clarified in s 43 as follows:

> 'Where the place of departure is specified by the policy, and the ship instead of sailing from that place sails from any other place, the risk does not attach.'

Sailing for a different destination

The same result would arise if the ship is to start on a voyage to a destination other than that contemplated by the policy.[28] In this instance, s 44 would prevent the attachment of risk. Section 44 states:[29]

> 'When the destination is specified in the policy, and the ship, instead of sailing for that destination, sails for any other destination, the risk does not attach.'

'At and from'

A ship may be insured 'at and from' a particular place; this is governed by r 3, which envisages two circumstances:

- Rule 3(a) states: 'Where a ship is insured "at and from" a particular place, and she is at that place in good safety when the contract is concluded, the risk attaches immediately'.

- Rule 3(b) states: 'If she be not at that place when the contract is concluded, the risk attaches as soon as she arrives there in good safety, and, unless the

---

26 *Sea Insurance Co v Blogg* [1898] 2 QB 398.

27 See *Way v Modigliani* (1787) 2 Term Rep 30 at p 31; *per* Buller J '... it certainly is not necessary that she should be in port at the time when it attaches, but she must have sailed on the voyage insured, and not on any other'.

28 See *Simon, Israel & Co v Sedgwick* [1893] 1 QB 303, CA and *Wooldridge v Boydell* (1778) 1 Doug KB 16.

29 Section 44 cannot possibly apply to an 'at and from' policy, for the risk would have already attached when the ship is 'at' the particular place. Any change of destination can only arise after the commencement of the risk, in which case s 45 on 'change of voyage' would apply: for a discussion on the law relating to a change of voyage, see below.

policy otherwise provides, it is immaterial that she is covered by another policy for a specified time after arrival'.

In both cases, the crucial moment for determination is 'when the contract is concluded'. According to s 21, a contract is 'deemed to be concluded when the proposal of the assured is accepted by the insurer, whether the policy be then issued or not ...'.

There is a, however, a third situation which is not covered by the Act, namely, that of a ship which has already sailed from the named port at the time when the contract is concluded.

Ship already at named port

The first instance covers the circumstance when the ship is already at the named port, the *terminus a quo*, at the time when the contract is concluded. If the word 'at' is given a literal interpretation, the risk would attach as soon as the ship arrives at the named port.[30]

But a ship well may be 'at' a particular place for a purpose other than for the insured voyage. If, for example, she is at the named port for another voyage or for a purpose (for example, repairs) which is unrelated to the insured voyage, it would be difficult to argue that the policy attaches the moment she arrived at that port.

If the ship is, at the time when the contract is concluded, at the named port for the purpose of sailing on another voyage, s 44 would apply. In such an event, the risk does not attach when a ship sails for a different destination.[31] In the same vein, there is no reason why a policy should attach to a ship which is undergoing preparations (at the particular port), not for the insured voyage but for another voyage. In *Tasker v Cunninghame*,[32] the House of Lords, citing *Lambert v Liddiard*[33] as authority, declared that:

'In the common case where it is "at and from" etc without any special words to restrict the meaning of the word "at", the beginning to load the cargo, or preparing for the voyage, seem to be the principal circumstances to determine the commencement of the risk.'

It is submitted that the keys words here are 'for the voyage', meaning the insured voyage. For the risk to attach, the ship must be at the named port either for or preparing for the insured voyage.

It has been suggested that as the word 'at' is lacking in precision, a presumption could be made that the policy attaches the moment the ship is 'at' that place in good safety. And unless it is rebutted, r 3(a) would apply, and the ship is insured during the whole of her stay at that port. The presumption, Arnould suggests, can always be rebutted with proof of the risk intended to be insured by the parties.[34]

---

30 See *Smith v Surridge* (1801) 4 Esp 25 where the ship was at the named port on the 13th, and the policy was effected on the 15th.

31 See *Simon Israel Co v Sedgwick* [1893] 1 QB 303; 7 Asp MLC 245.

32 (1819) 1 Bligh 87, HL.

33 (1814) 5 Taunt 480; 1 Marsh R 149.

34 Arnould, para 541.

Ship not at the named port

The standard words 'at and from' a particular place do not constitute a warranty or a representation that the ship is actually at the named port when the contract was concluded: this is clarified by s 42. Rule 3(b), however, is specially designed to cater for the event when the ship is not at the named port when the contract is concluded, but is expected to arrive there within a reasonable period of time. Naturally, the policy cannot attach until she arrives there in good safety.

In *Haughton v Empire Marine Insurance Co*,[35] for example, the vessel was damaged by coming into contact with an anchor after entering the harbour and whilst passing over a shoal up to her place of discharge. It was held that the policy attached as soon as the vessel arrived within the port named.

In *Foley v United Fire and Marine Insurance Co of Sydney*,[36] though the insurance was on chartered freight, nevertheless, the principle of law applied therein is equally relevant to a policy on ship. The policy was held to have attached soon after the arrival of the ship at the named port. The fact that the whole of the cargo of the previous voyage was not discharged did not prevent the attachment of the risk. The words 'at and from' (Mauritius), said Kelly CB, 'in their ordinary signification include the whole period the ship was actually at Mauritius'.[37]

Rule 3(b) has expressly declared that 'it is immaterial that she is covered by another policy for a specified time after arrival'. A degree of overlapping could arise, but this is inconsequential.

Ship already sailed from named port

The Act has omitted to cover a third situation, namely, when the ship had already sailed on the insured voyage at the time when the contract was concluded. Whether the policy had attached retrospectively is unclear. If it could be proved that the intention of the parties was to insure her for the voyage on which the ship had already set sail, there is no reason why the policy should not be allowed to attach retrospectively. But whether she would also have to comply with the 'good safety' requirement before she sailed on that voyage is another question which the court could one day be called upon to answer.

Meaning of 'good safety'

For an 'at and from' policy to attach, the ship must not only be 'at' the named port, but must also be there in a state of 'good safety'. This requirement has to be satisfied whether she is already at the named port when the contract is concluded, or arrives there after the contract has been concluded.

---

35   (1866) LR 1 Exch 206.

36   (1870) LR 5 CP 160.

37   *Ibid*, at p 162.

What constitutes 'good safety' is now well settled by cases such as *Parmeter v Cousins*[38] and *Bell v Bell*.[39] In the first case, the ship which was in a leaky condition, unfit to take in a cargo, and was kept afloat only by constant pumping was held not to be in a state of 'good safety'. The standard of 'good safety' is evidently lower than that of seaworthiness. So long as she exists as a ship and is physically capable of lying afloat, she is in good safety. She would still be classified as being in 'good safety' even if she is damaged. She does not even have to be safely moored to meet the requirement.[40]

In *Bell v Bell*,[41] the vessel, though leaky, was able to lie for a month loading in a river. The insurer's defence was to the effect that, as the ship was not in good political safety, having been seized and condemned on her arrival at the named port, the policy did not attach. This was rejected by the court, which held that the policy had attached, for the ship was in a state of good physical safety. The case is authority for the proposition that 'good safety' means good physical, and not political, safety.

Implied condition as to commencement of risk

From the moment a contract of marine insurance for a voyage is concluded, it is expected that 'the voyage insured shall be very shortly commenced, or is, at all events, in the near contemplation of the parties ...'.[42] It is understood by the insurer that the vessel would sail within a reasonable time from the date of the conclusion of the contract. However, the commencement of an insured voyage, whether under a policy 'from' or 'at and from' a particular place, could well be affected by delay. Any excessive delay would naturally vary the risk upon which the insurer has agreed to undertake.

Section 42, therefore, imposes upon the assured the duty to commence the adventure within a reasonable period of time. It applies to all voyage polices regardless of the subject-matter insured. As the wording of section calls for close examination, it would be helpful to cite it here in full:

> 'Where the subject-matter is insured by a voyage policy "at and from" or "from" a particular place, it is not necessary that the ship should be at that place when the contract is concluded, but there is an implied condition that the adventure shall be commenced within a reasonable time, and that if the adventure be not so commenced the insurer may avoid the contract.'

The first part of s 42 establishes the rule that it is not necessary in a 'from' and 'at and from' policy for the ship to be at the particular place when the contract is concluded. In so far as a 'from' policy is concerned, the risk attaches only when she starts on the voyage insured. As regards an 'at and from' policy, the fact that the ship may not be 'at' the particular place when the policy is concluded does not pose any problem, for r 3(b) allows for the risk to attach as soon as she arrives there in good safety.

---

38 (1809) 2 Camp 235.

39 (1810) 2 Camp 475.

40 See *Haughton v The Empire Marine Insurance Co* (1866) LR 1 Ex 206.

41 (1810) 2 Camp 475.

42 *Per* Tindal CJ, *Palmer v Marshall* (1832) 8 Bing 317 at p 318.

The second half of s 42 imposes on all voyage policies the implied condition that the adventure shall be commenced within a reasonable period of time. Before proceeding to examine the scope of this implied condition, it is necessary to point out the difference between a delay in the commencement of the adventure, and a delay arising during the course of the insured voyage; the former is governed by s 42, and the latter by s 48: they refer to different periods in time.

Delay in the attachment of risk and/or in the commencement of voyage

The commencement of the insured voyage in a policy 'from' a particular place could be delayed in either one or both of the following ways. The delay could arise in the course of the ship's (preliminary) voyage to the particular place and/or in the commencement of her insured voyage 'from' that particular place. In either case, the result is the same: there is delay hindering the commencement of the insured voyage 'from' the particular place, resulting in a delay in the attachment of the risk.

In an 'at and from' policy, a ship could encounter delay either during the course of the preliminary voyage to the particular place, and/or delay in the commencement of the insured voyage 'from' the particular place. In other words, a delay could occur either before and/or after the attachment of the risk. In the one case, there is a delay in the attachment of the risk, and in the other, a delay in the commencement of the insured voyage under a policy the risk of which had already attached. In either event, it would result in a delay in the commencement of the insured voyage.[43]

In a pre-statute case, *Mount v Larkins*,[44] Chief Justice Tindal expressed the rationale for the implied condition in the following terms:

'The underwriter has as much right to calculate upon the outward voyage, on which the ship is then engaged, being performed in a reasonable time, and without unnecessary delay, in order that the risk may attach, as he has that the voyage insured shall be commenced within a reasonable time, after the risk has attached. In either case the effect is the same, as to the underwriter who has another risk substituted instead of that which he has insured against; and in both cases, the alteration is occasioned by the wrongful act of the assured himself.'

It appears that, in this regard, no distinction need be made between a policy where the risk has attached and one where it has not. The key issue in each case is whether the delay has brought about a variation of the risk. It has to be emphasised that it is not a question of whether the risk has increased, but that '... the insured has, without necessity, substituted another voyage for that which was insured and, thereby varied the risk which the underwriter took upon himself'.[45]

---

43 See *Mount v Larkins* (1831) 8 Bing 121 at p 122 where the policy, 'at and from Singapore', was concluded on 28 February, but the ship did not arrive at Singapore till 30 March, and did not sail from there on her insured voyage till 3 May. There was delay all round, and Tindal CJ remarked that, 'But what is the difference ... whether this ... unjustifiable delay takes place in the course of the ship's voyage to Singapore, or after the ship is at Singapore ...'.

44 *Ibid.*

45 *Per* Tindal CJ, *Mount v Larkins, ibid.*

The defence of lawful excuse

It is noted that, unlike s 46 on deviation and s 48 on delay arising in the course of the voyage, s 42 does not say anything about lawful excuse. Take, for instance, the case of a ship which is unable, for causes beyond the control of the assured (for example, peril of the seas), to commence the insured voyage within a reasonable period of time. Would the assured be able to plead that, as the commencement of the voyage was delayed for necessary repairs to be effected on the ship, he should be excused?

The words 'without necessity' and the last few words of the above quotation are indeed interesting, for they are capable of being construed as embodying a defence for the assured. The main problem in this area of the law which requires consideration is whether the defence of lawful excuse is available to the assured.

In *De Wolf v The Archangel Maritime Bank Insurance Co Ltd*,[46] Mr Justice Blackburn, who delivered the judgment of the court, took time to explain the above comments made by Chief Justice Tindal, said:

'This may be relied on as an expression of opinion that the delay, if necessary, would not discharge the underwriters. It may be so, where the fact that the vessel is on a preliminary voyage is known and communicated to the underwriter, so as to make that the basis of the contract ...'

Naturally, if the delay or the likelihood of delay is known to the insurer before the contract is concluded, then the implied condition is negatived. The effect of notice, and of waiver, of the delay are both spelt out in s 42(2).[47]

Mr Justice Blackburn then went on to say:

'... there was no communication made to the underwriters as to where the ship was at the time when the policy was made. And we think it, under such circumstances, not material whether the delay which varies the risk was occasioned by the fault or the misfortune of the assured. In either case the risk is equally varied.'

Parliament, of course, if it had wanted, could have easily conferred the assured with the defence of lawful excuse, and inserted the words 'without lawful excuse' (after the word 'if') into s 42, as it had done so for ss 46 and 48.

But having said that, it has to be pointed out that there is a group of cases, decided before the *De Wolf* case, namely, *Smith v Surridge*,[48] *Palmer v Marshall*,[49]

---

46 (1874) LR 9 QB 451 at p 455-456.

47 See *Bah Lias Tobacco & Rubber Estates v Volga Insurance Co Ltd* (1920) 3 Ll L Rep 155 at p 202, KBD in which the insurer who had accepted an additional premium to cover a period during which the loss occurred were precluded from raising the defence of unreasonable delay.

48 (1801) 4 Esp 25, where the insurer was not discharged from liability by reason of the fact that the delay of about ... five months was involuntary; it was necessary for the ship to be repaired.

49 (1832) 8 Bing 318; where the insurer was discharged from liability because the delay was unexplained and not for the purpose of the voyage.

Palmer v Fenning[50] and *Mount v Larkins*,[51] which have made the defence of lawful excuse available to the assured. In *Smith v Surridge*,[52] the insurer was held bound by the contract, as the delay was involuntary; whereas in the remainder of the cases, the insurer was 'discharged' from liability because the delay was 'unaccounted'. There are obviously two points of view under the common law.

If s 42 is based on the ruling of the *De Wolf* case, the latest case on the subject, then there can be no doubt that there is no defence for a breach of the implied condition. Unless it is a case of sheer oversight, the fact that s 42 has omitted to incorporate the defence of lawful excuse goes a long way to support this view.

Legal effect of breach

At one time, there was some suggestion made by the common law that a breach of the implied condition would prevent the attachment of the risk under the policy. Words to the effect that the insurer was 'discharged from liability' were also used. Section 42, however, states that the insurer may 'avoid the contract'. This suggests that, even though the risk may have attached and/or the voyage has commenced, the contract must still be on foot, regardless of the delay. For if the position were otherwise, there would be no need to give the insurer the option of whether to proceed or not to proceed with the contract. Should the latter course of action be adopted, the contract is rendered void *ab initio*. Given this construction, the word 'condition' (as opposed to a 'warranty') appearing in s 42 has been awarded its traditional meaning, as understood in the law of contract, as giving rise to a right (at the election of the innocent party, the insurer) to treat the contract as repudiated.

Change of voyage

A 'change of voyage' is defined in s 45 as:

> 'Where, after the commencement of the risk, the destination of the ship is voluntarily changed from the destination contemplated by the policy ...'

As the section has not made any specific reference either to ship, goods or freight, it must apply to all voyage policies.

The underlying principle of the law on change of voyage was highlighted by the House of Lords in *Tasker v Cunninghame*, where the Lord Chancellor said:[53]

> 'When a ship is insured at and from a given port, the probable continuance of the ship in that port is in the contemplation of the parties to the contract. If the owners, or persons having authority from them, change their intention, and the

---

50   (1833) 9 Bing 460, in which there was no justification whatsoever for the delay. Alderson J (at p 46) said that for a delay to be justifiable it should be 'for the purpose of the voyage such as waiting for a wind, provisions, or the like'.

51   (1831) 8 Bing 121, where the insurer was discharged from the contract because the postponement of the voyage, occasioned by the wrongful act of the assured himself, was unreasonable and unjustified.

52   (1801) 4 Esp 25.

53   (1819) 1 Bligh 87, HL.

ship is delayed in that port for the purpose of altering the voyage and taking in a different cargo, the underwriters run an additional risk if such a change of intention is not to affect the contract.'

Any voyage policy could terminate prematurely because of a 'change of voyage' which has a specific meaning in the law of marine insurance. There are two important parts to the section; the first relates to the words 'after the commencement of the risk', and the second to 'voluntarily changed'.

'After the commencement of the risk'

First, it is pertinent to note that a change of voyage is a different concept altogether from that of sailing for a different destination referred to in s 44. In the case of sailing for another destination, the intention to sail for a destination different from that contemplated by the policy is manifested right from the very beginning when the ship sets sail. As the assured has no intention whatsoever of performing the insured voyage from the very inception, the risk does not attach.

A change of voyage can only arise 'after the commencement of the risk'. In a 'from' policy, the voyage must have started from the particular place named in the policy for the risk to attach. Any alteration of destination arising during the course of the insured voyage would attract s 45. In an 'at and from' policy, the risk must have attached when the ship arrives 'at' the particular place in good time and in good safety before s 45 can apply. In such a circumstance, the determination to change may be made either:

- in the interim period when the ship is 'at' the particular place (from which time the policy attaches) and before she sets sail on the insured voyage; or
- during the course of the insured voyage.

'Voluntarily changed'

To constitute a change of voyage, the destination of the ship must be 'voluntarily changed' by the assured. In other words, any change caused by an Act of God or *force majeure* would not discharge the insurer from liability. This point is illustrated in *Rickards v Forestal Land, Timber and Railways Co Ltd*,[54] where the master of the ship had to comply with an order from the German government to seek refuge in neutral ports or to return to Germany. One of the issues which was raised in the House was whether there was a change of voyage. To this, Lord Porter's response was:

> 'The master's act was both necessitated by moral force and reasonably necessary for the safety of the ship ... There was no voluntary change ... The master was acting, not on his own initiative, but on the orders which ... morally as a good subject he ought not to have resisted ... as the master's action was caused by circumstances beyond his and his employer's control, and was involuntary ... the voyage was not changed within the provisions of section 45 of the Act.'

---

54   [1941] 3 All ER 62 at p 96, HL.

Legal effect of change of voyage

Section 45(2) specifies the legal consequence of a change of voyage as follows:

'Unless the policy otherwise provides, where there is a change of voyage the insurer is discharged from liability as from the time of change, that is to say, as from the time when the determination to change it is manifested; and it is immaterial that the ship may not in fact have left the course of voyage contemplated by the policy when the loss occurs.'

Determination to change

In a somewhat roundabout fashion, the liability of the insurer is, by s 45, fixed at 'as from the time when the determination to change' is manifested. Whether the vessel has or has not actually departed from the course of the voyage contemplated by the policy is irrelevant. It is the mental state of the assured which is to be looked at, and not the actual physical act of change in course. In *Tasker v Cunninghame*,[55] it was argued by the assured that as nothing was done to alter the voyage, and no progress made in unloading the cargo, this was to be considered as resting in mere intention, and the loss must be considered as a loss under the policy. This defence was roundly rejected by the Lord Chancellor, whose reply was:

'Undoubtedly a mere meditated change does not affect a policy. But circumstances are to be taken as evidence of a determination, and what better evidence can we have, than those who were authorised had determined to change the voyage. In my opinion the voyage was abandoned.'

Change of voyage clause

Clause 2 of the IVCH(95), commonly referred to as the 'held covered' clause, states:

'Held covered in case of ... change of voyage ... provided notice be given to the Underwriters immediately after receipt of advices and any amended terms of cover and any additional premium required by them be agreed.'

Such a provision is allowed by s 45(2) by the words, 'Unless the policy otherwise provides'. Naturally, as the case of *Simon Israel Co v Sedgwick*[56] has pointed out, albeit a policy to goods, it is not possible to invoke a 'held covered' clause if the policy had not attached. This again reinforces the principle that a change of voyage can only arise after the risk has attached.

Deviation

Deviation is an important subject not only in marine insurance, but also in the law of contract of affreightment. The line between a deviation and a change of voyage may at first sight appear to be indistinct. In one case, it was said that, 'It is often a nice question on the facts whether an interruption of the voyage amounts to a deviation only or is a change of the voyage'.[57] Thus, it may be helpful at the outset to differentiate them.

---

55 (1819) 1 Bligh 87, HL.

56 [1893] 1 QB 303; 7 Asp MLC 245.

57 *Per* Lord Davey, *Thames & Mersey Marine Insurance Co v Van Laun* [1917] 23 Com Cas 104 at p 111, HL.

Deviation is defined by s 46(1) as follows:

'Where a ship, without lawful excuse, deviates from the voyage contemplated by the policy, the insurer is discharged from liability as from the time of deviation, and it is immaterial that the ship may have regained her route before any loss occurs.'

A deviation occurs when the ship leaves her prescribed or customary course, but with the intention of ultimately returning to that course to complete the insured voyage. The intention to arrive at the named port is never lost sight of. The *terminus ad quem* is not changed, but the proper and usual course of performing the voyage is changed. In *Wooldridge v Boydell*,[58] the learned Lord Mansfield, who clearly had a keen insight into the subject, with his usual lucid style, said:

'Deviations from the voyage insured, arise from after-thoughts, after-interest, after-temptation; and the party who actually deviates from the voyage described means to give up his policy. But a deviation merely intended but never carried into effect is no deviation. In all the cases of that sort, the *terminus a quo*, and *ad quem*, were certain and the same.'

A change of voyage, on the other hand, occurs when there is no intention of completing the insured voyage; the destination is changed. In each case, the test is whether there is any intention of sending the ship to the *terminus ad quem* specified in the policy. Lord Davey of the House of Lords in *Thames and Mersey Marine Insurance Co v Van Laun & Co* said that:[59] 'The usual test is whether the ultimate *ad quem* remains the same.'

The course of the voyage

That deviation can only be considered in the context of a voyage the course or route of which has already been mapped out either by the policy or by custom is obvious. To determine whether a ship has or has not deviated from its voyage, it is first necessary to ascertain what the course of the voyage contemplated by the policy is. The route which a ship may take for a voyage is either specified by the policy, or is the usual and customary course.[60]

If the course is specifically designated, it must be strictly complied with.[61] If it is not so designated, then the 'usual and customary' course has to be taken. What the usual and customary route of a vessel is, is of course, a question of fact. It could vary, *inter alia*, with the class of the vessel, and the trade in which is she engaged. It is generally recognised as the safest, most direct, and most expeditious course between the two destinations: it is a matter of common mercantile notoriety.[62]

The degree or extent of a deviation is irrelevant. Any alteration of course, however slight or trivial, constitutes a variation of the risk contemplated by the policy. That the risk may not have increased is also considered as immaterial.

---

58 (1778) 1 Doug KB 16 at p 18.
59 [1917] 23 Com Cas 104 at p 111, HL.
60 See s 47 for the position where several ports of discharge are specified in the policy.
61 See *Eliot v Wilson* (1776) 4 Bro Parl Cas 470.
62 See *Clason v Simmonds* (1741) cited in 6 Term Rep 533.

The matter of fact is, the new risk is not what the insurer had bargained for. It is for this reason that the insurer is discharged from his liability under the contract.

Intention to deviate is immaterial

Intention is all important in the case of a change of voyage, but is immaterial in deviation. According to s 46(3), '... there must be a deviation in fact to discharge the insurer from his liability under the contract'. A mere meditation to deviate has no effect on the contract.[63] The ship must have actually departed from its proper course before the insurer could discharge himself from liability.

Without lawful excuse

Section 46 has to be read with s 49, which spells out a list of excuses for deviation (and delay). It also provides that when 'the cause excusing the deviation or delay ceases to operate, the ship must resume her course, and prosecute her voyage, with reasonable despatch'.[64] These excuses have to an extent become of lesser importance because of the 'held covered' clause of the IVCH(95) and cl 8.3 of the ICC.

Legal effect of deviation

Section 46 states that, 'the insurer is discharged from liability as from the time of deviation ...'. The contract is not rendered void *ab initio*, and therefore any liability arising before the deviation remains in tact: the insurer is liable for all loss incurred prior to the deviation. The effect of this, however, may be displaced by a term in the contract such as a held covered clause.

Held covered

The heading of cl 2, though captioned as 'change of voyage', nevertheless provides cover in the case of deviation. It states:

'Held covered in case of deviation ... provided notice be given to the Underwriters immediately after receipt of advices and any amended terms of cover and any additional premium required by them be agreed.'

In *Greenock Steamship Co v Maritime Insurance Co*,[65] a held covered cl was held to apply even though the event for which the vessel was held covered was not discovered until after a loss had occurred.[66] The court also held that the extra reasonable premium which the insurer may levy has to be calculated as 'if the parties had known of the deviation at the time that it happened'.

---

63 See *Kingston v Phelps* (1795) cited in 7 Term Rep 165, where the master who had made up his mind to call at an unauthorised port was strangely enough forced by stress of weather into that very port. It was held that he had not deviated, as his intention was never carried into effect. The actual deviation was involuntary and would now fall within s 49(1)(b) as a circumstance 'beyond the control of the master'.

64 See *Delaney v Stoddart* (1785) 1 TR 22.

65 [1903] 1 KB 367.

66 The held covered cl read as: 'Held covered in case of any breach of warranty, deviation ... at a premium to be hereafter arranged.'

A similar problem arose in *Mentz, Decker & Co v Maritime Insurance Co*,[67] where Mr Justice Hamilton was asked to answer the question whether a notice given after a loss was effective under a held covered clause which specifies that 'due notice' must be given by the assured on receipt of advice of a deviation.[68] It was argued that the assured should not be allowed to claim the benefit of the clause because the notice given after a loss could not be said to be given with 'due notice'. The judge, applying the decision of the above case, held that the notice given by the assured, though given after loss, was sufficient to satisfy the terms of the clause.

Both the above cases have established the principle that a notice given after a loss is still valid. The question which arises from this is: can an assured afford to delay or postpone the giving of his notice on receipt of advice of a deviation, or of the event which is held covered?

'Immediately'

Mr Justice Hamilton expressed the view that a delay should not prevent an assured from recovering under the policy when 'nothing practicable' can be done on receipt of the notice.[69] Does this mean that, in such a circumstance, the assured may take his time in giving his notice?

In *Thames and Mersey Marine Insurance Co v Van Laun*, Lord Halsbury LC of the House of Lords appears to give the impression that an assured is allowed a reasonable period of time to give his notice. He remarked that:[70]

'... it is an implied term of the provision that reasonable notice should be given, that it is not competent to the assured to wait as long as he pleases before he gives notice and settles with the underwriter what extra premium can be agreed upon.'

It has to be pointed out that the his lordship was able to read this term into the contract because there was nothing in the held covered cl in question stipulating a time limit for the giving of the notice.[71] It is doubtful whether the same term may be implied in cl 2. It is submitted that there is no room for the application of the 'reasonable notice' rule under the IVCH(95). The word 'immediately' appearing in cl 2 connotes a sense of greater urgency than the words 'due notice' or a reasonable period of time. As soon as the assured is aware of the event he has to give his notice at once.

---

67 [1910] 1 KB 132 at p 135.
68 The cl read as: 'In the event of the vessel making an deviation ... it is mutually agreed that such deviation ... shall be held covered at a premium to be arranged, provided due notice be given by the assured on receipt of advice of such deviation ...'.
69 Cited with approval in *Hewitt v London General Insurance Co Ltd* (1925) 23 Ll L Rep 243.
70 (1917) 23 Com Cas 104 at p 109, HL.
71 The held covered cl was in the following terms: 'In the event of any deviation from the terms and conditions of this policy ... it is understood and agreed that notwithstanding such a deviation the interest hereby assured shall be held covered at a premium to be arranged.'

Delay in voyage

As in the case of a change of voyage and deviation, unreasonable delay in the prosecution of the insured voyage could also bring about a premature end to a voyage policy. The question of delay is dealt by s 48 in the following manner:

'In the case of a voyage policy, the adventure must be prosecuted throughout its course with reasonable despatch, and, if without lawful excuse it is not so prosecuted, the insurer is discharged from liability as from the time when the delay became unreasonable.'

Whether the ship has or has not prosecuted the voyage with reasonable despatch is, of course, a question of fact.[72] The excuses spelt out in s 49 for deviation are also applicable to delay.

Legal effect of delay

As there is nothing in the IVCH(95) on delay, the matter is governed by s 48. Clause 2 of the IVCH(95), the change of voyage clause, does not apply to delay and delay is, therefore, not held covered. The insurer is discharged from liability only as from the time the delay becomes unreasonable. This means that the right of the assured of recovery for any loss arising before such time is preserved. Reference, however, has also to be made to s 55(2)(b), which states that:

'Unless the policy otherwise provides, the insurer on ship or goods is not liable for any loss proximately caused by delay, although the delay be caused by a peril insured against.'

VOYAGE POLICY ON GOODS

Goods are almost invariably insured for a voyage in a policy incorporating either the ICC (A), (B) or (C). As they generally have to travel on land before and after a sea voyage – to be conveyed from the warehouse or place of storage to the port of loading, and from the port of discharge to the warehouse or place of storage – they are usually insured for both land and sea risks. Provided that the land risks are 'incidental' to the sea voyage, a policy of mixed sea and land risks may be taken out. This is permitted by s 2(1) of the Act and, as will be seen, the transit clause of the ICC is an example of such a policy.

The scheme of coverage set out in the ICC is complex and confusing. The duration of the cover is governed by cll 8, 9 and 10. Briefly:

- clause 8.1 sets out the general rules relating to attachment and termination of the insurance;
- clause 8.2 covers the particular circumstance where a change of destination occurs after the completion of the sea voyage;
- clause 8.3 in declaring that the insurance 'shall remain in force' confirms that the events listed therein will not terminate the insurance – its purpose is to dispel any doubts which one might have as regards the continuance of the cover should any one of the enumerated events arise;

---

72 See s 88.

- clause 9 relates specifically to a termination not of the contract of insurance, but of the contract of carriage and its effects on the contract of insurance; and,
- clause 10 – the 'change of voyage' clause – states that a change ordered by the assured is held covered.

Attachment of insurance

Under the ICC, the period of cover is contained in the 'transit clause,' clause 8 – sometimes referred as the 'warehouse to warehouse clause' – which reads as follows:

> 'This insurance attaches – from the time the goods leave the warehouse or place of storage at the place named herein for the commencement of the transit ...'

Though the provision is straightforward enough, nonetheless it is necessary to mention that the word 'leave' clarifies that the insurance does not attach whilst the goods are in the process of being loaded, nor whilst they are being conveyed other than with the intention of commencing the insured transit. The cover will only attach when the goods physically depart from the premises 'at the place named ... for the commencement of the transit'.[73]

Continuance of insurance

By cl 8.3, the insurer agrees to maintain cover should any one of the following circumstances arise: during delay beyond the control of the assured; any deviation; forced discharge; reshipment or transhipment during the voyage; and any permitted variation of the contract of carriage arising from the exercise of a liberty granted to shipowners or charterers under the contract of affreightment.

The objective of this clause is to remove any doubts which one might have regarding the validity of the cover should any one of these circumstances take place.

Delay beyond the control of the assured

A cargo owner does not, as a general rule, have control over the performance of the voyage. This necessarily means that the effect of delay, as laid down in s 48, could prove to be harsh on him. To mitigate the severity of this, cl 8.3 was inserted to preserve the cover during a delay; provided that the delay is beyond the control of the assured, the insurance continues to operate, presumably regardless of the period and the reasonableness or unreasonableness of the delay, as none of these considerations is mentioned in the clause.

The converse to the rule in cl 8.3 is that the policy will terminate if the delay is within the control of the assured. Thus, a cargo owner who has himself caused the delay (for example, in procuring or loading the cargo) would not be

---

73 The words 'at the place named herein for the commencement of the transit' were inserted to clarify the position and to avoid the problems encountered in *Re Traders & General Insurance Association Ltd* (1924) 18 Ll L Rep 450; see also *Symington & Co v Union Insurance Society of Canton Ltd* (1928) 3 Ll L Rep 280; 31 Ll L Rep 179.

able to plead the benefit of cl 8.3. Furthermore, he would also be in breach of cl 18, the 'avoidance of delay' or 'reasonable despatch' clause which declares that:

'It is a condition of this insurance that the Assured shall act with reasonable despatch in all circumstances within their control.'

The scope of this cl is wider than s 48; it is not confined to the sea voyage, for the words 'in all circumstances' include land transit. The penalty is presumably the same as that stated in s 48, namely that the insurer is 'discharged from liability as from the time when the delay became unreasonable'.

Loss proximately caused by delay

Clause 4.5 of the ICC (A), (B) and (C), which echoes the rule contained in s 55(2)(b), states:

'In no case shall this insurance cover –

loss damage or expense proximately caused by delay, even though the delay be caused by a risk insured against (except expenses payable under Clause 2 above).'[74]

Though the policy may remain in force, any loss proximately caused by delay is not recoverable.[75]

'Any deviation'

Clause 8.3 provides that the insurance shall remain in force during 'any deviation'. By this clause, the assured is neither required to give notice nor to pay any additional premium. Presumably, the reason for the rule is that, in practice, the deviation of a ship must almost invariably be beyond the control of a cargo owner.

Variation of the adventure

It is to be observed that cl 8.3 applies only when the variation of the adventure arises from the exercise of a liberty granted to shipowners or charterers under the contract of affreightment. Any unauthorised variation would not be covered by the policy. As the insurance 'shall remain in force,' the assured is not required to give notice to the insurer or to pay any additional premium.

Termination of insurance

Normal termination

In the normal course of events, the insurance will terminate when the goods arrive at any one of the three termini enumerated in cll 8.1.1 to 8.1.3. The phrase 'whichever shall first occur' qualifying all three clauses sets 60 days as the limit, or the cut-off point, of the cover. In the usual run of cases, the insurance would

---

74 The only claim for delay which may be recoverable is that arising from general average under cl 2. That the insurer will compensate the cargo owner's proportion of general average even though arising from delay has been preserved by this exception.

75 See *Pink v Fleming* (1890) 25 QBD 396.

have terminated in accordance with either cll 8.1.1, 8.1.2 or 8.1.3, before the expiration of the 60 days.

Premature termination

The 'ordinary course of the transit'[76] envisaged by cl 8.1 could, however, be shortened, or end prematurely, by reason of the occurrence of an event stipulated in cll 8.2, 9 or 10. The statutory laws on change of voyage (s 45); deviation (s 46); and delay during the voyage (s 48), described above, apply to all voyage policies. A cargo owner, however, is generally not in control of the voyage or of matters as to how it is to be prosecuted. A variation of the adventure, a change of destination or voyage, delay, and deviation could occur; and any of these events could be caused by the assured (the cargo owner) himself or, they could be beyond his control. Thus, clause 8.1 defining the duration of the risk – the points of attachment and termination – has to be read with cll 8.2, 9 and 10, all of which could affect the duration of the cover.

Change of final destination

Clause 8.2 is an example of a particular circumstance of a premature termination of the cover. For it to apply, the sea voyage must have terminated at the final port of discharge; the cargo discharged overside from the oversea vessel; and the goods 'forwarded to a destination other than that to which they are insured hereunder'. Strictly speaking, 'change of final destination of the cargo' would be a more suitable name for this provision, which is necessary because of the coverage for land transit. Whether such a change of destination is contemplated by s 45 (which relates to a change of voyage) is another question altogether. Section 45, it is observed, refers to the destination of the *ship* and not of the cargo.

As was seen, cl 8.2 is limited in scope; and unlike cl 9 on termination of the contract of carriage, and cl 10 on a change of voyage ordered by the assured, there is no held covered provision for such a change of destination. The clause provides for termination of the original insurance as from the time when the goods commence transit to its new destination.

It is interesting to note that the clause is silent as to the party who has instructed the change of destination. It simply states that, 'If ... the goods are to be forwarded to a destination other than that to which they are insured hereunder, this insurance ... shall not extend beyond the commencement of transit to such other destination'. It cannot apply to a change of destination (and of voyage) ordered by the assured, for this is specifically covered by cl 10.

Clause 8.2, it has been said, is 'intended to deal with the situation of a resale to a customer of the assured, and to make it quite clear which insurance would be in force (that of the original assured or his customer), the clause provides for termination of the original insurance ...'.[77] If this is the objective of the clause, more positive language should have been used to make this clearer. As it stands, it is not at all happily worded.

---

76 See *Safadi v Western Assurance Co* (1933) 46 Ll L Rep 140.

77 See NG Hudson, *The Institute Clauses* (1995, 2nd edn), p 24.

Termination of contract of carriage clause

Whether cl 9 applies to a change of destination which has been ordered not by the assured (cargo owner), but by the shipowner (or carrier) is the question which has to be considered, especially in the light of the fact that there is now no longer a held covered clause dealing directly with a change of voyage, as was previously available in the 1963 version of the ICC.[78] The relevant parts of cl 9 read as follows:

> 'If owing to circumstances beyond the control of the Assured ... the contract of carriage is terminated at a port or place other than the destination named therein ... then this insurance shall also terminate unless prompt notice is given to the Underwriters and continuation of cover is requested when the insurance shall remain in force ...'

Two elements have to be satisfied before a termination of the insurance can take place:

• 'the contract of carriage is terminated at a port or place other than the destination named therein'; and

• the circumstances are beyond the control of the assured.

A typical scenario contemplated by cl 9 is probably the case where a ship, unable to continue with the voyage because she has suffered severe damage, discharges her cargo at an intermediate port thereby causing a termination of the contract of carriage.[79]

A carrier (shipowner or charterer) who has, under a contract of carriage, agreed to carry cargo from A to B, for which the cargo owner (the assured) has accordingly insured them for the said voyage could, after the commencement of the voyage from A, terminate the contract of carriage by voluntarily sailing to C, a port other than the destination named in the said contract of carriage. Such a change of destination ordered by the carrier, though 'beyond the control of the Assured', would result not only in a termination of the contract of carriage, but also of the insurance 'unless prompt notice is given to the Underwriters and continuation of cover is requested ...'. As worded, cl 9 appears to be wide enough to embrace a change of voyage, with or without good reason, ordered by the carrier.[80]

It is to be observed that, unless prompt notice be given with a request for a continuation of cover and the payment of an additional premium, if so required by the underwriters, the policy will terminate.

Admittedly, the policy is not held covered, but the assured could prevent the termination of the insurance by issuing prompt notice with a request for a continuation of cover. Unlike a held covered clause, here, the assured has to

---

78   The 'Change of Voyage' Clause of the 1963 version of the ICC stated: 'Held covered at a premium to be arranged in case of change of voyage ...'.

79   Another obvious example is where the contract of carriage is prematurely terminated by unavoidable extraneous forces, eg, war.

80   However, Hudson, *The Institute Clauses* (1995, 2nd edn), p 26, holds the view that, 'there is now no provision in the Institute Cargo Clauses to hold the assured covered in the event of an illegal change of voyage by a shipowner or other carrier'.

take steps to forestall the termination of the insurance.[81] Further, it should be noted that cl 9 covers not only a termination of the contract of carriage, but also any termination of transit before the delivery of the goods as provided by cl 8. Like the sea voyage, land transit can also be terminated by circumstances beyond the control of the assured.

The continuation of cover granted is limited and will terminate as provided by either cll 9.1 or 9.2

Change of Voyage clause

Clause 10 is a departure from the general rule on change of voyage declared in s 45, by which the insurer is discharged from liability as from the time of change. Clause 10 states:

'Where, after attachment of this insurance, the destination is changed by the Assured, held covered at a premium and on conditions to be arranged subject to prompt notice being given to the Underwriters.'

Though named the 'change of voyage' clause, nevertheless it uses the word 'destination', and not 'the destination of the ship' as in s 45(1). As 'destination' is unqualified, it can refer to the destination of the ship at the named port, and also to the destination of the cargo which is to be delivered at the 'final warehouse or place of storage'. It has to be emphasised that this clause is applicable only when the 'destination' is changed by the assured himself. It clearly has no application to a change of voyage and/or destination which is beyond the control of the assured; such events are covered by cll 9 and possibly 8.2.

'Note' on 'held covered' clause

It is to be observed that in all the ICC,[82] there is, at the end of the policy, a 'Note' (in italics) emphasising that:

'It is necessary for the Assured when they become aware of an event which is "held covered" under this insurance to give prompt notice to the Underwriters and the right to such cover is dependent upon compliance with this obligation.'

Unlike cl 9, where the policy will automatically terminate unless it is prevented from so doing by prompt notice, a held covered clause has the opposite effect. The assured remains covered by the policy until such time as he becomes aware of the event for which he is 'held covered' and, on becoming aware of the event, fails to give prompt notice to the underwriters.

For completeness, it is necessary to refer to the case of *Simon Israel Co v Sedgwick*,[83] where the goods insured were intended to be shipped to Madrid when, by a blunder, they were shipped to Carthagena. Even though the policy in question contained a held covered clause, it did not help the assured, as the risk had not attached.

---

81 By this clause, the policy may be revived by the assured giving prompt notice and paying the additional premium. In a held covered clause, the policy continues to apply until such time as when the assured becomes aware of the loss and fails to give prompt notice to the insurer.
82 But not in the IVCH(95) or the ITCH(95).
83 [1893] 1 QB 303.

CHAPTER 5

VALUED AND UNVALUED POLICIES

A – VALUED POLICIES

A valued policy is defined in s 27(2) as 'a policy which specifies the agreed value of the subject-matter insured'. The purpose of fixing in advance the amount of compensation to be paid to the assured is to avoid disputes as to the value of the subject-matter insured. The validity of such a policy – whether it offends the principle of indemnity – was raised as early as 1761 in *Lewis v Rucker*,[1] where it was firmly established that it was not to be considered as a wager policy, or like an 'interest or not interest' type of policy. The learned Lord Mansfield remarked that, '... it must be taken that the value was fixed in such a manner as that the insured meant only to have an indemnity'. In *Irving v Manning*,[2] Mr Justice Patteson (who delivered the judgment of the Court of Appeal) had first to admit that a policy of insurance is not a perfect contract of indemnity before he could proceed to identify a valued policy as an example of its imperfection.[3] The convenience of a valued policy is, in the words of Mr Justice Gorell Barnes in *The Main*,[4] to save both parties the 'necessity of going into an expensive and intricate question as to the value in each particular case'. Of course, all is well and good if a fair and realistic figure is given as its valuation. But as to be seen, past cases have shown that the agreed values tended to be inflated and exorbitant.

AGREED VALUE IS CONCLUSIVE

In 1847, the question regarding the binding or conclusive nature of the agreed valuation was examined in *Irving v Manning*.[5] The House approved the decision of the lower court that, 'the agreed value is conclusive; each party has conclusively admitted that this fixed sum shall be that which the assured is entitled to receive in case of a total loss'. Lord Campbell expressed relief that this question, which had agitated Westminster Hall for 30 years, was at last solemnly resolved. The rule, confirmed by the highest authority of the land, is now embodied in s 27(3) of the Act, which states:

'Subject to the provisions of this Act, and in the absence of fraud, the value fixed by the policy is, as between the insurer and the assured, conclusive of the insurable value of the subject intended to be insured, whether the loss be total or partial.'

---

1   (1761) 2 Burr 1167 at p 1171.

2   (1847) 1 HL Cas 287.

3   He said, *ibid*, at p 287, '... it must be taken with [the] qualification that the parties may have agreed beforehand in estimating the value of the subject assured, by way of liquidated damages, as indeed they may in any other contract of indemnity'.

4   [1894] P 320 at p 327.

5   (1847) 1 HL Cas 287.

As can be seen, the section itself provides two exceptions to the general rule encapsulated in the phrases, 'subjection to the provisions of this Act' and 'in the absence of fraud'. Before proceeding to discuss the exceptions, some comments have to be made of the general rule.

In *Woodside v Globe Marine Insurance Co Ltd*,[6] a case decided before the Act, the binding nature of the valuation was said to apply regardless of any change in the actual value of the subject-matter insured. Justice Mathew took pains to describe the eventualities of a rise and fall in the actual value of the goods as follows:

'Whether the subject-matter of insurance be ship or goods, the valuation is the amount fixed by agreement at which in case of loss the indemnity is to be calculated. Where goods are assured the valuation may be low when the policy attaches; but the value to the owners may be enhanced when the goods have nearly reached their destination by the expenses of transit, etc. Yet the valuation is binding. And again, if the valuation be high, but the goods are depreciated in value from fall of market or other causes for which the underwriter is not liable, the valuation cannot be opened.'

The conclusive nature of the agreed valuation is binding even if, unbeknown to the parties, the ship was considerably damaged and the agreed value no longer reflects her real value. In this regard, *Barker v Janson*[7] and *Lidgett v Secretan*[8] are the leading and best illustrations on the subject. In *Barker v Janson*, at the time when the policy was made, but with the knowledge of the parties, the ship had sustained damage in a storm to such an extent that the expense of the repairs would have exceeded her value when repaired. She was, therefore, worth much less than the agreed valuation.[9] Notwithstanding this injury to the ship and the resulting substantial reduction in her value, the value stated in the policy was held conclusive as between the parties. The underwriters were not permitted to deduct from the valuation the sum it would have cost to make the vessel fit for sailing. Chief Justice Bovill observed that, 'both parties acting in good faith are willing to be bound by that valuation ... An exorbitant valuation may be evidence of fraud, but when the transaction is *bona fide*, the value agreed upon is binding'. It is fair to say that the agreed valuation, however largely in excess of the true value, is, in the absence of fraud, conclusive between the parties.

Whether the same rule applies to a voyage policy was considered in *Lidgett v Secretan*, where two policies were involved: the outward policy was from London to Calcutta and the homeward voyage was 'at and from Calcutta'. On the expiration of the first policy, the actual value of ship was, compared to the agreed valuation in the second policy, considerably reduced as a result of storm damage sustained by the ship during the first voyage. The real issue in the case

---

6   [1896] 1 QB 105; 1 Com Cas 237.

7   (1868) LR 3 CP 303.

8   (1871) LR 6 CP 616.

9   In *Barker v Janson* [1868] LR 3 CP 303 at p 307, Montague Smith J, said: 'A thousand things might lessen the value a vessel between the time of a policy being made and the time of its attaching, such as natural decay, worms, or the ship become drug in the market; and all the evils intended to be avoided by this kind of policy would arise again.'

was, as put by counsel for the insurers, '... whether the assured ... were entitled to recover under the second policy the full value of the ship as if she had been undamaged at the inception of the risk'. Counsel also argued that, as the policy was for a voyage, it should be treated differently from *Barker v Janson*, where the policy was for a period of time. The second insurer's main line of defence was to the effect that, as the implied warranty of seaworthiness applied to the policy in question, they should be allowed to deduct from the amount for which they are liable under that policy a sum which should (though not actually incurred) have been incurred in order to render the ship seaworthy for the homeward voyage: It was said that the nature of a voyage policy was such that the vessel should not depart on her voyage home until the repairs were effected to make the ship seaworthy.

This contention was roundly dismissed by Justice Willes, who could find no authority limiting the value to that extent. His justification for denying the insurer the deduction was as follows:

'If the vessel had been at sea, and the policy is a valued one, had been made after she had sailed, and the vessel had sustained damage, would the underwriters be entitled to say that the particular loss should be deducted from the value in the policy?'

With due respect, it is submitted that a more acceptable line of reasoning is that, because the policy was 'at and from Calcutta', it had attached when the ship arrived, albeit in a damaged condition, 'at' Calcutta. Further, the implied warranty of seaworthiness is applicable only at the commencement of the voyage, and as the vessel did not set sail from, but was destroyed by fire whilst undergoing repairs at Calcutta, no question of breach of the said warranty can arise.

Once a policy (voyage or time) has attached, the agreed value prevails whatever the actual value of the vessel might be at the time. Mr Justice Montague Smith said: 'It cannot depend upon the actual value at the time of the loss or at the time the risk attaches.' In so far as the conclusive nature of the valuation is concerned, no distinction is to be drawn between a time and a voyage policy. For better or for worse, the agreed value is conclusive.[10]

The most recent case to have tacitly confirmed the validity of an over-valued policy is *The Maira (No 2)*,[11] where the House of Lords indicated that the vessel, which was mortgaged twice over, should have been insured in accordance with the agreement for 130% of the mortgage debt.

---

10 By the time *Loders and Nucoline Ltd v The Bank of New Zealand* (1929) 33 Ll L Rep 70 at p 75 reached the court in 1929, the principle that the value of the subject-matter insured as stated in the policy is conclusive and cannot be re-opened was described as 'already very well established'.

11 *Glafki Shipping Co SA v Pinos Shipping Co (No 1)* [1986] 2 Lloyd's Rep 12, HL.

'As between the insurer and assured'

The valuation is, according to s 27(3), binding only 'as between the insurer and the assured', though Lord Campbell in *Irving v Manning*[12] was of the opinion that it enured for 'all purposes'. In *North of England Iron SS Insurance Association v Armstrong*,[13] the court, taking the agreed value of £6,000 into consideration, held that the insurers were entitled to recover from the assured the whole of the £5,000 which the assured had recovered from the owners of the ship responsible for the collision. On the effect of the agreement as to the value, Mr Justice Mellors commented:

> 'The basis of the contract is the agreed value of the vessel, and when, to avoid all questions as to the real value, the parties come to an agreement as to the value, it appears to me to follow as a matter of course that all those rights, which spring out of the payment by an underwriter for a total loss, must be governed by the agreed value.'

In *SS Balmoral v Marten*,[14] the insurers, who were asked by their assured to reimburse them their share of general average which they had contributed, were held liable to pay only that proportion of the salvage and general average losses which the policy value bore to the proved, or real, value of the ship.[15] Lord Shand was adamant that:

> 'In all questions of indemnity, therefore, the parties to the policy, insurers and insured, have agreed that though the ship may in truth be much more valuable, her value is to be taken at £33,000 only. There is no exception. The agreement is to apply in all cases of indemnity which may arise.'

Scrapping voyages

A vessel which has, during the course of a time policy, to make a journey (referred to as 'scrapping voyages') to a scrap yard or other place for the purpose of being 'broken up' or 'being sold for breaking up' will be governed by cl 1.5 of ITCH(95),[16] the relevant part of which states:

> '... any claim for loss of or damage to the Vessel occurring subsequent to such sailing shall be limited to the market value of the Vessel as scrap at the time when the loss or damage is sustained, unless previous notice has been given to the Underwriters and any amendments to the terms of cover, insured value and premium required by them have been agreed ...'

Unless previous notice and arrangements have been made, the scrap, and not the agreed value of the vessel at the time of loss, is to be taken as the figure for settlement of any claim for loss or damage. This is a contractual exception to the general rule contained in s 27(3) that the agreed value is conclusive.[17]

---

12   (1847) 1 HL Cas 287 at p 308, HL.

13   (1870) LR 5 QB 244.

14   [1902] AC 511, HL.

15   The agreed value was £33,000, but £40,000 was taken as the value in the salvage proceedings. The insurers were only bound to pay 33/40ths of the ship's contribution.

16   Previously cl 1.3 of the ITCH(83). There is no equivalent to cl 1.3 in the IVCH(95).

17   If the policy is unvalued, the scrap value, and not her value at the commencement of the risk (s 16(1)) is also to be applied.

EXCESSIVE OVER-VALUATION

The rule that the agreed value in a valued policy is binding and conclusive is firmly established. It was always thought that the value should never go beyond what is 'reasonable and fair,' and the assured is meant only to have an 'indemnity', the very basis of a contract of insurance.[18] Admittedly, it is, of course, difficult at any given time to be exact or precise about the value of the subject-matter insured. A margin of error is bound to occur, and the courts are generally prepared to overlook any difference between the real and the agreed value provided that it is not grossly or outrageously excessive. Not all over-valuations will be tolerated by the courts, and there are, as will be seen, more than ample grounds upon which the courts may set aside an agreed valuation which is excessive. What constitutes excessive over-valuation is a question of fact.

'In the absence of fraud'

The above phrase embodies the defence of fraud, which could be used to nullify an excessive agreed valuation. Section 27(3) specifically states that the valuation is conclusive only 'in the absence of fraud'. Thus, if a policy is tainted with fraud, the whole policy, and not just the agreed valuation, is at risk. According to Mr Justice Wright in *Loders and Nucoline Ltd v The Bank of New Zealand*,[19] the phrase 'in the absence of fraud' is simply 'a warning that if there is fraud, not only the valuation but the whole of the policy may be re-opened and avoided ... unless the policy is avoided the value is conclusive'.

The question of fraud was first considered in *Haigh v De la Cour*,[20] where it was held that fraud committed by the assured 'entirely vitiates the contract'. It was obvious from the circumstances of the case that, from the very beginning, the assured had intended to cheat the underwriters: fictitious invoices were issued; the bills of lading were interpolated after they were signed by the captain; the ship was run away with; and some of the cargoes were disposed of. It was held that the insurers were not liable even for the value of the goods that were actually on board.

More recently, in *The Gunford Case*,[21] Lord Shaw of Dunfermline, in an informative speech, dealt with the subject of fraud in the following way:

> 'Had this over-valuation been tainted by fraud the contract of insurance could not have been enforced. Where there is heavy over-valuation, fraud is, *a priori*, not very far to seek. But fraud is not here pleaded; and upon the general question it ought to be remembered that to the insurer using a ship as part of the going concern of a business a statement of value going much beyond the amount to be realised if the concern was stopped and the asset put upon the market in

---

18 In *Forbes v Aspinal* (1811) 13 East 323 at p 326, Lord Ellenborough's understanding was that the assured should keep 'fairly within the principles of insurance which is merely to obtain an indemnity' when fixing the agreed value.

19 (1929) 33 Ll L Rep 70 at p 76.

20 (1812) 3 Camp 319.

21 [1911] AC 529 at p 542, HL.

intelligible and legitimate It is not discountenanced by the Marine Insurance Act of 1906, but, on the contrary, is, apart from fraud held under s 27, sub-s 3, of the statute to be conclusive of the insurable value.'

It is, of course, possible for a valuation to be excessive without being fraudulent. As fraud is by no means easy to prove, this defence is rarely pleaded. It is true to say that '... it is much more easy to infer fraud from over-insurance of goods than from over-insurance of ship when both parties are in approximately the same position to know what the market value of the ship proposed to be insured is'.[22]

Breach of utmost good faith

Besides fraud, there is another defence which could be invoked by an insurer in order to avoid liability. Section 17 on the doctrine of *uberrimae fide*, or 'utmost good faith', is concerned with conduct of a lesser degree of impropriety than fraud. Conduct short of fraud could attract the operation of this principle; interestingly enough, the section has not, so far, been used for this purpose, and the reason for this could well be that the other defences available to the insurer have proved to be effective. It is to be noted that fraud would render a contract void *ab initio*, whereas a breach of the duty of utmost good faith would merely make the contract voidable.

The principle of utmost good faith is the golden thread running through the whole fabric of a contract of insurance.[23] A valuation known to the assured to be grossly excessive, but not revealed to the insurer, would surely offend the principle of disclosure and, very likely, constitute a breach of the duty of utmost good faith.

Wagering or gaming

A valued policy, as was seen, is not to be regarded as a wager policy. If it was, it would be void. Lord Mansfield in *Lewis v Rucker*,[24] after acknowledging the fact that there are many conveniences for allowing valued policies, nevertheless warned that 'if they are used merely as a cover to a wager, they would be considered as an evasion'. Gross over-valuation could be evidence of gaming or wagering. This was also recognised by Mr Justice Blackburn of the Court of Appeal in *Ionides v Pender*,[25] where he observed that, '... whether there is an excessive valuation or not, depends on whether the valuation was so high as to amount in part at least to a wager ...'. And a wagering policy is void by s 4. On the facts of the case, the court preferred to rest its decision on the ground of non-disclosure of a material fact. An assured who excessively over-values his insured property may well find that he has no policy upon which to base his claim: such a policy could be held to be void by reason of gaming or wagering.

---

22   *Per* Bailhache J, *General Shipping & Forwarding Co & Another v British General Insurance Co Ltd* (1923) 15 Ll L Rep 175 at p 176, further discussed below.

23   See Chapter 6.

24   (1761) 2 Burr 1167 at p 1171.

25   (1874) LR 9 QB 531 at p 536.

Non-disclosure of material fact

Excessive over-valuation could arise in one of two ways: an assured may take out one policy in which he has excessively over-valued the subject-matter insured or he could take out more than one policy on the same subject-matter insured, resulting in an over-valuation or, if preferred, over-insurance (by double insurance) of the subject-matter insured. In either case, the effect is the same.[26] An assured who fails to disclose to the insurer that the agreed valuation in a single policy, or the total sum of the agreed valuations of more than one policy, is excessive, would be guilty of a breach of the duty of disclosure.

Non disclosure of excessive over-valuation

Ionides v Pender[27] is the first case to consider non-disclosure of an excessive over-valuation as a ground for avoidance of a policy. In this case, the plaintiffs had insured goods at a value very greatly in excess of their real value without disclosing this fact to their underwriters. Justice Blackburn of the Court of Appeal adopted the questions which the trial judge had directed to the jury to consider upon the facts. As the order or sequence of the questions is particularly important, it is worthwhile citing them in full:[28]

- Were the valuations for insurance excessive?
- If excessive, were they so made with a fraudulent intent?
- Whether fraudulent or not, was it material to the underwriters to know that the valuation was excessive?
- Was it concealed from the underwriters?

He agreed with the trial judge that the valuations were excessive but that they were not made fraudulently. On the third question, of the materiality of the fact of the excessive over-valuation, he found that:

> '... there was distinct and uncontradicted evidence that underwriters do in practice act on the principle that it is material to take into consideration whether the overvaluation is so great as to make the risk speculative. It appears to us a rational practice.'

As this was regarded as a 'rational practice', he had no choice but to rule that the concealment of the fact of the excessive over-valuation constituted a breach of the duty of disclosure.

The defence of non-disclosure was also applied after the passing of the Act in three well-known cases, namely, *Gooding v White*,[29] *Piper v Royal Exchange*

---

26 In *The Gunford Case* [1911] AC 529 at p 536, HL, Lord Alverstone CJ thought that the over-valuation and over-insurance were in the circumstances of the case synonymous: 'Some distinction was attempted to be made between over-valuation and over-insurance, but, inasmuch as all the policies were valued policies, the question becomes immaterial.'

27 (1874) LR 9 QB 531.

28 It is observed that the same questions were raised in *Herring v Janson & Others* (1895) 1 Com Cas 177, but as all the answers were in the negative, judgment was accordingly awarded to the assured-plaintiffs.

29 (1913) 29 TLR 312.

Assurance[30] and *Berger and Light Diffusers Pty Ltd v Pollock*.[31] In the first of the trilogy, Mr Justice Pickford remarked that:

'It was unnecessary to say whether over-valuation that was effected for the purpose of defrauding the underwriters was done with too enthusiastic an idea of the profits likely to be realised from the cargo. It was sufficient that if there was, as he thought there was, such an over-valuation as ought to have been communicated there was a concealment of a material fact which avoided the policy.'

In the second case, Mr Justice Roche pointed out that the deterioration and the facts with regard to the value of the ship were matters which were known to the assured. As the assured was unable to show that the defendants knew or ought to have known of any facts material to the actual value of the yacht, judgment was awarded against them.

On the question of the knowledge of the insurer, either that he knew or ought to have known that the subject-matter insured was grossly over-valued, reference should be made to the case of *General Shipping and Forwarding Co v British General Insurance Co Ltd*,[32] where a distinction is drawn between over-insurance of goods and of ships. In this case, the vessel was valued at £5,000 in the policy when her actual market value was about £1,500. The insurers denied liability on the ground that the vessel was grossly over-valued. Mr Justice Bailhache awarded judgment in favour of the assured on the ground that the insurers themselves were in as good a position as the assured to gauge the market value of the ship. The judge pointed out that, if the policy be on goods, the matter would be on a different footing:[33] 'There the underwriter has no means of knowing the value of the goods except the statement of the assured. He has not, as in this case, all the information to his hand when he comes to insured goods ...'.

In *Berger and Light Diffusers Pty Ltd v Pollock*,[34] Mr Justice Kerr's remarks on the subject are particularly informative. He said:[35]

'Over-valuation is only one illustration of the general principle that insurers are entitled to avoid policies on the ground of non-disclosure of material circumstances. It must therefore always be shown that the over-valuation was such that, if it had been disclosed, it would have entitled the insurer to avoid the policy because it would have affected his judgment as a prudent insurer in fixing the premium or determining whether or not to take the risk.

The aim of this speech is to emphasis that the terms of s 18, namely, the test of materiality and of the prudent insurer, must be observed.

·

---

30 [1932] 44 Lloyd's Rep 103.

31 [1973] 2 Lloyd's Rep 442. See also *Visscherij Maatschappij Nieuw Onderneming Assurance Co Ltd v The Scottish Metropolitan* (1922) 27 Com Cas 198, CA.

32 (1923) 15 Ll L Rep 175, KBD.

33 *Ibid*, at p 176

34 [1973] 2 Lloyd's Rep 442.

35 *Ibid*, at p 465.

Non-disclosure of additional insurance

It is necessary to examine the position of an assured who has taken out legitimate insurances upon ship, cargo or freight, and also made additional separate insurance(s). An assured who takes out an additional valued policy or policies resulting in an over-valuation or over-insurance of the subject-matter insured, as in *The Gunford Case* and *Mathie v The Argonaut Marine Insurance Co Ltd*,[36] could also be caught by the rules of non-disclosure. In *The Gunford Case*, the assured, in addition to taking out a valued policy on hull for £18,500 (the actual value was £9,000) and on freight for £5,500 (actual value of about £5,000) took out additional policies in connection with the ship on disbursements for £6,500 and on hull and disbursements for £4,600.[37] Though these ppi policies on disbursements were void under s 4 of the Act, nonetheless, as 'they go to swell the sum which would be payable in the event of the ship being lost ... there was a very large over-valuation which might well make a prudent underwriters hesitate both as to undertaking the risk and consider the premium which he should be required before doing so'.

In the second case, additional policies were effected on freight or anticipated freight and also for disbursements. The issue was whether the assured was bound to disclose to the underwriter, with whom he had effected an insurance for £6,000 on a cargo of coal on his ship, the fact that he had already effected an insurance for freight, also for £6,000, which, in the circumstances, was higher than the freight that he could possibly earn. It was estimated that the actual freight upon the coal may have been something in the region of £1,800 to £2,000. The insurance of the cargo and freight added together (£12,000) was considerably in excess of the total value of the cargo and freight (£7,200). Lord Dunedin of the House of Lords held the view that there was a vital difference between this and *The Gunford Case*. Whilst the risk was said to be 'entirely speculative' in *The Gunford Case*, the assured in the case under consideration was entitled under the policy to insure freight up the limit of £6,000. In the circumstances of the case, it was held that there was no concealment of a material fact. Lord Sumner stressed that, 'The question is purely one of fact ...'. As there was nothing to change 'what was a perfectly usual and legitimate business transaction into a purely speculative one', the appeal of the insurer was dismissed.[38]

'Subject to the provisions of this Act'

In *Loders and Nucoline Ltd v The Bank of New Zealand*, Mr Justice Wright expressed the view that the words, 'Subject to the provisions of this Act' may

---

36 (1925) 21 Ll L Rep 145, HL.

37 [1911] AC 529, at p 543, *per* Lord Shaw of Dunfermline, '... the disbursements were the very things which had been already accounted for in the freight, and when the ship became a wreck the payment on these policies was not to be a payment of indemnity, but a present to the assured of this sum of money, a present falling to be made in the event of the wreck and loss of the vessel'.

38 *Per* Lord Dunedin, (1925) 21 Ll L Rep 145 at p 146, HL.

'perhaps refer to ss 29(4) and 75(2)'. As the former can be more appropriately discussed under 'unvalued policies', only the latter will be considered here.

Where subject-matter is not wholly or completely at risk

In the above case, Mr Justice Wright expressed the view that the words were 'not a qualification ... but a reminder of another rule which again is of essential importance in marine insurance'. The relevant parts of s 75(2) states that: 'Nothing in the provisions of this Act ... shall ... prohibit the insurer from showing that at the time of the loss the whole or any part of the subject-matter insured was not at risk under the policy'. This defence was raised in the case of *The Main*,[39] where the whole of the subject-matter insured, freight, was not at risk. The underwriters were entitled under the common law, the principle of which is now stated in s 75(2) of the Act, to show that a part[40] or the whole of the subject-matter was not at risk. Mr Justice Gorell Barnes said:

> 'In strictness, it is not an opening of the valuation, but is merely a reduction in proportion to the amount of cargo shipped, the valuation still being held binding as a valuation on that portion which is shipped.'

The policy covered only freight which was at risk on the voyage in question.[41]

B – UNVALUED POLICIES

An unvalued policy is defined in s 28 as 'a policy which does not specify the value of the subject-matter insured, but, subject to the limit of the sum insured, leaves the insurable value to be subsequently ascertained, in the manner hereinbefore specified'. Unvalued policies, sometimes referred to as 'open' policies, are nowadays rarely used. Whilst the valuation declared in a valued policy is accepted by both parties as binding and conclusive, in an unvalued policy, the value of the subject-matter insured, referred to as the 'insurable value', has to be subsequently ascertained in accordance with the rules set out in s 16.

INSURABLE VALUE

Policies on hulls and on goods are now always valued policies, but unvalued policies have also been used in the past for both hulls and goods.

Insurable value of ship

The method for ascertaining the insurable value of a ship is set out in s 16(1) as:

> '... the value, at the commencement of the risk, of the ship, including her outfit, provisions and stores for the officers and crew, money advanced for seamen's

---

39   [1894] P 320 at p 324.

40   *Forbes v Aspinall* (1811) 13 East 323 where the insurers were held liable for the loss of freight which was expected to be earned only from cargo which was actually on board.

41   The same rule applies to an unvalued policy: see *Williams & Others v North China Insurance Co* [1933] 1 KB 81, CA.

wages, and other disbursements (if any) incurred to make the ship fit for the voyage or adventure contemplated by the policy, plus the charges of insurance upon the whole. The insurable value, in the case of a steamship, includes also the machinery, boilers, and coals and engine stores if owned by the assured, and, in the case of a ship engaged in a special trade, the ordinary fittings requisite for that trade.'[42]

It is to be noted that in relation to a voyage policy, it is value of the ship at the commencement of the 'risk', not of the voyage, which is to be considered. Thus, in a voyage policy, reference has to be made to rr 2 and 3 of the Rules for Construction for the purpose of determining when the risk attaches. On the question as to what is included within the term 'ship,' s 16(1) has to be read with r 15. A policy simply on 'hull and machinery' does not cover stores and provisions because it is not as comprehensive as a policy on 'ship'.[43] It is to be observed that coals and engine stores are covered only if they are 'owned by the assured'.

Insurable value of freight

Section 16(2) states:

In insurance on freight, whether paid in advance or otherwise, the insurable value is the gross amount of the freight at the risk of the assured, plus the charges of insurance.

The word 'gross' covers working expenses to earn freight, and this is of 'great practical convenience in avoiding a troublesome, uncertain and possibly litigious inquiry into working expenses.'[44]

In relation to advance freight, it is to be recalled that the insurable interest lies not in the shipowner, but in the person who had paid the freight in advance.[45]

Insurable value of goods or merchandise

The insurable value of goods is 'the prime cost of the property insured, plus the expenses of and incidental to shipping and the charges of insurance upon the whole'. The expression 'prime cost' was examined in *Williams v Atlantic Assurance Co Ltd*[46] by the Court of Appeal with Lord Justice Scrutton stating that it is means the 'cost of manufacturing and would ... refer to the state of the goods at or about the time of their first being at risk, the time of commencing the adventure'. The invoice price is *prima facie* evidence of prime cost. He also clarified that it does not cover 'loss of a profit or rise in the market price which

---

42 *Hogarth v Walker* [1900] 2 QB 283 on dunnage mats and separating cloths on board a vessel engaged in the grain trade.

43 *Roddick v Indemnity Mutual Mar Insurance Co* [1895] 2 QB 380, CA.

44 *Per* Lord Robson, *The Gunford Case* [1911] AC 529 at p 549, HL.

45 Section 12.

46 [1933] 1 KB 81 at p 90, CA. For another example of an unvalued or open policy on goods, see *Berger & Light diffusers Pty Ltd v Pollock* [1973] 2 Lloyd's Rep 442.

was expected to be made or to occur in the future'. [47] Whether the loss be total or partial, the same principle applies. [48]

Floating or open policy on goods

A floating policy is defined in s 29. It is a policy on goods which leaves 'the name of the ship or ships and other particulars to be defined by subsequent declarations'. In the context of insurable value, s 29(4) states that:

> 'Unless the policy otherwise provides, where a declaration of value is not made until after notice of loss or arrival, the policy must be treated as an unvalued policy as regards the subject-matter of that declaration.'

The parties may, in view of the opening words to the subsection, insert a special clause in the policy as to valuation in the event of loss or arrival before a declaration is made. Clause 5 of the Institute Standard Conditions for Cargo Contracts (1/4/82) is an example of such a clause. It states:

> 'In the event of loss accident or arrival before declaration of value it is agreed that the basis of valuation shall be the prime cost of the goods or merchandise plus the expenses of and incidental to shipping, the freight for which the Assured are liable, the charges of insurance and … %.'

Insurable value of any other subject-matter

With respect to any other subject matter, s 16(4) states that the insurable value is simply the amount at the risk of the assured when the policy attaches, plus the charges of insurance.

---

47 In similar terms, Greer LJ, *ibid*, at p 103, noted that it means 'the prime cost to the assured at or about the time of shipment, or at any rate at some time when the prime cost can be reasonably deemed to represent their value to their owner at the date of shipment'.

48 *Usher v Noble* (1810) 12 East 673, the rule for estimating a partial loss is 'by taking the proportional difference between the selling price of the sound and that of the damaged part of the goods at the port of delivery, and applying that proportion (be it a half, a quarter, an eighth, etc) with reference to such estimated value at the loading port, to the damaged portion of the goods'.

CHAPTER 6

UTMOST GOOD FAITH, DISCLOSURE
AND REPRESENTATIONS

UTMOST GOOD FAITH

The very foundation of a contract of marine insurance sits on the principle of *uberrimae fidei*. 'Insurance is a contract *uberrimae fidei*'[1] and this is declared in s 17 of the Act as:[2]

> 'A contract of marine insurance is a contract based upon the utmost good faith, and, if the utmost good faith be not observed by either party, the contract may be avoided by the other party.'

The principle applies to all policies whatever the risk or the subject-matter insured.

'Utmost'

The word 'utmost' suggests that a high degree of good faith is required to satisfy s 17. In *Container Transport International Inc v Oceanus Mutual Underwriting Association (Bermuda)*,[3] Lord Stephenson, though he had reservations as to whether it was possible to go into degrees of good faith, was nevertheless prepared to accept that: 'It is enough that much more than an absence of bad faith is required of both parties to all contract of insurance'. Though he was reluctant to enter into a discussion on the different shades of good faith, he was clear of the minimum standard, that something more than the absence of bad faith is required. However, Mr Justice Steyn in *Banque Keyser Ullmann v Skandia*,[4] remarked that the duty is, '... not only to abstain from bad faith but to observe in a positive sense the utmost good faith ...'.

Disclosure and representations

Section 17 is the first of a group of sections falling under the heading 'Disclosure and Representations'. This arrangement of the sections had led some to deduce that the principle applies only to matters relating to disclosure and representations; and that as the duty of disclosure is by, s 18, only applicable 'before the contract is concluded', s 17 should likewise apply only to a pre-contract situation.

---

1   Chalmers, p 24.
2   See also s 86.
3   [1984] 1 Lloyd's Rep 476 at p 525, CA; reversing [1982] 2 Lloyd's Rep 178. Hereinafter referred to as *The CTI* case.
4   [1987] 1 Lloyd's Rep 69 at p 93.

The duty of disclosure is admittedly closely related to the doctrine of utmost good faith. The truth, however, is, as can be seen from the judgment of Lord Ellenborough in *Carter v Boehm*,[5] that the duty of disclosure stems from the principle of utmost good faith and not *vice versa*. But this, however, does not mean that the two notions are synonymous covering the same ground They may well overlap, but as the duty of utmost good faith is the source from which the duty of disclosure and the law of representation originate, it has to be the wider and more potent of the two concepts.

A breach of the duty of utmost good faith is generally established by proof of non-disclosure or misrepresentation. This has somehow, over the years, caused the line between the defences of non-disclosure and of utmost good faith to become less defined. The awakening that they are distinct principles came recently with the cases of *The CTI* case and, in particular, *The Litsion Pride*.[6]

An 'overriding duty'

In *The CTI* case, Lord Justice Kerr, sitting in the Court of Appeal, issued the reminder that the duty of utmost good faith is an 'overriding duty', of which the duty of disclosure is only an aspect thereof. In similar vein, Lord Justice Parker expressed the opinion that:[7] '... the duty imposed by s 17 goes ... further than merely to require fulfilment of the duties under the succeeding sections ...'. These comments have clarified that s 17 is independent of the duty of disclosure.

There are essentially two main legal issues in *The Litsion Pride*: the first, relating to time, raises the interesting question as to whether the duty of utmost good faith applies before and after the execution of the contract; and the second, as to whether the making of a fraudulent claim constituted a breach of the duty of utmost good faith. On the first issue, Mr Justice Hirst had no doubt whatsoever that the principle of utmost good faith applies before and after the execution of the contract. His observation was that: '... the authorities in support for the proposition that the obligation of utmost good faith in general continues after the execution of the insurance contract are very powerful'. In this sense, the duty of utmost good faith has to be wider than the duty of disclosure as defined in s 18, which states that the assured must disclose to the insurer 'before the contract is concluded' every material circumstance. Unlike s 18, there is no time limit imposed in s 17.

On the second question, Mr Justice Hirst held that: '... the duty not to make fraudulent claims and not to make claims in breach of the duty of utmost good faith is an implied term of the policy ...'. This is a demonstration of the fact that s 17 stands in its own right as a complete defence: it clearly does not have to rely on the defences of non-disclosure or misrepresentation for sustenance.

---

5   (1766) 3 Burr 1905, 1 Wm Bl 593.

6   *Black King Shipping Corpn v Massie* [1985] 1 Lloyd's Rep 437, QBD.

7   [1984] 1 Lloyd's Rep 476 at p 512, CA.

Reciprocal duties of utmost good faith

The words 'by either party' in s 17 have made it patently clear that the duty of utmost good faith is reciprocal. This principle of mutuality is adopted from the common law. If further confirmation be required, reference should be made to *Banque Keyser Ullmann v Skandia*,[8] where Lord Justice Slade, on appeal, remarked that:[9] '... the obligation to disclose material facts is a mutual one imposing reciprocal duties on insurer and insured. In the case of marine insurance contracts, s 17 in effect so provides'.

'May be avoided'

The legal effect of a breach of utmost good faith is spelt out in the words 'the contract may be avoided by the other party'. Here, the operative word is 'may'. Avoidance in s 17 means 'avoidance *ab initio*'.[10] As no other remedy, such as a right to damages, is sounded in s 17, avoidance of the contract is the only remedy available to the assured.

To conclude this discussion of the doctrine of utmost good faith, the very recent case of *The Star Sea*[11] should be referred to, for in there can be found a concise summary of the salient features of s 17 drawn out by Mr Justice Tuckey, who said:

> 'Three things are of note. First, the duty is not limited to the pre-contract stage (compare ss 18 – 21). Second, there is no requirement of materiality (*ditto*). Third, the only specified remedy for breach is avoidance. The courts have held that damages cannot be awarded for such a breach.'

DUTY OF DISCLOSURE

The duty of disclosure laid down in ss 18 and 20 is derived from s 17, the duty of utmost good faith. Section 18 relates to disclosure by the assured, and s 19 by agents effecting the insurance.[12] The underlying basis for the principle of

---

8   [1987] 1 Lloyd's Rep 69 at p 93, QBD.

9   [1988] 2 Lloyd's Rep 513 at p 544, CA.

10   *Per* Hirst J in *The Litsion Pride* [1985] 1 Lloyd's Rep 437 at p 515. A long time ago, it was thought that, as in the case of fraud, a breach of the duty of utmost good faith rendered the contract void: *Carter v Boehm* (1766) 3 Burr 1905.

11   *Manifest Shipping & Co Ltd v Uni-Polaris Insurance Co Ltd & La R Reunion Europeene* [1995] 1 Lloyd's Rep 651, QBD.

12   Knowledge of a material fact by his agent will be imputed to the assured. It is unnecessary to devote a section on the duties of a broker, as the law of disclosure of material facts basically applies in the same way to the agent as it is to the principal, the assured. For an excellent account of the rights and liabilities of a principal by the knowledge of his agent, see *Blackburn, Low & Co v Vigors* (1887) 12 QBD 531, HL. Other cases dealing with the duty of disclosure by agents effecting insurance are: *Lynch v Dunsford* (1811) 14 East 494; *Fitzherbert v Mather* (1785) 1 TR 12; *Gladstone v King* (1813) 1 M & S 35; *Proudfoot v Montefiore* (1867) Law Rep 2 QB 511; *Stribley v Imperial Marine Insurance Co* (1876) 1 QBD 507; *Sawtell v Loudon* (1814) 5 Taunt 359; *Morrison v Universal Insurance Co* (1872) LR 8 Exch 40; *Blackburn v Haslam* (1888) 21 QBD 144; and *Wilson & Others v Salamandra Assurance Co of St Petersburg* (1903) 8 Com Cas 129.

disclosure was, as early as 1766, clarified by Lord Mansfield in the celebrated case of *Carter v Boehm*.[13] He began first by noting that, 'Insurance is a contract upon speculation' and then proceeded to say that: 'Good faith forbids either party from concealing what he privately knows, to draw the other into a bargain, from his ignorance of that fact, and his believing the contrary ...'.[14]

Non-disclosure may be fraudulent or innocent. A fraudulent concealment of a material fact would obviously not only constitute a breach of the duty of utmost good faith, but also of the duty of disclosure. This explains why an eminent author has described it as a 'species of fraud'.[15] But not all non-disclosures are fraudulent: an assured may, by mistake or inadvertence, and without any fraudulent intention, conceal material information which he ought to have disclosed. An innocent concealment of a material fact, though it is not an infringement of the duty of good faith, will nonetheless entitle the insurer to avoid the contract. Although the suppression may be perfectly innocent, yet still the underwriter is misled. Furthermore, the risk run is really different from the risk understood and intended to be run, at the time of the agreement. There does not have to be fraud to constitute a breach of the duty of disclosure.[16] Thus, even an honest assured could, on the ground of non-disclosure, be denied of the right of recovery, if his insurer chooses to avoid the contract.

The duty of disclosure is a positive and not a negative duty; it is for the assured to take the initiative to reveal any material circumstance to the insurer, not for the insurer to inquire.[17]

It is necessary to mention that the right conferred to the insurer by s 18 to avoid the policy is based purely on the ground of a breach of the duty of disclosure. There is nothing in the sections, or in common law, requiring a causal link to be shown that the loss was caused by, or be related to, the fact of the undisclosed material circumstance. The question of the cause of loss does not arise when non-disclosure is pleaded as a defence.[18]

When to disclose

On a strict interpretation of s 18, the duty to disclose every material circumstance must take place 'before the contract is concluded'. According to

---

13 (1766) 3 Burr 1905 at p 1910.

14 Scrutton LJ in *Hoff Trading Co v Union Insurance Society of Canton Ltd* (1929) 45 TLR 466 at p 467, CA added that as '... the intending assured, knew everything, and the underwriter, the other party, knew nothing ... it was essential that the two parties should be put on equal terms, and it was the duty of the assured to disclose ...'.

15 In *Greenhill v Federal Insurance Co* [1927] 1 KB 65 at p 77, Scrutton LJ cited the following statement from Park's *Marine Insurance* with approval: 'The second species of fraud, which affects insurances, is the concealment of circumstances, known only to one of the parties entering into the contract'.

16 See *Joel v Law Union & Crown Insurance* [1908] 2 KB 863, CA, where the same principle was applied to a life policy. The assured had foolishly, but not fraudulently concealed a material fact; *Hoff Trading Co v Union Insurance Society* of Canton Ltd (1929) 45 TLR 466, CA, where the assured was unable to claim under the policy even though he did not consciously or deliberately over-value the ship.

17 A disclosure to the defendant's solicitor of the existence of a material circumstance is not notice of it to the defendant. See *Tate v Hyslop* (1885) 15 QBD 368.

18 See *Seaman v Fonereau* (1743) 2 Stra 1183.

s 21, 'A contract of marine insurance is deemed to be concluded when the proposal of the assured is accepted by the insurer, whether the policy be then issued or not ...'.[19]

A time limit is set by the words 'before the contract is concluded'. They give the impression that any material circumstance which comes to the knowledge of the assured *after* the contract is concluded need not be disclosed. The view that there is no continuing duty of disclosure was endorsed by a host of cases,[20] the most authoritative of which is *Niger Co Ltd v Guardian Assurance Co Ltd*,[21] where Lord Sumner in the House of Lords pointed out that, '... it would be going beyond the principle to say that each and every change in an insurance contract creates an occasion which a general disclosure becomes obligatory ...'. It was thought that once the duty had 'attached' there was no further duty of disclosure; whatever events may subsequently happen, the assured need not communicate to the underwriters.

As was seen, *The Litsion Pride*,[22] albeit at first instance, has categorically held that the obligation of utmost good faith continues even *after* the execution of the contract. Bearing this in mind, and working from the premise that s 17 'overrides' or prevails over s 18, it could be argued that s 17 has extended the duty of disclosure beyond the time limit imposed by s 18. The effect of s 17 on the duty of disclosure was described by Mr Justice Hirst as follows:[23]

> '... it seems to be manifest that, as part of the duty of utmost good faith, it must be incumbent on the insured to include within it all relevant information to him at the time he gives it; and in any event the self-same duty required the assured to furnish to the insurer any further material information which he acquires subsequent to the initial notice as and when it comes to his knowledge, particularly if it is materially at variance with the information he originally gave.'

As the assured in this case had, during the currency of the policy, failed to notify the insurer with 'relevant information' of the voyage,[24] they were held to be in breach of the duty of utmost good faith. It is to be noted that, by reason of the War Risk Trading Warranties, the assured were required to inform the insurers as soon as practicable of voyages to additional premium areas.

The above-cited remarks by Mr Justice Hirst seem to suggest that the duty of disclosure is a continuing one. If this is the case, then the words 'before the contract is concluded' in s 18 are superfluous. This perhaps explains the anxiety

---

19 See *Lishman v Northern Maritime Insurance Co* (1875) LR 10 CP 179, Ex Ch where the non-disclosure of a material fact coming to the knowledge of the assured after the acceptance of the risk, but before the execution of the policy was held not to be a concealment so as to avoid the policy.

20 See *Cory v Patton* (1874) LR 9 QB 577; *Lishman v Northern Maritime Insurance Co* (1875) LR 10 CP 179; *Ionides v Pacific Fire and Marine Insurance Co* (1871) LR 6 QB 674 at p 684; *Willmott v General Accident Fire & Life Assurance Corpn* (1935) 53 Ll L Rep 156; and *Berger v Pollock* [1973] 2 Lloyd's Rep 442.

21 (1922) 13 Ll L Rep 75, HL.

22 [1985] 1 Lloyd's Rep 437, QB.

23 *Ibid*, at p 512.

24 For example, her ETA, destinations etc, are likely to change as she proceeded with the voyage.

felt by Lord Jauncey in *Banque Keyser v Skandia*,[25] who was keen to restrict the scope of the duty of disclosure in accord with the terms of s 18. 'There is', he said, 'in general, no obligation to disclose supervening facts which come to the knowledge of either party after conclusion of the contract ... subject always to such exceptional cases as a ship entering a war zone or an insured failing to disclose all facts relevant to a claim'. Whether these are the only two exceptions to the general rule is not totally clear. But what is disturbing is that the range of information envisaged by the last part of this sentence is indeed very wide.

There are two points of view on the subject, both of which are of vital importance to the position of the assured. Needless to say, before an assured can comply with the duty of disclosure he has first to be made absolutely clear of the extent of his obligation. Until such a time as this matter is directly and conclusively clarified by a higher court, an assured would be well advised to take heed of the fact that the duty of utmost good faith is overriding. It is worthwhile to bear in mind that utmost good faith is the fountain-head from which all his other duties flow. So as not to compromise his position, he ought to disclose all 'material' circumstances and 'relevant' facts which can possibly affect the risks insured, coming to his knowledge before and after the conclusion of the contract.

Material circumstance

The duty imposed by s 18(2) on an assured to disclose 'every material circumstance' which is known to him places him in a dilemma of having to decide what information bearing upon the risk he ought to disclose.[26] The statutory requirement is that only 'material circumstances' which would 'influence the judgment of a prudent insurer in fixing the premium, or determining whether he will take the risk' need be disclosed.[27] It is the assured who has to decide, before the conclusion of the contract, what information he must disclose.[28]

The question whether a particular circumstance is or is not material resolves itself into one of pure fact. An undisclosed fact may be material in one case and not in another; it could be material at one period of time but not in another. As the matter is purely one of fact, it would be a futile exercise to examine all the

---

25 [1990] 2 Lloyd's Rep 377, HL.

26 When an insurer seeks to avoid a policy for non-disclosure, the arguments will naturally focus on the particular item of information which has been withheld. Seen from hindsight, this can be of little help or consolation to an assured who has to decide in advance which item of information he should disclose to the insurer. He could of course err on the side of caution and disclose everything to the insurer. But in the commercial world, this is not a practicable course to take. See *Ionides & Another v Pender* (1874) LR 9 QB 531 at p 539: '... it would be too much to put on the assured the duty of disclosing everything which might influence the mind of an underwriter. Business could hardly be carried on if this was required'.

27 See also s 20(2).

28 Note s 18(3) which spells out the circumstances which need not be disclosed.

cases which have held a particular circumstance material or not material.[29] This part will therefore examine only those aspects of the law which are either controversial or have been recently subjected to judicial scrutiny.

Materiality and avoidance

The test of materiality and the related question pertaining to the legal effect of non-disclosure are the two main topics in this area of law which have recently engendered a great deal of debate. For a period of time, it was thought that the matter relating to materiality and avoidance of the contract on the ground of non-disclosure had been put at rest by the Court of Appeal in *The CTI* case. These issues, however, were recently resurrected in *Pan Atlantic Insurance Co Ltd and Another v Pine Top Insurance Co Ltd*,[30] where the House of Lords finally resolved what it has regarded a 'long-standing controversy' with a history of more than 200 years.[31] Before proceeding to discuss the ruling of the House, it is necessary for a fuller understanding of the subject briefly to mention the law, laid down by *The CTI* case, as it stood before *The Pine Top* case.

The Court of Appeal in *The CTI* case held that there was only one test for determining the effect of non-disclosure of a material fact: The yardstick laid down by s 18(2) is the hypothetical, not the actual, or particular, insurer. It was held that a circumstance was material only if its disclosure would have *decisively* influenced the mind of a prudent insurer. Whether the actual or particular insurer was or was not induced by the undisclosed fact or misrepresentation to enter into the contract was considered irrelevant. The case decided that there was only one criterion which needed be applied. Materiality and the right of avoidance of the contract were both determined by proof of an actual effect of the undisclosed information on a prudent insurer. The principle of law propounded was that if the undisclosed information would have led a prudent insurer either to reject or to accept the risk on more onerous terms, that alone was sufficient to confer upon the particular insurer the right to avoid the contract. Whether the particular insurer himself was or was not actually induced by the undisclosed information to enter into the contract was considered of no consequence.

---

29 For a comprehensive study of examples of material circumstances, see Ivamy, pp 53–66. Excessive over-valuation of a ship is, of course, a classic example of non-disclosure of a material fact. As the law in this area is now well settled, it is unnecessary to go into the cases: see, eg, *Lewis v Rucker* (1761) 2 Burr 1167; *Haigh v De La Cour* (1812) 3 Camp 319; *Barker v Janson* (1868) LR 3 CP 303; *North of England Association v Armstrong* (1870) LR 5 QB 244; *Ionides v Pender* (1874) LR 9 QB 531; *Woodside v Globe Marine Insurance Co* [1896] 1 QB 105; *Thames & Mersey Insurance Co v Gunford Ship Co* [1911] AC 529, HL; *Visscherij Maatschappij v Scottish Metropolitan Assurance Co* (1922) 27 Com Cas 198, CA; *Mathie v The Argonaut Marine Insurance Co Ltd* (1925) 21 Ll L Rep 145; *Loders & Nucoline Ltd v Bank of New Zealand* (1929) 33 Ll L Rep 70; *Piper v Royal Exchange Assurance* (1932) 44 Ll L Rep 103, KBD; *Williams v Atlantic Co Ltd* [1933] 1 KB 81, CA; *Willmott v General Accident Fire & Life Assurance Corpn Ltd* [1935] 53 Ll L Rep 156; *Slattery v Mance* [1962] 1 Lloyd's Rep 60; and *Berger & Light Diffusers Pty Ltd v Pollock* [1973] 2 Lloyd's Rep 442. Most of these incidents of scuttling of grossly over-valued ships have occurred at a time when there was a recession in the market. Some of these cases are discussed in relation to the defence of wilful misconduct: see Chapter 10.

30 [1994] 2 Lloyd's Rep 427, HL. Henceforth referred to as *The Pine Top* case.

31 *Per* Lord Mustill, *ibid*, at pp 432 and 442.

Contrary to *The CTI* case, *The Pine Top* case has declared that there is not one, but two distinct stages to the inquiry. The first is to determine the *materiality* of the circumstance, and the second, the right of the insurer to *avoid* the contract. It is relevant, at the outset, to note that there is no difference between an allegation of non-disclosure and of misrepresentation: the same criterion of materiality is laid down in ss 18(2) and 20(2). Furthermore, the legal effect is also the same: In both cases, the insurer may avoid the contract.[32] The ensuing discussion of the ruling of the House is, therefore, relevant to both non-disclosure and misrepresentation, but for convenience this discussion will only refer to the former.

Test for materiality

It has, first and foremost, to be shown that the undisclosed fact is material in accordance with the terms laid down in s 18(2). That materiality must be judged by the response of a hypothetical prudent insurer is clear, for if this was not the case, the actual underwriter could, after the risk has matured, convince himself and the court that he would have rejected the risk or increased the premium. But how this prudent insurer test is to applied is a question which has caused some concern.

The hypothetical prudent insurer

The real problem was framed by Lord Goff thus: 'Is the insurer required to show that full and accurate disclosure would have led the prudent insurer either to reject the risk or at least to have accepted it on more onerous terms?' This is referred to as the 'decisive influence test'.

Section 18(2) is capable of two interpretations. One interpretation, which relies on the 'decisive influence test', requires proof that a prudent insurer would be decisively influenced by the undisclosed fact. The other was referred to by Lord Mustill as the lesser standard of the 'impact on the mind of the prudent underwriter test'. By the latter criterion, any information which a prudent insurer would have wanted to know or take into account has to be disclosed.

The decisive influence test adopted by *The CTI* case was roundly rejected by the majority of the House in *The Pine Top* case.[33] Lord Goff, relying on a literal interpretation of the wording of s 18(2), held that they:

> '... denote no more than an effect on the mind of the insurer in weighing up the risk. The subsection does not require that the circumstance in question should have a decisive influence on the judgment of the insurer.'

'Influence' and 'whether'

Treating the matter as simply one of statutory interpretation, both Lord Goff and Lord Mustill pointed to the fact that the legislature had left the word 'influence' unadorned. The latter was of the opinion that the legislature could have easily inserted a phrase such as 'decisively influence', 'conclusively

---

32 See ss 18(1) and 20(1).

33 With Lord Templeman and Lord Lloyd of Berwick dissenting on this issue.

influence', 'determine the decision' and the like if it had intended to promote the decisive influence test. 'Influence the mind', said Lord Mustill, is not the same as 'change the mind'.

Emphasis was also placed on the word 'whether', which Lord Mustill had decided:[34] '... clearly denotes an effect on the thought processes of the insurer in weighing up the risk, quite different from words which might have been used but were not, such as "influencing the insurer to take the risk".' Lord Goff took the approach that: 'A circumstance may be material even though a full and accurate disclosure of it would not in itself have had a decisive effect on the prudent underwriter's decision whether to accept the risk and if so at what premium.'

It is apparent from the above remarks that the decisive influence test is not to be applied. All that the assured need disclose is information which is objectively material; there is nothing in s 18(2) to suggest that materiality is to be confined to such circumstances as would definitely have changed the mind of a prudent underwriter.

Right of avoidance

The Pine Top case, after rejecting the decisive influence test, proposed an additional obstacle for the insurer: He has now not only to show that the undisclosed information is material in the sense described above, but also that he was in fact induced to enter into the contract on the relevant terms. The latter requirement, which was not adopted in *The CTI* case,[35] is referred to as the 'actual inducement test'.

The 'actual inducement' test

The House unanimously agreed that even though actual inducement is not expressly stipulated as a requirement by s 18(2), nonetheless it is an implied term of the contract. Lord Mustill phrased the issue as, '... the need, or otherwise, of a causal connection between the misrepresentation or non-disclosure and the making of the contract of insurance'. After conducting a thorough examination of the legal position, he concluded that:[36]

'... there is to be implied in the 1906 Act a qualification that a material misrepresentation will not entitle the underwriter to avoid the policy unless the misrepresentation induced the making of the contract, using "induced" in the sense in which it is used in the general law of contract.'

If the non-disclosure or misrepresentation did not actually induce the making of the contract, the insurer will not be allowed to rely on it as a ground for avoiding the contract. Lord Templeman's sentiments were:[37]

---

34 [1994] 2 Lloyd's Rep 427 at p 440, HL.

35 *Ibid*, at p 431, Lord Goff explained that it was thought in *The CTI* case that actual inducement was not required because it was already incorporated in the decisive influence test, though attributing it not to the actual insurer, but to the hypothetical prudent insurer.

36 [1994] 2 Lloyd's Rep 427 at p 452.

37 *Ibid*, at p 430.

'The law is already sufficiently tender to insurers who seek to avoid contracts for innocent non-disclosure and it is not unfair to require insurers to show that they have suffered as result of non-disclosure.'

It is evident from *The Pine Top* case that an insurer does not now have an unfettered or invariable right to avoid the contract. First, he has to prove the materiality of the undisclosed information, and secondly, that he was induced to enter the contract on the relevant terms. Lord Mustill has summed up the two stages of the legal inquiry as follows:[38]

'The materiality or otherwise of a circumstance should be a constant; and the subjective characteristics, actions and knowledge of the individual underwriter should be relevant only to the fairness of holding him to the bargain if something objectively material is not disclosed.'

The tests for materiality is *not* the same as that for inducement. If the insurance market had found the law as proposed in *The CTI* case 'remarkably unpopular',[39] they must surely now find the ruling of the House in *The Pine Top* case even more so: The two stages to the inquiry have rendered their burden of proof much more onerous.

REPRESENTATIONS

Like the duty of disclosure, the principles relating to representations made by an assured also stem from the doctrine of *uberrimae fidei* laid down in s 17. There are similarities and differences between the principles relating to disclosure and representation. As pointed out earlier, the tests for materiality and the legal effect of non-disclosure and misrepresentation are the same; the criterion of the hypothetical prudent insurer employed to determine the materiality of a fact or circumstance, and its twin, the 'actual inducement test' used for determining the right of avoidance, both enunciated by *The Pine Top* case,[40] apply to non-disclosure as well as misrepresentation.

Section 20, captioned as 'Representations pending negotiation of contract', defines the various types of representations and the legal effect of a misrepresentation. Representations are statements made by the assured or his agent, 'during the negotiations for the contract, and before the contract is concluded'.[41] The time when a contract is deemed to be concluded is spelt out in s 21.

Representations may be made orally or in writing. They are generally made spontaneously in answers to questions put to the assured by his insurer. If an assured is asked a question, he must answer truthfully regardless of the materiality of the question to the risk. If he gives a false or untruthful answer with the intention of deceiving the insurer, though it may not be a material fact, this would constitute a breach of the duty of utmost good faith, the effect of

---

38   *Ibid*, at p 442.

39   *Per* Steyn J, *The Pine Top* case [1993] 1 Lloyd's Rep 496 at p 505, CA.

40   [1994] 2 Lloyd's Rep 427, HL.

41   A disclosure of a material fact must also be made 'before the contract is concluded': s 18(1).

which would render the contract voidable at the option of the insurer under s 17.[42]

Unlike an express warranty, which must be 'included in, or written upon, the policy',[43] a representation is not a term of the contract of insurance, but a statement made during negotiations to induce the insurer to enter into the contract. By painting a favourable picture of the risk, the intention of the assured is to persuade the insurer to accept the risk, or to accept the risk at a lower premium. Non-disclosure, on the other hand, is a concealment of facts which tend to show the risk to be greater than it would otherwise appear.

Types of representations

Section 20(3) may initially give the impression that there are two types of representations, namely, as to a matter of fact and as to a matter of expectation or belief. Templeman, however, holds the view that there are three types of representation: a representation as simply of a fact; of a material fact; and a representation of expectation or belief.[44]

Section 20(1) states: 'Every material representation made by the assured ... must be true. If it be untrue the insurer may avoid the contract.' There are two main features to this statement. First, the materiality of the representation has to be determined, and secondly, the meaning of the term 'true' has to be ascertained.

The test for materiality spelt out in s 20(2) is the same as that for non-disclosure of a material fact. It is to be determined by using the yardstick of a prudent insurer. If the representation is not material, then it should have no legal effect. But should it be found to be material, in the sense that it would influence the mind of a hypothetical prudent insurer, then the next step of the inquiry is to ascertain whether the representation of fact is 'true'. For this, reference to s 20(4) has to be made: Whether a material representation is or is not true depends on whether it is 'substantially correct', that is to say, if the difference between what is represented and what is actually correct would not be considered material by a prudent insurer. The prudent insurer test is applied twice: First, as to the materiality of the representation, and then as to the truth of the representation. The classic authority on the subject of misrepresentation is *Pawson v Watson*,[45] where it was represented that the ship carried 12 guns and 20 men when in fact she carried only nine guns, six swivels, 16 men, and nine boys. As this was held to be substantially correct, the insurer was unable to avoid the contract.

Whether there is a third category of representation, simply of fact, is, it is submitted, with due respect, doubtful, for it could be argued that that which is not material cannot possibly induce the insurer to enter into the contract or to

---

42 Section 17.

43 Section 35(2).

44 Templeman, *Marine Insurance, Its Principles and Practice* (1986, 6th edn), p 34; hereinafter referred to simply as 'Templeman'.

45 (1778) 2 Cowp 785. *Cf De Hahn v Hartley* (1786) 1 TR 343.

enter the contract on different terms. In order to avoid the contract, the insurer must now satisfy the actual inducement test. It is contended that the purpose of s 20(4) is not to create a new class of representation, that of fact, but to define the meaning of the word 'true' when applied in relation to a material representation as set out in s 20(1). Section 20(4) has to be read with ss 20(1) and 20(2).[46] Moreover, it has always been said that the single feature which distinguishes a representation from a warranty is that a warranty does not have to be material to the risk: This is made clear by s 33(3).

A representation as to a matter of expectation or belief is true if it be made in good faith.[47]

The effect of a misrepresentation is the same as that for non-disclosure: the insurer may avoid the contract if the representation turns out to be untrue. The insurer has now to prove that he was actually induced to enter the contract.

---

46   The word 'material' should perhaps be read before the word 'fact' in s 20(4).
47   Section 20(3).

CHAPTER 7

WARRANTIES

A – GENERAL PRINCIPLES

There are two types of warranties identified by the Act: express and implied warranties.[1] A warranty in marine insurance, whether express or implied, is indeed a very special term of the contract. In the law of marine insurance, a warranty is also referred to as a promissory warranty and this is made clear by s 33(1), which defines a warranty to mean:

> '... a promissory warranty, that is to say, a warranty by which the assured undertakes that some particular thing shall or shall not be done, or that some condition shall be fulfilled, or whereby he affirms or negatives the existence of a particular state of facts.'

There are certain features, common to both express and implied warranties, laid down by case law and the Act relating to the nature of a marine insurance warranty and the effect of its breach. These qualities have bestowed upon it its undoubted strength and importance as a contractual term:

- A promissory warranty does not have to be material to the risk;
- A promissory warranty must be exactly complied with;[2]
- There is no defence for a breach of a promissory warranty;
- A breach of a promissory warranty is irremediable;[3]
- A causal connection between breach and loss need not be shown;
- A breach of a warranty automatically discharges the insurer from liability; and
- A breach of a warranty may be waived.

Each of the above general principles will be examined separately, followed by a discussion of some of the standard examples of express warranties, and then the implied warranties.

MATERIALITY TO THE RISK

There can be no question of querying the materiality of a warranty: a warranty does not have to be material to the risk. This is what distinguishes it from non-disclosure and misrepresentation. This aspect of the law is more appropriate to an express rather than to an implied warranty, the materiality of which cannot be called into question being implied by law. Section 33(3) states that it must be exactly complied with 'whether it be material to the risk or not'. The law on the subject is more than well-established.

---

1   Section 33(2).
2   Section 33(3).
3   Section 34(2).

In *Union Insurance Society of Canton, Ltd v George Wills & Co*,[4] Lord Parmoor in the Judicial Committee of the Privy Council, on appeal from a judgment of the Supreme Court of Western Australia, stated that: 'If the promise amounts to a warranty it is immaterial for what purpose the warranty is introduced.'

In *Newcastle Fire Insurance Co v MacMorran and Co*,[5] it was noted that:

'... if there is a warranty, the person warranting undertakes that the matter is such as he represents it; and unless it be so, whether it arises from fraud, mistake, negligence of an agent, or otherwise, then the contract is not entered into; there is in reality no contract ... Therefore the materiality or immaterality signifies nothing. The only question is as to the mere fact.'

Lord Justice Bankes in *Farr v Motor Traders Mutual Insurance Society*[6] went so far as to say that a warranty, 'however absurd', is still binding on the parties.

EXACT COMPLIANCE

The most demanding characteristic of a promissory warranty, whether express or implied, is that it must be *exactly* complied with. Unlike a representation,[7] s 33(3) insists upon a *literal* compliance: substantial observance is not good enough. The use of the word 'must' in s 33(1) strengthens this requirement. Thus, there is no room for the application of the maxim *de minimis non curat lex*; neither is a severance of the contract possible.

During the second half of the 18th century, a pair of indeed unforgettable cases, namely, *Pawson v Watson*[8] and *De Hahn v Hartley*,[9] both presided over by Lord Mansfield, discussed the differences between a representation and a warranty in a contract of marine insurance. In the first case, Lord Mansfield's remarks regarding the nature of an express warranty were *obiter*. As the statement of fact was not inserted into the policy, the judge had no choice but to construe it as a representation.[10] Though *obiter*, his comments are nevertheless lucid and revealing, and the principle there so expressed is still good law. He stated that:[11]

'Where it is a part of the written policy, it must be performed: as if there be a warranty of convoy, there it must be a convoy: nothing tantamount will do, or answer the purpose; it must be strictly performed, as being part of the agreement ...'

---

4   [1916] AC 281, Privy Council.

5   (1815) 3 Dow 255 at pp 259 and 262.

6   [1920] 3 KB 669 at p 673, CA.

7   A representation of fact need only be 'substantially correct' (s 20(4)) and a representation of expectation or belief is true if made in good faith (s 20(5)). See below.

8   (1778) 2 Cowp 785.

9   (1786) 1 TR 343.

10 The *Julius Caesar* was described to the underwriter as: 'she mounts 12 guns and 20 men'. When she was taken by an American privateer, she had on board 6 pounders, 4 three pounders, 3 one pounders, 6 half pounders which were called swivels, and 27 men and boys in all; but of them, 16 only were men (not 20 as the instructions mentioned) and the rest boys.

11 (1778) 2 Cowp 785 at pp 787-788.

In *De Hahn v Hartley*,[12] the clause which was written in the margin of a policy of insurance on the *Juno* stated that she had 'sailed from Liverpool with 14 six-pounders, swivels, small arms, and 50 hands or upwards; copper-sheathed'. On this occasion, as the statement was written into the policy, albeit it in the margin,[13] Lord Mansfield was able to classify it as a warranty. It is worthwhile setting out the words of the learned judge, as they accurately declare the legal position:

> 'There is a material distinction between a warranty and a representation. A representation may be equitably and substantially answered: but a warranty must be strictly complied with. Supposing a warranty to sail on 1st August, and the ship did not sail till the 2nd, the warranty would not be complied with. A warranty in a policy of insurance is a condition or a contingency ...'[14]

In a similar tone, Mr Justice Ashhurst stressed that[15] 'the very meaning of a warranty is to preclude all questions whether it has been substantially complied with: it must be literally so'.

The court was not, and correctly so, influenced in any way by the fact that the *Juno* was *as safe*, having set sail with 46 hands on board instead of 50 as required by the warranty. Whether the actual situation is for better or for worse makes no difference: the underwriter has the right to say, the truth of the case is not according to what he had bargained for.

The severity of the rule of literal compliance can also be seen in the case of *Overseas Commodities Ltd v Style*,[16] where the question of severance of contract was also discussed. The facts of the case involved a cargo of canned pork insured under an 'all risks' policy which contained a warranty: 'warranted all tins marked by manufacturers with a code for verification of date of manufacture'. The court held that there was a breach of warranty in that a substantial[17] number of tins were not marked with a code in accordance with the warranty.

Mr Justice McNair was not prepared to grant the assured indemnity even for the tins that were properly marked in compliance with the terms of the warranty. The whole basis of his decision rested upon the ground that there was only *one* policy of insurance for the whole consignment of the goods, and that the contract of insurance could not be severed into as many contracts as there were tins of pork that were covered by that policy. He was adamant that the

---

12 (1786) 1 TR 343.

13 See also *Bean v Stuppart* (1778) 1 Dougl 11.

14 The illustration with regard to dates clearly excludes the application of the *de minimis* rule.

15 (1786) 1 TR 343 at p 346.

16 [1958] 1 Lloyd's Rep 546.

17 How the court would have decided if only one or two tins were not properly marked is an interesting thought. Whether the *de minimis* rule could be invoked in such a situation is yet to be decided. On the application of the *de minimis* rule for the purpose of determining whether a loss is total or partial, see *Boon Cheah Steel Pipes Sdr Bhd v Asia Insurance Co* [1975] 1 Lloyd's Rep 452, where the Malaysia High Court refused to apply the *de minimis* rule. As exact compliance is required, any difference, however negligible or insignificant, is unlikely to be considered as inconsequential.

contract of insurance should not be re-written in order to provide coverage for some of the loss.

NO DEFENCE FOR BREACH

With the exception of the two excuses laid down in s 34, there is clearly no defence for a breach of an express or implied warranty. Though not specifically spelt out by the Act, the general principle that there is no defence for a breach of a warranty is firmly established by the common law. As there is nothing in the Act which is inconsistent with this rule, it 'shall continue to apply to contracts of marine insurance'.[18] Moreover, as only two excuses are laid down by the Act, they must be regarded as the only exceptions to the general rule allowed by law.

The application of the general rule is actually best illustrated in cases relating to a breach of the implied warranty of seaworthiness. The common law principle was first established in 1764 in the case of *Mills v Roebuck, The Mills Frigate*,[19] a prominent landmark in the legal history of marine insurance. Lord Mansfield's judgment was said to have 'hit the city of London like a thunderbolt'[20] when he held that an assured could not recover upon a policy on a ship which suffered from a latent defect unknown to both parties to the contract. The facts of the case involved the French-built *Mills Frigate* which was fastened together with bolts of iron that were liable to rust, causing the timbers of such ships to become loose without any visible signs of decay, rendering her incapable of bearing the sea. The court held that the assured could not recover even though the loss was caused by a latent defect unbeknown to both parties.

Similarly, pleas such as the exercise of care and due diligence, inevitable accident, and good faith are also of no avail. There is a long line of cases which had applied the rule.[21] To drive home the point, Lord Eldon in *Douglas v Scougall*,[22] in reference to the implied warranty of seaworthiness stressed that:

'It is not necessary to inquire whether the owners acted honestly and fairly in the transaction, for it is clear law that, however just and honest the intentions and conduct of the owner may be, if he is mistaken in the fact, and the vessel is in fact not seaworthy, the underwriter is not liable.'

In *Forshaw v Chabert*,[23] the position was stated as follows: 'Now it is clear that a ship must be seaworthy at the time when she sails; the assured warrants that, and whatever physical necessities may interpose, he is not allowed to deviate from the strict terms of his warranty'.

---

18 Section 91(2).

19 Reported in Park, *Insurance*, (7th edn), Chapter XI, p 334.

20 DEB Gibb, *Lloyd's of London*, 1957, p 67.

21 *Lee v Beach* (1792) Park, *Insurance*, (8th edn) at p 468; *Oliver v Cowley* (1792) *ibid*, at p 470; *Forshaw v Chabert* (1821) 3 Br & B 159; *Douglas v Scougall* (1816) 4 Dow 278; *Wedderburn & Others v Bell* (1807) 1 Camp 1; and *Quebec Marine Insurance Co v The Commercial Bank of Canada* (1870) LR 3 PC 234.

22 (1816) 4 Dow 278.

23 (1821) 3 Br & B 159.

These cases, which have firmly established that there is no defence for a breach of the implied warranty of seaworthiness, have led the said warranty to be described as being 'absolute' in nature. In this sense, the same may be said of all warranties

Excuses under section 34(1)

As mentioned earlier, there are only two statutory excuses contained in s 34(1) which may be pleaded as a defence for non-compliance of a warranty: a change of circumstance, and when compliance with the warranty is rendered unlawful by any subsequent law. The excuse of a change of circumstance is more relevant to an express warranty than to an implied warranty, though, as worded, the section applies to both. In respect of the defence of illegality, s 34(1) complements s 41, which implies a warranty of legality in all polices that not only the adventure but the performance of the adventure has to be lawful.[24]

BREACH IS IRREMEDIABLE

Another defence, to the effect that the breach of the warranty was remedied before the loss, was unsuccessfully pleaded in relation to the implied warranty of seaworthiness in *Quebec Marine Insurance Co v The Commercial Bank of Canada*,[25] the classic authority on the subject. Counsel for the assured suggested that as the defect was remedied before the loss occurred, the underwriters will remain liable. This defence, described as 'a proposition of perilous latitude', was rejected by the Privy Council. The principle of law, now contained in s 34(2), declares that: 'Where a warranty is broken, the assured cannot avail himself of the defence that the breach has been remedied, and the warranty complied with, before loss'.

CAUSAL CONNECTION NOT REQUIRED

The fact that a breach of a warranty has no causal connection with the loss whatsoever is also immaterial. In *Foley v Tabor*,[26] Chief Justice Erle's address to the jury on this point was:

'It is not necessary for the insurer to make out that the loss was caused by the unseaworthiness relied upon. The question depends upon the state of the ship at the time when she sailed upon her voyage.'

The fact that the breach of a warranty has not caused the loss is clearly of no consequence.

---

24 Discussed below.

25 (1870) LR 3 PC 234.

26 (1861) 2 F & F 683 at p 672.

AUTOMATIC DISCHARGE FROM LIABILITY

Section 33(3) states that, 'A warranty ... is a condition which must be exactly complied with'. Though called a warranty, it is in fact, as defined by the said section, a 'condition' of a promissory nature. Thus, 'promissory condition' would be a more suitable name for it. The word 'condition' is not defined in the Act. It is, however, capable of two meanings: it could be used in the lay or non-technical sense to mean a provision, a requirement or simply a term of the contract[27] which in this case must be exactly complied with; or it could be interpreted in a strict and purely legal sense, as understood in the general law of contract, as a particular type of contractual term, a condition as opposed to a warranty or innominate term.

Under ordinary contract law, a warranty is a term of a contract the breach of which would bestow upon the innocent party the right only to damages. That an insurance warranty does not belong to such a class of warranty known in the general law of contract was made clear in *The Cap Tarifa*,[28] where it was said:

> 'The term "warranty" is used in different senses and, in insurance law, special considerations are applicable to the problem under discussion, apart from the general principles of contract law. Thus the familiar distinction between condition and warranty in the general law of contract is not applicable in the discussion of warranties in policies of insurance.'

Traditionally, a marine insurance warranty has always been recognised as a condition. However, in the past, it has also been referred to as a condition precedent to the attachment of risk; a condition precedent to the liability or further liability of the insurer; and even a condition subsequent. Recently, in *The Good Luck*,[29] it was confirmed that it is a condition precedent to the liability or further liability of the insurer.

A condition precedent

It is interesting to note that it was only as late as 1991 that the nature of a marine insurance warranty became the subject of serious and intense scrutiny in the House of Lords in *The Good Luck*. It is clearly the definitive authority on the subject of marine insurance warranties. The central and decisive consideration of the case revolved around the issue regarding the legal consequences of a breach of a promissory warranty as defined in s 33(3) of the Act. It is to be noted that, though the case was concerned directly with an express warranty, the principles enunciated therein on the effects of a breach also applies to implied warranties.

---

27 In *Overseas Commodities Ltd v Style* [1958] 1 Lloyd's Rep 546 at p 558, McNair J endeavoured to explain the meaning of the word as follows: 'A condition of what? Surely, a condition of the contract of insurance'.

28 *Per* Walsh J [1957] 2 Lloyd's Rep 485 at p 490. In *W & J Lane v Spratt* [1970] 2 QB 480 at p 486, Roskill J clarified the position as follows, '... it is well known, particularly in the field of marine insurance law, that the word "warranty" is often used when those who use it in truth mean a "condition".

29 *Bank of Nova Scotia v Hellenic Mutual War Risks Association (Bermuda) Ltd* [1991] 2 WLR 1279; [1991] 2 Lloyd's Rep 191, HL.

The facts of the case may be briefly summarised as follows. *The Good Luck* was insured under a policy which contained, *inter alia*, an express warranty (a P&I club rule) prohibiting her from entering certain declared areas. These areas were of such extreme danger that it was considered not acceptable by the insurer that they should cover vessels entering them.[30] In breach of the warranty, the vessel entered the Arabian Gulf and was struck by a missile which so badly damaged her that she became a constructive total loss. One of the main questions which the House had to consider was the legal effects such a breach would have on the policy. The controversy was whether the club had 'ceased' to insure her at the time of the breach of the warranty. It was necessary to know the answer to this question because the insurers (the P&I club) had undertaken to notify the mortgagees only 'if the ship ceases to be insured'. The answer to this debate was largely dependent upon whether the insurer was automatically discharged from liability by reason of the breach, or whether he was required to take active steps to rescind or avoid the contract, as he would have to in the case of a breach of a condition under ordinary principles of contract law. Lord Goff, referring to the wording of s 33, held that:[31]

> '... if a promissory warranty is not complied with, the insurer is discharged from liability as from the date of the breach of warranty, for the simple reason that fulfilment of the warranty is a condition precedent to the liability or further liability of the insurer.'

For this pronouncement, Lord Goff relied heavily on the case of *Thomson v Weems*,[32] a non-marine case decided in 1884, as the authority which had proposed that '... compliance with that warranty is a condition precedent to the attaching of the risk'. In the said case, the judge stressed the fact that the insurer only accepted the risk conditional upon the warranty being fulfilled and that that was the whole rationale for its very existence.

As can be seen from Lord Goff's speech, a promissory warranty is today to be regarded as a 'condition precedent'. Whether a promissory warranty is also a 'condition' (the term used in s 33(3)) and the legal implications of being classed as a 'condition precedent' will now have to be examined.

'Condition' and/or 'condition precedent'

In the law of contract, the variety of senses in which the expression 'condition' has been used was described by Trietal[33] as 'one of the notorious sources of difficulty in the law of contract'. It is necessary for the sake of clarity to go over some of the old ground on the law relating to conditions and condition precedents. According to Trietal,[34] the term 'condition precedent' is normally used to describe an 'event' or 'order of performance' in the sense that the performance by one party may be a condition precedent to the liability of the

---

30 If the owner wanted cover whilst his vessel was in the prohibited area, special arrangements had to be made.
31 [1991] 2 Lloyd's Rep 191 at p 202, HL.
32 (1884) 9 App Cas 671 at p 684.
33 *Law of Contract*, (9th edn), p 703–707.
34 'Conditions' and 'Conditions Precedent' [1990] 106 LQR 185.

other'. A 'condition,' however, is simply a term of a contract which requires conformity. Trietal warns that, though they are distinct concepts, a clause may well be a condition and a condition precedent at the same time. Regrettably, the term 'condition precedent' has been loosely used to refer to both a term of a contract and an event, that is, the prior or concurrent performance by one party before that of the other became due. This indiscriminate use of terms has generated a great deal of confusion and problems not only in the law of contract, but also in this area of marine insurance law. In the light of its dual usage, it is necessary to inquire what Lord Goff meant exactly when he used the words 'condition precedent' in relation to a promissory warranty. The question whether he had one or both of these concepts in mind has to be explored.

Under general contract law, a breach of a condition precedent normally produces the following consequences:

- the injured party can simply refuse to perform his part of the bargain without having to make any previous election; and

- the injured party is only justified in refusing to perform for so long as the failure continues.

Whether the second effect is to be applied to a breach of a promissory warranty is a question which needs to be considered.

Automatic discharge

When Lord Goff ruled that an insurance warranty was a 'condition precedent', he did not clarify whether it was to be granted both the above characteristics of a condition precedent. There is no doubt that the first applies to a promissory warranty. The basis of his decision can be ascertained from the following remarks he had made:[35]

> 'They [referring to s 33] show that discharge of the insurer from liability is automatic and is not dependent upon any decision by the insurer to treat the contract or the insurance as at an end; though, under s 34(3), the insurer may waive the breach of the warranty.'

Section 33(3), however, merely states that, '... If [a warranty] be not so complied with ... the insurer is discharged from liability as from the date of the breach of warranty ...'. In the light of the above speech, the word 'automatically' has now to be read before the word 'discharged'.

A condition, as an ordinary contractual term, does not possess the quality of enabling the innocent party in the event of its breach to be automatically discharged from all future liability under the contract. The legal requirement that the innocent party has to exercise the option either to affirm or rescind the contract in the event of a breach of a 'condition' is obviously incompatible with Lord Goff's rule of automatic discharge. Viewed in this light, a promissory warranty cannot thus be regarded as a condition which by definition is a term the breach of which would allow the innocent party the right of choice, either to affirm or rescind the contract. As far as Lord Goff was concerned, once a breach of a promissory warranty has been committed, the result is automatic: the

---

35 [1992] 2 Lloyd's Rep 191 at p 202, HL.

insurer is *spontaneously* discharged from liability as from the date of the breach, but without prejudice to any liability incurred by him before that date.

The future of the contract

In relation to a warranty on geographical limits, the second of the above consequences of a breach of a condition precedent is particularly significant to the question of whether a ship which has entered and departed from a prohibited area is covered for a loss of or damage sustained whilst traversing outside the prohibited area during the currency of the policy. In other words: is the policy revived or restored on the ship leaving the prohibited area? As *The Good Luck* was a constructive total loss, this question did not arise for consideration. If she was able to sail out of the prohibited zone, would she then, once again, be covered by the policy?

In order to ascertain the effect such a breach has on the future of the contract, reference has to be made to another crucial statement made by Lord Goff:[36]

'Certainly, [s 33(3)] does not have the effect of avoiding the contract *ab initio*. Nor, strictly speaking, does it have the effect of bringing the contract to an end. It is possible that there may be obligations of the assured under the contract which will survive the discharge of the insurer from liability, as for example a continuing liability to pay a premium. Even if in the result no further obligations rest on either parties, it is not correct to speak of the contract being avoided ...'

It is noted that the emphasis here is that it is *liability* and not the contract which is brought to an end. With due respect, it is submitted that this statement is as ambiguous as it is confusing. If the contract is not brought to an end, then it must surely be still on foot or in force. Lord Goff may have perhaps intended to say that, though the insurer was automatically discharged from liability or future liability, the contract was, nevertheless, still operative for certain limited purposes, such as the payment of premium already accrued. The purpose of keeping the contract alive is, presumably, to give the insurer the opportunity, if he so desires, to waive the breach.

As was seen, certain parts of Lord Goff's judgment steered dangerously close to language which is more akin to a limitation of liability clause rather than a promissory warranty. The relevant parts read as follows:[37]

'... the insurer does not avoid liability ... it is only in the sense of repudiating liability (and not repudiating the policy) that it would be right to describe him as being entitled to repudiate. In truth the insurer, as the Act provides, is simply discharged from liability as from the date of the breach, with the effect that thereupon he has a good defence to a claim by the assured.'

But having said that, it has to be pointed out that he was careful in his judgment to distinguish between the two forms of warranty, *viz* 'those warranties which simply denote the scope of the cover ... and those which are

---

36   *Ibid.*

37   *Ibid*, at p 203.

promissory warranties, involving a promise by the assured that the warranty will be fulfilled'.[38] He clarified that it is with the latter type of warranty – the subject of ss 33–34 of the Act – that he was concerned with.

Suspension of the contract?

Is it possible that the contract is suspended whilst the insured vessel is in the prohibited area? The suspension theory is consistent with ordinary contract principles applicable to a condition precedent, but not a condition which 'justifies rescission in the sense of an outright or *permanent refusal* to perform and to accept further performance from the party in breach':[39] an election to rescind the contract is required to achieve this end. Thus, if an insurance warranty is to be construed as a condition precedent in its strict sense, it is possible that the risks under the policy could be turned on and turned off by the actions of the assured. To restore coverage, all that the assured has to do is to leave the prohibited zone, provided, of course, that the policy has not expired.

Whether an insurance warranty is also to be invested with the second of the above-mentioned characteristics of a condition precedent is doubtful. Such a legal position, though consistent with the nature of a condition precedent, is, it is submitted, untenable. It is clearly incompatible with another fundamental principle relating to a promissory warranty, namely, that a breach of a promissory warranty cannot be remedied and complied with even before loss.[40] It would not, therefore, be unreasonable to conclude from this that there is no place for the suspension theory in the event of a breach of a promissory warranty. Once a breach has been committed, the insurer is automatically discharged; and unless the breach is waived, the insurer is not liable for further losses under the policy. There is clearly no place for the suspension of contract theory in Lord Goff's rule of automatic discharge. If the rule of automatic discharge is to be carried to its logical conclusion, the insurer would be discharged from liability on taking the very first step of entering the prohibited zone. The moment she enters the prohibited area, the insurer is automatically discharged from liability or further liability. This would mean that, unless the breach was waived, any damage suffered by the vessel thereafter, wherever and however sustained, would not be covered by the policy. Unless such a clause is construed as a limitation of cover, there is no question of a suspension of the policy.

A 'new approach'

Lord Goff has apparently adopted a new approach in his treatment of a marine insurance warranty. In fact, he had borrowed the idea from Lord Justice Kerr of the Court of Appeal in the case of *State Trading Corpn of India Ltd v M Golodetz Ltd*[41] who had pre-empted the legal position as follows:

---

38 *Ibid*, at p 201.
39 Trietal, *Law of Contract*, (9th edn) p 703.
40 Section 34(2).
41 [1989] 2 Lloyd's Rep 277 at p 287, CA.

'... the correct analysis may lie in a new approach to the construction of the contracts in question. Thus ... upon the true construct of the contract, the consequence of the breach is that the cover ceases to be applicable unless the insurer subsequently affirms the contract rather than to treat the occurrence as a breach of the contract by the insured which the insurer subsequently accepts as a wrongful repudiation.'

When Lord Goff used the term 'condition precedent' to describe the effect of a breach of a promissory warranty, he was using it only in a limited sense: the first but not the second of the two features described above. A promissory warranty is thus a special kind of condition precedent, the breach of which automatically discharges the insurer from liability, without the insurer having to take steps to rescind the contact, which he would have to do so in the case of a breach of an ordinary 'condition'. This is probably what Lord Goff had in mind when he said:[42]

'Even if in the result no further obligations rests on either parties, it is not correct to speak of the contract being avoided; and it is, strictly speaking, more accurate to keep to the carefully chosen words in s 33(3) of the Act, rather than to speak of the contract being brought to an end, though that may be the practical effect.'

As the insurer is entitled to refuse to perform or accept performance from the party (the shipowner) in breach, the policy is, in practical terms, at an end. Unless the breach is waived, there is no future for the contract.[43] In this respect, the effect of a breach of a promissory warranty is no different from that of a breach of a condition. The difference is that, in the case of the former, it is not dependent upon a decision by the insurer to rescind the contract, whereas in the latter, he has to take steps to end the contract.

A 'cross' of two contract law concepts, namely, a condition and a condition precedent, is inherent in Lord Goff's proposal. The marriage of one strain from a 'condition' with another from a 'condition precedent' has produced a new hybrid of contractual term, yet to be given a name of its own in the general law of contract. In marine insurance law it is known as a promissory warranty.

The legal position is somewhat peculiar in the sense that in the event of a breach of a promissory warranty the contract is neither void nor avoidable. It is by no means void,[44] as rights and liabilities accrued before the breach are expressly preserved by the Act. Neither is it voidable,[45] as the insurer does not have to take the initiative to rescind the contract. Further, the contract is neither suspended nor brought to an end.

---

42 [1991] 2 Lloyd's Rep 191 at p 202, HL.

43 M Clarke, *Breach of Warranty in The Law of Insurance* [1991] LMCLQ, p 437, says that 'the only reasonable inference from silence on the part of the insurer is that the contract does not go on'.

44 In *Bond v Nutt* [1777] 2 Comp 601, Lord Mansfield explained that '... the policy was void; the contingency had not happened; and the party interested had a right to say, there was no contract between them.' In *Samuel v Dumas* [1923] 1 KB 592, HL, Viscount Cave remarked that as the insurer had waived the breach he was prevented from 'treating the marine policy on the vessel as void ...'.

45 A breach of a warranty against contraband of war was described as having avoided the whole insurance in *Seymour v London & Prov Marine Insurance Co* [1872] 41 LJ CP 193; 1 Asp MLC 323. This is no longer good law in the light of *The Good Luck* [1991] 2 Lloyd's Rep, 191, HL

One principle which the rule of automatic discharge has certainly taken care of is that of the implied waiver or affirmation of a contract brought about by reason of silence or delay. An insurer who does nothing after a breach of a promissory warranty can now no longer be accused of having, by his inactivity, impliedly waived or affirmed the contract. In the absence of some overt act on his part demonstrating an intention to waive the breach, the insurer is automatically discharged from all future liability.

WAIVER OF BREACH OF WARRANTIES

Section 34(3) permits an insurer to waive a breach of warranty. Such a course of action, which is normally achieved by the insertion of either a held covered or a waiver clause, is also recognised by the phrase 'subject to the provisions in the policy' in s 33(3).[46]

Waiver and estoppel

Clarke observed that the distinction between 'waiver' and 'estoppel' is 'not drawn easily and in insurance cases, not drawn often'.[47] This is true in *Provincial Insurance Co of Canada v Leduc*,[48] where the vessel was wrecked after she had entered the Gulf of St Lawrence in breach of an express warranty. Soon after loss, the assured gave notice of abandonment, which was accepted by the insurer with full knowledge of all the facts. It was held by the Privy Council that the acceptance of the notice under the circumstances was sufficient to 'estop' the insurer from denying liability for the loss which the vessel had sustained whilst in the prohibited area. The insurer argued that as the ship was not insured when she was lost – as the policy did not extend to a loss in the prohibited area – the notice of abandonment was of no avail because there was no insurance in existence at the time of the loss. This contention was curtly rejected by the Privy Council in a brief reply that: '... the vessel was in fact insured; the loss occurred during the time and upon a voyage described in the policy, but there was a breach of one of the warranties or conditions expressed.'

How the vessel could be described as having been engaged on a 'voyage described in the policy' when she was clearly trading within the prohibited area in breach of the warranty is baffling. Presumably, the court felt that it had to keep the policy alive in order that it may be waived. It has to be said that this is an old case decided at a time when it was thought that a breach of a promissory warranty gave the insurer the right to avoid the contract. As the insurer in this case had not only *not* avoided the contract, but had in fact affirmed its existence by accepting the notice of abandonment, the court had no choice but to hold that he had waived the breach. As the right of avoidance of a contract is no longer the legal effect of a breach of a warranty, the matter has now to be considered in the light of s 33(3), read with *The Good Luck*, which lays down the

---

46 It is to be noted that the implied warranty of legality laid down in s 41 cannot be waived; a discussion of this warranty can be found below.

47 M Clarke, *Breach of Warranty in The Law of Marine Insurance* [1991] LMCLQ 437 at p 439.

48 (1874) LR 6 PC 224, PC.

rule that the insurer is *automatically* discharged from liability or further liability as from the date of the breach. Arnould,[49] however, states that this change in the law has not solved the problem, as it is still open to the same objection: once an insurer is discharged, or even automatically discharged, from liability as from the date of breach, it would logically be almost impossible for him to waive the breach of a contract from which he has already been discharged.

It would appear that the doctrine of estoppel is obviously the tidiest way of removing these nagging problems: an insurer may not be able to affirm a contract by waiver because he has been discharged from liability as from the date of breach, but he can certainly, by his conduct, be estopped from pleading as having been discharged from liability. The decision would have stood on firmer foundation if the court were to justify it purely on the basis of estoppel. It was the conduct of the insurer – by his acceptance of the notice – which precluded him from relying on the breach of the express warranty to exonerate him from liability for the loss. Though the word 'waiver' was not used by the court, the effect is nonetheless the same. Whether called a waiver or an estoppel, such an interpretation of the law would not be inconsistent with Lord Goff's rule of automatic discharge, in particular, with his remarks that:

'... when, as s 34(3) contemplates, the insurer waives a breach of a promissory warranty, the effect is that, to the extent of the waiver, the insurer cannot rely upon the breach as having discharged him from liability.'

That the contract of insurance is not wholly brought to an end after a breach of a promissory warranty was a point which Lord Goff had repeatedly stressed in his judgment. Obviously, the contract of insurance had to be kept sufficiently alive for the assured to issue a notice of abandonment under it and, more importantly, for the insurer to be bound by his acceptance of it. This perhaps explains Lord Goff's relentless emphasis that the contract was not brought to an end by reason of the breach.[50]

Whilst on the subject of waiver of warranties, it is necessary to mention that each of the ICC has a waiver clause (cl 5.2) for the implied warranties of seaworthiness and fitness of the ship on which the insured cargo is carried. This will not be discussed here as it can be more appropriately examined later when the scope of the implied warranty of seaworthiness is considered.

Held covered clause

A held covered clause is a device which an assured could rely on to protect himself in the event of a breach of a warranty. Under cl 3 of the ITCH(95), breach of certain warranties, namely, 'as to cargo, trade, locality, towage, salvage services or date of sailing', is held covered by the policy, provided that the assured complies with the conditions laid down therein. In the case of the IVCH(95), 'any breach of warranty as to towage or salvage services' is held covered, provided that notice be given to the underwriters immediately after receipt of advices and any amended terms of cover and any additional premium

---

49 Arnould, para 708, fn 18.

50 If the contract was to be brought to an end, it was feared that there would be nothing left of the contract upon which the insurer could 'bite' on to waive the breach.

required by them be agreed.[51] Once the specified terms are complied with, the breach is waived and the assured is entitled to claim for the loss.

B – EXPRESS WARRANTIES

FORM OF WARRANTY

An express warranty, according to s 35(1) of the Act, 'must be included in, or written upon, the policy, or must be contained in some document incorporated by reference into the policy'.[52] Thus, provided that there is an intention to warrant, answers to questions contained in slips, proposal forms or covering notes; P&I Club rules; and declarations and statements of fact, can all become warranties if they are inserted or incorporated, either directly or indirectly by way of reference, into a policy. It is to be noted that this requirement is stated in mandatory terms, which means that oral statements made during the course of negotiations cannot be regarded as promissory warranties.[53] According to Lord Mansfield, 'if the parties had considered it as a warranty they would have had it inserted in the policy'.[54]

A representation made during the negotiations for the contract can also, by the same process of incorporation, be converted into an express warranty; it is often said that the mere fact that it has been inserted into a policy is indicative of its materiality and importance as a contractual term. The making of such a deduction is treading on dangerous ground because the materiality of the warranty to the risk is totally irrelevant.[55] Furthermore, it could mislead one to conclude that all express terms in polices are warranties.

Express warranties may be standard, such as those found in the Institute Hulls Clauses[56] and the Institute Warranties on trading limits,[57] or they may be transitory or custom-made in the sense that they were framed specially for the particular contract of insurance.[58]

A warranty may be expressed in 'any form of words'.[59] There is no special or formal wording in which it must be drafted. Thus, provided that an intention to warrant is manifested, any written statement may be construed as a warranty. The word 'warranted', however, is often used to preface an express

---

51 Notice given after a loss was held in *Greenock Steamship Co v Maritime Insurance Co Ltd* [1903] 1 KB 367, and *Mentz, Decker & Co v Maritime Insurance Co* [1901] 1 KB 132, sufficient to satisfy the proviso.
52 In *Bean v Stupart*, (1778) 1 Dougl 11, a warranty on the margin of a policy was considered as much as if it was written in the body of the policy.
53 They are representations: s 20.
54 *Pawson v Watson* (1778) 2 Cowp 785 at p 786.
55 Section 33(3).
56 Eg, cll 1.1 and 3 of the ITCH(95) and cl 1.1 of the IVCH(95).
57 See Appendix 17.
58 For this purpose, the Schedule to the Institute Clauses has provided space, under the heading 'Clauses, endorsements, special conditions and warranties', for their insertion as an express term of the contract.
59 Section 35(1).

warranty: but this does not mean that if the word 'warranted' is not used, an express term cannot be construed as a warranty. Unfortunately, the term 'warranted' has also been used to secure for the insurer exception or limitation of cover.

Like any other contract, the express terms in contracts of marine insurance are varied. They may be broadly divided into four categories:

- exception clauses;
- mere words of description identifying or qualifying the subject-matter;
- limitation of liability clauses defining the scope of the insurer's liability; and
- promissory warranties.

It is important to bear in mind that not all the express terms of a contract of insurance are warranties.

Exception clauses

Exception clauses in marine insurance are often prefaced with the words 'warranted free of'.[60] The use of the expression 'warranted' in exception clauses has in the past generated a degree of confusion as to whether such terms are in fact warranties. First, it is best that they be swiftly eliminated from the present discussion because, though they may look like express warranties, they clearly fall outside the realm of promissory warranties. (The purpose of an exception clause is to restrict the scope of the policy and to exempt the insurer from responsibility for a particular risk. As the intention of such a clause is not to warrant, but to except liability, they are clearly not promissory warranties.)

Perhaps it needs to be mentioned that in the case of an exception clause, causation plays an important role: only a loss proximately caused by the excepted peril is not covered by the policy, whereas in the case of a promissory warranty, the cause of a loss is totally irrelevant.[61] This is indeed a fundamental distinction between an exception clause and a promissory warranty. In *The Cap Tarifa*,[62] Mr Justice Walsh of the Supreme Court of New South Wales pointed out that 'the difference between a condition and an exception is that the former places some duty or responsibility on the assured, while the latter restricts the scope of the policy'.

---

60 Eg, 'warranted free of particular average'. In *Nova Scotia v Hellenic Mutual War Risks Association (Bermuda) Ltd, The Good Luck* [1991] 2 Lloyd's Rep 191 at p 201, Lord Goff distinguished between '... those warranties which simply denote the scope of the cover (as in the familiar fc and s clause – warranted free of capture and seizure) and those which are promissory warranties, involving a promise by the assured that the warranty will be fulfilled'.

61 With the exception of s 36(2). As a rule, a breach of a promissory warranty does not have to cause the loss. However, with regard to the implied condition of proper documentation, the loss has to occur 'through' a breach of this condition before the insurer is entitled to avoid the contract.

62 *Simons v Gale* [1957] 2 Lloyd's Rep 485 at p 491, Australia Supreme Court of New South Wales; on appeal to the Privy Council, [1958] 2 Lloyd's Rep 1.

Descriptive warranty

Words describing or qualifying the subject-matter insured are particularly susceptible to being classified as a promissory warranty. The distinction between a warranty and mere words of description is best illustrated in the case of *Overseas Commodities Ltd v Style*,[63] to which reference has already been made. Mr Justice McNair held that the identification number which the tins of pork butts were to be marked was not a warranty, but were mere words of description for the purpose of identifying the goods: 'the policy only attaches to such of the goods that comply with the description'. In contrast, the term expressed as 'warranted all tins marked by manufacturers with a code for verification of date of manufacture' was held to be a warranty.

Indeed, in the classic case of *Yorkshire Insurance Co Ltd v Campbell*,[64] Lord Sumner, delivering the judgment of the Privy Council, observed that: '*Prima facie*, words qualifying the subject-matter of the insurance will be words of warranty, which in a policy of marine insurance operate as conditions.' In this case, the learned judge felt compelled to give some legal significance to the words describing the pedigree of the horse[65] – the subject-matter insured. He was convinced that since the parties had chosen to import the description of the subject-matter insured into their contract, they must presumably bear some legal effect. And when that statement is in writing and is incorporated into the policy itself, the matter is beyond doubt.

According to Lord Sumner, unless proven otherwise, words describing or qualifying the subject-matter insured are as a general rule deemed to be warranties. To rebut this presumption, evidence of intent would have to be shown. On the question of evidence, he offered some guidelines as to what may be taken into consideration. He pointed out that:[66]

'... regard must be had, no doubt, to the surrounding circumstances, in order that the policy may be read as the parties to it intended it to be read ... but this means having regard to the nature of the transaction and the known course of business and the forms in which such matters are carried out ...'

As a rough guide, it is perhaps fair to say that a description inserted merely for the purpose of identifying the subject matter, having no relation whatsoever to the risks insured against in the particular policy, is not a promissory warranty. Each case, of course, has to be decided on its own facts.

Limitation of liability clause

The line between a clause limiting the liability of the insurer and a promissory warranty is sometimes not so easy to draw, and a degree of disarray is evident in this area of the law of marine insurance which will soon become obvious in the discussions to follow on warranties on trading or navigational limits.

---

63   [1958] 1 Lloyd's Rep 546 at p 559.
64   [1917] AC 218 at p 224, Privy Council.
65   The horse was described in detail as a 'Bay gelding by Soult X St Paul (mare), 5 yrs ... nr sh, 2 hind legs white, blaze on face, slight chip off knee, grey hairs nr side belly'.
66   *Ibid*, at p 225.

EXAMPLES OF EXPRESS WARRANTIES

As can be seen from the wording of s 33(1), an express warranty may be stated either in positive or negative terms, and may be divided into two broad categories:

- where the assured warrants the existence or otherwise of certain facts, or
- where he warrants that he would or would not perform certain acts.

The use of the word 'shall' in the earlier part of s 33(1) refers to future events, whilst the latter part of the section to facts existing at the date the contract was made. In any event, a duty or responsibility is placed on the assured: as he has given the promise or undertaking, he has to ensure that it is exactly complied with.

It is impossible, and a futile exercise, to describe all the different types of promissory warranties that are employed in marine policies. For the purpose of illustration, the two express warranties identified by the Act, namely, the warranty of neutrality and of good safety; the disbursements warranty, the towage and salvage warranty, the new Classification Clause of the ITCH(95) and the IVCH(95); and the well-known warranty on geographical limits of navigation will be examined.

Express warranty of neutrality

Where a policy on ship or goods contains an express warranty of neutrality, s 36 seeks to govern the express warranty by implying two terms to the express warranty, namely, that:

- 'there is an implied condition that the property shall have a neutral character at the commencement of the risk, and that, so far as the assured can control the matter, its neutral character shall be preserved during the risk'; and

- 'there is also an implied condition that, so far as the assured can control the matter, she shall be properly documented, that is to say, that she shall carry the necessary papers to establish her neutrality, and that she shall not falsify or suppress her papers, or use simulated papers. If any loss occurs through breach of this condition the insurer may avoid the contract.'

It is necessary to distinguish the effects of a breach of the two implied conditions. A breach of the first condition will naturally cause a breach of the express warranty of neutrality. This will trigger s 33(3) to *discharge* the insurer from liability as from the date of the breach. A breach of the second implied condition as regards proper documentation will, on the other hand, confer upon the insurer the right to 'avoid' the contract. But this can only take place if the loss has occurred through a breach of this condition. In other words, causation, though not generally relevant to a breach of a warranty, is relevant here. The insurer can avoid the contract only if the loss 'occurs through' or was caused by a breach of the condition.

Express warranty of good safety

Very little need be said about s 38 on the warranty of good safety except that the expression 'good safety' is also used in r 3 of the Rules for Construction. Section 38 states that, 'If the subject-matter insured is warranted "well" or "in good safety" on a particular day, it is sufficient if it be safe at any time during that day'.

Disbursements warranty

The ITCH(95) and the IVCH(95) each has a warranty relating to disbursements contained in cll 22 and 20 respectively. This warranty was originally introduced pursuant to *The Gunford Case*[67] discussed earlier. The purpose of the warranty is to limit the amount of insurance which the owner of a vessel may effect on disbursements, managers' commissions and a list of other items. It is now possible to insure up to 25% of the valuation stated in the policy in respect of these enumerated matters. The given percentage is to ensure that he does not over-insure by double insurance; thus, he may safely insure up to the percentage permitted without having to make a disclosure of the additional insurances to the insurer.

Clause 22.1.8 of the ITCH(95), however, permits the assured to insure 'irrespective of amount' against the risks excluded by the war, strikes, malicious acts, and the radio contamination exclusions (cll 24–27).[68]

The purpose of cl 22.2 of ITCH(95) is to protect an innocent mortgagee who has no knowledge of the breach of warranty from recovering under the policy. The insurer is prevented from setting up the breach committed by the shipowner as a defence against any claims made by a mortgagee.

Towage and salvage warranty

The above warranty on towage and salvage is tucked away in the Navigation clause, cl 1.1, of both the ITCH(95) and the IVCH(95). By cl 1.1, 'customary'[69] towage, and towage to the 'first safe port or place when in need of assistance' are excepted and, therefore, are not covered by the warranty. As the scope of cl 1.1 has already been fully discussed, very little need be said about the warranty here except that it is also governed by a held covered clause known as the Breach of Warranty clause (cl 3) in the ITCH(95), and the Change of Voyage clause (cl 2) in the IVCH(95). In the event of any breach of warranty as to towage and salvage services, the assured is held covered 'provided that notice

---

67 (1911) 16 Com Cas 270; 12 Asp MLC 49.

68 *Cf Samuel v Dumas* [1924] AC 431 it was held that additional insurance effected by the assured against loss of freight by war risks only in a sum exceeding the amount allowed by the warranty constituted a breach of the warranty, which stated that the amount 'insured' on freight should not exceed a certain percentage of the stated value of the hull and machinery. The House of Lords construed the word 'insured' to include insurances against marine and war risks

69 See *Russell v Provincial Insurance Co Ltd* [1959] 2 Lloyd's Rep 275, QBD for an interpretation of the words 'customary towage' in a similarly worded clause. Towing abreast was held to be common and customary in the trade for the vessels concerned.

be given to the Underwriters immediately after receipt of advices and any amended terms of cover and any additional premium required by them be agreed'.[70]

By the new cl 1.2 of the 1995 version of the ITCH,[71] any contracts entered into by the assured for towage or pilotage services which are either customary or compulsory will not prejudice the insurance. The clause acknowledges the fact that the assured (or their agents) may have to enter, or be compelled to enter into such contracts in 'accordance with established local law or practice'. The insurance shall not be prejudiced even if the said contracts entered into may have limited or exempted the liability of the pilots and /or tugs and/or towboats and/or their owners.

The classification clause

The new cl 4.1 the classification clause of the ITCH(95) requires that:

- the vessel be classed with a Classification Society agreed by underwriters and to remain in class, and

- the Classification Society's recommendations, requirements and restrictions regarding seaworthiness and of her maintenance thereof be complied with by the date(s) set by the Society.

One of the objectives of the clause is to improve safety standards of vessels; it also demonstrates the underwriter's support of the endeavours of Classification Societies in promoting the seaworthiness of ships. The intention of the clause is to not only to ensure that an assured complies with the rules of Classification Society, but more importantly that a reputable Classification Society, one agreed by the underwriters, be used.

A warranty

Though not described as a warranty, and the word 'warranted' does not appear in the clause, cl 4.1 can nevertheless be classified as a warranty if there is an intention to warrant. It is understood by the market to be a warranty.[72] Furthermore, in the event of breach of any of the duties set out in cl 4.1, the underwriters will be 'discharged from liability ... as from the date of the breach'.[73] Thus, the effect of a breach of cl 4.1 is the same as that stipulated in s 33(3) of the Act. The words 'unless the Underwriters agree to the contrary in writing' suggest that it is possible to waive the breach.[74] As a warranty, its terms must be exactly complied with, and its breach will attract the operation of the

---

70 Held covered clause is discussed above under the heading of 'Waiver of breach of warranties'.

71 This clause is similar to the pilotage and towage clause in the American Institute Hulls Clauses (2 June, 1977). Note also the new cl 1.3 where the use of helicopter for the transportation of personnel supplies and equipment to and/or from the Vessels shall not prejudice the insurance.

72 This clause was originally drafted as a 'Warranted that: the Vessel is classed with ... and existing class maintained': see document 'Joint Hull 131 (30.06.89)'.

73 See cl 4.2.

74 See s 34(3).

law as set out in the case of *The Good Luck*.[75] The failure to comply would automatically discharge the insurer from liability even if such failure does not result in a claim or its breach did not cause the loss. This is so unless the vessel is 'at sea' at the time of breach, in which case the underwriters are discharged from liability upon her arrival at her next port.[76]

It is to be noted that the 'duty' imposed on the 'assured, owners and managers' is a continuous duty, commencing from the inception of and running throughout the period of the insurance.

Class and maintenance of class

By cl 4.1.1, the vessel must be classed with a Classification Society *'agreed* by the Underwriters and that her class within that Society is maintained'. In other words, any change of class or of Classification Society without the agreement of the underwriters would constitute a breach. It is observed that the word 'that' is significant: the vessel has to maintain not only her class, but her class within *that* Society.

Recommendations, requirements and restrictions of Classification Society

It needs to be emphasised that only recommendations, requirements or restrictions imposed by the vessel's Classification Society pertaining to the vessel's seaworthiness or to her maintenance in a seaworthy condition have to be complied with. Whether or not a particular recommendation, requirement or restriction relates to seaworthiness[77] is a problem which is likely to arise. The meaning of 'seaworthiness' has thus to be clear in one's mind. What the position would be if an extension were to be granted to the assured by the Classification Society for compliance with their recommendation etc is not clarified. Presumably, there will be no breach if the date of the extension is complied with.

Reporting to Classification Society

Clause 4.3 imposes a duty upon the assured to report to the Classification Society '... any incident condition or damage in respect of which the Vessel's Classification Society might make recommendations as to repairs or other action to be taken by the assured, owners or managers'. The difficulty here lies in the word 'might'. It would appear that an assured is expected to be able to anticipate what his Classification Society might or might not do in a particular circumstance. Cl 4.3 is peculiar in the sense that there is no sanction spelt out for its non-compliance.

---

75 [1991] 2 Lloyd's Rep 191, HL.

76 The applicability of cl 5.1 of the ITCH(95), and the possibility of conflict between the effects of cl 4.1.1 (that of discharge) and of cl 5.1 (of automatic termination) of the ITCH(95) are discussed elsewhere.

77 The meaning of the word 'seaworthiness' is discussed below.

Authorisation for release of information

The purpose of cl 4.4 of the ITCH(95) is to enable the underwriter to obtain information directly from the Classification Society which, without necessary authorisation from the assured, is not obliged to divulge on the ground of the principle of privity of contract. Through this facility, the underwriter hopes to obtain vital information regarding the condition of the ship. Some thought may, perhaps, have to be given to the question of whether the assured has the power to make such an authorisation unilaterally without first obtaining the consent of the Classification Society. Again, as in the case of cl 4.3, there is no penalty given for a breach of this clause. What would be the legal effect if the Classification Society were to refuse to comply with an authorised request of the underwriter for information and/or documents?

Warranties on geographical limits of navigation

Colledge v Harty,[78] decided in 1851, appears to be the first case to have come before a court of law for a determination as to whether a clause restricting the geographical limits of navigation of a ship is, in legal terms, an exception or a warranty. The clause in question stated that ships were 'not to sail from any port on the east coast of Great Britain to any port in the Belts between 20th December and 15th February'. After hearing arguments from both sides, the court came to the firm conclusion that such a term was a warranty and not an exception. According to the judge:[79]

> 'The reason which induces me to construe this as a warranty and not an exception is that there is no time in which the vessel is to be on the policy again; and the consequence of holding this an exception would be that the policy would cease during the voyage within the prohibited period, and after that the ship would be again on the policy.'

Why the absence of a time stipulation should make any difference is unclear. The reason for holding this a warranty and not an exception is, it is submitted, unsatisfactory. If the clause was construed not as a warranty, but as a limitation of cover defining the scope of the liability of the insurer, there should be no problem regarding the time when the policy could come on again. There is no reason why a policy could not be 'turned off' when she enters the prohibited area, and 'turned on again' when she departs from it. If some form of trigger is required to revive coverage under the policy, it could be argued that the action of the assured in sailing into and out of the prohibited area speaks for itself, performing the same function as time which seemed to have so bothered the judge. The liability of the insurer could be made dependent upon the actions of the assured.

In 1874, when *Provincial Insurance Co of Canada v Leduc*[80] was heard, neither the Privy Council nor the lower courts spent any time in studying the nature of the clause which stated that the ship was 'not allowed ... to enter the Gulf of St Lawrence ...'. Without any discussion, and presumably relying on *Colledge v*

---

78   (1851) 6 Exch 205; 20 LJ Ex 146.

79   *Ibid*, at p 212.

80   (1874) LR 6 PC 224.

Harty, the Privy Council accepted without hesitation that the clause was a warranty. On this assumption, the judges proceeded with their investigation of whether there was a waiver of the breach of the warranty.

Ten years later, in *Birrell v Dryer*,[81] an identical clause was again regarded as a warranty. On this occasion, the House of Lords was completely absorbed in determining whether the words 'Gulf of St Lawrence' included both the gulf and river of the St Lawrence.

A century later, a further opportunity arose where the matter could have been reviewed, if the House wanted to, in *The Good Luck*.[82] Regrettably, the subject was not broached and the House this time was primarily concerned with the legal effects of a breach of a promissory warranty. Any suggestion of resurrecting the issue of whether such a clause was or was not a warranty would probably have been briskly dismissed by Lord Goff who was clear in his mind that he was dealing with a warranty. It is noted that Lord Goff drew a distinction between an exception and a warranty, but did not, however, distinguish a warranty with a limitation clause. An exception, as mentioned earlier, operates differently from a clause defining the scope of the liability of the insurer. In the case of the former, only a loss proximately caused by an excepted risk is not covered by the policy, whereas in the latter, causation is irrelevant in the sense that if a loss occurs within the prohibited geographical limits, the assured is, regardless of the cause of loss, simply not covered by the insurance.

The distinction between a warranty and a clause delimiting the use of the insured property has been clarified in a series of motor[83] and household[84] policies of insurance. Such a distinction, which has never been drawn in marine insurance cases, has obviously caused Arnould some concern, provoking him to devote a section of his work to this matter.[85] In *Re Morgan and Provincial Insurance Co*,[86] Lord Justice Scrutton, with commendable clarity, described the law as follows:

'In many cases of this class the question has arisen whether ... promises that a certain state of thing shall continue, or a certain course of conduct shall be pursued, during the whole period covered by the policy, so that if the particular promise is not kept the policy is invalidated; or whether these promises are merely *descriptive of the risk* so that if the accident happens while the promised state of thing subsists there is a valid claim, but if the accident happens while the state of thing has ceased or been interrupted there is no valid claim ...'

---

81   (1884) 9 App Cas 345, HL.

82   [1991] 2 Lloyd's Rep 191, HL.

83   See *Farr v Motor Traders Mutual Insurance Society Ltd* [1920] 3 KB 669, CA; *Dawsons, Ltd v Bonnin* [1922] 2 AC 413; *Roberts v Anglo Saxon Insurance Assocn Ltd* (1927) 10 Ll L Rep 313; *Re Morgan and Another & Provincial Insurance Co* [1932] 2 KB 7, HL; and *De Maurier (Jewels) Ltd v Bastion Insurance Co Ltd* [1967] 2 Lloyd's Rep 550, QBD.

84   *Shaw v Robberds* (1837) 6 A & E 75; *Dobson v Sotheby* (1827) Moo & M 90; and *Simmonds v Cockell* [1920] 1 KB 843.

85   See Arnould, para 692.

86   [1932] 2 KB 70 at p 79, CA.

The difference in simple terms is between 'clauses which are conditional and those which are merely descriptive'.[87]

Limitation of liability

Arnould has, in no uncertain terms, advocated that a clause restricting the navigation of ships to certain geographical limits is not a warranty in its strict sense, but a term which defines the risk covered by the policy. He was perturbed by the fact that the legal status of such an important clause has never been seriously debated or scrutinised by the courts. From 1851 to the present day, it has always been *assumed* to be a warranty. To understand fully Arnould's[88] point of view, it is necessary to refer to some of these well-known non-marine insurance cases he cited.

In *Farr v Motor Traders Mutual Insurance Society Ltd*,[89] the statement in the proposal that the cab was only to be driven in one shift per 24 hours was held by Mr Justice Rowlatt, whose decision was affirmed by the Court of Appeal, to be merely a limitation of the risk and not a warranty. Whilst the cab is driven in one shift per 24 hours the risk will be covered, but that if, in any one day of 24 hours, the cab is driven in more than one shift, the risk will no longer be covered and will cease to attach until the owner resumes the practice of driving the cab for one shift only.[90]

Also concerned with a motor car policy of insurance, the case of *Roberts v Anglo Saxon Insurance Association Ltd*[91] is particularly relevant, as the general principles of insurance law on warranties apply to all policies including marine. The policy in question contained the clause: 'Warranted used only for the following purposes: commercial travelling'. Lord Justice Bankes of the Court of Appeal held that whenever the vehicle was not being used in accordance with the terms prescribed by the said clause, it was not covered. His comments, which are particularly pertinent to this discussion, read as follows:

'... the parties had used that language as words descriptive of the risk, and that, as a result, when the vehicle is not being used in accordance with the description it is not covered; but it does not follow at all that because it is used on some one occasion, or on more than one occasion, for other than the described use, the policy is avoided. It does not follow at all ... If the proper construction, on its language, is a description of the limitation of the liability, then the effect would be that the vehicle would be off cover during the period during which it was not

---

87 *Ibid*, at p 82. The Court of Appeal's decision was affirmed by the House of Lords [1933] AC 234. The statement made by the assured that the insured vehicle will be used for delivery of coal was construed as a descriptive clause, accordingly, the assured were held to be covered by the insurance while the lorry was being used for carrying coal, but not covered while being used for other purposes.

88 Arnould, para 692.

89 [1920] 3 KB 669, CA.

90 While one of the cabs was undergoing repairs, the other cab was driven in two shifts per 24 hours for a very short period of time in August; and from that time until the accident happened (in November) the two cabs were driven in one shift only.

91 (1927) 10 Ll L Rep 313.

being used for the warranted purposes, but that it would come again on the cover when the vehicle was again used for the warranted purpose.'[92]

This speech clearly supports an 'on cover' and 'off cover' type of situation, that is, a suspension of the contract.

Similarly, it is interesting to note that certain parts of Lord Goff's judgment in *The Good Luck* had also steered dangerously close to language which is more appropriate to a limitation of liability clause than to a promissory warranty. He said:[93]

'... the insurer does not avoid the policy ... it is only in the sense of repudiating liability (and not repudiating the policy) that it would be right to describe him as being entitled to repudiate. In truth the insurer ... has a good defence to a claim by the assured.'

However, in fairness, it has to be said that he was careful in his judgment, taking pains to distinguish the two forms of warranty: those which 'simply denote the scope of cover ... and those which are promissory warranties involving a promise by the assured that the warranty will be fulfilled'.[94]

It is observed that the only judge who has ever really examined the character of a navigational limits clause is the learned Lord Justice Scrutton in the Court of Appeal in *Re Morgan and Provincial Insurance Co*[95] Though the case was not concerned with marine insurance, his comments, however, were with direct reference to a navigational limits clause. As his comments are most enlightening, it is worthwhile reciting the relevant passage:

'... if a time policy contains a clause "warranted no St Lawrence between 1st October and 1st April", and the vessel was in the St Lawrence on 2nd October, but emerged without loss, and during the currency of the policy in July a loss happens, the underwriters cannot avoid payment on the ground that between 1st October and 1st April the vessel was in the St Lawrence *(Birrell v Dryer)*. That is an example of a so-called warranty which merely defines the risk insured against.'

The choice of the word 'so-called' reveals his disapproval of the said clause being classified as a warranty. He was, in effect, stating that the clause was not a warranty in its true sense, but a term which defines the risk insured under the policy.

Lord Justice Scrutton, after analysing a host of cases on the law relating to limitation of liability clauses and promissory warranties, arrived at the same conclusion as Arnould. Their understanding of the legal position is, however, clearly in direct conflict with the reasoning of Parke B in *Colledge v Harty*, who had obviously found the uncertainty caused by any suspension of the contract disconcerting.

To complete the picture, it is necessary to mention that there are two other cases which have conspicuously refrained from describing such navigational

---

92 The choice of the word 'warranted' by Bankes LJ is indeed unfortunate; it is liable to cause confusion as it is clearly quite inappropriate to the point he was trying to make.

93 [1992] 2 Lloyd's Rep 191 at p 202, HL.

94 *Ibid*, at p 201.

95 [1932] 2 KB 70 at p 80, CA; [1933] AC 240, HL.

limit clauses as a warranty. In *Wilson v Boag*,[96] the clause relating to the use of a motor launch 'only on the waters of Port Stephens and within a radius of fifty miles thereof' was described by the Supreme Court of New South Wales as a 'limitation of the liability of the insurer to loss sustained while the launch is within a defined geographical area'. Nowhere in the judgment was the clause referred to as a warranty.

In similar fashion, the Court of Appeal in *Navigators and General Insurance Co Ltd v Ringrose*[97] held that the insurer's liability under the policy, which contained the clause that the vessel was insured 'whilst within the United Kingdom' was to be determined solely by the place where the accident occurred. The word 'warranty' was not mentioned in any of the judgments delivered by each of the Lords Justice.[98]

Suspension of the contract

A breach of a warranty cannot, in the light of *The Good Luck*, bring about a suspension of the contact of insurance, because the insurer is automatically discharged from liability in the event of a breach. The fundamental difference between a promissory warranty and a clause which defines the liability of the insurer is that a breach of the former discharges the insurer from liability, whilst in the case of the latter the contract is merely suspended.

If a clause restricting navigational limits were to be classed not as a warranty, but as a term which merely defines the scope of the cover, the policy would simply be suspended when the vessels enters the prohibited area. On the happening of such an event, the contract is not brought to an end, the assured is simply not covered by the policy. But when he leaves the prohibited area, coverage under the policy is restored.

One cannot help but notice that none of the marine insurance cases has queried what the understanding of the parties of the clause was. The purpose of inserting such a clause was never ascertained, and whether its wording was clear enough to permit an inference to be drawn that there was an intention to warrant was never explored. The question which should have been asked is whether it was the understanding of the parties that the future of the whole contract of insurance is conditional upon the assured not entering the prohibited area. However worded, it is the intention of the parties which is crucial.

If these issues had been debated before the courts, one would, perhaps, accept the current legal position with less resistance. However, it could be said that having been accepted as a warranty for almost 150 years, it is now probably too late in the day to turn the clock back. It has, by usage, come to be known as a warranty. The golden opportunity to address and, if necessary, redress this issue has now passed. Should an assured decide not to regard the clause as a

---

96 [1956] 2 Lloyd's Rep 564, Supreme Court of New South Wales.

97 [1962] 1 WLR 173.

98 See also *Winters v Employers Fire Insurance Co* [1962] 2 Lloyd's Rep 320, United States of Florida Civil Court, where the phrase 'within the limits of the continental United States of America' was simply referred to as a term and not a warranty.

warranty, but only as one descriptive of the risk, he would need to rephrase it in clearer terms manifesting an intention *not* to warrant. The decisive consideration has to be whether it is the intention of the parties to exact or to give a warranty. In this regard, it would be prudent to bear in mind the words of Lord Justice Scrutton that, 'a great deal turns upon the language of the particular policy; but it must be remembered that in contracts of insurance the word "warranty" does not necessarily mean a condition or promise the breach of which will avoid the policy'.[99]

The Institute Warranties

The Institute Warranties (1/7/76) contain a list of warranties relating to geographical limits of navigation. Navigation is prohibited during certain months of the year within certain areas the parameter of which is defined by degrees of latitude and longitude. In practice, a trading limits warranty is invariably accompanied by a held covered clause, the purpose of which is to allow an assured the right to obtain cover whilst navigating within the prohibited area, provided that prompt notice is given and additional premium arranged.

CONSTRUCTION OF WARRANTIES

Though the law is adamant that exact compliance is required of a warranty, a court of law is nevertheless sometimes prepared, where there is ambiguity, to give a warranty a reasonable construction in order to give effect to the term. Like any other contract, the terms of a contract of marine insurance have to be construed in order that their real meaning may be ascertained. But once a reasonable interpretation has been awarded to a warranty, it must be literally complied with. In *Provincial Insurance Co v Morgan*,[100] Lord Wright remarked that, '... it is clear law that in insurance a warranty or condition ... though it must be strictly complied with, must be strictly though reasonably construed'.

How a reasonable interpretation may be arrived at was considered by Lord Esher MR in *Hart v Standard Marine Insurance Co*,[101] in which he said:

'... a warranty like every other part of the contract is to be construed according to the understanding of merchants, and does not bind the insured beyond the commercial import of the words ... the words are not to be construed in the sense in which they would be used amongst men of science, but as they would be used in mercantile transactions. The next question then is, what is the ordinary sense in which the words used in this warranty would be accepted by mercantile men engaged in the business of insurance? If the words are capable of two meanings you may look to the object with which they are inserted, in order to see which meaning business men would attach to them.'

---

99 *Re Morgan and Provincial Insurance Co* [1932] 2 KB 70 at p 79, CA. The word 'avoid' will now have to be read as 'automatically discharge'.

100 [1933] AC 241 at p 254, HL.

101 [1889] 22 QBD 499 at pp 500 and 501, CA. See also *Bean v Stupart* (1778) 1 Dougl 11.

The rule of *contra proferentum*

The House of Lords in *Birrell & Others v Dryer & Others* ,[102] presided by the Earl of Selborne LC, in interpreting the term 'warranted no St Lawrence ...' stated that there was no ambiguity or uncertainty in these words sufficient to prevent the application of the ordinary rules and principles of construction. The House of Lords felt that as a 'fair and natural meaning' could be placed on the warranty, there was no justification for invoking the *contra proferentum* rule to free the underwriters from liability. The fair and natural meaning of the words 'St Lawrence' covered the whole of the St Lawrence, both gulf and river.

In *Winter v Employers Fire Insurance Co*,[103] an American case, we are reminded by Judge Tyrie A Boyer of another fundamental principle of construction:

'The law is well settled that an ambiguity in a policy of insurance must be construed most favourably to the insured and most strictly against forfeiture ... As in other policies, marine contracts are strictly construed against the insurer and favourably to the insured, and where two interpretations are possible, that which will indemnify the insured will be adopted. Any ambiguity in the policy will be resolved against the company ... Any construction of a marine policy rendering it void should be evaded.'

In similar vein, Mr Justice Roche in *Simmonds v Cockell*,[104] when awarding a reasonable interpretation to the term 'warranted that the said premises are always occupied' of a household insurance stated that:

'... it is a well-known principle of insurance law that if the language of a warranty in a policy is ambiguous it must be construed against the underwriter who has drawn the policy and has inserted the warranty for his own protection.'

Whenever there is ambiguity in a warranty, a court may employ any one or more of the above basic rules of construction to give it a sensible and plausible meaning. Rather than be the cause of bringing the contract to an end, a court would be more inclined to give a reasonable interpretation to a term. If necessary, the term would be construed against the underwriter for whose benefit it was inserted. A sensible balance has thus to be struck, but a court must never be seen to be re-writing the contract for the parties.

C – IMPLIED WARRANTIES

An implied warranty is a term of a contract regarded by law as so obviously essential and fundamental to the contract that the parties must have presumed that it applies without having to make any express provision for it. So indispensable is the term that it is tacitly understood that it is to be read into the policy even though it does not appear on the face of it. There are four warranties implied by the Act:[105]

---

102 (1884) 9 App Cas 345 at p 350, HL.

103 [1962] 2 Lloyd's Rep 320 at p 323, US Ct.

104 [1920] KB 843 at p 845.

105 The implied condition of proper documentation is only implied when the policy contains an express warranty of neutrality: s 36(2).

- Implied warranty of portworthiness (s 39(2));
- Implied warranty of seaworthiness (s 39);
- Implied warranty of cargoworthiness, that is, the fitness of the ship to carry the goods (s 40(2)); and
- Implied warranty of legality (s 41).

Curiously, parliament also considered it necessary to specify the negative in s 37, that there is no implied warranty as to the nationality of a ship or, that her nationality shall not be changed during the risk; and in s 40(1) that there is no implied warranty that the goods or moveables are seaworthy.

IMPLIED WARRANTY OF PORTWORTHINESS

As was seen, the subject-matter may in a voyage policy be insured either 'from' or 'at and from' a particular place.[106] In a 'from' policy, only a single warranty, that of the implied warranty of seaworthiness, applies at the commencement of the voyage. Whilst in an 'at and from' policy, the ship has, in addition to the implied warranty of seaworthiness, to comply with the implied warranty that she be reasonably fit to encounter the ordinary perils of the port, that is, she be seaworthy for the port[107] or 'portworthy'.

In a policy which attaches while the ship is *in* port, namely, an 'at and from' policy, the ship, according to s 39(2), has to comply with the implied warranty that she shall 'at the commencement of the risk, be reasonably fit to encounter the ordinary perils of the port. Section 39(2) is, obviously, not applicable when the subject-matter is insured 'from' a particular place, for the risk under such a policy does not attach whilst she is at that port.[108] Unless expressly excluded by the policy, s 39(2), like s 39(1), is worded to apply to all voyage policies, whether on ship, cargo or freight.

Whether a ship has to be fit enough to endure the ordinary perils of the port *throughout* the period of her stay whilst 'at' that port is an issue which has never been raised. Unlike the implied warranty of seaworthiness, there is no litigation concerning this implied term. As the implied warranty of seaworthiness is applicable only at the commencement of the voyage, it could be said that the implied warranty of portworthiness should, likewise, apply only at the commencement of the risk. The wording of s 39(2) is sufficiently clear to support the assumption that the ship need only be portworthy at a specific point in time.

---

106 See rr 2 and 3 of the Rules for Construction. Note that r 2 applies to all policies, whilst r 3 applies only to a policy on ship.

107 Lord Penzance in *Quebec Marine Insurance Co v Commercial Bank of Canada* (1870) LR 3 PC 234 at p 241 described this as 'seaworthiness for the port'.

108 To insure her for port risks, an assured could take out the Institute Time Clauses Hulls, Port Risks policy. See *Mersey Mutual Underwriting Association v Poland* (1910) 15 Com Cas 205 at p 209, where a policy on 'port risks' was construed to cover: '... a risk of a character peculiar to a port and which is involved in a vessel being in port for the ordinary purposes for which vessel is in port, as distinguished from the risks of a vessel on a voyage, subjecting herself to the ordinary perils of navigating on that voyage.'

In the case of an 'at and from' policy on a ship, the risk, according to r 3, attaches or commences only when she has arrived at that place in 'good safety'. The implied warranty of portworthiness thus coincides with the attachment of the risk, which occurs only when the ship is in a state of good safety at that port: At that particular moment when she is in good safety she has to be sound enough to be in port without being at risk from the ordinary perils of the port. Whether a ship is or is not 'reasonably fit' to encounter the ordinary perils of the port is, of course, a question of fact.

IMPLIED WARRANTY OF SEAWORTHINESS

The Act implies a warranty of seaworthiness in a voyage policy, but not in a time policy.[109] This does not, however, mean that the unseaworthiness of a ship insured under a time policy is totally irrelevant. A different set of rules declared in s 39(5) applies to time policies. To avoid confusion, the legal principles relating to seaworthiness applicable to a time policy will be dealt with separately later in this chapter. All the provisions contained in s 39 are derived from case law decided before the Act. There is a wealth of authorities in this area of law which, provided that they are not inconsistent with the express provisions of the Act, may be referred to for the purpose of clarifying or explaining the legal position.[110]

Implied warranty of seaworthiness in voyage policies

Section 39(1) declares in general terms that:

> 'In a voyage policy there is an implied warranty that at the commencement of the voyage the ship shall be seaworthy for the purpose of the particular adventure insured.'

Subject-matter insured

The section does not specify the nature of the subject-matter insured. As worded, it is wide enough to be construed as being applicable to *all* voyage policies regardless of the nature of the subject-matter insured, whether it be ship, goods, freight, or any property exposed to maritime perils.[111] In the case of a policy on goods or other moveables, however, there is also another section dealing specifically with this implied term, where the general rule declared in s 39(1) is reaffirmed in s 40(2) as follows:

> 'In a voyage policy on goods or other moveables there is an implied warranty that at the commencement of the voyage the ship is not only seaworthy as a ship, but also that she is reasonably fit to carry the goods or other moveables to the destination contemplated by the policy.'

---

109 The rationale for this difference in the law can be found in the celebrated case of *Gibson v Small* (1853) 4 HL Cas 353.

110 See s 91(2): The rules of the common law, including the law merchant, save in so far as they are inconsistent with the express provisions of this Act, shall continue to apply to contracts of marine insurance.

111 See ss 3 and 5.

'Ship'

The section refers specifically to the seaworthiness only of the 'ship'. The question as to whether the implied warranty of seaworthiness is also to be applied to lighters, crafts and the like, employed for the conveyance of the cargo to and from the ship has to be considered.

This question was raised in the case of *Lane v Nixon*.[112] The common law position is that the implied warranty of seaworthiness is not applicable to lighters employed to land or discharge the cargo. This decision is, of course, correct and logical because the warranty of seaworthiness is applicable only at the commencement of the voyage. Unless the process of the landing of cargo by means of lighters can be considered as a separate stage of the voyage, the implied warranty does not apply after the voyage has commenced. The judges could not regard it in any sense as a stage of the voyage.[113]

The fact that the word 'craft' appears in cl 5.1, but not in cl 5.2 of the ICC(A), (B) and (C), which deals specifically with waiver of the implied warranty of seaworthiness, must mean that it does not apply to craft.[114]

It is contended that, as is the position under the common law, there is, under the Act, no implied warranty of seaworthiness as to 'craft' or other means of conveyance. Section 39(1) has not expressly included other means of conveyance within its ambit. Clause 5.1 is an exclusion (not an imposition) clause laying down the rule that, if the assured or their servants are privy to such unseaworthiness of the vessel or craft at the time the subject matter is loaded onto the vessel or craft, he will not be able to claim under the policy for any loss damage or expense arising therefrom.

Meaning of seaworthiness

It may be helpful, before proceeding to analyse the nature and scope of this implied warranty, first to define the meaning of the term 'seaworthiness'.[115] Needless to say, this discussion of definition is also relevant to a time policy, as the word 'seaworthy' also appears in s 39(5). There are essentially two criteria by which the seaworthiness of a ship may be measured. The first is espoused in s 39(4), which determines the seaworthiness of a ship by her ability to encounter

---

112 (1866) LR 1 CP 412.

113 The damage to the goods sustained whilst they were in the lighter was held recoverable under the policy which covered 'all risks to and from the ship'.

114 Templeman, at p 49, holds the view that cl 5.1 'extends the implied warranties to craft or other means of conveyance ...'. It is submitted that such an interpretation of the clause is difficult to support, especially when it is compared with cl 5.2. Though 'craft' and other means of conveyance are mentioned in cl 5.1, it is concerned only with unseaworthiness other than that relating to the implied warranties of seaworthiness which is applicable only at the commencement of the voyage.

115 'Seaworthiness' has the same meaning in marine insurance as in the law relating to carriage of goods by sea: see *Ingram and Royle Ltd v Services Maritimes du Treport* (1913) 12 Asp Mar Law Cas 493; 108 LT Rep 304; 1 KB 538; *Firemen's Fund Insurance Co v Western Australian Insurance Co Ltd* (1929) 138 LT 108, following *Becker, Gray & Co v London Assurance Corpn* [1918] AC 101 at p 114, HL, *per* Lord Sumner. Cases on carriage of goods by sea interpreting the meaning of 'seaworthiness' may thus be referred for this purpose.

the ordinary perils of the sea. The second, a common law criterion, uses the standard of the ordinary, careful and prudent shipowner.

Ability to encounter the ordinary perils of the seas

Section 39(4) provides a broad and general definition that:

'A ship is deemed to be seaworthy when she is reasonably fit in all respects to encounter the ordinary perils of the seas of the adventure insured.'

This criterion is derived from the celebrated case of *Dixon v Sadler*,[116] where Baron Parke defined 'seaworthiness' in the following terms:

'... it is clearly established that there is an implied warranty that the vessel shall be seaworthy, by which it meant that she shall be in a fit state as to repairs, equipment, crew and in all other respects to encounter the ordinary perils of the sea of the voyage insured, at the time of sailing upon it.'

The ship's 'fitness to encounter the ordinary perils of the seas of the voyage' is universally accepted as the test for determining the seaworthiness of a ship.[117] The two words in the statutory definition which require elaboration are 'reasonably' and 'ordinary'. The former refers to the standard of fitness, whilst the latter describes the perils of the seas.

Standard of reasonable fitness

It is significant to note that the standard of fitness is not one of perfection, but only of 'reasonableness'. To be seaworthy, a ship is not expected to be able to weather every conceivable storm or withstand every imaginable peril of the sea. All that is required of her is that she be reasonably suitable for the particular voyage. For example, a ship which sets sail with an open port hole would clearly fail to satisfy the standard of perfection, but would be quite acceptable according to the standard of reasonable fitness.[118] Similarly, the fact that a master is not expected to be in a state of perfect health was appreciated in the case *Rio Tinto Co Ltd v The Seed Shipping Co Ltd*.[119]

Ordinary perils of the seas

That the ship need only be fit enough to encounter the 'ordinary', not extraordinary, perils of the seas[120] is another well-established aspect of the implied warranty. She need only to be capable of withstanding the normal vicissitudes of the voyage. What in each case is an 'ordinary' peril of the sea was

---

116 (1839) 5 M & W 414; affd, (1841) 8 M & W 895.

117 It was applied in *Kopitoff v Wilson* (1876) 3 Asp MLC 163; *Burges v Wickham* (1863) 3 B & S 669; and received the firm approval of the House of Lords in *Steel v State Line SS Co* (1877) 3 App Cas 72; 37 LT Rep; 3 Asp MLC 516, and *Elder Dempster & Co v Paterson Zochonis & Co* [1924] AC 522.

118 Provided, of course, that the port hole can be shut easily, speedily and without any inconvenience. On the subject of open port holes, see *Steel v State Line SS Co* (1877) 3 App Cas 72 HL and *Dobell & Co Steamship v Rossmore Co* [1895] 2 QB 408.

119 (1926) 134 LT 763; (1926) 24 Ll L Rep 316 at p 320. See also *Moore v Lunn* (1923) 39 TLR 526.

120 See r 7 of the Rules for Construction. The term 'perils of the seas' refers only to fortuitous accidents or casualties of the seas. It does not include ordinary action of the winds and waves.

explained in *Kopitoff v Wilson*[121] and *The Gaupen (No 3)*.[122] In the former, incidental risks to which a ship must, of necessity, be exposed in the course of the voyage were considered 'ordinary' perils of the seas. In the latter, heavy weather of the kind expected of the voyage was held to fall within the scope of an 'ordinary' peril of the seas. Thus, even severe weather, hurricanes, cyclones and strong gales could be considered as 'ordinary' perils of the seas if they are conditions expected of a particular region.

The ordinary, careful and prudent shipowner criterion

Another more recent determinant, which has often been employed to ascertain the seaworthiness of a ship, is that offered by Mr Justice Channel in *McFadden v Blue Star Line*,[123] where the yardstick was couched as follows:

'To be seaworthy, a vessel must have that degree of fitness which an ordinary, careful and prudent owner would require his vessel to have at the commencement of her voyage, having regard to all the probable circumstances of it'.

The test is direct, objective and simple to apply:[124] a ship is seaworthy if an ordinary, careful and prudent owner would send her to sea in her present condition. Though s 39(2) has provided its own test for the purpose of ascertaining 'seaworthiness', there is no reason why the common law standard of the prudent shipowner could not also be invoked. A combined application of both methods was employed by Mr Justice Earle in *Gibson v Small*[125] as follows:

'[Seaworthiness] expresses a relation between the state of the ship and the perils it has to meet in the situation it is in; so that a ship before setting out on a voyage is seaworthy, if it is fit in the degree which a prudent owner uninsured would require to meet the perils of the service it is then engaged in, and would continue so during the voyage, unless it met with extraordinary damage.'

A relative term

Both the above criteria have been criticised as being too broad to be useful. As guidelines, they do not dictate any positive rules or conditions which must be complied with for a ship to attain the standard of seaworthiness. The notion of seaworthiness has long been recognised by law as a concept which allows variables to be taken to consideration. This was made clear in *Burges v Wickham*[126] by Mr Justice Cockburn when he commented that:

'... the term seaworthiness is a relative and flexible term, the degree of seaworthiness depending on the position in which the vessel may be placed, or on the nature of the navigation or adventure on which it is about to embark.'

In *Foley v Tabor*,[127] Chief Justice Erle directed his jury in similar terms: '... seaworthiness is a word which the import varies with the place, the voyage,

---

121 (1876) 1 QBD 377; 3 Asp MLC 163.

122 24 Ll L Rep 355.

123 [1905] 1 KB 697 at p 706.

124 This test was applied in *Reed v Page* [1927] 1 KB 743.

125 (1853) 4 HL Cas 353.

126 (1863) 3 B & S 669.

127 (1861) 2 F & F 663.

the class of ship, or even the nature of the cargo.' In *The Queen v Freeman*,[128] 'the trade in which she was engaged, and the season of the year' were added to the list.

'Seaworthiness' is a relative and flexible term. It varies according to the nature of the voyage contemplated. Thus, a ship may be seaworthy for one voyage, but not for another. There is no fixed or absolute standard of seaworthiness, and the wording of s 39(1) itself makes this clear: it states that the ship shall be seaworthy for 'the purpose of the particular adventure insured'.

Specific matters relating to seaworthiness

An analysis of cases will reveal the fact that there are five aspects of a ship which can affect or impinge upon her seaworthiness. These matters relate to:

* design and construction;[129]
* machinery, equipment and navigational aids;[130]
* sufficiency and competence of crew;[131]
* sufficiency and quality of fuel;[132] and
* stability and stowage of cargoes.[133]

'At the commencement of the voyage'

It is important to remember that the implied warranty of seaworthiness is applicable only at a particular time, that is, 'at the commencement of the voyage'. Regardless of whether the policy is 'from' or 'at and from' a particular place, the implied warranty of seaworthiness applies only when the ship sets sail from that particular place. She does not have to be seaworthy for the voyage whilst she is lying in port. But once the warranty is fulfilled, 'the shipowner's obligation to the underwriter is at an end'.[134] There is no continuing warranty of seaworthiness. Whether a voyage has or has not commenced is, of course, a question of fact: A ship has to break ground and quit her moorings with the

---

128 (1875) 9 IR 9 CL 527.

129 *Anglis & Co v P & O Steam Navigation Co* [1927] 2 KB 456; *The Marine Sulphur Queen* [1973] 1 Lloyd's Rep 88, USCA; *The Torenia* [1983] 1 Lloyd's Rep 210, KBD; and *Coltman v Bibby Tankers Ltd, The Derbyshire* [1986] 1 WLR 751.

130 *The President of India* [1963] 1 Lloyd's Rep 1; *The Antigoni* [1991] 1 Lloyd's Rep 209, CA; *The Yamatogawa* [1990] 2 Lloyd's Rep 39, QBD; *The Theodegmon* [1990] 1 Lloyd's Rep 52, QBD; *The Subro Valour* [1995] 1 Lloyd's Rep 509, QBD; *The Maria* (1937) 91 Fed Rep (2d) 819; and *The Irish Spruce* [1976] 1 Lloyd's Rep 63.

131 *Wedderburn & Others v Bell* (1807) 1 Camp 1; *The Makedonia* [1962] 1 Lloyd's Rep 316; *Standard Oil Co of New York v The Clan Line Steamers Ltd* (1924) AC 100; 16 Asp MLC 273; and *The Hong Kong Fir* [1962] 2 QB 26; [1961] 2 Lloyd's Rep 478.

132 *Louis Dreyfus & Co v Tempus Shipping Co* [1931] AC 726, HL; and *Fiumana Societa Di Navigazione v Bunge & Co Ltd* [1930] 2 KB 47; *Thin v Richards & Co* [1892] 2 QB 141; *McIver & Co v Tate Steamers Ltd* [1903] 1 KB 362; and *Northumbrian Shipping Co v Timm & Son Ltd* [1939] AC 397.

133 *The Aquacharm* [1982] 1 Lloyd's Rep 7; *The Friso* [1980] 1 Lloyd's Rep 469, QBD; *Elder Dempster & Co Ltd v Paterson, Zochonis & Co* [1924] AC 522; and *Smith Hogg & Co v Black Sea & Baltic Insurance Co* [1940] AC 997.

134 Per Bigham J in *Greenock Steamship Co v Maritime Insurance Co* [1903] 1 KB 367 at p 373.

intention of embarking upon her voyage before she can be said to have commenced her voyage.[135] Thus, a mere intention to commence a voyage is inconsequential.

Seaworthiness by stages

The implied warranty of seaworthiness, though expressly stated to be applicable only at the commencement of the voyage – meaning the insured voyage – has to be read in the light of the doctrine of seaworthiness by stages as defined in s 39(3). This is yet another declaration of a well-founded common law principle which is also applicable in the law of contracts of affreightment. The rule of seaworthiness by stages was described as 'older than the age of steam'.[136] *Bouillon v Lupton*[137] is regarded as the creator of the rule, but in fact a hint of the concept can be sensed even earlier in 1815 in the case of *Oliver v Loughman*.[138] In *Quebec Marine Insurance Co v The Commercial Bank of Canada*,[139] Lord Penzance of the Privy Council states the rule as follows: '... there is seaworthiness for the port, seaworthiness in some cases for the river, and seaworthiness ... of a whaling voyage, for some definite, well-recognised, and distinctly separate stage of the voyage.'

A distinct and well-known stage of a voyage is that for the purpose of coaling or refuelling. One need only refer to the familiar cases of *Thin v Richards & Co*,[140] *The Vortigern*,[141] and *Northumbrian Shipping Co v Timm Son Ltd*[142] to ascertain the rationale for the formulation of the rule. It is clear that the rule, specially devised to meet practical commercial necessities and exigencies, is nothing but a relaxation of the implied warranty of seaworthiness. It modifies the responsibility of the shipowner to the extent that it permits compliance in stages or by instalments. Instead of demanding fulfilment of the warranty, all at once, at the commencement of the voyage, it allows the shipowner the right to stagger the performance of this duty, but only in relation to certain matters. It is to be understood that this laxity in the execution of the promise, sanctioned by law, does not in any measure diminish or enlarge the duty of the shipowner: it merely eases the performance of his obligation, leaving the obligation itself well intact.

It is observed that under British jurisdiction, the courts are reluctant to extend the boundaries of the doctrine of seaworthiness by stages. It has invariably been restricted to matters of necessity for commercial, physical or practical reasons. The courts have always jealously guarded the limits of its

---

135 See *Pittegrew v Pringle* [1832] 3 B & Ad 514; *Sea Insurance Co v Blogg* [1898] 3 Com Cas 218 CA; *Hunting v Boulton* [1895] 1 Com Cas 120; and *Mersey Mutual Underwriting Association v Poland* (1910) 15 Com Cas 205.

136 *Per* Lord Porter, *Northumbrian Shipping Co v E Timm & Son Ltd* [1939] AC 397 at p 411, HL.

137 (1863) 33 LJ CP 37.

138 (1815), reported as a footnote in *Weir v Aberdeen* (1819) 2 B & Ad 320 at p 322.

139 (1870) LR 3 PC 234 at p 241, PC.

140 [1892] 2 QB 141, CA.

141 [1899] P 140, CA.

142 [1930] AC 397, HL.

application, confining it only to cases of refuelling,[143] and when circumstances justify its application, such as 'when the ship requires different kinds of or further preparation or equipment'. There has to be a physical or commercial need to warrant a division of the voyage into stages.

Effect of breach of implied warranty of seaworthiness

As was seen earlier, the House of Lords in *The Good Luck* has pronounced that a promissory warranty in marine insurance is in fact a condition precedent, the breach of which automatically discharges the insurer from liability as from the date of breach. This rule applies to all promissory warranties including the implied warranty of seaworthiness.

In fact, as early as 1807, in *Wedderburn & Others v Bell*,[144] Lord Ellenborough had already referred to the implied warranty of seaworthiness as a 'condition precedent to the policy attaching'. His remark is certainly an accurate description of the legal position, but only in so far as regards a policy which insures the subject-matter 'from' a particular port. Such a policy does not attach until the ship has commenced the voyage in a seaworthy condition from that port. No liability can be incurred before the commencement of the voyage because the policy attaches only when the ship sets sail 'from' that particular port in compliance with the implied warranty. In this context, it is true to say that it is a condition precedent to the attachment of the risk.

In the case of an 'at and from' policy, however, the position is different in the sense that the policy had already attached when the ship arrived 'at' the particular port in good safety. Any loss occurring before the vessel sets sail – whilst the vessel is at that place – would thus fall upon the policy. Should a breach of the implied warranty of seaworthiness be committed later when she sets sail, the insurer is only discharged from liability as from the date of breach, but without prejudice to any liability incurred by him before the breach.

Exclusion of the implied warranty of seaworthiness

The warranty of seaworthiness – absolute in its nature and capable of producing a most disastrous effect upon a policy in the event of its breach – is an important safeguard for the preservation of life at sea. Yet its creator, regarding it to be the 'bounden legal duty' of the shipowner 'towards the mariners for the safety of their lives, and towards the merchants who load their goods' to furnish a seaworthy ship, has also deemed it fit to allow for its exclusion in a policy of marine insurance.[145]

---

143 In *Greenock SS Co v Maritime Insurance Co* [1903] 1 KB 367 at p 372, Bigham J remarked: 'But the warranty is one thing and the observance of it another. It is clear that in such an adventure it is practically impossible for the ship to sail with sufficient coal for the whole of the contemplated voyage. She would have to call at convenient ports on her route for the purpose of replenishing her bunkers, and therefore, though the warranty at starting is that she shall be seaworthy for the whole voyage, the warranty is sufficiently observed if the voyage is so arranged as that the ship can and shall coal at convenient ports *en route*.'

144 (1807) 1 Camp 1.

145 *Per* Baron Martin in *Gibson v Small* (1853) 4 HL Cas 353 at p 370. In a contract of affreightment, the parties are also permitted by means of a clearly worded exception clause to exclude the application of the implied warranty of seaworthiness: see *Nelson Line v James Nelson* [1908] AC 16.

To exclude the application of the implied warranty of seaworthiness in a voyage policy, the parties to the contract of insurance may either employ the use of an exception clause or waive the breach as allowed by s 34(3) of the Act. It is appropriate at this juncture to mention that a waiver of a breach generally operates as a subsequent assentment (after the breach) 'to maintain liability notwithstanding the violation of the warranty'.[146] An exclusion clause, on the other hand, is an antecedent agreement (incorporated into the policy) excepting the insurer from liability for a certain cause of loss. The result, however, is the same whether the implied warranty is excluded by an exception clause or a waiver of its breach: the effectiveness of the implied warranty is negated.

Exception clauses

Neither the common law nor the Act prohibits the use of exclusion clauses in a contract of insurance. Thus, the parties to the contract are at liberty to negotiate for a total or qualified dispensation of this implied term. In the celebrated case of *Quebec Marine Insurance Co v Commercial Bank of Canada*,[147] the Privy Council accepted the fact that:

> '... it is competent to parties by language in a contract to which, as an ordinary rule, the law attaches some implied condition, by express, pertinent, and apposite language to exclude that condition ...'

However, it was held that the stipulation in question, which excepts the underwriters from liability for 'rottenness, inherent defects and other unseaworthiness ...' was not clear enough to be construed as a statement that, the insurer had intended to surrender the implied warranty of seaworthiness. The court was of the view that the express clause had in fact strengthened, not weakened, the position of the underwriters, and was a particular effort to amplify, not nullify, the rule that the insurer is not liable for unseaworthiness. Like all exclusion or exception clauses, they have to be clear and unambiguous to be enforceable.

As can be seen below, there is a variety of clauses which have been used to exclude the implied warranty. They are basically variations of either the 'seaworthiness admitted' or the 'held covered' clause.

'Allowed to be seaworthy' and 'seaworthiness admitted' clauses

A clause stating that the ship was to be 'allowed to be seaworthy for the voyage' was used in *Phillips & Another v Nairne and Another*.[148] The effect of such a clause was held to have relieved the owner of the obligation to comply with the implied warranty of seaworthiness. It excluded any objection regarding the seaworthiness of the ship, whatever may be her state of repair the ship was considered seaworthy. Such a clause is an admission of fact and acts as an estoppel: it estops the insurer from pleading unseaworthiness as a defence. According to Pollock CB, who had to interpret the same clause in *Parfitt v*

---

146 *Per* Lord Penzance in *Quebec Marine Insurance Co v The Commercial Bank of Canada* (1870) LR 3 PC 234 at p 244, PC.

147 *Ibid*, at p 242.

148 (1847) 4 CB 343.

Thompson,[149] the admission 'enures for all purposes, and amounts to a dispensation of the usual warranty of seaworthiness'. The assumption of seaworthiness precluded the insurer from relying upon the fact of her unseaworthiness as a defence.

The 'allowed to be seaworthy' clause was later replaced with the 'seaworthiness admitted' clause which was more directly expressed.[150] Both have now fallen into disuse, but in relation to cargo, the 'unseaworthiness and unfitness exclusion clause' (cl 5) of the ICC (A), (B) and (C) could be described as the modern equivalent.

Held covered clause

A 'held covered' is also commonly used to protect an assured in the event of a breach of a warranty. In *Greenock Steamship Co v Maritime Insurance Co Ltd*,[151] Mr Justice Bingham had to interpret the effect of a wide clause which read as follows: 'held covered in case of *any* breach of warranty ... at a premium to be hereafter arranged'. The plaintiffs had breached the implied warranty of seaworthiness in sending the ship to sea with an insufficient supply of coal. As they were unaware of her unseaworthy condition until after the loss, no arrangement for the payment of additional premium was made. The judge had no doubt whatsoever that the clause applied to a breach of the implied warranty of seaworthiness. After acknowledging the importance of the warranty, he proceeded to explain the operation of the clause:[152]

> '... it entitles the shipowner, as soon as he discovers that the warranty has been broken, to require the underwriter to hold him covered ... But what is to happen if the breach is not discovered until a loss has occurred? I think even in that case the clause still holds good, and the only open question would be, what is a reasonable premium for the added risk.'

Whilst on the subject of the held covered clause, all that needs to be mentioned here is that cl 3 of the ITCH(95) and cl 2 of the IVCH(95) are of limited application and do not apply to the implied warranty of seaworthiness. Thus, a shipowner who wishes to protect himself from the consequences of a breach of this warranty would have to insert a clause specially for this purpose; otherwise, all he can hope for is for the insurer to waive the breach.

'Unseaworthiness and unfitness exclusion' clause

The held covered clause (cl 10) in the ICC(A), (B) and (C), applying to a change of destination, is not concerned with seaworthiness. The subject of

---

149 (1844) 13 M & W 393 at p 395.

150 The January 1912 and 1963 version read as follows: 'The seaworthiness of the vessel as between the assured and the underwriters is hereby admitted.' By admitting that the vessel is seaworthy, the insurer has precluded himself from relying on a breach of the implied warranty of seaworthiness as a defence. See *Firemen's Fund Insurance Co v Western Australian Insurance Co & Atlantic Insurance Co* (1927) 17 Asp MLC 332 for the effect of a 'seaworthiness admitted' clause in an original policy upon a policy of reinsurance.

151 [1903] 1 KB 367.

152 *Ibid*, at pp 374–375. See also *Mentz, Decker & Co v Maritime Insurance Co* [1910] 1 KB 132, where a notice given after a loss as a result of a barratrous deviation was held sufficient to satisfy a similar held covered clause.

seaworthiness is dealt with in cl 5, captioned as the 'unseaworthiness and unfitness exclusion clause' in all the ICC. Before proceeding to analyse the scope of cl 5, it would be helpful to understand the reasons for its insertion. As was seen, the implied warranty of seaworthiness declared in s 39(1) applies to all voyage policies, including a policy on goods even though it is obvious that shippers are generally not in a position to know, least of all exercise control over, the condition or fitness of the vessel on which his cargo is carried.[153] As cargo policies are normally for a voyage, it soon became clear that the statutory requirement as regards the seaworthiness of the carrying ship had to be altered. Thus, to mitigate the harshness of the application of the implied warranty of seaworthiness in relation to cargo, cl 5 is now a standard provision in all the ICC.

Clauses 5.1 and 5.2 may initially appear to be indistinct. Only cl 5.2 will be considered here as it is concerned with the implied warranty of seaworthiness and unfitness. Clause 5.2, sometimes called the 'waiver' clause, states:

> 'The Underwriters waive any breach of the implied warranties of seaworthiness of the ship and fitness of the ship to carry the subject-matter insured to destination, unless the Assured or their servants are privy to such unseaworthiness or unfitness.'

The reference to 'the implied warranties of seaworthiness and fitness' is indeed significant: cl 5.2 is specifically directed at the implied warranties. By agreeing *in advance* to waive a breach of the implied warranties, the effect is to nullify both ss 39(1) and 40(2) of the Act.

Clause 5.1, on the other hand, does not mention the implied warranties. Accordingly, it has to be said that, by contrast, it is not concerned with the implied warranty of seaworthiness which operates only at the commencement of a voyage, but only with seaworthiness arising *during the course of* a voyage.[154]

That the implied warranties are not completely dispensed with or negated by cl 5.2 is clear. It is the breach, not the warranties, which is waived. The breach, however, is only waived if the assured (or his agent) is not privy to *such* unseaworthiness or unfitness. The corollary of this is that if the assured (or his agent) is privy to such unseaworthiness, he will not be able to claim under the policy. It is to be recalled that as a general rule, the lack of knowledge or privity in a *voyage* policy has never been considered a relevant consideration for the purpose of determining the liability of the insurer in the event of a breach of the

---

153 Unless, of course, he is shipping his own goods on board his own ship.

154 Clause 5.1 is clearly not concerned with the implied warranty of seaworthiness. It is an exception clause excluding the insurer from liability for a loss arising from unseaworthiness to which the assured or his agents are privy at the time the subject-matter is loaded on board the ship. It maintains cover against loss for all other types of unseaworthiness which arise after the initial implied warranty of seaworthiness applicable at the commencement of the voyage has been complied with. If the implied warranty of seaworthiness is not fulfilled, there can be no question of excepting the insurer from liability, because he would have been automatically discharged from further liability under the contract as from the date of breach, that is, at the commencement of the voyage. The legal effect produced by cl 5.1 is as follow: provided that the assured or his servants are not privy to such unseaworthiness, at the time the subject-matter is loaded, he is insured for any loss arising from the unseaworthiness of the vessel.

implied warranty of seaworthiness. Therefore, in this sense, the implied warranty of seaworthiness has been modified by cl 5.2.

The position under the ICC as regards the warranties of seaworthiness and unfitness, implied by ss 39(1) and 40(2) may thus be summarised as follows: cl 5.2 has to an extent changed the character of the implied warranty of seaworthiness – it is no longer absolute in nature. Provided that the cargo owner, the assured (or his servants), is not privy to the vessel's condition of unseaworthiness (existing at the time when the vessel commences on her voyage), he would be able to recover from the insurer for any loss proximately caused by an insured peril. In this light, the position of the implied warranty of seaworthiness under the ICC has become more like the rules applicable to a time policy where 'privity' is also an essential ingredient as spelt out in s 39(5) which is discussed below

Unseaworthiness and the Inchmaree clause

A latent defect in hull or machinery could well render a vessel unseaworthy, resulting in a breach of the implied warranty of seaworthiness.[155] A latent defect is one which 'could not be discovered on such an examination as a reasonably careful skilled man would make'.[156] As the implied warranty of seaworthiness is absolute in nature, the assured would not be able to plead as a defence the lack of knowledge of the defect. Any claim that he had exercised due care would be of no avail.

However, cl 6.2.1 of the ITCH(95)[157] (and cl 4.2.1 of IVCH(95))[158] provides insurance cover against loss of or damage to the subject-matter insured caused by, *inter alia*, '... any latent defect in the machinery or hull' with the proviso that such a loss or damage must not have resulted from the 'want of due diligence by the Assured, Owners or Managers or *Superintendents or any of their onshore management*'.[159] This proviso would not be difficult to fulfil, as a latent defect is by definition a defect which is not discoverable by the exercise of due diligence or ordinary care. Whether cl 6.2.1 of the ITCH(95) could be construed in a manner so as to override the implied warranty of seaworthiness has to be considered. If it is to be given its full effect, an assured would be able to recover under the policy, even though the implied warranty of seaworthiness has been breached by reason of the latent defect. As this subject can be more conveniently examined in the discussion of the Inchmaree clause, it will not be considered here.

---

155 A classic example is *The Mills Frigate, Mills v Roebuck*, reported in Park, *Insurance* (7th edn), Chapter XI, at p 67.

156 *Brown v Nitrate Producer SS Co* (1937) 58 Ll L Rep 188. For other definitions of latent defect, see *The Dimitrios N Rallias* (1922) 23 Ll L Rep 363, CA; *The Caribbean Sea* [1980] 1 Lloyd's Rep 338; *Miss Jay Jay* [1987] 1 Lloyd's Rep 32, CA; *Sipowicz v Wimble* [1974] 1 Lloyd's Rep 593; and *Irwin v Eagle Star Insurance Co* [1973] 2 Lloyd's Rep 489.

157 Previously cl 6.2.2 of the ITCH(83).

158 Also known as the Inchmaree clause. See Chapter 12.

159 The words in italics are not in the ITCH(83) or the IVCH(83).

Burden of proof

An insurer would naturally wish, whenever possible, to plead a breach of the implied warranty of seaworthiness as a defence to exonerate himself from liability to a claim. As he is making the allegation that the ship is unseaworthy, it is only fair and natural that he should bear the burden of proof. This is in accordance with the general principle of the law of evidence: he who alleges must prove, and the burden normally lies on the party who asserts the affirmative of the issue or question in dispute. *Parker and Others v Potts*[160] may be cited as the authority which has enunciated the general rule that 'a ship is *prima facie* to be deemed seaworthy'; thus, it lies upon the insurer to prove the contrary.

However, the burden of proof may well shift to the assured in certain circumstances. The circumstances under which the general rule may be displaced have to be examined, as such a shift in the burden of proof is an advantage of tactical importance to the insurer who is now to be relieved of the duty, which originally lies in him, to provide evidence to show that the ship was unseaworthy when she set sailed. A court would, naturally, as far as possible, prefer to leave the initial burden where it lies, and it would rarely disturb the general rule of onus of proof unless the circumstances clearly permit.

The particular facts of a case could invoke a presumption of unseaworthiness, albeit a rebuttable one, resulting in the shifting of the burden to proof to the assured, who would have to adduce evidence to refute the presumption. It is then incumbent upon the assured to show that the ship was, in fact, seaworthy when she set sail and that her condition had arisen from cause or causes arising subsequent to the commencement of the voyage.

It has been said that an appropriate scenario to raise the presumption is when a ship has to return to port, or sinks very shortly after leaving port. When such a presumption may be raised is a question of fact, and a court of law would be most disinclined to allow its operation unless it falls within the legal guidelines which sanction its application. Some guidance was offered by Parke B in *Franco v Natusch*,[161] who observed that:

> 'It was laid down in the House of Lords in *Parker v Potts* ... that it must be taken *prima facie* that a ship is seaworthy at the commencement of the risk; but that if, soon after her sailing, it appears that she is not sound or fit for sea, without adequate cause of stress of weather, etc, to account for it, the rational inference is, that, notwithstanding appearances, she was not seaworthy when the voyage commenced.'

The reluctance of the Court of Appeal to raise the presumption of unseaworthiness can clearly be seen in *Pickup v Thames Insurance Co*,[162] where the ship had to put back to port 11 days after sailing. The court held that the facts of the case did not raise the 'irresistible inference' that the ship was

---

160 (1815) 3 Dow's R 23.

161 (1836) Tyr & Gr 401.

162 (1878) 3 QBD 594, CA.

unseaworthy when she set sail. The trial judge was held to have misdirected the jury when he instructed them that the mere fact that the ship had to return to port so soon after sailing was in itself sufficient to raise the presumption that she was unseaworthy at the time of sailing.

The crucial point, which was made patently clear by all the judges in the Court of Appeal, is that time is only *one* of the factors, and for that matter of 'a very limited extent only' and of 'secondary consideration'[163] that may be taken into account when determining whether the presumption could be raised. Time cannot of itself, without more, give rise to the presumption to shift the onus of proof.

All the judges emphasised the fact that if the circumstances of the case is such that, 'it is possible to ascribe the result to any other cause than the condition of the vessel on starting on the voyage', the presumption cannot be invoked. In the case, there was a possibility that the ship was unable to proceed with the voyage because of severe weather arising during the course of the 11 days which had elapsed between her leaving and returning to port. Further, a period of 11 days was considered not short enough in this case to denude the onus of proof from the underwriters. The court warned that it is in each case a question of fact, not of law, for the jury to draw the necessary inference.[164]

No implied warranty of seaworthiness in time policies

English law does not impose a warranty of seaworthiness on a time policy.[165] This was confirmed in 1853 by the House of Lords in *Gibson v Small*,[166] and the principle is now firmly consolidated in s 39(5) of the Act which declares that:

> 'In a time policy there is no implied warranty that the ship shall be seaworthy at any stage of the adventure, but where, with the privity of the assured, the ship is sent to sea in an unseaworthy state, the insurer is not liable for any loss attributable to unseaworthiness.'

Though there is no implied warranty of seaworthiness in a time policy, this does not, however, mean that the question of seaworthiness is irrelevant. Surprisingly, there is hardly any litigation on this section.

---

163 *Per* Cockburn J, *ibid*, at p 598.

164 The Court of Appeal took the opportunity to clarify the decision of *Watson v Clark* [1813] 1 Dow 336 which has sometimes been cited as having laid down the rule that the presumption was one of law, and that the mere fact that a ship had to return to port shortly after leaving it was in itself sufficient to raise a presumption of unseaworthiness. What Lord Eldon was, in fact, saying in that case was that, 'if a ship was seaworthy at the commencement of the voyage, though she became otherwise only one hour after, still the warranty was complied with and the underwriter was liable'.

165 In America, the implied warranty applies to both time and voyage policies.

166 (1853) 4 HL Cas 353. In this case, all the pros and cons for not implying a warranty of seaworthiness in a time policy were exhaustively canvassed. Later, in *Dudgeon v Pembroke* (1877) 2 App Cas 284, HL, the final nail was driven into the coffin confirming that there is no implied warranty of seaworthiness in a time policy.

'At any stage of the adventure'

The above phrase was inserted to foreclose any arguments, such as those raised in *Jenkins v Heycock*,[167] suggesting that a warranty of seaworthiness is applicable at the commencement of each and every intermediate voyage made during the currency of the time policy. These words have put at rest any doubts which one might have as to the applicability of the implied warranty at each intermediate voyage undertaken by the insured vessel.

'Privity'

The meaning of the word 'privity' was analysed in *The Eurysthenes*[168] by the Court of Appeal. This 'old-fashioned' word, said Lord Denning, embraces not only actual knowledge but also constructive knowledge, and knowledge means:[169]

'... not only positive knowledge, but also the sort of knowledge expressed in the phrase "turning a blind eye". If a man, suspicious of the truth, turns a blind eye to it, and refrains from inquiry – so that he should not know it for certain – then he is to be regarded as knowing the truth. This "turning a blind eye" is far more blameworthy that mere negligence. Negligence in not knowing the truth is not equivalent to knowledge of it.'

Lord Justice Roskill, who was of the same mind, said:[170]

'If the facts amounting to unseaworthiness are there staring the assured in the face so that he must, had he thought of it, have realised their implication upon the seaworthiness of his ship, he cannot escape from being held privy to that unseaworthiness by blindly or blandly ignoring these facts or by refraining from asking relevant questions regarding them in the hope that by his lack of inquiry he will not know for certain that which any inquiry must have made plain beyond possibility of doubt.'

The court also concluded that 'privity' is not the same as 'wilful misconduct' or 'actual fault or privity'. The court has clarified that 'privity' does not carry any connotation of fault, and negligence is not equivalent to privity.[171]

Here, it is appropriate to refer to the trenchant observations made by Mr Justice Kerr in *Piermay Shipping Co SA and Brandt's v Chester, The Michael*.[172] Though his comments were in respect of the requirement of consent and privity in relation to barratry, they are nevertheless relevant to the present discussion as they offer an insight as to what constitutes 'privity'. He said:[173]

---

167 (1853) 8 Moore's PC Cases 350.

168 [1977] 1 QB 49, CA. *The Eurysthenes* was very recently applied in *Manifest Shipping & Co Ltd v Uni-Polaris Insurance Co Ltd & La Reunion Europeene, The Star Sea* [1995] 1 Lloyd's Rep 651, QBD See also *Frangos v Sun Insurance Office* (1934) 49 Ll L Rep 354 and *Willmott v General Accident Fire and Life Assurance Corpn Ltd* (1935) 53Ll L Rep 35, KBD.

169 *Ibid*, at p 66.

170 *Ibid*, at p 76.

171 In *Compania Naviera Vazcongada v British & Foreign Mar Insurance Co Ltd, The Gloria* (1934) 54 Ll L Rep 35, it was held that mere omission to take precaution against the possibility of the ship being unseaworthy did not make the owner privy to any unseaworthiness which such precaution might have revealed.

172 [1979] 1 Lloyd's Rep 55, QBD; [1979] 2 Lloyd's Rep 1, CA.

173 *Ibid*, at p 66.

'It is clear that consent or privity can range from active complicity to mere passive concurrence. An owner who makes it clear that he would like to see his ship at the bottom of the sea, but does not want to know any more about it, is privy to its sinking just the same way as Henry II was privy to the murder of Thomas Becket when he said "Will no one rid me of this turbulent priest?" Even if the suggestion of scuttling comes from someone else, and the owner implies consent by saying nothing against it, he would be privy and could not say that the act was "to his prejudice".'

This colourful analogy is, in effect, no different from Lord Denning's notion of 'turning a blind eye'.

Another related question which the court considered was: what must the assured be privy to? Lord Justice Geoffrey Lane's answer was 'unseaworthiness' and 'not the facts which in the upshot prove to amount to unseaworthiness.'[174] On this point, Lord Denning's speech is particularly informative. He said:[175]

'To disentitle the shipowner, he must, I think, have knowledge not only of the facts constituting the unseaworthiness, but also knowledge that those facts rendered the ship unseaworthy, that is, not reasonably fit to encounter the ordinary perils of the sea.'

It needs to be said that it is the privity of the 'assured' which is relevant. Thus, 'the knowledge must be that of the shipowner personally, or of his *alter ego*, or in the case of a company, of its head men or whoever may be considered their *alter ego*'. In other words, the right people must have the relevant knowledge.[176]

'Attributable to unseaworthiness'

First, it is to be noted that s 39(5) does not use the words 'caused by' or 'proximately caused by' unseaworthiness. Instead the term 'attributable to' is used, the meaning of which will be discussed in greater depth later.[177] The cases of *Thomas and Son Shipping v The London and Provincial Marine and General Insurance Ltd*[178] and *Thomas v Tyne and Wear Steamship Freight Insurance Association Ltd*[179] are the two main authorities on causation relating to s 39(5). Suffice it is here to mention that if unseaworthiness is the sole proximate cause of a loss, the insurer does not have to rely on s 39(5) to free himself from liability. In a standard policy, unseaworthiness is not a peril insured against. Thus, regardless of whether the assured is or is not privy to the vessel's condition of unseaworthiness, such a loss is just not recoverable. To invoke s 39(5), the loss has first to be brought under the policy. This means that it has to

---

174 [1977] 1 QB 49 at p 81, CA.

175 *Ibid*, at p 68.

176 In *The Pacific Queen* [1963] 2 Lloyd's Rep 201, knowledge as to the condition of the vessel resting in one of the partners and the manager (also a partner) was sufficient to impute the company with privity. *Cf The Spot Pack* [1957] AMC 655, where acts of those in supervisory management and those in normal operation were distinguished.

177 *See* Chapter 8.

178 (1914) TLR 595, CA, hereinafter referred to as *The Thomas and Son Shipping Case*.

179 [1917] KB 938, hereinafter referred to as *The Thomas Tyne and Wear Case*.

be shown that the loss is caused by an insured peril and is, therefore, *prima facie* recoverable.[180] The insurer's defence would then be that the assured is to be disentitled of his right of claim by reason of his privity to the vessel's condition of unseaworthiness. As with the defence of wilful misconduct under s 55(2)(a), the expression 'attributable to' appearing in s 39(5) is specially chosen to cover the circumstance where unseaworthiness is either a remote cause of loss or where it is one of two or more proximate causes of loss at least one of which is an insured peril. There would be no need to apply s 39(5) if unseaworthiness is the sole proximate cause of loss or where unseaworthiness is one of two or more proximate causes of loss, none of which is an insured risk under the policy.

'Particular unseaworthiness'

The wording of s 39(5) does not state whether the insurer is to be exempted from liability for loss attributable to any kind of unseaworthiness or only to the particular unseaworthiness to which the assured is privy when he sent the vessel to sea. This uncertainty was clarified in *The Thomas Tyne and Wear Case*, where Mr Justice Atkin – who had to contend with a ship which was unseaworthy in two ways: unfitness of hull, to which the assured was not privy, and an insufficient crew, to which he was privy – observed that:[181]

'Where a ship is sent to sea in a state of unseaworthiness in two respects, the assured being privy to the one and not privy to the other, the insurer is only protected if the loss was attributable to the *particular* unseaworthiness to which the assured was privy.'[182]

As the assured was not privy to the particular unseaworthiness – unfitness of hull – which had caused the loss, the insurers were held liable for the loss.[183] An insurer is to be held not liable for a loss attributable to unseaworthiness only to which the assured was privy.

---

180 Eg, in *George Cohen, Sons & Co v Standard Marine Insurance Co* (1925) 21 Ll L Rep 30, the loss of the battleship was proximately caused by perils of the sea and/or restraint of princes but remotely by unseaworthiness. As the assured was not aware of the ship's condition of unseaworthiness, they were able to recover for the loss. See also *The Miss Jay Jay* [1985] 1 Lloyd's Rep 264; [1987] 1 Lloyd's Rep 32, CA.

181 *Ibid*, at p 941.

182 Arnould at para 719 suggests that the word 'such' should be read before the word 'unseaworthiness'.

183 It is interesting to note that the arbitrator (whose finding of fact was accepted by the court) found that the loss of the ship was attributable solely to the unfitness of the hull. In spite of the fact that unseaworthiness was not an insured peril under the policy in question, the insurer were held liable for the loss on the basis that the assured were not privy to this particular unseaworthiness It is submitted that the decision is on this ground difficult to support. A similar result occurred in *Ashwort v General Accident Fire and Life Assurance Corpn* [1955] IR 268, and in a Canadian case, *Coast Ferries Ltd v Century Insurance Co of Canada & Others, The Brentwood* [1973] 2 Lloyd's Rep 232. Cf *Fawcus v Sarsfield* (1856) 6 El & Bl 192 at p 204; and *Samuel v Dumas* [1924] AC 431 at p 468, HL, *per* Lord Justice Sumner.

IMPLIED WARRANTY OF CARGOWORTHINESS

Section 40(2) has imposed two implied warranties in a voyage policy on goods or other moveables. There is an implied warranty that the ship on which the cargo is carried is:

- seaworthy at the commencement of the voyage; and
- reasonably fit to carry the good or other moveables to the destination contemplated by the policy: that is, she is also cargoworthy.

As these provisions are now overridden by the 'unseaworthiness and unfitness exclusion clause' (cl 5) of the ICC (A), (B) and (C), which has already been discussed earlier, very little need be said here about them except that the former relates to seaworthiness pertaining to the ship's ability to encounter the ordinary perils of the sea, whilst the latter is concerned with her capability to carry the particular cargo in question, commonly referred to as the implied warranty of cargoworthiness in the law of carriage of goods by sea.

The familiar distinction between uncargoworthiness and bad stowage, however, needs to drawn here. Bad stowage can, of course, cause a ship to become unseaworthy, but only if it affects her stability and ability to encounter the ordinary perils of the sea. But bad stowage which does not interfere with the ship's capability to combat ordinary sea perils is just pure and simple bad stowage and will not offend the implied warranties of seaworthiness or cargoworthiness.[184]

Though the ship has to be seaworthy, there is no implied warranty that the goods or moveables have to be seaworthy, or that they have to be able to endure the stresses or vicissitudes of the sea voyage.[185]

IMPLIED WARRANTY OF LEGALITY

The implied warranty of legality is laid down in s 41 as follows:

> 'There is an implied warranty that the adventure insured is a lawful one, and that, so far as the assured can control the matter, the adventure shall be carried out in a lawful manner.'

It will be recalled that the subject of legality is also echoed in s 3, where the words 'lawful marine adventure' are used. As the wider word 'adventure' and not 'voyage' is used in s 41, it has to apply to all policies regardless of the nature of the subject-matter insured and the policy whether it be for time or voyage. Section 41 may be divided into two parts: the legality of the adventure and the performance of the adventure.

---

184 The distinction was made clear in *Kopitoff v Wilson* (1876) 1 QBD 377; *Elder, Dempster & Co Ltd v Paterson, Zochonis & Co* [1924] AC 522 and *Blackett, Magalhaes & Colombie v National Benefit Assurance Co* (1921) 8 Ll L Rep 293, CA.

185 Section 40(1).

Illegality under British law

As a general rule, the legality or otherwise of an adventure is determined according to the common and statute laws of England. If the adventure to be performed is wholly or partly illegal according to English law, the contract of insurance would be affected.

Illegality under foreign law

In the day when Lord Mansfield sat on the bench, the attitude towards foreign law was quite different. It was said that: 'The courts in this country do not take notice of foreign revenue law'.[186] Whether Lord Mansfield had just foreign revenue law or all foreign laws in mind was not made clear. Holding the view that, 'one nation does not take notice of the revenue law of another', the insurance on the adventure was held not to be illegal even though the outcome of the case would in effect lead to the defrauding of a foreign legal system. This privilege of not having to take notice of any foreign laws cannot nowadays be carried too far, especially when a 'friendly' state is involved. This was made clear by the House of Lords in *Regazzoni v KC Sethia (1944) Ltd*,[187] where Viscount Simonds declared that:

> 'Just as public policy avoids contracts which offend against our own law, so it will avoid at least some contracts which violate the laws of a foreign State and it will do so because public policy demands that deference to international comity.'

Any adventure contravening a foreign law which had not been acted upon or enforced by its own country would not constitute a breach of the implied warranty. This was held in *Francis, Times and Co v Sea Insurance Co*,[188] where insured goods, consisting of arms and ammunition, were sent to Persia where there was an edict issued by the Persian government prohibiting the importation of arms and ammunition into Persia. It was well-known that so long as duties were paid there was no prospect of interference by the authorities who were aware that the trade was open and notorious. As this law was never implemented, Mr Justice Bingham held that the voyage was not, according to the law of Persia, an illegal voyage.

Legality of the adventure

It has to be said that it is not always easy to answer the question whether a contravention of a particular rule or regulation would render an adventure illegal. Naturally, not all breaches of rules and regulations would automatically cause the adventure to become illegal. In *Redmond v Smith*,[189] Chief Justice Tindal cautioned that in each case, the objective of the particular legislation has to be considered. In the said case, the captain was by statute forbidden to take out seamen who were not under articles. The said judge observed that:

---

186 *Per* Lord Mansfield, *Planche v Fletcher* (1779) 1 Dougl 251 at p 253.

187 [1958] AC 301; [1957] 2 Lloyd's Rep 289, HL.

188 (1898) Com Cas 229.

189 (1844) 7 Man & G 457.

'... the [Act] was passed for a collateral purpose only; its intention being to give to merchant seamen a readier mode of enforcing their contracts and to prevent their being imposed upon ... but it is nowhere said that such non-compliance shall make the voyage illegal; the section merely provides a remedy against the master.'

As the aim of the legislation was to protect seamen from imposition, the defence of illegality raised by the insurer has to fail.

In the light of this, it is not surprisingly that the American court in *The Pacific Queen*[190] had declined to answer the question as to whether the fact that a wooden-hulled motor vessel which carried bulk gasoline without a certificate, in breach of the Tanker Act, rendered the voyage illegal.

Legality in the performance of the adventure

Not only must the adventure be lawful, but its performance must also be lawful. The second implied warranty of s 41 is qualified with the term 'so far as the assured can control the matter'. If the assured is in a position to control the matter, then, he has to do so. The case of *Pipon v Cope*,[191] concerning barratry, is apt for the purpose of illustrating this point. Here, the crew members had committed repeated acts of smuggling on three consecutive voyages. In such circumstances, it would be difficult for the shipowner to argue that the matter was beyond his control, for he could and should have taken positive steps (for example, by replacing the ship with a new crew) to prevent the repeated acts of smuggling, thereby enabling the adventure to be carried out in a lawful manner.

Supervening illegality

An adventure could well start off as lawful, but become unlawful later as a result of war or a change of events. *The Sanday Case*[192] is a classic example of a supervening illegality where, because of the outbreak of war, the prosecution of the voyage would be illegal; in compliance with the law the assured had no choice but to be abandon the voyage. The insurer pleaded illegality as their defence to the assured's claim for indemnity for the loss or frustration of the adventure. The House held that the loss was caused by an insured peril, 'restraint of princes', and that the act by the assured of the compliance with the law did not constitute illegality. However, should the assured choose to flout the law by continuing with the voyage, he would be in breach of s 41 in having failed to exercise control over the matter to ensure that 'the adventure shall be carried out in a lawful manner'.

Legal effect of breach

The legal effect of a breach of the implied warranty of legality is not spelt out in s 41. It would appear that under ordinary contract law, no court, either of law or equity, will lend its assistance to give effect to a contract which is illegal.

---

190 [1963] 2 Lloyd's Rep 201, US Ct of Appeals, Ninth Circuit.

191 (1808) 1 Camp 434.

192 [1915] 2 KB 781, HL.

Language to the effect that such a contract is void, void *in toto*, nugatory, ineffective and unenforceable have been used to describe its effect. It has been said that if the illegality is 'so reprehensible', the contract is void *in toto*. But if the illegality is merely undesirable, the taint of illegality will not destroy all legal remedies. In the pre-statute case of *Redmond v Smith*,[193] the effect of illegality was considered by the Chief Justice, who expressed the legal position in the following terms:

> 'A policy on an illegal voyage cannot be enforced; for it would be singular, if, the original contract being invalid and therefore incapable to be enforced, a collateral contract founded upon it could be enforced. It may be laid down, therefore, as a general rule, that, where a voyage is illegal, an insurance upon such voyage is invalid. Thus, during the war, policies effected on vessels sailing in contravention of convoy acts were held void.'

The general rule, said the judge, is that the contract of insurance is void. However, it is to be noted that this case was decided before the Act, and should therefore not be applied if the law contained therein is inconsistent with the Act.[194]

It is submitted that, couched in terms of a warranty, reference should be made to s 33(3) for the purpose ascertaining the effects of its breach; the consequence that the insurer is to be 'discharged from liability as from the time of the breach of the warranty' is applicable to all warranties.[195] Support for this contention can be drawn from the Canadian case of *James Yachts v Thames & Mersey Marine Insurance Co Ltd and Others*,[196] where Mr Justice Ruttan had no doubt whatsoever that, pursuant to the equivalent to our s 41, the insurers were to be *discharged* from liability as the plaintiffs had carried out an unlawful business of boat-building contrary to the by-laws and regulations of the municipality.[197]

There is a whole world of difference in saying that a contract is void, or voidable, or that the insurer is 'discharged' from liability. In the case of a 'discharge' under s 33(3), which is now to be read as 'automatic discharge' in the light of *The Good Luck*,[198] the insurer is discharged from liability only as from the date of the breach: all rights and liability accrued before the breach are preserved. When an assured 'avoids' a contract, he is avoiding the contract from the very beginning.

---

193 (1844) 7 Man & G 457 at p 474.

194 Section 91(2).

195 But Chalmers, p 63, states: 'A contract to do a thing which cannot be done without a violation of the law is void, whether the parties know the law or not. But if a contract is capable of being performed in a legal manner, it is necessary to show clearly the intention to perform it in an illegal manner to enable the insurer to avoid it.' With regard to the former case, as the contract is illegal right from the very beginning, no rights or liabilities can accrue. The practical effect of a discharge in such a case is probably the same as that of holding the contract void. In relation to the latter, it has to be pointed out that totally different effects arise from the avoidance of a contract and from the discharge of liability.

196 [1977] 1 Lloyd's Rep, 206 at p 212, British Columbia Supreme Court.

197 The assured was also found guilty of non-disclosure of a material fact by which the insurers were entitled to avoid the policy.

198 [1991] 2 Lloyd's Rep 191, HL.

Breach of the implied warranty of legality cannot be waived

Though s 34(3) states that a breach of warranty may be waived, nevertheless, it has to be pointed out that a breach of the implied warranty of legality is an exception to the rule. In this sense, the use of term 'warranty' in s 41 is incongruous when read with s 34(3).

Gedge v Royal Exchange Assurance Corpn[199] is often cited as the authority which has established the principle that a breach of the implied warranty of legality cannot be waived. In this case, the policy was null and void by the presence of the ppi clause.[200] The insurer could have simply pleaded illegality as an absolute and complete defence to the claim brought by the assured, but instead he alleged concealment of material facts as the ground for their denial of liability. By taking this course of action, it could be argued that the insurer was, in effect, waiving the breach by pretending that the policy was valid and may be sued upon.

The court, however, was not prepared to allow the parties to treat the contract as if it was valid, and accordingly refused to enforce it. The fact that illegality was not pleaded made no difference whatsoever to the outcome of the case. The court's decision was not actually premised on waiver, but on the more direct basis that it would not lend its hand to such a plaintiff. It held that:[201]

'No court ought to enforce an illegal contract or allow itself to be made the instrument of enforcing obligations alleged to arise out of a contract or transaction which is illegal, if the illegality is duly brought to the notice of the court, and if the person invoking the aid of the court is himself implicated in the illegality.'

---

199 [1900] 2 QB 214.
200 Sections 4 (1) and 4 (2)(b).
201 [1900] 2 QB 214 at p 221.

CHAPTER 8

THE CAUSE OF LOSS

INTRODUCTION

The legal theory of causation has always been regarded as one of the most troublesome areas of the law. This was pointed out in *Ashworth v General Accident Fire and Life Assurance Corpn*[1] by Mr Justice Black, who said: 'I know of no problem in the whole science of the law more abstruse than that of causation. The philosophers have had much to say about it.' Furthermore, the matter is aggravated by the fact, as one Law Lord has observed, that 'the terminology of causation in English law is by no means ideal. It would be the better for a little plain English'.[2] The excessive use of Latin terms to describe the legal principles has not helped matters.[3]

It is necessary at the outset to mention that this chapter is concerned with the case where only one single loss is sustained during one accident or casualty, and that loss is brought about by the operation of more than one cause, that is to say, by a combination of causes. We are not concerned here with the problem of separate successive losses, each caused by a distinct peril operating independently to occasion the losses. In short, damage or loss sustained in two distinct incidents is outside the scope of the ensuing discussion.

THE RULE OF PROXIMATE CAUSE

The law on the subject of causation in marine insurance is contained in s 55(1) which declares in a somewhat tediously repetitive manner that:

'Subject to the provisions of this Act, and unless the policy otherwise provides, the insurer is liable for any loss proximately caused by a peril insured against, but, as subject as foresaid, he is not liable for any loss which is not proximately caused by a peril insured against.'

According to Chalmers:[4] 'No principle of marine insurance law is better established than the rule of *causa proxima, non remota, spectatur*'. Section 55(1), which is a statutory declaration of this principle,[5] has been translated to mean that 'the immediate, not the remote, cause is to be considered'.[6]

---

1 [1955] IR 268 at p 295, Supreme Court, hereinafter referred to simply as *The Ashworth Case*.

2 *Per* Lord Sumner in Becker, *Gray & Co v London Assurance Corpn* [1918] AC 101 at p 114, HL.

3 Eg, *causa proxima non remota spectatur, causa causans, causa sine qua non*, and *novus actus interveniens*.

4 Chalmers, p 78.

5 See Lord Brightman's judgment in *The Salem* [1983] 1 Lloyd's Rep 342 at p 350, HL.

6 As defined in PG Osborn, *A Concise Law Dictionary*; a similar definition given in Mozely & Whiteley, *Law Dictionary*. The word 'immediate' has been used in two senses, as a synonym to 'proximate' and also to denote the cause which is last in point of time. See eg, *Ionides v The Universal Marine Insurance Co* (1863) 14 CB (NS) 259, where both words were used without any explanation as to their meanings.

In marine insurance, the law of causation has 'in the course of years had a remarkable history'.[7] For a considerable period of time the principle of *causa proxima* was applied in different ways. However, the turning point in its history occurred in 1918 in the celebrated case of *Leyland Shipping Co Ltd v Norwich Union Fire Insurance Society Ltd*,[8] where the House of Lords conclusively settled the law of proximate cause under s 55(1). Before proceeding to analyse the legal principles laid down in *The Leyland Case*,[9] it is necessary for the purpose of comparison (and to avoid confusion when reading earlier cases) briefly to comment on the law which existed before 1918.

The law before 1918

Before *The Leyland Case*, there were essentially two methods used by judges to ascertain 'the' cause of a loss. As in the Act, the common law has always recognised that only the *causa proxima* is to be considered; however, over the years, two sets of rules have been employed for determining the proximate cause in marine insurance.

According to one point of view, that applied in *Pink v Fleming*,[10] 'the *last* cause only must be looked to and the others rejected, although the result would not have been produced without them'. Worded in a different way, Lord Justice Lindley stated that:[11] 'It has long been the settled rule of English law with regard to marine insurance that only the *causa proxima* or *immediate* cause of the loss must be regarded.'[12] The last or immediate cause in point of time was for convenience selected as the *causa proxima*: simply taking the last event in point of time as the proximate cause is not a judicious, but a mechanical, process of making a selection. Rejecting all preceding links, the *last* link in the chain of causation was regarded as *the* cause of loss. This appears to be the rule favoured by most of the earlier judges.

Instead of using *time* as the criterion, another school of thought had looked for what was 'efficient' and 'predominant' as the *causa proxima*. This was applied by the Court of Appeal in *Reischer v Borwick*.[13] For a proper understanding of the rule, it is necessary briefly to refer to the facts of the case. As a result of a collision, the insured vessel, which sprang a leak, was anchored and temporarily repaired in order to take her out of immediate danger. Later, the effect of the motion of the water created by a tug sent to tow her to the

---

7   *Athel Line Ltd v Liverpool & London War Risks Insurance Association Ltd* [1946] 1 KB 117 at p 122, *per* Lord Greene MR.

8   (1918) AC 350, HL, hereinafter referred to as *The Leyland Case*.

9   *Ibid*.

10 (1890) 25 QBD 396 at p 397, CA, *per* Lord Esher MR.

11 *Ibid*, at p 398.

12 This rule, it would appear was founded upon the well-known maxim of Lord Bacon, cited in *De Vaux v Salvador* (1836) 4 Ad&E 420 at p 431 by Chief Justice Lord Denman: 'It were infinite for the law to judge the cause of causes, and their impulsions one of another; therefore it contenteth itself with the immediate cause, and judgeth of acts by that, without looking to any farther degree.'

13 (1894) 2 QB 548, CA; 7 Asp MLC 493.

nearest dock for repairs caused the leak to resume, and the vessel sank and was abandoned.

Lord Justice Lopes, firmly rejecting the 'last' cause, perils of the seas, which was not an insured peril under the policy in question, held that 'the cause of the damage ... was the collision, and the consequences of the collision ... never ceased to exist, but constantly remained the efficient and predominating peril to which the damage now sought to be recovered was attributable'.[14]

One cause of loss

There can be no problem when only one cause is identifiable to have occasioned a loss. For example, in *Ballantyne v Mackinnon*,[15] the defects in the design and construction of the vessel; and in *Wadsworth Lighterage and Coaling Co v Sea Insurance Co*,[16] the general debility of the barge was held to be the sole cause of loss. Obviously, the only question to be determined in such a case is whether such a cause of loss is covered by the policy.

Under this heading, reference must next be made to *Atlantic Maritime Co Inc v Gibbon*,[17] which has been discerned as the authority illustrating the fact that it is possible for a single cause of loss to be covered by two heads of claim.[18] The Court of Appeal held that the 'real' and 'efficient' cause of the loss was the restraint of princes and not civil war, and that it was 'immaterial that the restraint was also an incident of a civil war, as the civil war, *per se*, was not responsible for the loss'. Whether regarded as one cause falling within two heads of claim or as two causes, the effect is the same: a court has still to decide which one of the two heads of claim (or two causes) is the proximate cause of loss. In effect, the same matter is being looked at, but from a different angle.

More than one cause of loss

A casualty at sea is more often than not precipitated by a combination of causes. Perils of the seas, for instance, may initially appear to have caused a loss, but there is generally another force (or forces) which could oust or prevail over perils of the seas, or any insured peril, as the proximate cause of loss. It has been said that a cause rarely operates by itself to occasion a loss: there is almost invariably an array of contributing factors and influences working behind the

---

14 *Ibid*, at p 553. O'May, *Marine Insurance* (1993, 1st edn), p 320, hereinafter referred to simply as O'May, following Arnould, para 775, has, it would appear, erroneously reported that collision and perils of the sea were both held as proximate causes. Lord Lindley pointed out that the loss was 'proximately, though not exclusively, caused by the collision'. None of the judges, though they had acknowledged the fact that perils of the seas was a cause of loss, had attributed it as another proximate cause of the loss. If perils of the seas was held also as a proximate cause, the loss would not have been recoverable because it was expressly excepted under the policy.

15 (1896) 2 QB 455.

16 (1929) 34 Ll L Rep 285. See also *Fawcus v Sarsfield* (1856) 119 ER 836, where unseaworthiness was the sole cause of loss.

17 [1953] 2 All ER 1086, CA.

18 See Arnould, para 77; and O'May, p 320.

scene, and this has led to metaphors such as 'beads in a row' and 'links in a chain' being used to describe the successive events leading to the loss.

In *The Leyland Case*,[19] Lord Dunedin had aptly described the situation as follows: 'But there are certain perils which, so to speak, pray in aid the perils of the sea.' Unseaworthiness, for example, 'which may assume according to the circumstances an almost infinite variety, can never be the sole cause of the loss'. According to the learned Lord Wright, it must 'always be only one of several co–operating causes'.[20] A peril is required in order to evince that the vessel, or some part or quality of it, is less fit than it should have been and hence the casualty ensues.[21] A combination of causes can often be expected to be responsible for a casualty.[22]

When two or more causes are seen to operate to occasion a loss, controversies and differences in opinion often arise as to how one cause is to be singled out, in preference to another cause (or causes), as 'the' cause of the loss. By what criterion is the choice to be based on? The common law (and s 55(1)) has always employed the rule of *causa proxima* to resolve such a dispute. But, as the above discussion has revealed, different rules have been applied in the law of marine insurance for the purpose of determining the proximate cause of a loss. The question which has now to be considered is: which of the two theories, namely that proposed in *Pink v Fleming*[23] or that in *Resicher v Borwick*,[24] is to be applied to s 55(1)?

Meaning of 'proximately'

What exactly does the word 'proximately', appearing in s 55(1), mean? The perplexed question as to whether a judge should trouble himself with 'distant causes' and 'go into a metaphysical distinction between causes efficient and material and causes final' or 'look exclusively to the proximate and immediate cause of the loss'[25] again reared its head, but this time in the House of Lords in *The Leyland Case*,[26] the facts of which are as follows: *The Ikaria* was insured, *inter alia*, for perils of the seas, but was warranted against 'all consequences of hostilities'. After she was torpedoed, she was taken alongside a quay in the outer harbour. There she sustained more damage when she bumped against the quay and sprang a leak. She was then ordered to a berth where she was moored. But eventually, her bulkheads gave way, she sank and became a total

---

19 [1918] AC 350 at p 363, HL.

20 *Per* Lord Wright, *Smith, Hogg & Co Ltd v Baltic Insurance Co* (1940) 19 Asp MLC 382 at p 384, HL.

21 *Per* Lord Wright, *A/B Karlshamns Oljefabriker & Another v Monarch SS Co Ltd* 82 Ll L Rep 137 at pp 155-156, HL.

22 According to Arnould, para 775, a hint that more than one cause could be attributed to a loss is traceable, as early as 1774, to the celebrated case of *Vallejo v Wheeler* (1774) 1 Cowp 143; but *Hagedorn v Whitmore* (1816) 1 Stark 157, however, has been identified as the first case to recognise this possibility.

23 (1890) 25 QBD 396.

24 (1894) 2 QB 548, CA; 7 Asp MLC 493.

25 *Per* Willes J, *Ionides v The Universal Marine Insurance Co* (1863) 14 CB (NS) 259 at p 289.

26 [1918] AC 350, HL.

loss. The shipowners claimed for a loss by perils of the seas. In ascertaining the relative rights of the parties, the court had to determine the proximate cause of loss. The obvious choices were 'perils of the seas' and 'consequences of hostilities'.

Lord Shaw, in a graphic and informative speech, illustrated his understanding of the law of proximate cause with the following comment:[27]

'To treat *proxima causa* as the cause which is nearest in time is out of the question. Causes are spoken of as if they were as distinct from one another as beads in a row or links in a chain, but – if this metaphysical topic has to be referred to – it is not wholly so. The chain of causation is a handy expression, but the figure is inadequate. Causation is not a chain, but a net. At each point influences, forces, events, precedent and simultaneous, meet; and the radiation from each point extends infinitely. At the point where these various influences meet it is for the judgment as upon a matter of a fact to declare which of the causes thus joined at the point of effect was the proximate and which was the remote cause ... What does "proximate" here mean? To treat proximate cause as if it was the cause which is proximate in time is, as I have said, out of the question. The cause which is truly proximate is that which is proximate in efficiency.'[28]

Though proximity in time was emphatically rejected, 'this does not mean, however, that the last cause necessarily can never be the real cause of any loss or injury'.[29]

Lord Dunedin further clarified matters by stating that the solution lay in:[30]

'... settling as a question of fact which of the two causes was what I will venture to call (though I shrink from the multiplication of epithets) the dominant cause of the two. In other words, you seek for the *causa proxima*, if it is well understood that the question of which is *proxima* is not solved by the mere point of order in time.'

The principle of *The Leyland Case* was subsequently applied[31] in two more House of Lords decisions, namely, *Board of Trade v Hain SS Co*[32] and *Yorkshire Dale SS Co Ltd v Minister of War Transport, The Coxwold*,[33] both of which were concerned with war risks. In the latter, Lord Wright was again given the opportunity to refer to his hobby-horse:[34]

'This choice of the real or efficient cause from out of the whole complex of the facts must be made by applying common-sense standards. Causation is to be understood as the man in the street, and not as either the scientist or metaphysician, would understand it. Cause here means what a business or

---

27 *Ibid*, at p 369.

28 *Resicher v Borwick* (1894) 2 QB 548, CA; 7 Asp MLC 493 was approved by the House of Lords.

29 *Per* Salmon LJ, *Gray & Another v Barr* [1971] 2 Lloyd's Rep 1 at p 14, CA.

30 [1918] AC 350 at p 363.

31 For a concise summary of the legal position before and after *The Leyland Case*, see *Gray and Another v Barr* [1971] 2 Lloyd's Rep 1 at p 5, CA; and *Wayne Tank & Pump Co Ltd v Employer's Liability Assurance Corpn Ltd* [1974] QB 57 at pp 66–67, CA.

32 [1929] AC 534, HL.

33 (1942) 73 Ll L Rep 1 at p 10, HL.

34 See also Lord Wright's comments on causation in *Smith, Hogg & Co Ltd v Baltic Insurance Co* (1940) 19 Asp MLC 382 at p 384, HL.

seafaring man would take to be the cause without too microscopic analysis but on a broad view ... The question always is what is *the* cause, not merely what is *a* cause.'

Both cases have confirmed beyond doubt that *The Leyland Case* had stated the correct legal principle of causation in marine insurance. For emphasis, reference may be made to the succinct words of Lord Shaw in the said case:[35]

'... proximate cause is an expression referring to the efficiency as an operating factor upon such the result. Where various factors or causes are concurrent, and one has to be selected, the matter is determined as one of fact, and the choice falls upon the one to which may be variously ascribed the qualities of *reality, predominance, efficiency*.'

It is now conclusively settled that 'proximately' in s 55(1) denotes that which is proximate in efficiency rather than in time.[36]

For completeness, it has to be mentioned that under the rule of *causa proxima* as defined by *The Leyland Case*, there is no room for the application of the principle of the *novus actus interveniens*. In *Wayne Tank and Pump Co Ltd v Employers Liability Assurance Corpn Ltd*,[37] Lord Denning MR showed his intolerance of this concept in the following comment:

'I must say that I do not care for this emphasis on *novus actus interveniens*. It seems to me to be going back to the old and forsaken test of the latest in time. I would reject *novus actus*. I would ask, as a matter of common sense, what was the effective or dominant cause ...?'

A common sense approach

Adjectives such as 'direct', 'directly caused',[38] 'dominant',[39] 'effective', 'efficient',[40] 'predominant', and 'real' have been used by judges to assist them in their task of identifying the proximate cause of a loss. At best, they serve merely as a guide or yardstick, for ultimately, and most of the judges are in agreement on this, common sense has to prevail and this seems to be the best, and perhaps most reliable, measure for determining the proximate cause of a loss.

In *Athel Line Ltd v Liverpool & London War Risks Insurance Association Ltd*,[41] Lord Greene MR was resigned to the fact that: 'the point at which it appears to

35 [1918] AC 350 at p 370.

36 More light is shed on the subject in *The Ashworth Case* [1955] IR 268 at p 289, where Black J of the Irish Supreme Court said that: 'It was made clear in *The Leyland Case* that proximate cause has a special connotation in marine insurance cases. It does not mean the cause nearest in time. The cause which is truly proximate is that which is proximate in efficiency ...'

37 (1974) QB 57 at p 67, CA, hereinafter referred to as *The Wayne Tank Case*.

38 Lord Sumner in *Becker, Gray and Co v London Assurance Corpn* [1918] AC 101 at p 113, (decided three months before *The Leyland Case*) thought that 'direct cause' would be a better expression than *causa proxima*. In *JJ Lloyd's Instruments Ltd v Northern Star Insurance Co Ltd, The Miss Jay Jay* [1987] 1 Lloyd's Rep 32 at p 39, Slade LJ stated that the same meaning must be attributed to the phrase 'directly caused' as to the phrase 'proximately caused' in s 55(1).

39 See *Gray & Another v Barr* [1971] 2 Lloyd's Rep 1 at p 5.

40 See *Atlantic Maritime Co Inc v Gibbon* [1953] 2 All ER 1086 at p 1099, CA, where restraint of princes, and not civil war, was held to be the 'real, efficient' cause of the loss.

41 [1946] 1 KB 117 at p 122.

have come to rest at the moment, is that which lays it down that this type of question of causation is really a matter for the common sense and intelligence of the ordinary man ...'.

More recently, in *Gray v Barr, Prudential Assurance Co Ltd (Third Party)*,[42] Lord Denning MR summarised the legal position thus:

'Ever since [*The Leyland Case*] in 1918 it has been settled in insurance law that the "cause" is that which is the efficient or dominant cause of the occurrence or, as it is sometimes put, what is in substance the cause; even though it is more remote in point of time, such cause to be determined by commonsense.'

In *Heskell v Continental Express Ltd and Another*,[43] Mr Justice Devlin, though clear about the fact that common sense is a 'blunt instrument', nevertheless, had a great deal of faith in it. He said:

'... I cannot believe that if the ordinary man thinks that two causes are of approximately equal efficacy, he cannot say so without being interrogated on fine distinctions.'

The last word on the subject has to be as expressed by Lord Shaw in *The Leyland Case*:[44]

'In my opinion ... too much is made of refinements upon this subject. The doctrine of cause has been, since the time of Aristotle and the famous category of material, formal, efficient, and final causes, one involving the subtlest of distinctions ... I will venture to remark that one must be careful not to lay accent upon the word "proximate" in such a sense as to lose sight of or destroy altogether the idea of cause itself.'

It is probably easier to state the legal principles relating to causation than to apply them. As 'questions of causation are mixed questions of fact and law' differences in opinion are bound to arise.[45]

More than one proximate cause of loss

That it would only be necessary to invoke *The Leyland* rule when there are several causes operating to occasion a loss is obvious. By equating the proximate cause with that which is efficient, real and dominant, the law has in effect invited judges to weigh the causes of a loss to determine their strength, influence and predominance. Under the old rule of taking the event which is last in point of time, there could only be one proximate cause of loss.[46] Under *The Leyland* rule, however, it is possible for there to be more than one proximate

---

42 [1971] 2 Lloyd's Rep 1 at p 5, CA. The words uttered by Lord Sumner in *Canada Rice Mills Ltd v Union Marine & General Insurance Co Ltd* [1941] AC 55 at p 71 that '*causa proxima* in insurance law ... is "in substance" the cause ... or the cause "to be determined by common-sense principles" ...' were cited with approval.

43 [1950] 1 All ER 1033 at p 1048.

44 [1918] AC 350 at p 370.

45 *Per* Lord Brightman, *Shell International Petroleum Co Ltd v Caryl Anthony Vaughan Gibbs, The Salem* [1983] 1 Lloyd's Rep 342 at p 350, HL.

46 In this context, one can appreciate the advantages and convenience of choosing the immediate or last event as the proximate cause.

cause; and this was perceived by Mr Justice Black (dissenting) in *The Ashworth Case*, where he pointed out that:[47]

> '... the word 'dominant' was applied ... as denoting persistence and not exclusiveness. The dominance of the first cause, so understood, did not prevent the action of the sea from being also a real and effective co-operating cause.'

Two proximate causes of equal or nearly equal efficiency

That it is possible for there to be two proximate causes which are of equal or nearly equal efficiency was recently confirmed in *JJ Lloyd's Instruments Ltd v Northern Star Insurance Co Ltd, The Miss Jay Jay*,[48] where unseaworthiness due to design defects and an adverse sea were both held to be the proximate causes for the loss. In *The Wayne Tank Case*,[49] Lord Denning MR had also acknowledged the fact that it was possible for there to be 'not one dominant cause, but two causes which were equal or nearly equal in their efficiency in bringing about the damage'. In such a case, the problem which is likely to arise is when one of the proximate causes is covered by the policy and the other is not.

One included loss and one not expressly excluded loss

In recognising that it is possible for there to be two proximate causes of loss, the law has generated a further problem for itself. This was encountered in *The Miss Jay Jay*,[50] where Lord Justice Lawton observed that:

> 'It now seems settled law, at least as far as this court is concerned, that, if there are two concurrent and effective causes of a marine loss, and one comes within the terms of the policy and the other does not, the insurers must pay.'

And as the defendants did not expressly provide for the exclusion of unseaworthiness or design defects, the plaintiffs were able to recover under the policy.

In much simpler terms, Lord Justice Slade phrased the legal position as follows:[51]

> 'As there were no relevant exclusions or warranties in the policy the fact that there may have been another proximate cause did not call for specified mention since proof of a peril which was within the policy was enough to entitle the plaintiffs to judgment.'

Halsbury's *Laws of England* has summarised the law in a concise statement as follows: 'If one of these causes is insured against under the policy, and none of the others is expressly excluded from the policy, the assured will be entitled to recover.'[52]

---

47 [1955] IR 268 at p 299.

48 [1987] 1 Lloyd's Rep 32 at p 36, CA. See also *Heskell v Continental Express Ltd & Another* [1950] 1 All ER 1033 at p 1048, though the dispute was in relation to a bill of lading, the remarks uttered by Devlin J on causation regarding 'co-operating' causes and causes of 'equal efficacy' are nevertheless relevant. See also the first instance judgment of *Wood v Associated National Insurance Co Ltd* [1984] 1 Qd R 507.

49 (1974) QB 57 at p 67, CA.

50 [1987] 1 Lloyd's Rep 32 at p 36, CA.

51 *Ibid*, at p 37.

52 4th edn, vol 25, para 181.

It has to be pointed out that the insurance under consideration in *The Miss Jay Jay* was a time and not a voyage policy. This fact was, of course, critical to the defendant's case. As distinct from a voyage policy, there is no implied warranty of seaworthiness in a time policy, which meant that unless the insurers were able to prove that *The Miss Jay Jay* was sent to sea in an unseaworthy state with the privity of her owners, and that that unseaworthiness caused the loss, they were liable for the loss. In so far as unseaworthiness is concerned, causation is of utmost importance in a time policy. Under a voyage policy, however, whether unseaworthiness did or did not cause the loss is irrelevant: the defense is essentially premised on a breach of a warranty, rather than on unseaworthiness as having caused the loss.

One included loss and one expressly excluded loss

The other side of the coin can be seen in the case of *Board of Trade v Hain SS Co Ltd*,[53] where Viscount Sumner of the House of Lords, in relation to a dispute under a charterparty, expressed the view that if a loss is 'the product of two causes, joint and simultaneous', and one of the causes is expressly excluded by an exception clause, the insurers are not liable. As they have expressly stipulated for freedom, the loss is not apportionable, and 'hence no part of it can fall on the policy'.

In a case concerned directly with insurance, albeit not marine, *The Wayne Tank Case*,[54] an exception was held to take priority over the general words of a policy. Lord Denning MR said that 'general words always have to give way to particular provisions'. In more positive terms, Lord Justice Roskill remarked:[55] 'I think the law in this respect is the same both for marine and non-marine, namely, that if the loss is caused by two causes effectively operating at the same time and one is wholly expressly excluded from the policy, the policy does not pay'. Arnould's observation that the above principle is now established 'virtually beyond doubt' has to be correct.[56]

The celebrated pre-statute case of *Cory v Burr*[57] is, of course, an authority directly in point, as a marine policy of insurance was under scrutiny. The House of Lords was confronted with the problem of having to determine which of the following causes was the proximate cause of the loss – barratry and/or seizure.[58] As the case was decided at the time when the rule of the immediate or

---

53 [1929] AC 534. Lord Sumner said much the same thing in his dissenting speech in *Samuel v Dumas* [1924] AC 431 at p 467: 'Where a loss is caused by two perils operating simultaneously at the time of loss and one is wholly excluded because the policy is warranted free of it, the question is whether it can be denied that the loss was so caused, for if not the warranty operates'. This passage was approved by Morris LJ in *Atlantic Maritime Co Inc v Gibbon* [1954] 1 QB 88, at p 138.

54 [1973] 2 Lloyd's Rep 237; [1974] QB 57. *Board of Trade v Hain SS Co Ltd* [1929] AC 534 was cited with approval by Lord Denning MR.

55 (1974) QB 57 at p 75, CA.

56 See Arnould, para 777.

57 (1883) 8 App Cas 393, HL.

58 The insured vessel was seized by Spanish revenue officials because of the barratrous acts committed by the crew who were engaged in smuggling.

last in point of time prevailed, seizure, which was an excepted peril, was declared as the proximate cause of the loss. Today, a court could well hold both as the proximate causes of loss. The result, however, would be same: as seizure was *expressly* excepted, the loss would not have been recoverable even if barratry was held as another proximate cause of loss.[59]

The first step is to determine what the proximate cause(s) of loss is. If, after weighing the relative efficiency of the causes, only one proximate cause is identified, the next step is to determine whether it is a peril insured against. If, however, more than one proximate cause of equal efficiency is ascertained, the progression from here is to determine whether either of the proximate causes is expressly excluded by the policy. Naturally, if none of the two proximate causes is expressly excluded by the policy, the loss would be recoverable. On the other hand, if one or both of the proximate causes is expressly covered by an exclusion, the loss would not be recoverable.[60]

The 'Paramount Clause'

The War Exclusion, Strikes Exclusion, and Malicious Acts Exclusion of the ITCH(95) and the IVCH(95); the Radioactive Contamination Exclusion of the ITCH(95); and of the IVCH(95) are all made subject to a clause, referred to as the paramount clause, which states:[61] 'The following clauses shall be paramount and shall override anything in this insurance inconsistent therewith'. The aim of this clause is to clarify that, in the event of a conflict between any of these exclusion clauses and 'anything' in the insurance, the exclusion clauses are to prevail.

More than two proximate causes of equal or nearly equal efficiency

The question as to whether it is possible for there to be more than two proximate causes, all of equal or nearly equal efficiency, has yet to be considered by a court of law. There does not appear to be any reason why this should not be possible or why such a case could not be resolved by invoking the principle proposed in *The Wayne Tank Case*. Should one of the proximate causes (be it out of three or more) be expressly excluded by the policy, an insurer should not, for the same reasons given above, be made responsible for the loss.

'Subject to the provisions of this Act'

The general rule of proximate cause under s 55(1) is subject to two overriding considerations. It is subject to the provisions of the Act and to any express term

---

59 Suffice it is to mention here that as seizure is expressly excluded by the War Exclusion Clause of the ITCH(95) and the IVCH(95), a loss caused by a barratrous seizure is not recoverable even if barratry is considered as another proximate cause of loss. It would appear that the loss would be recoverable only if barratry is the sole proximate cause of loss in which case the war exclusion clause and its paramount clause are inapplicable. See *The Hai Hsuan* [1958] 1 Lloyd's Rep 578.

60 In the court of first instance in *Wood v Associated National Insurance Co Ltd* [1984] 1 Qd R 507, the judge held unseaworthiness and wilful misconduct as the proximate causes for the loss; on appeal [1985] 1 Qd R 297, only the latter finding was affirmed.

61 But not in the ICC.

of the policy which provides otherwise. This necessarily means that the general rule may well be displaced by statutory and/or contractual exceptions.

Section 55(2)(a) uses a different causative expression, 'attributable to', to qualify the exception of wilful misconduct of the assured. The wording of this provision has to be compared with those in s 55(2)(b) which spells out that an insurer is not liable for any loss 'proximately' caused by delay. Whether any significance should be placed upon the difference in the use of terminology has to be explored. It is noted that s 39(5) has also, in relation to unseaworthiness under a time policy, employed the term 'attributable to' to describe the cause of loss. Does this mean that the general rule of proximate cause is to be set aside whenever the term 'attributable to' appears in the Act?

'Attributable to' wilful misconduct

The phrase 'attributable to' may at first sight appear to be 'neutral'[62] and innocuous. But as the following discussions will reveal, the matter is far from straightforward. Surprisingly, there is hardly any post-1906 authority dealing directly with the causative aspects of the defence of wilful misconduct: *Samuel v Dumas*[63] appears to be the only case which has shed some light on the subject, albeit from the dissenting judgment of Lord Sumner.[64]

Wilful misconduct as the proximate cause of loss

The majority of the House of Lords in *Samuel v Dumas*, after having firmly established that scuttling is not a peril of the sea, held that, as the loss was *proximately* caused by an act of wilful misconduct committed by the shipowner,[65] the loss was not recoverable.[66] As this was essentially the basis of the decision, there was no need for the majority of the House to examine the meaning of the words 'attributable to' in s 55(2)(a). The insurers' defence was based simply on the fact that the loss was not caused by an insured peril.[67] They could not rely on s 55(2)(a) because the plaintiff-mortgagee was not in any way involved in scuttling the ship.

---

62 *Per* Kerr LJ in *The Salem* [1982] 1 Lloyd's Rep 369 at p 381.

63 [1924] AC 431, HL.

64 In a different context, Kerr LJ of the Court of Appeal in *The Salem* [1982] 1 Lloyd's Rep 369 at p 381, in reference to the old 'seaworthiness admitted clause' (where the word 'attributable' was used to qualify the wrongful act or misconduct of the shipowners), was content with simply stating that 'these are neutral words which cannot be read as intended to alter the well established principles of causation in this field'. It is submitted that this remark should not be taken at its face value: what the judge had probably intended to say was that the proximate cause of a loss has first to be determined before any question relating to the applicability of the above clause can be considered.

65 See also *Wood v Associated National Insurance Co Ltd* [1985] 1 Qd R 297, where the Australian Appeal Court held that an act of reckless disregard could constitute wilful misconduct.

66 And this is so whether the action is brought by the shipowner, who is himself guilty of wilful misconduct, or by an innocent assured (such a mortgagee or a cargo owner) who is not in any way to be blamed for the loss.

67 If the shipowner was bringing the claim, the insurer would have an added reason for not settling the claim. The insurer would also plead the general defence that no man can take advantage of his own wrong. But in so far as an innocent party is concerned, the insurer can only rely on the ground that the loss was not covered by the policy.

Wilful misconduct as a remote cause of loss

The dissenting judge, Lord Sumner, however, appears to be the only member of the House to have taken a keen interest in the wording of s 55(2)(a).[68] He had to rely on the difference in wording between ss 55(1) and 55(2)(a) to support his point of view. In a lengthy speech, the most part of which need not concern us here, he alone held that the loss was proximately caused by perils of the seas, even though sea water was deliberately let into the ship by the orders of her owners and there was nothing accidental or fortuitous about the loss. Boldly he asked:[69] 'Why is the language varied and the words "attributable to" used instead of "proximately caused by"?' He pointed out that the legislature, if it had wanted to, could have easily added (in s 55(2)(b)) wilful misconduct to delay as a proximate cause of loss, for which it expressly states that the insurer is not liable. After holding that the loss of the ship was proximately caused by a peril of the seas, which meant that the loss was recoverable, he then went on to explain how the defence of wilful misconduct, as stated in s 55(2)(a), was to be employed'.[70]

First, he rationalised that parliament did not have to legislate for the event of a loss proximately caused by the wilful misconduct of the assured. Such a loss is never recoverable because it can never be an insured peril.[71] Furthermore, in relation to an assured who is himself guilty of wilful misconduct, the loss is also governed by the cardinal principle that a man cannot take advantage of his own wrong. From this he concluded that s 55(2)(a) could not have been enacted to cover the case where wilful misconduct was the proximate cause of the loss. On this point, it is necessary to refer to a concise and perceptive statement made by Arnould to the effect that: '... the misconduct need not be the proximate cause in order for the subsection [s 55(2)(a)] to operate, for if this were so it would be largely superfluous.'[72]

Lord Sumner was, however, also conscious of the fact that a loss proximately caused by an insured peril (for example, fire or perils of the seas) could also be attributed to an act of wilful misconduct committed by the assured. He had no doubt that such a loss, though proximately caused by an insured peril, would not be recoverable if the assured himself was guilty of wilful misconduct. He had carefully avoided describing the assured's act of wilful misconduct as a remote cause, and his reason for so doing can be gleaned from the following comment he made:[73]

---

68 See also his remarks in *Britain SS Co v King (The Petersham)* and *Green v British India Steam Navigation Co Ltd (The Matiana)* [1921] 1 AC 99 at p 131, HL, where the term 'attributable' was interpreted as referring to a remote cause.

69 [1924] AC 431 at p 471.

70 Naturally, the majority view does not have to involve itself with such arguments, as once scuttling is held not to be a peril of the seas, the subject is immediately brought to a close. No one, not even an innocent party, such as a mortgagee, would be able to recover for such a loss which is not insured against.

71 Note that s 55(2)(a), unlike (b) and (c), is not qualified with the term 'unless the policy otherwise provides'.

72 Arnould, para 786.

73 [1924] AC 431 at p 472.

'It is to be observed that the whole section is framed to state for what an insurer is liable ... and is not framed as a definition of proximate or of remote causes .... the object of the section is to declare for what the insurer is liable and for what he is not.'

Lord Sumner obviously held the view that s 55(2)(a) was concerned with liability rather than causation. Nevertheless, his interpretation of s 55(2)(a) is informative:

'As a matter of construction s 55 seems to me to prescribe that the assured's wilful misconduct is a ground for refusing to him, but to him only, the indemnity, which the proximate origin of the loss would otherwise have brought about ... I cannot see any need for introducing this question of misconduct, unless it is first assumed that the loss has been brought within the policy by being proximately caused by perils mentioned therein.'

According to Lord Sumner, a loss has to be *prima facie* recoverable before the assured could be disentitled of his right to indemnity under the policy: the giving with the one hand and taking away with the other was Lord Sumner's perception of the section.

He had earlier in the House, in *The Petersham and The Martiana*,[74] postulated that there was no connection between ss 55(1) and 55(2)(a). The latter, he said, 'precludes the implication of resort to the origin, to which a loss is "attributable" ...'. He then went on to say that:

'I see no connection between expressly disabling an assured from recovering for a loss which, though in itself the proximate consequence of perils by the seas, is really self-inflicted by his ulterior wilful misconduct, and interfering with the statutory rule prescribed in s 55(1) in a case where an event has happened without fault in any one, and the only question is whether or not it is within the insurance effected.'

If one is to go a little further back in time,[75] a more cogent explanation of the law in this regard can be found in the judgment of Lord Campbell in another important case, *Thompson v Hopper*,[76] where he pronounced that:

'We are of opinion that the maxim relied upon can never be applied where it contravenes the fundamental rule of insurance law that the assurers are not liable for a loss occasioned by the wrongful act of the assured ...

The most forceful and instructive part of his judgment, however, lay in his rhetorical question:

'Is it to be said, then, that, to exempt the assurers from liability, the misconduct of the assured must be the direct and proximate cause of the loss? We think that, for this purpose, the misconduct need not be the *causa causans*, but that the assured cannot recover if their misconduct was *causa sine qua non*.'

---

74 [1921] 1 AC 99 at p 132, HL.

75 One should not be too hasty in referring to pre-1906 case law for the purpose of aiding in the construction of the provisions of the Act. However, unless a particular section (eg, s 60) has gone further than simply to consolidate the pre-existing law, reference to antecedent law may indeed be necessary if there is a doubt about what the language of the statute means. As s 55(2)(a) has not gone further, but is an enactment of pre-existing law, one is justified in referring to past cases: See *Bank of England v Vagliano Brothers* [1891] AC 107, at pp 144–145.

76 (1856) 6 E & B 937 at p 949; (1858) EB & E 1038.

The *causa sine qua non* or remote cause of a loss is, as a general rule, irrelevant. This is embodied in the heart of the maxim *causa proxima non remota spectatur*. But when a remote cause takes the form of an act of wilful misconduct, the rule of *causa proxima* has to give way, and rightly so, to another fundamental principle of English law, that a man shall not take advantage of his own wrong.

This was later made clearer in *Trinder, Anderson & Co v Thames & Mersey Marine Insurance Co*,[77] where Lord Justice Smith, after acknowledging the fact that remote causes were generally inconsequential, reminded the court that the maxim *causa proxima non remota spectatur* was qualified by a well established legal maxim, *dolus circuitu non purgatur*. This simply means that a loss, even though proximately caused by a peril insured against, would not be recoverable if it was also occasioned, albeit remotely, by the wilful misconduct of the assured.

The above discussion has clearly demonstrated the fact that the rule of proximate cause does not fit neatly within the scheme of things under s 55(2)(a). The arguments proposed in the pre-1906 cases cited above are equally relevant to the statutory defence under s 55(2)(a) as they were to the same defence under the common law. Lord Sumner's interpretation of the section, though it has not as yet been endorsed by a full court as stating the correct principle of law, is nonetheless rational and convincing. Its logic will become more apparent if one is to consider the case of a ship which has been intentionally set alight by or at the instigation of the shipowner. In such a circumstance, fire would invariably be regarded as the proximate cause,[78] and wilful misconduct of the shipowner, the remote cause of the loss.[79] Provided that the plaintiff himself is not guilty of wilful misconduct, he would be able to claim under the policy. For example, an innocent mortgagee would be able to recover for such a loss, but not the shipowner who is instrumental in causing the loss.[80]

Section 55(2)(a) does not say that an insurer is not liable for a loss proximately caused by the wilful misconduct of the assured; such a provision would be stating the obvious. If wilful misconduct committed by the shipowner is regarded as the sole proximate cause of a loss, the insurer would not be liable by reason of the fact that such a cause of loss is not a peril insured against. No one, not even a blameless plaintiff, will be able to claim for such a loss. Should the assured himself be guilty of wilful misconduct, the insurer would have an added reason for not settling the claim. He would also plead the maxim *dolus circuitu non purgatur* to free himself from liability.

The word 'attributable', which is not as specific or as direct as the term 'proximately caused by', was chosen for a purpose: the contingency which the

---

77 [1898] 2 QB 114 at p 124, CA.

78 See *Gordon v Rimmington* (1807) 1 Camp 123, *per* Lord Ellenborough: '... if the ship is destroyed by fire .... Fire is still the *causa causans* and the loss is covered by the policy'. See also *Slattery v Mance* [1962] 1 All ER 525; and *Schiffshypothekenbank Zu Leubeck AG v Norman Philip Compton, The Alexion Hope* [1988] 1 Lloyd's Rep 311, CA.

79 There is no reason why wilful misconduct cannot be regarded as 'a' (one of two or more) proximate cause of loss. But so far, there is no direct authority on this point.

80 See *The Alexion Hope* [1989] 1 Lloyd's Rep 311, CA.

section was specifically enacted to cover is where the proximate cause of the loss is a peril insured against, and the remote cause is wilful misconduct. Such a loss is only *prima facie* recoverable, as the assured would be stripped of his right to claim under the policy if his act of wilful misconduct is found to have remotely caused the loss. Viewed in this light, one could say that the phrase 'attributable to' was specifically chosen by parliament in order to displace the general rule of *causa proxima*.

Wilful misconduct as a proximate cause of loss

None of the above comments has touched upon the possibility of wilful misconduct acting as a proximate cause of loss. In the light of recent developments in this area of the law,[81] there is no reason why, for example, fire and wilful misconduct could not both be regarded as the proximate causes of a loss. Is s 55(2)(a) applicable to such a circumstance?

The last part of Lord Sumner's remark, cited earlier, could well accommodate the situation where an insured peril and wilful misconduct are both proximate causes of a loss. Such a loss would be brought within the policy by being proximately caused by the former. Even though one of the proximate causes (fire) may be covered by the policy, the loss is, nonetheless, irrecoverable. It could be argued that if wilful misconduct operating as a remote cause is sufficient to deprive an assured of his right to indemnity, he would, *a fortiori*, be denied recovery if it was a proximate cause of the loss.

Whether the section has contemplated the legal position of a loss where there are two proximate causes, one of which is wilful misconduct and the other a peril insured against, is doubtful. The term 'attributable to', however, is wide and neutral enough to apply to such a contingency. It would appear that if wilful misconduct of the assured can be ascribed to a loss, whether acting as a remote cause or as one of two or more proximate causes, the loss would not be recoverable. In any causative form, it is fatal to the case of an assured who has himself committed an act of wilful misconduct.[82]

The above reasons have obviously influenced the draftsman of the Institute Cargo Clauses to adopt the expression 'attributable to' in relation to the exception of a loss occasioned by the wilful misconduct of the assured.[83]

---

81 See, eg, *The Ashworth Case* [1955] IR 268; *The Wayne Tank Case* (1974) QB 57, CA; and *The Miss Jay Jay* [1987] 1 Lloyd's Rep 32, CA discussed above.

82 It is significant to note that s 55(2)(a) will only prevent recovery for a loss attributable to the wilful misconduct of the 'assured'. Thus, an innocent mortgagee, whether suing as an original assured or as assignee, would not be able to recover under the policy, if the wilful misconduct of the shipowner is held to be the sole proximate cause of the loss: such a cause of loss is not insured peril. This is so even though he himself may have been free from blame. However, the position is different if one of the proximate causes of the loss is an insured peril; such a loss would, in so far as an innocent mortgagee is concerned, be recoverable even though the wilful misconduct of the shipowner in scuttling the ship may have operated as a remote cause or as another proximate cause of loss.

83 See cl 4.1 of the ICC (A), (B) and (C): 'In no case shall this insurance cover loss damage or expense attributable to wilful misconduct of the Assured.'

'Attributable to' unseaworthiness

Whether the above interpretation of the causative effect of the term 'attributable to' given to s 55(2)(a) in relation to the defence of wilful misconduct should also be given to s 39(5) on the issue of unseaworthiness in a time policy is another question which has to be examined.[84] In a time policy, the insurer is not liable for any loss 'attributable to' such unseaworthiness to which the assured is privy. The scope of s 39(5) and, in particular, the legal implications and causative effects of the term 'attributable to' have to be analysed.

Section 39(5) is of general application. It applies to all subject-matter insured under a time policy. As the Institute Hulls Clauses, both for voyage and time, do not have a specific clause on the subject of seaworthiness, s 39 applies. In all the ICC, however, there is the unseaworthiness and unfitness exclusion clause which bears a principle similar to that stated in s 39(5). As its name suggests, it is worded as an exception of liability for unseaworthiness and unfitness of the vessel. As cl 5 of the ICC has taken the matter out of s 39(5), it is best that it be left for discussion separately. This part will, therefore, concentrate only on the scope of s 39(5) as applied to a standard time policy on hulls.

Unseaworthiness, whether in a voyage or time policy, can occasion a loss either as:

- the sole proximate cause;
- a proximate cause; or
- a remote cause.

Unseaworthiness as the sole proximate cause of loss

One has to begin with the premise that a policy of insurance is to provide an assured with indemnity for losses caused by 'risks', and only for risks which are insured against. Unless specifically insured, a loss solely caused by unseaworthiness is not an insured risk under the Institute Hulls Clauses. As such, it should not be recoverable whether the assured is or is not privy to such condition of unseaworthiness.

This was the law before the passing of the Act. In *Fawcus v Sarsfield*,[85] the vessel, insured under a time policy, without encountering any more than ordinary risks, was obliged, owing to her defective state when she set sail, to put into a port for repair. The court ruled that, 'unless this loss arose from perils insured against, it cannot be cast upon the underwriters'.[86] The assured, although he was unaware of the existence of the defect and was not in any way blameworthy, could not recover the expenses of such repairs as were rendered

---

84 Under a voyage policy, an insurer would simply rely on breach of the implied warranty of seaworthiness (s 39(1)) to defend his case: the insurer is discharged from liability as from the date of the breach and does not, as in a time policy, have to show that the loss, or for that matter, any loss was caused by unseaworthiness.

85 (1856) 6 El & Bl 192 at p 204.

86 See also *Ballantyne v Mackinnon* [1896] 2 QB 455, where the Court of Appeal held that, 'the loss complained of arose solely by reason of the inherent vice of the subject-matter insured ...'.

necessary in consequence of the unseaworthy state of the vessel. As the sole proximate cause of loss was unseaworthiness, which was not a peril insured against, the plaintiffs failed in their claim.

Another reason why a loss solely caused by unseaworthiness is not recoverable is that, as pointed out by Lord Justice Sumner of the House of Lords in *Samuel v Dumas*,[87] such a cause of loss is not a risk:

'So it is in cases on time policies, where the loss is directly caused by unseaworthiness, for then it is plain that the loss was a certainty, whatever the state of the weather or the sea ...'.[88]

The next question which arises is whether s 39(5) has altered the common law existing before 1906. More pointedly, can an assured now, by reason of s 39(5), recover under a time policy for a loss which is solely caused by 'such'[89] or the particular aspect of unseaworthiness to which he is not privy?

The three main English authorities concerned with s 39(5) are: *The Thomas and Son Shipping Case*,[90] *The Thomas Tyne and Wear Case*,[91] and more recently, *The Eurysthenes*.[92] Though not directly relevant to the issue at hand, these cases are, nevertheless, informative. In the first pair of cases, the loss was not exclusively caused by unseaworthiness, and in the last case, the policy under consideration was special, as by the Rules of the Association, the Club had agreed to indemnify the shipowner (a member) even for damage to cargo 'arising out of ... unseaworthiness or unfitness of the entered ship'. This case has, therefore, no bearing to the present discussion, as unseaworthiness which caused the loss was specifically covered by the said Rules.[93]

The Supreme Court of Ireland, however, in *The Ashworth Case*,[94] was squarely confronted with this problem. The facts of the case were not very much in controversy: as a result of unseaworthiness the vessel had to be beached during the course of a voyage. The trial judge found that she was sent to sea in an unseaworthy state with the knowledge of her owners, but as he had regarded a peril of the seas as the proximate cause of loss, the shipowners were to able to recover for the loss. On appeal, all the judges were in agreement that the loss was proximately caused by unseaworthiness and not by a peril of the

---

87 [1924] AC 431 at 468, HL.

88 Cited with approval by the trial judge in *Coast Ferries Ltd v Century Insurance Co of Canada and Others, The Brentwood* 23 DLR (3d) 226 at p 230, who said: '... due only to unseaworthiness, water had to come in, not by accident or by chance, but to be expected.' His decision was reversed on appeal on a different finding of fact; on appeal [1973] 2 Lloyd's Rep 232.

89 It is now accepted that s 39(5) has to be read as if the word 'such' had been inserted before the word 'unseaworthiness': see *Thomas & Son Shipping v The London & Provincial Marine & General Insurance Ltd* (1914) TLR 595, CA; and *Thomas v Tyne & Wear SS Freight Insurance Association* [1917] KB 938.

90 (1914) TLR 595, CA.

91 [1917] KB 938.

92 *Compania Maritime San Basilio SA v Oceanus Mutual Underwriting Association (Bermuda) Ltd* [1977] 1 QB 49, CA.

93 As the loss which was caused by unseaworthiness was specifically insured against the shipowner's claim was prima facie recoverable.

94 [1955] IR 268.

sea, but differed in their finding as regards the question of privity. The majority, which found that the assured was aware of the condition of the ship in all the aspects which made her unseaworthy, held that the loss was not recoverable.[95]

The majority could have rested its decision on either or both of the following grounds:

- that unseaworthiness was not an insured risk under the policy in question; and/or

- that the assured was privy to the vessel's condition of unseaworthiness when she was sent to sea.

Mr Justice O'Byrne, in somewhat imprecise terms, said that, 'the unseaworthy condition of the ship was the dominant and effective cause of the loss ... and that the loss is attributable to that condition within the meaning of s 39(5) ...'. Regrettably, the judgment delivered by Chief Justice Maguire is equally vague. What is clear, however, is that all the judges had taken great pains to inquire whether the ship was 'with the privity of the assured' sent to sea in an unseaworthy condition. From this, one can only deduce that if they were of the opinion that the first ground alone was sufficient to disentitle the assured of the right of recovery, it would not have been necessary for them to investigate further on the question of privity. From the tenor of the majority judgment, one is somehow led to believe that the decision was based on the second, rather than the first, of the two grounds. Otherwise, the inquiry as regards the question of privity would be superfluous. It would not be unreasonable to assume that, like Mr Justice Black, dissenting, the majority would have awarded judgment in favour of the plaintiffs if they had not been privy to the vessel's condition of unseaworthiness. 'Privity' was obviously the decisive consideration.

A similar approach was taken by the trial judge in the Canadian case *Coast Ferries Ltd v Century Insurance Co of Canada and Others, The Brentwood*.[96] Even after acknowledging the fact that it was unseaworthiness 'alone' which had occasioned the loss; that it was 'the proximate cause' of the loss; and (agreeing with Lord Sumner) that a loss 'directly caused by unseaworthiness ... was a certainty',[97] he nevertheless deemed it fit to award judgment in favour of the plaintiffs because they were found not to be privy to the vessel's condition of unseaworthiness. Surely, the corollary of this is that if the plaintiffs were aware of the vessel's condition, they would not be allowed to recover for the loss.

It is interesting to note neither of the cases has placed any importance on the fact that unseaworthiness was the sole proximate cause of loss, or that it was not

---

95 The dissenting judge, Mr Justice Black, held that, as the assured was not privy to the vessel's condition of unseaworthiness, which was the dominant cause of the loss, the loss was recoverable. It is important to note that he was not averse to holding both peril of the sea and unseaworthiness as 'co-operating proximate' causes of the loss. This aspect of his decision is discussed below.

96 [1973] 2 Lloyd's Rep 232, hereinafter referred to as *The Brentwood*.

97 Lord Sumner's comments were cited earlier.

an insured peril under the policy, or to the words 'attributable to' appearing in s 39(5) (or its equivalent).

Admittedly, with the exception of this first instance Canadian judgment, which has been overturned on a different finding of fact and on, what seems to be, a different ground,[98] none of the above decisions has expressly pronounced, though they might have implied, that provided that an assured is not privy to the vessel's condition of unseaworthiness, a loss solely caused by unseaworthiness is recoverable.

Arnould, citing *The Thomas and Son Shipping Case*[99] as authority, has, however, interpreted s 39(5) as follows:[100]

'It is not necessary, in order to exonerate the insurer from liability under the above proviso, that the unseaworthiness should be the sole cause of the loss; it is sufficient that the unseaworthiness was a *proximate* cause of the loss.'

The second part of this statement is supportable. But, with due respect, it is submitted that the opening words are by no means easy to sustain, as they seem to suggest that the section is applicable not only when unseaworthiness is a proximate cause of loss, but also when it is the sole cause of loss. Indeed, no British judge has yet directly ruled that a loss caused solely by unseaworthiness, to which the assured is not privy to, is recoverable under a standard form time policy on hull.

Section 39(5), it is observed, does not openly state that an insurer is to be made liable for a loss proximately caused by a condition of unseaworthiness of which an assured has no knowledge. Nor does it say, from the point of view of the assured, that he is to be conferred with the right to be indemnified for a loss which is solely caused by unseaworthiness. It is argued that such a loss, unless specifically insured against, is not indemnifiable, regardless of whether the assured is or is not privy to the vessel's condition of unseaworthiness.

On this point, the dissenting judgment of Mr Justice Black in *The Ashworth Case* is clearly worthy of attention:[101]

'... whether the action of the sea upon the ship in question at any material time constituted a peril of the sea at all; for if it did not, no time need be wasted on the other question, since the loss would not be covered by the policy.'

Any statutory provision stating that an insurer is not to be made liable for any loss proximately caused by unseaworthiness would, as in the case of the defence of wilful misconduct discussed earlier, be superfluous for stating the obvious. If Parliament had intended to render an insurer liable for a loss 'proximately caused' by unseaworthiness in the event that the assured is not privy to such unseaworthiness, it would have said so in much clearer and more

---

98 The Appeal Court found that because the assured (shipowner) was guilty of the want of due diligence, and was therefore in breach of the proviso to the Inchmaree clause, they could not rely on the said clause.

99 (1914) TLR 595, CA, and see *George Cohen, Sons & Co v Standard Marine Insurance Co Ltd* (1925) 21 Ll L Rep 30.

100 Arnould, para 718.

101 (1955) IR 268 at p 293.

positive language.[102] The expression 'attributable to' must have been chosen for a good reason.

This area of law is in urgent need of clarification. It is submitted that s 39(5), as worded, should not be read as capable of imposing a liability upon an insurer for a risk which he has not, under the contract of insurance, specifically agreed to insure. Its use, as the next part of this discussion will reveal, has to be limited to the particular case where the loss is prima facie recoverable under the policy in question.

Unseaworthiness as a proximate cause of loss

An observation of Lord Justice Buckley of the Court of Appeal in *The Thomas and Son Shipping Case*[103] is particularly pertinent to this aspect of s 39(5). In terms very similar to that used by Arnould, he said: 'The question was not whether it was the sole cause, but whether it was a cause, in the sense of being a *proximate* cause'.

Briefly, the facts of the case are as follows. The ship was unseaworthy in two respects: first, the condition of her hull was defective – a fact to which the assured was not privy; and secondly, her crew was insufficient, of which the assured was aware. On this occasion,[104] the court held that unseaworthiness arising from the insufficient crew was 'a' cause of the loss. What the other proximate cause(s) of loss was was not discussed. The circumstances of the accident, however, seem to point to perils of the sea, an insured risk, as another proximate cause. If such were the case, the decision would clearly be supportable; the loss was *prima facie* recoverable by virtue of the fact that it was caused by a peril of the seas, but as the assured was privy to the particular aspect of unseaworthiness, namely, the insufficiency of her crew, which was another proximate cause of the loss, he had, because of his own blameworthy conduct, to be disentitled of his right to indemnity.

Lord Justice Buckley clearly supported the view that it was possible for there to be more than one proximate cause for a loss.[105] Mr Justice Black, the dissenting judge in *The Ashworth Case*,[106] was of the same mind; both perils of the sea and unseaworthiness were held as proximate causes of the loss. His application of s 39(5) was as follows:

'... if the action of the sea – a peril of the seas – was a proximate cause of the loss, that loss was covered by the policy, notwithstanding that the unseaworthiness of

---

102 If this was the intention of parliament, it could have easily used the term 'proximately caused by', rather than 'attributable to' in s 39(5).

103 (1914) TLR 595, CA.

104 *Cf The Tyne and Wear Case* [1917] KB 938 where, in a suit arising out of the same accident, the court arrived at a different finding of fact: the loss was held to have been caused by reason of her defective hull.

105 In *Wood v Associated National Insurance Co Ltd* [1984] 1 Qd R 507, the trial judge found both unseaworthiness and wilful misconduct as the proximate causes of the loss. However, on appeal, [1985] 1 Qd R 297, only the latter was affirmed as the proximate cause of the loss.

106 (1955) IR 268 at p 300. Black J said that: '... Mr Justice Davitt [trial judge] seems to me to have thought that if the action of the sea was a proximate cause of the loss (as he held it was), the unseaworthiness of the ship could not have been equally a proximate cause (as I think it was).'

the ship was a co-operating cause, unless the plaintiff shipowner was privy to the unseaworthiness at the time of sailing.'

Having attributed one of the proximate causes of the loss to a peril insured against, a recoverable loss, he felt justified in investigating further to determine whether the assured could be deprived of the right of recovery under the policy by reason of being privy to the vessel's condition of unseaworthiness, which was another proximate cause of loss.

That two proximate causes of loss can exist side by side to occasion a loss is now an accepted rule of law. Recently, it was applied in *The Miss Jay Jay*,[107] where both perils of the seas and unseaworthiness were held to be proximate causes of equal or nearly equal efficiency. As the former was an insured peril and the latter was not expressly excluded, the assured was able to recover under the time policy. The court would not have hesitated to strip the assured of his right to claim under the policy if he had been found to have been privy to the vessel's condition of unseaworthiness. Similar issues will also arise if negligence covered by cl 6.2.2 (the Inchmaree clause) of the ITCH(95) and unseaworthiness are both proximate causes of the loss.[108]

Such a construction would not only place s 39(5) in harmony with s 55(1) on the rule of proximate cause, but also in line with s 55(2)(a) on the defence of wilful misconduct. After all, s 39(5) is a specie of the defence of wilful misconduct. The difference in the law before and after the enactment of the Act was pointed out by Mr Justice Atkin in *The Tyne and Wear Case* as follows:[109] 'It was always necessary to show that the loss was the result of some misconduct. Now the statute has defined the degree of misconduct required as sending the ship to sea in an unseaworthy state with the privity of the assured.' It is submitted that, as in the case of s 55(2)(a) discussed earlier, s 39(5) should rightly be brought into play only if the proximate cause or one of the proximate causes of the loss is a peril insured against.

Unseaworthiness as a remote cause of loss

None of the above cases has considered the possibility of unseaworthiness conducing as a remote cause of loss. Would an insurer be exempted from liability for a loss which is proximately caused by a peril insured against, but remotely by unseaworthiness to which the assured was privy when the ship was sent to sea?

One could easily dismiss this question with the reply that the law of proximate cause is not concerned with remote causes: the very essence and objective of the rule of proximate cause is to eliminate remote causes when determining 'the' cause of the loss. But as the rule on proximate cause contained in s 55(1) is made 'subject to the provisions of this Act', of which s 55(2)(a) is one, it is necessary to inquire whether s 39(5), with identical causative language, is to be construed as another exception to the general rule.

---

107 [1987] 1 Lloyd's Rep 32, CA.
108 See *The Brentwood* [1973] 2 Lloyd's Rep 232, BC CA.
109 [1917] KB 938 at p 941.

The courts have not, since the passing of the Act, been asked to make a ruling on this question. A pair of pre-1906 authorities, namely *Thompson v Hopper*[110] and *Dudgeon v Pembroke*,[111] have, however, dealt with this point. But as the principles laid down in s 39(5) were not then in existence,[112] these cases are not relevant to the present discussion.[113]

Perhaps, the answer can be found in the remarks made by Mr Justice Roche in *Cohen, Sons and Co v Standard Marine Insurance Co Ltd*,[114] who had given the decision of *The Thomas and Son Shipping Case*[115] a broad and generous interpretation:

> '... it is enough if a matter of unseaworthiness, being a matter to which the assured is privy, is a cause or part of the cause of the loss. I adopt the principle of Thomas's case ... that it is enough if the unseaworthiness to which the assured forms part of the cause of the loss.'

No qualification or restriction – that unseaworthiness has to be a proximate cause – has been imposed.[116]

Arnould states that, 'the proximate cause rule does not apply to a loss occasioned by the wilful act of the assured'. And as s 39(5) has been regarded by him as 'analogous' to s 55(2)(a) and by Mr Justice Atkin as an off-shoot of the defence of wilful misconduct, there is no reason why the same cannot be said about s 39(5).[117]

A time policy insurer does not have to rely on s 55(2)(a) to exempt himself from liability.[118] To free himself from liability for a loss which is 'attributable to' unseaworthiness, he does not have to go so far as to prove the commission by the assured of an act of wilful misconduct. Proof of a lesser degree of fault, that

---

110 (1856) 6 E & B 172, 937; (1858) EB & E 1038, where perils of the seas was held to be the proximate cause of loss. The Exchequer Chamber was, however, prepared for the sake of argument to assume that unseaworthiness had contributed as a remote cause of the loss. And even then, it held that such a remote cause was, regardless of whether the assured was or was not privy of the defect which rendered the ship unseaworthy, inconsequential.

111 (1877) 2 App Cas 284, HL. In this case, unseaworthiness was not even a remote cause.

112 Before the enactment of s 39(5), only the defence of wilful misconduct (now contained in s 55(2)(a)) was available to an insurer. In *Thompson v Hopper* (1856) 6 E & B 172, 937; (1858) EB & E 1038, the Appeal Court had correctly held the view the act of knowingly sending an unseaworthy ship to sea did not, *per se*, constitute an act of wilful misconduct.

113 In fact, Roskill LJ in *The Eurysthenes* [1977] 1 QB 49 at pp 74–75, had issued serious warning of the danger of relying on pre-1906 cases for the purpose of interpreting sections of the Act.

114 (1925) 21 Ll L Rep 30.

115 (1914) TLR 595, CA.

116 *Frangos & Others v Sun Insurance Office Ltd* (1934) 49 Ll L Rep 354, decided after the passing of the Act, is of little help: Even though the proximate cause of the loss was a peril insured against, the assured was not privy to the vessel's condition of unseaworthiness, the remote cause of the loss.

117 Arnould, para 718: 'It is submitted that, as in the analogous case of s 39(5), it is only necessary that the misconduct of the assured should be one of the effective causes of the loss.' Read in its proper context, it is clear that the word 'effective' was used in a general sense to mean a contributing (but not necessarily a proximate) cause.

118 In fact, an insurer would not be able to rely on this defence unless there is proof of fraud, a violation of the law, a breach of contract, an evil or a sinister intention, or reckless disregard.

of just being 'privy' to the particular feature of the vessel's condition of unseaworthiness to which the loss is attributable, will be sufficient to disentitle an assured of his right to recovery under the policy.

Just as unseaworthiness and perils of the seas are capable of generating problems relating to causation, so can unseaworthiness and negligence operating as contributory causes of loss.[119] Undoubtedly, these issues which have so far eluded judicial attention will one day have to be settled by a firm ruling from the bench.

'Unless the policy otherwise provides'

Lord Justice Slade in *The Miss Jay Jay*[120] pointed out that the words 'unless the policy otherwise provides' in s 55(1) have left the matter open to the draftsman of a policy to restrict or exclude the application of the subsection. The Institute Clauses have used a variety of causative expressions to qualify the terms of some of their perils: words such as 'attributable to'; 'reasonably attributable to'; 'arising from'; 'caused by'; 'proximately caused by'; and 'resulting from' are employed.[121] The question which has to be considered is whether such terms are to be awarded a meaning different from 'proximately caused', referred to in s 55(1). One could argue that because a different expression has been chosen, a different meaning must be intended. However, most judges would probably adopt the same approach as Mr Justice Scrutton and 'start with the consideration that to all policies of insurance, whether marine or accident, the maxim *causa proxima non remota spectatur* is to be applied if possible'. Another point he made is that when in doubt – where vague words have been used – they must be 'strictly' read 'in accordance with the ordinary maxim'.[122]

'Caused by'

Both the ITCH(95)[123] and the IVCH(95)[124] employ the term 'caused by' in the opening words of the 'perils' clause. In fact, this term is commonly used in all the Institute Clauses. Even though the words 'directly' or 'proximately' do not appear, it has always been understood that it has to be read as if the word 'proximately' was inserted before it.

In support of this, reference could be made to a speech delivered by Mr Justice Scrutton in *Coxe v Employers' Liability Assurance Corpn Ltd*:[125] 'The words ... "caused by" and "arising from" do not give rise to any difficulty. They are words which always have been construed as relating to the proximate cause.'

---

119 See, eg, *The Brentwood* [1973] 2 Lloyd's Rep 232, BC CA.

120 [1987] 1 Lloyd's Rep 32, HL.

121 See cll 1, 3, 5, 6, & 7 of the ICC(B).

122 *In Coxe v Employers' Liability Assurance Corpn Ltd* [1916] 2 KB 629 at pp 633 and 634.

123 Clause 6.1 and 6.2.

124 Clause 4.1 and 4.2.

125 [1916] 2 KB 629 at p 634. The same applies to the expression 'traceable to', but not 'indirectly caused by'.

To go beyond or exclude the maxim *causa proxima non remota spectatur*, more precise language would have to be used.[126]

The expression 'directly caused by' was previously used in the earlier versions of some of the provisions of the Inchmaree clause.[127] The word 'directly' does not add anything, and has the same meaning as 'proximately'.

'Attributable to'

As was seen, the expression 'attributable to' appearing in ss 39(5) and 55(2)(a) has been subjected to a great deal of intense judicial scrutiny. The same term also appears in the ICC (B) and (C), but there does not seem to be any reported case on the Cargo Clauses. There is no reason why the meaning given to the term 'attributable to' used in the Act should not also be given to the ICC (B) and (C) or that the addition of the word 'reasonably' should make any difference to the meaning of the term 'attributable to'.

'Consequences thereof'

The expressions 'consequences thereof' and 'consequent on' used in relation to war risks and insurance on freight, respectively, had caused some interest of whether they should be construed as having displaced the general rule of proximate cause.

The old 'warranted free of capture and seizure' clause had, *inter alia*, excepted the marine risks insurer from liability for 'consequences of hostilities or warlike operations ...'.[128] Whether the words 'consequences of' are wide enough to oust the general rule of proximate cause was considered by the House of Lords in a trilogy of war risks cases beginning with the classic authority of *The Petersham and The Matiana*;[129] *Yorkshire Dale SS Company Ltd v Minister of War Transport, (The Coxwold)*;[130] and *Liverpool & London War Risks Association Ltd v Ocean SS Co Ltd, (The Priam)*.[131] Though the legal principles set out in these cases are now redundant in so far the 'fc and s' clause is concerned, nevertheless, the comments made by the law lords on causation are still relevant for the purposes of the present discussion.

---

126 The term 'directly or indirectly' caused by was held effective for excluding the rule of *causa proxima*. As Scrutton J was unable to understand what was meant by the expression 'indirect' proximate cause, he felt that it had to be interpreted to mean that a more remote link in the chain of causation was envisaged

127 The term 'caused through' was also used in an earlier version of the negligence cover of the Inchmaree clause; see Lord Justice Scrutton's interpretation of this term in *Lind v Mitchell*, (1928) 45 TLR 54, CA.

128 Commonly referred to as the 'fc and s' clause: 'Warranted free of capture, seizure, arrest, restraint, or detainment, and the consequences thereof or of any attempt thereat; also from the consequences of hostilities or warlike operations ...'. The objective of the clause was to remove the war perils from the scope of the standard marine policy.

129 *Britain SS Co v The King (The Petersham)* and *Green v British India Steam Navigation Co Ltd (The Matiana)* [1921] 1 AC 99, HL.

130 (1942) 73 Ll L Rep 1, HL.

131 [1948] AC 243, HL.

The natural starting point in considering these cases has to be *The Petersham and The Matiana*. Although the main issue of the case was concerned with whether the loss of the vessels fell within the war or marine policies, some of the judges of the House, in particular Viscount Cave and Lord Sumner, took pains to examine the legal implication of the term 'consequences of'. One of the arguments raised by counsel in the case was to the effect that any loss attributable to warlike operations fell within the war risk policy. To this, Lord Sumner curtly replied:

'If that means that a loss, not proximately caused by warlike operations but (remotely) attributable to them, is one for which the insurers are liable, in a case like the present, it is contrary to s 55(1) of the Marine Insurance Act, for the policy contains no special provision to this effect, unless the words "consequences of warlike operations" are pressed beyond anything that they will bear.'

Viscount Cave, however, was content summarily to dismiss the issue with the following remark:[132]

'The rule, long established in cases relating to marine insurance ... that an insurer is not liable for any loss which is not proximately caused by a peril insured against, applies with full force to a clause such as that which is now under consideration ...'.

It has been made clear by these statements that the term 'consequences of' does not alter the fact that the rule of proximate cause applies.

In *The Priam*, the crux of the decision, interestingly enough, lies obscurely in Lord Porter's explanation for taking so much time on the subject. As his remarks on causation are particularly informative, it is sensible to quote them:

'I have, however, dealt with the question somewhat at length, lest it should be thought that the insurance of the *consequences* of hostilities or of warlike operations or, for the matter of that, of capture seizure arrest restraint or detainment by the King's enemies and the *consequences* thereof in any way abrogated or lessen the effect of the rule stated in s 55 of the Marine Insurance Act that the insurer is not liable for any loss which is not proximately caused by a peril insured against or that it widens the insurance so as to cover the consequences of consequences.'

The House of Lords was given another bite of the cherry to express its opinion on the subject of causation in *The Coxwold*,[133] where Lord Wright, another enthusiast of the law of causation, expressed the view that there was no causative connotation in the term 'consequences'. The remarks made by Mr Justice Willes in the ancient case of *Ionides v Universal Marine Insurance Co*,[134] to the effect that the words 'all consequences of hostilities' refer to the totality of causes, not to their sequence, or their proximity or remoteness, were cited with approval.[135]

---

132 [1921] 1 AC 99 at p 107.

133 (1942) 73 Ll L Rep 1, HL.

134 (1863) 14 CB (NS) 259 at p 290.

135 Also cited with approval by Lord Sumner in *The Petersham* and *The Matiana* [1921] 1 AC 99 at p 131, HL.

That the word 'consequences' does not have the effect of reducing or nullifying the rule of proximate cause is now firmly established.[136]

'Consequent on'

Clause 15 of the current Institute Time Clauses (Freight) excepts the insurer from liability for any claim 'consequent on loss of time whether arising from a peril of the sea or otherwise'.[137] This clause was in use even as early as the latter half of the 19th century, as the case of *Bensaude and Others v Thames and Mersey Marine Insurance Co Ltd*[138] bears witness. None of the Law Lords, however, discussed the clause in causative terms. Lord Herschell said:

'The whole basis of the claim, of course, must be the loss of the subject-matter insured – that is, the freight. That loss must arise from one of the perils insured against. What is the meaning of saying that the underwriter is not to be liable for any claim consequent upon loss of time? It must mean that although the subject-matter insured has been lost, and although it has been lost by a peril insured against, if the claim depends on loss of time in the prosecution of the voyage so that the adventure cannot be completed within the time contemplated, then the underwriter is to be exempt from liability.'

Later, in *Naviera de Canarias SA v Nacional Hispanica Aseguradora SA, (The Playa de las Nieves)*,[139] the subject again came before the House for consideration. Lord Diplock, whose judgment was adopted by all the other law lords, postulated that:

'... we are not concerned in the instant case with whether the loss of hire was "proximately caused" by a peril insured against in the sense in which that expression is used in s 55(1) of the Marine Insurance Act 1906. What we are concerned with is the construction of an exceptions clause which does not even use the word "cause". It contemplates a chain of events expressed to be either "consequent on" or "arising from" one another ... the clause is concerned with an intermediate event between the occurrence of a peril insured against and the loss of freight for which the peril was, in insurance law, the proximate cause.'

The term 'consequent on' was not regarded as a causative, but as a descriptive expression defining the scope or extent of the exception. That it does not have a bearing on causation is now firmly accepted.[140]

---

136 Three further House of Lords' decisions on war risks, namely, *Attorney-General v Ard Coasters Ltd (The Ardgantock Case)* and *Liverpool & London War Risks Insurance Association Ltd v Marine Underwriters of SS Richard De Larrinaga (The Richard De Larrinaga Case)* [1921] 2 AC 141; *Attorney-General v Adelaide SS Co Ltd (The Warilda)* [1923] AC 292, and *Board of Trade v Hain SS Co Ltd* [1929] AC 534; and a Court of Appeal decision, *Athel Line Ltd v Liverpool & London War Risks Insurance Association Ltd* [1946] 1 KB 117, CA, have all applied the rule of proximate cause without making an issue of the matter.

137 Commonly known as the 'time charter clause'.

138 [1897] AC 609 at p 614, HL, hereinafter referred to as *The Bensaude Case*. Later in *Turnbull, Martin & Co v Hull Underwriters' Association Ltd* [1900] 2 QB 402, the decision of *The Bensaude Case* was applied.

139 [1978] AC 853, HL.

140 See also *Russian Bank For Foreign Trade v Excess Insurance Co Ltd* [1918] 2 KB 123 at p 127, where the term 'claims due to delay' was held to mean the same thing as 'consequent on loss of time'.

It would appear from the above discussion that expressions such as 'consequences of' and 'consequent on' are evidently not specific enough to cut down or nullify the rule of proximate cause. In fact, the principle of *contra proferentum* is relevant here: In the case of *Coxe v Employers' Liability Assurance Corpn Ltd*,[141] Mr Justice Scrutton did not hesitate to point out that, 'if the defendants choose to employ very vague words of that kind, the words must be read strictly against them and in accordance with the ordinary maxim'.

---

141 (1916) 2 KB 629 at p 634.

CHAPTER 9

MARINE RISKS

INTRODUCTION

In marine insurance, the insured risks on hulls and cargo may be divided into two broad categories, namely, marine risks and war and strikes risks. The term 'marine risks' is a handy expression commonly used to refer to any risks other than war and strikes risks. Marine risks may be further sub-divided into:

- The traditional risks, such as perils of the seas, fire, theft, jettison, and piracy insured under the old SG policy; together with other recent additions, which are not strictly speaking marine risks,[1] they are now insured under cl 6.1 of the ITCH(95) and cl 4.1 of the IVCH(95); in relation to cargo, some of these perils are specially insured under the ICC (B) and (C), and are generally covered by the ICC (A) by reason of the policy being for all risks. This chapter examines the risks insured under cl 6.1 of the ITCH(95) and cl 4.1 of the IVCH(95); their counterparts in the ICC (B) and (C); and the scope of the 'all risks' cover of the ICC (A);

- Additional or special risks insured under cl 6.2 of the ITCH(95) and cl 4.2 of the IVCH(95), commonly referred to as The Inchmaree clause[2] which was introduced as a result of the case of the same name;[3] and

- The 3/4ths Collision Liability of cl 8 of the ITCH(95) and cl 6 of the IVCH(95) previously known as 'the running down clause'.[4]

A separate chapter is also devoted to the statutory excluded losses;[5] the problematic but important area of the law on burden and standard of proof in relation to a claim of loss by perils of the seas, barratry, and fire, and the defence of wilful misconduct;[6] and war and strikes risks.[7]

A – PERILS OF THE SEAS RIVERS LAKES OR OTHER NAVIGABLE WATERS

The very purpose of marine insurance is obviously to secure the assured with an indemnity for loss of or damage sustained by the subject-matter insured during the course of a marine adventure. A 'marine adventure', as defined in s 3, occurs when any ship, goods, or other moveables are exposed to 'maritime perils' of which 'perils of the seas' is not surprisingly named as one of the perils.

---

1   Eg, 'contact with land conveyance, dock or harbour equipment or installation'; earthquake volcanic eruption or lightning' and 'accidents in loading discharging or shifting cargo or fuel.'

2   Also sometimes called the negligence clause; discussed in Chapter 12.

3   *Thames & Mersey Marine Insurance Co v Hamilton, Fraser & Co* (1887) 12 App Cas 484, HL.

4   See Chapter 13.

5   See Chapter 10.

6   See Chapter 11.

7   See Chapter 14.

'Perils of the seas' was specifically insured against under the old SG policy applying to both ship and goods, and is also an insured peril under the current Institute Hulls Clauses.

Clause 6.1.1 of the ITCH(95) and cl 4.1.1 of the IVCH(95) provide coverage for loss of or damage to the subject-matter insured caused by 'perils of the seas rivers lakes or other navigable waters'. We are now no longer left in doubt that loss or damage caused by perils of the 'rivers, lakes or other navigable waters' are also covered by the said Clauses.

With regard to insurance of cargo, perils of the seas, and of rivers lakes and other navigable waters are under the ICC (A) covered by virtue of the policy being for all risks. The ICC (B) and (C), however, have adopted a different scheme in this regard: instead of employing the traditional concept of 'perils of the seas', as understood under the common law, the old SG policy and the Institute Hulls Clauses, the ICC (B) and (C) do not provide for insurance against 'perils of the seas' as such. As the words 'perils of the seas' are not used, it is best in order to avoid confusion that they be left for discussion separately.

The vast number of cases which have come before the courts for the purpose of determining the meaning and scope of the phrase 'perils of the seas' has clearly demonstrated the fact that the term is not as simple or as straightforward as it may seem. Distinctions have been drawn, and the line between 'perils of the seas' and other concepts such as unseaworthiness, wear and tear, negligence, barratry and wilful misconduct, is sometimes, as will be seen later, not so readily apparent.

Sea water could be intentionally let into a ship, with or without the connivance of the shipowner. It could also be allowed entry into the ship by the negligence of the crew, as, for example, in leaving a valve or port hole open when it should have been kept closed. The sea could also find its way into a ship by reason of her unfit condition due to wear and tear, unseaworthiness, or a latent defect. That the ingress of sea water into a ship need not necessarily be the result of a peril of the seas is clear. In order to be able to discern 'perils of the seas' from other causes, it is necessary to elicit the characteristics of the concept. Interestingly, judges have employed various means for the purpose of determining whether a loss was caused by a peril of the seas; these devices will be discussed after a study of the legal definitions of the term has been undertaken.

DEFINITIONS OF 'PERILS OF THE SEAS'

Rule 7 of the Rules for Construction is the statutory definition of 'perils of the seas'. It is restricted:

> '... only to fortuitous accidents or casualties of the seas. It does not include the ordinary action of the winds and waves.'

Terms such as 'marine risks', 'the hazards of the sea' and 'external accidental means'[8] have been used in the past in non-standard marine polices to describe either an exception of liability or a risk insured against under the policy. All these terms have been construed by the courts as synonymous with 'perils of the seas'.[9]

However, the most comprehensive of the judicial definitions is that approved by Lord Bramwell in *Thames and Mersey Marine Insurance Co v Hamilton, Fraser and Co, The Inchmaree* to the effect that:[10]

> 'Every accidental circumstance not the result of ordinary wear and tear, delay, or of the act of the assured, happening in the course of the navigation of the ship, and incidental to the navigation, and causing loss to the subject-matter of insurance.'

The term 'perils of the seas' naturally conjures up in one's mind a picture of a turbulent sea, violent storms, forceful gales,[11] hurricanes, excessive squalls, large washes of waves, tempestuous weather and the like. In this context, Mr Justice Mustill (as he was then), in the court of first instance, in *The Miss Jay Jay*[12] gave an interesting meteorological account of the range of weather conditions which a ship could encounter during the course of a voyage. The types of weather which a ship may be exposed to were categorised as follows:

- abnormally bad weather;
- adverse weather;
- favourable weather; and
- perfect weather.

Indeed, it would almost be impossible to attribute a loss to 'perils of the seas' if the weather conditions to which the ship was exposed to, at the time of loss, were favourable or perfect. Inevitably, in such a situation, some other cause or causes of loss, for example, unseaworthiness, wear and tear, or the wilful misconduct of the assured would most probably be found to be responsible for the loss.

The distinction between 'abnormally bad' and 'adverse' weather, according to Mr Justice Mustill, lies in the fact that the former falls 'outside the range of

---

8   See *E D Sassoon v Western Assurance Co* [1912] AC 563, PC, where insurance was effected against marine risks. In *Miss Jay Jay* [1985] 1 Lloyd's Rep 264 at p 271; [1987] 1 Lloyd's Rep 32, CA, Mustill J remarked that there is 'no material distinction between 'perils of the seas' and 'external accidental means'.

9   See *Trinder, Anderson & Co v Thames and Mersey Mar Insurance Co* [1898] 2 QB 114, where it was said that 'perils of the seas' has the same meaning in marine insurance as in the law of carriage of goods by sea.

10 (1887) 12 App Cas 484 at p 492, HL: Lord Bramwell also approved the definition provided by Lopes LJ in the *Hamilton, Fraser and Co v Pandorf & Co*, 16 QBD 629 at p 633: 17 QBD 670, CA; (1887) 12 App Cas 518, HL: 'In a seaworthy ship damage to goods caused by the action of the sea during transit not attributable to the fault of anybody, is a damage from a peril of the sea.'

11 In *Willmott v General Accident Fire & Life Assurance Corpn Ltd* (1935) 53 Ll L Rep 156, the court pointed out that even if the vessel was 'tight' (ie, seaworthy), she still could not have ridden out the considerable gale.

12 [1985] 1 Lloyd's Rep 264 at p 271; [1987] 1 Lloyd's Rep 32, CA.

conditions which the assured could reasonably foresee that the vessel might encounter on the voyage in question', whilst the latter, 'within the range of what could be foreseen, but at the unfavourable end of that range'.

Ordinary action of the winds and waves

The exclusion of 'ordinary action of the winds and waves' from the definition of the 'perils of the seas' in r 7 could tempt one to deduce that only weather which is extraordinary or abnormal falls within the scope of the definition. This is clearly a mistaken point of view. In *Skandia Insurance Co Ltd v Skoljarev*,[13] Mr Justice Mason, who was aware of this misconception, pointed out that: 'The old view that some extraordinary action of the wind and waves is required to constitute a fortuitous accident or casualty is now quite discredited.'

In *The Miss Jay Jay*,[14] Mr Justice Mustill, who was not quite so direct, observed that the fact that the 'adverse' weather could reasonably have been anticipated makes no difference, if the action of the wind or sea is the immediate cause of the loss. In his survey of weather conditions, he explained that the adjective 'ordinary' qualifies the word 'action', not the winds and waves. Thus, not only extraordinary, but also ordinary winds and waves could fall within the ambit of 'perils of the seas'.

In the recent case of *CCR Fishing Ltd and Others v Tomenson Inc and Others, The La Pointe*,[15] the Canadian court pointed out that there are two elements to the term 'perils of the seas': the cause of the loss must be 'fortuitous' and it must be 'of the seas'.

The word 'fortuitous' clearly excludes any loss which has been intentionally caused by any person,[16] and any loss resulting from inevitable deterioration generated by the ordinary action of the winds and waves.[17] The cause of the loss must not be intentional or inevitable.

For the purpose of determining whether an event is or is not fortuitous, the distinction between, on the one hand, what is regular and normal, and on the other, the unusual and unexpected, was used in *Popham and Willett v St Petersburg Insurance Co*.[18] The issue at hand was whether obstruction by ice was or was not a peril of the seas. It was held that, as the annual regular obstruction of the port by ice in winter was in 'no sense an accident being part of the ordinary course of things, like the ebb and flow of the tides – the loss was not caused by a peril of the seas'. Thus, to fall within the scope of this peril, the ice encountered has to be 'unusual' at that time of the year, creating extraordinary difficulty or danger to navigation.

---

13 [1979] 142 CLR 375 at p 385, High Court of Australia.

14 [1985] 1 Lloyd's Rep 264.

15 [1991] 1 Lloyd's Rep 89, Supreme Court of Canada.

16 See *Samuel v Dumas* [1924] 18 Ll L Rep 211 HL, which has overruled *Small v United Kingdom Marine Mutual Insurance Association* [1897] 2 QB 311, CA on the issue of perils of the seas.

17 See *Existological Laboratories Ltd v Century Insurance Co of Canada (The Bamcell II)* (1983) 2 SCR 47.

18 (1904) 10 Com Cas 31 at p 34.

To amplify this point, the ancient case of *Magnus v Buttemer*[19] needs to be mentioned. The ship in question was in the harbour for unloading when she was damaged as a result of taking the ground on the natural falling and rising of the tide. The court held that as there was 'nothing unusual, no peril, no accident'; the damage fell within the description of ordinary wear and tear.

Reference should also to be made to the House of Lord's decision of the case *Mountain v Whittle*,[20] where damage sustained as a result of an influx of water into the ship caused by a wash of extraordinary size and dimension, created by the tug employed to tow the insured vessel, was held to be a loss through a peril of the seas.

Distinction between sea and land risks

A comparison which has frequently been drawn to facilitate the understanding of the concept is that between sea risks and land risks. It has been said that the requirement of 'of the seas' will be met if the loss would not have occurred on land. The test may be simply expressed as whether the accident is one which could only occur at sea. *The Inchmaree*[21] is, of course, the classic case on this subject. Lord Bramwell's description of the position read as follows:

'The damage to the donkey-engine was not through its being in a ship or at sea. The same thing would have happened had the boilers and engines been on land, if the same mismanagement had taken place. The sea, waves and winds had nothing to do with it.'

The reverse position was encountered in *The Stranna*,[22] where the sea had everything, and the land had nothing to do with the loss. The heeling of the ship was 'wholly unexpected' and was just an 'unfortunate accident'. The court noted that the loss was not only a peril of the seas, but also a peril *on* the seas. But as 'it could not have happened on land' the court had to hold that the loss was caused by a peril of the seas.

The same line of argument was recently applied in *The La Pointe*.[23] As the ship sank as a consequence of the ingress of sea water into the ship – an event which could not occur on land – the accident was held to be 'of the seas'. The fact that the accident would not have occurred but for the negligent act of the crew in leaving a valve open did not detract the loss from being caused by a peril of the seas.

The case of *Grant, Smith & Co v Seattle Construction and Dry Dock Co*[24] is a particularly important case for the purpose of illustrating the point that the sea,

---

19   (1852) 11 CB 876.

20   [1921] AC 615, HL.

21   *Thames & Mersey Insurance Co v Hamilton, Fraser & Co* (1887) 12 App Cas 484, HL. Lord Halebury LC at (p 491) remarked that, 'Sea perils or the like become enlarged into perils whose only connection with the sea is that they arise from machinery which gives motive power to ships'.

22   [1937] P 130; [1938] P 69.

23   [1991] 1 Lloyds Rep 89.

24   [1920] AC 162 at p 171.

wind or wave has to play a part in causing the loss. After acknowledging the fact that it was 'not desirable to attempt to define too exactly a "marine risk" or a "peril of the seas"', Lord Buckmaster proceeded to lay down the law as follows: 'it is some condition of sea or weather or accident of navigation producing a result which, but for these conditions would not have occurred'. It was not at all difficult for the court in this instance to find that a peril of the seas did not cause the loss of the dry dock which had capsized in the harbour by reason of her inherent unfitness for the work.

In similar, but more graphic terms, the Privy Council in *Sassoon & Co v Western Assurance Co*[25] pointed out that 'there was no weather, nor any other fortuitous circumstances, contributing to the incursion of the water; the water merely gravitated by its own weight through the opening of the decayed wood', the damage to the opium was not a loss caused by a peril of the seas.

That the sea or land criterion is neither fool-proof nor altogether easy to apply may be gathered from a speech delivered by Lord Atkinson of the House of Lords in *Stott Steamers Ltd v Marten*:[26]

> 'A peril whose only connection with the sea is that it arises on board ship is not necessarily a peril of the seas nor a peril *ejusdem generis* as a peril of the sea. The breaking of the chain of a crane, or of a shackle of that chain, if overloaded or subjected to too severe a strain, is not more maritime in character when it occurs on board a ship than when it occurs on land.'

The celebrated case of *Hamilton, Fraser & Co v Pandorf & Co*,[27] a case in relation to a contract of affreightment (which excepted the carrier from liability from 'dangers and accidents of the seas') is frequently referred to as the authority laying down the rule that damage caused by sea water, which escaped because rats had gnawed a hole in a pipe connecting the bath-room with the sea, is a loss caused by a peril of the seas. As sea-water, and not tap-water, had caused the mischief, albeit with the help of rodents, the loss was accidental and fortuitous. The outcome of the case would almost certainly have been different if the damage had been caused by the escape of tap-water from a water-closet, such an incident could also occur on land.

Perils *of* the seas and perils *on* the seas

The subtle distinction between a peril of the seas and a peril on the seas has invariably been ascribed to the case of *The Xantho*.[28] But, in fact, the distinction was referred to, though not in such bold terms, as early as 1816 in *Cullen v Butler*.[29] This case is better known as the authority which has established the rule that a ship which is sunk due to being fired upon by another ship (mistaking her for an enemy) is not a loss caused by a 'peril of the seas', but one

---

25 [1912] AC 561 at p 563.
26 [1916] AC 304 at p 311.
27 (1887) 12 App Cas 518; 6 Asp MLC 212, HL.
28 *Wilson, Sons & Co v Owners of Cargo per The Xantho* (1887) 7 HL Cas 504, HL.
29 (1816) 5 M & S 461.

which falls within the general words of 'all other perils, losses'. The logic of Lord Ellenborough's arguments is, indeed, worthwhile noting:

> 'If it be a loss by perils of the sea, merely because it is a loss happening upon the sea, as has been contended, all the other causes of loss specified in the policy are, upon that ground, equally entitled so to be considered; and it would be unnecessary as to them ever to assign any other cause of loss, than a loss by perils of the sea.'

Therein lies the beginning of the distinction between a peril *of* the seas and a peril *on* the seas.

In *The Xantho*,[30] Lord Herschell of the House of Lords, though he did not approve the outcome of *Cullen v Butler*,[31] nevertheless emphasised the importance of the word 'of ' in the term 'perils *of* the seas'. It would seem that no work on the subject can be described as complete without a quotation of the famous words of Lord Herschell:

> 'I think it clear that the term "perils of the sea" does not cover every accident or casualty which may happen to the subject matter of the insurance on the sea. It must be a peril "of" the sea. Again it is well settled that it is not every loss or damage of which the sea is the immediate cause that is covered by these words. They do not protect, for example, against that natural and inevitable action of the winds and waves which results in what may be described as wear and tear.'

Frost damage

It would be difficult to argue that damage by frost is a peril of the seas because it could also occur on land. Thus, with the exception of the ICC (A), it would not, unless specifically otherwise stated, be covered under any of the standard Institute Clauses.

Collision is a peril of the seas

The Xantho[32] is also to be credited for laying down the rule that a collision is a peril of the seas. The House declared that a collision, whether 'caused by a sunken rock, or by an iceberg, or by another vessel, or whether that other vessel is or is not in fault', is a peril of the seas.

To be accurate, it was *Smith v Scott*[33] (a less well-known case) in 1811, which had pronounced that a loss occasioned by another ship running down the insured ship, through the gross negligence of the crew of that other ship, is a loss by a peril of the seas: that 'still the sea did the mischief' was a fact which Mr Justice Mansfield found difficult to ignore.

The rationale for the common law rule is best explained in the case of *Davidson v Burnard* as follows:[34]

---

30 (1887) 7 HL Cas 504 at p 517.

31 (1816) 5 M & S 461.

32 (1887) 11 PD 170.

33 (1811) 4 Taunt 126.

34 (1868) LR 4 CP 117 at p 121.

'... unless some distinction can be made between a loss from an accident happening through the negligence of the crew of another vessel and a loss from an accident happening ... from such negligence of the crew ... the loss would be a loss occasioned by the perils of the sea.'

Thus, no distinction is drawn between a loss caused by the negligence of the crew of the insured vessel and one caused by the negligence of the crew of another vessel.[35] With regard to the former, the assured is protected by the words 'even though the loss would not have happened but for the misconduct or negligence of the master or crew' in s 55(2)(a).[36]

Unascertainable peril of the seas

There is a species of loss known as an 'unascertainable' or 'unspecified' peril of the seas described in *Lamb Head Shipping Co Ltd v Jennings, The Marel*.[37] It is a form of loss which is proved by the drawing of inferences when a shipowner is unable to pinpoint an event or an accident to show that the loss was accidental or fortuitous. Unlike the usual claim for a loss by a peril of the seas (as traditionally understood), the courts would allow an inference to be drawn, where the loss is unexplained or where the ship is missing, that the ship was lost by reason of an unascertainable peril of the seas.[38] The manner and extent of proof in such cases can be more appropriately discussed elsewhere.[39]

PERILS OF THE SEAS AND NEGLIGENCE

A loss proximately caused by a peril of the seas could well be precipitated by the negligence of the master, crew, pilot, charterer, shipowner, repairer, engineer, stevedore, or any person.[40] Provided that the loss is proximately caused by a peril insured against, an assured may, by reason of s 55(2)(a), recover for the loss 'even though the loss would not have happened but for the misconduct or negligence of the master or crew'.[41] Attention has to be drawn to the following: first, that only the conduct of the 'master or crew', and not that of the assured, is expressly excused under the said section; and secondly, that the first limb of s 55(2)(a) prevents recovery for any loss 'attributable to the wilful

---

35   See *The Woodrop Sims*, (1815) 2 Dod 83, on collision.

36   The assured would, of course, be claiming for the loss of or damage sustained by his vessel as a loss by a peril of the seas. With regard to the damage sustained to the other vessel for which the assured, if held responsible, would be able to claim under the 3/4ths collision liability clause: cl 8 of the ITCH(95) and cl 6 of the IVCH(95). The assured's liability to a third party arising out of a collision at sea will be discussed later: see Chapter 13.

37   [1992] 1 Lloyd's Rep 402.

38   In *Munro, Brice & Co v War Risk Association Ltd & Others* [1918] 2 KB 78 at p 86, Bailhache J held the view that, 'A plaintiff who alleges that his vessel was lost by a peril of the sea cannot be ordered to state how the sinking came about'.

39   See Chapter 11.

40   Even rodents can cause the entry of sea water into the ship: see *Hamilton, Fraser & Co v Pandorf & Co* (1887) 12 App Cas 518, where rats gnawed a hole in a pipe which passed through the cargo of rice, with the result that sea water entered and damaged the rice.

41   A loss proximately caused by an act of wilful misconduct committed by the master or crew would be recoverable as barratry: cl 6.2.4 of the ITCH(95) and cl 4.2.4 of the IVCH(95).

misconduct of the assured' but is silent on a loss attributable to the negligence of the assured.

Negligence of the master or crew

Negligence as a remote cause of loss

It is interesting to note that even before the promulgation of the Act, as early as 1821 in the case of *Walker v Maitland*,[42] it was decided that insurers were liable for a loss proximately caused by a peril of the seas, but remotely by the negligence of the master and crew.[43] Chief Justice Abbott held that 'the winds and waves caused the loss'; and the fact that they 'would not have produced that effect, unless there had been neglect on the part of the crew' was considered irrelevant.[44]

Seven years later, the same principle was again applied in *Bishop v Pentland*[45] when the vessel stranded as the rope with which she was fastened broke; although the stranding was occasioned indirectly or remotely by the negligence of the crew in not providing a rope of sufficient strength, the loss was nonetheless held recoverable.

In another much celebrated case, *Davidson and Others v Burnand*,[46] the court was prepared to overlook the negligence of the crew who, in having left some cocks and valves opened when they should have been kept shut, caused water to enter the ship and damaged a cargo of produce. Mr Justice Willes, who could see no distinction between a loss caused by the negligence of the crew of the vessel insured and one caused by the negligence of the crew of another vessel, decided that the damage was caused by a peril of the seas.

Similarly, in *Redman v Wilson*,[47] the insurers were also held responsible, as the judges felt that they could not 'distinguish between the negligence of the master and mariners, and the negligence of the natives (if they were negligent, and remotely gave occasion to the loss) who were employed to put the cargo on

---

42 (1821) 5 B & Ald 171 at p 175.

43 The sloop being left to herself, as the entire crew were asleep, ran ashore and was beaten to pieces by the sea.

44 An earlier case which had applied the same principle, but in relation to a loss by fire started by the negligence of one of the crew, is *Busk v The Royal Exchange Assurance Co* (1818) 5 B & A 171.

45 (1827) 7 B & C 219.

46 (1868) LR 4 CP 117. The same rule applies in the law of carriage of by sea: see, eg, *Blackburn & Another v Liverpool, Brazil & River Plate Steam Navigation Co* [1902] 1 KB 290 where damage to cargo caused by the influx of sea water by an engineer opening of a wrong valve was held to have been due to a peril of the seas. Similarly, in *The Stranna* [1938] 1 All ER 458, the lost of a cargo of wood which shot overboard during loading was held to have been occasioned by a peril of the seas, and 'none the less so because it was the negligence of those who were concerned with the work of loading the ship that brought the peril into operation'.

47 (1845) 14 M & W 482.

board'. The loss of the ship was held to have been caused by perils of the seas even though she was, to prevent her from sinking, deliberately ran ashore.[48]

Another often cited authority is *Dixon v Sadler*,[49] which explained the basis for the rule as follows:

'... an assured makes no warranty to the underwriters that ... the master and crew shall do their duty during the voyage, and their negligence or misconduct is no defence to an action on a policy, where the loss has been immediately occasioned by the perils insured against.'

In this case, the master and mariners threw overboard so much of the ballast that the vessel became unseaworthy, and was lost by perils of the seas. She would have encountered and overcome the perils of the seas if it were not for the wrongful, negligent and improper act of the master and crew.

In the more recent case of *Lind v Mitchell*,[50] the unreasonable conduct of the master in prematurely abandoning and setting fire to a ship, which leaked badly after a collision with ice, was held to constitute negligence. On these facts, the Court of Appeal had no doubt that the loss was caused by a peril of the seas. It, however, preferred to rely on s 55(2)(a), rather than the Inchmaree clause,[51] as the main ground for its decision. According to Lord Justice Sankey:[52]

'... those perils of the sea were the dominant cause, and, having regard to section 55(2) ... I think the underwriters are liable in this case, because there was a loss proximately caused by a peril insured against, although perhaps the loss would not have happened but for the misconduct and negligence of the master or crew.'

Once again, the negligence of a master acting as a remote[53] cause of the loss was considered inconsequential.[54]

A slightly different approach was, however, taken by the court in *Baxendale v Fane, The 'Lapwing'*,[55] where bottom-damage sustained by a yacht, as a result of having been negligently docked, was held as a loss caused by stranding, a peril of the seas. Interestingly, s 55(2)(a) was not mentioned by the judge, who chose to rest the matter simply on the basis that the loss was fortuitous. Fortunately for the assured, the negligence committed by those responsible for the docking operation was the 'intervention' which provided the fortuitous circumstances which entitled them to recover under the terms of the policy: the loss was indemnifiable as a loss by a peril of the seas.

---

48 See *McAllister & Co v Western Assurance Co of the City of Toronto* (1926), 27 Ll L Rep 109, where a loss was held to have been caused by a peril of the seas even though the opening in the ship, which allowed the entry of the sea, was made by the negligence of stevedores in unloading the ship.

49 (1839) 5 M & W 405 at p 414; (1841) 8 M & W 895, Ex Ch.

50 (1928) 45 TLR 54, CA.

51 The current equivalent is cl 6.2 of the ITCH(95) and cl 4.2 of the IVCH(95).

52 (1928) 45 TLR 54 at p 57, CA.

53 Describing negligence as a remote cause of loss was considered by Arnould as a 'misuse of language'. He thought that it would be more appropriate to regard negligence as 'part of the chain of events': see para 763A. However described, it has to be distinguished from the proximate cause of the loss.

54 But 'if necessary', Scrutton LJ was prepared to offer recovery under the then equivalent to cl 6.2 of the ITCH(95). On this point, see Chapter 12.

55 (1940) 66 Ll L Rep 174.

Negligence as the proximate cause of loss

A master or member of crew could also, by his negligence, and without the aid of the sea or the elements, directly or proximately cause the loss of a ship and/or her cargo. If negligence, and not perils of the seas, is regarded as the proximate cause of loss, then the above discussion on s 55(2)(a) is irrelevant. Such a cause of loss is now specifically insured under cll 6.2.2 and 4.2.2 (commonly referred to as the Inchmaree clause) of the ITCH(95) and the IVCH(95) respectively. These provisions are more fully discussed elsewhere.[56]

Negligence of the assured

Negligence as a remote cause of loss

As pointed out earlier, s 55(2)(a) expressly overlooks the negligence (and wilful misconduct) of the 'master or crew', but not that of the assured. The question which now arises is: what is the position as regards a loss proximately caused by a peril insured against, for example, a peril of the seas, but remotely caused by the negligence of the assured? Can an assured, whether or not acting as master or crew, be prevented from claiming under a policy for a loss proximately caused by a peril of the seas, which he himself has remotely occasioned by his negligence?[57] Section 55(2)(a) expressly forbids recovery only for 'any loss attributable to the wilful misconduct of the assured'. No mention, however, is made of a loss 'attributable to' the negligence of the assured. As both the Act and the Institute Hulls Clauses are silent on this point, reference to case law has to be made in order to ascertain the legal position under the common law.

Assured acting as master or crew

In the old days, before corporate ownership became established, it was not uncommon for a shipowner, whether a sole or part-owner, to act as the master (or member of crew) of his own ship. Acting in this capacity, he could, through negligent navigation or the mishandling or mistreatment of the cargo, indirectly cause the loss of property.

Trinder, Anderson & Co v Thames and Mersey Marine Insurance Co,[58] decided before the enactment of the Act, is by far the most illuminating authority on the subject. The stranding of the vessel, which brought about the loss of freight sued for, was caused by the negligent navigation (though not the wilful act) of one of the assured who was a part-owner and captain of the ship. One of the main issues was whether an assured, who was personally guilty of negligent navigation during the voyage covered by the policy, could recover for the loss.

---

56   A loss caused by 'the negligence of master officers crew or pilots'; and of 'repairers or charterers provided such repairers or charterers are not an Assured hereunder' are now specifically insured against. For a study of these clauses, see Chapter 12.

57   Short of holding a position on board the ship, it is difficult to envisage how an assured, such as a mortgagee, can negligently or otherwise, cause the loss of the insured property.

58   [1898] 2 QB 114, CA, hereinafter referred to as *The Trinder Case*.

Lord Justice Smith in the Court of Appeal was adamant that the loss was 'none the less a peril of the sea though brought about by negligent navigation'. 'Negligent navigation', he said, 'has never been held to be equivalent to *"dolus"* or ... *"misconduct"'*.

In similar vein, Lord Justice Collins, referring to the act of the assured (who was shipowner and master) remarked that: 'His negligence does not, any more than that of his servants, alter the character of the sea peril, which still remains the *causa proxima* ...'. In unequivocal terms, he concluded that:

'Nothing short, therefore, of *dolus* in its proper sense will defeat the right of the assured to recover in respect of a loss of which but for such *dolus* the proximate cause would be a peril of the sea.'

The legal position may be briefly summarised as follows: provided that the act of the assured is negligently and not wilfully committed, the loss would retain its 'fortuitous' character which is essential to constitute a peril of the seas. As far as navigational matters are concerned, his act is no different from that of any other master.

It is necessary, at this juncture, to refer to *Westport Coal Company v McPhail*,[59] which, though a bill of lading case, is nonetheless useful for the purpose of highlighting the difference between the conduct of the shipowner acting in the capacity of master and of owner. *The Trinder Case*,[60] decided in the same year and also by the Court of Appeal, was cited with approval.

The Court of Appeal in *The Westport Case*, relying on the fact that as 'it was the negligence of the master in the sphere of his duty as master which caused the loss', held that the exception[61] was adequate to protect the defendant shipowner for the loss of the cargo. According to Lord Justice Collins, 'the negligence which caused the damage was exclusively master's, as distinguished from part-owner's, negligence, within the meaning of the exception'.

The above remarks, however, imply that if the conduct of the shipowner was committed in the capacity of owner or part-owner, and not as master or crew, the result could well be different. In the particular circumstance when a shipowner-assured acts as master, or a member of crew, of his own ship, as in *The Trinder Case*,[62] the position is straightforward: wearing the hat of the master, his act of neglect falls squarely within the terms of the said section.[63] The question which now has to be considered is whether the outcome would be different if the assured did not hold any position on board the ship, but has, through his neglect, remotely caused the loss of the subject-matter insured. Arnould, relying on the *The Trinder Case* and by drawing an inference from the

---

59 [1898] 2 QB 130, CA.

60 [1898] 2 QB 114, CA.

61 The exception was in respect of 'the neglect and default of master in navigating the ship'.

62 [1898] 2 QB 114, CA.

63 The distinction between a negligent and a wilful act has to be borne in mind: any loss attributable to the wilful act committed by an assured (in this case a shipowner acting as master) would in relation to his co-owners (if any) constitute barratry. As far as he (the assured shipowner) is concerned, such a loss is not recoverable for two reasons. First, the loss is not caused by a peril insured against; but more importantly, it is specifically excluded by s 55(2)(a).

language of s 55(2)(a), is of the view that the assured would be able recover for such a loss.[64]

Such a cause of loss clearly does not fall within the wording of the last limb of s 55(2)(a), namely, 'even though the loss would not have happened but for the ... negligence of the master or crew'; and the principle laid down in *The Trinder Case* has, it is contended, to be confined to the special circumstances of the case: the fact that the assured was acting as master when the act of neglect was committed was the main reason for the decision. There are, however, other grounds upon which the court could have applied to support its decision. First, the rationale for disregarding negligence operating as a remote cause lies in the law of causation – though this was not pointed out in any of the cases cited above, remote causes, whether committed by an assured (acting in whatever capacity), a member of crew or any person(s), have never played a part in the equation of the rule of *causa proxima*. The only remote cause of loss which would prevent an assured from recovering under a policy is that of the wilful misconduct of the assured. The term 'attributable to' in s 55(2)(a) has made this very clear;[65] Secondly, s 55(2)(a) expressly excludes recovery only for any loss attributable to the wilful misconduct, but not for the negligence, of the assured. This is probably the inference Arnould had in mind.

In conclusion, a loss proximately caused by a peril insured against, but remotely by the negligence (whether or not committed whilst acting in the capacity of master) of an assured is, as a general rule, recoverable. He could, however, be precluded from recovery if the insurer is able to rely upon s 39(5)[66] or s 78(4) of the Act.[67]

PERILS OF THE SEAS AND WILFUL MISCONDUCT

Scuttling is not a peril of the seas

Before the decision of the House of Lords in *Samuel v Dumas*,[68] it was at one time thought that any loss or damage caused by the entry of sea water into a ship was a loss caused by a peril of the seas.[69] The celebrated case has, however, dispelled this mistaken belief by declaring that a loss caused by the wilful

---

64 Arnould at para 763A: '... it may be inferred from the language of the subsection [referring to s 55(2)(a)], although it is not expressly so provided therein, that, even where the peril occasioning the loss has been due to the negligence (not amounting to wilful misconduct) of the assured himself, the underwriter will not, on account of such negligence, be relieved from liability. It was so decided before the passing of the Act, in *Trinder, Anderson & Co v Thames and Mersey Marine Insurance Co* [1898] 2 QB 114 (CA)'.

65 See Chapters 8 and 10.

66 See Chapter 7.

67 See Chapter 17.

68 [1924] 18 Ll L Rep 211, HL.

69 See *Small v United Kingdom Marine Mutual Insurance Association* (1897) 2 QB 311, CA; *Chartered Trust & Executor Co v London Scottish Assurance Corpn Ltd* (1923) 39 TLR 608, which had held that an innocent mortgagee is entitled to succeed for a loss caused by scuttling is now overruled; and *Graham Joint Stock Shipping Co Ltd v Merchants' Marine Insurance Co* (1923) 17 Ll L Rep 44, 241, HL.

misconduct of the shipowner in scuttling his ship is not a loss caused by a peril of the seas, even though the sea may have played a part or lent a helping hand in causing the loss.

The reasons for the rule that scuttling is not a peril of the seas are twofold. First, the loss or damage is, in so far as the wrongdoer is concerned, clearly not fortuitous: a deliberate and an intentional act has caused the loss, and the sea was able to play its part only because it was allowed to do so by man. Such a loss is neither accidental nor fortuitous: it is a certainty. Secondly, equity would not allow a wrongdoer to take advantage of his own wrongful act.[70]

The position of an innocent cargo owner and of an innocent mortgagee

One could, however, be tempted to argue that, in relation to an innocent third party, such as a cargo owner or a mortgagee, the wilful act committed by the shipowner is fortuitous. The act of the shipowner is *vis-à-vis* a cargo owner or a mortgagee that of a stranger. In *Small v United Kingdom Marine Mutual Insurance Association*,[71] it was held that, in so far as the mortgagee, an innocent party, was concerned, the loss was recoverable as a loss by perils of the seas. *Samuel v Dumas*[72] has, however, overruled this aspect of the judgment of the case.[73]

In this regard, a cargo owner is in the same position as a mortgagee; this was pointed out by Lord Justice Scrutton in the Court of Appeal in *Samuel v Dumas*[74] in the following terms:

'... I know of no case ... where an owner of goods has recovered for damage to his goods by sea water intentionally admitted by the owner of the ship, either for perils of the sea or barratry.'

A loss or damage caused by sea water intentionally admitted into a ship, whether by a shipowner, master or crew, or even a stranger, is not a loss by perils of the seas. The 'wilful' nature of the act negates 'fortuity' which is an essential ingredient of the peril. Regardless of whether the claim is brought by a shipowner, cargo owner or mortgagee, the nature or character of the act is the same:[75] as there is no 'element of chance or ill-luck', the loss cannot be described as accidental or fortuitous.[76] Nobody can recover for such a loss as a loss by a *'peril of the seas'*.

---

70 One of the maxims of equity is 'he who comes into equity must come with clean hands'.
71 (1897) 2 QB 311, CA.
72 [1924] 18 Ll L Rep 211, HL.
73 To protect himself from being excluded for such a loss, a mortgagee should take up the Institute Mortgagees' Interest Clauses Hulls: see Appendix 23.
74 [1923] 1 KB 592 at p 620. Scrutton LJ's remarks in reference to goods must be confined to a cargo policy in which 'perils of the seas' is an insured risk. It has, it is submitted, no relevance to an all risks policy. The position of a cargo owner whose cargo (insured under the ICC(A)) has been damaged or lost as a consequence of scuttling is discussed below.
75 In *Pateras & Others v Royal Exchange Assurance* (1933) 49 Ll L Rep 400 at p 407, Roche J, relying on *Samuel v Dumas* [1924] 18 Ll L Rep 211, HL, held that 'nobody could recover because the wilful throwing away of the ship was not a fortuitous circumstance ...'.
76 Naturally, the position is different in the case of a loss caused by fire which, as a matter of construction, does not contain the element of 'fortuity'. As such, a loss caused by fire is recoverable even if it was deliberately started by a stranger, a third party to the contract of insurance. For a discussion on the right of a cargo owner or a mortgagee to sue for a loss by a fire deliberately started by a shipowner, see below.

The ICC (A), (B) and (C)

With regard to cargo insured under the ICC (B) or (C), a loss caused by a wilful act committed by any person is expressly excluded by cl 4.7. The words 'any person or persons' are wide enough to include a loss caused by the shipowner in scuttling the ship.

In contrast, the absence of the deliberate damage or destruction exclusion clause in the ICC (A) could be read to mean that, as there is no express exclusion for such an event, a loss resulting from scuttling is covered. Moreover, the fact that the ICC (A) is an all risks policy supports this assumption. It is important to bear in mind that the claim of the cargo owner is not based on 'perils of the seas', but on the term 'risks'. It is submitted that in so far as the cargo owner is concerned, the loss, though not caused by a 'peril of the seas', is recoverable as a 'risk' which may or may not happen during the course of transit. In the words of Lord Sterndale of the Court of Appeal in *The Gaunt Case*,[77] 'it is a danger or contingency which might or might not arise'. As far as the cargo owner is concerned, the loss is not a certainty, but a risk.

PERILS OF THE SEAS AND BARRATRY

Whenever a ship is lost at sea by reason of the entry of sea water, barratry and a peril of the seas are often pleaded in the alternative as causes of loss.[78] This is because sea water could accidentally or fortuitously enter a ship and cause a loss, or could be 'invited' to enter a ship to cause a loss.[79] In the case of the former, the action of the winds and waves – that is, perils of the seas – would be regarded as the proximate cause of loss; whilst in the latter, either barratry or wilful misconduct on the part of the shipowner would be considered as the proximate cause of loss. In any event, scuttling[80] a ship, whether done with or without the knowledge or consent of the shipowner, is not a peril of the seas: this has been settled beyond doubt by *Samuel v Dumas*.[81] It is suffice to mention here that the distinction between a peril of the seas and barratry is well defined. The former is a fortuitous act, whilst the latter is an intentional act committed by man, the master or crew:[82] they are mutually exclusive.

---

77   (1920) 1 KB 903 at p 910.

78   See eg, *La Compania Martiartu v Royal Exchange Assurance* [1923] 1 KB 650, CA; *The Michael*, [1979] 2 Lloyd's Rep 1, CA – where the shipowners originally claimed for loss by a peril of the seas, but when fresh evidence came to light, the plea was changed to barratry; and *Banco de Barcelona & Others v Union Marine Insurance Co Ltd* (1925) 30 Com Cas 316.

79   Sea water could be intentionally admitted by the master or crew, with or without the knowledge or consent of the shipowner. Such an act is known as scuttling. In the case of the former, the cause of loss is wilful misconduct, whilst in the latter, it is barratry.

80   Defined in *The Concise Oxford Dictionary* as: 'let water into (a ship) to sink it, esp by opening the seacocks'.

81   [1924] 18 Ll L Rep 211, HL.

82   For a discussion of the law of barratry, see Chapter 12.

PERILS OF THE SEAS AND WEAR AND TEAR

Unless the policy otherwise provides, loss or damage caused by 'ordinary wear and tear' is as a general rule excluded by s 55(2)(c) as a risk insured against.[83] Clause 4.2 of all the ICC expressly provides that ordinary wear and tear of the subject-matter insured is not covered.

Loss or damage caused by the ordinary actions of the winds and waves, which has been expressly excluded by r 7 of the Rules for Construction from the definition of 'perils of the seas', is a loss caused by ordinary wear and tear. As mentioned earlier, the word 'ordinary' qualifying the actions of the winds and waves appearing in r 7 was inserted for the purpose of eliminating losses resulting from ordinary wear and tear. In *The Miss Jay Jay*,[84] Mr Justice Mustill pointed out that 'the principal object of the definition (r 7) is to rule out losses resulting from wear and tear.'

Loss or damage caused by ordinary wear and tear is not covered by reason of the fact that it is an inevitable loss – a certainty – and, therefore, not a peril.

The difference between a loss caused by a peril of the seas and one by wear and tear is best illustrated by Mr Justice Lush in his direction to the jury in *Merchants' Trading Co v The Universal Marine Insurance Co*:[85]

'... "perils of the sea" denoted all marine casualties resulting from the violent action of the elements of the wind and waters, lightning, tempest, stranding, striking on a rock, and so on – all casualties of that description as distinguished from the silent natural gradual action of the elements upon the vessel itself, though the latter properly belonged to wear and tear, and that what the underwriters insured were casualties that might happen, not consequences which must happen, casualties which might occur and were incident to navigation arising from the violent action of the elements upon the ship.'

In *Wadsworth Lighterage and Coaling Co Ltd v Sea Insurance Co Ltd*,[86] the sinking of the ship, through general debility, was held not to have been occasioned by perils of the seas, although she had been sunk by the entry of sea water.

PERILS OF THE SEAS AND UNSEAWORTHINESS

The seaworthiness of a ship is frequently brought into question and raised as a defence by an insurer whenever a claim is made for loss of or damage sustained by the subject-matter insured by reason of either the entry of sea water into the ship or the violent action of the elements. It is to be noted that, regardless of the nature of the subject-matter insured, an insurer has always the right to plead

---

83 See Chapter 10.

84 [1987] 1 Lloyd's Rep 264 at p 271, QBD; [1987] 1 Lloyd's Rep 31, CA.

85 (1870), reported in a footnote in *Anderson v Morice* (1870) 2 Asp MC 431n, cited in (1876) 1 App Cas 713 at p 716, HL. The defence raised by the underwriter was that the loss resulting from the sudden eruption of water into the ship was caused by the unseaworthy condition of the vessel, the subject-matter insured. For an analysis of this defence, see Chapter 7.

86 (1929) 45 TLR 597, CA. For a discussion of law relating to the exclusion of ordinary wear and tear, see Chapter 10.

unseaworthiness as a defence to an action brought by an assured claiming that perils of the seas has caused the loss or damage.[87]

The general legal principles relating to seaworthiness vary with whether the policy is a voyage or a time policy. Furthermore, they could be modified by the terms of the policy, as in the case of the ICC.[88] In view of the fact that there is a fundamental distinction under English law between time and voyage policies in so far as the issue of seaworthiness is concerned,[89] it is necessary, in order to avoid confusion, to divide the ensuing discussion of the relationship between perils of the seas and unseaworthiness into three parts. The first part will deal with voyage policies; the second, with time policies; and the third, with the position under the ICC. But before so doing, it would be helpful to illustrate the relevance of seaworthiness in relation to the subject of perils of the seas.

A seaworthy ship, as defined by case law[90] and s 39(1), is one which is 'reasonably fit in all respects to encounter the ordinary perils of the seas of the adventure insured'. This necessarily means that if she is incapable of enduring even the most 'ordinary' of sea perils, she cannot be said to be seaworthy and, consequently, the loss cannot be attributed to perils of the seas.[91]

On the subject of weather conditions, a ship is expected to be able to 'deal adequately with adverse as well as favourable weather'.[92] 'Adverse' weather falls within the scope of 'ordinary' perils of the seas if it is weather which could reasonably be foreseen that the vessel might encounter on the voyage in question. In this context, the definition proposed in *Steel v State Line SS Co*[93] is perhaps preferable: a vessel is unseaworthy if she is unfit to endure all the hazards which 'a ship of that kind, and laden in that way, *may fairly be expected to encounter*' on the voyage.

It would be very difficult indeed to argue that a loss is proximately caused by the sea if the ship is unable to endure the 'expected', 'ordinary', and 'foreseeable' perils of the seas of the adventure insured. In such a case, a judge would be more inclined to find that some aspect of her physical condition – for example, latent defect, wear and tear or unseaworthiness – must have caused the loss. The case of *Merchants' Trading Company v The Universal Marine Insurance Co*[94] may be referred to illustrate this point. The defence of a breach of the implied warranty of seaworthiness was, in this action, successfully raised by the insurer, as the ship lying quietly at anchor was unable to keep herself afloat in still water. Accordingly, the court had no alternative but to rule that her unfit

---

87 As a general rule, it is for the insurer relying on unseaworthiness as a defence to prove that the vessel was unseaworthy: see *Lamb Head Shipping Co v Jennings, The Marel* [1992] 1 Lloyd's Rep 402, at p 412. For a fuller discussion of the subject of burden of proof, see Chapter 11.

88 See cl 5 of the ICC (A), (B) & (C).

89 For a discussion on this aspect of the law, see Chapter 7.

90 See Chapter 7.

91 *A fortiori*, if her structure or condition is unfit to withstand perfect weather conditions, she would undoubtedly be classified as unseaworthy.

92 *Per* Mustill J in *The Miss Jay Jay* [1985] 1 Lloyd's Rep 265 at p 271, QBD; [1987] 1 Lloyd's Rep 32, CA.

93 (1877) 3 App Cas 72 at p 77. Emphasis added.

94 (1870) 2 Asp MLC 431 at p 432.

condition caused the loss. The test used by the trial judge, which was approved by the Appeal Court, was worded as follows: 'whether the leak was attributable to injury and violence from without or to weakness within.'

Similarly, in *E D Sassoon & Co v Western Assurance Co*,[95] a cargo of opium, the subject-matter insured, stored on a wooden hulk was damaged by sea-water percolating through a leak. The Privy Council held that as the damage was not caused by perils of the seas, but by the decayed and infirm condition of the vessel, which was not an insured risk, the insurer could not be held responsible for the loss.

The latest comment on the subject was expressed by Lord Justice Croom-Johnson in *The Miss Jay Jay*[96] to the effect that:

'If at the start of a voyage a vessel is in such a state of general debility that the ordinary action of the winds and waves in any type of sea is bound to cause her damage and such action duly causes her damage, common-sense may dictate that the condition of the vessel rather than the action of the winds and waves shall be treated as the sole proximate cause of the damage.'

To conclude this discussion, reference should be made to the case of *Dudgeon v Pembroke*,[97] where Lord Coleridge, Chief Justice, who clearly had a deep and profound understanding of this branch of the law, summarised the position as thus:

'Seaworthiness and power to encounter ordinary perils are convertible terms. But the underwriter does not insure against ordinary perils; he indemnifies only against the extraordinary and unforeseen perils of the sea ... He does not insure against inherent vice, or – what is the same thing in other words – against ordinary perils.'

Voyage policies

Section 39(1) of the Act, relating to the implied warranty of seaworthiness, is applicable to all voyage policies regardless of the nature of the subject-matter insured. If the ship is unseaworthy 'at the commencement of the voyage', this would constitute a breach of the implied warranty of seaworthiness for which the insurer is automatically discharged from liability as from the date of breach. On such an occasion, it would not be necessary for a hulls insurer to show the cause of loss or, for that matter, that unseaworthiness caused the loss.[98] His defence would simply rest on the premise that a warranty has been breached and, consequently, he could not be made liable for any loss or damage however caused.[99]

95 [1912] AC 563, PC.

96 [1987] 1 Lloyd's Rep 32 at p 41, CA. Citing as authority *Fawcus v Sarsfield* (1856) 6 E & B 192; and *Wadsworth Lighterage & Coaling Co v Sea Insurance Co* (1929) 45 TLR 597, CA.

97 (1875) 1 QBD 96 at p 127.

98 Now automatically discharged from liability in the light of the ruling in *The Good Luck* [1991] 2 Lloyd's Rep 191, HL.

99 See s 33(3).

This matter was raised in *The Miss Jay Jay*[100] by Mr Justice Mustill who, with commendable clarity, analysed the relationship between perils of the seas and the defence of unseaworthiness in voyage and time policies. As his comments are particularly succinct and helpful, it is worthwhile reciting them in full:

'Under a voyage policy, the assured warrants that the vessel will be seaworthy *at the commencement of the voyage*. If the warranty is broken, any claim in respect of a casualty occurring during the voyage will inevitably fail, without the need for any complex analysis of the nature of a peril of the sea, or of the doctrine of causation.'

It is observed that these remarks are relevant only in relation to unseaworthiness constituting a breach of the implied warranty which is applicable only 'at the commencement of the voyage'. An insurer would not be able to plead breach of the implied warranty of seaworthiness as a defence, if the condition of unseaworthiness arises *after* the commencement of the voyage. On the occurrence of such an event, his plea can only rest on the ground that the unfit or infirm condition of the vessel caused the loss. In this regard, the court would have to determine whether perils of the seas or unseaworthiness was the proximate cause of the loss.

Time policies

According to Mr Justice Mustill, the defence of unseaworthiness is liable to raise problems of causation in time policies. He warned that:

'Certainly the absence of an implied warranty of seaworthiness, combined with the principle that a "peril of the seas" involves an element of fortuity, does create difficult problems in the field of causation ...'

The reasoning of the trial judge was as follows:[101]

'... when the vessel succumbs to debility, the claim fails, not because the loss is quite unattended by fortuity, but because it cannot be ascribed to the fortuitous action of the wind and waves.'

In the final analysis, the consideration is really one of fact: the court has to find, as it would have to in any other cause of action, the proximate cause of loss, be it perils of the seas, unseaworthiness, or any other cause. Even though *Miss Jay Jay* was found to be 'plainly' unseaworthy by reason of defects in design and construction, her physical condition did not cause the loss.[102]

In each case, the task is purely one of determining the proximate cause of loss: Inert or passive unseaworthiness is inconsequential. Bramwell B in

---

100 In the court of first instance [1965] 1 Lloyd's Rep 265 at p 270. In similar terms, Lord Coleridge CJ in *Dudgeon v Pembroke* (1874), 1 QBD 96 at p 128 said: 'In a voyage policy it is true the assured warrants power to encounter ordinary perils. Such perils, therefore, are not perils which, if they cause loss, give a right of recovery under such a policy, not merely because they are not within the words of the policy, but because a condition has not been complied with, *viz*, that the ship shall be fit to meet them.'

101 [1965] 1 Lloyd's Rep 265 at pp 270 and 271.

102 The assured had no idea that she was unseaworthy because the defects in design were latent. In *Frangos & Others v Sun Insurance Office Ltd* (1934) 49 Ll L Rep 354, the fact that the vessel was unseaworthy was held to be inconsequential because perils of the seas was held to have *proximately* caused the loss.

Thompson v Hopper[103] illustrated this point effectively with a series of rhetorical questions:

'How, on any theory of causation, can that [unseaworthiness] be a cause with or without which the effect would equally have happened? Suppose she had been struck by lightning while lying there, would the plaintiff have caused her loss by unseaworthiness?'

As perils of the seas was held the 'immediate'[104] cause, the loss was recoverable, in spite of the fact that the plaintiffs had knowingly, wilfully, and improperly sent the ship to sea in a condition which was dangerous to go to sea. The decisive consideration rested in the finding that unseaworthiness was in no sense a cause of the loss.[105]

A similar approach was adopted after the passing of the Act in *Willmott v General Accident Fire and Life Assurance Corpn Ltd*,[106] where the insured vessel, which sank in harbour during a strong gale, was held to have been lost by perils of the seas. The court relied heavily on the fact that, as there was evidence to the effect that the vessel could not have ridden out the sea even if she had been fit, it would be difficult to hold that her defective condition was in any way responsible for the loss.

The 'Unseaworthiness and Unfitness Exclusion Clause' of the ICC

The implied warranty of seaworthiness, declared in s 39(1) of the Act, has been expressly waived by cl 5.2 of the ICC. The position regarding seaworthiness (and unfitness) of the carrying ship is now governed by cl 5.1. By cl 5.1, any loss or damage arising from the unseaworthiness or unfitness of the vessel or craft is covered unless the 'Assured or their servants are privy to such seaworthiness or unfitness, at the time the subject-matter is loaded therein.'[107]

THE INSTITUTE CARGO CLAUSES

The ICC (A)

The ICC (A) is an all risks policy and, therefore, unlike the ICC (B) and (C), there is no specific provision enumerating the perils insured against. As the policy covers *all* risks of loss or of damage to the subject-matter insured, there is no need to provide a specific clause for perils of the seas. Provided that the loss does not fall within one of the exclusions listed in cll 4 to 7, a loss caused by a

---

103 On appeal, (1858) El Bl & El 1033 at p 1045. See also *Ballantyne v Mackinnon* (1896) 2 QB 455 at pp 460–461, CA.

104 It is to be noted that the last or 'immediate' cause of loss was the law applicable before the decision of *The Leyland Case* [1918] AC 350, HL.

105 Unseaworthiness here was not even a remote cause.

106 (1935) 53 Ll L Rep 156.

107 See Chapter 7.

peril of the seas is recoverable. Though a loss caused by an intentional act, such as scuttling, is not a loss caused by a 'peril of the seas', it is nonetheless a 'risk' in so far as a cargo owner who has taken out an all risks policy is concerned. And as there is no express exclusion clause prohibiting recovery for loss caused by deliberate damage or destruction of the subject-matter insured, other than the exclusion of wilful misconduct of the assured, such a loss should be recoverable.

The ICC (B) and (C)

A legal regime somewhat different from the conventional notion of 'perils of the seas' operates under the ICC (B) and (C). Both sets of Clauses have conspicuously avoided the use of the expression 'perils of the seas' which, over the years, has been awarded an almost precise meaning in law. In view of the fact that the draftsmen of the said Clauses have deliberately chosen not to adopt the term in any of their provisions, it is fair to say that 'perils of the seas', as commonly understood, is not an insured peril under them. Accordingly, the whole system of law associated with the concept should not, strictly speaking, apply or be allowed to apply in relation to these Clauses.

Instead of examining the conditions to which the ship is exposed to at sea, as is the case whenever 'perils of the seas' is pleaded as the cause of loss, cl 1.1.2 of the ICC (B) and (C) gives importance to certain events, namely, the act of being 'stranded, grounded, sunk, or capsized' for the purpose of determining liability. Under cl 1.1.4, 'collision or contact of vessel ... with any external object other than water' is another peril insured against in both sets of the Cargo Clauses. Whereas 'jettison or washing overboard' is a peril insured against under the ICC (B), only 'jettison' is insured under the ICC (C). 'Entry of sea lake or river water into vessel ...' is insured under the ICC (B), but not under (C).

But as these clauses are concerned with the 'entry of sea', 'water', 'collision'[108] and incidents of navigation such as 'stranding, grounding, sinking and capsizing', all of which are traditionally associated with the concept of 'perils of the seas', it would be appropriate to discuss them under this part.

'Stranded grounded sunk or capsized'

Clause 1.1.2 of the ICC (B) and (C) insure against any '... loss of or damage to the subject-matter insured reasonably attributable to vessel or craft being stranded grounded sunk or capsized'.

First, it is observed that 'craft' is included in this peril, and therefore any loss sustained by cargo whilst being conveyed in a lighter which has stranded is covered.[109] Secondly, it would appear that the scope of this clause is in one

---

108 Collision is a peril of the sea: *The Xantho*, (1887) 12 App Cas 503.

109 See *Hoffman & Another v Marshall* (1835) 2 Bing NC 383, where a particular average loss incurred by the stranding of a lighter conveying goods from ship to shore was held not recoverable: a stranding of craft was not mentioned in the common memorandum. *Cf The Thames & Mersey Marine Insurance Co v Pitts, Son & King* [1893] 1 QB 476, a policy which covered all risks in craft, and contained a warranty against particular average, unless, 'the ship or craft should be stranded'.

sense wider, but in another narrower, than the concept of 'perils of the seas'. This, it is hoped, will become apparent from the ensuing discussion.

The last four words of the above clause denote the requirement of simply the occurrence of an event or incident. On a strict interpretation, it would seem that a vessel, even if seriously damaged in a storm, but which does not actually strand, ground, sink or capsize, would not attract the operation of this clause. Under common law, however, such damage is, provided that the element of fortuity is satisfied, generally regarded as a loss caused by a peril of the seas.

The facts of *The Stranna*[110] are particularly suitable to illustrate the restrictive aspect of the clause. The vessel heeled temporarily as a result of the negligence of those involved with the loading of the ship. The loss of the cargo, which shot overboard, was held to have been occasioned by a 'peril of the seas'. Under the ICC (B) and (C), such a loss is unlikely to be considered as falling within the scope of cl 1.1.2 because the ship did not actually 'strand, ground, sink or capsize'. In this sense, its scope is narrower than 'perils of the seas'. Unless one of the events stipulated actually occurred, any loss of or damage to insured cargo caused by the mere rolling of a ship in a storm will not fall within the clause.

By not calling the risk insured against 'perils of the seas', the element of 'fortuity' – an essential feature of the concept – should be irrelevant. In the majority of cases, the element of fortuity would probably be satisfied. However, as pointed out earlier, a ship may strand, ground, sink or capsize as a result of causes other than perils of the seas: Unseaworthiness, wear and tear, wilful misconduct of the shipowner, barratry, fire, and negligence are but a few examples of causes which could lead to the stranding, grounding, sinking or capsizing of a ship. On a literal construction, cl 1.1.2 is not concerned with the cause of, but rather with the fact of, the stranding, grounding, sinking or capsizing of the ship. Provided that the loss does not fall within one of the exceptions listed in the general exclusions clause,[111] it would appear that it will be recoverable, regardless of whether a 'peril of the seas' or 'fortuity' plays a part.

To illustrate the converse, that the peril insured under cl 1.1.2 is wider in scope than the term 'perils of the seas', the situation encountered in *Magnus v Buttemer*[112] could be cited. Whilst in harbour, the ship took to the ground on the falling of the tide. The loss was held not to have been due to a peril of the seas, as nothing unusual or fortuitous happened. It is usual and natural for a ship in the ordinary course of a voyage to rise and fall with the tide. But because the ship did in fact strike the ground (but did not strand), it would not, in such a case, be difficult to argue that the loss falls within the named peril of 'grounding'. Under common law, stranding has always been regarded as a peril

110 [1938] 1 All ER 458, CA.

111 *Wadsworth Lighterage & Coaling Co Ltd v Sea Insurance Co Ltd* (1929) 45 TLR 597, CA is particularly relevant for this point. Though loss or damage caused by 'sinking' was a peril insured against, nevertheless, the insurers were held not liable: she had been sunk by the entry of sea water by reason of her general debility.

112 (1852) 11 CB 876.

of the seas, but not grounding occurring in the usual course of a voyage without the occasion of an extraordinary casualty. Under cl 1.1.2, there is no need to distinguish between the two, as both are risks insured against.

As the words 'perils of the seas' are not used, one could be tempted to argue that the element of fortuity is not an essential element for this insured risk. Furthermore, support for this could be drawn from the fact that the clause itself does not state that the events have to occur accidentally. Does this mean that if a ship is wilfully 'stranded grounded sunk or capsized' by the shipowner, the cargo owners would be able to claim for the loss of their cargo? In such a circumstance, the exclusion relating to 'deliberate damage or deliberate destruction of the subject-matter insured or any part thereof by the wrongful act of any person or persons' would apply. The words 'any person or persons' are wide enough to include the shipowner. Thus, it would appear that by reason of cl 4.7, such a loss is not recoverable under the ICC (B) and (C). These arguments do not apply to a claim for a loss under the ICC (A) because such a cover is for all risks; moreover, there is no exclusion for deliberate damage under the ICC (A).

In the light of this, the deletion of the Seaworthiness Admitted clause, in particular the second part of the clause,[113] which was specially framed in the aftermath of *Samuel v Dumas*[114] for the protection of an innocent cargo owner, is indeed most damaging to the cause of a cargo owner who has taken out the ICC (B) or (C). However, to overcome these problems he can now take out the Institute Malicious Damage Clause to cover for such a loss – in which case cl 4.7 would be deemed to be deleted from the policy, and he would also be insured for 'malicious acts vandalism or sabotage'.

'Stranded'

The common memorandum of the old SG policy,[115] – the equivalent of the current deductible clause (cl 12 of the ITCH(95)) – had used the word 'stranded' for the purpose of excepting certain losses from the 'free from average' warranty. The word 'stranded' is defined in r 14. But the definition therein provided was to be used in relation to the legal effects of a loss under the memorandum occasioned by the stranding of a ship, and not as to the factual meaning of the word.

There is, however, no scarcity of case law interpreting the meaning of the word 'stranded' used in relation to the memorandum.[116] One of the earliest cases to comment on the word is *Harman v Vaux*[117] where 'merely touching the

113 The relevant part of the clause read as follows: 'In the event of loss the Assured's right of recovery hereunder shall not be prejudiced by the fact that the loss may have been attributable to the wrongful act or misconduct of the shipowners or their servants, committed without the privity of the Assured.'

114 [1924] AC 431, HL.

115 'Corn, fish ... are warranted free from average, unless general, or the ship be stranded ...'. See Appendix 1.

116 There is no reason why the word 'stranded' when used in relation to describe a risk insured against should be given a different meaning from that under the memorandum.

117 (1813) 3 Camp 429.

ground' was held not to constitute a stranding. It was pointed out that, 'If the ship touches and runs, the circumstance is not to be regarded. There she is never in a quiescent state. But if she is forced ashore, or is driven on a bank and remains for any time upon the ground, this is stranding, without reference to the degree of damage she thereby sustains'.

The case of *M'Dougle v Royal Exchange Assurance Co*[118] provides the most comprehensive description of the term. A ship must be aground for an *appreciable* period of time before she can be considered to have 'stranded'. If it was merely a case of 'touch and go' without the ship remaining 'fixed' upon an obstructing object (whether rock, bank, reef, or of whatever other nature) for a period of time, that will not constitute a stranding.[119]

'Grounded'

A ship touching ground is generally regarded as a phenomenon which is expected to occur during the ordinary course of navigation. In the absence of some accidental occurrence or extraneous cause, any damage sustained by a ship as a result of an ordinary grounding is, as far as a hull policy is concerned, a loss by wear and tear of the subject-matter insured.[120] Whether the same rule should be applied to the ICC is, it is submitted, questionable. First, it is noted that the exception of 'wear and tear' refers to the subject-matter insured and not the wear and tear of the carrying ship.[121] Secondly, as pointed out earlier, in view of the fact that 'fortuity' is not a part of the equation of this risk, any loss or damage suffered by cargo caused by the ship touching ground should be recoverable regardless of whether the loss was or was not fortuitous.[122] And even if fortuity is to be considered as an essential requirement for this risk the loss is, as far as a cargo owner is concerned, fortuitous.

'Sunk or capsized'

The word 'sunk' is self-explanatory. This, perhaps, explains the absence of authority offering a definition of the word. In *Bryant and May v London*

---

118 (1816) 4 Camp 283; 4 M & S 503.

119 See also *Carruthers v Sydebotham* (1815) 4 M & S 77 where the 'tumbling over' of a ship was held to have stranded; *Baker v Towry* (1816) 1 Stark 436, where the vessel which struck a rock and remained fixed for about 20 minutes was held to have stranded; *Hearne v Edmunds* (1819) 1 Brod & B 381; *Rayner v Godmond* (1821) 5 B & Ald 225, where a vessel by accident, and not in the ordinary course of the voyage was rendered immovable on the strand; *Kingsford v Marshall* (1832) 8 Bing 458; *Corcoran v Gurney* (1853) 1 E & B 456; *De Mattos v Saunders* (1872) LR 7 C 570; and for a thorough study of case law on stranding, see *Letchford v Oldham* (1880) 5 QBD 538.

120 See *Wells v Hopwood* (1832) 3 B & Ad 20 at p 23 where it was accepted that stranding is a peril of the seas, but not 'where a ship takes the ground in the ordinary and usual course of navigation and management in a tidal river, upon the ebbing of the tide, or from natural deficiency of water, so that she may float again upon the flow of the tide'. See also *Popham & Willett v St Petersburg Insurance Co* (1904) 10 Com Cas 31; and *Magnus v Buttemer* (1852) 11 CB 876, where a ship taking ground during unloading on the natural falling and rising of the tide was also held to be a loss by wear and tear.

121 Clause 4.2 of the ICC (A), (B) and (C) refers to '... ordinary wear and tear of the subject-matter insured'.

122 Provided, of course, that the loss does not fall within one of the exclusions listed in the policy or the Act.

Assurance Corpn,[123] the matter was considered, albeit in a most superficial and unsatisfactory manner, in relation to a clause which warranted the insurer from liability from particular average 'unless the ship were stranded, sunk or burnt'. The fact (admitted by the assured) that the ship could have gone down further in the water seems to have influenced the jury in arriving at its decision that the ship had not sunk

'Capsized' is a relatively modern concept in marine insurance law and has not, as yet, been subjected to judicial scrutiny. In lay terms, it is used to describe a ship which has overturned or completely heeled over. A ship which has capsized does not necessarily mean that she has 'sunk'.[124]

'Collision or contact of vessel ... with any external object other than water'

Clause 1.1.4 of the ICC (B) and (C) cover 'collision or contact of vessel craft or conveyance with any external object other than water'.

As discussed earlier, the classic case of *The Xantho*[125] has ruled that a collision is a peril of the seas. Consequently any loss or damage sustained by cargo caused by a collision was under the old SG policy brought as a claim based on a peril of the seas. But as 'collision' is expressly stated as a peril insured against under cl 1.1.4, it now stands in its own right as a head of claim.[126] The fact that the vessel did not actually strand, ground, sink or capsize, as a result of the collision, is irrelevant.

Contact of a vessel with a lighthouse, iceberg, wreck, jetty, pier, cable, or any other external object 'other than water' is covered. The word 'external' has to be in relation to the ship: that is, an object outside the ship.[127] Thus, any damage sustained by cargo caused by contact of the cargo with the hold of the ship, parts of the ship, or her equipment, would not fall within the meaning of the words 'contact with any external object'.

The exception of 'contact with water' may, on first reading, appear to be incongruous and peculiar: in a marine adventure, contact of the vessel with water is an inevitable phenomenon. If this exception were not inserted, one could be tempted to argue that any damage brought about by the mere contact of the vessel with sea water – an 'external object' – which is a natural and obvious course of events, is covered. The exception is worded to exclude damage arising from the ordinary action of the sea coming into contact with the vessel. It is significant to note that it is the contact of the vessel – *not of the cargo* – with water which is not covered under the policy.

---

123 (1866) 2 TLR 591.

124 O'May, p 177, cited an American case, *Share & Triest Co v Fireman's Fund Insurance Co* (1919) 261 F 777, to illustrate the point that a barge which was towed upside down to port was held not to have 'sunk'.

125 (1887) 12 App Cas 503.

126 This necessarily means that any doubts as to the correctness of the decision of *The Xantho* (1887) 12 App Cas 503 can no be longer an issue.

127 In *Reischer v Borwich* [1894] 2 QB 548, CA, the ship was insured against damage from 'collision with any object ...'. The Court of Appeal held that damage sustained as a result of a collision with a snag was covered by the policy.

It is important to recall that damage to cargo caused by contact with 'derelict mines, torpedoes, bombs or other derelict weapons of war' is expressly excluded by the war exclusion clause (cl 6.3) of the ICC.[128]

'Jettison or washing overboard'

The ICC (B) provide coverage for loss of or damage to the subject-matter insured caused by 'jettison or washing overboard' whilst the ICC (C) insure only against a loss by 'jettison'. Jettison is also a peril insured under the old SG policy, the ITCH(95) and the IVCH(95).[129]

At a time of emergency, cargo is often thrown overboard for the safety of the whole adventure. The jettison of cargo, or part of a vessel's equipment or furniture, is commonly associated with general average; as such, the loss is invariably recovered as general average sacrifice.[130] In view of the fact that a peril of the seas is responsible for causing the ship to be at risk, it should not come as a surprise for such a claim to be declared upon as a loss by 'perils of the seas'.

As 'jettison' is insured as a separate and independent peril, it is not dependent upon other heads of claim for sustenance: it is neither confined to circumstances of general average nor to an action based on 'perils of the seas'.

The fundamental distinction between 'jettison' and 'washing overboard' lies in the fact that the former is a deliberate act committed by man throwing cargo overboard, whilst the latter is an act of the sea. A loss of cargo which falls overboard as a result of rolling in heavy sea or of a sudden listing of the ship does not constitute 'jettison'. The act of throwing the cargo overboard has to be performed by man, not by natural forces.

The word 'jettison', though unqualified, does not cover the throwing of cargo overboard *without lawful cause*. In *Butler v Wildman*,[131] Mr Justice Bayley remarked that:

'Jettison, in its largest sense, means any throwing overboard ... But its true meaning, in a policy of insurance, seems to me to be any casting over board *ex justa causa*.'

In the said case, a quantity of money was deliberately thrown overboard by the master of the vessel in order to prevent it falling into the hands of the enemy. The court held that in the circumstances of the case, the master was in fact under a 'duty' to throw the money overboard. The loss was held to be

---

128 This was specially inserted to clarify the situation encountered in *Costain-Blankevoort (UK) Dredging Co v Davenport, The Nassau Bay* [1979] 1 Lloyd's Rep 395 where 'contact with any fixed or floating object (other than a mine or torpedo)' was expressly excluded from the then fc and s warranty. The loss of the dredger, which exploded after having sucked up a number of Oerlikon shells (derelict weapons of war), was held not to fall within the warranty and was therefore recoverable as a marine risk. As the dredger was in contact with a 'fixed or floating object' which was neither a mine nor a torpedo, the marine insurers were held liable for the loss.

129 See cl 6.1.4 of the ITCH (95) and cl 4.1.4 of the IVCH(95). Jettison is a 'maritime peril': see s 3.

130 See s 66 & cl 2 of the ICC (B) and (C).

131 (1820) 3 B & Ald 398 at p 403.

recoverable within the perils of 'jettison', enemies, and the general words of 'all other losses and misfortunes'.

The case of *Taylor v Dunbar*[132] has often been cited as authority for establishing the rule that the loss of a cargo which has been jettisoned because it had become putrid as a result of delay in the voyage (brought upon by tempestuous weather) is not recoverable as a loss by the peril of 'jettison'. It is submitted that this is not an accurate interpretation of the outcome of case. The loss of the meat was not recoverable by reason of the fact that delay, which was not a peril insured against, and not jettison or a peril of the seas, was held to have proximately caused of loss.

Livestock and perishable cargoes are often thrown overboard *after* they have perished. In such a case, the act of jettison cannot be regarded as the cause of loss, as the loss had already been sustained before the cargo is jettisoned. Throwing overboard in such a case is simply an act of disposal of decayed property.

The act has to be justifiable. If not, it would, as far as the ICC (B) and (C) are concerned, fall within the exclusion of 'deliberate damage' under cl 4.7. There is no equivalent to cl 4.7 under the ICC (A). This and the fact that it is an all risks policy suggest that such a loss, though committed without lawful excuse, is recoverable. In so far as the innocent cargo owner is concerned, the loss is a 'risk' insured against.[133]

'Entry of sea lake or river water into vessel '

Loss or damage sustained to cargo caused by the entry of sea-water into the ship is recoverable under the ICC (B), but not (C). This clause may be invoked when a loss is caused by the mere entry of sea-water into the vessel without necessarily the occurrence of a casualty such as a 'stranding, grounding, sinking or capsizing', or a 'collision or contact of vessel ... with any external object'.

Damage caused by the *intentional* admission of sea-water in the ship would be governed, as in the case of cl 1.1.2, by the exception of deliberate damage or destruction under cl 4.7 of the ICC (B) and ICC(C).

The question which arises is whether the loss of or damage to cargo has to be caused by the physical contact of sea water with the cargo. Under common law, the position in relation to a cargo claim under 'perils of the seas' is clear. A few well-known cases have established the rule that actual contact with sea water is not an essential ingredient for an action under 'perils of the seas'. It is submitted that the same rule should apply to a claim under this clause.

In *Gabay v Lloyd*,[134] for example, horses, in consequence of the agitation of the ship in a storm, kicked and wounded each other so much so that they all died. This was held to be a loss by a peril of the seas.

In *Montoya and Others v The London Assurance Co*,[135] a cargo of hide and tobacco was shipped; the entry of sea water into the hold caused the hides to

---

132 (1869) LR 4 CP 206.

133 See *The Gaunt Case* [1921] 2 AC 41, HL.

134 (1825) 3 B & C 791; see also *Lawrence v Aberdein* (1821) 5 B & Ald 107.

135 (1851) 6 Exch 451, hereinafter referred to simply as *The Montoya Case*.

ferment. The putrefaction of the hides imparted an ill flavour and thereby damaged the tobacco. Though sea water did not come into contact with the tobacco, nonetheless it was held to be a loss by perils of the seas. The court applied the 'mischief' rule to arrive at its decision. In the words of Pollock CB:[136]

'As a general rule, where mischief arises from perils of the seas, and the natural and almost inevitable consequence of that mischief is to create further mischievous results, the underwriters in such case, are responsible for the further mischief so occasioned.'

That it was not necessary that the sea-water be in 'absolute contact' with the injured article was the view held by Martin B.

The case of *Cator v Great Western Insurance Co of New York*[137] may initially appear to be in conflict with the decision of *The Montoya Case*.[138] In *The Cator Case*, 449 packages out of 1,711 packages of teas shipped were damaged as a result of contact with sea-water. The remaining packages, which had not been in contact with sea-water, were sold for less than their market value by reason of the fact that buyers were suspicious that they might also be tainted. The court held that the assured could only recover in respect of the packages which had actually been in contact with sea-water, but not in respect of the loss of the remainder, which did not suffer any actual physical injury, but only injury to reputation.

The case should not be interpreted as having laid down the principle that actual physical contact of sea-water with the damaged cargo is essential for a loss to be recoverable as by a peril of the seas. Chief Justice Bovill took pains to stress that the cases are distinguishable on the ground that 'here there was no damage whatever to the [remaining] packages of teas, which arrived perfectly sound and untouched, and altogether unaffected by the sea-water'.[139] In contrast, in *The Montoya Case*, the tobacco itself was actually injured, as the stench had affected the flavour and consequently the value of the tobacco.

In the final analysis, it is in each case a question of causation and remoteness of damage: whether the damage arose proximately from sea-water has to be determined. Indirect, collateral and consequential liability arising from suspicion and prejudice are matters which are obviously too remote to be considered. By no stretch of imagination can they be described as the 'natural and almost inevitable consequence' created by the mischief of sea-water.

Loss caused by preventive action

Loss or damage sustained by the subject-matter insured due to action necessarily and reasonably taken to prevent a loss by a peril insured against is recoverable. Such a loss is considered as if it had been caused by that peril and is recoverable as such. For example, in *Canada Rice Mills Ltd v Union Marine and*

---

136 *Ibid*, at p 458. In similar vein, Platt B stated that, 'whatever mischief is occasioned to the cargo by the shipping of sea-water, is a loss occasioned by the perils of the seas, and that the insurers are liable to make the loss good'.

137 (1873) 8 LR 8 CP 552.

138 (1851) 6 Exch 451.

139 (1853) 8 LR 8 CP 552 at p 558.

General Insurance Co Ltd,[140] a cargo of rice which was damaged by heat caused by action taken to prevent the incursion of the sea was held recoverable as a loss by a peril of the seas. This is the first case in marine insurance to make a ruling on this point of law.[141] That the Privy Council had arrived at its conclusion by applying the rule of proximate cause established by *The Leyland Case*, (now contained in s 55) was made clear: the proximate cause of the loss of the rice was held to be perils of the seas and not the action taken to prevent the loss.[142]

B – FIRE AND EXPLOSION

'Fire' and 'explosion' are specifically insured under cl 6.1.2 of the ITCH(95), cl 4.1.2 of the IVCH(95]), and the ICC (B) and (C). As explosion is now specially named as an insured peril, the question which had so troubled the courts in the past as to whether it was included within the term 'fire' is now academic.[144] These perils are also covered under the ICC (A) by virtue of the policy being for all risks.

ACCIDENTAL, FORTUITOUS AND DELIBERATE FIRE

Unlike perils of the seas, violent theft and barratry, there is no statutory definition of 'fire'.[144] *Gordon v Rimmington*[145] is, perhaps, the first case to describe the limits or, more appropriately, the lack of limits of the peril of 'fire'. Lord Ellenborough said:

> '... if the ship is destroyed by fire, it is of no consequence whether this is occasioned by a common accident, or by lightning, or by an act done in duty to the state. Nor can it make any difference whether the ship is thus destroyed by third persons, subjects of the King, or by the captain and crew acting with loyalty and good faith. Fire is still the *causa causans*, and the loss is covered by the policy.'

---

140 [1941] AC 55 at p 76, PC.

141 The Privy Council had in fact applied the principle as laid down in carriage of goods by sea in *The Thrunscoe* [1897] P 301, where the facts were almost identical.

142 The same principle applies to the peril of 'fire'. *Canada Rice Mills Ltd v Union Marine and General Insurance Co Ltd* [1941] AC 55 approved the decision of *Stanley v Western Insurance Co* (1868) LR 3 Ex 71 at p 74, where a loss caused by spoiling goods by water, as a result of a necessary and bona fide attempt to put out a fire, was held to be a loss caused by fire and recoverable as such. With regard to a claim for a loss caused by preventive actions taken to prevent the spread of a fire, see below

143 Only 'fire' was insured under the old SG Policy. It is now no longer necessary to determine which one of the four types of loss associated with fire and explosion, categorised by Scrutton LJ in *Re Hooley Hill* [1920] 1 KB 257, CA, is the cause of loss. See also *Stanley v The Western Insurance Co* (1868) LR 3 Ex 71 at p 74.

144 Cases on fire such as *Pelly v Royal Exchange Assurance* (1757) 1 Burr 341; *Australian Agriculture Co v Saunders* (1875) LR 10 C. 668; *Niger Co v Guardian Assurance Co of Yorkshire Insurance Co* (1922), 13 Lloyd's Rep 75, HL; and *George Kallis v Success Insurance Ltd* [1985] 2 Lloyd's Rep 8, PC, were mainly concerned with the issue as to whether goods which were destroyed by fire breaking out at the warehouse at which they were stored were covered by a marine policy of insurance.

145 (1807) 1 Camp 123 at p 124.

In *The Alexion Hope*,[146] Lord Justice Lloyd of the Court of Appeal referred to 'fire' as one of the 'intermediate perils ... which can be caused either accidentally or deliberately, and are not subject to the limitation imposed on the meaning of perils of the seas by the definition in the Act'. He also pointed out that the term included '... as a matter of construction, a fire started deliberately by a stranger to the insurance'.[147] As a general rule, the term 'fire' is wide enough to cover all forms of fire, accidentally or deliberately started by any person or persons. But, as can be seen later, a general rule may be modified, qualified or even displaced by the Act (for example, s 55), or by an express term in the policy,[148] if so permitted by the Act.

Fire negligently started by the master or crew

The question as to whether a loss or damage sustained as a result of a fire which has been negligently started by the master or crew is covered by the peril of 'fire' was examined in *Busk v Royal Exchange Assurance Co*[149] by Mr Justice Bayley, who observed that:

'... there is no authority which says that the underwriters are not liable for a loss, the proximate cause of which is one of the enumerated risks, but the remote cause of which may be traced to the misconduct of the master and mariners ...'

Applying the same principle, the judge in *The Belle of Portugal*[150] held that the electrician's negligence did not defeat the plaintiffs' right of recovery under the policy.

These cases have demonstrated that if a fire has proximately caused a loss, any negligence committed by the master or crew is irrelevant. This rule is now encapsulated in s 55(2)(a). A shipowner could also rely on cl 6.2.2 of the ITCH(95)[151] and cl 4.2.2 of the IVCH(95) to claim for such a loss. However, if he wishes to plead that the loss was proximately caused by the 'negligence of Master Officers Crew or Pilots ...' he would have to satisfy the terms of the proviso to the said clause.[152]

A cargo owner who has insured his goods under the ICC (B) or (C) would plead cl 1.1.1 to claim for his loss. An assured who has subscribed to a policy under the ICC (A) would simply plead that it is covered by reason of the policy being for all risks.

---

146 [1988] 1 Lloyd's Rep 311 at p 317.

147 Cited with approval by Cresswell J in *National Justice Compania Naviera SA v Prudential Assurance Co Ltd, The Ikarian Reefer* [1993] 2 Lloyd's Rep 68 at p 71.

148 Eg, the General Exclusions clause of the ICC (A), (B) and (C), in particular, cl 4.7 of the ICC (B) and (C).

149 (1818) 2 B & Ald 73 at p 80.

150 [1970] 2 Lloyd's Rep 386, US Court of Appeals.

151 Previously cl 6.2.3 of the ITCH(83).

152 Commonly known as the Inchmaree clause, discussed in detail in Chapter 12.

Fire wilfully started by the master or crew

The position of a shipowner and an innocent mortgagee

Under the ITCH(95) and the IVCH(95), loss of or damage caused by a fire which has been deliberately started by the master or crew, without the connivance of the shipowner, is recoverable under both counts of 'fire' and 'barratry'.[153] Obviously, if the fire was started with the connivance of the shipowner, it would not constitute barratry because barratry is, by definition, an act committed 'to the prejudice of the shipowner'.[154] Neither would the shipowner be able to recover for a loss by fire, for being himself guilty of wilful misconduct, he would be barred from so doing by s 55(2)(a) of the Act.

Like a shipowner, a mortgagee, provided that he himself did not set the ship alight or was a party to the ship being set alight, would also be able to recover for a loss or damage caused by a barratrous fire. He has a right of claim whether he sues as an assignee (of the shipowner's policy) or as an original assured under his own hulls policy or the Institute Mortgagee's Interest Clauses.

The position of an innocent cargo owner

A cargo owner, however, is in a different position. Even though fire is specifically named[155] as a peril insured against under the ICC (B) and (C), nonetheless, he would not be able to recover by reason of cl 4.7. It is to be noted that, though s 55(2)(a) excuses not only negligence but also the misconduct of the master or crew, the provision is prefaced with the words, 'unless the policy otherwise provides'. The ICC (B) and (C) have, through cl 4.7, otherwise provided that loss or damage caused by 'deliberate damage to or deliberate destruction of the subject-matter insured or any part thereof by the wrongful act of *any* person or persons' is not covered.[156]

A master or crew member who deliberately starts a fire and thereby causes damage to the ship, clearly commits a barratrous act *vis-à-vis* the shipowner. However, in relation to a cargo owner who has taken out a policy in the form of either the ICC(B) or (C), his loss to cargo is not covered for two reasons, First barratry is not a peril insured against under the ICC (B) and (C) and, secondly, cl 4.7 excludes losses caused by deliberate damage or destruction. To insure himself against a loss caused by malicious damage, he would have to take out

---

153 See Chapter 12.

154 See r 11 of Rules of Construction.

155 Clause 1.1.1 of the ICC(B) & (C).

156 A cargo owner would probably argue that if the intention of the master or crew was to damage or destroy only the ship, and not the cargo, cl 4.7 does not apply. Though it is difficult to see how it is possible to destroy or inflict deliberate damage to a ship without causing damage to the cargo, each case has, of course, to be decided on its own facts. Whether such a strained and narrow interpretation – that it applies only to deliberate damage or destruction aimed directly at the cargo – may be placed on the clause is, it is submitted, doubtful, for the wording of cl 4.7 is wide in scope.

the Institute Malicious Damage Clause, the purpose of which is to 'delete' the exclusion contained in cl 4.7 of the ICC (B) and (C).[157]

The position under the ICC (A) is, however, different. First, as this is an all risks policy, and there is nothing in cl 4 to exclude a barratrous fire, the loss is recoverable. Secondly, support could be drawn from the fact that there is no equivalent to cl 4.7 of the ICC (B) and (C) in the ICC (A). Thirdly, a case could be made of the fact that the Institute Malicious Damage Clause is available to be used only with a policy, such as the ICC (B) and (C), which contains an exclusion for deliberate damage and deliberate destruction of the subject-matter insured. Admittedly indirect and somewhat tenuous, the inference which could be drawn from this is that the Institute Malicious Damage Clause is unnecessary in the case of the ICC (A) because such a loss is already covered by reason of the policy being for all risks. Provided that the assured cargo owner himself is not guilty of any wilful misconduct, a loss by fire, however caused, is a 'risk' insured under the ICC (A). The only defence which could be used by the underwriters to refute a claim for a loss caused by such a deliberate fire is that, though the policy may be for all risks, such a loss is not a risk but a certainty. Against this, it could be argued that though it is not a risk *vis-à-vis* the arsonist, it is a risk in so far as an innocent cargo owner is concerned.[158]

Fire negligently started by the assured

It is difficult to envisage how an assured such as a cargo owner or a mortgagee could negligently start a fire on board a ship. A shipowner, however, could negligently cause a fire if he was to act as master of the ship at the time of loss. Section 55(2)(a) denies an assured the right of recovery only if he was guilty of misconduct, but not negligence.

As early as 1898, in *Trinder Anderson & Co v Thames and Mersey Marine Insurance Co*,[159] Lord Justice Smith pointed out that:

'It is not disputed at the bar that negligence of an assured upon a fire policy, whereby the fire was occasioned which caused the loss, affords no defence to the insurer. Why so? Because loss by fire is what is insured against ...'

The law in relation to the peril of fire is in this regard the same as that relating to negligent navigation: the loss would still be considered as having

---

157 The relevant part of the Institute Malicious Damage Clause reads: '... it is hereby agreed that the exclusion 'deliberate damage to or deliberate destruction of the subject-matter insured or any part thereof by the wrongful act of any persons or persons is deemed to be deleted and further that this insurances loss of or damage to the subject matter caused by malicious acts vandalism or sabotage ...'.

158 It is important to be reminded of the fact that the ICC (A) do not insure against 'fire' or 'perils of the seas' as such, but against 'all risks'. Thus, provided that the event or casualty which caused the loss is a 'risk' *vis-à-vis* the cargo owner, the damage to or loss of his cargo is recoverable. In so far as the cargo owner is concerned, such a loss is not a certainty, but is unexpected and, therefore, a risk. Support for such a construction of the ICC (A) can be found in *London and Provincial Leather Process Ltd v Hudson* [1939] 3 All ER 857 at p 861, and *Nishina Trading Co Ltd v Chiyoda Fire and Marine Insurance Co Ltd* [1969] 2 All ER 776, discussed below.

159 [1898] 2 QB 114 at p 124, CA.

been proximately caused by perils of the seas even though the assured, who acting as master, was negligent in navigating the ship.

Fire wilfully started by the assured

It is pertinent to note that s 55(2)(a) excuses only the misconduct of the master or crew, but not that of the assured. Any loss brought about by the wilful misconduct of the assured, whether he be the shipowner, a cargo owner, or a mortgagee, is clearly excluded by s 55(2)(a).[160] The *modus operandi* of scuttling a ship by setting it on fire is a story which is all too familiar with the courts. The defence that the plaintiff has wilfully caused or connived at the destruction of his own vessel is invariably raised whenever fire is pleaded as the cause of loss: *Slattery v Mance*;[161] *The Alexion Hope*;[162] *Continental Illinois National Bank and Trust Co of Chicago and Xenofon Maritime SA v Alliance Assurance Co Ltd, The Captain Panagos DP*;[163] and *The Ikarian Reefer*[164] are classic examples. As these cases are primarily concerned with the issue of burden of proof, it would be more convenient to discuss them in detail later in another chapter.[165]

For the present purposes, it is adequate to cite the lucid remarks made by Mr Justice Salmon in *Slattery v Mance*:[166]

'Of course the plaintiff cannot recover if he was the person who fired the ship or was a party to the ship being fired. This result, however, does not depend on the construction of the word "fire" in the policy but on the well known principle of insurance law that no man can recover for a loss which he himself has deliberately and fraudulently caused. It is no more than an extension of the general principle that no man can take advantage of his own wrong.'

Fire wilfully started by a stranger

In *The Alexion Hope*,[167] Lord Justice Lloyd remarked that a fire would still be the proximate cause of loss even if it was deliberately started by a 'stranger' to the insurance. Any person who is not a party to the contract of insurance is a 'stranger'. The same principle, but worded in terms of the 'mischievous person', was proposed by Mr Justice Salmon in *Slattery v Mance*,[168] who pointed out that: 'The risk of fire insured against is quite obviously not confined to an accidental

---

160 And by cl 4.1 of all the ICC.

161 [1962] 1 All ER 525.

162 [1988] 1 Lloyd's Rep 311, CA.

163 [1989] 1 Lloyd's Rep 33, CA.

164 [1993] 2 Lloyd's Rep 69; [1995] 1 Lloyd's Rep 455, CA. It is observed that the Court of Appeal overturned the finding of Cresswell J, who held that the vessel was lost as a result of a peril of the seas, and that if she had been deliberately set on fire by a member of the crew, the defendants had failed to prove that the owners in any way consented or were privy to that action. After spending a great deal of time examining the evidence given by the master and the expert witnesses, the Court of Appeal found that the vessel was deliberately run aground with the consent of her owners. For a further discussion of this case, see Chapter 11.

165 For the law on the burden and standard of proof , see Chapter 11.

166 [1962] 1 All ER 525 at p 526, QBD.

167 [1988] 1 Lloyd's Rep 311, CA.

168 [1962] 1 All ER 525 at p 526, QBD.

fire. If the ship had been set alight by some mischievous person[169] without the plaintiff's connivance, there could be no doubt that the plaintiff would be entitled to recover'.[170]

The position of an innocent mortgagee

Whether a shipowner could be classed as a 'stranger' *vis-à-vis* a mortgagee was considered in *The Alexion Hope*,[171] where the plaintiffs were mortgagees suing under a mortgagees' interest policy issued by the defendant underwriters. The question raised was whether they could recover under the policy for a loss caused by a fire deliberately started by the shipowner.[172] The Court of Appeal (and Mr Justice Staughton in the court of first instance) held that so long as the plaintiffs-assured-mortgagee were not themselves guilty of any wilful misconduct, they were entitled to succeed under the policy. For all intents and purposes, the act of a shipowner is in relation to a mortgagee the act of a stranger. But, as discussed earlier, if the shipowner himself were to claim for the loss of his ship under his own policy of insurance, he would fail in his action.

It is necessary to recapitulate that the position would be different if a peril of the seas were to cause the loss.[173] To elicit this distinction, it would be helpful to recall the remarks made by Mr Justice Evans in *The Captain Panagos DP*[174] that: '... "Fire", unlike "perils of the sea", does not itself connote a fortuity ...'. As fortuity is not an essential ingredient for the peril of 'fire', it means that all forms of fire are covered regardless of whether they were started accidentally or deliberately. In terms of proof, the assured does not have to prove, as in the case of perils of the seas, that the loss is fortuitous. All that he has to show is that the loss is proximately caused by fire, or by precautionary actions taken to prevent the ignition of or the spread of a fire.[175]

To conclude this part of the discussion, it would be helpful to refer to the lucid and instructive summary – describing the position of a mortgagee – delivered by Lord Justice Purchas in *The Alexion Hope*:[176]

'... as between the mortgagee and the mortgagee's interest insurer, it matters not whether the fire was started by an independent agent, or whether by or with the connivance of the shipowner, the master or the crew, or indeed whether it occurred fortuitously.'

---

169 Eg, a vandal, a stowaway, or a stevedore who is not a crew member.

170 See also the remarks of Purchas LJ in *The Alexion Hope* [1988] 1 Lloyd's Rep 311 at p 322, CA.

171 *Ibid*.

172 It is to be noted that, with the exception of the wilful misconduct of the assured, there is no exclusion for deliberate damage or deliberate destruction of the subject-matter insured caused by the wrongful act of any person(s) under the ICC (A) and the Institute Hulls Clauses. *Cf* cl 4.7 of the ICC (B) and (C).

173 For a discussion of the position of a cargo owner or mortgagee in relation to a claim for a loss of loss by perils of the seas, see above.

174 [1986] 2 Lloyd's Rep 470 at p 511, QBD.

175 See below.

176 [1988] 1 Lloyd's Rep 311 at p 322, CA.

The position of an innocent cargo owner

A cargo-owner who takes out a policy of insurance under the ICC (B) or (C) is, unfortunately, not placed in the same position as an innocent mortgagee described above. Even though the fire may have been started by a stranger to the contract of insurance subscribed by the cargo owner, he is, for the same reason as in the case of fire wilfully started by master or crew, barred from recovery by cl 4.7. To insure himself against such a cause of loss, he would have to take up the Institute Malicious Damage Clause.

As regards the ICC (A), the reasoning given to the case of a fire wilfully started by the master or crew, discussed earlier, also applies here.

LOSS CAUSED BY PREVENTIVE ACTION

Cargo often suffer damage as a result of actions taken to prevent a loss (by a peril insured against) from taking place.[177] In *Symington and Co v Union Insurance Society of Canton Ltd*,[178] a cargo of cork was damaged when the local authorities, to prevent a fire from spreading, threw some of the cork into the sea and poured water on the rest of the cargo. Even though the cork was not actually on fire, the Court of Appeal was prepared to allow indemnity under the policy. In the words of Lord Justice Scrutton:[179]

'... there being a fire, goods are damaged not by the fire but by the water used to extinguish the fire, or the water used to prevent the fire from spreading, and that such damage can be claimed as a damage resulting from fire, and in my view, can be claimed under a marine policy as a damage caused by fire.'

Lord Justice Greer expressed his approval of the following remarks made by Kelly CB in *Stanley v Western Insurance Co*:[180] 'I agree that any loss resulting from an apparently necessary and *bona fide* effort to put out a fire ... every loss that clearly and proximately results, whether directly or indirectly, from the fire, is within the policy'. Though the case was concerned with a business premise policy of insurance, nevertheless, the principles in relation to insurance for fire were regarded as of general application.

To recover for such a loss, there has to be either:

* a fire actually in existence, if not in the cargo, near the cargo; or
* 'an actual existing state of peril of fire, and not merely a fear of fire'.[181]

A mere apprehension that a fire might break out is not sufficient proof. It has to be shown that the risk had begun to operate and there was danger.[182] This requirement that there be real and not imaginary danger stems also from

---

177 In relation to perils of the seas, see above.

178 (1928) 34 Com Cas 23, CA.

179 *Ibid*, at p 31.

180 (1868) LR 3 Ex 71 at p 74.

181 *Per* Gorell Barnes J, *The Knight of St Michael* [1898] P 30 at p 35.

182 See *Kacianoff v China Traders Insurance Co Ltd* [1914] 3 KB 1121, CA, where the risk of capture raised a similar question; *The Knight of St Michael* [1898] P 30; and *Butler v Wildman* (1820) 3 B & Ald 398, were referred to.

the fact that such a claim is often premised as a loss by way of general average.[183] Under the law of general average,[184] it is well established that not only must the loss be incurred for common safety, but that actual danger must exist at the time of loss.[185]

EXCEPTIONS OF LIABILITY

Even though an insurance against fire is wide and does not have, as in the case of 'perils of the seas', the element of fortuity as a component, it is nevertheless governed by the exceptions spelt out in s 55(2) and in the policy.[186] The exception of a loss caused by a fire deliberately started by an assured has already been discussed.[187] Another example which is of particular relevance to fire is when damage is caused to cargo by the inherent vice or nature of the subject-matter insured.

Inherent vice

The inherent vice of the subject-matter insured could be raised as a defence to a claim of loss by fire.[188] This was made clear in *Boyd v Dubois*,[189] where it was queried whether the fire which damaged a cargo of hemp (the subject-matter insured) was generated by the condition of the cargo. But as there was no proof that the fire had originated from the state of the hemp, the plaintiffs succeeded in their claim.

For the purpose of comparison, it is necessary to refer to *The Knight of St Michael*,[190] where the plaintiffs had effected insurances on freight upon the ship against 'fire and all other ... losses ...'. During the course of the voyage, a portion of a cargo of coal, which was over-heating and liable to combust and cause destruction to both ship and cargo, was discharged and sold entailing a consequent loss of freight. Though no part of the coal was ever actually on fire, it was reasonably obvious to all concerned that if the ship were allowed to continue on her direct voyage, both ship and cargo would almost certainly be destroyed by fire. As the subject-matter insured was not the cargo of coal, but freight, the question of 'inherent vice or nature of the subject-matter insured' could not arise in relation to such an insurance. Thus, the court held that the

---

183 See *Symington & Co v Union Insurance Society of Canton Ltd* (1928) 34 Com Cas 23 at p 31; and, in particular, *The Knight of St Michael* [1898] P 30, where a claim for a partial loss and for a general average loss of freight were discussed. See also *Papayanni & Jeromia v Grampian SS Co Ltd* (1896) Com Cas 448 where the ship was scuttled after a fire had broken out on board the ship; the scuttling of the ship under such circumstances was held to be a general average act.

184 General average in relation to the law of marine insurance is examined in Chapter 17.

185 Particularly relevant is *Watson v Firemen's Fund Insurance Co* [1922] 2 KB 355.

186 See cll 4 to 7 of the ICC (A), (B) and (C).

187 See above.

188 Clause 4.4 of the ICC (A), (B), and (C) excludes 'loss damage or expense caused by inherent vice or nature of the subject-matter insured'; see also s 55(2)(c).

189 (1811) 3 Camp 133.

190 [1898] p 30.

partial loss of freight was recoverable, if not as a loss by fire, as a loss *ejusdem generis* falling within the general words 'all other losses ...'.

C – VIOLENT THEFT BY PERSONS OUTSIDE THE VESSEL

DEFINITION OF THEFT

Clause 6.1.3 of the ITCH(95) and cl 4.1.3 of the IVCH(95) insure against theft in terms of 'violent theft by persons from outside the vessel'. Theft is not an insured risk under the ICC (B) and (C): to provide coverage for this peril, the assured must seek either an all risks policy in the form of the ICC (A) or the Institute Theft, Pilferage and Non-Delivery Clause.[191]

Rule 9 of the Rules for Construction of Policy states: 'The term "thieves" does not cover clandestine theft, or a theft committed by any one of the ship's company, whether crew or passengers'. The provision in the ITCH(95) and the IVCH(95) is in fact a restatement of this definition. There are essentially two components to the peril: first, it has to be 'violent', and secondly, it has to be committed by 'persons from outside the vessel'.

Violent theft

The exclusion of 'clandestine' theft from the statutory definition is now made clearer by the use of the word 'violent' in the Hulls Clauses. *La Fabrique de Produits Chimiques v Large*[192] is the authority for this requirement. Mr Justice Bailhache had no doubt that, 'in a policy of marine insurance pure and simple the risk of loss by thieves does not cover an ordinary clandestine theft, but only theft accompanied with violence'. In this case, the thieves had smashed two sets of doors in order to gain entry into a warehouse. The case is also an illustration of the fact that to constitute theft, there does not have to be an assault upon some person; violence to property will suffice. To exclude furtive theft, American policies employ the term 'assailing thieves' to describe the risk.

Athens Maritime Enterprises Corpn v Hellenic Mutual War Risks Association (Bermuda) Ltd, The Andreas Lemos[193] illustrates the point that the time at which violence is used or displayed is crucial. On this occasion, the gang armed only with knives used force to make good their escape. As the act of appropriation had already been completed when force or a threat of force was used, the theft was held to be clandestine in nature.[194] Any force or violence demonstrated after the crime had been accomplished does not constitute theft or, for that matter, a riot or piracy.

---

191 See Appendix 19.

192 [1923] 1 KB 203. As the requirement of violence was satisfied in this case, it was unnecessary for the judge to answer the question which he had raised as to whether in a warehouse to warehouse policy the word 'theft' is also to be limited to theft by violence. He felt inclined that it ought to be so limited.

193 [1982] 2 Lloyd's Rep 483.

194 As violence was not displayed before or during the commission of the crime, the acts of the gang did not constitute a riot, theft, or piracy.

Persons from outside the vessel

Even as early as 1874, the term theft had already acquired a certain fixed meaning in the law of marine insurance. In *Taylor v Liverpool and Great Western Steam Co*,[195] all the judges pointed out that even though the word 'theft' was ambiguous, as to policies of insurance it had always been associated with theft by 'persons outside the ship and not belonging to it'.

The most instructive case on the subject, however, is *Steinman & Co v Angier Line*,[196] where an excellent historical account was given by Lord Justice Bowen, who gave the rationale for the rule as follows:

'The broad principle of commercial law was and is that the ship, in the absence of express provision to the contrary, was liable to the cargo owner for losses occasioned by theft committed on board ... Insurers ... are not responsible for simple theft committed on board the vessel, because it is presumed with reason, that the accident has happened through some default of the captain or crew.'

The concept of 'theft' in marine insurance refers to acts of depredators outside the ship, the thief who 'breaks through and steals'.

Dishonest intention

Another requirement, which is not expressly spelled out, but is obviously implied in the statutory definition, is dishonest intention. In *Nishina Trading Co, Ltd v Chiyoda Fire and Marine Insurance Co Ltd*,[197] though the main issue was concerned with the peril of 'taking at sea',[198] the Court of Appeal nevertheless offered its opinion on the subject of theft, as the Institute Theft, Pilferage and Non-delivery Clause was incorporated into the policy. Lord Denning MR had no doubt that the act committed by the shipowner did not constitute theft. He pointed out that:[199]

'They only raised money on mortgage. They may have thought that they had some sort of lien on the goods ... but if they honestly believed it, they would not be guilty of "theft". No ordinary person would call it "theft" if they honestly thought they had a right to do it.'

All the judges agreed that dishonesty is an essential ingredient for the offence of theft; and 'unless dishonesty is shown, no one should be branded as having committed a theft'.

---

195 (1874) LR 9 QB 546 at p 551. A dispute in relation to an exception of theft under a bill of lading.

196 [1891] 1 QB 619, CA.

197 [1969] 2 All ER 776, CA.

198 The court's ruling that the act of master and owner in mortgaging the goods constituted 'taking at sea' is now overruled by the House of Lords in *The Salem* [1983] 1 Lloyd's Rep 342. It is now established beyond doubt that 'takings at sea' does not cover a 'wrongful misappropriation by a bailee, just as much as by anyone else'. In fact, 'any loss damage or expense arising from insolvency or financial default of the owners managers charterers or operators of the vessel' is now expressly excluded by cl 4.6 of the ICC (B) and (C). Such a loss would naturally be covered by an all risks policy.

199 [1969] 2 All ER 776 at p 779, CA.

INSTITUTE THEFT, PILFERAGE AND NON-DELIVERY CLAUSE

The above clause insures against not only violent, but also furtive theft, and non-delivery of cargo.[200] Cargo could, of course, just simply disappear without trace or explanation. In *Cleveland Twist Drill Co (GB) Ltd v Union Insurance of Canton*,[201] the plaintiff's claim was for the loss of a number of drills which they had shipped from London to New York. When the ship arrived in New York, six cases were missing, eight cases were completely empty and two were partly empty. The drills were insured under a marine policy with a clause covering all risks of theft and pilferage. As no force or violence was used, it was evident that the theft was secret, and on this Lord Justice Scrutton of the Court of Appeal noted that: 'It is one of the peculiarities of secret theft that you do not see it happen; and that being so, when the article has disappeared, how are you going to prove that it is a loss by theft as distinct from a loss by wrong delivery?'

In relation to cargo which has not been delivered at its proper destination or which has mysteriously disappeared, it is necessary in each case to explore the possibility of jettison, pilferage, and misdelivery as the cause of loss. A wrong delivery by accident, mistake or negligence is clearly not theft; and the mere fact that goods are not delivered, or are delivered to the wrong person, will not *per se* found a claim for theft. However, under the circumstances of the case, the court was able to make the inference that they were all pilfered by the same people.

In *Forestal Land, Timber and Railways Co Ltd v Rickards*,[202] Mr Justice Hilbery had occasion to examine the scope of the term 'non-delivery' appearing in a clause which insured against 'damage by hook, oil, theft, pilferage and non-delivery'. He pointed out that the term 'non-delivery' following enumerated perils insured against was not an insurance against an entirely new risk, but is limited by the context in which they are found. He said:

'Where such words occur in such a context, the insured need not prove loss by theft or pilferage. It is enough if he proves non-delivery and gives *prima facie* proof that the goods were not lost in any way other than by theft or pilferage.'

Under the current Institute Theft, Pilferage and Non-Delivery Clause, 'non-delivery' is confined to the entire package, and does not apply to a case where a part of the contents of a case or container is missing.

D – JETTISON

Very little need be said about jettison, save that cl 6.1.4 of the ITCH(95) and cl 4.1.4 of the IVCH(95) refer to the jettison of part of a vessel's equipment or furniture. The general principles discussed earlier in relation to cargo are also relevant here. As in the case of goods, a ship's equipment or furniture may have

---

200 See Appendix 19.
201 (1925) 23 Ll L Rep 50, CA.
202 [1940] 4 All ER 96 at p 110.

to be jettisoned at a time of danger, such a loss incurred by the shipowner is recoverable as a general average sacrifice.[203]

E – PIRACY

'Piracy' has, over the years, been shuttled back and forth – first, as an insured peril under marine risks, then under war risks, and has now reverted back to marine risks policies of insurance. It was an insured peril under the old SG policy, but was later excluded from it by the 'warranted free of capture and seizure clause'.[204] It is now specifically insured under cl 6.1.5 of the ITCH(95), cl 4.1.5 of the IVCH(95), and under the ICC (A) by reason of the policy being for all risks, but is not insured under the ICC (B) and (C). It is to be noted that 'piracy' (and barratry) is specifically *excepted* from the War Exclusion Clause (cl 24.2) of the ITCH(95) and cl 21.2 of the IVCH(95), and cl 6.2 of the ICC (A), but not from the War Exclusion Clause (cl 6.2) of the ICC (B) and (C) because it is unnecessary to do so.[205]

Definition of 'piracy'

Rule 8 of the Rules for Construction states that: 'The term "pirates" includes passengers who mutiny and rioters who attack the ship from the shore.' The definition, as suggested by the word 'includes', is by no means exhaustive, and case law has to be referred to for a fuller understanding of the concept.

Nesbitt v Lushington[206] is perhaps the earliest of cases to touch upon the subject of piracy. In a violent and unlawful manner, an armed mob attacked, boarded and arrested the ship, and forced the master to sell to them a cargo of corn at a reduced price. The court had no doubt that such an act was piratical in nature. In *Palmer v Naylor*,[207] a group of emigrants murdered the captain and part of the crew, and carried away the ship. The court held that 'the seizure of the vessel ... the taking her out of the possession and control of the master and crew, and diverting her from the voyage insured, were either direct acts of piracy or acts so entirely *ejusdem generis*, that ... they are clearly included within the general words at the end of the peril clause'.

The *locus classicus* on the subject is *Republic of Bolivia v Indemnity Mutual Marine Assurance Co Ltd*,[208] where the Court of Appeal, which had to interpret the meaning of the word 'piracy' – an insured peril under the policy in question – held that it meant 'piracy in a popular or business sense'. A pirate is a man who plunders 'indiscriminately for his own ends, and not a man who is simply

---

203 See cl 10 of the ITCH(95) and cl 8 of the IVCH(95) on the right of recovery for general average losses

204 Staughton J in *The Andreas Lemos* [1982] 2 Lloyd's Rep 483 at p 486, described this whole process by which war risks insurance was put together as 'convoluted'.

205 It is unnecessary to exclude piracy from the War Exclusion Clause of the ICC (B) and (C) because it is not an insured peril under these policies.

206 (1792) 4 TR 783.

207 (1854) 10 Ex 382.

208 [1909] 1 KB 785, CA.

operating against the property of a particular State for a public end ...'. Such a man would satisfy 'his personal greed or his personal vengeance by robbery or murder ...'. As the goods intended for the Bolivian government were seized by Brazilian malcontents who were acting purely for public and political motives, the loss was held not to have been caused by pirates.

Later, in *The Andreas Lemos*,[209] it was declared that force or the threat of force is an essential element of piracy, and this has to occur at such a time as to cause the loss. Another issue which concerned the court was whether piracy had to occur within territorial waters.[210]

On the first issue, Mr Justice Staughton held that 'theft without force or a threat of force is not piracy under a policy of marine insurance'. Furthermore, because the act of appropriation had been completed when the force or a threat of force was used, the loss was not a loss by piracy. He pointed out that, 'the very notion of piracy is inconsistent with clandestine theft'. In the light of the fact that both the perils of 'theft' and 'piracy' require the use of force, it may be difficult to distinguish between them. In fact, he acknowledged that 'most, if not all, pirates are also thieves, but the exclusion of the piracy from the marine cover by the fc & s clause refers to pirates who are thieves as well as any other pirates'.[211]

On the second question, as regards the place for the commission of the act, it was decided that there was no reason to limit piracy to acts outside territorial waters. In the context of marine insurance, 'if a ship is, in the ordinary meaning of the phrase, "at sea" ... or if the attack upon her could be described as "a maritime offence" ... then for the business purposes of a policy of insurance she is ... in a place where piracy can be committed'.

An assured who has subscribed to the ICC (B) or (C), but wishes to seek cover for 'piracy,' would have to do so specially, as neither the Institute War Clauses (Cargo) nor the Institute Strikes Clauses (Cargo) insure against 'piracy'.[212] To protect himself against 'piratical' theft (and all other types of theft), he would have to take up the Institute Theft, Pilferage and Non-delivery Clause.[213] And as for malicious damage caused by pirates and others, he would have to take up the Institute Malicious Damage Clause. In this regard, the scope of cover provided by the ICC (B) and (C) is clearly inadequate.

---

209 [1982] 2 Lloyd's Rep 483, QB.

210 For a definition of the crime of piracy under public international law, see In *Re Piracy Jure Gentium* (1934), 49 Ll L Rep 411, PC; [1934] AC 586.

211 Under the old SG policy, it was unnecessary to distinguish between the three forms of forcible robbery, as 'pirates, rovers and thieves' were all insured risks. Under the ITCH(95) and the IVCH(95), piracy and violent theft are both insured marine risks.

212 See Chapter 14.

213 See Appendix 19.

F – CONTACT WITH LAND CONVEYANCE, DOCK OR HARBOUR EQUIPMENT OR INSTALLATION

This was previously part of a larger provision which included 'contact with aircraft or similar objects, or objects falling therefrom' which has now been moved to cl 6.2.5 of the ITCH(95).[214] If it were not for this clause, any loss or damage sustained by a vessel which collides into fixtures or landed objects such as a 'land conveyance, dock or harbour equipment or installation' would not be recoverable, for strictly speaking, such risks are not maritime in character and therefore do not fall within the cover for perils of the seas nor the 3/4ths Collision Liability Clause. If a vessel were to incur damage by toppling over in a graving dock, repair yard, or by colliding into a dock wall, such a loss would be recoverable.[215]

G – EARTHQUAKE, VOLCANIC ERUPTION OR LIGHTNING

Clause 6.1.7 of the ITCH(95) and cl 4.1.7 of the IVCH(95) are self-explanatory, covering damage caused by earthquake, volcanic eruption or lightning. The cost of the removal of volcanic dust immediately comes to mind as a loss falling within this cover.

H – ACCIDENTS IN LOADING DISCHARGING OR SHIFTING OF CARGO OR FUEL

The above clause, now contained in cl 6.1.8 of the ITCH(95)[216] and cl 4.1.8 of the IVCH(95) was originally inserted as a result of the decision of *Stott (Baltic) Steamers Ltd v Marten and Others*,[217] where the House of Lords decided that damage caused to the hull, when a part of the crane's tackle broke causing the boiler, which was being lowered, to fall into the hold of the ship, was not recoverable as a loss by peril of the seas or a peril *ejusdem generis* therewith. As neither sea perils nor any of the then enumerated additional perils of the Inchmaree clause had caused the loss, it was held not indemnifiable. Having been moved from cl 6.2 of the ITCH(83) to cl 6.1 of the ITCH(95) means that it is now no longer subject to the due diligence proviso.

---

214 Discussed in Chapter 12.
215 See N Hudson, *The Institute Clauses* (1995, 2nd edn), p 91.
216 Previously cl 6.2.1 of the ITCH(83).
217 [1916] AC 304, HL.

I – ALL RISKS: THE ICC (A)

Meaning of 'all risks'

The Institute Cargo Clauses (A) provides, but with exceptions, coverage for 'all risks' of loss of or damage to the subject-matter insured.[218] The meaning of the term 'all risks' was examined in a number of cases,[219] the most notable of which are *Schloss Brothers v Stevens*,[220] and *The Gaunt Case*.[221] Before proceeding to discuss these authorities, it is relevant to note that the statutory and contractual exclusions have to be borne in mind when considering the scope of an 'all risks' or a similarly worded policy. Whether the wording of such a policy is clear and precise enough to override the statutory exceptions listed in s 55(2)(b) and (c),[222] – in which the Act itself allows exceptions to be made to the general rule – is a matter which has to be raised. To put the question in a more direct way: is an insurer of an 'all risks' cargo policy liable for 'ordinary wear and tear';[223] 'ordinary leakage and breakage';[224] 'inherent vice or nature of the subject-matter insured';[225] and for any loss proximately caused by delay,[226] or by rats or vermin?[227]

In the leading authority on the subject, *The Gaunt Case*, Lord Sumner's oft-cited explanation of the term is instructive. After giving examples of what would and would not fall within the concept of 'all risks', he said:[228]

'There are, of course, limits to "all risks". There are risks and risks insured against. Accordingly, the expression does not cover inherent vice or wear and tear or British capture. It covers a risk, not a certainty; it is something which happens to the subject-matter from without, not the natural behaviour of that

---

218 The exceptions are contained in cll 4, 5, 6 and 7.

219 See, eg, *Jacob v Gailler* (1902) 7 Com Cas 116 and *Theodorou v Chester* [1951] 1 Lloyd's Rep 204.

220 [1906] 2 KB 665.

221 [1921] 2 AC 41, HL.

222 Which are reproduced in cl 4 of all the ICC.

223 Discussed in Chapter 10,

224 See s 55(2)(b). An assured may, of course, by means of an express clause, insure specifically against ordinary leakage. In *Traders & General Insurance Association Ltd* (1921) 38 TLR, barrels of soya-bean oil were insured as 'To pay average, including the risks of leakage in excess of 2 per cent'; in *De Monchy v Phoenic Insurance Co of Hartford & Another* (1929) 34 Ll L Rep 201, turpentine was insured against 'Leakage from any cause in excess of 1 per cent'; and in *Dodwell & Co, Ltd v British Dominions General Insurance Co Ltd* (note) in [1955] 2 Lloyd's Rep 391, barrels of oil carried in one vessel were insured to include 'risks of leakage irrespective of FPA', and in another, to include '... risk of leakage from any cause whatever'. These cases, and the exception of loss by ordinary leakage, are discussed in Chapter 10.

225 See s 55(2)(c). An assured may insure specifically against a loss by inherent vice: see *Overseas Commodities Ltd v Style* [1958] 1 Lloyd's Rep 54, where the policy on a cargo of canned pork butts was insured against 'all risks of whatsoever nature and/or kind ... including inherent vice and hidden defect'. For a discussion of this case, and the exception of inherent vice, refer to Chapter 10.

226 Section 55(2)(b).

227 Section 55(2)(c).

228 [1921] 2 AC 41 at p 57, HL.

subject-matter, being what it is, in the circumstances under which it is carried. Nor is it a loss which the assured brings about by his own act, for then he has not merely exposed the goods to the chance of injury, he has injured them himself. Finally, the description of "all risks" does not alter the general law; only risks are covered which it is lawful to cover ...'

That ordinary wear and tear and inherent vice are not insured under an 'all risks' policy has been made patently clear in the above remarks. However, should a more pointed statement be required, the words of Lord Birkenhead LC may be referred to: '[all risks] cannot, of course, be held to cover all damage however caused, for such damage as is inevitable from ordinary wear and tear and inevitable depreciation is not within the policies.'

In *Schloss Brothers v Stevens*,[229] the insurance was against 'all risks by land and by water'. Mr Justice Walton, whose decision was approved by the Court of Appeal, was clear in his mind that 'effect must be given to the expression "all risks"' and that it 'must be read literally as meaning all risks whatsoever', but proceeded to say that it has also to be qualified:[230] '... they were intended to cover all losses by any accidental cause of any kind occurring during the transit' and that 'there must be a casualty'. On this occasion, the goods which were damaged as a result of exposure to damp, because of an abnormal delay in the transit arising from unusual and accidental causes, were held to be covered by the policy. The abnormal character of the delay rendered the loss fortuitous.[231]

Thus, it would appear that the exclusion under s 55(2)(b) and cl 4.5 excepting the insurer from liability for 'loss damage or expense proximately caused by delay' applies only to normal, but not unusual and abnormal delay.[232] The question as to whether the same holds true for abnormal or extraordinary (as opposed to ordinary) leakage and wear and tear has never been raised. There does not appear to be any reason why such exceptional losses should not be covered by an 'all risks' policy. Guidance on this point may be drawn from an observation made by Lord Sterndale of the Court of Appeal in *The Gaunt Case*:[233]

'... where the evidence shows damage quite exceptional and such as has never in a long experience been known to arise under normal conditions of such a transit, there is evidence of the existence of a casualty, or something accidental, and of a

---

229 [1906] 2 KB 665.

230 *Ibid*, at p 673.

231 See also *E D Sassoon & Co Ltd v Yorkshire Insurance Co* (1923) 16 Ll L Rep 129, CA.

232 The ancient cases of *Tatham v Hodgson* (1796) 6 Term Rep 656; *Taylor v Dunbar* (1869) LR 4 CP 206; and *Pink v Fleming* (1890) 25 QBD 396 on delay have to be read with caution. First, they were decided in the days when the last cause in point of time was prevalent; secondly, and more significantly, the policies under consideration were not for 'all risks' and as such, any loss caused by delay, normal or otherwise, was not covered. Unless delay is specifically enumerated as a peril insured against, the loss would not be recoverable however fortuitous the circumstances of the loss may be. This is also true of the ICC (B) & (C). See also *E D Sassoon & Co Ltd v Yorkshire Insurance Co* (1923) 16 Lloyd's Rep 129, CA, where 'mould or mildew', which was specifically insured against under the policy in question, was held to be the proximate cause of loss of the cigarettes which, after a considerable period of delay during transit, arrived badly mildewed.

233 (1920) 1 KB 903 at p 910, CA; [1921] 2 AC, HL.

danger or contingency which might or might not arise, although the particular nature of the casualty was not ascertained.'

A loss may be rendered fortuitous and accidental by reason of the *exceptional* or *extraordinary* character of the delay.

It is to be noted that even if a policy is worded as generously as to insure against 'all and every risk whatsoever however arising', the element of fortuity is still required. This was held to be so by the case of *London and Provincial Leather Process Ltd v Hudson*[234] where the insurance in question, though described as the 'widest possible policy', was nevertheless held to be bound by the requirement that the loss has to be *accidental*. Lord Justice Goddard said that, 'there must be in some form or another a casualty'. And as the firm to which the assured had sent their undressed skins of leather to be processed had become insolvent, and their affairs were taken over by an administrator according to German law, the assured was held to have been deprived by 'some unexpected acts of his property in the goods or of his possession of the goods'.[235]

The same is true, said the judge, with regard to embezzlement by an agent. Feeling somewhat uneasy about the fact that the act which had occasioned the loss was consciously and wilfully committed, and there was nothing therefore fortuitous or accidental about it, nonetheless, he rationalised (citing fire as an example) that in so far as the assured was concerned, the loss was unexpected and fortuitous.

In *F W Berk & Co v Style*,[236] a similar restrictive interpretation was also given to an almost identical clause in a policy insuring against 'all risks of loss and/or damage from whatsoever cause arising'. It was held not to be wide or clear enough to cover a loss, damage or expense proximately caused by inherent vice, a loss which can by no means be described as accidental or fortuitous.

It is evident from the above discussion that the critical and operative word is 'risks', which is commonly understood to be associated with fortuitous and accidental events. In the light of this, one has then to consider whether a clause which refrains from using the word 'risks', but simply states that the insurance covers 'all loss or damage howsoever caused' would be adequate to impose liability on an insurer for all losses, whether fortuitous or not. There is no authority directly in point. It is submitted that in each case, it is a question of interpretation and all the terms of the policy (including exceptions, if any) would have to be considered, together with the intention of the parties, commercial realities and practice. But one point which is clear is that no clause, however widely phrased, would be construed so as to allow an assured the right of recovery for a loss which he has brought about by his own wilful act of misconduct.[237]

---

234 [1939] 3 All ER 857 at p 861, KBD.

235 The skins were insured against 'all risks' during carriage; and while in Germany, against 'all and every risk whatsoever'.

236 [1955] 1 QB 180. Not surprisingly, a month later, in *Gee Garnham Ltd v Whittall* [1955] 2 Lloyd's Rep 562, a similar interpretation was given to the same clause by the same judge.

237 Note that s 55(2)(b) and (c), but not s 55(2)(a), expressly allow a policy to 'otherwise provide'. This necessarily means that the defence of wilful misconduct can never be overridden by an express term of a policy.

Misappropriation and conversion of cargo

In *Integrated Container Service Inc v British Traders Insurance Co Ltd*,[238] the subject-matter of insurance was containers which were leased to a firm that subsequently became bankrupt. Some of the containers belonging to the assured were lost, some damaged, and some were made the subject of a lien for port dues and warehouse charges. The Court of Appeal could 'see no reason why the risk of unlawful sale by a third party should be excluded. The plaintiffs effectively lose their containers whether the sale is lawful under a lien – port regulations or a process of judicial execution – or unlawful'. The loss caused as a consequence of the insolvency of the lessee of the containers was held to be covered by the 'all risks' policy. The same result was arrived at in *London and Provincial Leather Process Ltd v Hudson*[239] discussed earlier.

Insolvency and financial default of the owners, manager, charterers or operators of the vessel

Whilst on the subject of insolvency, the cases of *Nishina Trading Co Ltd v Chiyoda Fire and Marine Insurance Co Ltd (The Mandarin Star)*[240] and *The Salem*[241] deserve a mention. By reason of a financial dispute over the payment of charter hire, which were in arrears, between the owners and the charterers of *The Mandarin Star*, the shipowners converted cargo belonging to the assured to their own use. Such a circumstance was held to amount to a 'taking at sea'.[242] This decision has, for reasons which need not concern us here, been overruled by *The Salem*.[243] However, a comment which is particularly relevant to the present discussion is that made by Lord Roskill, who took the opportunity to point out that 'if cargo interests require cover for such a loss, they must seek either an "all risks" policy or some other appropriate form of cover'.[244] But as can be seen in the next paragraph, the truth of this statement was short-lived.

Today, an 'all risks' cover in the form of the ICC (A) would not be adequate to protect an assured for an event such as that which occurred in *The Mandarin Star*. It would now be ensnared by the exclusion of cl 4.6 which appears in all the ICC: the insurer is excepted from liability for 'loss damage or expense arising from insolvency and financial default of the owners managers charterers

238 [1984] 1 Lloyd's Rep 154 at p 162, CA. The second issue of the case on the recoverability of sue and labour charges is discussed in Chapter 17.

239 [1939] 3 All ER 857 at p 861, KBD.

240 [1969] 2 All ER 776, CA.

241 [1983] 1 Lloyd's Rep 342, HL.

242 The Court of Appeal had erroneously held that the peril of 'taking at sea' was not confined to capture and seizure, but covered a case of conversion of cargo provided that it was not committed 'in harbour, nor in port, but "at sea"'. The act of the shipowner could not be classified as 'theft' because, first, there was no violence involved, and secondly, there was no dishonest intention on the part of the shipowners.

243 [1983] 1 Lloyd's Rep 342 at p 349, HL. *The Salem* has re-established the rule that 'taking at sea' involved the deprivation of possession whether by seizure or capture of cargo: the peril did not include the risk of the shipowner misappropriating the goods.

244 It would now have to be an 'all risks' policy but without an exclusion such as cl 4.6 of the ICC (A), (B) and (C).

or operators of the vessel'. The objective of this clause is, obviously, to encourage cargo owners to use reputable, reliable and financially-sound carriers to transport their goods. The terms 'insolvency' and 'financial default' are indeed wide.[245] To be insolvent, one does not have to be declared a bankrupt: simply not being able to pay debts would suffice. The clause, as worded, does not apply to a case where the financial position of a third party is responsible for the loss.

Burden of proof

One of the main advantages of an 'all risks' cover, as opposed to an enumerated risks policy in the form of the ICC (B) and (C), relates to the important question of proof. In the words of Lord Sumner in *The Gaunt Case*:[246]

'When [the assured] avers loss by some risk coming within "all risks" ... he need only give evidence reasonably showing that the loss was due to a casualty, not to a certainty ... I do not think that he has to go further and pick up one of the multitude of risks covered, so as to show exactly how this loss was caused. If he did so, he would not bring it any the more within the policy.'

In similar vein, the Lord Chancellor said:[247]

'... the plaintiff discharges his special onus when he has proved that the loss was caused by some event covered by the general expression and he is not bound to go further and prove the exact nature of the accident or casualty which in fact occasioned his loss.'

Though the burden of proof is, in some respects, lighter than a policy of enumerated risks, this does not mean that the assured will not be required to disprove any counter theory that may be put forward by the insurer designed to show that the loss was not fortuitous, for example, wear and tear or inherent vice. In *Theodorou v Chester*,[248] the plaintiffs were required to rebut the insurer's defence that the damage sustained by the sponges were due to ordinary and normal risks of transit. As the plaintiffs were able to show that the cargo was damaged as a result of an accidental and extraneous cause, they succeeded in their action.

As regards the standard of proof, we are recently reminded by the case of *Fuerst Day Lawson v Orion Insurance Co Ltd*[249] that the standard is the same as in all civil actions, that of the balance of probabilities.

---

245 For a detailed account of the pressures put forward by the Federation of Commodity Associations to modify the wording of particular commodity contracts, and other aspects of the clause, see *O'May*, pp 201– 203.

246 [1921] 2 AC 41 at p 58, HL.

247 *Ibid*, at p 47.

248 [1951] 1 Lloyd's Rep 204.

249 [1980] 1 Lloyd's Rep 656.

CHAPTER 10

EXCLUDED LOSSES

INTRODUCTION

The main statutory excepted losses set out in s 55(2) of the Act are examined in this chapter. They are of particular relevance to the Institute Hulls Clauses for, unlike the ICC, the ITCH(95) and the IVCH(95) do not have a general exclusion clause. It is noted that all the statutory exclusions are expressly reiterated in the ICC.[1] The excluded losses in s 55(2) are of general application; and the opening phrase 'in particular' serves to reinforce the fact that they are specific examples flowing from the general rule spelt out in s 55(1) that an insurer is only liable for 'any loss proximately caused by a peril insured against, but ... he is not liable for any loss which is not proximately caused by a peril insured against'. With the exception of the defence of wilful misconduct under s 55(2)(a), all the other causes of loss, though expressly excluded by the said section, may nevertheless be insured under a policy. This is allowed by the opening words to s 55(2)(b) and (c), 'unless the policy otherwise provides'. This chapter will focus only on the main exceptions, namely, a loss 'attributable to the wilful misconduct of the assured'; a loss 'proximately caused by' delay;[2] ordinary wear and tear; ordinary leakage and breakage; and inherent vice or nature of the subject-matter insured.

WILFUL MISCONDUCT OF THE ASSURED

Section 55(2)(a) excepts an insurer from liability for any loss attributable to the wilful misconduct of the assured. Unlike the other exceptions contained in s 55(2), the parties cannot contract out of this exception. In other words, this statutory exception cannot be overridden. Though the section is of general application, nevertheless, each of the ICC has its own provision on the subject worded as follows: 'In no case shall this insurance cover loss damage or expense attributable to wilful misconduct of the Assured'.[3]

The rationale for the rule is based primarily on 'the general principle that no man can take advantage of his own wrong'.[4] Furthermore, the wilful character of the act takes the fortuitous element out of the cause of loss. Thus, such a cause cannot be regarded as a risk: that the purpose of insurance is to protect an assured against risks, perils and accidents, and not against deliberate and intentional acts which would inevitably result in the damage or destruction of the subject-matter insured, must be borne in mind at all times.[5]

---

1   Additional exclusions can be found in cl 4 of the ICC (A), (B) and (C).

2   For the legal effect of the words 'attributable to' and 'proximately caused by' in s 55(2)(a), see Chapter 8.

3   Note that the 'Assured' here is the cargo owner, not the shipowner.

4   *Per* Salmon J, *Slattery v Mance* [1962] 1 All ER 525 at p 526.

5   See the remarks made by Collins LJ in *Trinder, Anderson & Co v Thames Mersey Marine Insurance Co* [1898] 2 QB 114 at p 127, CA.

Meaning of 'wilful misconduct'

'Wilful misconduct' is not defined by the Act, but was a well-known concept in the law of marine insurance even before the passing of the said Act. The scuttling of a ship at the behest of her owner is, of course, the most obvious and common example of an act of wilful misconduct.[6] The success of any claim for a loss, whether based on fire, barratry or perils of the seas, is dependent upon the critical fact that the assured himself has not procured the loss of his own ship. Any evidence to the effect that the shipowner had connived at or was privy to the deliberate sinking of the vessel would be proof adequate for the defence of wilful misconduct. But, as 'ships are not cast away out of lightness of heart or sheer animal spirits',[7] the court must be satisfied that the allegation has been proved, if not to the highest criminal standard of beyond reasonable doubt, at least to a high standard of proof.[8]

The defence of wilful misconduct was frequently referred to as being embodied in the maxim *dolus circutu non purgatur*. In a well-known speech by Mr Justice Willes in *Thompson v Hopper*,[9] he said that:

'*Dolus* ... stands for *dolus malus*, and cannot mean simply any thing which may lead to the damage of another ... if *dolus*, in the sense in which it is used in the maxim, can exist independent of evil intention, it cannot so exist without either the violation of some legal duty, independent of contract, or the breach of a contract, express or implied between the parties.'[10]

Words such as 'fraud', 'wrong', 'a sinister intention', 'a breach of contract' and 'a violation of some legal duty' were employed by Mr Justice Willes to explain the meaning of the term.

In *The Trinder Case*,[11] Lord Justice Collins issued the caution that: 'Nothing short, therefore, of *dolus* in its proper sense will defeat the right of the assured to recover ...'. An element of wilfulness, a conscious determination to bring about a loss, and a design to achieve a certain result are the familiar characteristics of an act of wilful misconduct. Merely carrying out an act which is usual and expected under the contract of insurance is not such an act. For instance, in *Papadimitriou v Henderson*,[12] a case of an insurance on war risks, Lord Goddard

---

6   This explains the scarcity of judicial comment on the meaning of the term, and for the observation made by McPherson J in *Wood v Associated National Insurance Co Ltd* (1985) 1 Qd R 297 at p 301, CA that '... there is remarkably little authority on the meaning of the expression "wilful misconduct"'. Indeed, it is interesting to note that the dispute in nearly all the reported cases on wilful misconduct pleaded by the insurer as a defence to a claim by a shipowner for a loss either by perils of the seas, barratry, or fire was in relation to the question of the burden and standard of proof. These cases are fully discussed in Chapter 11.

7   *Per* Lord Sumner in *La Compania Martiartu v The Corpn of the Royal Exchange Assurance* (1924) 19 Ll L Rep 95 at p 99, CA. This case is discussed in greater depth in Chapter 11.

8   For a discussion on the standard of proof required in a case where wilful misconduct is pleaded as a defence to a claim for loss caused by perils of the seas, barratry, and fire, see Chapter 11.

9   In the Exchequer Chamber, (1858) El Bl & El 1038 at p 1047.

10   Cited with approval by Collins LJ in the Court of Appeal in *The Trinder Case* [1898] 2 QB 114 at p 127, CA.

11   *Ibid*, at p 128.

12   (1939) 64 Ll L Rep 345.

held that a shipowner was not guilty of wilful misconduct even if he had tried to proceed with his contract voyage in the presence of danger. 'There must always,' he said, 'be a risk of capture during a war, which is the very reason why shipowner and merchants insured against war risk'. The position, however, would be different if the shipowner had deliberately sent his ship forward in order to run a blockade. In such a circumstance, an inference may be drawn that 'he was not endeavouring to carry out the voyage, but was endeavouring to get his ship captured, and that, of course, would be wilful misconduct'.

The defence of wilful misconduct is invariably pleaded by an insurer in the form of an allegation that the shipowner was guilty of procuring and/or conniving at the casting away of the ship or setting her alight. It is employed as a means of rebutting the plaintiff's claim that the loss was fortuitous by reason of perils of the seas, or that it was barratrous by reason of the wilful and deliberate act by the master or crew.

If an act of wilful misconduct is proved, a loss by perils of the seas is automatically negated. According to Viscount Finlay in *Samuel v Dumas*:[13] 'Scuttling is not a peril of the sea; it is a peril of the wickedness of man.' The line between a negligent and a wilful act was drawn by Viscount Cave as follows: 'the expression "perils of the sea", while it may well include a loss by accidental collision or negligent navigation, cannot extend to a wilful and deliberate throwing away of a ship by those in charge of her'.[14]

Act of reckless disregard

The next question to be considered is whether an act which is something less than positive, less than intentional, such as an act of reckless disregard or indifference, can amount to 'wilful misconduct' within the meaning of the section. The facts of the Australian case of *Wood v Associated National Insurance Co Ltd*[15] are particularly suitable for this discussion, as the conduct of the shipowners, though flagrant, was short of wilful. They had sent the ship to sea knowing full well of the potential danger to which she was exposed, and that her crew (none of whom was competent) would not be able to cope in an emergency.

It is clear from the evidence that the plaintiffs had never intended by their conduct to cause the loss of the vessel. Nonetheless, their reckless disregard in exposing the vessel to the perils of navigation, knowing that it was not in a condition fit to encounter the possible risks, was held by the Australian Court of Appeal to constitute an act of 'wilful misconduct'. The facts of the case are indeed interesting, for they are capable of generating a host of related legal issues, namely, causation, unseaworthiness under a time policy, and the defence of wilful misconduct. Even though both wilful misconduct and

---

13 [1924] AC 431 at p 459. Also discussed in Chapter 9.

14 *Ibid*, at p 448. Scuttling, though not a peril of the seas, may nevertheless constitute barratry, if it be committed against the wishes of the owners. The concepts of barratry, perils of the seas and wilful misconduct are mutually exclusive.

15 (1985) 1 Qd R 297, hereinafter referred to as *The Wood Case*.

unseaworthiness were pleaded by the insurers in justification of their refusal to pay under the policy, the Court of Appeal, however, chose to analyse only the issue as to whether the behaviour of the assured amounted to 'wilful misconduct' under the Australian section corresponding to s 55(2)(a) of our Act.

Mr Justice McPherson, whose judgment was adopted by all the other judges, relied heavily on American cases to arrive at his decision. He had also, interestingly enough, cited with approval an obscure *obiter* remark made by Mr Justice Kennedy of the lower court in *The Trinder Case*[16] to the effect that the term 'wilful' included 'a reckless disregard of possible risks'. Furthermore, he thought that Lord Denning MR, from the remarks he had made in *The Eurysthenes*,[17] would find his interpretation of the section acceptable. To this collection of cases, Mr Justice McPherson could have also added a comment, in support of his decision, made in passing by Lord Wrenbury in *The Warilda*[18] that: '... if the loss occurs through the wilful negligence or wilful act of the assured', the loss would not be recoverable.

The Wood Case has brought within the concept of 'wilful misconduct' a lesser form of misbehaviour – that of 'an act of reckless disregard'. That the circumstances of the case played a significant role in influencing the decision of the court has to be emphasised. The conduct of two of the three owners was, to say the least, blatantly irresponsible and careless to the extreme; their behaviour was of total disregard for the safety of the lives of those on board. As the judge astutely observed, they would probably not have run the risk had she not been insured. Thus, the principle laid down has, it is submitted, to be read in its proper context. It has to be stressed that 'privity' alone is not sufficient to convert the act of an assured to one of wilful misconduct. All the facts of the case point to a very high degree of recklessness and indifference, so much so that it was more than just turning a blind eye.

There does not appear to be any authority in this country which has directly held that an act of reckless disregard *per se* amounts to wilful misconduct. Under British law, all the cases in relation to time policies were mainly concerned with s 39(5) of the Act, where just being 'privy' to sending an unseaworthy ship to sea is sufficient to disentitle the assured of his right to indemnity for any loss 'attributable to' such unseaworthiness.[19] As discussed earlier, s 39(5) is applicable only if such unseaworthiness to which the assured is privy to is a cause or 'forms part of the cause of the loss'.[20]

---

16 8 Asp MLC 300 at p 301; on appeal [1898] 2 QB 114, Kennedy J said: '... as regards conduct of the assured exonerating the underwriters ... the line is to be drawn as regards the conduct of the assured at acts which are done knowingly and wilfully, including in the term wilfully a reckless disregard of possible risks ...'.

17 *Compania Maritima San Basilio SA v Oceanus Mutual Underwriting Association (Bermuda) Ltd* [1977] 1 QB 49 at p 66, CA. But a close examination of the speech made by Lord Denning will reveal that this supposition is difficult to sustain, as his comments were all made in reference to the concept of 'privity' under s 39(5), and not to 'wilful misconduct' under s 55(2)(a).

18 *Attorney-General v Adelaide SS Co Ltd* [1923] AC 292 at p 308, HL.

19 See Chapters 7 & 8.

20 *Per* Roche J, *Cohen, Sons & Co v Standard Marine Insurance Co Ltd* (1925) 21 Ll L Rep 30.

As different terms are used in ss 39(5) and 55(2)(a), it is not unreasonable to assume that there must be a difference in meaning between 'privity' and 'wilful misconduct'.[21] In *The Eurysthenes*,[22] Lord Justice Roskill was content with merely stating that 'privity' was not the same as 'wilful misconduct'; whilst Lord Geoffrey Lane left the matter open with the remark that: 'In many cases, no doubt, sending a ship to sea knowing that it is unseaworthy will amount to wilful misconduct, but not necessarily so'. Regrettably, he did not elaborate when such an act would amount to wilful misconduct. However, Arnould, who shares the same view, has provided an illustration:[23]

> 'It is possible to conceive cases where, with the privity of the assured, an unseaworthy ship may be sent to sea without any real misconduct on his part. For instance, in time of war, a shipowner fearing an attack upon a naval port may very properly order his vessel to sail at once, although he knows that she is not perfectly seaworthy in all respects.'

The above remarks have clarified that the notions of privity, negligence, and wilful misconduct are separate, but may overlap in certain circumstances. They have been described by Arnould as follows: '... "privity" in this subsection [s 39(5)] does not necessarily carry any connotation of fault: it is not the same as negligence, nor is it the same as wilful misconduct, although in many cases sending to sea in an unseaworthy state may also be either negligence or misconduct'.

It has been said that if privity and wilful misconduct were to mean the same thing, then s 39(5) would be rendered otiose or superfluous. Such a deduction is not quite correct: s 39(5), which applies only to a time policy, is concerned with 'privity' of sending an unseaworthy ship to sea, whilst s 55(2)(a) on wilful misconduct is wider in scope. Section 55(2)(a) applies to all policies, and the ship which the assured has wilfully scuttled does not have to be unseaworthy. As was seen, in a time policy, the assured simply being 'privy' to the particular unseaworthiness which the loss is 'attributable to' is sufficient to free the insurer from liability for that loss. The result would still be same if he had wilfully cast away the ship whether she be seaworthy or not. In a voyage policy, however, both privity and unseaworthiness are immaterial in so far as s 55(2)(a) is concerned.

Sending a ship to sea merely with knowledge that the ship is unseaworthy is not in itself sufficient to amount to an act of wilful misconduct. Proof of something more – an intention to commit something sinister – is required to constitute wilful misconduct. The fact that a shipowner has knowledge of the vessel's condition of unseaworthiness does not necessarily mean that he intends to scuttle her, or intends to commit an act of wilful misconduct, when he sends her to sea in that state. Whether an inference could be drawn from a particular set of facts that the assured must have intended to commit an act wilful of misconduct is a question of fact to be determined by looking at all the

---

21 Section 55 applies to both voyage and time policies, whereas s 39(5) is relevant to a time policy only.

22 [1977] 1 QB 49 at p 66, CA.

23 Arnould, para 720, footnote 62.

circumstances of the case. The line between privity and wilful misconduct may in certain circumstances be difficult to draw, but nevertheless, it has to be drawn.

It is interesting to note that the trial Judge in *The Wood Case* held that the loss was attributable to both unseaworthiness *and* wilful misconduct,[24] whilst Mr Justice McPherson of the Court of Appeal came to the firm conclusion that the latter was the proximate cause of the loss.[25] This finding is by itself sufficient to dispose of the case, without the need for recourse to be made to s 39(5). Such a cause of loss is not a peril insured against.[26]

The Wood Case should not be construed as having established the rule that the act of knowingly sending an unseaworthy ship to sea *on its own* is sufficient to constitute wilful misconduct. More than just being 'privy' to the sending of an unseaworthy ship to sea is required, before such an act would be classified as wilful misconduct.

Wilful misconduct of 'the assured'

It has to be emphasised that it is the wilful misconduct only of the 'assured' which is relevant. This raises the interesting question of whether an act of wilful misconduct committed by the shipowner could affect the right of an innocent party (such as a mortgagee or a cargo owner), who is himself not guilty of any wilful misconduct, from recovering under a policy of insurance.[27] Starting from the premise that if the proximate cause of the loss is wilful misconduct, then, the loss, being not fortuitous, is not recoverable as a loss by a peril of the seas. This should logically hold true whether the claimant is the shipowner himself or any person, whether suing as original assured or as an assignee, claiming under a policy of marine insurance.

The innocent mortgagee

A mortgagee could bring an action against an insurer either as an original assured or as assignee of a policy. As an original assured, his rights against the insurer are separate and independent of those of the shipowner – as it is not a joint interest;[28] his claim cannot, as a rule, be tainted by the misconduct of

---

24 The trial judge held that loss was attributable to unseaworthiness *and* wilful misconduct; in consequence the insurer was entitled to rely on the defences provided by ss 39(5) and 55(2)(a). It is submitted that the decision of the trial judge is preferred; a sensible treatment was given to the facts of the case, and the conclusion drawn as regards the cause of the loss was fair and realistic. Also, the legal principles were accurately described and correctly applied.

25 In *Thompson v Hopper* (1858) El Bl & El 1038; 120 ER 796; a pre-statute case, the shipowner was alleged to have knowingly sent an unseaworthy ship to sea; but as neither unseaworthiness nor the act of wilful misconduct had occasioned the loss, and perils of the seas was held to have proximately caused the loss, the plaintiffs succeeded in their claim.

26 See *Samuel v Dumas* [1924] AC 431, HL, where the deliberate casting away of a ship was held not to be a peril of the sea and the loss was, therefore, not recoverable.

27 See cl 4.1 of the ICC (A), (B) and (C); and cl 4.7 of the ICC (B) and (C).

28 A mortgagee and a shipowner, though they may share the same policy, may be separately insured: see s 14(2), which allows any person having an interest in the subject-matter insured to insure on behalf of or for the benefit of other persons.

another party, in this case the shipowner. An assignee, on the other hand, is not in such a privileged position, as he does not have any better right than the assignor; this necessarily means that should the assignor be guilty of wilful misconduct, he would certainly be prevented from recovering under the policy.

In *Samuel v Dumas*,[29] however, the mortgagee's interest under the policy was separate, thus falling within the first of the above two classes. Thus his interest, which was original and not by way of assignment, should not be affected by the fraud of the shipowner. Viscount Finlay in the House of Lords raised the legal issue as thus:[30]

> 'Can the innocent mortgagee recover? Can he, in virtue of his independent right as one of the assured under the policy, claim in respect of the loss of the vessel? This will be found to resolve itself into the inquiry whether the loss can be considered as a loss by perils of the sea. It follows that, to recover, the mortgagee must show that the sinking of the vessel by the entrance of the sea which followed from the scuttling can be considered as a loss by perils of the sea, as otherwise, the loss would not be from a peril covered by the policy.'

As there was no loss in this case by a peril insured against, the appeal of the mortgagee must fail, regardless of the fact that he was a perfectly innocent party. As the loss was not *prima facie* recoverable under the policy that was the end of the matter: the fact that the mortgagees themselves, as an original assured, were not guilty of wilful misconduct is irrelevant. As a loss by scuttling is not a peril of the seas, any claimant, however pure and innocent, will not be able to recover under the standard hulls policy.[31]

For a different reason, the mortgagees in *Graham Joint Stock Shipping Co Ltd v Merchants Marine Insurance Co Ltd*[32] were also unable to claim under their policy. As they were suing as assignee, they had no better right than the assignor, the shipowners. As the shipowners themselves were unable to recover for their loss because they were guilty of wilful misconduct, the mortgagees, though innocent, were also barred from recovery.

Wilful misconduct of a co-owner

Whether an innocent owner could be prevented from recovering under a policy by an act of wilful misconduct committed by a co-owner was considered on appeal, though not seriously, in *The Wood Case*.[33] As only two of the Wood family were involved in the control and management of the ship, it was queried whether the loss could be said to be attributable to the wilful misconduct of all three so as to taint the claim of the third member of the family.

It is interesting to note that instead of saying that the loss was not caused by a peril insured against, as scuttling was not a loss by a peril of the seas,[34] the Appeal Court preferred to rely on the finding that the third assured, having left

29 [1924] AC 431, HL.
30 *Ibid*, at p 451.
31 *Cf* dissenting judgment of Lord Sumner, *ibid*, at p 470–471.
32 (1923) 17 Ll L Rep 44 and 241, HL.
33 (1985) 1 Qd R 297.
34 *Samuel v Dumas* [1924] AC 431 was neither cited by the lower court nor the Appeal Court.

the control of the vessel with his two co-owners, was 'not now in a position to urge that the loss was not attributable to any wilful misconduct on his own part'.[35] It is also observed that the Appeal Court had decided that the conduct of the two active members of the family was committed in the capacity of owners and not as master of the ship. The purpose of this was to clarify that their conduct was not barratrous in nature.[36]

The position in relation to a claim by a co-owner for a loss by barratry is different. The case of *Jones v Nicholson*[37] has established that an owner may recover for a loss caused by the barratrous act of a co-owner acting in the capacity as master of the insured ship. As a loss by barratry is *prima facie* recoverable, there is no reason why an innocent co-owner may not claim for a loss under a policy. Provided that he himself (as an 'assured') is not guilty of the want of due diligence, the loss is recoverable as a loss by barratry.[38]

As 'fortuity' is not an essential element for the peril of fire, an innocent co-owner is in the same position as an innocent single shipowner whose ship has been barratrously scuttled. Provided that the party who is bringing the action is himself not in any way involved in setting the ship on fire, he should be able to claim under the policy as a loss by fire.[39]

Proof of wilful misconduct

Discovery of ship's papers

A trilogy of cases – namely, *Astrovlanis Compania Naviera SA v The Linard, The Gold Sky*,[40] *Palamisto General Enterprises SA v Ocean Marine Insurance Co Ltd, The Dias*,[41] and *Probatina Shipping Co Ltd v Sun Insurance Office Ltd, The Sageorge*,[42] – all decided in the early 1970s, have clarified the legal position regarding the question of discovery of ship's papers. It would appear from the interesting historical account given by Lord Denning in *The Sageorge* that the practice in marine insurance as regards discovery before the delivery of defence is an exception to the general rule. The justification which was given for the rule was that, 'The underwriters have no means of knowing how a loss was caused: it occurs abroad and when the ship is entirely under the control of the assured'. It was thought that the practice, which arose 'in the days of sailing ships when underwriters in Lloyd's Coffee House were completely in the dark as to the loss of the vessel', was no longer appropriate 'in the present day when underwriters at Lloyd's get information as soon as anyone of a loss, and of the circumstances in which it occurred'.

---

35   (1985) 1 Qd R 297 at p 308.

36   *Westport Coal Co v McPhail* [1898] 2 QB 130 CA was cited by the Appeal Court.

37   (1854) 10 Exch 28 at p 38; see also *Westport Coal Co v McPhail*, *ibid*.

38   See the proviso to cl 6.2 of the ITCH(95). The law of barratry is discussed in Chapter 12.

39   Loss by fire is examined in Chapter 9.

40   [1972] 1 Lloyd's Rep 331, CA.

41   [1972] 2 Lloyd's Rep 60, CA.

42   [1974] 1 Lloyd's Rep 369, CA.

The Court of Appeal was prepared to continue with the practice of discovery because it may serve a useful purpose in scuttling cases, but it was not prepared to make the order automatically. In each case, 'The judge should see whether or not it is a proper case for it'. In other words, it is now in the discretion of the judge whether to make the order and whether to order a stay pending compliance with an order for ships papers. The right to an order for discovery and stay of proceedings are no longer automatic rights.[43]

Burden and standard of proof

It would appear that the burden and standard of proof for the defence of wilful misconduct vary according to the nature of the plaintiffs' claim. As the matter of wilful misconduct is generally pleaded as a defence, the burden of proof, as a general rule, lies with the defendants. The law, at least in relation to a loss caused by a peril of the seas and fire, is clear that the burden lies with the defendants. The plaintiffs would, of course, have to present a *prima facie* case that the loss was fortuitous in case of perils of the seas, and that there was a fire on board in the case of fire, before the defendants would be called upon to give their defence. At the end of the day, the plaintiffs have to prove only on the balance of probabilities that the loss was so caused. The defendants are not required, even if the defence of wilful misconduct was alleged as the cause of loss, to prove the criminal standard of beyond a reasonable doubt.[44]

However, in relation to a claim for loss by barratry, the legal position both as regards the burden and standard of proof is less clear. There are two points of view on the subject, which may be more conveniently discussed elsewhere.[45]

DELAY

Section 55(2)(b) states:

'Unless the policy otherwise provides, the insurer on ship or goods is not liable for any loss proximately caused by delay, although the delay be caused by a peril insured against.'

Like the other exceptions listed in s 55(2)(c),[46] it is possible for the parties to contract out of this statutory exception. Except for expenses payable by reason of cl 2 in relation to general average and salvage charges, the ICC has, through cl 4.5, retained this exception in almost identical terms.[47] As only ship and goods are mentioned, one could be tempted to deduce that the exception does not apply to freight; consequently, a freight insurer would be liable for loss of freight caused by delay. However, the loss of time clause, cll 15 and 11 of the Institute Time Clauses Freight and Institute Voyage Clauses Freight respectively,

---

43 See Orders 18, r 12 and 72, r 7 of the Rules of the Supreme Court.

44 See Chapter 11.

45 See Chapter 11.

46 But not s 55(2)(a).

47 Clause 4.5: In no case shall this insurance cover – loss damage or expense proximately caused by delay, even though the delay be caused by a risk insured against (except expenses payable under cl 2 above).

provides that: 'This insurance does not cover any claim consequent on loss of time whether arising from a peril of the sea or otherwise.' It is observed that 'consequent on' is used here, whereas 'proximately caused by' is used in s 55(2)(b).[48] The term 'proximately caused by' signifies that a loss remotely occasioned by delay is neither affected by s 55(2)(b) nor cl 4.5.

The principle embodied in the rule, in particular, that an insurer is not liable even though the delay may be caused by a peril insured against, may be traced to a very old case, *Tatham v Hodgson*,[49] where a cargo of slaves who were insured upon a voyage died as a result of insufficient provisions occasioned by extraordinary delay in the voyage because of bad weather. Even though perils of the seas, a peril insured against, was responsible for the delay, the court identified mortality by natural death as the proximate cause of loss. As public policy appears to be the underlying consideration for the decision of the court, this case cannot be said to be the true origin of the rule.[50]

The other two well-known cases on delay are *Taylor v Dunbar*[51] and *Pink v Fleming*.[52] In the case of the former, the loss, if it were decided under the Act, would fall squarely within the terms of s 55(2)(b). Delay was held the proximate cause for the loss of the cargo of meat which was rendered putrid during the voyage. That the delay was occasioned by tempestuous weather was not regarded as relevant. Justice Keating feared that if he were to allow recovery, he would be establishing a dangerous precedent, as many cargoes are necessarily affected by the voyage being delayed. In the second case, citing *Taylor v Dubar* with approval, the proximate cause was also held to be delay when the ship on which the goods were carried was damaged in a collision which caused her to be laid up for a considerable period of time for repairs.

The decision of *Pink v Fleming* has to be distinguished from that in *Schloss Brothers v Stevens*.[53] The fact that the latter was an all risks, as opposed to an enumerated risks, policy was crucial to the outcome of the case. Mr Justice Walton pointed out that, 'if all accidental causes of damage were included ... all that has to be considered is whether the damage that happened was the direct result of some such accidental cause, and I consider that it was the direct result of an accidental cause'. As the delay occasioned was abnormal and extraordinary, the loss was recoverable. This necessarily means that the word 'ordinary' has to be read into cl 4.5 of the ICC (A); in so far as the ICC (B) and (C) are concerned, being for enumerated perils, all forms of delay, whether ordinary or extraordinary are excepted.

---

48 For the meaning of the words 'consequent on', see Chapter 8.

49 (1796) 6 Term Rep 656.

50 The judges felt that if they were to hold the insurer liable for the loss, it would encourage the captains of slave ships to take an insufficient quantity of food for the sustenance of their slaves.

51 (1869) LR 4 CP 206.

52 (1890) 25 QBD 396, CA.

53 [1906] 2 KB 665.

ORDINARY WEAR AND TEAR

Section 55(2)(c) of the Act, which is of general application, declares that 'the insurer is not liable for ordinary wear and tear'.[54] However, its opening words allow exceptions to be made to the general rule; but so far there is no reported case where a policy is found to have departed from the general rule.[55] Each of the ICC, including the ICC (A), which insures against 'all risks', has its own express provision, cl 4.2, excepting the insurer from liability for such a loss. An insurer of the ITCH(95) and the IVCH(95), however, has to rely on s 55(2)(c) for this exclusion.

Why a loss caused by ordinary wear and tear is made an exception is not difficult to understand. If one were to begin with the premise that insurance is against risks, accidents and fortuitous events, the answer becomes obvious. A loss caused by ordinary wear and tear is not a risk, but an inevitable phenomenon: that things will deteriorate with age, usage, and wear and tear is a natural and expected progression of events. There is nothing fortuitous or accidental about a loss generated by general or inherent debility. And as the very essence of insurance is to insure against risks and not certainties, such a loss is not covered, not even in an all risks policy. Furthermore, it is expressly excluded by r 7 of the Rules for Construction from the notion of 'perils of the seas': loss or damage caused by the 'ordinary action of the winds' does not fall within the scope of 'perils of the seas'.[56]

Whether the adjective 'ordinary' qualifying 'wear and tear' adds anything to the definition has never been discussed. It was inserted, presumably for emphasis, in contradistinction with an 'extraordinary' loss. The answer to this query can be found in *Soya GmbH Mains Kommanditgesellschaft v White*,[57] where Lord Justice Donaldson of the Court of Appeal, who delivered a most comprehensive judgment on the subject of risk, referred to the following passage of an early edition of Arnould with approval:[58]

'No ship can navigate the ocean for any length of time, even under the most favourable circumstances, without suffering a certain degree of decay and diminution in value, which is generally comprised under the term wear and tear; for this, however considerable, if it arises merely from the ordinary operation of the usual casualties of the voyage, the underwriter is never liable: he is only liable when the damage sustained is something beyond this, and has been caused by the direct and violent operation of one of the perils insured against.'

---

54 Note that whereas no qualification is made in s 55(2)(c); the exception of delay in s 55(2)(b) is expressly stated to be applicable only to 'ship or goods'.

55 In *Wadsworth Lighterage & Coaling Co Ltd v Sea Insurance Co Ltd* (1929) 45 TLR 597, CA, Scrutton LJ thought that it would be 'very unusual' for a policy to provide otherwise.

56 In *Sassoon & Co v Western Assurance Co* [1912] AC 563, PC; water had percolated through a leak caused by the rotten condition of the hulk causing damage to a cargo of opium, the subject-matter insured. The Privy Council held that the loss sustained by the cargo was not caused by perils of the seas.

57 [1982] 1 Lloyd's Rep 136 at pp 145–146, CA; on appeal to the House of Lords [1983] 1 Lloyd's Rep 122, hereinafter referred to simply as *'The Soya Case'*.

58 Arnould, *Marine Insurance* (1857, 2nd edn), para 285.

Any abnormal or exceptional damage sustained under an enumerated risks policy will be recoverable only if the assured is able to refer to a specific peril as the proximate cause of loss. In an all risks policy, he need only give evidence to show that, by reason of the exceptional character of the damage, the loss must have arisen fortuitously.

In *Wadsworth Lighterage and Coaling Co Ltd v Sea Insurance Co Ltd*,[59] the assured failed to recover for the loss of a barge which, although she had been sunk by the entry of sea water, was held not to have been occasioned by perils of the seas: a loss by ordinary wear and tear was the proximate cause for her loss.

Recently, in *The Caribbean Sea*,[60] the subject of wear and tear was raised in relation to the Inchmaree clause. Before proceeding to discuss the legal implications, it would be helpful to be familiar with the relationship between s 55(2)(c) and the Inchmaree clause. Unless the policy otherwise provides, s 55(2)(c) excepts an insurer from liability for any loss or damage caused by 'ordinary wear and tear' and 'inherent vice or nature of the subject-matter insured'. In the case of the latter, cl 6.2.1 (the Inchmaree clause) of the ITCH(95)[61] and cl 4.2.1 of the IVCH(95) have 'otherwise provided' that, *inter alia*, 'loss of or damage to the subject-matter insured caused by ... any latent defect in the machinery or hull' is covered: whereas, any loss or damage caused by wear and tear is not so otherwise provided and is, consequently, not an insured risk. Mr Justice Goff, relying on the reasoning given by Mr Justice Scrutton in the case of *CJ Wills and Sons v The World Marine Insurance Co Ltd* confirmed that:[62] '... the balance of authority indicates that, where the defect is attributable to ordinary wear and tear, there can be no recovery under the Inchmaree clause.'

The distinction between 'ordinary wear and tear' and 'latent defect' in machinery or hull is of utmost importance: the former is an excluded loss, whilst the latter is an included loss. Thus, a judge has in each case to determine whether latent defect or ordinary wear and tear in machinery or hull is responsible for the loss. In *The Caribbean Sea*,[63] the defective design of a nozzle, which was held to constitute a latent defect,[64] developed fatigue cracks at a welded joint causing water to enter the ship which led to her sinking. The ship was clearly lost through a combination of causes, namely, latent defect and the ordinary working of the ship (which caused the fracture to open up before the end of her natural life).

The court had to apply the rule of *causa proxima* to determine whether latent defect or ordinary wear and tear was the proximate cause of the loss. Mr Justice Goff held that the former was the proximate cause of the loss, even though the

---

59   (1929) 45 TLR 597, CA.

60   [1980] 1 Lloyd's Rep 338, QBD.

61   Previously cl 6.2.3 of the ITCH(83).

62   (1911) *The Times*, 14 March; (Note) in [1980] 1 Lloyd's Rep 350.

63   [1980] 1 Lloyd's Rep 338, QBD. See also the recent case of *Promet Engineering (Singapore) Pte Ltd v Sturge and Others, The 'Nukila'* [1996] 1 Lloyd's Rep 85 QBD.

64   It would be more convenient and appropriate to examine this aspect of the case when the Inchmaree clause is discussed: see Chapter 12.

'defective design has had the effect that defects would inevitably develop in the ship as she traded'.[65] The claim was held recoverable under the Inchmaree clause.

The solution in each case lies in a proper determination of the proximate cause of the loss.[66]

In relation to cargo, ordinary wear and tear would refer to damage or loss sustained through the ordinary stresses and vicissitudes of the voyage: chafing, normal transit risks of dust and dirt combined with atmospheric moisture,[67] or any inevitable damage caused by the handling of the cargo would constitute ordinary wear and tear.

ORDINARY LEAKAGE AND BREAKAGE

An insurer is excepted from liability for ordinary leakage and breakage, a natural and inevitable loss, by s 55(2)(c) of the Act. Under cl 4.2 of the ICC, only 'ordinary' leakage is expressly excepted. Why 'breakage' has been omitted from the list is unclear; but this does not mean that it is not an excepted risk because, unless the policy otherwise provides, s 55(2)(c) prevails.

Ordinary leakage

The meaning of 'leakage' was considered in *De Monchy v Phoenic Insurance Co of Hartford & Another*,[68] where it was argued that to constitute 'leakage' there had to be visible signs or stains on the casks. This contention was swiftly dismissed by the House of Lords with the comment that leakage meant, 'any stealthy escape either through a small hole which might be discernible, or through the pores of the material of which the casks is composed'. The loss of the turpentine, which has the propensity to vaporise and disappear even through the material of sound and tight receptacles, without any external sign, was held to have been lost by leakage.

It is observed that only 'ordinary' leakage is excepted both by the Act and by the ICC. This necessarily means that if the loss is by exceptional leakage, it would be covered if it could be shown that it was accidentally or fortuitously

---

65 In *CJ Wills & Sons v The World Marine Insurance Co Ltd* (1911), *The Times*, 14 March; (Note) [1980] 1 Lloyd's Rep 350, a defective weld which resulted a link in a chain breaking was also held to have been caused by latent defect. The rationale was that if the weld had been sound and without the defect in the link, though worn, would have ample strength to stand the strain.

66 In *The Popi M* [1985] 2 Lloyd's Rep 1, HL, the decayed and deteriorated condition of the vessel was raised as a defence, but as the plaintiffs were unable to discharge the burden of proof which was on them and had left the court in doubt as to the cause of loss, the House had no choice but to apply the 'third alternative' to dismiss their claim. For a discussion of the 'third alternative' rule, see Chapter 11.

67 See *Theodorou v Chester* [1951] 1 Lloyd's Rep 204; and *Whiting v New Zealand Insurance Co Ltd* (1932) 44 Ll L Rep 179 at p 140, where Roche J said: 'Moist atmosphere is not an accident or peril that is covered. It is more or less a natural test or incident which the goods have to suffer and which underwriter has not insured against.'

68 (1929) 34 Ll L Rep 201.

caused.[69] Under the ICC (B) and (C), loss by leakage, whether ordinary or extraordinary is not recoverable.

Insurance against leakage

There are only two reported cases of leakage, both of which were concerned with the interpretation of a clause in the policy insuring specifically against leakage. In *Traders & General Insurance Association Ltd*,[70] barrels of soya-bean oil were insured as: 'To pay average, including the risks of leakage in excess of 2%'. During the voyage, the vessel met with stormy weather and a considerable quantity of oil was found to have been lost. Whether the word 'leakage' meant leakage as a peril insured against, or merely as a cause of loss from a peril insured against was the main issue in the case. Mr Justice Bailhache held that the word was intended to cover leakage *simpliciter*, that is, 'leakage of any kind whatever might be the cause of it. Leakage caused by a peril insured against would be covered in any event, and it would have been unnecessary to say anything about it'.

In *Dodwell & Co Ltd v British Dominions General Insurance Co Ltd*,[71] barrels of oil carried in *The Glenstrae* were insured to include 'risks of leakage irrespective of FPA', and in *The Protesilaus* to include 'risk of leakage from any cause whatever'. When the vessels arrived at their destinations, it was found that 12% and 60% of the oil carried in *The Glenstrae* and *The Protesilaus*, respectively, had leaked. In the case of the former, Mr Justice Bailhache held that the underwriters were liable only for the extra leakage due to sea transit. The normal or ordinary leakage of five%, out of the total of 12%, was deducted from the amount recoverable; the rationale being that these barrels would have leaked even if there had been no sea transit at all. As regards the 60% loss, no deduction was made: because of the comprehensive wording of the clause, the whole of the leakage to which these barrels of oil were subjected to was recoverable.

The above authorities illustrate that an express clause insuring simply against leakage would not be adequate to protect an assured for a loss caused by 'ordinary leakage'. To contract out of the statutory exception, a wide and comprehensive clause would have to be used.

Ordinary breakage

The risks of ordinary breakage of fragile goods is a matter which both parties to the contract of insurance must surely expect to occur during the course of even the most ordinary of voyages. As such a loss is inevitable it is, 'unless the policy otherwise provides' excepted in all the ICC.

---

69   Such as when the barrels or casks have been mishandled.
70   (1921) 38 TLR 94.
71   (Note) in [1955] 2 Lloyd's Rep 391.

In an all risks policy, however, breakages which are not ordinary in character would be covered if accidentally or fortuitously caused. Unlike the case of an enumerated risks policy, the assured does not have to prove that a specific peril had caused the loss. He is required only to give evidence reasonably showing that the loss was due to an accident or casualty. Provided that there is nothing 'ordinary' about the breakage, it would be recoverable.

INHERENT VICE OR NATURE

Section 55(2)(c) of the Act excepts an insurer from liability for 'inherent vice or nature of the subject-matter insured'. In relation to insurances on hulls and machinery the term 'latent defect' is generally employed to describe such a cause of loss, but with regard to cargo, the expression 'inherent vice' is more appropriate and has, therefore, been retained by cl 4.4 of all the ICC. As cover for a loss of or damage caused by latent defect in machinery or hull under the Inchmaree clause, cl 6.2.1 of the ITCH(95) and cl 4.2.1 of the IVCH(95) will be discussed later, this part will consider only insurance of cargo.

An examination of the meaning of the term 'inherent vice' has first to be undertaken before any worthwhile study of case law can be made regarding the interpretations of the clauses which have been inserted into policies providing for insurance against damage to or loss of cargo occasioned by inherent vice.

Meaning of 'inherent vice'

What constitutes inherent vice? To the layman, the matter is simple: the natural process of fruit decaying;[72] flax loaded in a damp condition which are liable spontaneously to combust; wine turning sour; hemp effervescing and generating a fire;[73] meat becoming putrid; flour heating; the growth of mould and mildew; and the heating sweating and spontaneous combustion of certain commodities are common examples of inherent vice. Decay, corruption and internal decomposition are its characteristics. But, as can be gleaned shortly, the legal aspects of the term has caused some confusion.

Though the leading authority on the subject is clearly *The Soya Case*,[74] it is best, because of the complexity of the issues raised, to reserve its discussion to a later stage. The distinction between an external and internal cause is the criterion used for the purpose of determining whether a loss has or has not been caused by inherent vice. To elicit this distinction, the two cases relating to the

---

72　In *Bradley v Federal Steam Navigation Co* (1927), 27 Ll L Rep 221 at p 395, Lord Sumner, in a case dealing with a contract of carriage, described the inherent nature of the apples which were damaged as follows: 'whether they were simply weaker than their neighbours or had some idiosyncrasy – was such that they could not stand the voyage. They decayed, not because of the ship or of the sea or of the route, but because they were apples which were not fit to make the voyage in an ordinary way.'

73　See *Boyd v Dubois* (1811) 3 Camp 133; as there was no proof that the fire had originated from the damaged state of the hemp, the plaintiffs were able to claim under the policy.

74　[1983] 1 Lloyd's Rep 122, HL.

growth of mould and mildew on cigarettes, namely, *Birds Cigarette Manufacturing Co Ltd v Rouse and Others*[75] and *Sassoon and Co v Yorkshire Insurance Co*[76] will first be discussed.

In *The Birds Cigarette Case*,[77] a cargo of cigarettes, which was insured, arrived badly mildewed; some of them were found to be soaking wet with salt water which obviously came from without – that is, an external source; and others were wet with fresh water, apparently as a result of evaporation from within. Mr Justice Bailhache without question allowed the claim for the former,[78] but the loss of the latter, which he had described as being foredoomed to mildew and were practically rendered useless by the excess of moisture that was in them, was held to have been caused by inherent vice and, therefore, not recoverable. But where sea water had accelerated the destruction of these cigarettes, he was prepared to apportion the loss.[79]

Following from this, the next logical question which arises is that considered in *The Sassoon Case*,[80] namely, whether a clause insuring against 'mould and mildew' *simpliciter* was adequate to render an insurer liable for a loss by mould and mildew, but resulting from inherent vice. In this case, cigarettes insured for damage by 'mould and mildew' arrived at its destination, after a considerable period of delay, badly mildewed. The plaintiffs claimed that as the loss was caused by mould and mildew, it was covered by the express term. The defendants, however, pleaded that the goods were not damaged by any peril insured against, but by inherent vice.

That mould and mildew are liable to grow on certain commodities for any number of reasons is common knowledge: it could be produced by an internal or an external cause. Lord Justice Atkin agreed with the trial judge, Mr Justice Roche, that a distinction had to be drawn between 'mould and mildew which are the result of inherent vice or the nature of the subject-matter of the insurance, and mould and mildew which are produced by some external fortuitous cause'.[81] On the evidence adduced, all the judges of the Court of Appeal were in agreement that the loss was 'the result of some fortuitous circumstance and not the result of inherent vice'. And as the defendants were unable to prove that the growth of mould and mildew was due to the inherent nature of the goods, judgment was awarded against them.

Lord Justice Atkin took the opportunity to query, even though it was unnecessary for him to do so because the loss in question was fortuitously

75   (1924) 19 Ll L Rep 301, KBD.

76   (1926) 16 Lloyd's Rep 129, CA, hereinafter referred as *The Sassoon Case*.

77   (1924) 19 Ll L Rep 301, KBD.

78   See also *Whiting v New Zealand Insurance Co Ltd* (1932) 44 Ll LRep 179, where the insurers were held liable for mould damage to paper hats which were incurred because of the wooden cases in which they were stored were left standing in pools of water on the quay: damage caused by moisture from without is not a loss by inherent vice.

79   The breach of the warranty ('warranted no complaints') in the warehouse policy was by itself sufficient to defeat the plaintiff's claim.

80   (1923) 16 Ll L Rep 129, CA.

81   *Ibid*, at p 133.

caused, whether the clause covered a loss by mould and mildew generated by inherent vice. He expressed his sentiments as follows:[82]

> 'It seems to me conceivable if apt words are used that an assured might cover a loss occasioned by mould which he does not know enough about ... In this particular case ... there is something to be said for the view that the intention of the parties here was to cover mould or mildew arising from *any cause whatsoever*;[83] that is one of the matters that was in the mind of the assured.'

It has, however, to be stressed that the above remarks were *obiter*. According to this interpretation, the said clause performed two functions: it not only provided insurance coverage for mould and mildew however caused, but also served to operate as an exception to the general rule as stated in s 55(2)(c) that an insurer is not liable for inherent vice or nature of the subject-matter insured.

Lord Justice Scrutton, however, appears to have held a different point of view. This can be ascertained from the following proposal he made:[84]

> '... if it could be shown that this mould or mildew resulted entirely from the condition of the goods when shipped and must have resulted from that condition when shipped as an ordinary incident of the voyage then the underwriters would not be liable ...'

It is interesting to note that Lord Justice Scrutton did not treat the clause as providing an exception to the general rule that an insurer is not liable for inherent vice. He regarded it only as a provision for insurance coverage against 'mould or mildew' fortuitously caused. His views on this matter are more clearly expressed when he later said:[85]

> '... where you are insuring against a specific peril and have to show some damage caused by that specific peril, subject to that reservation that if the peril results from the condition of the thing itself, the underwriter is relieved.'

The third Judge, Lord Justice Bankes, also could not resist the temptation of raising the question,[86] but he, however, stood firm in refusing to provide an answer.

The most recent case on the subject is *Noten BV v Harding*,[87] where mould and mildew was responsible for damage sustained by a cargo of gloves. The Court of Appeal reversed the factual finding of the trial judge,[88] and held that

---

82 *Ibid.*

83 Emphasis added. These words would include mould and mildew arising from inherent vice. But whether they would construed as being wide enough to cause an insurer to be liable for inevitable damage occasioned by inherent vice has to be considered.

84 (1923) 16 Ll L Rep 129 at p 132.

85 *Ibid.*

86 *Ibid*, at p 131. The question being whether: 'the assured are entitled to go so far as to say when an underwriter takes such a risk he cannot be held to contend the damage complained of was due to inherent vice'.

87 [1990] 2 Lloyd's Rep 283, CA.

88 [1989] 2 Lloyd's Rep 527, QB. The trial judge, Phillips J, found that the damage was caused by the dropping of water from a source external to the goods on to the goods; he did not consider significant the fact that the moisture originally came from the goods before being placed in the container, which moisture escaped only to fall back onto the goods later.

the loss was caused by inherent vice or nature of the subject-matter. The outcome was summarised by Lord Justice Bingham as follows:[89]

'The goods deteriorated as a result of their natural behaviour in the ordinary course of the contemplated voyage, without the intervention of any fortuitous external accident or casualty. The damage was caused because the goods were shipped wet ... I regard it as immaterial that the moisture travelled round the containers before doing the damage complained of.'

As the moisture originated from the gloves and not from other cargo or sources independent of any cargo, it was held that the gloves were in effect the author of their own misfortune.[90] Once again, the distinction between an internal and external cause was drawn.[91]

Lord Justice Bingham took the opportunity to comment on the phrase 'inherent vice or nature of the subject-matter insured'. He thought that the words 'inherent vice', taken alone, were misleading, implying some defect in the goods when, in fact, there was nothing defective about the gloves, only that its (hygroscopic) nature or natural behaviour was such that it will absorb moisture when placed in a humid atmosphere.

With the exception of The Sassoon Case, all the above cases, though they have to a certain extent defined the concept of inherent vice, have not, however touched upon the issues pertaining to inevitable damage caused by inherent vice, and the possibility of providing coverage therefor. These problems were exhaustively discussed in the Court of Appeal in The Soya Case[92] and The Sassoon Case. Lord Diplock, sitting in the House of Lords in the former case, acknowledged the existence of the problem, but preferred not to provide a solution, as it was unnecessary for him to do so.

For a proper understanding of the legal issues, it is necessary to set out the details of the facts of The Sassoon Case. A cargo of soya beans insured under an HSSC (Heat, Sweat and Spontaneous Combustion) policy arrived in a heated and deteriorated condition. At the risk of being tedious, it is necessary to mention that the House had accepted the fact that soya beans containing a moisture content of:

---

89   [1990] 2 Lloyd's Rep 283 at p 288, CA.

90   The remarks uttered by Wright J in C T Bowring & Co Ltd & Another v Amsterdam London Assurance Co Ltd (1930) 36 Ll L Rep 309 at p 327 KBD, to the effect that even if the moisture (which caused damage to a cargo of nuts) came from the particular cargo that were insured to later cause damage to itself, must now surely be considered as erroneous in the light of the Court of Appeal's ruling in Noten BV v Harding [1990] 2 Lloyd's Rep, 283. That Bingham LJ was not at all impressed with this comment made by Wright J can be seen at p 288 of his judgment. Whereas it was impossible in The Bowring Case to trace the origin of the moisture which damaged the nuts, it was in The Noten Case directly traceable to the insured cargo of gloves.

91   In Bowring & Co Ltd & Another v Amsterdam London Assurance Co Ltd , ibid, 'sweat' damage which resulted from an external cause was held to be covered; whereas the 'heating' damage due to the wet condition of the nuts (an internal cause) when shipped was not.

92   [1983] 1 Lloyd's Rep 122.

- more than 14% will inevitably deteriorate during the course of even a normal voyage;[93]
- between 14 and 12%, (for convenience referred to as the 'grey area') suffer a risk of heating, and may or may not deteriorate during the course of an ordinary voyage; and
- less than 12% are not at risk of heating[94]

The soya beans shipped fell within the 'grey area', and as nothing untoward happened during transit, the assured could not argue that the loss was caused by a casualty or by an external cause. Thus, the main issues were whether the loss was caused by inherent vice and, if so, whether it was covered by the HSSC policy.

'Inherent vice' was defined by Lord Diplock in general terms as:[95]

'... the risk of deterioration of the goods shipped as a result of their natural behaviour in the ordinary course of the contemplated voyage without the intervention of any fortuitous external accident or casualty.'

The operative word in this definition is 'risk'. He then continued to say:

'Prima facie, this risk is excluded from a policy of marine insurance unless the policy otherwise provides ... and the question of construction ... is whether the standard HSSC policy does otherwise provide.'

The House had no problem whatsoever in arriving at the conclusion that the loss was caused by inherent vice and that the standard HSSC policy did 'otherwise provide', so as to perform the function of displacing the prima facie rule laid down in s 55(2)(c) that the insurer is not liable for 'inherent vice or nature of the subject-matter insured'. The insurers were accordingly held liable for the loss.

The above enunciation of the law appears to be simple enough, but leaves unanswered an important question relating to losses falling within the first category, namely, where the occurrence of a loss is not a risk or a casualty, but a certainty. What would have been the outcome of the case 'if, unknown to the assured, the moisture content of the beans on shipment had been so high as to make such deterioration inevitable'?

Known certainty of loss

Before the decision of The Soya Case,[96] it was at one time thought that 'inherent vice' pertained only to damage or loss (of cargo) which were bound to occur by

---

93 According to Waller LJ, underwriters would not carry a risk when the moisture is over 14%, because 'it would not be a risk it would be a certainty'.

94 As no risk is involved, the shipper as a matter of common sense would not insure for such a loss.

95 [1983] 1 Lloyd's Rep 122 at p 126, HL.

96 Certain remarks made by some of the Law Lords in The Gaunt Case [1921] 2 AC 41 at p 57, have brought about this misconception of the law: Lord Sumner, for instance, had tarred inherent vice with the same brush as certainty when he stated that the assured need only give evidence reasonably showing that the loss arose due to 'a casualty, not a certainty or to inherent vice or wear and tear'. See Waller LJ's interpretation of this statement in the Court of Appeal in The Soya Case [1982] 1 Lloyd's Rep 136 at p 141.

reason of the vice or nature of the subject-matter. Lord Justice Waller of the Court of Appeal noted that:[97] 'In some of the authorities inherent vice is used to describe a certainty and is used in contradistinction to a risk'. Inherent vice was regarded as something which will inevitably cause damage. The understanding was that because such a loss was a certainty, no risk was involved and, therefore, it could not be covered by a policy of insurance, and was hence expressly excluded by s 55(2)(c). This had led the trial judge, Mr Justice Lloyd, to describe 'the relationship between inherent vice and inevitably of damage, as defences to a claim under the Marine Insurance Act' as 'elusive'.[98] Equally sharp and accurate in his observation was Lord Justice Donaldson when he expressed surprise in *The Soya Case* that the subject had never really been considered 'in isolation'. 'Cross currents', he said, 'which may or may not be relevant to the defence of inherent vice *simpliciter*' have caused the matter to be pushed aside.[99]

That there are essentially two types of inherent vice is deducible from the judgments of all the Law Lords. One type of inherent vice will inevitably cause a loss, rendering the loss a certainty; and the other belongs to a class (the grey area) which may or may not cause damage to or loss of the subject matter insured. The latter does not create problems: such a risk[100] is as a general rule excluded by s 55(2)(c), and whether the general rule is to be displaced is in each case a question of construction of the terms of the policy. Whether the former, described as a 'known certainty of loss' is insurable will now be considered.

Section 55(2)(c) itself, through its introductory words 'unless the policy otherwise provides', allows insurance against loss or damage by inherent vice. But whether insurance against a loss by inherent vice of that specie which is bound to occur, that is, against a certainty of loss, is contemplated by these opening words is indeed an interesting legal point.

In the Court of Appeal, Lord Justice Waller in *The Soya Case* and Lord Justice Scrutton in *The Sassoon Case*[101] held the view that insurance coverage for losses of known certainty was not possible. Disapproval was expressed by Lord Justice Waller as follows:[102]

'If inherent vice means something that will certainly happen, it is not a risk but a certainty. It is therefore not something against which insurance can be taken. If, however, it is a cause of damage which may or may not happen because of conditions within the substance itself, then it will be excluded unless the risk is specifically covered.'

The basis of his objections lies in the rudimentary principle of insurance law that a contract of insurance is against risks, and not certainties. If one were to

---

97   [1982] 1 Lloyd's Rep 136 at p 141, CA.

98   [1980] 1 Lloyd's Rep 491.

99   [1982] 1 Lloyd's Rep 136 at p 144, CA.

100 Such a risk of loss by inherent vice was described by Bingham LJ in *The Noten Case* [1990] 2 Lloyd's Rep 283 at p 287, CA, as capable of being 'as capricious in its incidence as damage caused by perils of the seas'.

101 (1926) 16 Lloyd's Rep 129 at p 130, CA.

102 [1982] 1 Lloyd's Rep 136 at p 141, CA. The passage from the judgment of Atkin LJ, cited earlier, seems to imply that only insurance where there is an element of risk may be undertaken.

return to basics and cite the remarks of Chief Justice Cockburn in *Paterson v Harris*, the premise becomes clear:[103]

'But the purpose of insurance is to afford protection against contingencies and dangers which may or may not occur; it cannot properly apply to a case where the loss or injury must inevitably take place in the ordinary course of things.'

The word 'inevitably', followed by 'ordinary course of things', clearly refers to a loss which in the ordinary course of events is bound to arise.

Lord Justice Donaldson in *The Soya Case* was, however, more liberal in his thinking; he was prepared to accept the fact that it was possible to insure against a 'known certainty', but as this was highly unlikely to occur in practice, he was not too perturbed by it. He stated:[104]

'This is not to say that known certain losses cannot be the subject matter of a contract of indemnity; merely that very clear words will be required since it is highly improbable contract for someone to make in the course of his business as an insurance underwriter.'

It would appear from the above discussion that the problem is reducible into three categories, two of which were raised by Lord Justice Donaldson,[105] and the third by Mr Justice Lloyd (in the court of first instance) in *The Soya Case*:[106]

- If the certainty of the loss is known to the assured and not to the underwriter, there is really no problem, as other defences such as non-disclosure and even fraud, will be available to the underwriter.

- Where the certainty of loss is known to both parties, it would be difficult, except on the principle that insurance is about risks and not known certainties, to refuse exemption for loss.

- Where the certainty of loss is unknown to both parties, it would be difficult to argue that no risk is involved. Mr Justice Lloyd could see no reason why this could not be the legitimate subject-matter of a policy of insurance.[107] As its propensity to self-destruct is unknown to both parties, it could be argued that that in itself is an element of risk. But whether known or unknown to the parties, a loss resulting from inherent vice is, unless specifically insured against, not recoverable.

In conclusion, it is fair to say that the legal position in this regard is unclear. Two schools of thought have been offered by the Court of Appeal, and the House of Lords has refused to provide an answer to the question. But the preponderant view seems to be that if the vice or nature of the cargo is such that it will in the course of time inevitably destroy or damage itself, the loss is not fortuitous but a certainty, and would not, therefore, be recoverable under any of the standard forms of cargo policies of insurance, not even one for 'all risks'.

---

103 (1861) 1 B & S 336, where the claim was made for injury to a cable by sea water. The defence raised was that the damage was the necessary result of the exposure of the cable to sea water. This passage was cited with approval by Bankes LJ in *The Sassoon Case* (1923) 16 Lloyd's Rep 129 at p 130, CA.

104 [1982] 1 Lloyd's Rep 136 at p 149, CA.

105 *Ibid.*

106 [1980] 1 Lloyd's Rep 491 at p 504.

107 *Ibid.*

The reason being, as discussed earlier, an 'all risks' policy insures only against risks of, and not inevitable, losses. These problems await judicial ruling.

Insufficiency or unsuitability of packing

Berk v Style[108] is the authority which has extended the concept of inherent vice to include its packaging. The defective paper bags in which the cargo of kieselghur was packed were held to constitute inherent vice. This aspect of the decision was much criticised, but the problem is now academic, as cl 4.3 of all the ICC excepts the insurer from liability for 'insufficiency or unsuitability of packing or preparation of the subject-matter insured'.[109]

A month later, in *Gee and Garnham Ltd v Whittall*,[110] Mr Justice Sellers invoked the same principle which he had formulated in *Berk v Style*,[111] and held that damage sustained by a part of a cargo of kettles caused by water-staining due to the use of unseasoned wood wool (inadequate packing) was a loss which came within the exception of 'inherent vice' and was, therefore, not recoverable.[112]

'Unless the policy otherwise provides'

As discussed above, even an unqualified clause insuring against:

- 'all risks';[113]

- 'all and every risk whatsoever however arising';[114]

- 'all risk and every risk whatsoever and all loss or damage from whatsoever cause arising';[115] and

- 'all risks of loss and/or damage from whatsoever cause arising',[116]

have all, for one reason or another, been held to be insufficient to protect an assured for damage to or loss caused by inherent vice. In the main, they were construed as not being sufficiently clear or precise to cover damage to or loss of cargo by reason of inherent vice. The critical word is 'risks' implying that only accidental or fortuitous causes of loss are covered. The reasons why a loss caused by the first type of inherent vice, that which will inevitably occur, is not recoverable under such a policy are twofold. First, such a loss is neither accidental nor fortuitous: because it is a loss of known certainty, no risk is

---

108 [1955] 3 All ER 625, QBD.

109 In fact, for the purpose of cl 3, 'packing' shall be deemed to include stowage in a container or liftvan but only when such stowage is carried out prior to attachment of this insurance or by the Assured or their servants.

110 [1955] 2 Lloyd's Rep 562, QBD.

111 [1955] 3 All ER 625, QBD.

112 Some of the kettle which were damaged by rain while on the quay were held recoverable.

113 See *Schloss Brothers v Stevens* [1906] 2 KB; *The Gaunt Case* [1921] 2 AC 41; and *T M Noten BV v Harding* [1990] 2 Lloyd's Rep 283, CA.

114 See *London & Provincial Leather Process Ltd v Hudson* [1939] 3 All ER 857 at p 861, KBD.

115 See *Gee & Garnham Ltd v Whittall* [1955] 2 Lloyd's Rep 562, QBD.

116 See *Berk v Style* [1956] 1 QB 180, QB.

involved. Secondly, inherent vice is expressly excepted by s 55(2)(c) of the Act and cl 4.4 of the policy. The second type of loss arising from inherent vice, that which may or may not occur, though a risk, is not recoverable because of the second reason.

Even a clause as wide as that found in *Overseas Commodities Ltd v Style*[117] is liable to be given a narrow construction. A cargo of canned pork was insured against 'all risks of whatsoever nature and/or kind. Average irrespective of percentage. Including blowing of tins. Including inherent vice and hidden defects. Condemnation by authorities to take place within three months of the date of arrival in final warehouse ...'.

Mr Justice McNair, after having acknowledged that the parties had contracted out of the statutory protection, nevertheless, felt that in view of the peculiar nature of the subject-matter insured – namely, pasteurised and not wholly sterilised pig produce – some limitation must be placed on the said clause. He stated that:[118]

'...it seems inconceivable that the underwriters should, with their eyes open, have accepted liability for loss by inherent vice developing at any time in the future, since such a produce must inevitably, if not consumed within a limited period, suffer loss from inherent vice, for, being perishable, it necessarily contains the seeds of its own ultimate destruction.'

Unless the intention of the parties is unambiguously expressed, the courts would be inclined, taking into account commercial realities, practice of the trade, the nature of the subject-matter insured and any other factors relevant to the case, to give a sensible construction to any clause which endeavours to impose liability on an insurer for a loss which he has been given statutory exemption. Unless clear words are used, a court would be reluctant to strip him of this protection.[119]

An assured, desirous of insuring his cargo specifically against inherent vice, would, in the light of the above cases, have to be selective in his choice of words. In particular, he should take heed of the advice given by Mr Justice Sellers in *Berk v Style*:[120]

'Having regard to the established law in the matter, if the plaintiffs had wished to insure against inherent vice – if, indeed, they could have done so at any reasonable premium – they should have used specific words to that effect, or at least have had cl 6 or the relevant part of it struck out.'[121]

---

117 [1958] 1 Lloyd's Rep 547.

118 *Ibid*, at p 560.

119 A clause insuring against damage from 'sweating and/or heating when resulted from external cause' would not, of course, be adequate to insure against inherent vice: see *Bowring & Co Ltd & Another v Amsterdam London Insurance Co Ltd* (1930) 36 Ll L Rep 309.

120 [1956] 1 QB 180 at pp 186–187.

121 The equivalent to cl 4.4 of the current ICC. In *Biddle, Sawyer & Co Ltd v Peters* [1957] 2 Lloyd's Rep 339, QBD, a clause 'against all risks of whatsoever nature from whatsoever cause arising including condemnation and blowing of tins or decomposition of meat. Excluding inherent vice unless causing blowing of tins' read in isolation could be interpreted (in view of the double negative) to have included inherent vice if it had caused blowing of tins. But as the exception clause, one similar to cl 4.4, was not struck out, it was held that the effect was to exclude from the risks covered any form of inherent vice.

CHAPTER 11

BURDEN AND STANDARD OF PROOF

INTRODUCTION

A ship with cargo on board sinks to the bottom of the sea, and whereupon a claim for the loss is instituted under the policy either by a shipowner, cargo owner, mortgagee, assignee and/or other interested parties is a scenario all too familiar in shipping. In such an event, should the circumstances of the case so permit, the plaintiffs would almost invariably plead fire, barratry and/or perils of the seas as the cause or causes of loss;[1] and the defendants, with the same degree of predictability, would rest their defence on the ground that there was no case to answer and/or that the loss was caused by the wilful misconduct of the plaintiffs – the two strings to their bow.

This pattern of proceedings is evident in a large number of cases all dealing with the thorny but important question as to the burden of proof. As the following discussion of the authorities will reveal, a case could be won or lost simply on this premise. Lord Brandon in *Rhesa Shipping Co SA v Edmunds, The Popi M* warned that:[2]

'No judge likes to decide cases on burden of proof if he can legitimately avoid having to do so. There are cases, however, in which, owing to the unsatisfactory state of the evidence or otherwise, deciding on the burden of proof is the only just course for him to take.'

The notion of 'burden of proof' carries two obligations: the burden of producing evidence and the burden of persuasion.[3] The former refers to the practical process of adducing enough evidence to allow the trier of fact to find for him on the issue in question. This burden may shift from one party to the other during the trial.[4] The latter, however, which is what Lord Brandon was referring to in the above remark, remains constant on one side throughout the litigation. The burden of persuasion requires the burdened party to persuade the trier of fact to find for him on the issue. In simple terms, it means that he must prove his case.

The general rule on the burden of proof in marine insurance is stated by Mr Justice Greer in *Banco De Barcelona and Others v Union Marine Insurance Co Ltd* as follows:[5]

'It is indisputable that marine insurance cases afford no exception to the general rule that before a plaintiff can become entitled to judgment he must prove his

---

1 The most recent case to have received the attention of the Court of Appeal on these issues is *The Ikarian Reefer* [1995] 1 Lloyd's Rep 455, CA in which the decision of the trial judge was overturned on a different finding of fact.

2 [1985] 2 Lloyd's Rep 1 at p 6, HL.

3 The distinction was drawn in *Northwestern Mutual Life Assurance Co v Linard, The Vainqueur* [1973] 2 Lloyd's Rep 275, USDC.

4 In *The Vainqueur, ibid*, at p 280, the burden of producing evidence shifted to the defendants after the plaintiffs had made out a *prima facie* case.

5 (1925) 30 Com Cas 316 at p 317. See also *The Vainqueur, ibid*, at p 279, *per* Ward, DJ: 'Generally, the burden of proof in an action on marine insurance is to show that a loss arose from a peril covered by the policy is on the plaintiff.'

case, that is to say, he must establish his cause of action to the reasonable satisfaction of the tribunal.'

Where the defendants are concerned, all that they have to do is to deny the plaintiffs' allegations; they are by no means obliged to plead an affirmative defence. This was made perfectly clear in *The Popi M* by Lord Brandon as thus:[6]

'Although it is open to underwriters to suggest and seek to prove some other cause of loss, against which the ship was not insured, there is no obligation on them to do so. Moreover, if they chose to do so, there is no obligation on them to prove, even on a balance of probabilities, the truth of their alternative case.'[7]

With these general principles in mind, it is proposed that the burden and standard of proof in relation to a plaintiff's claim for a loss by perils of the seas, barratry, or fire will each be discussed separately. In the process, the burden of proof in relation to the defence of wilful misconduct would, needless to say, also arise naturally for consideration.

A – PROOF OF LOSS BY PERILS OF THE SEAS

Like any other civil action, the burden of proof of a claim under a marine policy of insurance lies with the plaintiffs. They have to prove to the satisfaction of the court that the loss was caused by a peril insured against. Where perils of the seas is asserted as the proximate cause of loss, they would have to make out a *prima facie* case of an accidental or fortuitous loss before the defendants would be called upon to present their defence. As a general rule, the plaintiffs have to provide direct proof pointing to a *specific* accident or casualty responsible for the loss. However, as will be seen, this may not always be possible in which case they would wish to rely on the presumption of a loss by an unascertainable peril of the seas.

This part on perils of the seas will first discuss the burden of proof of the plaintiffs and then of the defence. As regards the position of the plaintiffs, first, the general principle of proof will be discussed; secondly, the presumption of a loss by an unascertainable peril of the seas – by which an unexplained loss and the case of a missing ship may be proved – will be examined; and finally, the standard of proof will be considered. The position of the defendants requires a consideration of the defence of wilful misconduct and the application of a rule known as the 'third alternative'.

BURDEN OF PROOF ON THE PLAINTIFFS

That the plaintiffs have to prove that the loss was proximately caused by a peril of the seas is incontrovertible. In *The Tropaioforos*,[8] Mr Justice Pearson remarked:

---

6   [1985] 2 Lloyd's Rep 1 at p 3, HL. See also *The Lakeland* (1927) 28 Ll L Rep 293, US Court of Appeals.

7   Except, it would appear, when he pleads the defence of wilful misconduct as a defence to a claim of loss by barratry: see *Elfie A Issaias v Mar Insurance Co Ltd* (1923) 15 Ll L Rep 186, CA which is fully discussed below.

8   *Compania Naviera Santi SA v Indemnity Marine Assurance Co Ltd* [1960] 2 Lloyd's Rep 469 at p 473. See also *The Vainqueur* [1973] 2 Lloyd's Rep 275 at p 279, USDC.

'As to the burden of proof, the whole question has been reserved in the House of Lords; but, subject to that reservation, it has been established decisions of courts of first instance and the Court of Appeal (with some support from dicta in the House of Lords) that the plaintiffs have the burden of proving, in a case such as this, that there was an accidental loss by perils of the seas ...'

Mr Justice Brandon in *Compania Naviera Vascongada v British and Foreign Marine Insurance Co Ltd, The Gloria*[9] was also clear in his mind that 'the onus of proof that the loss was fortuitous lies upon the plaintiffs ...'. And recently, the same was reiterated by Mr Justice Bingham in *The Zinovia*[10] to the effect that: 'To succeed in their claim for a loss by perils of the seas, the owners must prove that the loss of the vessel was proximately caused by such a peril.'

In 1985, the long-awaited House of Lords ruling arrived with *The Popi M*,[11] which has established beyond doubt that, in relation to a claim for a loss by perils of the seas, the burden of proof is and remains throughout on the plaintiffs.[12] This necessarily means that they have to satisfy the court, regardless of the nature of the defence raised, that the subject matter-insured was lost by a peril of the seas. If the court is, at the conclusion of the hearing, left in doubt as to whether the loss was or was not so caused, the plaintiffs have failed to prove their case.[13]

That the mere entry or incursion of sea water is not in itself sufficient proof of a loss by perils of the seas is now a well established rule of law.[14] Thus, in order to succeed in a claim for a loss by such a peril, an assured has to adduce evidence to prove that the loss was accidental or fortuitous. And if he is unable to provide clear proof of a casualty or accident to demonstrate this fact, he has failed to prove his case. The facts and circumstances of a loss may sometimes render it difficult, if not impossible, for a shipowner to provide direct, affirmative or positive proof[15] of a loss by a peril of the seas. Should he find himself in such a dilemma, he has another route by which he could take to prove his case: he could, by the process of elimination of other possible causes, endeavour to persuade the court to draw the inference that the loss was caused by an 'unascertained' or 'unspecified' peril of the seas.

---

9   (1936) 54 Ll L Rep 35 at p 50.

10 [1984] 2 Lloyd's Rep 264 at p 271, QBD.

11 [1985] 2 Lloyd's Rep 1, HL.

12 The Court of Appeal had earlier in *Miceli v Union Marine & General Insurance Co Ltd* (1938), 60 Ll L Rep 275 applied the same rule. See also *La Compania Martiartu v The Corpn of the Royal Exchange Assurance, The Arnus* [1923] 1 KB 650, CA: it would appear that all the insurer has to do is to offer a reasonable explanation of the loss and show that it was probably due to an event not insured against; *The Lakeland* (1927) 28 Ll L Rep 293, US Court of Appeals; *The Gloria* [1936] 54 Lloyd's Rep 55; and *The Vainqueur* [1973] 2 Lloyd's Rep 275.

13 A justification for this rule can be found in *Compania Naviera Santi SA v Indemnity Marine Assurance Co Ltd, The Tropaioforos* [1960] 2 Lloyd's Rep 469 at p 473, discussed below.

14 *Samuel & Co v Dumas* (1924) 18 Ll L Rep 211, HL.

15 As opposed to inferential evidence.

Presumption of loss by an unascertainable peril of the seas

The concept of 'perils of the seas' is wide enough in scope to embrace a class of loss known as an unascertainable or unspecified peril of the seas. Proof of this type of loss is achieved by way of inference drawn by reason of the circumstances relating to the loss. An assured has to adduce sufficient relevant circumstantial evidence for the court to make the inference that the loss was caused by an unascertainable peril of the seas.[16]

There are two sets of circumstances under which a court may be prepared (in the absence of direct proof) to depart from the general rule as regards the burden of proof in order to draw the inference that the loss was due to an unascertainable peril of the seas. One relates to unexplained losses and the other to missing ships. As an exception to the general rule of proof, the plaintiffs, on satisfying certain conditions, are allowed to rely on the drawing of an inference to prove his case.

Unexplained loss

The problems on the question of proof and the principles relating to the presumption of loss by an unascertainable peril of the seas in relation to unexplained losses of ships were examined in detail in the recent case of *The Marel*.[17] The owner of a ship which sinks at sea in unexplained circumstances would find it extremely difficult to provide concrete proof that the loss was caused by a peril of the seas. If the loss occurred shortly after sailing or happened in calm ordinary weather conditions,[18] his task is even all the more onerous, as a presumption of unseaworthiness is likely to be raised against him if no other explanation is forthcoming to account for the loss.

Mr Justice Mason in *Skandia Insurance Co Ltd v Skoljarev*[19] was prepared to draw the presumption on the ground that it:

> '... arises from the fact that the immediate cause of the loss is the foundering of the ship and, if that is not due to unseaworthinesss at the inception of the voyage, it is difficult to perceive how the foundering could have been caused otherwise than by a fortuitous and unascertained accident of the seas, or perhaps a latent defect.'

In the light of *The Marel*,[20] a shipowner in such a case has to adduce proof to eliminate not only unseaworthiness, but also all other possible causes of loss. With regard to the former, he has to rebut any presumption of unseaworthiness that, by reason of the facts of the case, may be raised against him.

---

16 *Per* Mason J, in *Skandia Insurance Co Ltd v Skoljarev* [1979] 142 CLR 375 at p 393, High Court of Australia: 'The extensive concept of "perils of the sea" is an important element in the existence of the presumption.'

17 [1992] 1 Lloyd's Rep 402.

18 See eg, *Skandia Insurance Co Ltd v Skoljarev* [1979] 142 CLR 375, [1979] 26 ALR 1; High Court of Australia, where the vessel sank in a calm sea after rapid entry of sea water into the engine room. The point and cause of entry of sea water into the ship were unknown.

19 *Ibid*, at p 377, hereinafter referred to as *The Skandia Case*.

20 [1992] 1 Lloyd's Rep 402.

Elimination of unseaworthiness

As a general rule, the unseaworthiness of a ship has to be proved by the insurer if he wishes to raise this as a defence.[21] The general principle (of he who alleges must prove) may, however, be set aside if a presumption of unseaworthiness is made available to him. There are essentially two occasions in which a plaintiff may be confronted with a presumption of unseaworthiness:

- In the absence of any external circumstances to account for the loss or damage, a presumption that the ship must have set sail in an unseaworthy condition may be drawn if she is by reason of her disability unable, soon after sailing, to proceed with her voyage; this is the presumption of a breach of the implied warranty of seaworthiness in a voyage policy.

- The 'irresistible' presumption that unseaworthiness has *caused* the loss – as discussed by Mr Justice Brett (as he then was) in *Anderson v Morice*.[22]

These presumptions would have to be rebutted by the plaintiff if he wishes to rely on the presumption of a loss by an unascertainable peril of the seas to prove his case.

Rebuttal of the presumption of breach of the implied warranty of seaworthiness in a voyage policy

An attempt to elicit a presumption of unseaworthiness at the commencement of the voyage, on the basis of the maxim *res ipsa loquitur*, was successfully made in *Pickup v Thames Insurance Co*,[23] where the vessel (insured under a voyage policy) unable to prosecute her voyage had to return to port 11 days after sailing. On the subject of burden of proof, Lord Justice Brett of the Court of Appeal summarised the legal principles as follows:

'The burden of proof upon a plea of unseaworthiness to an action on a policy of marine insurance lies upon the defendant, and ... it never shifts, it always remains upon him. But when facts are given in evidence, it is often said certain presumptions, which are really inferences of fact, arise, and cause the burden of proof to shift; and so they do as a matter of reasoning, and, as a matter of fact, for instance, where a ship sails from a port, and soon after she has sailed sinks to the bottom of the sea, *and there is nothing in the weather to account for such a disaster*, it is a reasonable presumption to be made that she was unseaworthy when she started ...'

Later, in the case of *Ajum Goolam Hossen & Co v Union Marine Insurance Co*,[24] heard before the Privy Council, the shipowner, who was able to rebut the presumption of unseaworthiness, recovered for a total loss even though the loss did not appear to be traceable to any specific or particular peril of the seas. The legal position was described as follows:

'The real cause of the loss is unknown, and cannot be ascertained from the evidence adduced in this action. But underwriters take the risk of loss from

---

21 'It has been universally stated that the onus of proof of unseaworthiness is on the insurer': *per* Mason J, in *The Skandia Case* [1979] 142 CLR 375 at p 387.

22 (1874) LR 10 CP 58. See below.

23 (1878) 3 QBD 594, CA. Emphasis added.

24 [1901] AC 362, PC.

unascertainable causes; and after carefully weighing all the evidence and bearing in mind the presumption of unseaworthiness on which the underwriters rely, their Lordships have come to the conclusion that unseaworthiness at the time of sailing is not proved.'

It has to be said that it is generally not for the shipowner to prove that his ship was seaworthy.[25] However, where the facts of the case warrant the drawing of the presumption of unseaworthiness, he would have no choice but to furnish proof of the condition of his ship if he is effectively to rebut this presumption. A judge cannot draw the inference (that the loss was caused by an unascertainable peril of the seas) upon which the assured relies on in order to make out his case unless he is satisfied that the ship was seaworthy at the commencement of the voyage. The possibility of unseaworthiness as a cause of loss has to be eliminated. If the plaintiffs are able to show that the ship was seaworthy at the commencement of the voyage, the court may well find that she was lost by a peril of the seas.

In *The Skandia Case*,[26] Chief Justice Barwick in the High Court of Australia remarked that the shipowners:

'... not being able to point to any contribution of the elements to account for the entry of water into the hull of the vessel, had perforce to rely on the inference that that entry into a seaworthy vessel was due to, or itself amounted to, a peril of the sea. That is to say, to attribute the loss of the vessel to a peril of the sea necessarily involved ... a conclusion that the vessel was seaworthy.'

Such a presumption of unseaworthiness at the commencement of the voyage is to the insurer, under a voyage policy, *prima facie* proof of a breach of a warranty which is his defence to the shipowner's claim for indemnity. But as there is no implied warranty of seaworthiness in a time policy, 'the mere fact that the vessel was unseaworthy at the commencement of the voyage will not afford any defence to the underwriters'.[27] The issue is not one of determining whether the ship was unseaworthy when she set sail or, to put it in another way, whether a warranty of seaworthiness has been breached (as there is none in a time policy), but one of identifying whether unseaworthiness or a peril of the seas (ascertainable or unascertainable) is the proximate cause of loss.

Rebuttal of the presumption of unseaworthiness as the cause of loss

A similar presumption of unseaworthiness, but drawn under a different set of circumstances was advocated by Mr Justice Brett in *Anderson v Morice*:[28]

'... in the absence of any other evidence as to the condition of the ship, the fact of her sinking in smooth water without any apparent cause would create an irresistible presumption of unseaworthiness.'

Again, it is clear from this statement that it is only upon proof of seaworthiness[29] that a court is able to prevent the operation of the presumption

---

25 In law, there is no *prima facie* presumption of seaworthiness in favour of the assured on the issue of causation.

26 [1979] 26 ALR 1; [1979] 142 CLR 375 at p 377.

27 *Per* Judge Diamond in *The Marel*, [1992] 1 Lloyd's Rep 402 at p 426.

28 (1874) LR 10 CP 58.

29 As a general rule, it is not the duty of the assured to prove that his ship is seaworthy.

of unseaworthiness, and to make the necessary inference of a loss by an unspecified peril of the seas.

In *The Skandia Case*,[30] the above process of elimination was applied by Mr Justice Mason, whose comments on the subject are indeed lucid and helpful. They read as follows:

'Although there is nothing in all this to throw the burden of proof of seaworthiness onto the insured, there is one class of case in which the insured will find it necessary to establish seaworthiness in order to prove his case. This is where the insured, having no direct evidence of loss due to a fortuitous event, seeks to establish by inference a case of loss due to an *unascertained peril of the sea*. To justify this inference he will seek to exclude the possibility of loss caused by unseaworthiness by calling evidence as to the condition of the ship.'

The purpose of adducing evidence to establish that his ship was seaworthy is obviously to eliminate unseaworthiness as the proximate cause of loss. Unseaworthiness, however, is not the only cause of loss which the shipowner is required to eliminate. According to *The Marel*,[31] he would also have to discount other possible causes of loss not covered by the policy before he would be allowed to claim the benefit of the presumption of a loss by an unascertained peril of the seas.

Elimination of all other possible causes

In *The Marel*,[32] Judge Diamond pointed out that a court may be prepared to draw the inference that a ship was lost through an unascertainable peril of the seas only if it is satisfied that all other possible relevant causes of loss, including unseaworthiness, which are not insured by the policy, such as ordinary wear and tear and wilful misconduct, are not responsible for the loss. He explained that the concept of 'perils of the seas', though wide, does not cover loss by wear and tear or a case where the vessel has been deliberately sunk by her owner.[33]

A rebuttable presumption of fact

It is pertinent to note that, though it is possible to achieve with the aid of inference (if direct proof is not available) that the vessel was lost due to some unascertained peril of the seas, the burden of proof still remains throughout with the plaintiffs: it remains their duty to satisfy the court on the balance of probabilities, even if the evidence be circumstantial, that the ship was lost by an unascertained peril. And if in the end a court is, as in *The Marel*,[34] doubtful as to whether the casualty was caused by some unascertainable peril or accident, it would be disinclined to draw the inference in favour of the shipowner.

---

30 [1979] 26 ALR 1 at p 13; [1979] 142 CLR 375 at p 390, High Court of Australia. Emphasis added. A most enlightening and exhaustive summary of all the relevant cases pertaining to the law of perils of the seas and the burden of proof in respect thereof can be found in this interesting case.

31 [1992] 1 Lloyd's Rep 402.

32 *Ibid*, at pp 424 and 425.

33 If she was deliberately sunk by the master or crew without the connivance of the owner, it would constitute an act of barratry which in any event is a peril insured against, unless specifically excepted by the policy.

34 *Ibid*, at p 427.

The inference of fact, if drawn, is only *one* factor amongst others which the court has to consider. It is to be taken into account with all the other circumstances of the case that the loss of the vessel was due to an unascertainable peril of the seas. *The Marel*[35] has also made it clear that the inference is a rebuttable one. This means that an insurer is always entitled to adduce evidence to negate it.

At a trial, the sequence of events would basically be as that described by Lord Anderson in *The Spathari*.[36] First, the plaintiffs have to prove that the ship sank by reason of the influx of sea water; the defendants would then have to adduce evidence to explain how that inflow might have been occasioned. If they are unable to do so, the plaintiffs would have been regarded as having proved the proximate cause of the sinking, and 'they would have been entitled to found on the presumption that the unascertained peril which occasioned the inflow of water was a peril covered by the policy'. On the other hand, if the evidence led by the defenders is of 'such potency as to create a doubt which the Court is unable to solve as to the cause of the influx of water, the presumption which favours the pursuers is displaced'.

Missing ships

Green v Brown[37] is the case responsible for the formulation of the rule that 'a ship never heard of is presumed to be foundered at sea'. That the vessel sailed out of port on her intended voyage and was since never heard of was all the evidence available to the court. Under the circumstances, the Chief Justice felt that 'it would be unreasonable to expect certain evidence of such a loss, as where everybody on board is presumed to be drowned; all that can be required is the best proof the nature of the case admits of, which the plaintiff has given'. This case was approved by Lord Justice Scrutton of the Court of Appeal in *La Compania Martiartu v Royal Exchange Assurance*.[38]

It is important to note that a court has to be satisfied that the ship had, in fact, sailed on her intended voyage before it would allow the plaintiffs to pray the aid of the presumption. Though this was not distinctly couched as a legal prerequisite in *Green v Brown*,[39] nevertheless, the rule was confirmed by Lord Abbott CJ in *Koster v Innes*.[40] As no evidence was adduced to prove that the vessel had ever sailed for the port of destination, it was not possible for him, in this case, to invoke the presumption.

A year later, the presumption was applied in *Koster v Reed*,[41] where it was proved that the ship sailed on the voyage insured with the goods on board, but

---

35 *Ibid*.

36 (1923) 17 Ll L Rep 66, Court of Session.

37 (1743) 2 Str 1199.

38 [1923] 1 KB 650 at p 657; hereinafter referred to as *The Martiartu Case*. 'The presumption may well be, when nothing is known except that the ship has disappeared at sea, that her loss was by perils of the sea': *Green v Brown, ibid*.

39 (1743) 2 Str 1199.

40 (1825) Ry & Mood 334. See also *Cohen v Hinckley*, (1809) 2 Camp 51.

41 (1826) 6 B & C 19.

never arrived at her port of destination; shortly after sailing, a report was heard at the port of departure indicating the ship had foundered at sea but that the crew were saved.[42] These facts were considered sufficient *prima facie* evidence of a loss by perils of the seas.[43] Though the crew members survived, they were not called to give evidence. The court held the view that it was not incumbent on the plaintiffs to scour all over Europe in search of the crew, who were presumed to be foreigners, as the ship was foreign and was trading between foreign ports. Moreover, it was impossible to compel the attendance of witnesses resident abroad.

As the evidence is regarded only as *prima facie* proof it is of course rebuttable. One of the judges, however, was careful to remind us of this in his judgment, and another pointed out that his decision was influenced by the fact that 'the plaintiff was owner of the goods, not of the vessel, and the underwriters might have just as good means of inquiring about the crew as the plaintiff had'.

As the decision was delivered in 1826, it has, of course, to be viewed with a degree of caution. With the advancement of technology in means of communication, it is unlikely that the presumption will in the present day be applied lightly; unless there are strong reasons for so doing, it would not be unreasonable to say that judges would be more inclined to enforce the general principles on the burden of proof. Naturally, it would be easier, in conjunction with the presumption of an actual total loss provided for by s 58 in relation to missing ships, to invoke the presumption in a case where there are no survivors.

Standard of proof

Having established that the burden of proof rests with the plaintiffs, it is now necessary to consider the degree or standard of proof required to satisfy the court. The law in this regard is no different from the general rule applicable to all civil actions: The plaintiff has to prove *on a balance of probabilities* that the ship was lost by a peril of the seas. That this legal requirement of proof on a balance of probabilities is to be applied with common sense was advocated by the Law Lords in *The Popi M*.[44] Thus, a judge must, on the evidence, be satisfied that the event, as alleged, is more likely to have occurred than not; if the occurrence of the event is extremely improbable, he would, on the basis of common sense, have to find for the defendant. In *The Tropaioforos*,[45] Mr Justice Pearson stated that: '... the degree of proof required is only to show a balance of probabilities in favour of an accidental loss by perils of the seas.'

---

42 See also *Twemlow v Oswin* (1809), 2 Camp 85, where Mansfield, CJ held that 'it is enough to prove that she was not heard of in this country after she sailed, without calling witness from her port of destination to shew that she never arrived there'.

43 If the ship should by chance turn up after the underwriters have paid up as for a lost ship, she is to be considered as abandoned, and will belong to the underwriters: *Houstman v Thornton* (1816) Holt NP 242; 171 ER 229.

44 [1985] 2 Lloyd's Rep 1, HL.

45 [1960] 2 Lloyd's Rep 469 at p 473.

The principle enunciated in *The Popi M* was recently applied in *The Ikarian Reefer*[46] when it went to the Court of Appeal. After spending a great deal of time examining the evidence given by the master and the expert witnesses, the Court of Appeal decided to make its own finding of facts. It overturned the decision of Mr Justice Cresswell, who held that the loss was caused by the grounding of *The Ikarian Reefer* due to the negligent navigation of the master. Lord Justice Stuart-Smith summarised the law on the burden of proof as follows:[47]

'For the shipowners to succeed, the evidence has to establish that the grounding probably was fortuitous; this conclusion can co-exist with a residual possibility that it was deliberate (or in scientific terms, a low order of probability) because the plaintiffs are required to prove their case on "balance of probabilities" only.'

The order of probability may be 'low', but the court must never be left in doubt as to the cause of loss; otherwise, it may be forced to invoke the rule of the 'third alternative,' discussed below, to dismiss the plaintiffs' case.

The 'Third Alternative'

In *The Popi M*, Lord Brandon reminded the court that a judge is clearly not obliged to make a finding one way or the other with regard to the facts adduced by the parties. He pointed out that in reality the position is often 'not just a simple choice between the cause of loss relied on by the shipowners and the alternative cause of loss put forward by underwriters'. There is a third alternative always available to him:[48]

'He has open to him the *third alternative* of saying that the party on whom the burden of proof lies in relation to any averment made by him has failed to discharge that burden.'

If the evidence as regards the proximate cause of loss is at the conclusion of the trial doubtful and uncertain, a judge would have no choice but to find for the defendants. The reason being that the plaintiffs have failed to discharge the persuasive burden of proof which rests on them throughout.[49]

It is to be noted that in *The Popi M*,[50] the plaintiffs' claim was based on perils of the seas (alternatively negligence of the crew), and the defence was essentially one of denial that the loss was so caused. The defective condition of the ship was also raised, though not seriously. It is also to be noted that scuttling with the connivance of the shipowner was not pleaded as a defence. Thus, whether the decision of *The Popi M*, and the rule of the third alternative therein proposed is to be confined to its own facts, and should not be applied to a case where scuttling with the connivance of the shipowner is pleaded as defence, is a matter which has to be considered. In other words, is the third

---

46   [1995] 1 Lloyd's Rep 455, CA.

47   *Ibid*, at p 459.

48   [1985] 2 Lloyd's Rep 1 at p 6, HL. Emphasis added.

49   In *The Vainqueur* [1973] 2 Lloyd's Rep 275, judgment was awarded to the insurers even though the proof adduced by them was not sufficient to find that the vessel was scuttled. The plaintiffs failed to discharge the burden of proving that the loss fell within the policy. See also *The Lakeland* (1927) 29 Ll L Rep 293 at p 296.

50   [1985] 2 Lloyd's Rep 1, HL.

alternative applicable when the defence of wilful misconduct of the assured is pleaded by the defendants?

THE DEFENCE

The defendants would be called upon to answer only if the plaintiffs have made out a *prima facie* case of a fortuitous or accidental loss by perils of the seas. Should there be a case to meet, the defendants, according to Lord Justice Cairns of the Court of Appeal in *The Dias*, can either:[51]

> '... simply traverse the allegations in the points of claim or they can make an affirmative allegation of scuttling. If they adopt the former course they can cross-examine and call evidence to show that the vessel was not lost by a fortuitous accident, but cannot set up an affirmative case that she was cast away with the privity of the owner.'

If the case for the defendants is to rest solely on the first ground, they would not be allowed to surprise the plaintiffs at the trial with allegations of fraud and criminal conduct. Provided that the defences are properly pleaded, there is nothing to prevent a defendant from taking both courses, denying that the vessel was lost as a result of perils of the seas *and* alleging that the vessel was wilfully cast away with the connivance of the owner. A defendant has two strings to his bow and both may be put into use at the same time.[52]

That the 'third solution' may only be invoked if the court is, at the end of the trial, doubtful as to the cause of loss is obvious. It has, of course, no relevance to a case such as *Samuel v Dumas*,[53] where the defence of scuttling with the connivance of the owner was conclusively proved by the defendants.

The defence of wilful misconduct

Case law has demonstrated that the defence of wilful misconduct is invariably pleaded by underwriters as a defence to a claim for a loss by perils of the seas. Whether the third alternative may be employed by the court when an allegation of scuttling is raised against a claim of loss by perils of the seas has to be explored. For the purpose of comparison and for a proper understanding of the ensuing discussions in relation to a claim of a loss by barratry and of fire, an insight into this area of law is necessary.

The problem began in 1923 with an *obiter dictum* uttered by Lord Justice Scrutton of the Court of Appeal in *The Martiartu Case*.[54] In a suit by a shipowner against the underwriters on a policy of marine insurance, perils of the seas and barratry were alleged as alternative causes of loss. The defence was that the

---

51   [1942] 2 QB 625 at p 647.

52   See, eg, *The Gold Sky* [1972] 2 Lloyd's Rep 187 at p 192; appeal on a procedural issue [1972] 1 Lloyd's Rep 331; *The Michael* [1979] 1 Lloyd's Rep 55; [1979] 2 Lloyd's Rep 1; and *Michalos (N) & Sons Maritime SA v Prudential Assurance Co Ltd, The Zinovia* [1984] 2 Lloyd's Rep 264.

53   [1924] AC 431; 29 Com Cas 239. See also *The Cruz, Banco De Barcelona & Others v Union Marine Insurance Co Ltd* (1925) Com Cas 316, where scuttling with the connivance of the plaintiffs was also proved; *The Tropaioforos* [1960] 2 Lloyd's Rep 469; and *The Eftychia, Bank of Athens v Royal Exchange Assurance* (1937) 57 Ll L Rep 37, on appeal, 59 Ll L Rep 67.

54   *Ibid*, at p 657.

vessel had been intentionally scuttled by the master and crew with the connivance of the plaintiffs. Both the trial and appeal courts had no doubt whatsoever that, on the evidence, the vessel was deliberately scuttled with the connivance of her owners. In the light of this, it was really quite unnecessary for the court to make any comment on the burden of proof. Nevertheless, Lord Justice Scrutton could not restrain himself from offering his opinion on the matter. He said:[55]

> '... if ... an examination of all the evidence and probabilities leaves the court doubtful what is the real cause of the loss, the assured has failed to prove his case ... for he has not proved a loss by perils insured against.'

As the defendants in this case were able to offer a *reasonable explanation* showing that the loss was probably due to the scuttling of the ship with the connivance of the owners, the court found in their favour.

It is interesting to observe that the above comments made by Lord Justice Scrutton were given express approval by Lord Brandon in *The Popi M*,[56] even though the defence of wilful misconduct was not raised as a defence in the case. The seeds of the 'third alternative' were obviously sown in *The Martiartu Case*. Lord Brandon had apparently considered Lord Justice Scrutton's *dictum* to be of general application.

In *Pateras and Others v Royal Exchange Assurance, The Sappho*,[57] Mr Justice Roche, citing *The Martiartu Case*[58] with approval, stated that:

> '... although there is, of course, and must be a strong presumption against the commission of an act so criminal as the wilful throwing away of a ship, yet if the matter be really uncertain as between that explanation of the loss and a fortuitous explanation of the loss, the onus is on the plaintiffs.'

The third alternative was also applied, perhaps unwittingly,[59] by Mr Justice Branson in *The Gloria*.[60] As his remarks are well known and were frequently cited by judges, it would be helpful to cite them:

> 'The onus of proof that the loss was fortuitous lies upon the plaintiffs, but that does not mean that they will fail if their evidence does not exclude all reasonable possibility that the ship was scuttled. Before that possibility is considered, some evidence in support of it must be forthcoming ... If ... the Court ... is not satisfied that the ship was scuttled, but find that the probability that she was is equal to the probability that her loss was fortuitous, the plaintiff will fail.'

Following the usual sequence of play, the plaintiffs alleged that *The Gloria* was lost by a peril of the seas, to which the defendants pleaded, *inter alia*, that she was scuttled with the privity of her owners. As the plaintiffs had

55 *Ibid*, at p 657.

56 [1985] 2 Lloyd's Rep 1 at p 3, HL.

57 (1934) 49 Ll L Rep 400 at p 407, QBD. Here, wilful misconduct was pleaded as a defence to a claim of loss by perils of the seas.

58 [1923] 1 KB 650.

59 Branson J did not cite any authority to support his opinion.

60 (1936) 54 Ll L Rep 35 at p 50, KBD. See also *The Eftychia, Bank of Athens v Royal Exchange Assurance* (1937) 57 Ll L Rep 37 at p 56, where Branson J referred to his own judgment in *The Gloria*.

successfully discharged the onus of showing that the loss was fortuitous, judgment was awarded against the defendants. The evidence adduced by the defendants was clearly not strong enough to cast sufficient doubts upon the plaintiffs' claim.

An equally instructive authority is *The Dias*,[61] where Mr Justice Cairns, citing some of the above cases[62] with approval, succinctly summarised the legal position as follows:

'If scuttling is alleged and the insurers are going to ask the court to find positively that the vessel was scuttled, then they must discharge the onus of proving their allegation ... If, where loss by peril of the seas is alleged by the plaintiff and scuttling by the defendant, the court at the end of the day is not satisfied that either story is more probable than the other, then the plaintiff fails ...'

Another recent authority on the subject is *The Zinovia*,[63] where the plaintiffs' action for loss by perils of the sea was met with the defence of wilful misconduct with the connivance of the owners. On this occasion, the defendants were unable to satisfy the court, according to the high standard of proof required, that the vessel was deliberately cast away. Judgment, however, was entered for the plaintiffs, not because the defendants had failed to prove their case, but because the plaintiffs themselves were able to convince the court that the loss was proximately caused by a peril of the seas, namely, by grounding. By way of *obiter*, Mr Justice Bingham stated his view in the following manner:[64]

'Nonetheless, if at the end of the case the court considers a loss by perils of the sea to be no more probable than a loss caused by another, uninsured peril, then the owners must fail'.

It would seem that Mr Justice Bingham, if he had to, would not be adverse to applying the third alternative.

In *The Gold Sky*,[65] however, the plaintiffs could not discharge the onus of proving that the loss was fortuitous. Wilful misconduct was pleaded as an affirmative defence to the plaintiffs' claim of loss by perils of the seas. After declaring his support for *The Gloria* and *The Dias*, Mr Justice Mocatta applied the third alternative to resolve the dispute.

The best explanation of all is perhaps that offered by District Judge Ward in *The Vainqueur*.[66] In a short but helpful comment, he pointed out that 'if the evidence of scuttling is in balance or equipoise ... it becomes crucial which party

---

61 *Palamisto Geberal Enterprise SA v Ocean Marine Insurance Co Ltd* [1972] 2 Lloyd's Rep 60 at pp 75 and 76, CA.

62 Cairns, LJ relied on *La Compania Martiartu v Royal Exchange Assurance* [1923] 1 KB 650; *The Tropaiforos* [1960] 2 Lloyd's Rep 469; and *The Gloria*, 54 Ll L Rep 35.

63 [1984] 2 Lloyd's Rep 264, QBD.

64 He also expressed his approval of the remarks made by Cairns, LJ in *The Dias, Palmisto General Enterprises SA v Ocean Marine Insurance Co Ltd* [1972] 2 Lloyd's Rep 60 at pp 75 and 76, CA.

65 [1972] 2 Lloyd's Rep 187 at p 192; appeal on a procedural issue, [1972] 1 Lloyd's Rep 331, CA.

66 [1972] 2 Lloyd's Rep 60, CA. Judgment was awarded to the insurers even though the proof adduced by them was not sufficient to find that the vessel was scuttled. The plaintiffs failed to discharge the burden of proving that the loss fell within the policy. See also *The Lakeland* (1927) 28 Ll L Rep 293 at p 296.

has the burden of persuasion that the loss was an insured event'. Unlike *The Gloria*,[67] the evidence of scuttling which the defendants had tendered, though found not to be substantial enough for the court to make a positive finding that the vessel was scuttled, was nevertheless perfectly adequate for the purpose of throwing doubts on the plaintiffs' case (of a loss by perils of the seas or an explosion). The defendants had obviously done enough, in a manner of speech, to tip the scale in their favour; and as the ultimate burden of persuasion lies with their opponents, judgment was awarded against the plaintiffs.

To use the words of Lord Justice Bankes in *The Martiartu Case*,[68] the defendants had 'put forward a reasonable explanation of the loss' causing the 'superstructure' of the plaintiffs' case to collapse. Even more generous is the judge in *The Lakeland*,[69] who was prepared to accept 'any evidence of circumstances tending to support [the defendants'] theory of scuttling with the connivance of the owners'.

There was clearly a group of judges who supported the rule of the 'third alternative' even when the defence of wilful misconduct was pleaded. The rule of the third alternative complements the general principle of proof that the ultimate burden of persuasion lies with the plaintiffs. In relation to a claim of loss by perils of the seas, it is pertinent to recall that 'fortuity' is an essential ingredient.[70] Thus, any evidence suggesting that the cause of loss is other than fortuitous would result in the plaintiffs having failed to prove their case.

The most recent pronouncement as to the standard of proof required for the defence of wilful misconduct pleaded in relation to a claim of loss by perils of the seas can be found in *The Ikarian Reefer*,[71] where the Court of Appeal, through Lord Justice Stuart-Smith, expressed the opinion that:

> 'If the plaintiffs fail to discharge this burden, however, their claim under this head [referring to perils of the seas] must fail, even if the insurers have alleged but fail to prove that the grounding was deliberate and the cause, therefore remains uncertain: *The Popi M* ...'.

Having determined that the standard of proof is the *balance of probabilities*, he then proceeded to say that, whether the measure of 'the balance of probabilities is different in practice from the criminal standard of "beyond reasonable doubt" and if so by how much' is a question of semantic. He refused to provide a direct answer to the question but took the safe course by saying that:

> 'The burden of proof is not discharged ... if the evidence fails to exclude a substantial, as opposed to a fanciful or remote possibility that the loss was accidental. But we bear in mind that, on the authorities, the burden which rests upon the insurer is derived from the civil, not the criminal standard ...'

The only clarification that can be derived from the above observations is that the degree of proof is clearly not the criminal standard, but what the precise standard is remains unclear.

---

67 (1936) 54 Ll L Rep 35.
68 [1923] 1 KB 650 at p 655, CA 23 1 KB 650.
69 (1927) 28 Ll L Rep 293 at p 296, USCA.
70 For a discussion of fortuity as an essential characteristic of perils of the seas, see Chapter 9.
71 [1995] 1 Lloyd's Rep 455 at p 459, CA.

To conclude this discussion, it is worthwhile referring to the carefully chosen words of Mr Justice Mason of the High Court of Australia in *The Skandia Case*[72] . Citing *The Martiartu Case* as authority, he said:

'... the insured will fail in an action ... if he does no more than adduce evidence of facts which are equally consistent with the hypothesis that the loss occurred from the defective, deteriorated or decayed condition of the vessel or the inevitable act of the sea, as with the supposition that the loss resulted from a peril of the sea.'

Scuttling with the connivance of the shipowner is, it is observed, conspicuously left out of the above list of possible causes. Reserving this for special treatment, he cautiously pointed out that:[73] 'The onus of proof in such a case has its own difficulties and they have not yet been completely resolved'. Mr Justice Mason obviously had the maze of confusion relating to proof of connivance in cases of barratry in mind when he made this statement.

It is to be noted that none of the above cases has declared that, if wilful misconduct is pleaded as a defence to a claim of a loss by perils of the seas, the standard of proof required to be discharged by the defendant is, as it is sometimes alleged in the case of barratry, to be of the criminal standard of beyond reasonable doubt. On the contrary, the Court of Appeal in *The Ikarian Reefer* seemed to think that it is the civil standard of the balance of probabilities – the same as that expected of the plaintiffs.

There is no cogent reason why the third alternative cannot be invoked merely because wilful misconduct is pleaded as a defence to an action based on perils of the seas. But, as can be seen shortly, it would appear that the law in relation to the burden and standard of proof is different if scuttling with the connivance of the ship owner is pleaded as a defence to barratry. Why and whether this should be so will now be explored.

B – PROOF OF LOSS BY BARRATRY

One of the most problematic areas of the law of barratry is in relation to the question of the burden of proof. There are two sides to the problem: first, as to proof of the ingredients of the peril; and secondly, as to proof of the defence that the loss was caused with the connivance of the shipowner – that the ship was deliberately scuttled – the defence of wilful misconduct. The plaintiffs, of course, have to bear the burden of having to prove that the loss was deliberately caused by the master or crew.[74] But a ship could be intentionally cast away by the master or crew with or without the connivance of her owners. The former is clearly not recoverable, as such an act constitutes wilful misconduct (of the assured) which is not a peril insured against.[75] The latter, however, is a barratrous act and is recoverable if barratry is a peril insured against under the policy.[76] These two forms of loss are distinguishable purely upon the fact of

---

72 [1979] 142 CLR 375 at pp 391 and 392.

73 *Ibid*.

74 *The Michael* [1979] 1 Lloyd's Rep 55 at p 66, QBD. Proof of scuttling would negate a loss by peril of the seas.

75 See s 55(2)(a).

76 See cl 6.2.4 of the ITCH(95) (previously cl 6.2.5 of the ITCH(83)) and cl 4.2.4 of the IVCH(95).

whether the shipowner has or has not consented to the commission of the act by the master or crew.

With the exception of refuting that the act of the master or crew was not intentionally committed – to which there is always the danger that a peril of the seas could then be regarded as the cause of loss – it is difficult to envisage what other defences the defendants could raise to resist a plaintiff's claim of a loss by barratry other than to plead connivance on the part of the shipowners to the act of scuttling.[77] A claim that a ship has been barratrously scuttled by the master or crew is, therefore, almost certainly to be met with the defence that it occurred with the consent of the shipowners. What the defendants are in effect alleging is that the loss was caused by the wilful misconduct of the shipowner. This has caused the law of barratry and of the defence of wilful misconduct to become inextricably inter-related.

PROOF OF CONSENT OR ABSENCE OF CONSENT

The absence of consent or privity on the part of the shipowners is, as case law has established, an essential ingredient of the peril of barratry.[78] This is entrenched in the definition of barratry in r 11 of the Rules for Construction. For an act to be barratrous, it has to be 'to the prejudice of the owner'. It has also to be proved, whether the act takes the form of delay, deviation, fire,[79] intentional breach of blockade,[80] or scuttling, that it was committed without the privity or complicity of the shipowner.

A 'serious and important question' which now arises is, which party has to prove the issue of consent. Is it for the plaintiffs to prove the absence of consent on their part, or is it for the defendants to prove the plaintiffs' complicity in the loss? The answer to this question is of vital importance, as the outcome of a case is critically dependent upon which party bears the initial persuasive onus of proof.

77　The defendants do not have a real choice, as they would have if perils of the sea had been pleaded as the cause of loss. In such a case, as mentioned earlier, they can either simply deny the plaintiffs' allegation that a peril of the seas caused the loss and/or resist the claim by providing the court with an alternative affirmative theory as to the proximate cause of loss.

78　See Chapter 12.

79　In the case of a loss by fire, the plaintiffs are strongly advised to rely on fire (rather than barratry) as the cause of loss, as the term 'fire' is wide enough to include all forms of fire, whether or not it was deliberately started by a member of crew. The only defence which the defendants could plead is that the fire was started with the connivance of the owners, in which case they [the defendants] would have to bear the onus of proof: see *The Ikarian Reefer* [1993] 2 Lloyd's Rep 68 at p 71; [1995] 1 Lloyd's Rep 455, CA; *The Alexion Hope* [1988] 1 Lloyd's Rep 311; and *The Captain Panagos* [1986] 2 Lloyd's Rep 470. Though the act of the crew in deliberately setting the ship on fire also constitutes barratry, it would not be in the interests of the plaintiffs to plead barratry, for in so doing they could well be called upon to prove the absence of privity or consent on their part if the view of Kerr J in *The Michael* [1979] 1 Lloyd's Rep 55 at p 66; was adopted. See also *The Martiartu Case* [1923] 1 KB 650.

80　In *Everth v Hannam* (1815) 6 Taunt 375 the vessel was condemned for breach of a blockade. The plaintiffs' action for the loss of their vessel by barratry failed, as the court was of the view that merely proving that the master had violated the blockade (without more) was not sufficient proof of barratry. It was held that in order to succeed in their claim for barratry, the owners had to disaffirm their privity and consent to the breach: the plaintiffs' had to show that it was not done under their order or direction.

The law in this regard is indeed controversial and unsettling, as there are two conflicting points of view on the matter. For convenience, I shall refer to one school of thought, that expressed by the Court of Appeal in *Elfie A Issaias v Marine Insurance Co Ltd*[81] as *The Issaias* Rule, and the other, as expressed by Lord Justice Scrutton (by way of *obiter*) in the Court of Appeal in *The Martiartu Case*[82] and by Mr Justice Kerr (as he then was) in *The Michael*,[83] as the *The Martiartu-Michael* Rule.[84]

The Issaias Rule

A great deal of controversy centres around the decision of the Court of Appeal in *The Issaias Case*,[85] the facts of which are as follows. The plaintiffs, the shipowners, claimed for a total loss of their vessel by perils of the seas: the defence was a denial with the plea that the ship was wilfully scuttled by the orders and with the concurrence of her owners. Of importance, however, is the fact that it was not contested that the ship was intentionally sunk by the acts of the master and crew. The decision of the case thus hinged primarily upon whether the shipowners had or had not consented to the acts of the master and crew and, more significantly, which party was to prove this fact.

The fact that barratry was not specifically pleaded as an alternative cause of loss did not seem to concern the court, which was prepared to allow the plaintiffs, if it was necessary to do so, to amend their statement of claim during the trial to incorporate barratry as a cause of loss.[86]

All the judges of the court were firmly of the view that the burden of proof of the fact that the owners were privy to the acts of the master rested with the defendants. According to Lord Justice Atkin: 'The charge of privity against the owner makes against him an allegation of what would be a crime ... and in any case a charge of very serious dishonesty'.[87] Due to the seriousness of the

---

81 (1923) 15 Ll L Rep 186, CA, hereinafter referred to as *The Issaias Case*. Roskill LJ of the Court of Appeal in *The Michael* [1979] 2 Lloyd's Rep 1 at pp 12 and 13 expressed some support for *The Issaias* Rule.

82 [1923] 1 KB 650 at p 657.

83 [1979] 1 Lloyd's Rep 55 at p 66, QB (Com Ct).

84 Support for *The Martiartu-Michael* Rule can be found in *The Spathari, Demetriades & Co v Northern Assurance Co* (1923) 17 Ll L Rep 66; *The Cruz, Banco de Barcelona & Others v Union Marine Insurance Co Ltd* (1925) 30 Com Cas 316, *per* Greer J at pp 317–318; *The Gloria, Compania Naviera Vascongada v British & Foreign Marine Insurance Co Ltd* (1936) 54 Ll L Rep 35 at p 51, QBD; *The Eftychia, Bank of Athens v Royal Exchange Assurance* (1937) 9 Ll L Rep 67, at pp 77 and 83; *The Tropaioforos, Compania Naviera Santi SA v Indemnity Marine Assurance Co Ltd* [1960] 2 Lloyd's Rep 469, *per* Pearson J at p 473, QBD; *The Gold Sky, Astrovlanis Compania Naviera SA v Linard* [1972] 2 Lloyd's Rep 187 at p 192, QBD; *The Dias* [1972] 2 Lloyd's Rep 60 at p 76, CA; *The Vainqueur* [1973] 2 Lloyd's Rep 275, *per* Ward, D at p 282, USDC; *The Zinovia* [1984] 2 Ll L Rep 264, *per* Bingham J at p 272, QBD; and *The Captain Panagos DP* [1986] 2 Lloyd's Rep 470, QBD at p 511, *per* Evans J; [1989] 1 Lloyd's Rep 33 at p 40, *per* Neil, I.J.

85 (1923) 15 Ll L Rep 186, CA.

86 The plaintiffs succeeded in the Court of Appeal without having to amend the pleadings; but in *The Zinovia* [1984] 2 Lloyd's Rep 264 at p 271, Bingham J thought it preferable that an amendment should be made.

87 (1923) 15 Ll L Rep 186 at p 191, CA.

accusation, the judge felt that he had to treat the matter as if it was a criminal charge.[88] Relying on a well established principle of English (criminal) law – the presumption of innocence – Lord Justice Atkin formulated the legal rule as follows:[89]

> 'We have then a case, now admitted by the plaintiff, to be one where the master, intentionally and successfully, let water into the ship for the purpose of sinking her. Unless done with the privity of the owner, this would be barratry ... The only issue is whether the owner was privy to the act of the master. I entertain no doubt that the onus of proving this fact rests upon the defendant underwriters ... The plaintiff is entitled to invoke in his favour a principle of English law ... the principle of presumption of innocence. I will cite from *Stephen on Evidence* ... "The burden of proving that any person has been guilty of a crime or wrongful act is on the person who asserts it, whether the commission of such act is or is not directly in issue in the action".'

Stating the same principle but with a different slant, the Master of the Rolls invoked the rule that there is *no presumption of complicity* in English law: the fact that a ship has been proven to have been scuttled does not automatically raise a presumption that it took place with the complicity of her owners. In the words of Lord Justice Warrington:[90]

> '*Prima facie* it was an act of barratry and would be one of the perils insured against; and it is for the underwriters to show that the wrongful act of the master was not committed "to the prejudice" of the owner inasmuch as it was connived at by him. I apprehend that to cast away a man's ship without his consent is "to his prejudice"...'

The Issaias Rule, it should be pointed out, has to be confined to its own facts: that is, where the fact that a barratrous act has been committed was *not* an issue, and the defence raised was one of wilful misconduct on the part of the shipowners. In fact, the Law Lords had emphasised that as the cause of loss (a deliberate sinking of the ship by the master or crew) was no longer in dispute, privity was the only issue outstanding.

Lord Justice Atkin has, in the following comment, given us an insight of his opinion on the matter: 'This is not the case of an unexplained loss. I do *not* think the onus would be altered if it were, if the issue raised was scuttling.'[91] He was prepared to apply *The Issaias* Rule regardless of whether the loss was explained or not; he would invoke the Rule whenever wilful misconduct is pleaded as a defence to a claim of loss by barratry.

According to *The Issaias* Rule, the burden of proof shifts to the defendants once the court is satisfied, either by admission or proof, that the ship has been deliberately scuttled. The Court of Appeal has deemed it fit to put the defendants to a strict proof because the nature of the defence was an allegation of the commission of a crime.

---

88 See *The Tropaioforos* [1960] 2 Lloyd's Rep 469 at p 473, *per* Pearson J '... that scuttling a ship would be fraudulent and criminal behaviour'.

89 (1923) 15 Ll L Rep 186 at p 191.

90 *Ibid*, at p 189.

91 *Ibid*, at p 191.

Some faint support for *The Issaias* Rule can be found in the cautious remarks of Lord Justice Roskill of the Court of Appeal in *The Michael*.[92] It would, however, be more befitting to say that the matter was left open as the issue was not argued on appeal.

The Martiartu–Michael Rule

In an *obiter dictum* expressed by Lord Justice Scrutton of the Court of Appeal in *The Martiartu Case*,[93] where perils of the sea and barratry were pleaded as alternative causes of loss, the burden of proof was said to lie with the plaintiffs. Regrettably, the judge did not, in the context of barratry, make it explicitly clear in his judgment which party has to prove the issue of consent. His Lordship did not go so far as to lay down the rule (as it was unnecessary for him to do so) that it was for the plaintiffs to prove not only that the ship was deliberately scuttled, but that it was scuttled without the connivance of her owners. But this is implicit in his judgment, for he held the view that it is the plaintiffs who have to prove a loss by a peril insured against, and proof of this in relation to barratry would entail proof of the absence of connivance.

The twin burden of proof

The Michael[94] has categorically imposed a twin burden of proof on the shipowner. Mr Justice Kerr, the trial judge, approached the problem, first, without considering any of the authorities. He said:

'Apart from authority, the answer seems obvious in principle. The owners must establish a loss by the insured peril of barratry, which involves establishing both a deliberate sinking *and* the absence of the owners' consent. If at the end of the day the court is left in doubt whether the owners consented or not, then it seems to me that the claim must fail.'

Interestingly, Mr Justice Kerr preferred to rely on the Court of Session's decision in *Demetriades v Northern Assurance Co, The Spathari*,[95] rather than *The Martiartu Case*,[96] which was not even mentioned in his judgment, to buttress his stand on the matter. Courageously, he dismissed *The Issaias* Rule as being incorrect in principle.

In *The Spathari*,[97] the ship was proved to have been scuttled by the engineer. As the outstanding fact was not left in doubt – that is, that the ship was scuttled with the connivance of her owners – the statements made by Lord Justice Clerk and Lord Anderson were *obiter*. Lord Justice Clerk said that:[98]

92 [1979] 2 Lloyd's Rep 1 at p 13, CA.

93 [1923] 1 KB 650, CA; The decision of the Court of Appeal was affirmed by the House of Lords (1924) 19 Ll L Rep 95.

94 [1979] 1 Lloyd's Rep 55; [1979] 2 Lloyd's Rep 1, CA.

95 (1923) 17 Ll L Rep 65, Court of Session. When *The Spathari* reached the House of Lords, (1924) 21 Ll L Rep 265, the appeal failed without the question of scuttling, privity or onus being further considered.

96 (1923) 1 KB 650, CA.

97 (1924) 21 Ll L Rep 265.

98 *Ibid*, at p 334.

'If the evidence establishes that the ship was scuttled, as I think it clearly does, and leaves it in doubt whether or not the pursuers were parties to the plot, then their actions must fail ... If [The Martiartu Case and The Issaias Case] be irreconcilable, then I prefer the former and I am prepared to follow it. I respectfully agree with Lord Justice Scrutton ...'

Lord Anderson, who held the same view, showed his preference in the following terms:[99]

'If these two decisions are inconsistent with one another I prefer the law laid down in the former case [The Martiartu Case] as it seems to me to rest upon the fundamental rule of proof which denies a pursuer success unless he proves his case.'

In The Zinovia,[100] the problem was considered by Mr Justice Bingham, albeit in the court of first instance. His sentiments were vividly described in a concise statement: '... it would still seem to me wrong in principle that the onus should be laid on underwriters of disproving an essential ingredient of the owner's claim'. Not surprisingly, following the strategy in The Issaias Case,[101] the plaintiffs, though they did not specifically put forward barratry as a head of claim, nevertheless, reserved their right to do so if the evidence turned out to support such a claim. But as the owners had succeeded in showing that the loss was proximately caused by a peril of the seas, namely, the grounding of the vessel, judgment was awarded to them.

To ensure that his decision covered all possible grounds and, more significantly, to pre-empt appeal on the basis of burden of proof, the learned judge delivered a guarded judgment:[102]

'The insurers ... have not satisfied me, according to the high standard of proof required, that the owners wilfully cast away the vessel. I am on the contrary satisfied that the owners did not do so ... If, contrary to my conclusion, the vessel ... was deliberately run aground by the master or crew, the insurers had not proved that the owners in any way consented, or were privy, to that action. If the burden of disproving privity lay on the owners, I should hold that they had discharged it.'

The learned judge, who expressed some reservation about The Issaias Rule, nevertheless felt bound by it.[103]

---

99 Ibid, at p 352.

100 [1984] 2 Lloyd's Rep 264 at p 272.

101 (1923) 15 Ll L Rep 186, CA.

102 [1984] 2 Lloyd's Rep 264 at p 303.

103 Ibid, at p 272, Bingham J said: '... once the owners have proved a casting away by the deliberate act of the master or crew, it is for the insurer to establish to the high standard required for proof of fraud in a civil case that the owners consent to, or connived at the casting away.'

In *The Captain Panagos DP*,[104] Lord Justice Neill of the Court of Appeal found himself in the same predicament of being bound by authority. However, in the following comment with reference to barratry, he intimated his view on the subject as follows:

'... it is a necessary ingredient of the definition that the wilful act should have been committed "to the prejudice of the owner". Accordingly, if the primary contention of the owner of a vessel is that the loss was a loss by barratry, I can see great force in the argument that it is for the owner to prove that the wrongful act was committed "to his prejudice" and therefore that it was committed without his consent or connivance.'

Lord Justice Neill would have adopted Mr Justice Kerr's approach in *The Michael*,[105] if he were free to do so.

In *The Tropaioforos*,[106] Mr Justice Pearson offered his opinion on the question of the onus of proof in connection with scuttling in the following terms:

'... due weight must be given to the consideration that scuttling a ship would be fraudulent and criminal behaviour. No doubt one reason for placing the burden of proof on the shipowners in such a case as this is that they are likely to have all or almost all, the relevant information, and the insurers are likely to have virtually no information initially.'

That these remarks relate to a claim for a loss by a peril of the seas is clear. But, scuttling a ship is criminal behaviour whether it is pleaded as a defence to an action for loss by perils of the seas or by barratry. Admittedly, with regard to the availability of information in relation to the shipowner, there is an element of truth in this statement. The same, however, cannot be said of the position of an assignee, a cargo-owner, a mortgagee or any interested party who is not in any way involved in the management of the affairs of the ship.

Interestingly, Mr Justice Salmon in *Slattery v Mance*[107] was of the opinion that: 'There is no principle of the common law and no authority ... for the proposition that, when the facts are peculiarly within the knowledge of the person against whom the assertion is made, the onus shifts to that person.'

A solution?

There are clearly two contradictory points of view on the question of the burden of proof when scuttling with the connivance of the shipowner, or effectively the

---

104 [1989] 1 Lloyd's Rep 33 at p 40, CA. Evans J in the court of first instance [1986] 2 Lloyd's Rep 470 at p 511 who shared the same sentiments stated that: '... if it were necessary to decide the issue in the present case ... I doubt whether it would be my conclusion if unaided by authority. The definition of barratry includes "to the prejudice of the owner" which suggests that the assured must prove that he was an innocent victim. The burden might not be heavy, unless the plaintiff's own evidence raised doubts about his innocence, or the defendant insurer adduced evidence which had that effect.' See also *The Ikarian Reefer* [1993] 2 Lloyd's Rep 68, QBD, a case on similar facts where Cresswell J, who also felt bound to apply *The Issaias* Rule, held that the burden of proof that it was deliberately set on fire by or with the connivance of the ship owner was on the defendants. On appeal [1995] 1 Lloyd's Rep 455, the decision of Creswell J was over-turned on a different finding of fact.

105 [1979] 1 Lloyd's Rep 55.

106 [1960] 2 Lloyd's Rep 469 at p 473.

107 [1962] 1 All ER 525 at p 526, QBD.

defence of wilful misconduct, is pleaded as a defence to a claim for a loss by barratry. On one side, there is a host of authorities of first instance judgments and Court of Appeal *dicta* supporting *The Martiartu-Michael* Rule; on the other, an affirmative but almost solitary and much tolerated Court of Appeal ruling of *The Issaias Case*.

In 1924, a year after *The Issaias* Rule was declared, the Earl of Birkenhead of the House of Lords in *Anghelatos v Northern Assurance Co Ltd, The Olympia*[108] predicted that: '... it is almost certain that this matter will one day require careful consideration by your Lordships when it arise as an issue which actually requires decision in this House ...'.[109] Lord Sumner, however, in a rather subtle, but most enlightening speech, offered some indication of his perception of the law:[110]

> 'If it is the case that loss by wilful misconduct by the assured is a mere *exception* out of a *prima facie general liability* from loss by stranding or by foundering, then I can well understand why the law says those who allege that exception must prove it, namely, the underwriters, but if it be that the law as I understand it lays down finally that an assured is insured against accidental stranding, but not against designed stranding, then it may well be that the assured only brings himself within the proposition that he has proved a loss by perils insured against, if he proves the circumstances of the loss were circumstances of accidental stranding.'

The distinction as stated lies, on the one hand, between an exception 'out of a *prima facie* general liability' and, on the other, between a peril which is insured and one which is not, (as illustrated by his example of accidental and designed stranding); though fine and intriguing it is, nevertheless, instructive, as it may well be the answer to the problem.

Without reading too much between the lines, it would seem that Lord Sumner, though he had made it perfectly clear that the point should be explicitly kept open for future decision, is supportive of *The Martiartu–Michael* Rule. Approaching the matter in another way, it is submitted that the nature and characteristics of an insured peril have to be closely examined for the purpose of determining whether it falls within the '*prima facie* general liability' class of an insured peril. For example:

- In the case of fire (of which there is no definition), other than proof of loss or damage caused by fire, there is no other requirement such as fortuity or absence of consent for the plaintiffs to prove.[111] There is, thus, a '*prima facie* general liability' for loss by fire, and if wilful misconduct is pleaded, it is pleaded as an 'exception out of a *prima facie* general liability'.

---

108 (1924) 19 Ll L Rep 255 at p 256, HL.

109 Neill LJ in *The Captain Panagos DP* [1989] 1 Lloyd's Rep 33 at p 40 CA, was also resigned to the fact that, '... the judgments ... in *The Elias Issais* make it impossible for any court below the House of Lords to conclude that where it is common ground ... that a stranding was caused by a deliberate act, the onus of proving an absence of consent or connivance rests on the owners'.

110 (1924) 19 Ll L Rep 255 at p 262. Emphasis added.

111 See *Slattery v Mance* [1962] 1 All ER 525; *The Alexion Hope* [1988] 1 Lloyd's Rep 311, CA; *The Captain Panagos DP* [1989] 1 Lloyd's Rep 33, CA; and *The Ikarian Reefer* [1993] 2 Lloyd's Rep 68, QBD; [1995] 1 Lloyd's Rep 455, CA.

- Where a peril of the seas is concerned, the requirement of 'fortuity' or 'accidental' loss (as set out in r 9) clearly rules out from its scope all forms of loss caused by a deliberate or an intentional act. Proof of fortuity would necessarily entail proof of the absence of consent. The second distinction drawn by Lord Sumner between 'accidental' and 'designed' stranding relating to perils of the seas and wilful misconduct on the part of the ship respectively, highlights this point.[112] In the case of fire, the defendants have to prove connivance.

- In the case of barratry, the absence of consent or privity is an inherent feature of the peril. As an integral element of the peril, it has to be proved by the shipowner as a part of the claim, otherwise, the act committed by the master or crew is not barratrous.

Unlike fire, there is no general liability for a loss by a peril of the seas or barratry. Thus, it does not seem unreasonable to expect the party who seeks to rely on such a peril as the cause of loss to adduce proof to satisfy the specifications of the insured peril, namely, fortuity in the case of perils of the seas, and the absence of connivance in the case of barratry.

It would appear that when one applies the *The Issaias* Rule, there is always a possibility that a plaintiff could win a case by default: the fact that the defence may have failed to prove (to the high standard expected of a criminal proceeding) that the ship was scuttled with the connivance of her owners, does not necessarily mean that the plaintiffs have successfully discharged their duty of proving that the loss was barratrous – that it occurred *without* their connivance – or, in the case of a peril of the seas, that it was fortuitous. Once the defence of wilful misconduct is pleaded, it triggers a series of consequences: first, the burden of proof, according to *The Issaias* Rule, shifts to the defendants to prove that the loss was caused with the connivance of the plaintiffs; and, secondly, as can be seen shortly,[113] the standard of proof changes from a balance of probabilities to one of a higher standard, if not beyond reasonable doubt, almost as high as that standard, depending on the gravity of the allegation of fraud.[114]

In *The Issaias Case*, the Master of the Rolls attempted to distinguish *The Martiartu Case* from the case he had to deal with at hand. *The Martiartu Case*,[115] he said, was not relevant because the issue there was in relation to the cause of loss, and 'it was to that issue that the remarks in question were addressed'; whilst in *The Issaias Case*, however, the cause of loss had been ascertained and was no longer in dispute.

Using the same analogy, Lord Justice Neill in *The Captain Panagos DP*[116] tried to distinguish the cases in the following way: he observed that in *The Issaias*

---

112 A loss by stranding, if designed by the master or crew, would constitute barratry. Lord Sumner could not have had barratry in mind, as barratry is not an accidental loss.

113 See below.

114 See also *Anonima Petroli Italiana SpA and Neste Oy v Marlucidez Armadora SA, The Filiatra Legacy* [1991] 2 Lloyd's Rep 337, CA.

115 See below.

116 [1989] 1 Lloyd's Rep 33 at p 40, CA.

Case[117] the sinking was 'held', whilst in *The Michael*,[118] it was 'admitted' by the owners, to be deliberate. Why this should make any difference was not explained.

The distinction is difficult to fathom: it is not quite accurate to say that mere proof of the commission of a deliberate act of scuttling by the master or crew is sufficient to make out a *prima facie* case of barratry. Barratry, by definition, is not only an act which is 'wilfully committed' but also one which is committed 'to the prejudice of the owner'.

From hindsight, it would appear that the defendants in *The Issaias Case* would have been better off if they had not averred wilful misconduct as their defence. After all, as was seen earlier,[119] a defendant is not obliged to provide the court with an affirmative theory for the cause of loss. But, as *The Issaias* Rule has demonstrated, if a defendant elects to take the course of alleging that the ship was scuttled with the connivance of the shipowner, the burden will be cast upon him to prove the allegation, failing which the plaintiffs would succeed in their claim. It would therefore seem that a defendant, unless he is in possession of strong evidence of the commission of a fraudulent or criminal act, would be better off if he were to refrain from pleading the defence of wilful misconduct, and simply endeavour to deny the plaintiffs' claim by whatever other means available to him.

To illustrate this point, reference could be made to the American case of *The Lakeland*,[120] where the defendant simply denied the plaintiffs' allegations (of a loss by a peril of the seas) without pleading any affirmative defence. As this point was summarised with admirable clarity by the judge, it is advisable to quote from it:[121]

> 'The ultimate burden did not shift by reason of the evidence of scuttling presented by defendants; that evidence was not offered in support of any affirmative defence, because there was none; it was offered to sustain the denial of liability to raise at least a question in the jury's mind as to whether or not the sinking was in fact due to a peril covered by the policies; it bore only upon the question as to whether or not plaintiffs had affirmatively made out their case of liability under the policies.'

On this occasion, the defendants, without going so far as to 'accuse' the plaintiffs of wilful misconduct, merely supplied the court with evidence sufficient to throw doubts upon the plaintiffs' claim which was that a peril of the seas caused the loss. Through cross-examination of witnesses, the defendants' strategy was to bring to light some evidence of unseeming conduct so as to implicate the plaintiffs, that they were in some way responsible for the loss: such evidence, the defendants had hoped, as would be sufficient to expose or show up the weaknesses of the plaintiffs' case.[122]

---

117 (1923) 15 Ll L Rep 186, CA.

118 [1979] 1 Lloyd's Rep 55; [1979] 2 Lloyd's Rep 1, CA.

119 See above.

120 (1927) 28 Ll L Rep 293, US Court of Appeals.

121 *Ibid*, at p 296.

122 As the issues on the burden of proof were not properly defined at the trial, the Appeal Court ordered that the case be retried.

Whether a British court of law would allow a defendant, who has not pleaded the defence, to proceed with evidence of wilful misconduct is doubtful. In the light of the comments made by Lord Justice Cairns in *The Dias*,[123] direct proof would almost certainly be ruled out. It is, however, anticipated that skilful cross-examination of witnesses is as far as the defendants would be allowed to go.

The Martiartu–Michael Rule is consistent with the general principles of the law relating to burden of proof.[124] As the absence of privity or consent is an essential feature of barratry, the party who alleges that an act of barratry has been committed should therefore have to bear the burden of having to prove this requirement. And if, at the end of the day, the court is uncertain as to the cause of loss, it should apply the 'third alternative', as proposed by the House of Lords in *The Popi M*,[125] to arrive at a decision.

It is submitted that 'barratry' and 'perils of the seas' should be placed in the same category in so far as the crucial question of proof of privity or consent is concerned; 'fire' on the other hand could then be seen as an exception to the rule. There would not then be the added advantage of pleading barratry, in preference to perils of the sea, as the cause of loss.

Under current law, the burden of proof varies not only according to the nature of the claim, but also, to the nature of the defence raised. This matter has to be settled, and a general authoritative pronouncement from the House of Lords is now long overdue.

STANDARD OF PROOF OF COMPLICITY

The onus and standard of proof of complicity (or the defence of wilful misconduct) should logically be the same whether the claim of the assured be based on fire, barratry or perils of the seas. But as the preceding discussion has demonstrated, barratry (and fire)[126] is placed in a different category from perils of the seas. In view of the fact that there are two points of view on the question of the onus of proof with the regard to the issue of connivance in relation to barratry, it should not come as a surprise that the standard of proof would vary according to which point of view one adopts.

In *The Issaias Case*,[127] the Court of Appeal, after equating the casting away of a ship by a shipowner as a crime, a fraud and a charge of the gravest kind, had perforce to invoke the criminal standard of proof of beyond reasonable doubt. Accordingly, the Master of the Rolls ruled that: 'Fraud must be brought home to a man with reasonable certainty'; and in an equally informative speech, Lord Justice Warrington said that, 'when the defendants charge the plaintiff with the very serious misconduct of conniving at the casting away of his ship, in other

---

123 [1972] 2 Lloyd's Rep 60 at p 75, CA.

124 The same general principle applies to perils of the seas: see Chapter 9.

125 [1985] 2 Lloyd's Rep 1.

126 See below.

127 (1923) 15 Ll L Rep 186, CA.

words of being a party to that act, it is incumbent on them to bring his guilt home without reasonable doubt'.

Subsequently, in *Hornal v Neuberger Products Ltd*,[128] the Court of Appeal again had the opportunity to re-examine this question. Though not an insurance case, the principles enunciated therein have been regarded as of general application in civil actions. Lord Justice Denning, after reviewing all the cases and relying on the judgment which he had delivered in *Bater v Bater*[129] arrived at the conclusion that:

> '... the standard of proof depends on the nature of the issue. The more serious the allegation the higher degree of probability that is required; but it *need not* in a civil case, reach the very high standard required by criminal law.'

Recently, the Court of Appeal in *The Filiatra Legacy*[130] reiterated, albeit in a case relating to carriage of goods by sea, that in a case where the assertion of a serious crime is involved, the manner of proof has to be appropriate to the case.

The Issaias Case, amongst others, was criticised as having laid down too high a standard of proof.

No absolute standard of proof

It is fair to say that judges do recognise that there is no 'absolute' standard of proof in a civil case. It would be safer to say that the standard of proof in a civil case is variable from case to case depending on the gravity of the issue or charge.[131] The allegation of a commission of a crime in a civil action would raise the standard from the balance of probability to that of a higher standard. That the highest ceiling of proof of beyond reasonable doubt is not ruled out as a possibility can be seen in the carefully chosen words of Lord Justice Denning.[132] The more serious the charge the higher is the standard of proof.

It is thus not surprising that the judges who felt bound to apply *The Issaias* Rule, such as Mr Justice Branson in *The Gloria*,[133] and Mr Justice Bingham in *The Zinovia*,[134] had no choice but to apply the higher standard of proof attendant to the Rule.

---

128 [1957] 1 QBD 247 at p 258.

129 [1951] P 35. He spoke of 'a degree of probability which is commensurate with the occasion' and of 'a degree of probability which is proportionate to the subject-matter'. Emphasis added.

130 [1991] 2 Lloyd's Rep 337 at p 373, CA.

131 See *The Captain Panagos DP* [1989] 1 Lloyd's Rep 33 at p 41, *per* Neill LJ: 'That the burden of proof, though not quite equivalent to that required in a criminal case is a heavy burden commensurate with the gravity of the matter'.

132 He has used the words 'need not' as opposed to 'cannot'.

133 (1936) 54 Lloyd's Rep 35 at p 50, *per* Branson J: 'Scuttling is a crime, and the court will not find that it has been committed unless it is proved with the same degree of certainty as is required for the proof of a crime'.

134 [1984] 2 Lloyds' Rep 264 at p 272, *per* Bingham J, '... it is for the insurer to establish to the high standard required for proof of fraud in a civil case that the owners consented to, or connived at, the casting away'.

On the other hand, as to be expected, supporters of *The Martiartu–Michael* Rule would naturally apply the standard of proof which is consistent with their theory of the onus of proof. Mr Justice Kerr held that 'common sense' required that the plaintiffs satisfy him on a 'clear balance of probability' that the vessel was sunk without their knowledge or consent. As the burden of proof does not shift, but remains with the plaintiffs throughout – regardless of the nature of the defence – they have to satisfy the courts on a balance of probability that the loss was caused by an insured peril.

C – PROOF OF LOSS BY FIRE

The fact that 'fortuity' is not an essential ingredient for the peril of 'fire' renders the onus of proof for the assured that much easier to fulfil. To capture the words of Mr Justice Evans in *The Captain Panagos DP*:[135]

> '"Fire", unlike "perils of the seas", does not itself connote a fortuity ... there is no statutory definition which gives grounds for arguing that the possibility of connivance must be disproved. I therefore conclude that the plaintiffs would have proved a loss by fire, if their claim had not been defeated by the defence of owners' connivance.'

Thus, in comparison with 'perils of the seas', an assured in a claim for loss by fire has a *lesser* burden of proof: *Slattery v Mance*[136] is the authority which has established the rule that '... once it is shown that the loss has been caused by fire, the plaintiff has made out a *prima facie* case, and the onus is on the defendant to show on a balance of probabilities that the fire was caused or connived at by the plaintiff'. Accordingly, if at the end of the day the jury comes to the conclusion that the loss is equally consistent with arson as it is with an accidental fire, the onus being on the defendant, the plaintiff would win on that issue.[137]

The above statements have clarified that the initial proof of loss by fire lies with the plaintiffs, but proof of the defence of connivance, and of wilful misconduct, rests with the defendants. It is not for the plaintiffs to prove the absence of connivance, but for the defendants to prove its presence.

In *The Ikarian Reefer*,[138] Mr Justice Cresswell, after citing the above case and *The Captain Panagos DP*[139] with approval, summarised the legal position as regards the burden of proof as follows:

> 'Where the owners have proved a loss by fire, the burden of proving a deliberate fire and connivance lies upon the insurer. If the evidence leaves the court in doubt then the assured is entitled to succeed. Thus the assured in a claim for loss by fire has a lesser burden than one claiming for loss by perils of the sea (who

---

135 [1986] 2 Lloyd's Rep 470 at p 511, QBD; on appeal [1989] 1 Lloyd's Rep 33.

136 [1962] 1 All ER 525 at p 526.

137 It has to be said that the standard of the 'balance of probabilities' advocated by Salmon J is now, in the light of the Court of Appeal's ruling in *The Captain Panagos DP* [1989] 1 Lloyd's Rep 33 at p 41 *per* Neill LJ, no longer good law.

138 [1993] 2 Lloyd's Rep 68 at p 71, CA. The fact that his decision was overturned on a different finding of facts does not affect his observations on the law on the burden of proof.

139 [1986] 2 Lloyd's Rep 470 at p 510. The remarks of the trial judge, Evans J, were approved.

must prove fortuity); though he is in the same position in this respect as the claimant for loss by barratry.'

In what way the plaintiffs' position is the same as that of a claimant for a loss by barratry is unclear. Admittedly, the burden of proof of a plaintiff claiming a loss by fire is lighter than in the case of a perils of the seas: he does not have to prove fortuity. The similarity referred to by Mr Justice Creswell presumably relates to the question of the burden of proof of connivance as laid down in *The Issaias Case*, to the effect that the defendants have to bear the burden of proof that the ship was wilfully set on fire, or was scuttled by the plaintiffs. In the case of a peril of the seas, however, as the need to prove fortuity entails proof of an absence of connivance, the burden of proof lies with the plaintiffs. In this sense, fire is said to be in the same class as barratry.

Standard of proof

An insurer who alleges that a ship was deliberately set on fire with the connivance of the assured has to prove this fact. This is in conformity with the general principle of the common law: he who asserts must prove.

That the burden of proof of the defence of wilful misconduct, in a case where fire is alleged to have caused a loss, lies upon the defendants is also an indisputable principle of the law of marine insurance.[140] As the peril of 'fire', unlike perils of the seas, does not contain the element of fortuity, the burden of proof of connivance must rest with the defendants. The question which now arises is: what is the standard of proof as regards this defence?

That 'fire' is in the same class as 'barratry' in relation to the onus of proof as regards the defence of wilful misconduct is made clear in the above observations. Lord Justice Neill of the Court of Appeal in *The Captain Panagos DP*[141] was clear that 'the burden of proof, though not quite equivalent to that required in a criminal case is a heavy burden commensurate with the gravity of the matter'. The same criterion was applied by Mr Justice Cresswell in *The Ikarian Reefer*[142] who was, of course, bound by this and the other similar rulings of the Court of Appeal. It is interesting to note that when *The Ikarian Reefer* went on appeal, the Court of Appeal, relying on *The Filiatra Legacy*[143] held that:

> On this issue, the burden of proof rests unequivocally on the insurers, and the degree or standard of proof which the law requires makes the burden heavier than that which rests upon the shipowners. Although the same "balance of probabilities" test applies, the standard of proof required is commensurate with the gravity of the allegation made; and no more serious allegation can be made against the master of a ship, a trained and experienced professional who was responsible for its safety and for the lives and welfare of its crew.'

---

140 The comments made by the Court of Appeal in *The Ikarian Reefer* [1995] 1 Lloyd's Rep 455 are concerned with the burden and standard of proof in relation to a claim for a loss by perils of the seas.

141 [1989] 1 Lloyd's Rep 33 at p 41, CA.

142 [1993] 2 Lloyd's Rep 68 at p 71, QBD.

143 [1991] 2 Lloyd's Rep 337 at p 373, CA.

In the light of these remarks which are the most recent on the subject, one could safely say that the degree or standard of proof ranges from at its lowest, the balance of probabilities, to its highest, which may come close to, but not quite, the standard of beyond reasonable doubt. The Court of Appeal was quick to remind us that, '... we bear in mind that, on the authorities, the burden rests upon the insurers is derived from the civil, *not* the criminal standard' of proof.

CHAPTER 12

THE INCHMAREE CLAUSE

INTRODUCTION

Clause 6 of the ITCH(95) and its counterpart, cl 4 of the IVCH(95), provide cover not only for some of the traditional perils of the old SG Policy,[1] but also for other perils some of which are excluded by s 55(2)(c), for example, 'any injury to machinery not proximately caused by maritime perils'.[2] Clauses 6.1.6 and 6.1.8 of the ITCH(95) insuring against loss of or damage to the subject-matter insured caused by 'contact with land conveyance, dock or harbour equipment or installation'[3] and 'accidents in loading and discharging or shifting cargo or fuel'[4] respectively can by no stretch of imagination be said to arise from a marine peril.[5] With the exception of barratry, the same holds true for the other losses enumerated in cl 6.2.

Clause 6.2 is commonly referred to as 'the Inchmaree clause'. It has derived its name from the vessel of the same name in the case of *Thames and Mersey Marine Insurance Co v Hamilton, Fraser and Co, The Inchmaree*[6] because of which it was introduced. It is sometimes called the 'Negligence Clause' by reason of the fact that it (cll 6.2.2 and 6.2.3) also insures against loss of or damage to the subject-matter caused by the negligence of two groups of persons, namely, employees on board – 'master, officers, crew or pilots'; and outsiders – 'repairers or charterers'. It has earned its third name – the 'additional perils clause'[7] – from cl 6.2.1, which insures against loss of or damage to the subject-matter insured caused by the 'bursting of boilers, breakage of shafts or any latent defect in the machinery or hull'. Unless the policy otherwise provides, such losses are generally governed by s 55(2)(c), which states that the insurer is not liable for 'any injury to machinery not proximately caused by maritime perils'.

It is to be noted that cl 6.2, but not cl 6.1, is made subject to a proviso which has to be complied with before the assured can recover for any of perils

---

1   Namely, perils of the sea, fire, theft, jettison, piracy and barratry.

2   Note that 'breakdown of or accident to nuclear installations or reactors' previously covered by cl 6.1.6 is no longer covered by the ITCH(95). See also cl 27 of the ITCH(95) on the exclusion for radioactive contamination.

3   Note that 'contact with aircraft or similar objects falling therefrom' previously part of cl 6.1.7 of the ITCH(83) has been moved to cl 6.2.5 of the ITCH(95) and is now subject to the due diligence proviso.

4   'Accidents in loading discharging or shifting of cargo or fuel' was previously insured under cl 6.2.1 of the ITCH(83) and was subjected to the due diligence proviso. As it is now moved to cl 6.1 of the ITCH(95), it is not longer governed by the proviso.

5   Loss of or damage caused by 'breakdown of or accident to nuclear installations or reactors' was previously covered by cl 6.1.6 of the ITCH(83). They are now no longer covered by the ITCH(95). See also cl 27 of the ITCH(95) for the exclusion of loss caused by or contributed to by or arising from radioactive contamination.

6   (1887) 12 AC 484, HL.

7   To avoid confusion, it is best that this name be not used, as it could be mistaken for the Institute Additional Perils Clauses – Hulls.

enumerated therein. The proviso will be examined later; and the relationship between s 55(2)(c) and cl 6.2, and between s 39 and cl 6.2, will be studied as and when appropriate.

Before embarking upon an analysis of the scope of cl 6.2, reference should first be made to *The Inchmaree Case*,[8] the facts of which are as follows. *The Inchmaree* was insured by a time policy. During the voyage, an engineer had negligently left a valve closed when it should have been kept opened. This caused the air-chamber of a pump worked by a donkey-engine to burst. The sole question which the House had to consider was whether the loss – that is, the cost of repairing the engine – was one of the losses or misfortunes against which the insurer had agreed to indemnify the owners of *The Inchmaree*. The House held that as the perils of the seas was not in any way responsible for the loss, her owners could not claim for the loss under the policy.[9]

As a result of the decision of the House, cl 6.2 was specially formulated in order to allow a shipowner to recover for such a loss. Only cll 6.2.1 and 6.2.2 appeared in the original version, the rest were added later. If the 1906 Act was then in existence, the House would have been able to cite s 55(2)(c) as a ground for excepting the insurer from liability: the basis for its refusal would simply be that an insurer is not liable for 'any injury to machinery not proximately caused by maritime perils'.

'CAUSED BY'

The opening words of cl 6.2, 'caused by', have been subjected to a considerable amount of litigation. Leaving aside for the moment the provision relating to negligence, one would have thought that cl 6.2.1, by itself, would be adequate to provide a shipowner with indemnity for a loss such as that which occurred in *The Inchmaree Case*. After all, it was the very reason why the clause was formulated. But the words 'caused by' have been awarded an interpretation which has limited its scope. Two Court of Appeal decisions have conclusively settled the rule that the repair or replacement cost for a boiler which has burst, for a shaft which has broken, or for any part of the machinery or hull suffering from latent defect, is not recoverable.

The first case, *Oceanic SS Co v Faber*,[10] involved a flaw in the tail-shaft caused by imperfect welding. Some years later the flaw, which was not visible on the surface at previous surveys, developed a crack and the shaft had to be replaced by a new one. The assured claimed for its replacement cost only to be turned down by the Court of Appeal which held that the clause did not cover such a loss; it did not cover latent defects in the machinery, but only for a loss *'through'*

---

8   *Thames & Mersey Marine Insurance Co v Hamilton, Fraser & Co* (1887) 12 AC 484, HL.
9   Overruling *West India & Panama Telegraph Co v Home & Colonial Marine Insurance Co, The Investigator* (1880), 6 QBD 51. The House was not prepared to hold that the loss was of the same genus as 'perils of the sea'.
10 (1907) 13 Com Cas 28, CA.

(the then current wording of the clause) a latent defect.[11] Lord Justice Fletcher Moulton explained that:[12]

> 'A defect initially latent, but spreading until it becomes a patent defect, is an ordinary incident in all machinery ... that is a case of a latent defect developing into a patent defect ... I do not believe for one moment that this clause means that the machinery is insured against the existence of latent defects. It only means that, if through their latency those defects have not been guarded against, and actual loss of the hull or machinery, or damage to the hull or machinery arises, from those defects, the insurers will bear the burden of that loss.'

A few years later, the Court of Appeal was again confronted with the same problem in *Hutchins Brothers v Royal Exchange Assurance Corpn*,[13] where a latent defect in the stern frame became visible as a result of wear and tear during the currency of the policy. The cost of a new stern frame was held not recoverable under the policy. Lord Justice Vaughan Williams cited the following remarks made by Mr Justice Walton, the trial judge in *Oceanic SS Co v Faber*, with approval:[14]

> '... the effect and sense of this clause is not that the underwriters guarantee that the machinery of the vessel is free from latent defect, or undertake, if such defects are discovered during the currency of a policy, to make such defects good.'

In similar terms, Lord Justice Fletcher Moulton stressed that:[15]

> 'To hold that the clause covers it would be to make the underwriters not insurers, but guarantors, and to turn the clause into a warranty that the hull and machinery are free from latent defects, and, consequently, to make all such defects repairable at the expense of the underwriter.'

Subsequently, in *Scindia Steamships Ltd v The London Assurance*,[16] the same principle was applied in relation to the breakage of a shaft.[17]

To throw more light on the subject, reference should be made to a remark uttered by Mr Justice Wright in *Maccoll and Pollock Ltd v Indemnity Mutual Marine Assurance Co Ltd*.[18] Even though the policy under consideration was non-marine, his comments on the Inchmaree clause are, nonetheless, pertinent:

> '... the latent defect itself is not something covered by the policy as a casualty; it is simply a case of an inherent fault or defect which may indeed cause damage to the rest of the thing insured, and for that damage there will be a claim, but it will not be a claim in itself because in this as in other cases the original vice of the subject-matter is not covered.'

---

11 The use of the words 'caused by' instead of 'through' in the current version does not make any difference as regards the intention of the clause.

12 (1907) 13 Com Cas 28 at pp 34–35, CA.

13 [1911] 2 KB 398, CA.

14 *Ibid* at p 408.

15 *Ibid*, at p 411.

16 [1937] 1 KB 639. For a further discussion of this case, see below.

17 The principle of consequential damage laid down in *Oceanic SS Co v Faber*, (1907) 13 Com Cas 28, CA; *Hutchins Brothers v Royal Exchange Assurance Corpn* (1911) 2 KB 398, CA; and *Scindia Steamships Ltd v The London Assurance* [1937] 1 KB 639, was recently applied in *Promet Engineering (Singapore) Pte Ltd v Sturge and Others, The 'Nukila'* [1996] 1 Lloyd's Rep 85, QBD.

18 (1930) 38 Ll L Rep 79, KB.

The mere discovery of a latent defect is not recoverable under the clause. Moreover, an insurer is, as a general rule, by s 55(2)(c) not liable 'for' inherent vice or nature of the subject-matter insured.

To complete this part of the discussion, it is necessary to mention *Wills and Sons v The World Marine Insurance Ltd*,[19] which so far appears to be the only case where a claim made under this clause has been successful. On this occasion, damage was caused to the hull of an insured dredger when a link of the hoisting chain of the bucket ladder gave way. The latent defect in the welding of the link, and not wear and tear, was held to have caused the loss.

BURSTING OF BOILERS

Loss of or damage to the subject-matter insured 'caused by' the bursting of boilers is recoverable, but not the cost of repairing or replacing the boiler which had burst. To recover for the latter, the assured has to identify a specific peril insured against, for example, perils of the seas, fire, explosion or negligence of the crew as the cause for the loss. Any consequential damage sustained as a result of the bursting of a boiler or an explosion would also be covered by cl 6.1.2 regardless of whether it was or was not accompanied by fire.

BREAKAGE OF SHAFTS

This limb of cl 6.2.1 is best illustrated by the case of *Scindia Steamships Ltd v The London Assurance*,[20] where the ship was in dry dock undergoing an operation which required the removal of the propeller and tail shaft. Owing to latent defect, the shaft broke and a propeller to which it was attached to also fell, causing a blade of the propeller to break. The insurer admitted liability for the replacement blade, but refused to pay for the replacement of the shaft. As the loss of the shaft was not 'caused through' (now 'caused by') a latent defect, but was the latent defect itself, the insurers were held not liable for this loss. Mr Justice Branson said that the clause, by reason of the words 'caused through' envisaged 'a state of affairs in which the main cause produces damage which has an effect on something else'.[21]

In *Jackson v Mumford*,[22] Mr Justice Kennedy, whose decision was approved on appeal, had to consider, *inter alia*, whether the breakage of a connecting-rod was so closely akin to the breakage of a shaft that the *ejusdem generis* principle should be applied to the clause. On finding that a connecting-rod and a shaft were always distinguished in the language of engineers, and that the functions performed by them were different, the clause was held inapplicable.

---

19 Decided in 1911, reported as a 'Note' in [1980] 1 Lloyd's Rep 350.
20 [1937] 1 KB 639.
21 *Ibid*, at p 649.
22 (1902) 8 Com Cas 61; (1904) 9 Com Cas 114, CA.

LATENT DEFECT IN THE MACHINERY OR HULL

Here, it is necessary to establish the relationship between the statutory exception of s 55(2)(c) and this part of the cl 6.2.1. First, the precise wording of the section is important. It states: 'Unless the policy otherwise provides, the insurer is not liable *for* ... inherent vice or nature of the subject-matter insured...'.[23] This relationship was referred to by Mr Justice Branson in *Scindia Steamships v The London Assurance* as follows:[24]

'... except under those words of this clause which deal with latent defects, damage *caused by* latent defects is excluded from this clause by virtue of section 55(2)(c) of the Marine Insurance Act 1906.'

This is echoed by Arnould, who states that:[25]

'The cover in respect of latent defect would be virtually meaningless if this were not to be construed as applying even in cases of inherent vice. Where this part of the clause applies, therefore, a defence of inherent vice is not open to underwriters.'

With due respect, it is submitted that these comments are not quite so accurate. First, it is to be noted that s 55(2)(c) does not state that the insurer is not liable for any loss 'caused by' (or proximately caused by) inherent vice or nature of the subject-matter insured.[26] As worded, it only excludes a loss 'for', and not 'caused by', inherent vice or nature of the subject matter insured. That s 55(2)(c) and this aspect of the clause do not overlap or contradict one another is clear. They are mutually exclusive applying to different types of loss; the former to the latent defect itself, and the latter to losses 'caused by' a latent defect.[27] That the defence in s 55(2)(c) is not available to the insurer is correct, but the reason is not that to hold otherwise would render the clause meaningless, but that the section, by reason of its wording, has no relevance to a loss 'caused by' latent defect. In fact, the defence which would have been available to the insurer, if the policy had not otherwise provided, is the last exception contained in s 55(2)(c) which states that: 'Unless the policy otherwise provides, the insurer is not liable ... for any injury to machinery not proximately caused by maritime perils.'[28]

Meaning of latent defect

In *Sipowicz v Wimble & Others, The Green Lion*,[29] an American court defined a latent defect as one which 'a reasonably careful inspection would not reveal. It

---

23 See Chapter 10.

24 [1937] 1 KB 639 at p 648. Emphasis added.

25 Arnould, para 829.

26 Such a cause of loss is now covered by cl 6.2.1 which, as discussed earlier, employs the term 'caused by'.

27 Arnould, para 829.

28 A loss of or damage to the subject-matter insured against caused by a latent defect in the machinery or hull cannot be described as a loss caused by 'maritime perils'. The clause has to be construed as falling with the words 'unless the policy otherwise provides'. Why 'hull' has been left out of s 55(2)(c) is unclear.

29 [1974] 1 Lloyd's Rep 593, USDC (SDNY) contains a comprehensive historical account of American cases on the subject.

is not a gradual deterioration but rather a defect in the metal itself.' The plaintiffs had asserted, *inter alia*, that the sinking of *The Green Lion* had resulted from a latent defect in the vessel's machinery or hull. Water had entered the ship because the metal fastening, which secured the keel and keelson to the hull, had weakened, causing a separation to occur. These fastenings were worn out because of age, wear and lack of maintenance.

The court held that as the metal fastenings were not inherently defective in their original construction, the defect was not latent. Moreover, as the plaintiffs themselves were aware of the condition of these metal supports, the defects were clearly not latent, but patent. Any defect which is 'observable', 'accessible', 'not hidden', and not unknown, but fully revealed will not be classified as latent.

In *Jackson v Mumford*,[30] Mr Justice Kennedy expressed, by way of *obiter*, the view that weakness in the design of a connecting-rod was not a latent defect; his view is evident from his comments that a latent defect did 'not cover the erroneous judgment of the designer as to the effect of the strain which this machinery will have to resist, the machinery itself being faultless, the workmanship faultless, and the construction precisely that which the designer intended it to be'.[31]

Error in design

The above remarks give the impression that a 'latent defect' is concerned only with defects in the material used and not with error in design.[32] This conception of the term has now to be read in the light of the recent decision of *Prudent Tankers Ltd SA v Dominion Insurance Co Ltd, The Caribbean Sea*[33] in which the vessel sank as a result of the entry of sea water. The owners asserted, *inter alia*, that the loss was caused by a latent defect in the hull, owing to fatigue cracks initiated at the circumferential weld joining the nozzle to the vessel's plate. In fact, the loss was attributable to a combination of two factors: first, the manner in which the vessel was designed and, secondly, the effect upon the nozzle on the ordinary working of the vessel, causing the fracture to open up a significant period of time before the end of the life of the vessel. Basically, the issue was whether such a loss was caused by a latent defect.

---

30 (1902) 8 Com Cas 61.

31 *Ibid*, at p 69.

32 An American case, *Irwin v Eagle Star Insurance Co Ltd, The Jomie* [1973] 2 Lloyd's Rep 489, USCA, has held that to constitute a latent defect, there has to be a defect in the metal: it does not cover a mistake made by the air conditioning firm in joining iron and brass in an under-sea-waterfitting.

33 [1980] 1 Lloyd's Rep 338. It is to be noted that the view expressed by Kennedy J was *obiter*, and when the case went on appeal this issue was not considered. Further, it is pertinent to observe that the views expressed by Goff J (as he then was) in *The Carribean Sea* was also in the court of first instance. The American position as stated in *Irwin v Eagle Star Insurance Co Ltd, The Jomie* [1973] 2 Lloyd's Rep 489 is in line with the opinion of Kennedy J.

Applying a well-known test used in contracts of affreightment, he arrived at the conclusion that, as the cracks 'could not be discovered on such examination as a reasonably careful skilled man would make', they were latent defects.[34] The most instructive part of his judgment reads as follows:

> '... in considering whether there was a defect *in* the hull or machinery which directly caused the loss of or damage to the ship, one is concerned with the actual state of the hull or machinery and not with the historical reason why it has come about that the hull or machinery is in that state.'

Accordingly, the loss was held to have been caused by a latent defect even though it had originated and developed as a result of an error or defect in design. The cause for the defect was considered irrelevant. This interpretation, which has yet to be approved by a higher court, has the support of Arnould.[35]

Latent defect and unseaworthiness

A defect, whether latent or patent, in hull or machinery would render a vessel unseaworthy but only if it impinges upon her ability to encounter the ordinary perils of the sea. Thus, not all latent defects existing in the hull or machinery of a ship will automatically cause her to become unseaworthy. The defect has to be in relation to a matter which affects her capability to combat ordinary sea perils. A defect in loading equipment, for example, would not affect a ship's ability to encounter the ordinary perils of the sea.[36] In each case, the nature of the defect has to be examined.

It has been pointed out by Arnould, citing American cases in support, that there is a 'conflict' between this part of the clause (6.2.1) which insures against a loss caused by latent defect, and s 39(1) which implies a warranty of seaworthiness in a voyage policy.[37] As the law relating to seaworthiness is different in time and voyage policies, it is necessary to divide this study into two parts:[38] voyage policies will first be discussed, and then time policies.

Voyage policy

Arnould, in a brief statement, submits that:[39]

> '... the latent defect cover, must ... be regarded as overriding the implied warranty of seaworthiness in voyage policies, to the extent that there is a conflict between the implied warranty and this head of cover. The point has not been decided in this country, but the majority of the American cases proceed on the basis that unseaworthiness is no answer to a claim in respect of "latent defect".'

---

34 The test propounded in *Brown v Nitrate Producers' SS Co* (1937) 58 Ll L Rep 188, a contract of affreightment case, was applied. Goff J showed preference for this definition rather than the American definition declared in *Parente RA v Bayville Marine Inc & General Insurance Co of America* [1975] 1 Lloyd's Rep 333, USNY.

35 Arnould, para 831.

36 For the meaning of seaworthiness, see Chapter 7.

37 Park, *Marine Insurance and Average*, Chapter XIV, p 387, also relying on American authorities describes this 'conflict' as an 'anomaly'.

38 Discussed in Chapter 7.

39 Arnould, para 829.

The legal position, as can be seen shortly, is not as straightforward as described above.

Breach of the implied warranty of seaworthiness

It has to be stressed that the implied warranty of seaworthiness, spelt out in s 39(1), is applicable only 'at the commencement of the voyage'. In the event of a breach the insurer is discharged, now 'automatically' discharged, from liability as from the date of breach, that is, at the commencement of the voyage. Regardless of the cause of loss, and even if no loss has occurred, the insurer is automatically freed from liability as from the time of breach.[40] Thus, unless the breach has been waived, it is submitted that there can be no question of referring to the Inchmaree clause or, for that matter, any of the enumerated perils in the policy as the basis of a claim. More significantly, the House of Lords has recently in *The Good Luck*[41] emphasised that a promissory warranty in marine insurance is actually a condition precedent to the further liability of the insurer. Unless the 'condition precedent' (or the warranty) is fulfilled, the insurer is automatically discharged from liability. Thus, if the implied warranty of seaworthiness is not complied with, the insurer is automatically discharged from liability as from the date of breach, which is 'at the commencement of the voyage', at which point of time the warranty is applicable. Once a breach of the implied warranty has been committed, any loss occurring *after* the commencement of the voyage would not be covered.

Having been automatically discharged from liability or further liability as from the commencement the voyage, it is indeed difficult to see how this clause, or for that matter any of the insured perils, could be invoked. Consequently, it is submitted that the clause cannot override or prevail over the implied warranty of seaworthiness. Naturally, in an 'at and from' policy, he would be able to recover for any loss sustained whilst the ship is 'at' the named port, after the attachment of the risk but before the commencement of the voyage. Any loss suffered before the commencement of the voyage is unaffected by a breach of the warranty.

It is, of course, always possible to exclude the implied warranty by means of an express clause. However, it can be overridden only by 'express, pertinent, and apposite language'.[42] There is, however, nothing in the IVCH(95) excluding the implied warranty of seaworthiness, and the 'held covered' clause (clause 2) does not cover such a breach.[43] Thus, unless a clear and express clause is specially inserted in the policy,[44] the implied warranty of seaworthiness will prevail. The purpose of cl 4.2.1 is to provide cover for a loss caused by latent defect, not for excluding or negativing the implied warranty of seaworthiness

---

40 See s 33(3) and *The Good Luck* [1991] 2 Lloyd's Rep 191, HL.

41 *Ibid*. The effects of a breach of a warranty are discussed in Chapter 7.

42 See *Quebec Marine Insurance Co v Commercial Bank of Canada* (1870) LR 3 PC 234 at p 242.

43 By cl 2 only a 'breach of a warranty as to towage or salvage services' are held covered.

44 See ss 35(2) and (3). Under common law, only three clauses, namely, the 'allowed to be seaworthy'; the 'seaworthiness admitted' clause; and the 'held covered in case of any breach of warranty at a premium to be hereinafter arranged' clause were found acceptable by the court as capable of excluding the implied warranty of seaworthiness from the contract of insurance. For a detailed study of this subject, see Chapter 7.

Unseaworthiness under a time policy

In a time policy, the legal principles relating to seaworthiness are more complex. Unlike a voyage policy, there is, under British law, no implied warranty of seaworthiness in a time policy. Whereas causation and privity are irrelevant in a voyage policy, they are of utmost importance in a time policy. The relevant part of s 39(5) states that: '... where with the privity of the assured, the ship is sent to sea in an unseaworthy state, the insurer is not liable for any loss attributable to unseaworthiness'. All three factors, namely, (a) the vessel has to be unseaworthy; (b) the loss has to be attributable to unseaworthiness; and (c) the assured has to be privy to such unseaworthiness which has caused the loss, have to be satisfied before the insurer can be exonerated from liability.[45]

To determine whether there is an anomaly between s 39(5) and cl 6.2.1, the elements of privity and causation have to be considered in relation to the terms of, and to the proviso to, cl 6.2. First, it is to be noted that the very essence of a latent defect is that it is not discoverable even with the exercise of due diligence. As such, it is a defect which the assured cannot be privy to, and if he has knowledge of such a defect, then the defect cannot be 'latent'.

Should a shipowner be privy to the vessel's condition of unseaworthiness to which the loss is attributable, he would not only be unable to recover under s 39(5), but also under cl 6.2.1 by reason of the fact that the defect is not latent in character.[46] On the other hand, should he be not privy to the (latent) defect to which the loss is attributable to, the insurer would be liable under s 39(5). A loss 'caused by' a latent defect is 'attributable to' unseaworthiness, if unseaworthiness is a cause of the loss.[47] Provided that the loss has 'not resulted from the want of due diligence by the assured, owners, managers or superintendents,' it would also be recoverable under cl 6.2.1. The non-discovery of the latent defect would not by itself constitute a breach of the proviso, for no amount of due diligence exercised would reveal the defect. It is incapable of being discovered even with the exercise of due diligence.

There is, therefore, no conflict between the terms of s 39(5) and the latent defect cover of cl 6.2.1. In fact, they complement each other. In conclusion, it is submitted that caution should be exercised when relying on American authorities, especially in this area of law when British and American law differ. There is an implied warranty of seaworthiness in a time policy under American law, but not under British law.

NEGLIGENCE OF MASTER OFFICERS CREW OR PILOTS

Section 55(2)(a) and cl 6.2.2 of the ITCH(95) together provide considerable coverage to an assured for any loss or damage, proximately or remotely, caused by the negligence of master or crew. A loss proximately caused by a peril

---

45 For a detailed discussion of the law relating to seaworthiness in a time policy, see Chapter 7.
46 It is necessary to be reminded of the fact that s 39 is not restricted to unseaworthiness by reason of latent defect; it applies to all forms of unseaworthiness.
47 See Chapter 8.

insured against but remotely caused by the negligence of the master or crew is covered by s 55(2)(a).[48] This part of the discussion is concerned with negligence operating as the proximate cause of loss; such a cause of loss is governed by cl 6.2.2 which provides indemnity for 'loss of or damage to the subject-matter insured caused by ... negligence of master, officers, crew or pilots'.[49] Of course, these words refer to personnel on board the insured vessel.[50]

It is to be noted that only negligence, not misconduct, incompetence or error in judgment, is insured by cl 6.2.2[51] However, on payment of an additional premium, the insurance could be extended to cover 'loss of or damage to the vessel caused by any accident or by negligence, incompetence or error of judgment of any person whatsoever'.[52] In so far as the misconduct of master or crew is concerned, the assured would be able to recover as for a loss by barratry, if the act was wilfully committed 'to the prejudice of the owner, or, as the case may be, the charterer'.[53] But if the misconduct of master or crew which has proximately caused the loss does not amount to barratry, the loss would not be recoverable. Moreover, s 55(2)(a) would be of no assistance to the assured as it applies only to misconduct (and negligence) of master or crew operating as a remote cause of loss.[54]

Negligence as the proximate cause of loss

Though the word 'proximately' has not been used to qualify the term 'caused by' appearing in the opening words of cl 6.2 (and 6.1) of the ITCH(95), it has always been understood that the rule of proximate cause has to be read into it.[55] Thus, cl 6.2.2 can only be invoked when the negligence of the master, officer, crew or pilot is *the* or *a* proximate cause of loss. Surprisingly, there is hardly any British authority directly concerned with this provision. Only two reported cases, namely, *Lind v Mitchell*[56] and *Baxendale v Fane, The Lapwing*,[57] have been identified to be concerned with this point of law. In both cases, the court was prepared to invoke the negligence cover of the Inchmaree clause but only as an alternative ground for its decision.

---

48 The law in this regard has already been discussed in depth earlier, see Chapter 9.

49 As a pilot is specifically named, the question of whether or not he is a member of crew is now academic. Ship's engineers would now fall within the category of 'officers' or 'crew'.

50 The 1931 version of this clause insured against the negligence of 'Master mariners, engineers or pilots'. The word 'mariners' was interpreted in an American case, *Rosa and Others v Insurance Co of the State of Pennsylvania, The Belle of Portugal* [1970] 2 Lloyd's Rep 386, USCA (Ninth Circuit) as wide enough to cover a loss caused by the negligence of the crew of another vessel.

51 *Cf* American Liner Negligence Clause.

52 See cl 1.1.2 of the Institute Additional Perils Clauses (Hulls); see Appendix 16.

53 For a discussion of the law of barratry, see below.

54 The law of causation is fully discussed in Chapter 8.

55 See *Coxe v Employers' Liability Assurance Corpn Ltd* [1916] 2 KB 629 at p 634. For a thorough examination of the law of proximate cause, see Chapter 8.

56 (1928) 45 TLR 54, CA.

57 (1940) 66 Ll L Rep 174.

In the first case, the facts of which have already been referred to earlier,[58] the plaintiff, a mortgagee, claimed that the ship was lost by a peril of the seas and/or fire and, alternatively, through the negligence of the master in unreasonably abandoning her prematurely. On the question of fact, the Court of Appeal agreed with the finding of the trial judge that: 'The ship sank ... because she had been holed in the ice. That was the real and only cause of her loss'. As such, the negligence of the master, whose conduct only came afterwards, could only be regarded as a remote cause of the loss.

Lord Justice Sankey was content with simply relying on perils of the seas and s 55(2)(a) as the grounds for his decision. Lord Justice Scrutton, however, the only judge in the case who made an effort to examine the wording of the clause (which in this case stated that the underwriter insures against loss of the vessel 'caused through the negligence of master') pointed out that, as the word 'directly' which appeared in another part of the clause had been left out of the negligence cover, negligence as a remote cause of loss was covered. Such a construction cannot be applicable to cl 6.2.2 which is worded differently.

In *The Lapwing*,[59] instead of 'caused through' the expression 'directly caused by' was used in the clause in question. Mr Justice Hodson decided that as the loss was fortuitously caused (by the intervention of the negligence of those responsible for the docking operation), it was recoverable as a peril of the seas or as a peril *ejusdem generis* with a peril of the seas, *viz*, stranding. He then proceeded to ascertain whether the negligence cover could be invoked as an alternative ground for his decision.

On the issue of negligence, he had to consider whether the manager of the ship-repairing company, by whose conduct the ship was negligently docked and as a result of which she sustained damage to her bottom, was the 'master' of the ship. Citing the definition of 'master' from the Merchant Shipping Act 1894 as authority, he held that as the manager was in 'command or charge' of the ship at the time of loss he was *pro hac vice* the 'master' of the ship. From this, he concluded that the said clause applied.

Regrettably, the judge had overlooked the phraseology of the clause. The word 'directly', although superfluous, has emphasised that only the negligence of the master or crew which has 'directly' or proximately caused the loss was covered. As worded, its legal effect is no different from that of cl 6.2.2. Thus, unless the negligence of the master was the only proximate cause, or one of two or more proximate causes of loss, it is difficult to see how the clause in question could be invoked.

In the event where there is no marine peril operating as the proximate cause of loss, cl 6.2.2 would be of particular use to the assured. It would be especially useful in a case such as *The Inchmaree*[60] where perils of the seas was not in any way responsible for the loss.

---

58 See Chapter 15.
59 (1940) 66 Ll L Rep 174.
60 (1887) 12 AC 484, HL, see Chapter 9.

Another case which, it would appear, has also misapplied this cover is the Canadian case of *The Brentwood*,[61] the facts of which have already been briefly stated elsewhere. The time policy in this case contained a clause similar to that in *The Lapwing*.[62] Bearing in mind the finding of the trial judge that unseaworthiness 'alone' was the proximate cause of loss,[63] a finding which the Appeal Court did not disturb, it is difficult to justify the application of the clause. Unless the negligence of the master was held to be another proximate cause of loss,[64] it is submitted that the Appeal Court had no justification for invoking the clause.

It would appear that the confusion which had arisen in these cases regarding the applicability of cl 6.2.2 (and s 39(5)) is largely due to the issue of causation. They were decided at a time when the law was unclear as to whether it was possible for there to be more than one proximate cause of loss.[65] A proper finding of the proximate cause or causes of a loss is critical to the outcome of a case. It is pertinent to note that cl 6.2.2 applies only if the negligence of the master, officers, crew or pilot is *the* or *a* proximate cause of a loss.[66]

Negligence of the assured

It is observed that an assured is not named in the list of persons for whose neglect is covered by cl 6.2.2.[67] It would not, therefore, be unreasonable to assume that any loss proximately caused by the negligence of an assured is not recoverable.[68] Moreover, as the assured has himself committed an act of neglect, he would not be able to satisfy the terms of the proviso that the damage or loss has not resulted from the want of due diligence on his part. The position, however, is different if an assured-shipowner were to be employed on board as 'master, officer, crew, or pilot': any loss proximately caused by his neglect committed whilst acting in any of these capacities would be covered by cl 6.2.2 read with cl 6.3.

---

61 [1932] 2 Lloyd's Rep 232; also discussed below and in Chapters 7 and 8.

62 (1940) 66 Ll L Rep 174.

63 The trial judge, relying on the Canadian counterpart to our s 39(5), awarded judgment in favour of the plaintiffs. As submitted earlier such a cause of loss is not a peril insured against and, therefore, should not be recoverable, regardless of whether the assured was or was not privy to such unseaworthiness. See Chapters 7 and 8.

64 There is no reason why unseaworthiness and the negligence of the master cannot both be held to be proximate causes. See *The Miss Jay Jay* [1987] 1 Lloyd's Rep 32, CA.

65 See, in particular, *The Miss Jay Jay, ibid*, and the cases discussed in Chapter 8.

66 Section 55(2)(a) applies to negligence of master or crew occasioning as a remote cause.

67 To dispel all doubts, the draftsman of the clause could have easily, as in a Canadian version of the clause, inserted the words 'other than an assured' into cl 6.2.2: see *The Brentwood* [1932] 2 Lloyd's Rep 232.

68 Though a case on insurance of cargo, *M R Currie & Co v The Bombay Native Insurance Co* (1869) LR 3 PC 72 may be cited to support this principle. The assured who had failed to act upon the advices of various surveyors that the cargo could be saved was prevented from recovering for the loss. The Privy Council (at p 81) said: '... how can the Assured recover from the Underwriters a loss which was made total by their own negligence?'. It would appear that the loss was held not recoverable on two grounds: first, the loss was proximately caused by the negligence of the assured which was not a peril insured against and, secondly, as the assured had failed to sue and labour, he was 'precluded' from claiming for the loss of the cargo. Further discussions of the law on sue and labour can be found in Chapter 17.

Shipowner acting as master, officer, crew or pilot

A shipowner acting as master, officer crew or pilot on board his own ship can, of course, by negligent navigation cause damage to or the loss of his own ship. In this regard, there are two clauses which would have to be read with cl 6.2.2. First, cl 6.3 states that 'master officers, crew, or pilots' are 'not to be considered as Owners within the meaning of cl 6 should they hold shares in the Vessel'. Secondly, the proviso to cl 6.2 has to be complied with before the shipowner would be allowed to recover for any loss falling within one of the perils enumerated therein. The relationship between cll 6.2.2, 6.3 and the proviso is not at all clear. In fact, on first reading, they could well appear to be contradictory but, as can be seen shortly, they could also be interpreted so as to complement each other. There is no litigation in the British courts on this subject. Nonetheless, the wording, scheme and objective of the clauses will have to be examined.

Part owner and co-owner

First, the last few words of cl 6.3 connote part ownership. Read with cl 6.2.2 and its proviso, a part owner acting in the capacity of master (officer, crew or pilot) is not in relation to the proviso to be considered as 'owner'.This necessarily means that his neglect or want of due diligence is to be regarded as irrelevant in so far as the proviso is concerned.

The objective of cl 6.3 is to enable a part owner to claim for any loss which he has negligently (and proximately) caused whilst acting in the capacity as master etc, of the vessel.[69] But for cl 6.3, it would not have been possible for him to recover for the loss under the policy, because his act of neglect would constitute a want of due diligence under the proviso. In the absence of cl 6.3, his co-owners would also be prejudiced by his act of neglect. Clause 6.3 was therefore framed to circumvent the problems generated in the event of a shipowner wearing two hats, one as owner and the other as master (or crew) of his own ship. It serves to provide not only the part owner (who has been negligent), but also his co-owner(s) with the right to recover for a loss under cl 6.2.2. Notwithstanding the fact that one of the owners has through his neglect or want of due diligence caused damage to or loss of the vessel, cl 6.3 has allowed all the owners the right claim for the loss under cl 6.2.2. The effect of cl 6.3 is to prevent an act of neglect committed by a part owner whilst acting as master from tainting not only his own claim, but also that of his co-owner(s).

Sole owner

Whether a sole owner who, whilst acting as master, has negligently caused damage to or the loss of his own ship is able to recover for a loss has to be considered, even though such a contingency might appear to be unlikely in this

---

69 In *The Trinder Case* [1898] 2 QB 114, CA, perils of the sea was held the proximate cause and the negligence of the owner-master, a remote cause of the loss.

day of corporate ownership.[70] Whether this was in the minds of the draftsmen when these clauses were framed is doubtful.[71]

On a literal interpretation of cl 6.3, a sole owner does not appear to be covered. This could create an anomalous situation whereby a part owner acting as master is able to recover for any loss which he has caused by his own neglect, but not a sole owner in the same position. Should this be the case, a sole owner should leave well alone matters relating to navigation, and appoint a third party to crew his ship. Presumably, as only one person is involved and, consequently, there being only one directing mind, difficulties may be encountered when distinguishing the roles in which he was acting at the time of loss.[72]

There is, however, no reason why judges should not be able to differentiate between an act committed by the master *qua* master and *qua* owner. The making of such a distinction, which is carried out all the time in petitions for limitation of liability, would permit a sole owner to recover under cl 6.2.2 for a loss caused by him whilst acting in the capacity of master but not of owner.

This anomaly in the law has inspired authors to draw a line between the duties which have to be performed *before* and *during* the voyage. Arnould holds the view that, 'the proviso would probably be restricted to failure to exercise due diligence to prepare or equip the ship for the voyage'.[73] And it has been said that in practice, it has been recognised that 'the lack of due diligence during the voyage is not usually treated by underwriters as being within the proviso ...'.[744]

Such a division of duties would remove the anomaly and prevent the conflict between cl 6.2.2 and the proviso from arising. It would give each of the clauses its own respective sphere of coverage: the proviso reserved for responsibilities pertaining to the preparation of the ship *before* the voyage, and cl 6.2.2 for duties to be performed *during* the voyage.

On cl 6.3, Arnould states that:[75]

'The stipulation that a master, etc, who holds shares in the vessel is not to be considered as part-owner would appear to narrow the scope of the proviso, so as to preserve the cover in cases where members of the ship's complement who hold shares in the vessel are negligent in preparing her for sea.'

The above approach of separating the duties to be performed before and during the voyage by the shipowner would also prevent cl 6.3 from 'narrowing' down the scope of the proviso.

---

70 In small coastal vessels and fishing vessels it is not uncommon for a sole owner to act as master of his own vessel.

71 If the intention was to include a sole owner, it could have worded the clause in clearer terms. It could have used words to the effect that, 'should they own or holds shares in the vessel', or 'should they hold all or any shares in the vessel'.

72 Such was the position under the common law of limitation of liability law (see *The Spirit of the Ocean* (1865) 34 LJ Ad 74; B & L 336) until the enactment of s 3 of the MS (Liability of Shipowners and Others) Act 1958. See *The Annie Hay* [1968] 1 Lloyd's Rep 141.

73 Arnould, para 832.

74 See O'May, p 137.

75 Arnould, para 832.

If the neglect in the performance of his duties as master was to cause the loss, cl 6.2.2 would apply; and provided that he (whether sole or part-owner) was not guilty of the want of due diligence in discharging his responsibility as owner, the proviso would be fulfilled. The shipowner's claim should not be invalidated merely by reason of him being both owner and master of the same ship. The solution to the problem is to determine which hat the assured was wearing at the time when his was negligent: if the loss was caused whilst carrying out the duties of master, it would be covered by cl 6.2.2, but if he was acting as owner cl 6.2.2 would not apply, as a loss caused by the negligence of an assured is not covered.

Negligence of the master or crew and unseaworthiness

The difference in the law relating to seaworthiness between voyage and time policies once again dictates that this discussion be divided into two parts: the first part will examine the application of the concept of seaworthiness and privity in a time policy, and the second, the implied warranty of seaworthiness in a voyage policy.

Time policy

The relationship between s 39(5) on seaworthiness in a time policy and cl 6.2.2 on negligence is not as distinct as that between s 39(5) and cl 6.2.1 on the latent defect cover described earlier. It has been said that there is somewhat of an anomaly evident in these relationships. A ship can be rendered unseaworthy as a result of an act of negligence committed by the master and/or crew. In such an event, both cl 6.2.2 (and its proviso) and s 39(5) would have to be considered.

To illustrate this relationship, the Canadian case of *The Brentwood* may again be referred to, the facts of which are as follows. As a consequence of improper loading, the vessel was rendered unseaworthy. This affected her stability causing her to roll over and later to be abandoned when she was found to be taking in water. The trial judge decided that:

- the proximate cause of the loss was unseaworthiness 'alone' due to improper loading; or
- the improper loading was due to the negligence of the master; and
- the owner was not privy to the negligence of the master.

Using this set of facts for the purpose of discussion, there are four possibilities which have to be considered. First, if the negligence of the 'master officers, crew, or pilots' is held to be the sole proximate cause of the loss, then, provided that such loss or damage has not resulted from the want of due diligence by the assured, etc, the insurer is liable.

Secondly, if unseaworthiness is the sole proximate cause of loss, then the loss, as submitted above, is simply not recoverable because unseaworthiness is not a peril insured against.[76] In such an event, it should be unnecessary to

---

76 See Chapter 7.

invoke s 39(5) to ascertain whether the assured was or was not privy to such unseaworthiness which caused the loss.[77]

Thirdly, it is also possible that negligence and unseaworthiness may both be regarded as proximate causes of the loss. In such a case, as unseaworthiness is not an insured peril, on this ground alone the loss is not recoverable. But as negligence is also another proximate cause, cl 6.2.2 has to be brought into play. It has to be mentioned that, as a loss proximately caused by unseaworthiness is generally not *expressly* excepted in a standard hull policy, there is still room for the application of the terms of the included loss, that is, cl 6.2.2; and provided that the due diligence proviso is fulfilled, it would appear that the assured would be allowed to recover for the loss.

Finally, if negligence alone is found to be the proximate cause of loss and unseaworthiness a remote cause, then both cl 6.2.2 and s 39(5) will apply.[78] The latter is applicable by reason of the fact that the loss is, by virtue of its wording, 'attributable to' unseaworthiness. In such a circumstance, a conflict could arise in which case it may be necessary to determine which provision, cl 6.2.2 or s 39(5) is to prevail. It is interesting to note that in *The Brentwood*, the decision of the Appeal Court was based almost primarily, if not exclusively, on cl 6.2.2. Though the assured, having found not to have been privy to the unseaworthiness, had complied with the proviso to our s 39(5), they were nevertheless found wanting in due diligence in not seeing that the vessel was properly loaded. Their appeal was dismissed because they had failed to satisfy the terms of cl 6.2.2. It would appear from this decision that an assured has to satisfy both the 'privity' and the 'due diligence' proviso to s 39(5) and cl 6.2.2 respectively. Needless to say, if they were found privy to the vessel's condition of unseaworthiness, that is, the improper loading, they would also be found guilty of the want of due diligence in failing to take action to remedy the fault.[79]

---

77 *Cf The Brentwood* [1973] 2 Lloyd's Rep 232, the lower court, after accepting that it was 'unseaworthiness alone' which had caused the loss proceeded immediately to determine whether the assured was 'privy' to the master's negligent act of overloading the ship. As the assured was able to satisfy the proviso to the Canadian equivalent to our s 39(5), judgment was awarded in their favour. Regrettably, the court failed to consider the fact that unseaworthiness was not an insured peril in the policy under consideration. Interestingly, the court also took time to determine whether the due diligence proviso to the negligence cover (our cl 6.2.2) was satisfied. And as the assured was found not guilty of the want of due diligence, they were able also on this ground to recover their loss.

78 Negligence of master or crew operating merely as a remote cause is always inconsequential: s 55(2)(a).

79 Arnould, at para 831, in fn 80, states: 'It was held in *Lemar Towing v Fireman's Fund Insurance Co* (1973) AMC 1843 that the negligence cover in the Inchmaree clause does not apply where the proximate cause of loss is crew-incompetence amounting to unseaworthiness; but it is submitted that this is unsound and that the Inchmaree clause covers negligence by incompetent crew members except in so far as defences based on breach of the warranty of seaworthiness in a voyage policy, or on the due diligence proviso, or s 39(5) of the 1906 Act may be open'. It is the author's submission that the above statement is correct but only if negligence is 'the' or 'a' (in the sense of one of two or more) proximate cause of loss. It is significant to note that in *The Lemar Towing Case*, the incompetence of the captain was held to have rendered the vessel unseaworthy at the commencement of the voyage; and unseaworthiness, and not the negligence of the master or crew, was the proximate cause of the loss. It was clearly on these findings of fact that the court was able to, and rightly so, dismiss the relevance of the negligence cover in the Inchmaree clause. Moreover, as there is an implied warranty of seaworthiness in a time policy under American law, *(continued ...)*

Summing up, whether s 39(5) and/or cl 6.2.2 applies in each case is dependent upon what is regarded as the proximate cause or causes of the loss.

Voyage policy

In a voyage policy, the position is less complex because of the absolute special nature of the implied warranty of seaworthiness in a voyage policy: a breach of the implied warranty of seaworthiness under s 39(1) would simply, regardless of the cause of loss, automatically discharge the insurer from liability. Questions relating to causation do not arise, as breach of the warranty *per se* is sufficient to free the insurer from liability. The guilt or innocence of the assured is also immaterial.

It is, however, also important to bear in mind that the implied warranty applies only at the commencement of the voyage. Once it has been complied with, there is no continuing warranty of seaworthiness and, therefore, any loss arising after the commencement of the voyage, proximately or remotely caused by unseaworthiness, will not affect the warranty which has by then already been spent.[80] Any loss proximately caused by the subsequent unseaworthiness is not recoverable because such a cause of loss is not a peril insured against. And if unseaworthiness is found to be the remote cause then one has to ascertain what the proximate cause of loss is to determine the liability of the insurer.

NEGLIGENCE OF REPAIRERS OR CHARTERERS

Clause 6.2.3 of the ITCH(95) and cl 4.2.3 of the IVCH(95) insure against loss of or damage to the subject-mater caused by 'negligence of repairers or charterers provided such repairers or charterers are not an assured hereunder'. Very little need be said about this cover except that if the repairers or charterers are themselves the assured under the policy, they would not be able to claim for the loss the reason being that the underwriters would not be able to recover by way of subrogation from the negligent repairers or charterers as they are also the assured. It is important to be reminded of the fact that the cover is for physical loss of or damage to the subject-matter insured caused by the repairers' or charterers' negligence.

(cont'd)

the breach of the warranty itself would be sufficient, regardless of the cause of loss, to discharge the insurer from liability for the loss as from the date of the breach, that is, at the commencement of the voyage. Even if an express cover for 'incompetence' were to be included in the Inchmaree clause, as in the American liner negligence clause, incompetence has still to proved to have proximately caused the loss before it could be applied.

80   See *Redman v Wilson* (1845) 14 M & W 476, where the court held that as the ship was seaworthy when she sailed from London, the loss, though remotely caused by the negligence of the natives in loading her, was proximately caused by a peril of the seas.

BARRATRY OF MASTER OFFICERS OR CREW

INTRODUCTION

The peril of 'barratry of master officers or crew' is specifically insured under cl 6.2.4 of the ITCH(95)[81] and cl 4.2.4 of the IVCH(95) both of which are subject to the proviso that such loss or damage must not have not resulted from the 'want of due diligence by the assured, owners, managers or *superintendents or any of their onshore management*.'[82]

Barratry was an insured peril under the old SG policy which was applicable to both ship and goods. Under the ICC (A) it is an insured peril by reason of the fact that such a policy covers all risks. It is, however, not an insured peril under the ICC (B) and (C). Moreover, it is excluded by cl 4.7 of the general exclusions clause[83] which, in broad terms, states that the policy does not cover 'deliberate damage to or deliberate destruction of the subject-matter insured or any part thereof by the wrongful act of *any person or persons*'. The words 'any person or persons' are wide enough to include the acts of the master and crew. The ensuing discussion is thus relevant only to the ITCH(95), the IVCH(95) and to a policy in which barratry is expressly insured.

DEFINITION OF BARRATRY

The common law

Before proceeding to elicit the essential requirements of the term 'barratry' through an analysis of the wording of the statutory definition contained in r 11 of the Rules for Construction, it would be helpful at this juncture to revert to the judgments of some of the classic authorities which have shed light on the subject. Barratrous conduct may be broadly divided into three groups: fraud, neglect of duty and criminal conduct.

Knight v Cambridge[84] is perhaps the first reported case to define 'barratry'. Equating it with fraud, the judge remarked that: 'And he that commits a fraud, may properly be said to be guilty of neglect ... of his duty .... its imports any fraud'. The same was reiterated in *Boehm v Combe*[85] to the effect that: 'The word barratry was large enough to include every species of fraud or *malus dolus*'. On neglect of duty, Lord Ellenborough pointed out in *Heyman v Parish* that[86] 'a gross malversation by the captain in his office is barratrous'. Later, in *Stamma v*

---

81 Previously cl 6.2.5 of the ITCH(83).

82 Words in italics are inserted by the ITCH(95) and the IVCH(95); they are neither in the ITCH(83) nor the IVCH(83).

83 There is no such provision as cl 4.7 (or its equivalent) in the ICC (A). The principle that barratry cannot be committed against a cargo owner is reflected in the ICC (B) and (C).

84 (1724) 2 Ld Raym 1349.

85 (1813) 2 Maule & Selwyn 172; 105 ER 172.

86 (1809) 2 Camp 149.

Brown,[87] the element of criminality was introduced; it was said that 'to make it barratry there must be something of a criminal nature, as well as a breach of contract ...'.

In 1774, the learned Lord Mansfield in *Vallejo v Wheeler*[88] referred to the Italian Dictionary for the meaning of the word *'barratrare'*. In strong, unflattering language, his translation into English defined the conduct as: 'to cheat, and whatsoever is by the master a cheat, a fraud, a cozening, or a trick ... nothing can be so general'. Another judge depicted the act as one of 'knavery of the masters or mariners'.

Finally, in *Earle v Rowcroft*[89] all three elements were combined in one definition to the effect that '... a fraudulent breach of duty by the master, in respect to his owners ... with a criminal intent, or *ex maleficio*, is barratry'. In this case, the main issue which the court had to consider was whether the conduct of the master in going to an enemy's settlement to trade (as cargo could be more speedily and cheaply obtained there) consequently causing the ship to be seized and confiscated was barratrous. It was clear that even though the act of the master was criminal in nature his intention was not dishonourable. On the subject of criminality, the court firmly ruled that:

'For it is not for him [master] to judge in cases not intrusted to his discretion, or to suppose that he is not breaking the trust reposed in him, but acting meritoriously, when he endeavours to advance the interests of his owners by means which the law forbids, and which his owners also must be taken to have forbidden, not only from what ought to be, and therefore must be presumed to have been, their own sense of public duty, but also from a consideration of the risk and loss likely to follow from the use of such means.'

The law as declared in *Earle v Rowcroft*[90] is regarded by some of the modern day judges as the most acceptable of the judicial definitions of barratry.

Later, however, the Chief Justice presiding in the Privy Council in *Australian Insurance Co v Jackson*[91] pointed out that the most comprehensive definition of barratry can be found in the 1st edn of Arnould on *Marine Insurance*.[92] Incorporating all the features described, it states that:

'Barratry then in English law may be said to comprehend not only every species of fraud and knavery covinously committed by the master with the intention of benefiting himself at the expense of his owners, but every wilful act on his part of known illegality, gross malversation, or criminal negligence, by whatever motive induced, whereby the owner or charterers of the ship (in cases where the latter are considered as owners *pro tempore*) are in fact damnified.'

---

87 (1742) 2 Stra 1173.

88 (1774) 1 Cowp 143 at p 154. The Chief Justice was of the opinion that before this, 'the nature of barratry had not been judicially considered or defined in England with accuracy'.

89 (1806) 8 East 126.

90 *Ibid*.

91 (1875) 33 LT 286, PC.

92 Arnould, para 820.

The most recent case to have analysed and traced the historical development of barratry is *The Salem*.[93] Mr Justice Mustill in the court of first instance remarked that: 'This strange word, which has featured in policies of marine insurance since mediaeval times, originally had the connotation of "trickery"'.

A modern American definition of barratry can be found in *The Hai Hsuan*[94] to the effect that:

'Barratry is one of the enumerated perils against which the defendants insured the plaintiff. This is a generic term which includes many acts of various kinds and degrees. It comprehends any unlawful, fraudulent or dishonest act of the master or mariners and every violation of duty by them arising from gross and culpable negligence contrary to their duty to the owner of the vessel, and which might work loss or injury to him the course of the voyage insured.'

Statutory definition of barratry

Compared to the common law, r 11 has adopted a more general approach in its definition of barratry. It states that:

'The term "barratry" includes every wrongful act wilfully committed by the master or crew to the prejudice of the owner, or, as the case may be, the charterer.'

As almost every word of the definition is significant, each will be discussed separately. First, it has to be pointed out that the word 'includes' suggests that the definition is not exhaustive.

'Wrongful act'

The word 'wrongful' used to describe the barratrous act is wide enough to embrace all the three aspects of barratry mentioned earlier, namely, fraud, breach of duty and criminal conduct. *Stamma v Brown*,[95] however, has given the impression that barratry is a criminal act and, therefore, the commission of a crime has to be proved before an act could be held barratrous. But an act can be 'wrongful' without being criminal in nature and thus criminality is not a mandatory requirement. This is confirmed in *Compania Naviera Bachi v Henry Hosegood & Co Ltd*,[96] where the pertinent part of the judgment read as follows:

'I do not think that for the purpose of barratry the commission of a crime is necessary. It must be a wilful act deliberately done, and to the prejudice of the owners. It is not necessary that the person doing it should desire to injure the owners if in fact there is an intention to do an act which will cause injury, even if the act be done to the benefit of persons who are guilty of barratry.'

93 [1981] 2 Lloyd's Rep 316 at p 324, QBD.
94 *Republic of China, China Merchants Steam Navigation Co Ltd and United States of America v National Union Fire Insurance Co of Pittsburgh, Pennsylvania* [1958] 2 Lloyd's Rep 578.
95 (1742) 2 Stra 1173.
96 [1938] 2 All ER 189. The court had, in relation to a dispute under a charterparty, to consider whether the conduct of the crew was barratrous under the terms of a clause which excepted the carrier from liability for acts of barratry of the master or crew. As the law on barratry in charterparties is the same as that in marine insurance, the comments of Porter J are thus also relevant here.

The commission of a crime is not an essential ingredient in the scheme of barratry. But, of course, if a crime has been committed by the master or crew, that is the best form of proof of barratry because such an act would undoubtedly be prejudicial to the interests of the shipowner. On the other hand, if the act is not criminal in nature, all that is required is that it be 'wilfully' and 'deliberately' committed, and that the shipowner is injured or harmed as a consequence. To avoid such arguments, the word 'wrongful' (and not criminal) was chosen to define barratry in r 11.

It is impossible, not to mention that it would serve no useful purpose, to describe all the various forms of barratrous conduct. For illustration, reference to a few examples would suffice in order that more time may be spent on examining in greater depth the problematic areas of the law such as deviation, scuttling and smuggling.

Running away with the ship and cargo was in the old days a rather common occurrence. In *Falkner v Ritchie*,[97] a partial loss sustained by the shipowner was held to have been caused by barratry when the crew carried the ship away to a distant country, plundered her cargo and deserted her.[98] The most recent case where such an event took place is the *Marstrand Fishing Co Ltd v Beer, The Girl Pat*.[99] Though the act of taking the ship by the master and crew was considered barratrous, the shipowners were, however, unsuccessful in their claim because they were unable to prove that the loss was irretrievable so as to constitute an actual total loss.

In *Havelock v Hancill*,[100] the master and crew, in defiance of their duty, took on board certain commodities which caused the ship to be seized. It was decided that the conduct of the master and crew (committed without the consent of the owner) fell within the general definition of barratry against which the underwriter had agreed to insure. The 'lawful trade' clause was held inapplicable, as it was construed to apply to the adventure or trade in which the shipowners had employed her, and not to the legality of the conduct of the master or crew. The barratrous act of the master did not render the adventure or voyage illegal.[101] Similarly in *Australian Insurance Co v Jackson*,[102] the act of the master in carrying native labourers in his ship without a licence, knowing that it was an illegal act, was held to be barratrous because it was committed without the knowledge of the shipowners.

---

97 (1814) 2 M & S 290. The loss was not regarded as a total loss so as to give the assured the right of abandonment because she was recaptured and part of the cargo was retrieved.

98 See *Jones v Nicholson* (1854) 10 Exch 28, where the master, who was also part owner, ran away with the ship and cargo. In relation to the other part owners, the master's act constituted barratry.

99 [1937] 1 All ER 158. Further discussed in Chapter 15.

100 (1789) 3 Term Rep 277. By the terms of the policy the ship was insured in any 'lawful trade'.

101 Section 41 relating to the implied warranty of legality refers to the conduct of the assured. In a policy on ship, it is the propriety of the shipowner which is under consideration, not that of the master or crew. See *Toulin v Anderson* (1809) 1 Taunt 227 where trading without licence was held to be a breach of the implied warranty.

102 (1875) 33 LT (NS) 286, PC.

Any act committed by the master and/or crew to defeat the performance of the voyage is barratrous being to the prejudice of his owners. In *Moss v Byrom*,[103] the captain, contrary to the instructions of his owners, took a prize which resulted in the loss of the vessel. The court held that it was an act of barratry even though the prize may have been for the benefit of his owner as well as himself, yet if he acted contrary to his duty to them, it was barratry. The fact that the captain might have conceived that his conduct was to the benefit of his owners is irrelevant. As he had acted contrary to his duty, and his act had in fact increased the risk of the shipowner,[104] the captain was held to have committed a barratrous act.

An intentional breach of a blockade;[105] trading with the enemy;[106] changing sides in a civil war;[107] breach of an embargo;[108] and causing a ship to be captured by a privateer,[109] are a few less well known examples of barratry. The classic examples of barratry, such as a deviation, scuttling, and smuggling, have engendered some interesting points of law and will therefore be given closer attention.

Smuggling

A species of barratry which also constitutes a crime is smuggling. The act of smuggling is, in itself, in a sense, 'harmless' until it comes to the knowledge of the customs authorities which could then cause the ship to be seized. In *Cory v Burr*,[110] the leading authority on the subject, the House of Lords considered two main issues: first, whether the barratrous act of the master or the seizure (by the Spanish revenue officers) was the proximate cause of loss; and secondly, whether the loss fell within the meaning of the word 'seizure' under the 'warranted free from capture and seizure' clause.

Seizure as the proximate cause of loss

It is clear from the remarks made by all the Law Lords that they regarded seizure, not barratry, as the 'proximate' cause of loss.[111] Lord Blackburn justified his stand on the matter with the following explanation:[112]

> '... but the barratry would itself occasion no loss at all to the parties insured. If it had not been that the Spanish revenue officers, doing their duty ... had come and seized the ship, the barratry of the captain ...would have done the assured no harm at all.'

---

103 (1795) 6 Term Rep 379.

104 Should any loss or accident happen to the ship during that time, his owners would have been responsible for it to the freighters of the ship.

105 *Goldschmidt v Whitemore* (1811) 8 East 126; and *Everth v Hannam* (1815) 2 Marsh R 72; 6 Taunt 375.

106 *Earle v Rowcroft* (1806) 8 East 126.

107 [1958] 2 Lloyd's Rep 578.

108 *Robertson v Ewer* (1786) 1 Term Rep 127.

109 *Arcangelo v Thompson* (1811) 2 Camp 620.

110 (1883) 8 AC 393, HL.

111 For a discussion of the law of causation, see Chapter 8.

112 (1881) 8 AC 393 at p 400.

In similar vein, Lord FitzGerald expressed his views as follows:

> 'Now it is obvious that with so large a definition as that, there may be instances of barratry which may be either harmless or effect but a small loss – for instance a deviation, or wilful delay; but barratry may also consist in a very small matter over which the owners or freighters have no control, the effects or consequences of which may be very serious .... The barratry created a liability to forfeiture or confiscation, but might in itself be quite harmless; but the seizure, which was the effective act towards confiscation, and the direct and immediate cause of the loss, was not because the act of the master was an act of barratry but that it was a violation of the revenue laws of Spain.'[113]

That seizure is to be considered the proximate cause of loss in such circumstances appears to be well accepted. The law as laid down in *Cory v Burr*,[114] has not been overruled; it is thus still good law, and more so when one considers the fact that it emanated from the highest court in the land. Whether the actual decision of the case on the issue of causation would be held differently in the light of the law set out in *The Leyland Case*[115] is doubtful. It is contended that on similar facts the court would probably, for the reasons given above, still regard seizure either as the sole proximate cause or, together with barratry, as another proximate cause of loss.[116]

Warranted free from capture and seizure

As seizure was held the proximate cause of loss, the next question which the House had to decide was whether it fell within the clause which excepted the insurer from liability for seizure. And as the word 'seizure' was interpreted as being wide enough to embrace 'every act of taking forcible possession either by a lawful authority or by overpowering force',[117] the shipowner's claim fell squarely within the exception, and was therefore not recoverable. Needless to say, if barratry had been found to have been the proximate cause of loss, the shipowner would have succeeded in his claim.

It has to be stressed that the fact that the policy in question contained an *express* exception of liability for capture and seizure was critical to the outcome of the case. As seizure was held the proximate cause of loss, the House had no choice but to give legal effect to the express term. In the light of this, the modern equivalent of the 'warranted free from capture and seizure' clause contained in

---

113 As the case was decided before *The Leyland Case*, the word 'proximate' was not used in the judgments. Under the old law, words such 'immediate' and 'ultimate' were used for the purpose of determining the cause of loss.

114 (1881) 8 AC 393. See also *Lockyer v Offley* (1786), 1 TR 252.

115 (1918) AC 350, HL; discussed in depth in Chapter 7.

116 See Chapter 7.

117 See *Cory v Burr* (1881) 8 AC 393. The definition was later developed in *The Hai Hsuan* [1958] 1 Lloyd's Rep 351 at p 358, by the United States, Court of Appeals, where it was pointed out that: '... "seizure" in a contract of insurance is always to be understood in a restricted and limited sense as signifying only the taking of a ship by the act of governments or other public authority for a violation of the laws of trade or some rule or regulation instituted as a matter of municipal policy, or in consequence of an existing state of war'. That 'seizure' does not include a violent taking of possession of the ship by a mutinous crew was the *ratio decidendi* of the case.

the war exclusion clause of the ITCH(95) and the IVCH(95) has to be considered.

The war exclusion clause of the ITCH(95) and the IVCH(95)

The main objective of the war exclusion clause is, as in the case of the 'free from capture and seizure' warranty, to except an insurer from liability for loss or damage liability or expense caused by 'capture seizure arrest or detainment ...'. Barratry and piracy are, however, specifically excluded from the exclusion.

On first reading, this exception within an exception may appear to confer a significant advantage to the assured. The implications of withdrawing barratry and piracy from the 'capture seizure arrest restraint or detainment' exclusion are: first, it confirms that they are not war risks, but marine risks. Secondly, and more importantly, it serves to clarify that, though a loss proximately caused by 'capture seizure arrest retain or detainment' is generally excepted, such a cause of loss resulting from a barratrous (or piratical) act is, however, not to be considered as an excepted loss falling within the scope of the war exclusion. An assured could well be misled by this into thinking that any loss proximately caused by, for example, a barratrous seizure, is recoverable by virtue of the fact that barratry is excepted from the war exclusion. However, further reflection will reveal that this is not the case.

The fact that a loss is not expressly excepted by the policy does not mean that it automatically becomes an included loss.[118] Thus, if seizure, though resulting from a barratrous act, is, as in the case of *Cory v Burr*,[119] held as the sole proximate cause, the loss is still not recoverable – the reason being that a loss proximately caused by seizure, barratrous or hostile, is not an insured risk under the ITCH(95)[120] The withdrawal of barratry (and piracy) out of the war exclusion simply means that a barratrous seizure is not an expressly excluded loss: it does not thereby imply that it has become an included or insured loss.[121]

---

118 However, in *The Hai Hsuan* [1957] 1 Lloyd's Rep 428, Thomsen CJ in the court of first instance expressed the opinion that if seizure was *not* expressly excluded by the policy the shipowner would be able, provided that barratry was *a* cause of the loss, to recover under the policy. He said: '...where barratry was a cause of loss, if the ultimate cause [eg, stranding or capture] was not excluded from coverage by a warranty or an exclusion clause, recovery might be had on the grounds of barratry, whether or not the ultimate cause was an insured peril; but that where the ultimate cause was excluded, recovery might not be had on the grounds of barratry.' Assuming the word 'ultimate' to mean 'proximate', the judge has given the impression that provided that the proximate cause (seizure) is not expressly excluded, barratry operating even as a remote cause is recoverable; and this is the case whether the proximate cause is or not is an insured peril. With due respect, it is submitted that unless barratry is another proximate cause, it is difficult to see how a remote cause of loss could ever be made recoverable simply because the proximate cause is not expressly excluded. Unless the proximate cause or one of the proximate causes of loss is a peril insured against, it is difficult to see how a loss remotely caused by barratry may be recoverable under the policy. Under common law and s 55(1) of the Act, a remote cause of loss has never been given any legal effect or consequence. Moreover, it is significant to note that s 55(2)(a) excuses the 'misconduct ... of the master or crew' only in cases where the 'loss is proximately caused by a peril insured against'.

119 (1881) 8 AC 393.

120 It is an insured risk under cl 1.2 of the IWSC(H), see Chapter 14.

121 The same applies to piracy.

The barratry exception is thus of limited use. It may be brought into play only in the case where both barratry and seizure are held to be the proximate causes of the loss. In such event, the loss is recoverable for two reasons: first, barratry, one of the proximate causes, is a peril insured against under cl 6.2.4; and secondly, as a barratrous seizure (unlike a hostile seizure) is not an *expressly* excluded loss, there is nothing in the policy to prevent the assured from recovery.[122]

It is significant to note that a barratrous seizure resulting from a breach of a custom regulation is also not covered by the Institute War and Strikes Clauses Hulls (IWSC(H)) falling within the exception of 'any loss damage liability or expense arising ... by reason of infringement of any customs or trading regulations' of cl 5.1.4. Thus, if seizure is held as the sole proximate cause, the loss is neither covered by the ITCH(95) nor the IWSC(H). This is a gap which a shipowner has to address; he is in a vulnerable position, for should the barratrous conduct of the master and/or crew cause the ship to be seized by the custom authorities, and seizure be held by the court as the proximate cause of loss, he would not be able to recover for the loss.

The death blow theory

If the seizure of a ship, in consequence of an act of smuggling committed by the master during the currency of the policy, is to take place *after* the expiration of the policy, the loss is not recoverable, regardless of whether the seizure is or is not an insured peril. The authority for this principle is *Lockyer v Offley*[123] where the ship, which was seized 24 hours after the termination of the voyage policy, was held not to be covered by the policy even though such seizure was in consequence of a barratrous act of smuggling committed by the master *during* the insured voyage.

In such a case, one could be tempted to resort to the 'death blow' or 'death wound' theory to argue that as the 'death blow' – that is, the barratrous act of smuggling – was sustained during the currency of the policy, the loss is recoverable.[124] The reply to such a contention is that the 'death blow' (barratry), though inflicted during the currency of the policy, did not cause the 'death': seizure is the proximate cause of loss. The rule that an insurer is not liable for any loss (whether or not caused by an insured peril) which occurs after the risk has terminated has to be strictly adhered to.

Repeated acts of smuggling

The proviso to cl 6.2 of due diligence would now apply to a situation such as that encountered in *Pipon v Cope*[125] to exonerate the insurer from liability. The purpose of the proviso is to ensure that not only the assured, the owners, and managers but also '... *superintendents or any of their onshore management*' have

---

122 For a discussion of included and excluded losses, see Chapter 8.

123 (1786) 1 TR 259.

124 For a more comprehensive study of the death blow theory, see Chapter 16.

125 (1808) 1 Camp 434.

acted responsibly in the management of the ship.[126] Lord Ellenborough decided that:

> 'It was the plaintiff's duty to have prevented these repeated acts of smuggling by the crew. By his neglecting to do so, and allowing the risk to be so monstrously enhanced, the underwriters are discharged.'

One has, of course, to remember that barratry is, by definition, an act committed *without* the consent or knowledge of the shipowner. Thus, an owner who has condoned repeated acts of smuggling committed by his crew would find it difficult to argue that he has not assented to the risk of the ship being seized. In not taking any action, he is himself guilty of the want of due diligence.

In *Trinder, Anderson & Co v Thames & Mersey Co*,[127] Lord Justice Collins in the Court of Appeal expressed the view that the decision in *Pipon v Cope*[128] can be supported on the grounds that 'the owners who were claiming in respect of loss by seizure for smuggling for the third time in three consecutive voyages must be taken to have *assented* to the barratrous acts of their servants. It was at all events *crassa negligentia aequiparata dolo*.'

Furthermore, in such a circumstance, the proviso has to be read with s 41 in which the implied warranty of legality is qualified with the words 'so far as the assured can control the matter'. A shipowner who is aware of the repeated acts of smuggling committed by his master or crew would find it difficult, if not impossible, to argue that the matter is beyond his control. By condoning the illegal acts of the master or crew it can be said that he has himself carried out the adventure in an unlawful manner.

'Wilfully committed'

To constitute barratry, the act of the master and/or crew has to be 'wilfully' committed. Thus, an act of mere neglect, ignorance, incompetence, or improper treatment, though it tended to the destruction of the vessel, is not barratrous. According to Lord Ellenborough in *Todd v Ritchie*:[129] '... the captain must be proved to have acted against his better judgment ...'. The element of 'wilfulness' has to be proved as a part of the plaintiffs' case. There are, however, two groups of cases, namely, those concerning deviation and scuttling, which are particularly useful for the purpose of illustrating this point.

Mere deviation and barratrous deviation

There is a whole ocean between a mere or common deviation and a barratrous deviation. Whether the loss of a ship which has been taken out of her course by the master or crew is to be attributed to barratry is an issue which has arisen on a number of occasions in some of the older cases. A master and/or crew who deliberately carries a ship on a course contrary to the orders of the shipowner

---

126 Words in italics were recently added to the ITCH(95) and the IVCH(95). Further discussion of the proviso to cl 6.2 of the ITCH(95) and cl 4.2 of the IVCH(95) can be found below.

127 [1898] 2 QB 114 at p 129.

128 (1808) 1 Camp 434.

129 (1816) 1 Stark 240.

clearly commits a barratrous act: he has intentionally committed a breach of duty.

In *Ross v Hunter*,[130] Mr Justice Buller said that, 'in one sense of the word, it is a deviation by the captain for fraudulent purposes of his own; and that is the distinction between deviation, as it is generally used, and barratry'. For deviation to amount to barratry the master or crew has to deviate with a fraudulent intent. The ship must be taken out of its direct or normal course 'for the purpose of his own private advantage, and ... for a fraudulent purpose ...'.[131] There must be a barratrous intention.[132]

Similarly in *Mentz, Decker & Co v Maritime Insurance Co Ltd*,[133] the master in breach of his orders and for his own private benefit took the ship on two occasions several hundred miles out of its course. Whilst trading at one of the port she stranded and became a total loss. These acts of deviation were held by the court to be barratrous.

The circumstances of the above two cases have to be compared with those in *Phyn v The Royal Exchange Assurance*,[134] where the vessel was carried out of its course by strong currents, and was later captured and condemned as prize. As there was no evidence of criminal intent, fraud or criminality, the deviation was held not to be barratrous. More importantly, the act was clearly not 'wilfully' committed, as the sea was responsible for her change of course.

If a ship has to return to port because of her unseaworthy condition, such a deviation does not constitute barratry.[135] The act of the captain being necessary for reasons of safety was not only not barratrous but was also justifiable.[136] It would appear that 'unless they be accompanied with fraud, or crime no case of deviation will fall within the true definition of barratry.'

Barratrous scuttling

Scuttling a ship is a deliberate and an intentional act; proof of the wilful casting away of a ship, whether committed with or without the connivance of the

---

130 (1790) 4 Term Rep 33.

131 *Ibid*, at p 37.

132 In *Stamma v Brown* (1742) 2 Stra 1173, the conduct of the master in calling at a port out of the direct route, in order to deliver cargo, was held to be a mere act of deviation and not barratry. The court found that his conduct was not inconsistent with his duty to his owners, but was in fact for their benefit. In a very old and peculiar case, *Elton v Brogden* (1747) 2 Str 1264, the act of the crew in forcing the master to go out of the course of the voyage was held to be neither a deviation nor barratry: it was not deviation by reason of the excuse of necessity; and it did not amount to barratry as the ship was not run away with in order to defraud the owners. The plaintiffs were awarded the sum insured, presumably, because she was captured.

133 [1910] 1 KB 133; (1909) 101 LT 808. The central issue of the case was whether the notice given by the assured, after he became aware of the loss, was sufficient to satisfy the held covered clause.

134 (1798) 7 Term Rep 505.

135 See *Hibbert v Martin* (1808) 1 Camp 538.

136 See s 49(1)(d). In the law relating to carriage of goods by sea, see *Kish v Taylor* [1912] AC 604, HL.

shipowner, would negative a loss by a peril of the seas which is an accidental and fortuitous loss.[137] The concepts are mutually exclusive.

Whether a loss can be said to have been attributed to barratry is dependent upon whether it has been wilfully or deliberately committed by the master and/or crew. Once that has been ascertained, the next question which arises for consideration is whether the shipowner is privy to the act of the master or crew which caused the sinking of the ship. If the shipowner was privy or had procured to the sinking of the ship, then the wilful misconduct of the shipowner, and not barratry, would be regarded as the cause of loss.

That the plaintiffs have to bear the burden of proving that the act of the master or crew was deliberate is not in dispute.[138] But the question as to which party has to prove the issue of privity or consent, that the shipowner was or was not privy to the acts of the master or crew, is not so easy to answer. This problem can be more conveniently discussed elsewhere.[139]

To the prejudice of the shipowner

Barratry is by definition an act committed by the master or crew to the prejudice of the shipowner. This necessarily means that if a shipowner consents or is privy to the barratrous act, he would not be in a position to claim that he has been prejudiced. This aspect of the law has been settled beyond doubt by the classic authorities of *Vallejo v Wheeler*[140] and *Nutt & Others v Bourdieu*[141] In the latter case, Lord Mansfield had to decide on the vital issue as to whether barratry can be committed against any but the owner/owners of a ship. His opinion which has never been challenged reads as follows:

'It is clear beyond contradiction that it cannot. For barratry is something contrary to the duty of the master and mariners, the very terms of which imply that it must be in the relation in which they stand to the owners of the ship ... The point is too clear to require any further discussion.'

In spite of the clarity and firmness of this statement, the matter was again raised in *Soares v Thornton*[142] only to be reaffirmed by the court with the following remark: ' ... the very definition of barratry is a fraud by the master and mariners against the owner of the ship'. In *Elfie A Issaias v Marine Insurance Co Ltd*,[143] the Master of the Rolls issued the reminder that ' ... to cast away a man's ship without his consent is 'to his prejudice' although the pecuniary effect may be to his advantage'.

---

137 That scuttling is not a peril of the seas is discussed in Chapter 9.
138 See eg, *The Michael* [1979] 1 Lloyd's Rep 55 at p 66, QBD.
139 See Chapter 11.
140 (1774) 1 Cowp 143. Lord Mansfield said that ' ... if the owner of a ship insures and brings an action on the policy, he can never set up as a crime a thing done by his own direction or consent'.
141 (1786) 1 Term Rep 323.
142 (1817) 7 Taunt 627 at p 639.
143 (1923) 15 Ll L Rep 186 at p 189, CA.

Nothing can be clearer than these statements. However, if more recent authority be required, the case of *Samuel v Dumas*[144] could be cited, as Lord Sumner has stressed that, 'it is of the very essence of barratry that the shipowner is wronged, and he is not wronged when he consents'. Subsequently, Mr Justice Kerr in the court of first instance in *The Michael*[145] reiterated the rule as follows:

'... "to the prejudice of the owner" means, in effect, without his consent, or, to use an expression which is sometimes used in other contexts, "without his privity" ... It is clear that consent or privity can range from active complicity to mere passive concurrence.'

The most complete and succinct recent account of barratry, however, was delivered by Mr Justice Mustill (as he then was) in the court of first instance in *The Salem*:[146]

'It is not enough to show fraudulent conduct by the master and crew directed against the interests of the person insured. Barratry necessarily involves a damnification of the shipowner whether he or someone else is the person insured under the policy ... It follows that if the shipowner is privy to the dishonesty of the crew, there can be no recovery under a policy on either ship or goods. Under a hull policy the assured fails for two reasons: (a) because the loss is not by barratry, since the act is not contrary to his interests, and (b) because he cannot recover for the consequence of his own wrongful act.'[147]

As the above cases have demonstrated, the absence of consent or privity on the part of the shipowner is an essential ingredient of the peril of barratry. The prickly question is: which party has to prove this fact? Is it for the plaintiffs to prove the absence, or the defendants to prove the presence, of privity? This difficult but interesting question involving the burden and standard of proof is discussed elsewhere.[148]

The owner

The word 'owner' appearing in r 11, though unqualified, is traditionally understood in the context of barratry to mean the *shipowner*. It is indeed regrettable that the word 'ship' is not inserted before the word 'owner' as this would dispel all doubts, particularly, as to whether a cargo owner who has been prejudiced by the act of the master or crew could successfully claim for barratry. But read as a whole and in conjunction with the words 'or, as the case may be, the charterer,' the implication that it refers only to a shipowner, and not a cargo owner, is clear. Moreover, the above cases have clarified this point beyond doubt.

144 [1924] AC 431 at p 463, HL. Even though he was the dissenting judge, Lord Sumner's opinion on this particular issue is nevertheless relevant. See also *Rickards v Forestal Land, Timber and Railways Co Ltd* [1941] 3 All ER 62, HL where the issue as to whether barratry could be committed against a cargo owner was again resurrected only to be quashed. As barratry is no longer a peril insured against under the ICC (B) & (C), the question is now academic.
145 [1979] 1 Lloyd's Rep 55 at p 67.
146 [1981] 2 Lloyd's Rep 316 at p 324, QBD.
147 Under a policy on goods the assured fails for the single reason that there is no loss by barratry.
148 See Chapter 11.

Owner of a chartered ship

A shipowner who has let out his ship on charter continues to have an insurable interest in her, even though the charterparty may contain a term to the effect that the charterer shall compensate the owner for any loss or damage sustained to the ship. He is not bound to 'trust exclusively to the credit of the charterer, but might likewise protect himself by a policy of insurance'.[149]

It would seem that if a wrongful act was committed under the direction of the charterer, the shipowner would also be prevented from claiming for the loss by barratry.[150] According to Lord Ellenborough in *Hobbs v Hannam*,[151] applying the law of agency, the reasoning is as follows:

'If I give the dominion of my ship to a charterer, his acts are my acts: and in this case Kendal [the charterer] whose orders the master implicitly obeyed, according to his instructions, was, in point of law, the agent of the plaintiff. Therefore, the loss arose from following his own orders; and there is no pretence for imputing it to barratry.'

Master a part-owner

That a master who is the sole owner of a ship cannot commit barratry is obvious: a man cannot commit a fraud against himself. There is, however, no reason why an innocent part-owner should not be allowed to claim under a policy – the act of the master (another part-owner) is in relation to him barratrous.

In *Jones v Nicholson*[152] it was held that 'if the master, being himself a part-owner, commits the barratry, that is equally a fraud upon the other part-owners'. The reasoning lies in the rhetoric: are the other owners the less injured because the master happens to be a part owner? There is, *vis-à-vis* the other owners, equally a fraudulent act in violation of his duty as master. The prejudice lies in the fact that his act renders the owners liable to the charterers for a breach of contract. Thus, barratry can be committed by a master who is also a part-owner of the ship.[153]

The demise charterer

The words 'or, as the case may be, the charterer' have been added to protect the position of a person who is, for all intents and purposes, the owner of the ship at the relevant time. A demise charterer is such a person, for he is by reason of his contractual relationship with the shipowner in possession and control of the ship.[154] This is well established in the law relating to charterparties, and in

---

149 *Per* Lord Ellenborough in *Hobbs v Hannam* (1811) 3 Camp 93. See also s 14(3).

150 The charterer himself would not be to claim under a policy, as he cannot complain of a wrong which he himself has ordered for its commission.

151 (1811) 3 Camp 93 at 95. In this case, the charterer himself had sent smuggled goods on board the ship for which she was seized by the authorities. The master was required by the shipowner to implicitly obey the orders of the charterer. Thus, the master in obeying the charterer's orders were in effect obeying the shipowner's orders.

152 (1854) 10 Exch 28 at p 38, *per* Alderson B.

153 See *Westport Coal Co v McPhail* [1898] 2 QB 130 CA for a dispute on the same point in the law of carriage of goods.

154 *Colvin & Others v Newberry & Benson* (1828) 8 B & C 166.

marine insurance the issue was first raised in 1774 in *Vallejo v Wheeler*.[155] The master, for his own convenience, took the ship out of her course in order to load a cargo of brandy and wine for his own account. The goods on board the ship, which were damaged as a result of this iniquitous scheme of the master, belonged to a freighter; his action was on a policy upon goods, and the legal issue raised was whether a barratrous act had been committed against him. It was argued that the deviation being with the knowledge of the shipowner could never be barratrous.

The court held that as the assured was the owner of the goods, as well as temporary owner of the ship, the act of the master was barratrous. The assured was regarded as owner *pro hac vice*, and in the light of this the conduct of the master was clearly barratrous.

It would seem that even if the original owner was privy to the wrongful act committed by the master or crew, it would nonetheless constitute barratry *vis-à-vis* the demise charterer, as he is *pro tempore* the owner of the ship. The position was explained in *Soares and Another v Thornton*[156] as follows:

'Then the act of the original owner and master together was a complete act of barratry. If the right of the original owner was then at an end, the right of the freighter must be in existence. The concurrence of the freighter was then the only thing that would prevent the act of the master from being an act of barratry.'

Provided that the demise charterer himself is not privy to the act of the master, he would be able to claim for a loss by barratry.

In *The Salem*,[157] Mr Justice Mustill observed that, 'owner ship of a vessel may be divisible, and that the proprietors of the hull may charter it out on terms which give the charterer a right of control sufficient to put him in the same position, for many purposes, as if for the time being he were himself the shipowner'.

A charterer who is not in possession or control of the ship would not be able to claim the status of owner *pro hac vice* or owner *pro tempore*, and as such is in the same position as a mere shipper of cargo discussed below.[158]

The cargo owner

It is significant to note that the above and older cargo-claim cases[159] would now have to be read with caution, as the legal principles proposed in them are only relevant to a policy in which 'barratry' is a peril insured against.[160] Obviously,

---

155 (1774) 1 Cowp 143.

156 (1817) 7 Taunt 627 at p 639.

157 [1981] 2 Lloyd's Rep 316 at 324, QBD.

158 For a fuller account of the law relating to a demise charter, see Mustill J's judgment in *The Salem* [1981] 2 Lloyd's Rep 316 at p 324, QBD.

159 Eg, *Stamma v Brown* (1742) 2 Stra 1173; *Vallejo v Wheeler* (1774) 1 Cowp 143; *Nutt v Bourdieu* (1786) 1 TR 323; *Ross v Hunter* (1790) 4 Term Rep 33; *Goldschmidt v Whitmore* (1811) 3 Taunt 508; *Soares v Thornton* (1817) 7 Taunt 627; and *Dixon v Reid* (1882) 5 B & Ald 597.

160 In the more recent cases of *Rickards v Forestal Land, Timber and Rlys Co Ltd* [1940] 4 All ER 96; [1941] KB 225 CA; [1941] 3 All ER 62, HL; *Commercial Trading Co v Hartford Fire Insurance* [1974] 1 Lloyd's Rep 179; and *The Salem* [1983] 1 Lloyd's Rep 316, HL, the cargo was insured under the old Lloyd's form where barratry was specifically named as an insured peril.

only if barratry is an insured peril is the conduct of the master or crew relevant for the purpose of determining whether it falls within the legal definition of the term. The older cases have, however, established that even in a cargo policy, the act committed by the master or crew must be against the *shipowner*, or, as the case may be, the charterer.[161] The fact that it was directed against the interests of, or was done in bad faith towards, only the cargo owners is not sufficient to render the act barratrous. This means that if the loss was assented to by the shipowner, the cargo owner would not be able to recover for barratry.[162] Such issues are now academic, as barratry is not only not an insured peril under the ICC (B) and (C), but it is also specifically excluded by the general exclusions clause, cl 4.7, excepting cover for 'deliberate damage to or deliberate destruction of the subject-matter insured or any part thereof by the wrongful act of any person or persons'.

A barratrous act would fall within the coverage of the ICC (A) by reason of the fact that the policy is for all risks, and barratry is not specifically excluded by the general exclusions clause. Under the scheme of an all risks policy, the assured does not have to prove the ingredients of barratry, but merely that the loss was fortuitous. Provided that the event which caused the loss was a risk,[163] and does not fall within one of the enumerated exclusions, the loss is recoverable.

The innocent mortgagee

The question of whether an innocent mortgagee may recover for a loss caused by barratry was examined by the Court of Appeal in *Small v United Kingdom Marine Mutual Insurance Association*.[164] The facts of the case are as follows. Using the ship as security, one Wilkes, a part-owner and master of the ship, borrowed a sum of money from Small. The ship was wilfully cast away by Wilkes, and the plaintiffs, who were the executors of Small, instituted an action (not as assignee) on a policy which had been subscribed on Small's behalf. Perils of the seas[165] and, alternatively, barratry were alleged as the causes of loss. The issue was

---

161 The legal principle first enunciated by Lord Mansfield in *Nutt v Bourdieu* (1786) 1 TR 323 at p 330, that barratry cannot be 'committed against any but the owners of the ship' could, if read out of context, be misleading. On first reading, it could give the impression that a cargo owner can never claim for a loss by barratry. But read in its proper context, it is clear that a cargo owner can succeed in his claim for barratry if it is proved that the act of the master or crew was committed against the interests of the shipowner. If only the interests of the cargo owner is prejudiced, then the act does not fall within the definition of barratry. Naturally, such an issue can only arise if barratry is an insured peril under the policy in question.

162 The clearest explanation for this rule is Lord Sumner's statement made in the House of Lords in *Samuel v Dumas* [1924] AC 431 at p 463, HL, which read as follows: '... there is very old authority for saying that cargo owners cannot recover as for barratry, when the barratrous act leading to the loss was *assented to by the shipowner*, for it is of the essence of barratry that the shipowner is wronged, and he is not wronged, when he consents ...'. In *The Salem* [1983] 1 Lloyd's Rep 342, the House of Lords held that as the master and crew were acting in conspiracy with the shipowner, their conduct was not barratrous.

163 See *British & Foreign Marine Insurance Co v Gaunt* [1920] 1 KB 903; [1921] 2 AC 41, HL.

164 [1897] 2 QB 311, CA, hereinafter referred to as *The Small Case*.

165 The law on perils of the seas and scuttling is examined in Chapter 9.

whether the act of Wilkes was in relation to Small, who was not a part-owner of the ship but a mortgagee, barratrous in nature.[166]

The Court of Appeal held that as Small 'took part in placing Wilkes in the position of captain'. Wilkes was to be regarded as the master for Small and the other part-owners. On this footing, the loss was held to be covered by the policy. Small, though not a part-owner, was nonetheless treated as one for the purpose of enabling him to recover for the loss on the ground of barratry. It would appear that the court, in its desire to allow the innocent mortgagee the right to recover under the hull policy, has, it is submitted, relied on a rather tenuous ground to support its decision. The court's interpretation of the facts is somewhat artificial and contrived, and therefore difficult to accept.

As was seen, case law and rule 11 have defined that to constitute 'barratry', the wilful act of the master or crew has to be committed to the prejudice of the owner or owner *pro hac vice*. Except for having a say in the appointment of Wilkes, Small's position did not in any other way resemble that of an owner or of a charterer by demise, who by reason of being in possession and control of the ship is for all intents and purposes the owner *pro hac vice*. The court should have taken into consideration the fact that Small did not employ Wilkes or pay his salary. Surely, simply being involved in the appointment of the master is not, in itself, sufficient to make Small owner or owner *pro hac vice* of the ship.

Howbeit, it is submitted that there was really no need for the court to make believe that Small was a part owner merely because he was able, as a condition of the loan, to insist that Wilkes be made master. The court could have arrived at the same decision by examining the definition of barratry. The law (common and statutory) does not say that to constitute barratry the act has to be committed to the prejudice of the *assured* who, in this case, were the mortgagees.[167] Lord Justice Smith acknowledged the fact that 'the act of Wilkes was barratrous as against Small just as it was against the co-owners'. Thus, it could be argued that, as Wilkes's conduct was barratrous *vis-à-vis* the other part owners, the legal requirement – 'to the prejudice of the owner'– was satisfied.

Once it is proved that the shipowners are in fact prejudiced, barratry is proved to have been committed. There is nothing in law to say that the wilful act has to be committed to the prejudice of the *assured*, whether he be a mortgagee or a cargo owner.[168]

To protect his interest fully, a mortgagee would be well-advised to take out the Institute Mortgagees Interest Clauses (Hulls).[169] It would be highly dangerous for him to rely solely on the precarious ground upon which of *The Small Case* was founded, as it could be overruled.

---

166 The House of Lords in *Samuel v Dumas* [1924] AC 431 has overruled the Court of Appeal's decision in *The Small Case* (1897) 2 QB 311, CA, on the claim based perils of the sea, but has left its ruling based on barratry undisturbed. As such, the judgment on barratry still stands as good law. For a discussion on *The Small Case* in relation to perils of the sea, see Chapter 9.

167 Since the assured has suffered a loss, he would also, of course, be prejudiced by the barratrous act.

168 This is the legal position in relation to cargo.

169 See cl 6.1.2 of the Institute Mortgagees Interest Clauses: see Appendix 23.

CONTACT WITH AIRCRAFT, HELICOPTER OR SIMILAR OBJECTS, OR OBJECTS FALLING THEREFROM

With the exception of the new addition of 'helicopter', cl 6.2.5 of the ITCH(95) was previously a part of a larger clause which included 'land conveyance, dock or harbour equipment or installation'.[170] This latter part of the clause remains in cl 6.1.6 of the ITCH(95) which is not subject to the due diligence proviso, whereas the above peril, having been moved from cl 6.1 to 6.2 is now subject to the proviso.

The first 'objects' must presumably be read *ejusdem generis* with aircraft and helicopter to include flying objects and machines such as air ships and satellites.[171] They obviously refer to civilian aircraft; but whether they also include military aircraft causing damage whilst performing military exercises is unclear. Provided that the loss does not fall within the scope of the war exclusion clause of the ITCH(95), there is no reason why such a loss should not be recoverable.

The second 'objects' refer to anything, for example, bombs, rockets, missiles, and satellites, falling from these flying objects.[172]

THE DUE DILIGENCE PROVISO

Any claim based on cl 6.2 of the ITCH(95) is subject to what is commonly referred to as the due diligence proviso, which is now worded as follows:

'provided such loss or damage has not resulted from want of due diligence by the Assured, Owners, Mangers or *Superintendents or any of their onshore management.*'[173]

There are two main problems which are likely to arise from this proviso: the first is in connection with the question of onus of proof, and the second in relation to the words 'resulted from'. Before preceding to examine these issues and the nature of the proviso, it is convenient first to consider the notion of due diligence.

Want of due diligence

The concept of due diligence is borrowed from art 3 r 1 of the Carriage of Goods by Sea Act 1971 where the term, which has been subjected to a considerable amount of judicial scrutiny, has acquired a rather specific meaning in law.[174]

---

170 Previously cl 6.1.7 of the ITCH(83) which is identical to cl 4.1.7 of the IVCH(83).
171 Whether a hot-air balloon is a 'similar object' is an interesting thought.
172 Whether substances such oil and chemicals falling from aircraft are 'objects' is unclear.
173 The words in italics have been added by the ITCH(95).
174 The failure to exercise due diligence under art 3, r 1 of the Carriage of Goods by Sea Act 1971 was construed in *Riverstone Meat Co Pty v Lancashire Shipping Co Ltd* [1961] 1 All ER 496 as non-delegable: the carrier was held liable by the House of Lords even for the negligence of the servants of a reputable firm of ship repairers.

Whether the same meaning is to be awarded to the term in the law of marine insurance has yet to be considered by the courts. The proviso could be interpreted to mean that only the *personal* want of due diligence of the 'owners, managers or superintendents or any of their onshore management' would prejudice the claim of the assured. In other words, only if any one of these persons is *personally* guilty of the want due diligence would the claim be irrecoverable. On the other hand, it could also be given a wider construction, as in the law of carriage of goods by sea, to include the want of due diligence on the part of the subordinates, employees, servants and agents of the 'assured, owners, mangers or superintendents or any of their onshore management'. It has been pointed out that in the United States, the rule of the *personal* want of due diligence is applied; and should the point arise in this country, the same is likely to be adopted.[175] As a list of persons is specified in the proviso, this assumption is probably correct.[176]

In *The Brentwood*,[177] the Court of Appeal held that as the plaintiffs, the assured, had failed to provide the master with the necessary standing instructions concerning minimum freeboard, they were guilty of the want of due diligence under the proviso. The exercise of due diligence means the exercise of due care and attention.[178]

Assured, owners, managers or superintendents or any of their onshore management

The proviso refers to the want of due diligence by the 'assured, owners, managers or superintendents or any of their onshore management'. The want of due diligence of any *one* of these persons would defeat the claim of the assured. A mortgagee, for example, whether suing as an assignee or as an original assured of a hull policy, who is himself free from blame, could well lose his right to indemnity under the policy should any one of these persons be found guilty of the want of due diligence. Thus, it is not sufficient merely to show that the assured themselves are free from blame, for the want of due diligence committed by any *one* of these listed persons would forfeit their right to recovery. The objective of the proviso is to ensure that members of the higher level of the corporate ladder are themselves vigilant and free from blame in the carrying out of their duties in the management of the vessel.

---

175 See Arnould, para 832.

176 If the intention of the clause was to include the want of due diligence of servants and agents, it could have easily added the words 'and of their servants and agents' at the end of the clause.

177 *Coast Ferries Ltd v Century Insurance Co of Canada* [1973] 2 Lloyd's Rep 232.

178 The test of culpable negligence, gross negligence or culpable inattention as propounded in earlier cases such as *Toulmin v Inglis* (1808) 1 Camp 421, and *Pipon v Cope* (1808) 1 Camp 434, cannot now be good law.

Proof of breach of proviso

Arnould,[179] relying on a rather tenuous statement made by the court of first instance in *The Brentwood*,[180] states that it is the assured who has to prove that the requirement of the proviso is satisfied. The opposite view, however, can be found in O'May, where it is also said that one should not be too perturbed with this issue as, for want of a better expression, it will all in the end come out in the wash with discovery and exchange of pleadings.[181] With due respect, it is submitted that the question of burden of proof is a matter of great tactical importance, especially in the light of the fact that a judge could dismiss a case purely on the ground of the plaintiffs having failed to prove their case. We were recently reminded by the House of Lords in *The Popi M*[182] of the principle that if the party upon whom the burden of proof lies in relation to any averment is unable to discharge that burden, the plaintiffs' case would be dismissed. If the persuasive burden lies with the assured, it is for them to discharge that burden; and not for the underwriters to prove or show how the loss occurred. It is contended that whether the burden of proof lies with the assured or with the underwriters is largely dependent upon how one regards the terms of the proviso: Is it a condition of the claim or is it a defence?

A condition or a defence?

The due diligence requirement of cl 6.2 could be seen either as an integral part or an ingredient of the assured's claim, or as providing the underwriters with a defence to the assured's claim. The question as to which party is to bear the initial burden of proof is critically dependent upon how the proviso is construed. If the exercise of due diligence is considered as a *component* of the assured's claim, then it is for them to satisfy the court that it has been complied with. On the other hand, if it is regarded as providing the underwriters with a defence to the claim of the assured, then, it would have to be proved by the underwriters.[183]

If the onus originally falls with the assured, their failure to prove the exercise of due diligence would naturally result in a failure on their part to prove their case. Having failed to prove an essential requirement of the claim, this would necessarily mean that there would be no case for the defence to answer. But should the initial burden lie with the underwriters, then all that the assured need prove as their case are the ingredients of the insured peril which they have alleged has proximately caused the loss. In practice, it is generally accepted as providing a defence to the underwriters; as such, it is expected of

---

179 Arnould, para 832.

180 [1973] 2 Lloyd's Rep 232. The Canadian Court of Appeal has conveniently left the matter open.

181 O'May, p 138.

182 *Rhesa Shipping Co SA v Edmunds* [1985] 2 Lloyd's Rep 1, HL. See Chapter 11.

183 As was seen, the same problem arises in the law of barratry: is it for the assured to prove the absence of connivance, or for the underwriters to prove that the assured had consented to the loss? See Chapter 11.

them to prove the want of due diligence, not for the assured to prove they were not guilty of the want of due diligence.

Clause 6.2 of the ITCH(95) has not only failed to clarify where the burden of proof lies,[184] but also whether the rule of proximate cause applies.

'Resulted from'

The introductory words to cl 6.2 (and 6.1) of the ITCH(95) use the term 'caused by' which, as was seen earlier, has always been understood to mean 'proximately' caused by. The proviso to the clause, however, uses the expression 'resulted from'. Whether the rule of proximate cause is to be applied to this term has yet to be considered by a court of law.

It is, however, the view of one author that,[185] 'The words "resulted from" are the equivalent of "proximately caused by"'. Whether the rule of proximate cause should be applied to the proviso is, it is submitted, doubtful. The rule of proximate cause, as laid down by s 55(1), is applicable, as can be seen by its wording, *only as regards a loss caused by a peril insured against.* Construed as a defence, its function is to *disentitle* the assured of the right to indemnity for a loss which is *prima facie* recoverable by reason of being *proximately* caused by one of the perils enumerated in cl 6.2. There is no reason why the underwriters should be required to prove the more onerous burden, that the loss was proximately caused by the want of due diligence. Used as a defence he need only adduce sufficient proof (as a remote cause) to cast a doubt upon the case of the assured. It is submitted that the words 'resulted from' must refer to the want of due diligence (by any of the persons named) as a remote cause of the loss, and should be construed as having the same legal effect as the term 'attributable to' appearing in ss 39(5) and 55(2)(a) of the Act, as discussed earlier.[186]

---

184 The matter was apparently considered when the proposals for the amendment to the proviso to cl 6.2 of the ITCH(95) were recently debated. It was, however, decided not to disturb the *status quo*, whatever that might be.

185 O'May, p 137. It would appear that in holding the view that it is the insurer who has to prove that the loss is 'proximately' caused by the want of due diligence under the terms of the proviso. O'May is in fact going against the grain of his own interpretation of the proviso to the effect that it provides a defence to the claim of the assured.

186 See Chapter 11.

CHAPTER 13

3/4ths COLLISION LIABILITY

INTRODUCTION

When two ships collide, both are bound to sustain some degree of damage, and this raises questions as to the rights and liabilities of their owners which, assuming that one or both of them are insured, could in turn actuate legal issues relating to marine insurance. There are two aspects to the problem: first, the matter has to be looked at from the position of the owner of the insured vessel in relation to the damage sustained by his own vessel and, secondly, in relation to his liability to the third party whose vessel has been damaged as a result of the collision with the insured vessel.

The insured vessel

The owner of an insured vessel (vessel A), should be able to recover from his own insurer for any damage sustained by his own vessel as a loss caused by a peril of the sea.[1] The fact that the master or crew of the insured vessel, vessel A, may have been negligent in the navigation of the ship and is partly or wholly responsible for the collision is immaterial, for s 55(2)(a) provides that the insurer is liable for any loss proximately caused by a peril insured against, 'even though the loss would not have happened but for the ... negligence of the master or crew'. Moreover, both the ITCH(95) and the IVCH(95) (cll 6.2 and 4.2 respectively, also known as the Inchmaree Clause) expressly states that:

> 'This insurance covers loss of or damage to the *subject-matter insured*[2] caused by – negligence of master, officers, crew or pilots.'

The 'subject-matter insured' refers to the assured's own vessel (vessel A), not the vessel which vessel A has collided with.

In so far as the insured vessel is concerned, there has never been any problem as regards recovery: subject to the limits set out in his policy, the assured is entitled to recover the full extent of the loss sustained by his own vessel as a loss caused by a peril of the seas.[3]

The Pollution Hazard Clause

Clause 7 of the ITCH(95)[4] on pollution hazard allows an assured to recover for any loss of or damage to the insured vessel caused by 'any governmental authority acting under the powers vested in it to prevent or mitigate a pollution hazard or *damage to the environment or threat thereof*, resulting directly from

---

1 Collision is a peril of the sea: *The Xantho*, (1887) 7 HL Cas 504.

2 Emphasis added.

3 It needs to be recalled that in so far as the policy subscribed by the owner of vessel A is concerned, the subject-matter insured is his own vessel (vessel A), and not the vessel (vessel B) belonging to the third party.

4 Cl 5 of the IVCH(95). Cl 7 was introduced in the ITCH in 1983; but it was in use since 1973 following *The Torrey Canyon* disaster of 1967.

damage to the Vessel for which the Underwriters are liable under this insurance ...'.[5]

The purpose of this clause is to provide additional cover for the assured in the event of action taken by any governmental authority, to avoid or reduce a pollution hazard and damage to the environment or threat thereof, which has caused loss or damage to the insured vessel.

First, it needs to be mentioned that cl 7 is not restricted to a claim in connection with the 3/4ths collision liability clause. It is of general application, allowing the assured the right to recover for any loss of or damage to the insured vessel sustained in the course of action taken for the prevention or mitigation of pollution. Nevertheless, it is convenient to discuss this clause here because such loss or damage could well arise when a collision occurs; furthermore, it is particularly relevant to the new amendments made to the exclusion clause (cl 8.4.5) of the 3/4ths collision liability clause (cl 8) of the ITCH(95) which will be discussed in this chapter.

Secondly, it is to be noted that the wording of the clause is precise: recovery for such a cause of loss of or damage to the insured vessel will only be allowed if it resulted 'directly from damage to the Vessel for which the underwriters are liable under this insurance ...'. This means that the original damage to the vessel must be proximately caused by an insured peril. Provided that the underwriters are liable for the original damage, they will also be liable for any loss or damage suffered by the insured Vessel caused by governmental action taken to prevent or mitigate a pollution hazard or damage to the environment or threat thereof.

Finally, it is also to be noted that there is a proviso to cl 7 to the effect that the action taken by the governmental authority must not have resulted from the want of due diligence by the 'assured, owners, or managers' to prevent or mitigate such hazard or threat thereof.[6] This proviso is similar to the old proviso in cl 6.2 of the ITCH(83). It is observed that the want of due diligence by 'Superintendents or any of their onshore management' is not included in this proviso, whereas it has recently been included in the proviso to cl 6.2 of the ITCH(95).[7]

Third party liability

Assuming for convenience that the insured vessel (vessel A) is wholly to be blamed for the collision, her owners would be legally liable to pay damages to the third party (owner of vessel B) for the damage sustained by vessel B. This then raises the following question: has the owner of the insured vessel (vessel A) the right to recover from his own insurer his liability to the third party? This question was answered in 1836 in the case of *De Vaux v Salvador*,[8] where the

---

5 The words in italics were added by the ITCH(95).

6 Clause 7: 'Masters Officers Crew or Pilots not to be considered Owners within the meaning of this Clause 7 should they hold shares in the Vessel.'

7 Whether the failure to amend cl 7, so that it may be brought in line with cl 6.2, is an oversight is unclear.

8 (1836) 4 A & E 420.

court decided that liability for collision damage incurred by an assured was not recoverable under the terms of what was then an ordinary form of marine policy on a ship. The effect of the decision meant that an assured would be out of pocket to the extent of the amount of damages which he had to pay to the third party.

As a consequence of *De Vaux v Salvador*, the running down clause was introduced which over the years was developed and enlarged. Its present form is now contained in the 3/4ths collision liability clause, often referred to simply as the 'collision liability clause', and can be found in both the ITCH(95) and the IVCH(95).[9]

THE COLLISION LIABILITY CLAUSE

Insurance against liability to a third party is expressly countenanced by s 3(2)(c) of the Act, the relevant parts of which state:[10]

> 'In particular there is a marine adventure where – Any liability to a third party may be incurred by the owner of, or other person interested in or responsible for, insurable property, by reason of maritime perils.'

It may be helpful to divide this study of the clause into two main parts. First, the meaning of the word 'collision' will be considered, followed by a discussion on the extent of the liability of the insurer and matters relating thereto.

Collision

The assured will only be indemnified under cl 8 of the ITCH(95) and cl 6 of the IVCH(95)[11] when the liability of the assured arises in consequence of the insured vessel 'coming into collision with any other vessel'. The two words here that require close examination are 'collision' and 'vessel'.

The word 'collision' conjures in one's mind a picture of two vessels coming into direct physical contact with one another, and some impact on the hulls is generally expected.[12] However, actual bodily contact of hulls is not necessary, and this was made clear in *The Niobe*[13] and *Re Margetts v Ocean Accident*,[14] both cases relating to damage caused by a tug whilst towing another vessel.

In the first case, the tug which was towing *The Niobe* came into collision with and sank another vessel, *The Valetta*. The owners of *The Valetta* recovered damages both from *The Niobe* and the tug, whereupon the owners of *The Niobe* instituted this action against their insurer seeking an indemnity for the amount which they had to pay to the owners of *The Valetta*. The insurer's defence was

---

9   Clauses 8 and 6 respectively.

10   See also s 74.

11   As cl 8 of the ITCH(95) and cl 6 of the IVCH(95) are identically worded, it would be more convenient simply to refer only to cl 8 for this discussion.

12   In *Union Mar Insurance Co v Borwick* [1895] 2 QB 279, at p 281, Mr Justice Mathew said: 'I cannot distinguish collision with from striking against'.

13   *David M'Cowan v Baine & Johnstone & Others* [1891] AC 401, HL.

14   [1901] 2 KB 792.

that under the policy he was only liable for damage arising from a 'collision'.[15] They argued that because *The Niobe* herself did not at any time come into physical contact with *The Valetta*, there was no 'collision' and, therefore, the collision liability clause did not apply.

The above contention was rejected by the House of Lords which held that the tug and tow must be regarded as – one and the same vessel – a single entity. The accident, albeit indirect, was nonetheless, a 'collision'. As regards the words 'come into collision with any other vessel', the Earl of Selborne said:[16]

> 'I should also hold them to cover an indirect collision, through the impact of the ship insured upon another vessel or thing capable of doing damage, which might by such impact be driven against the ship suffering damage.'

Lord Morris considered the tug as a 'part of the apparatus for moving the ship *Niobe*, and that a collision by the tug whilst so towing *The Niobe* was a collision of *The Niobe*' within the meaning of the clause in the policy.[17] Whether tug and tow be considered as one single item, or as a part of the other, the result is the same.

In *Re Margetts v Ocean Accident*,[18] the court had to consider whether an accident caused by a tug striking upon a vessel's anchor was a 'collision'. Though an anchor may be a considerable distance away from the vessel, it is 'not the less a portion of the vessel'.[19] Citing *The Niobe* as authority, the court held that the tug had come into collision with a 'vessel'.

In *Bennett SS Co v Hull Mutual SS Protecting Society*,[20] an assured took the matter one step further by arguing that fishing nets, which were attached to and extending from a fishing vessel about a mile away from the steamship, were part of a ship. The argument was along the lines that as a tug and an anchor have been considered as parts of a ship, there was no reason why fishing nets could not be considered likewise. This submission was rejected by Lord Reading CJ, who said that, 'Nets ... are not a part of the ship in that sense, nor are they things which it is necessary for her to have and without which she could not prudently put to sea'.[21]

The navigation clause

The principle laid down in the above authorities in relation to tug and tow must be applied with caution. It is noted that in the first two cases, it was made clear to the insurer from the terms of the cover that the insured vessel could be under tow: that the insured vessel could at some stage of the adventure be towed or be

---

15 The term of cover was, 'If the ship hereby insured shall come into collision with any other ship or vessel and the insured shall in consequence thereof become liable to pay, and shall pay, to the persons interested in such other ship or vessel, any sum or sums of money ...'.

16 [1891] AC 401 at p 404, HL.

17 *Ibid*, at p 411.

18 [1901] 2 KB 792.

19 *Per* Ridley J, *ibid*, at p 795.

20 [1914] 3 KB 57, CA.

21 *Ibid*, at p 61.

under tow was understood between the parties to the contract of insurance. In this regard, the position in these cases is different from that under the ITCH(95) and the IVCH(95) where each contains a warranty to the effect that:

'... the vessel shall not be towed, except as is customary or to the first safe port or place when in need of assistance, or undertake towage ... under a contract previously arranged by the Assured and/or Owners and/or Managers and/or Charterers.'

In such an event, the insurer does not have to rely on the collision liability clause, or the arguments raised in the above cases, to refute liability under the policy. All that they need plead is that a breach of a warranty had been committed the effect of which is that they are automatically discharged from liability as from the date of breach.[22]

'Vessel'

The collision liability clause can only be invoked if the insured vessel collides with another 'vessel'. Thus, a collision with a brick wall, lighthouse, dock, buoy, pier or quay will not attract the operation of the clause.

Sunken vessels and wrecks

Whether a sunken vessel or wreck can still be called a 'vessel' was considered in *Chandler v Blogg*,[23] and *Pelton SS Co v North of England P&I Association*,[24] respectively. In the former, the test of navigability was applied, and a sunken barge lying at the bottom of the sea was held to be a 'vessel', because she was capable of being raised and navigated. In the latter case, the test of navigability was rejected by Mr Justice Greer who preferred to apply his own test of 'whether or not any reasonably minded owner would continue salvage operations in the hope of completely recovering the vessel by those operations and subsequent repair'. He said:

'A ship may remain a ship or vessel even though she be damaged and incapable of being navigated, if she is in such a position as would induce a reasonably minded owner to continue operations of salvage ...'

A pontoon with a crane fixed in it was held in *Merchants Marine Insurance Co v North of England P&I Association*[25] to be neither a ship nor a vessel. A host of considerations were taken into account before the members of the Court of Appeal were prepared to come to their decision. Both Lords Justice Bankes and Scrutton did not think that it was possible to give an exhaustive definition or an exhaustive test which will be of assistance to each and every case. Whether a particular object is or is not a vessel is a question of fact.[26]

---

22   Section 33(3) read with *The Good Luck* [1991] 2 Lloyd's Rep 191, HL.

23   [1898] 1 QB 32.

24   (1925) 22 Ll L Rep 510 at p 512.

25   (1926) 32 Com Cas 165, CA.

26   See *Gas Float Whitton (No 2)* [1897] AC 337, in which a gas float used as a floating beacon was held neither a ship nor a vessel; *The St Macher* (1939) 64 Ll L Rep 27; (1939) 65 Ll L Rep 119 CA, where a newly constructed but unfinished ship was held to be a 'vessel used in navigation' within the meaning of the Merchant Shipping Act 1894; and *Polpen Shipping Co v Commercial Union* [1943] 1 All ER 162, where a flying boat on the water was held neither a 'ship' nor a 'vessel'.

A third vessel

A collision could involve more than two vessels: the insured vessel (vessel A) could collide with vessel B which could in turn collide with vessel C. Such an accident took place in *France, Fenwick & Co Ltd v Merchants Marine Insurance Co Ltd*,[27] where the third vessel, vessel C, suffered the most damage as a consequence of the collision between the insured vessel A and vessel B. Though there was no actual physical contact between the insured vessel A and vessel C, nevertheless, the Court of Appeal held that there was a 'collision' attracting the operation of the running down clause. The insurers were held liable to pay the assured the damages arising out of both collisions. Lord Justice Swinfen Eady said:[28]

> '... according to the true construction of a clause such as the present, an assured may become liable to pay damages in consequence of a collision between his ship and another ship, although the damage is not immediately and directly caused by the actual impact between the two colliding vessels.'

Provided that there is no *novus actus interveniens* to break the chain of causation, the collision between vessels B and C may be regarded as 'the attendant incidents of the collision' between vessels A and B. In the words of the Lord Justice,[29] 'although not the direct and immediate consequence of the impact – although one ship was not, by the force of the impact, driven directly against the other,' the damage occasioned to vessel C arose in consequence of the collision between vessels A and B. In other words, as the 'first collision was the cause of the second collision', the insurers were liable under the said clause for both.

Liability

Some of the details of the collision liability clause require close examination and it is necessary therefore to highlight the relevant parts of the clause:

> 'The underwriters agree to indemnify the assured for *three-fourths* of any sum or sums *paid* by the Assured to any other persons or persons by reason of the assured becoming legally *liable by way of damages* ...'[30]

Three-fourths of damages

The insurer is not liable for the full amount, but only three-fourths of the sum paid by the assured to the third party. It was thought that by compelling the assured to run one-fourth of the risks, that might encourage him to exercise due care and attention. This is now, of course, meaningless, for, in practice, the remaining one-fourth is absorbed by P&I cover.

---

27 [1915] 3 KB 290, CA.

28 *Ibid*, at p 301.

29 *Ibid*, at p 302.

30 Emphasis added.

Three-fourths of the insured value

There is, however, an overall ceiling up to which the insurer may be made liable, and this is set out in cl 8.2.2:

'In no case shall the Underwriters' total liability under cll 8.1 and 8.2 exceed their proportionate part of three-fourths of the *insured value* of the Vessel *hereby insured* in respect of any one collision.'[31]

It is to be observed that it is three-fourths of the insured value of the insured vessel, and not the value of the third party vessel, which is to be considered.

Three-fourths of the legal costs

Clause 8.3 provides that:

'The Underwriters will also pay three-fourths of the legal costs incurred by the Assured or which the Assured may be compelled to pay in contesting liability or taking proceedings to limit liability, with the prior written consent of the Underwriters.'

The word 'also' is to emphasise the fact that, in addition to third party liability for the collision damage, the insurer is liable to pay three-fourths of the legal costs incurred by the assured. Like most of the special provisions of the Institute Clauses, cl 8.3 was inserted in the aftermath of a judicial ruling – on this occasion, that of *Xenos v Fox*,[32] which categorically held that legal costs do not fall within the sue and labour clause, because they are not incurred to avoid or minimise the damage sustained by the insured vessel. Furthermore, as they do not fit within the description of 'damages', they are not recoverable under the then running down clause.[33] Clause 8.3 was thus inserted into the collision liability clause to overcome this difficulty.

Costs of attack and costs of defence

Legal costs may be divided into two broad categories: 'costs of attack' and 'costs of defence'. Costs of attack are legal costs incurred by the assured in instituting or prosecuting an action against the owners of the colliding vessel, for the purpose of recovering the loss sustained by his vessel. Such costs are in fact of no concern to this clause because they have very little, if anything, to do with third party liability. Provided that they are incurred in relation to loss or damage which is recoverable by the assured under the policy, either by way of particular average or otherwise, such costs, it has been said,[34] are generally recoverable in full from the underwriters. To this, it is contended, an additional condition should perhaps be added, to the effect that prior consent of the underwriters should first be obtained by the assured before he commences legal proceedings against the owners of the other vessel. Whether he could bind his

---

31 Emphasis added.

32 (1868) LR 3 CP 630.

33 See also *Cunard v Marten* [1902] 2 KB 624. Now cl 11.2 and cl 9.2 of the ITCH(95) and of the IVCH(95) on sue and labour, expressly states that '... collision defence or attack costs are not recoverable under this cl 11'.

34 See Templeman, pp 408-409, and O'May, p 236; it is the view of both authors that such legal costs are recoverable in full. Nothing, however, is said about whether prior consent of the underwriters is a necessary pre-requisite to recovery.

own underwriters with expenses, without first obtaining their consent, is questionable.[35] Further, unless the policy otherwise provides, it is difficult to see how legal costs of attack can ever be considered as an inherent part of a partial or total loss sustained by the subject-matter insured, or, more significantly, as a loss having been 'proximately' caused by a peril insured against.

'Costs of defence' are legal costs incurred by the assured in defending an action brought by the third party for collision damage. Unlike costs of attack, it appertains directly to third party liability for collision damage. It is the only cost which is relevant to and governed by the collision liability clause.

There are two parts to cl 8.3: the first relates to 'legal costs incurred by the assured', and the second to costs which he may be forced to pay in defending the action instituted by the third party in respect of the collision damage. As a rule, the successful litigant is entitled to his costs: the expenses incident to a suit or action are generally paid by the defeated party. Thus, should the assured wholly fail in his defence, he will be 'compelled to pay' legal costs for contesting liability. This is covered by the latter part of the clause which relates to costs as between party and party (the third party's costs). Needless to say, he would also have to bear his own legal costs, which is covered by the first part of the clause. All in all, an assured who has failed in his defence is entitled to recover from the underwriters three-fourths of the total legal costs for defending the suit.

A court of law has, of course, the power to award legal costs to reflect the degree of blame to be apportioned to the parties.[36] Thus, depending on the degree of the apportionment of blame, the assured may have to bear some of his own costs and also some of the third party's costs.[37] However apportioned, the assured is entitled by cl 8.3 to recover from the underwriters three-fourths of his over-all legal costs of defence.[38]

Unlike liability for damages, cl 8.3 has not set an upper limit for which an insurer could be made liable for legal costs. As prior written consent from the underwriters is required, they would naturally have some control over the amount that may be expended. In the light of this, it would be difficult for the underwriters to argue at a later date that a particular sum is exorbitant.

'In addition to'

It is significant to note that cl 8.2 also states that:

> 'The indemnity provided by this cl 8 shall be *in addition to* the indemnity provided by the other terms and conditions of this insurance ...'

The insurer could be made liable not only for the full extent (of the insured value) of the damage sustained by his own vessel, but also up to three-quarters of the insured value in relation to third party liability. All in all, the insurer

---

35 With the exception of sue and labour expenses. If costs of defence are not recoverable as sue and labour, costs of attack are likely to be treated in the same way. See *Xenos v Fox* (1868) LR 3 CP 630.

36 The right of apportionment of blame is conferred by the Maritime Conventions Act 1911.

37 The third party would also have to bear a share of the costs.

38 In practice, however, no distinction is likely to drawn between costs of attack and costs of defence; costs is generally awarded as a single sum.

could be made liable in respect of up to 175% of the insured value of the vessel which he has agreed to insure. To this, an additional sum of three-quarters of the legal costs incurred by the assured has to be added.

'Legally liable by way of damages'

These words have been interpreted to mean liability in tort and not in contract. This interpretation of the words was first suggested in the case of *Furness Withy and Co Ltd v Duder* in which Mr Justice Branson said:[39]

> '... the clause means that where in consequence of a collision there arises a legal liability upon the shipowners to pay a sum which can properly be described as damages for a tort, then the underwriters will indemnify them. The expression "... by way of damages" indicates ... a liability which arises as a matter of tort, and not as a matter of contract.'

Later, in *Hall Brothers SS Co Ltd v Young*,[40] the above principle was confirmed and applied with approval by the Court of Appeal. As the payment made by the assured was not made by way of damages in tort, but in consequence of the application of French law, it was held not recoverable.

Exclusions

In addition to the 'paramount' exclusions listed in cll 24 to 27 of the ITCH(95)[41] in relation to war, strikes, malicious acts and radioactive contamination, cl 8.4 stipulates five payments which are not covered by the 3/4ths collision liability clause. They relate to sums which the assured shall pay for or in respect of:

- removal or disposal of obstruction, wrecks, cargoes or any other thing whatsoever;[42]
- any real or personal property or thing whatsoever except other vessels or property on other vessels;[43]
- the cargo or other property on, or the engagements of, the insured vessel;
- loss of life, personal injury or illness;[44] and
- pollution or contamination, and damage to the environment.[45]

Damage to the environment or threat thereof

The new cl 8.4.5 of the ITCH(95) has excluded from the scope of the 3/4ths collision clause any sum which the assured shall pay for or in respect of not only pollution or contamination but also for 'threats thereof'. 'Damage to the environment or threat thereof' has been added to complement cl 7, the pollution

---

39 [1936] 2 KB 461 at p 468.

40 [1939] 1 KB 748, CA.

41 Clauses 21–24 of the IVCH(95).

42 Clause 8.4.1 of the ITCH(95). See *The North Britain* [1894] P 77; and *The Engineer* (1898) AC 382.

43 Clause 8.4.2 of the ITCH(95).

44 Clause 8.4.3 of the ITCH(95). See *Coey v Smith* (1860) 22 Dunlop 955; and *Taylor v Dewar* (1864) 5 B & S 58. Liability for loss of life and personal injury is generally covered by P&I Clubs.

45 Clause 8.4.5 of the ITCH(95).

hazard clause, which allows recovery for 'loss of or damage to the Vessel caused by any governmental authority acting under the powers vested in it to prevent to mitigate a pollution hazard or *damage to the environment or threat thereof ...'.[46]

It is to be observed that cl 7 allows recovery for loss of or damage to the insured vessel, whereas cl 8.4.5 excludes recovery for any sum which the assured may pay for or in respect of pollution or contamination (or threats thereof) or for damage to the environment (or threat thereof).

The new cl 8.4.5. has also taken pains to clarify that it (the exclusion) does not apply to any sum which the assured shall pay for or in respect of salvage remuneration where salvors have worked to prevent or minimise damage to the environment as is referred to in art 13(1)(b) of the International Convention on Salvage 1989. This qualification has been inserted to tie in with the new cl 10.6 on general average and salvage of the ITCH(95), under which it is specifically declared that such an enhanced salvage award made under the said art 13(1)(b) is not excluded from recovery as general average or salvage.[47]

'Paid by the Assured'

It is apparent from the opening words of cl 8.1 that there is a prerequisite which has to be satisfied before the assured could be indemnified for third party liability for collision: the assured has to provide proof of payment before he would be indemnified. He has to 'pay to be paid'. This principle which is well-known in P&I cover is, as can be seen shortly, of crucial importance not only to the assured, but also to the third party in relation to his rights under the Third Parties (Rights Against Insurers) Act 1930.[48]

THIRD PARTIES (RIGHTS AGAINST INSURERS) ACT 1930

A third party, though he may legally have a right of claim against 'the insured'[49] for the damage sustained by his ship, may well find himself unable to recover his loss because of the insolvency of the insured. This problem of the unsatisfied third party is addressed in the above-named Act which third parties had believed, for a period of time, was enacted to aid them in the recovery of their losses. This Act describes its objective as:

'An Act to confer on third parties rights against insurers of third party risks in the event of the insured becoming insolvent, and in certain other events.'

Section 1(1) of the 1930 Act states that the rights of the insured (against the insurer under the contract in respect of the liability) 'shall ... be transferred to and vest in the third party to whom the liability was so incurred ...'. Subsection

---

46 The words in italics were added by the ITCH(95).

47 When clause 8.4.5 is read with clause 10.6, it becomes clear that an enhanced salvage award made under art 13(1)(b) of the International Convention on Salvage Convention 1989, is recoverable: further discussed in see Chapter 17.

48 Hereinafter referred to simply as the '1930 Act': see Appendix 3.

49 In accordance with the 1930 Act, and for consistency, the expression 'the insured' will under this part be used to refer to the owner of the insured vessel who is legally liable to pay damages to the third party.

(4) then proceeds to spell out the effect of the transfer thus: 'Upon a transfer under subsection (1) ... of this section, the insurer shall ... be under the same liability to the third party as he would have been under to the insured ...'. Until one examines the finer points and implications of the whole scheme of things, this may initially appear, from the point of view of the third party, to be an attractive and generous concession. But, when read in the light of the decision of the House of Lords in *The Fanti and Padre Island*,[50] the position of the third party is not as rosy as it might seem. The question is essentially: exactly what rights against the insurers are transferred from the insured to the third party?

As is revealed by its name, two cases, namely, *The Fanti*[51] and *The Padre Island*,[52] were heard together in the House of Lords (and in the Court of Appeal) because the legal issues raised in them were the same. The facts of the cases were similar and may be briefly summarised as follows. In both cases, the cargo owners had instituted claims against the shipowners for the loss of their cargoes. Though judgments were entered in their favour, the shipowners did not honour them: nothing was paid in or towards the satisfaction of the judgment. Later, as a result of the claimants' petitions, the shipowners' businesses were ordered to be wound up, whereupon the claimants commenced arbitration proceedings against the association (of which the shipowners were members) pleading their rights under the 1930 Act.

Lord Brandon of the House of Lords, in a most methodical manner, condensed the issues into three main questions, though it is noted that the whole controversy of the case can effectively be said to have revolved around a single issue, that of the effect of the 'pay to be paid' rule. In the light of this it would be helpful, before proceeding to consider these questions, to say something here about that rule.

'Pay to be paid'

The rules of most, if not all, P&I associations (clubs) are based on what is commonly known as the 'pay to be paid' system. This means that, to be entitled to an indemnity in respect of liabilities or expenses incurred by a member (the insured), he must first prove that he himself has discharged the liabilities or expenses. In other words, before he could be paid by the association, he has first to prove that he had paid the third party.

The relevance of the above authority, relating to P&I association rules and the 1930 Act, to the question of collision liability may not at first be obvious. It is noted that, though not couched in so many words, the scheme of the collision liability clause is, in effect, also based on a 'pay to be paid' basis of indemnity: only if the assured had in fact paid the third party would he be indemnified for the loss under cl 8. In this respect, its scheme of operation is similar to the P&I 'pay to be paid' rule and, therefore, the comments made in *The Fanti and Padre*

---

50   [1990] 2 Lloyd's Rep 191, HL.

51   [1987] 2 Lloyd's Rep 299, on appeal [1989] 1 Lloyd's Rep 239, CA; [1990] 2 Lloyd's Rep 191 HL.

52   *Ibid.*

Island (No 2) pertaining to the said rule and the scope of the 1930 Act are also relevant to the collision liability clause.

If a case be required to confirm this point, it can be found in *Re Nautilus Steam Shipping Co Ltd*,[53] where the Court of Appeal had settled beyond doubt that the 1930 Act was applicable to the running down clause, the predecessor of the collision liability clause. Moreover, there is nothing in the 1930 Act prohibiting its application to a claim arising under the collision liability clause.

Rights of the insured

Lord Brandon started on the right footing, first, by questioning what rights, if any, the members had (before they were ordered to be wound up) against the clubs under their contracts of insurance in respect of their liabilities to the third parties.[54] In order to determine the nature of the rights which the third party is to derive from the insured under the 1930 Act, it is first necessary to ascertain the rights of the insured.

The answer to this question is to be found in the 'pay to be paid' rule, but in the words of Lord Brandon:[55]

'... the members were not entitled to be indemnified by the clubs in respect of liabilities to third parties which they had incurred, unless and until the members had first discharged those liabilities themselves. In other words, payment by the members to the third parties was a condition precedent to payment by the club to the members.'

The rights of the insured before they were ordered to be wound up were only contingent rights: until the condition precedent, that is, payment to the third party, is fulfilled, the insured has no claim under the policy. In similar terms, Lord Goff said:[56]

'That right is, at best, a contingent right to indemnity, the right being expressed to be conditional upon the member having in fact paid the relevant claim or expense. Here the relevant claim or expense was never paid, by the member or indeed by anybody else on his behalf. That condition not having been fulfilled, the member had no present right to indemnity ...'

The same can be said of the position of an assured under the collision liability clause. By cl 8.1, he must show that a sum of money has been 'paid by the assured to any other person or persons by reason of the assured becoming legally liable by way of damages ...'.

Relevance of the 'pay to be paid' rule

To respond to the contention raised by the third party, Lord Brandon was forced to address the problem regarding the relevance of the 'pay to be paid' *vis-à-vis* the 1930 Act. It was submitted by counsel for the third party that the

---

53   (1935) 52 Ll L Rep 183, CA.

54   In the context of the collision liability clause the word 'members' should be substituted for 'the insured', and the 'clubs', for 'the insurer'.

55   [1990] 2 Lloyd's Rep 191 at p 197, HL.

56   *Ibid*, at p199.

condition of prior payment offended s 1(3) of the 1930 Act, the relevant parts of which state that:

> 'In so far as any contract of insurance ... in respect of any liability of the insured to third parties purports, whether directly or indirectly, to avoid the contract or to alter the rights of the parties ... the contract shall be of no effect.'

Lord Goff, who confessed that he was 'startled' by this proposal, could not see how the condition of prior payment could be rendered of no effect by s 1(3) of the 1930 Act. He said:[57] 'The rights of the parties remained exactly the same; all that happened was that, following the member's insolvency, and *a fortiori* following the winding-up, the member was no longer able to fulfil the condition of prior payment ...'. There is clearly no merit or substance in this contention.

Admittedly, upon being ordered to be wound up, a member is prevented from discharging his liability to a third party. But in no sense does this '... result, directly or indirectly, from any alteration of the member's rights under his contract of his insurance', but rather from 'the member's inability, by reason of insolvency, to exercise those rights.'[58] The same holds true of the collision liability clause.

Rights of the third party

The rights of the third party is by far the most important aspect of the case. Lord Brandon proceeded to ask the question of what rights against the clubs, if any, were transferred from the members to third parties upon the members being ordered to be wound up. Referring to ss 1(3) and 1(4) as authority, Lord Brandon's reply was:[59]

> 'The effect of these provisions is that, in a case where the insurer would have had a good defence to a claim made by the insured before the statutory transfer of his right to the third party, the insurer will have precisely the same good defence to a claim made by the third party after such a transfer.'

The statutory rights of the third party is dependent on the rights of the insured. He definitely has no better rights than the insured. According to Lord Goff,[60] 'The statutory transferee of the member's right is in no better position than the member; and so, if the condition is not fulfilled, he too has no right to be indemnified.' In this sense, his position is similar to that of an assignee.

Before the delivery of this decision of the House, third parties had high hopes that the 1930 Act would promote their cause and protect their interests in relation to the insurer. The decision of the House is in one sense welcomed, because it had settled a 'central question' which had troubled maritime lawyers since 1930. Its outcome, however, must leave many a third party disappointed. Its effect on the collision liability clause is equally damaging; there is now no chance of a third party ever recovering their loss directly from the insurer of the shipowner whose vessel is legally liable for the collision.

---

57 *Ibid*, at p 203.

58 *Per* Lord Brandon, *ibid*, at p 197.

59 *Ibid*, at p 198.

60 *Ibid*, at p 200.

In the final analysis, it can to be said that it is not the 1930 Act itself which has fallen short; it is the interaction between the 'pay to be paid' rule with the terms of the 1930 Act which has rendered its application impossible. To conclude this part of the discussion, reference should be made to the colourful and perceptive remarks of Lord Jauncey on the matter:[61]

> '... it is difficult to see how it could be said that a condition of prior payment would drive a coach and horses through the Act; for the Act was not directed to giving the third party greater rights than the insured had under the contract of insurance.'

THE PRINCIPLE OF CROSS-LIABILITIES

There are two methods by which claims for collision damage may be adjusted: single liability and cross-liabilities. The latter is imported into the collision liability clause; and provided that both vessels are to be blamed for the collision and that the liability of one or both vessels is not limited by law, this method of calculation is to be used. Though the mathematical formula is not spelled out by the clause, nonetheless it appears to be well-known, even in the early days when the principle of single liability was in favour, as is evident in the cases of in *Stoomvaart Maatschappy Nederland v Peninsula & Oriental Steams Navigation Co, The Khedive*[62] and *London SS Owners' Insurance Co v The Grampian SS Co, The Balnacraig*.[63] For a proper understanding of the subject, a comparison between these two methods of adjustment has to be made. As will be seen, each method produces a different result.

Single liability

In legal terms, the basis of single liability was explained by Lord Esher MR in *The Balnacraig* in the following terms:[64]

> 'But if the damage to one ship exceeds the damage to the other, there will be a monition that the owners of the ship least damaged shall pay to the owners of the other ship half the difference between the amounts of damage sustained by the two ships respectively. The case determines point blank that there is only one liability, and therefore there can be only one payment.'

The basis of the principle is one liability, one payment. In the end, only one sum of money passes from one owner to the other: the owner who has suffered the lesser of the damage shall have to pay. Employing this method of calculation, the assured in this case did not have to pay anything to the third party; by reason of this fact, his claim under the policy failed. Consequently, this led to the introduction of the principle of cross-liabilities in the collision liability clause.

---

61   *Ibid*, at p 204.
62   (1882), 7 App Cas 795.
63   (1889) 24 QBD 663, CA.
64   (1889) 24 QBD 663 at pp 666 and 667, CA.

Adopting the figures used by Arnould,[65] the mathematical formula for single liability is to be worked out as follows:

'Assuming that ship A and ship B have come into collision, and both are equally to blame –

A sustains damage to the extent of £10,000

B sustains damage to the extent of £ 6,000

As each is liable for 50% of the damage sustained by the other –

A is liable for 50% of B's damage [50% of £6,000 = £3,000]

B is liable for 50% of A's damage [50% of £10,000 = £5,000].

The net result is that B, the owner of the ship which has suffered the lesser of the damage, has to pay A £2,000 [£5,000 – £3,000]. The single liability of B to A is £2,000. A owes B nothing.'

Liability of A's insurer

A's insurer would pay A £10,000 for the damage sustained by vessel A, whereupon the insurer would, by way of subrogation, receive the £2,000 from B. As A does not have to pay anything to B for the collision, he cannot recover anything (except the £10,000) from his insurer under the 3/4th collision liability clause. Net loss to A's insurer is £10,000 - £2,000 = £8,000.

Liability of B's insurer

B's insurer would pay B £6,000 for the damage sustained by vessel B *and* 3/4ths of the £2,000 which B has had to pay A [3/4 of £2,000 = £1,500]. Net loss to B's insurer is £6,000 + £1,500 = £7,500.

B himself will have to bear a loss of £500 which amount is usually recoverable from his P&I association.

Cross liabilities

Liability of A's Insurer

A's insurer would pay A, for the damage sustained by –

Vessel A –   £10,000
Vessel B –   £ 2,250 [3/4 of half of B's damage (£3,000) = £2,250]
Total   **£12,250**

A's insurer to recover from B, by way of subrogation, 50% of A's damage (£10,000) = £5,000. Net loss to A's insurer is £12,250 – £5,000 = £7,250.

---

65   Arnould, para 801.

Liability of B's insurer

B's insurer would pay B, for the damage sustained by –

Vessel B –	£6,000
Vessel A –	£3,750 [3/4 of half of A's damage (£5,000) = £3,750]
Total	**£9,750**

B's insurer to recover from A, by way of subrogation, 50% of B's damage (£6,000) = £3,000. Net loss to B's insurer is £9,750 – £3,000 = £6,750.

B himself will have to bear a loss of £1,250 which amount is usually recoverable from his P&I association.

THE SISTERSHIP CLAUSE

When two ships belonging to the same owner collide with each other, the shipowner would find himself in a difficult position in so far as suing the 'other' ship or party for the loss: for under the common law a person cannot bring an action against himself.[66] The same applies to salvage services rendered to a sistership; he cannot claim salvage in respect of the services to the ship and freight, but can claim salvage from the owner of the cargo.[67]

As he is unable to sue himself, this means that he can only recover for the loss of or damage sustained by each of his ships from the insurers under the respective policy which he has taken out for each ship. The claim under each policy, however, is subject to the deductible clause, meaning that he has to suffer two separate sets of deductions, one from each policy.

The objective of the sistership clause is to put the assured in exactly the same position as if their vessel had collided with, or rendered salvage services to, a vessel belonging to a third party. The assured are conferred with: '... the same rights under the insurance as they would have were the other entirely the property of owners not interested in the vessel hereby insured'. In addition to stating how the matter may be resolved, it also lays down that the dispute should be referred to a sole arbitrator to be agreed upon between the underwriters and the assured.

THE PARAMOUNT CLAUSE

A collision, whether between sisterships or ships belonging to different owners, could, of course, occur during a time of war, as a result of an act of hostility, or, for that matter, under any one of the circumstances enumerated in the war; strikes, malicious act, or radioactive contamination exclusion of the ITCH(95).[68] One need only refer to the long line of cases on the construction of the term 'warlike operations' of the old 'f c and s' clause to realise that it is not always

---

66   See *Simpson v Thompson* (1877) 3 Asp MLC 567.

67   See *Cargo ex Laertes* (1887) 6 Asp MLC 174.

68   The nuclear exclusion of the IVCH(83) and the ITCH(83).

easy to classify a loss as a marine or a war risk. It is necessary to inquire whether such a loss is covered by 3/4ths collision liability clause or is excluded by the relevant exclusion clause of the ITCH(95) or the IVCH(95).[69]

The answer to the above question can be found in a clause (in bold print, commonly referred to as the paramount clause) appearing before the said exclusion clauses (cll 24-27). It declares that the exclusion clauses 'shall be paramount and shall override anything contained in this insurance inconsistent therewith'.

It should also be noted that each of the exclusion clauses commences with the phrase: 'In no case shall this insurance cover loss, damage, liability or expense[70] caused by ...'. The words which are relevant to the present discussion are 'liability' and 'caused by'. The former would cover collision liability; and, the phrase 'caused by' has to be construed to mean 'proximately' caused by.

The paramount clause is of relevance only when there are two proximate causes of loss: an included loss and an excluded loss falling within the terms of one of the enumerated risks of the war, strikes, malicious acts or radio active contamination exclusion of the ITCH(95).[71] Only in the event of such a conflict is the paramount clause applicable. The said exclusions will prevail to disentitle the assured from recovering for the loss. Thus, even though a collision is a peril of the seas and, as such, recoverable as a marine risk under the standard hulls policy, nevertheless, the assured will not be able to claim for the loss if one of the risks enumerated in the exclusions is also regarded as a proximate cause of loss. Needless to say, if collision is the sole proximate cause of loss, the paramount clause will not come into play.

---

69   But may be covered by the Institute War and Strikes Clauses, Hulls, discussed in Chapter 14.

70   'Expense' relates to sue and labour charges.

71   The nuclear exclusion under the IVCH(83) and the ITCH(83).

CHAPTER 14

WAR AND STRIKES RISKS

INTRODUCTION

The law of insurance on war and strikes risks has had a colourful and interesting, but somewhat tumultuous history. Dragged through the war years, it has endured many changes most of which were made as a result of lessons learnt from hindsight. It was only through trial and error that insurance on war risks has now settled itself in the form of the Institute War and Strikes Clauses for Hulls (IWSC(H)).[1] There is a set of Institute War and Strikes Clauses Hulls for time[2] and one for voyage. As for cargo, insurance for war and for strikes is contained in separate clauses, namely, the Institute War Clauses (Cargo) (IWC(C))[3] and the Institute Strikes Clauses (Cargo) (ISC(C))[4] respectively.

The current versions of the IWSC(H) and the IWC(C) have, fortunately, rendered much of the complex case law on the subject of war risks of academic interest. Thus, it is unnecessary to spend time on historical perspective,[5] except, perhaps, on those aspects which are relevant for a proper understanding of the modern clauses. Naturally, cases interpreting the meaning of familiar terms which are still being used in the current clauses will have to be examined.

For a great many decades, marine and war risks were insured under one policy: the old SG policy covered a host of perils, the majority of which, interestingly enough, were concerned with hostile acts of men rather than of the seas. Insurance of war risks is, in fact, sanctioned by s 3 of the Act, which defines 'maritime perils' as including '... war perils ... captures, seizures, restraints and detainments of princes and peoples ...'.

Warranted free of capture and seizure

In the old days, when both marine and war risks (and insurance for ship and goods), were covered by a single policy, an assured who did not wish to insure his ship against war risks had to attach a clause, known as the 'warranted free of capture and seizure' clause, to the policy. Used in this context, the word 'warranted' has no relation whatsoever to a promissory warranty as defined by s 33; it is understood to mean an exclusion or exception of liability for the risks enumerated.[6] This method of excluding insurance against war risks was later found inconvenient by the market.

---

1   As the main clauses of the IWSC(H) for time and voyage are identical, it is unnecessary to refer to both; the abbreviation 'IWSC(H)' is used in this chapter as referring to both the Institute War and Strikes Clauses Hull–Time, and the Institute War and Strikes Clauses Hulls–Voyage.

2   See Appendix 20.

3   See Appendix 21.

4   See Appendix 22.

5   For a full historical account of insurance on war risks, see Arnould, para 880; M D Miller, 2nd edn, Chapter 1; and D O'May, *War Risks* [1976] LMCLQ 180.

6   See Chapter 7.

Instead of having to affix the 'fc & s' clause to policy as and when the need arose, it was thought more convenient to have it printed in the policy; with the fc & s clause constituting a standard term of the policy, cover for war risks was automatically excluded. For a period of time, it was understood by all concerned that if an assured wanted to include war risks as part of the cover, he would have to take steps to have the clause deleted.

In its various forms, the use of the fc & s clause was found to be a contrived and an unsatisfactory way of excepting or excluding liability for war risks. Even its final version, drafted in 1943 after the decision of *Yorkshire Dale SS Co Ltd v Minister of War Transport, The Coxwold*,[7] was described as 'convoluted' and 'tortuous and complex in the extreme'.[8] Attempts to employ the fc & s clause both as an exception to, and positive cover for, war risks in one policy proved to be unworkable. Not surprisingly, it was eventually abandoned and replaced, thankfully, by the current clauses, which have adopted a tidier and more effective means of excluding war risks from the standard hull and cargo clauses, and of providing positive cover therefor. A 'back to back' method of coverage now applies and the whole subject is now made easier to understand. The war perils which are excluded by the ITCH(95), the IVCH(95), and all the ICC are now specifically insured by the IWSC(H) and the IWC(C). Additional risks have also been added to the positive cover. The cover for war and strikes risks will be discussed in the order as they appear in the IWSC(H); but before so doing, it is necessary to say something about the paramount clause to the war, strikes, malicious acts, and radioactive contamination exclusions of the ITCH(95) and the IVCH(95).

WAR, STRIKES, MALICIOUS ACTS AND RADIOACTIVE CONTAMINATION EXCLUSIONS OF THE ITCH(95) AND OF THE IVCH(95)

The paramount clause

The above-named exclusion clauses are 'paramount and shall override anything' contained in the 'insurance'[10] which is inconsistent with the said exclusion clauses. The question which arises is under what circumstances the paramount clause applies. It is to be noted that there is no paramount clause in any of the ICC.

---

7   (1942) 73 Ll L Rep 1, HL.

8   *Per* Mocatta J, in *Panamanian Oriental SS Corpn v Wright, The Anita* [1970] 2 Lloyd's Rep 355.

9   Replacing the nuclear exclusion clause of the ITCH(83).

10   It is to be noted that it is not just anything inconsistent with the Institute Clauses which is overridden; anything which is inconsistent with the 'insurance', eg, an express warranty, is also overridden.

The rule of proximate cause

Any of the perils insured by the ITCH(95) and the IVCH(95) can occur in time of peace as well as of war. A loss arising as a result of, for example, a peril of the seas, stranding, collision, or fire, can take place in a circumstance enumerated in the war exclusion or, for that matter, any of the other exclusion clauses. In the context of war (or warlike operations), the Lord Chancellor, Viscount Simon, in *The Coxwold*[11] was very much concerned with the problem of the possibility of dual causes of loss. His remarks, though they were made in reference to the subject of 'warlike operations' of the fc & s clause which no longer exists, are, nonetheless, pertinent to the present discussion. He said:

'It is not correct to say that, because a vessel is engaged in a warlike operation, therefore everything that happens to her during her voyage is proximately caused by a warlike operation or is a proximate consequence of a warlike operation. Neither is it correct to say that because the accident of a kind which arises from a marine risk (eg, stranding or collision), therefore the particular accident can in no circumstances be regarded as the consequence of a warlike operation. The truth lies between these two extremes.'

In such a situation, the question for determination is whether the marine or the war insurer is liable for the loss. In each case, the matter is to be resolved by applying the principle set out in s 55, the rule of proximate cause.[12] Using collision[13] as an example, the issue is: is the loss proximately caused by a peril of the seas, a marine risk, or a war risk? If the former is regarded as the proximate cause of loss, it would be covered by the marine policy, and therefore it would be unnecessary to inquire further. On the other hand, if one of the circumstances enumerated in the exclusion clause is held to be the proximate cause, the loss would be excluded. In the words of the Lord Chancellor,[14] 'one has to ask oneself what was the effective and predominant cause of the accident that happened, whatever the nature of that accident may be'.

If the matter may be so easily resolved by a straightforward application of the rule of proximate cause, one could then ask: what function does the paramount clause perform? When only a single cause is discerned as the proximate cause of the loss, there would be no need to refer to the paramount clause. But, as was seen,[15] a loss may well result from a combination of causes. It is possible for there to be two (or more) proximate causes of loss of equal (or nearly equal) efficiency. If collision and war are both regarded as the proximate causes of a loss, the former which is a peril insured against is an included loss, whereas the latter is not, by reason of the fact that it is expressly excluded by the war exclusion clause. In the absence of the paramount clause, a predicament would arise for the loss is recoverable under one clause, but not in another. The paramount clause was inserted to put this problem at rest. As each of the exclusion clauses is supreme, the loss is not recoverable; the fact that it may be

---

11 (1942) 73 Ll L Rep 1, HL.

12 See Chapter 8.

13 Collision is a peril of the sea: *The Xantho* (1887) 11 PD 170.

14 (1942) 73 Ll L Rep 1 at p 6, HL.

15 See Chapter 8.

recoverable as a marine risk is inconsequential. The need to refer to the paramount clause will only arise when there is a conflict as to which of the clauses is to prevail.

It has been suggested that the paramount clause was inserted for the purpose of avoiding the problem which arose in *Attorney-General v Adelaide SS Co Ltd, The Warilda*,[16] and also to deal specifically with the collision liability clause and the sue and labour clause.[17] In *The Warilda*, the hospital ship which was requisitioned by the Admiralty collided with vessel P which was proceeding with only dimmed sidelights. The House of Lords held that *The Warilda* was solely to blame for the collision and further, that she was engaged on a warlike operation of which the collision was a direct consequence. As the Admiralty had, under the terms of the charter, agreed to be responsible for war risks, they were held liable for the damage suffered by *The Warilda*.

As regards the damage sustained by the P, it was held by the House, in a different action, that the collision was due to the negligence of *The Warilda* in not giving way or slackening speed. The loss sustained by the P was as a direct consequence of negligent navigation of the master of *The Warilda*. As damage by negligent navigation was not excluded by the policy on marine risks,[18] the marine underwriters were liable for the loss under what was then the running down clause.[19]

O'May has pointed out that the marine insurers were held liable for the loss only because there was no paramount clause in the policy in question.[20] With due respect, it is difficult to see how a paramount clause would have made any difference to the case. A clause to the effect that the fc & s warranty is paramount would be of no relevance to the damage sustained by vessel P which was proximately caused by negligent navigation.

But, of course, if both war and collision were regarded as the proximate causes of the loss, then the presence of a paramount clause would have made a difference. The objective of a paramount clause is precisely to resolve such a conflict. By expressly declaring that the exclusion clauses prevail, it removes all doubts that if war is *the* proximate cause or one of the proximate causes of loss the marine risks insurer is not liable, even if the damage sustained by the P may also have been caused by an insured peril. But as the negligent navigation of *The Warilda* alone was held to have proximately caused the damage sustained by the P, the absence or presence of a paramount clause would have been of no consequence.

The view of the common law is that, if one of the proximate causes is expressly excepted, the exception must prevail. The courts are of the view that,

---

16 [1923] AC 292, HL.

17 See O'May, p 259 and JK Goodacre, *Institute Time Clauses Hulls* (1983, 1st edn), p 26.

18 See cl 6.2.2 of the ITCH(95) and cl 4.2.2 of the IVCH(95).

19 Now the 3/4ths collision liability clause.

20 He said, at p 259, that, 'It followed from this finding that such damages were not excluded by the fc & s clause and had to be paid by the marine underwriters under the running down clause, which was not, at that time, made subject to the fc & s clause'.

as the parties had taken pains to stipulate for freedom from liability, their express wishes must be enforced.[21]

In support of his contention, O'May relied on the word 'liability' in relation to collision liability, and 'expense' to suing and labouring. It is, however, submitted that these words have to be read with 'caused by' which means 'proximately' caused by the said risks. In short, only a loss 'proximately' caused by an event stipulated in the exclusion clauses would prevail and override another proximate cause which is covered by the policy.

WAR AND STRIKES COVER

The risks covered by cll 1.1. 1.2 and 1.3 of the IWSC(H) are worded in identical terms to the risks excluded by the war exclusion clause of the ITCH(95) (cl 24) and the IVCH(95) (cl 21). There are essentially three main categories of risks which are excluded by the war exclusion clause of the ITCH(95), the IVCH(95) and all the ICC, but are covered by cll 1.1, 1.2 and 1.3 of the IWSC(H) and the IWC(C). Each of these classes will be examined separately. As insurance for war risks for cargo (IWC(C)) is couched in almost identical terms as the IWSC(H), the following discussion is, it is needless to say, also relevant to cargo. Attention to the differences between them will be drawn as and when convenient.

'War civil war revolution rebellion insurrection or civil strife arising therefrom, or any hostile act by or against a belligerent power'

Clause 1.1 of the IWSC(H) and the IWC(C) states that it covers loss of or damage to the vessel caused by 'war, civil war, revolution, rebellion, insurrection, or civil strife arising therefrom, or any hostile act by or against a belligerent power'.

These risks are apparently graded in terms of gravity in descending order beginning with 'war' as the most serious of the risks insured. As none of the terms is defined, it can be assumed that they are to be given their popular or ordinary meaning. This scale of conflict may be divided into four groups:

(1) War;

(2) Civil war, revolution, rebellion, insurrection;

(3) Civil strife arising therefrom, meaning from (1) and (2) above; and

(4) Any hostile act by or against a belligerent power.

'War'

A 'war' can only be waged against another nation(s);[22] it involves hostilities between belligerent nations conducted by military, naval and/or air attacks or series of attacks. A formal declaration of war, *per se*, is not conclusive evidence

---

21 See Chapter 8.

22 It is interesting to note that 'war' itself was not expressly mentioned in the fc & s clause as an excluded risk.

that a state of war exists; neither is a statement to the opposite effect conclusive evidence that no state of war exists. The question as to whether there is or there is not a state of war in existence at a particular time is in each case one of fact.

'Civil war revolution rebellion insurrection'

All the above named events relate to internal conflict within one nation or country; it involves an uprising of rival factions or groups. The most serious of the list is civil war, followed by revolution, rebellion, and insurrection, all of which clearly fall short of a civil war; they are just gradations of unrest, tumult and turbulence. Revolution and rebellion involve the use of armed force in an attempt to overthrow the ruling power or established government of one's country in order to take control of the country or a part of it. An insurrection, however, which manifests itself as an uprising of the people against the established authority, is generally less organised than a revolution or rebellion. Though the line between one and the other may be fine, fortunately, it is unnecessary to distinguish between them because they are all insured risks.

'Riots' and 'civil commotions' could well fit within this class of perils, but have been included in the strikes clause. They will be discussed when that clause is examined.

'Civil strife arising therefrom'

A 'civil strife' is the weakest form of the internal disturbance listed. However, it is significant to note that the only type of civil strife which is covered is that which arises as a consequence of the preceding perils, namely, 'war, civil war, revolution, rebellion, insurrection'.

'Any hostile act by or against a belligerent power'

It is necessary at this juncture to discuss the historical events which have led to the formulation of this last limb of cl 1.1. The appearance of the fc & s clause in a standard marine policy meant that a clear line had to be drawn between marine and war risks. In each case, it had to be determined whether a loss was caused by a peril insured against or by a peril excluded by the fc & s clause. In this regard, particularly troublesome were the words 'warranted free ... from the consequences of hostilities or warlike operations'.[23] It is interesting to note that none of the versions of the fc & s clause had mentioned anything about a loss caused by a direct act of war or an act of hostility. It excluded only losses which were the result or consequence of hostilities or warlike operations. The expression 'warlike' suggests that a vessel does not have to collide with an enemy vessel to attract the operation of the fc & s clause; coming into collision with a warship would be sufficient to bring home liability to the insurer of war risks. Interestingly, it was not the consequence of war operations, but of 'warlike' operations which were relevant.

---

23 Described by MacKinnon LJ as 'ten infamously obscure words' in *The Coxwold* (1942) 1 KB 35 at p 43.

'Consequences of ... warlike operations'

A long and persistent line of cases dating from 1921 to 1946, nearly all emanating from the House of Lords, took the stand that, even though the insured vessel or the vessel with which she had collided with may not, at the time of loss, be directly engaged in an act of war, nevertheless, if she or the other vessel was engaged in 'warlike' operations, that alone was sufficient to take the loss resulting therefrom out of the cover of marine risks .

The main authorities on the subject of the fc & s clause were primarily concerned with the interpretation of the expression 'consequence of ... warlike operations'. Nearly all the cases were in connection with ships which were requisitioned by the government, using the familiar charterparty form 'T 99', during the First World War. One of the terms of the charter was that the government undertook the risk of damage resulting from 'all consequences of hostile or warlike operations', and her owners, marine risks. The government was, for all intents and purposes, acting as war risks underwriters of the chartered vessel. Insurance for marine risks was left to marine risks underwriters.

In the main, the judges in the House did not appear to have any difficulty in each of the cases in deciding whether a particular ship was or was not engaged in 'warlike operations'. In seven out of the nine leading authorities on the subject, either the injured ship herself and/or the other ship was engaged in warlike operations at the time of the loss. The following are examples of ships held to have been engaged in warlike operations:

- collision with a destroyer which was patrolling in an area for submarines;[24]
- collision with a warship proceeding on a voyage to pick up another convoy;[25]
- the carriage of war stores from one war base to another;[26]
- the employment of a ship as ambulance for the transportation of wounded solders;[27]
- using a ship as a mine planter;[28]
- proceeding in convoy on a zigzag course under the orders of the naval officers;[29]
- the discharge of oil into a naval vessel;[30] and
- travelling at high speed and taking a zigzag course in order avoid the possibility of submarine attack.[31]

---

24 *Attorney General v Ard Coasters Ltd* [1921] 2 AC 141, HL.
25 *Ibid.*
26 *Commonwealth Shipping Representative v P & O Service, The Geelong* [1923] AC 191, HL.
27 *Attorney General v Adelaide SS Co Ltd, The Warilda* [1923] AC 292, HL.
28 *Board of Trade v Hain SS Co Ltd* [1929] AC 534, HL.
29 *Yorkshire Dale SS Co Ltd v Minister of War Transport, The Coxwold* (1942) 73 Ll L Rep 1, HL.
30 *Athel Line Ltd v Liverpool & London War Risks Insurance Association Ltd, The Atheltemplar,* [1946] 1 KB 117, CA.
31 *Liverpool & London War Risks Assocn Ltd v Ocean SS Co Ltd, The Priam* [1948] AC 243, HL.

Marine risks insurers became perturbed by this trend and felt that marine risks were slowly but surely being converted into war risks. Much disquiet was experienced by the insurance market, which thought that the distinction between marine and war risks was becoming more and more faint and was gradually being eroded, so much so that Viscount Simon LC in *The Coxwold* had to issue the reminder cited earlier.[32]

The real problem, it is submitted, lies not so much in the question of causation, but in the use of the term 'warlike' operations. The expression is wide, and one could easily lose sight of the real issue, which is the determination of the proximate cause of loss.

It was said that the decisions of these cases had 'upset the balance between marine and war risks underwriters, to the extent that the fc & s clause should be further revised'.[33] After the decision of *The Coxwold*, it was revised and the relevant parts of the 1943 revision read as follows:

> '... but this warranty shall not exclude collision, contact with any fixed or floating object (other than mine or torpedo), stranding, heavy weather or fire unless caused directly (and independently of the nature of the voyage or service which the vessel concerned or, in the case of collision, any other vessel involved therein, is performing) by a hostile act by or against a belligerent power ...'

This part of the clause was introduced evidently to redress the balance. Unless the events enumerated are 'directly' (meaning proximately) caused by a hostile 'act' by or against a belligerent power, they are not to be excluded by the fc & s warranty: they are marine risks and continue to be covered by the policy. The words in the second pair of brackets were inserted with the above-mentioned line of cases in mind. The objective of these words is to dismiss the relevance of warlike operations and conduct which are only incidental to acts of hostility.

'Caused by'

Before the efficacy of this clause could be tested, it was redrafted and streamlined in the current version of the IWSC(H). Clause 1.1 states that the IWSC(H) covers 'loss of or damage to the vessel caused by ... any hostile act by or against a belligerent power'.[34] The term 'consequences of'[35] has been replaced by the expression 'caused by' which has to be read to mean 'proximately caused by'. In positive terms, it means that any loss proximately caused by a hostile 'act' by or against a belligerent power is excluded by the war exclusion clause but is covered by cl 1.1 of the IWSC(H).

The nature of the operation which the ship is engaged in at the time of loss is now irrelevant. It is observed that it is not so much the phrase 'consequences of', but the word 'warlike' in the old clause which had clouded the issue. Put in

---

32 (1942) 73 Ll L Rep 1 at p 6, HL.

33 See NG *Hudson, The Institute Clauses* (1995, 2nd edn), p 222.

34 See also cl 1.1 of the IWC(C).

35 The words 'all consequences of' were interpreted to mean the 'totality of causes, not to their sequence, or their proximity or remoteness': *per* Willes, J in *Ionides v The Universal Marine Insurance Co* (1863) 14 CB (NS) 259 at p 290.

the right perspective, the governing principle is the rule of proximate cause. Even with regard to the old fc & s clause, this point was in fact stressed by the Lord Chancellor in *The Coxwold* who said:[36] 'It is well settled that a marine risk does not become a war risk merely because the conditions of war may make it more probable that the marine risk will operate and a loss will be caused.' This comment is also relevant to cl 1.1.

With the demise of the expression 'consequence of ... warlike operations', it matters not, to borrow the imagery used by one author, whether a ship is carrying a cargo of war ammunition or a cargo of bibles for missionaries at the time of loss; no longer is it necessary to separate the 'marine sheep' from the 'warlike goats'.[37] It is worthwhile remembering that the term 'warlike' has been replaced with 'hostile', and 'operation' with 'act'. The test which has now to be applied is: is the loss proximately caused by a 'hostile act'?

'Hostile act'

Only a hostile act 'by or against a belligerent power' is excluded by the war exclusion clause and is covered by the IWSC(H). A hostile act committed by an individual does not count. The nearest explanation of the term can be gleaned from the definition given to the word 'hostilities' by Viscount Cave in *The Matiana and The Petersham* who said that:[38] 'The word 'hostilities' connotes operations of war, which may be either offensive or defensive ...'. Lord Wrenbury in the same case observed that:[39] '... the word "hostilities" does not mean "the existence of a state of war" but means "acts of hostility" or ... "operations of hostility"'. Both judges acknowledged the fact that 'warlike operations' has a wider reach than 'hostilities'. It would appear from the above comments that there does not have to be a war in progress for one belligerent power to levy a hostile act against another.

'Capture seizure arrest restraint or detainment, and the consequences thereof or any attempt thereat'

The above risks are covered by the IWSC(H), but in relation to the IWC(C) they are qualified with the words 'arising from risks covered under 1.1 above' which means that any 'capture seizure arrest restraint or detainment' must arise from one of the war risks enumerated in cl 1.1 discussed earlier.

'Capture' and 'seizure'

'Capture' and 'seizure', which also appeared in the fc & s clause, are derived from s 3 of the Act. These terms are defined in *Cory v Burr*,[40] a well-known barratry case. The words 'capture' and 'seizure' mean different things. In lay terms, 'capture' is often prefaced with the word 'enemy' and is generally

---

36 (1942) 73 Ll L Rep 1 at p 6, HL.
37 Arnould, para 895.
38 [1921] 1 AC 99, at p 108, HL.
39 *Ibid*, at p 133.
40 (1883) 8 App Cas 393.

understood to mean capture by an enemy or belligerent. 'Seizure', on the other hand, is a wider concept; it relates to any forcible act of dispossessing another of his/her property either by 'lawful authority or by over-powering force'. In the said case, the seizure of the vessel by the Spanish authorities in consequence of an act of smuggling was held to constitute 'seizure'.[41] Another example of a seizure is when diseased cattle are seized by health authorities.[42]

The word 'seizure' connotes a taking by a third party from another who is in possession of the ship or cargo. One cannot seize something from oneself; it implies forcible dispossession of property by another person. Thus, crew members on board a ship who are already in possession of the ship cannot seize the possession of her.

Barratrous and piratical seizures

A seizure of ship or goods as a consequence of a barratrous act (eg smuggling) committed by the master and/or crew was considered earlier.[43] It is observed that 'barratry and piracy' are specifically excepted from the war exclusion clause of the ITCH(95) and the IVCH(95). The purpose of the barratry (and piracy) exception within the war exclusion is to clarify that a loss caused by, for example, a barratrous seizure is not an excluded loss. This does not, however, mean that it has thereby become an included or insured loss under the Institute Hulls Clauses. Unless specifically insured, a loss solely and proximately caused by seizure, albeit barratrous, is not recoverable.[44]

In each case, the proximate cause of the loss has to be ascertained. There are three possibilities:

- if barratry is held as the sole proximate cause, there is no problem – it is covered by cl 6.2.4 of the ITCH(95) and cl 4.2.4 of the IVCH(95);

- if seizure is regarded as the sole proximate cause of loss, the loss is not, for reasons given earlier, recoverable under the Institute Hulls Clauses. Whether it is recoverable under the IWSC(H) is also unclear. Though the word 'seizure' in cl 1.2 of the IWSC(H) is unqualified, it could be argued that it relates only to hostile seizures occuring under war conditions. Further, if the seizure is by reason of infringement of customs regulations, the exception contained in cl 5.1.4 of the IWSC(H) would apply, thus preventing recovery. This could be described as a case of a loss falling between two stools.

- if both barratry and seizure are held to be the proximate causes of loss, it would appear that the loss is recoverable under the ITCH(95) for two reasons: first, barratry is an insured risk under cl 6.2.4, and, secondly, a barratrous seizure, having been excepted from the war exclusion clause, is no longer an *expressly* excluded loss.

---

41 Within the then fc & s clause under the policy. Under cl 5.1.4 of the IWSC(H) (but not the IWC(C)), 'arrest restraint detainment confiscation or expropriation ... by reason of infringement of any customs ... regulations' are excluded.

42 *Miller v Law Accident Insurance Soc* [1903] 1 KB 712.

43 See Chapter 12.

44 The same applies to piratical seizures.

The same line of argument applies to piratical seizures. If 'piracy' is regarded as the proximate cause, the loss is covered by cl 6.1.5 of the ITCH(95) and cl 4.1.5 of the IVCH(95). To ensure that there is no overlapping,[45] and to clarify that the loss is not also covered by the IWSC(H), 'piracy' is expressly excluded by cl 5.1.6 of the IWSC(H).

In so far as cargo is concerned, neither a loss proximately caused by barratry or by piracy is an insured peril under the ICC (B) and (C). For this reason, it is unnecessary expressly to except 'barratry' and 'piracy' from the war exclusion clause of the ICC (B) and (C). 'Piracy' has, however, to be expressly excepted from the war exclusion clause of the ICC (A) by reason of it being an all risks policy. Why barratry is not excepted from the war exclusion clause of the ICC (A) is unclear.[46]

'Arrest restraint or detainment '

All the above-named perils are derived from the old SG policy and the fc & s clause. Only 'restraints and detainment', but not 'arrest', appear in s 3 of the Act. Under the SG policy, 'arrests, restraints, and detainments' were qualified with 'of all kings, princes, and people, of what nation, condition, or quality soever ...'.[47] The meaning of the whole of this expression is defined in r 10 of the Rules for Construction as:

'The term "arrests etc of kings, princes, and people" refers to political or executive acts, and does not include a loss caused by riot or by ordinary judicial process.'

Following from this, the question which has to be considered is whether the same meaning is to be attributed to the current clause, which is unqualified.

The clause, in failing to incorporate the words 'of all kings, princes and people' or the like, has left the matter in doubt. But as there is nothing in the policy suggesting that a different interpretation be awarded to the expression, the definition in r 10 should apply.[48]

Meaning of 'arrest restraint or detainment'

Rule 10 has made it clear that the term 'arrests etc ...' refers to political or executive acts of governments or authorities. That force is not an essential ingredient for this peril was established in *Miller v Law Accident Insurance Co*,[49] where a ship carrying a cargo of cattle was prevented from entering port by the order of the administration – the executive authority at Buenos Aires. That the object of the assured in shipping cattle to the said port was altogether defeated

---

45 See also cl 5.3 of the IWSC(H).

46 For a fuller discussion on barratry, see Chapter 12; and for piracy, see Chapter 9.

47 See *The Sanday Case* [1915] 2 KB 781, HL, where as a consequence of 'restraint of princes,' the insured cargo suffered a loss of the adventure.

48 See s 30(2): '... unless the context of the policy otherwise requires, the terms and expressions mentioned in the First Schedule to this Act shall be construed as having the scope and meaning in that schedule assigned by them.'

49 [1903] 1 KB 712.

was not disputed.[50] The insurers, however, refused to pay for the loss on the ground that it was not due to 'arrest, restraint, or detainment', arguing that it implied the use of direct force and none had in fact been employed. The Court of Appeal unanimously held that the issue of the decree by the Argentine government, under which the landing of the cattle was forbidden, was an act of State falling within the words of the policy 'restraint of people'. Actual force was not used in this case because there was no opposition by the master; but force would have been used if he had not submitted.

The most recent authority on the subject of detainment, the use of force, and the exclusion of cl 5.1.4 is *The Wondrus*,[51] in which the policy in question incorporated the IWSC(H). The vessel was prevented (for some 18 months) from sailing from Bandar Abbas because of the impecuniosity of the charterers, who were unable to pay port due and freight tax, or provide certain necessary documents. In order to recover under the policy for the loss of hire, the assured had to show that the vessel was 'detained' within the meaning of cl 1.2 of the IWSC(H). The insurers rested their defence on cl 5.1.4, which excludes from cover detainment '... by reason of infringement of any custom or trading regulations'. Thus, the issue in the case was whether there was any detainment within the meaning of cl 1.2, and if so whether it was by reason of infringement of any customs regulation.

Applying r 10 and on the strength of *Miller v The Law Accident Insurance Co*,[52] the trial judge, Mr Justice Hobhouse, held that there was in *a sense*[53] a detention: though the vessel was not in fact physically detained, she would have been detained if she had tried to leave the port without paying her port dues and local tax. Provided that the detainment was not the result of 'ordinary judicial process' he felt that the words 'restraint' and 'detainment' have to be given 'a wide commercial interpretation'. On the question of the insurer's defence, he said that, 'In a commercial sense she was detained by reason of infringement of customs regulations'.

In the Court of Appeal, Lord Justice Lloyd, while upholding (albeit somewhat reluctantly) this part of the decision of Mr Justice Hobhouse, expressed his sentiments on the issue of detainment as follows:[54]

'... I would hold in agreement with the judge that if there was a detainment within the meaning of cl 1.2 then there was an infringement within the meaning of cl 4.1.5. But putting it in my own words, I would prefer to say that, reading the two clauses together, there was no detainment within the meaning of cl 1.2 at all.'

Nevertheless, he and Lord Justice Nourse upheld the decision of the trial judge who decided that the plaintiff's claim failed because the loss fell within

50 Applying *The Sanday Case* [1916] 1 AC 650, HL.

51 *Ikerigi Compania Naviera SA & Others v Palmer & Others, Globas Transeeas Corpn & Another v Palmer* [1992] 2 Lloyd's Rep 566, CA. For a discussion of *The Wondrus*, see P Foss, *Institute War and Strikes Clauses, Detainments and Exclusions* [1993] LMCLQ 22.

52 [1903] 1 KB 712, CA.

53 In another sense, she was not detained at all, because she was not physically restrained.

54 [1992] 2 Lloyd's Rep 566 at p 572, CA.

the exclusion of detainment by reason of infringement of any customs regulations.

Lord Justice McCowan, on the other hand, had no doubt whatsoever that the vessel was detained,[55] '... in the same sense that a man under house arrest could be properly described as detained, since, although free within his house, he would immediately be apprehended if he tried to leave it'. He agreed with Mr Justice Hobhouse on this point, but disagreed with him and the rest of the Appeal Court on the applicability of the exclusion. He confessed that he was puzzled as to how the judge had arrived at his conclusion that there was detainment by reason of infringement of custom regulations when the vessel did not at any time make any attempt to leave the port. Obviously, he held the view that nothing short of an actual infringement would trigger the exclusion.

The Wondrus, though not actually detained, could be described as having been 'constructively' detained; and her owners having 'constructively' infringed the custom regulations, if such a notion could be applied to an important matter such as breach of the law. Though not said in so many words, this appears to be the view of the trial judge. The former may be easier to accept, but not the latter. As there are clearly two points of view on the subject, this matter is in need of further judicial clarification.

Whilst on the subject of the exclusion of custom infringement, it is perhaps appropriate here briefly to mention *Panamanian Oriental SS Corpn v Wright, The Anita,*[56] where unmanifested goods were found when she was boarded by a Vietnamese custom official. A special military court acquitted the master of smuggling offences, but convicted some of the crew. The vessel was ordered to be confiscated, upon which her owners claimed for a constructive total loss, whereupon the insurers repudiated liability on the ground that the exclusion (worded in almost identical terms as cl 5.1.4 of the IWSC(H)) applied. That the vessel was in fact detained and that there was infringement of the Vietnam custom regulations were never in dispute. The main issue centred on the question of the integrity of the special court and the burden of proof in respect thereof. The Court of Appeal held that the burden of proof lies with the shipowners, and as they were unable to prove that the order of the special court was made under political direction and without jurisdiction, the loss fell within the exclusion. It was for the shipowners, not the insurers, to convince the Court of Appeal that the special Vietnamese court was not acting *bona fide* as an independent judicial body, but as a puppet court following the directions of the government or knowingly exceeding its power.

'Riot' and 'ordinary judicial process'

According to r 10 of the Rules of Construction, a loss caused by riot or by ordinary judicial process is not recoverable under this clause. As noted earlier, riot is excluded by the strikes exclusion of the ITCH(95) and the IVCH(95), but is now an insured loss under cl 1.4 of the IWSC(H). Whether the term 'riots' under these provisions may be given a meaning which has no connection

---

55   *Ibid*, at p 577.
56   [1971] 2 All ER 1028, CA; [1971] 1 Lloyd's Rep 487, CA.

whatsoever with its preceding words, namely, 'strikers, locked-out workmen or persons taking part in labour disturbances' is a question which has to be addressed. In other words: is a loss caused by an arrest, restraint, or detainment resulting from a riot covered by the IWSC(H)?

What are 'ordinary' and not 'ordinary' (extraordinary) judicial processes is unclear. In *Panamanian Oriental SS Corpn v Wright, The Anita*,[57] Mr Justice Mocatta in the court of first instance thought that the former related to civil, whilst the latter to criminal, proceedings. As his decision was overruled on other grounds, the validity of his civil and criminal distinction remains to be confirmed.

Clause 5.1.5 expressly excludes 'loss, damage liability or expense arising from the operation of ordinary judicial process, failure to provide security or to pay any fine or penalty or any financial cause'. The same problem as regards the meaning of 'ordinary judicial process' arises here.

'And the consequences thereof or any attempt thereat'

The phrase 'consequences of',[58] as was seen,[59] has been held not to be specific enough to abrogate or diminish the rule of proximate cause declared in s 55 of the Act. To recapitulate, they refer to 'the totality of causes, not to their sequence, or their proximity or remoteness ...'.[60] As such, they do not affect the general principles of causation and the same must apply here to the term 'consequences thereof'.

The provision of 'attempts thereat' has been inserted to clarify that a loss arising from attempts at 'capture seizure arrest restraint or detainment' are also covered.

The detainment clause

The detainment clause, cl 3 of the IWSC(H), applies only to 'capture seizure arrest restraint detainment confiscation or expropriation' of the vessel. It states that if the assured:

> '... shall thereby have lost the free use and disposal of the vessel for a continuous period of 12 months then for the purpose of ascertaining whether the vessel is a constructive total loss the assured shall be deemed to have been deprived of the possession of the vessel without any likelihood of recovery.'

The purpose of this clause is to aid an assured in his claim for a constructive total loss when he is deprived of the possession of the vessel without any likelihood of recovery.[61] It has thus to be read with s 60(2)(i) of the Act. The case which immediately springs to mind is *The Bamburi*,[62] which, though it cannot be said to be responsible for the introduction of the clause, nevertheless illustrates

---

57 [1970] 2 Lloyd's Rep 365.

58 And also 'consequent on' used in relation to insurance to freight.

59 For a fuller discussion on the law of causation.

60 *Per* Willes J in *Ionides v Universal Marine Insurance Co* (1863) 14 CB (NS) 259 at p 290.

61 For a thorough historical survey of the detainment clause, see O'May, p 276.

62 [1982] 1 Lloyd's Rep 312.

the usefulness of such a clause.[63] It is fair to say that a period of 12 months (from the date of the tendering of the notice of abandonment) was considered by the case as a 'reasonable time' for establishing that a constructive total loss, on the basis of unlikelihood of recovery, has occurred.

Exclusions

The terms of some of the exclusion clauses (cl 5) of the IWSC(H) are of particular relevance to this cover on capture, seizure, arrest, restraint or detainment.

Any loss, damage, liability, or expense arising from 'requisition ... or pre-emption' are excluded by cl 5.1.2. The need for this exclusion is particularly well illustrated by the case of *Robinson Gold Mining Co v Alliance Marine & General Insurance Co Ltd*.[64] In the absence of this exclusion, a vessel which, for example, has been requisitioned by the state may be recoverable under the heading of 'seizure, arrest, restraint or detainment'. There is no legal definition for the word 'requisition', but it is generally understood to mean the taking over of possession and ownership of merchant ships by the government during an emergency – for example, wartime.

The word 'pre-emption' is apparently a concept used in the American Institute Clauses. O'May has pointed out that it is 'probably covered by requisition', but 'to avoid narrow and irrelevant distinctions being made' both terms are used in the Institute and American Institute Clauses.[65]

Clause 5.1.3 excludes 'loss damage liability or expense arising from capture seizure arrest restraint detainment ... by or under the order of the government or any public or local authority of the country in which the vessel is owned or registered'.[66]

The exclusion under cl 5.1.4 relating to infringement of customs or trading regulations has already been discussed.

'Derelict mines torpedoes bombs or other derelict weapons of war'

Loss resulting from any of the above perils are excluded by the war exclusion clause of the ITCH(95), the IVCH(95) and all the ICC, but are now covered by cl 1.3 of the IWSC(H) and of the IWC(C). It is to be noted that an 'explosion' which is not connected with any of the above forms of ammunition is covered by cl 6.1.2 of the ITCH(95); cl 4.1.2 of the IVCH(95); cl 1.1.1 of the ICC (B) and ICC (B) under the peril of 'fire or explosion'; and under the ICC (A) by virtue of this being an all risks policy.

---

63 For further discussion of the clause, see Chapter 15.

64 [1901] 2 KB 919; 6 Com Cas 244. See also *France Fenwick & Co v The King* [1927] 1 KB 458; and *The Steaua Romana* (1944) P 43.

65 See O'May, p 274.

66 As regards war risks insurance for cargo, there is no equivalent to this exclusion in the IWC(C).

The case which is relevant to this risk is *The Nassau Bay*,[67] which was decided in 1978, when the fc & s clause was still in use. The court held that the damage sustained by the dredger, which had sucked up a number of derelict shells that exploded, was recoverable from the marine risks insurer because it was not excluded by the fc & s clause. Mr Justice Walton found it impossible to classify the dumping of ammunition, at the end of the war, a warlike operation.[68] Such a loss is clearly now not a marine risk, but a war risk falling within cl 1.3 of the IWSC(H) and the IWC(C).

'Strikers, locked-out workmen, or persons taking part in labour disturbances, riots or civil commotions'

The above clause appears in both the IWSC(H) and the ISC(C). As can be seen, it is a mirror image of the strikes exclusion clause of the ITCH(95), the IVCH(95) and all the ICC, though in the case of the ICC there is an additional exclusion for loss, damage, or expense *'resulting from* strikes, lock-outs, labour disturbances, riots or civil commotions' which has not been reproduced in the ISC(C).

It is noted that whilst the positive cover of the IWSC(C) and the ISC(C) insure against 'loss of or damage to' the vessel, the exclusion clause excludes 'loss damage or *expense* ...' from the ITCH(95), the IVCH(95) and the ICC. The positive cover is thus narrower than the exclusion.

The ISC(C) has, however, included under its wing a clause relating to loss of or damage to the vessel caused by 'any terrorist or any person acting from a political motive'. This appears as a separate clause (cl 1.5) in the IWSC(H).

Strikes

Neither the Act nor the Clauses have defined any of the above terms. In so far as strikes are concerned, the case closest to the subject is *The New Horizon*,[69] which involved a charterparty, where Lord Denning MR was prepared to accept the dictionary meaning of the word adopted by Mr Justice Sankey in *William Brothers (Hull) Ltd v Naamloose Vernootschap WH Berghuys Kolanhandel*[70] to the effect that a 'strike' is 'a general concerted refusal by workmen to work in consequence of an alleged grievance'. He then proceeded to amplify the term as follows:

> '... a strike is a concerted stoppage of work by men done with a view to improving their wages or conditions, or giving vent to a grievance or making a protest about something or other, or supporting or sympathising with other workmen in such endeavour. It is distinct from a stoppage which is brought about by an external event such as a bomb scare or by apprehension of danger.'

---

67 [1979] 1 Lloyd's Rep 395.

68 *Ibid*, at p 404, Walton J said: ' In the circumstances ... it itself is the very reverse of a warlike operation ... It involves the very opposite: the destruction of war stores, which surely is an act of pacification'.

69 [1975] 2 Lloyd's Rep 314 at p 317, CA.

70 21 Com Cas 253 at p 257.

Lord Justice Stephenson stressed that,[71] 'There cannot be a strike without a cessation of work by a number of workmen agreeing to stop work ... It must be a stoppage intended to achieve something, to call attention to something ...'.[72]

A 'labour disturbance', on the other hand, is something less specific than either a strike or a lock-out. It covers any industrial or employment dispute giving rise to a 'disturbance' which is less serious in nature than a rebellion or insurrection.

'Riots'

The term 'riot' has a fixed meaning in criminal law. In *The Andreas Lemos*,[73] Mr Justice Staughton adopted the criminal law definition of a 'riot' spelled out in *Field v the Receiver of Metropolitan Police*,[74] which was later approved by the House of Lords in *London & Lancashire Fire Insurance Co v Bolands Ltd*.[75] To constitute a riot, the following elements have to be complied with:

- a number of persons not less than three (now 12);[76]

- pursuing a common purpose;

- execution or inception of the common purpose;

- an intent on the part of the number of persons to help one another, by force if necessary, against any person who may oppose them in the execution of the common purpose;

- force or violence, not merely used in and about the common purpose, but displayed in such manner as to alarm at least one person of reasonable firmness and courage.

Even though a riot in fact took place in *The Andreas Lemos*, nonetheless, the loss was held not recoverable because the riot took place only after the loss, and therefore it could not have caused the loss. In the colourful words of Mr Justice Staughton, it should be given its 'current and popular meaning', and not what a 'sloane ranger' would consider a 'riot'; 'The word today means the sort of civil disturbance which has recently occurred in Brixton, Bristol or Wormwood Scrubs'.[77]

Incorporated as part of the cover on strikes and, particularly, in relation to cargo, under the heading of the Institute Strike Clauses (Cargo), it is liable to cause confusion – for one could validly ask the question: is the word 'riots' (and 'civil commotions') to be read *ejusdem generis* with the preceding words 'labour

---

71   [1975] 2 Lloyd's Rep 483 at p 317.

72   *Cf* cl 3.7 of the ISC(C): Absence, shortage, or withholding of labour *per se* does not amount to a strike.

73   [1982] 2 Lloyd's Rep 483, QBD.

74   [1907] 2 KB 853 at p 860.

75   (1924) 19 Ll L Rep 1; [1924] AC 836, HL.

76   The Public Order Act 1986 which came into force on 1 April 1987 has increased the number from three to 12 or more persons: s 10(2) of this 1986 Act expressly provides that rr 8 and 10 of the Rules for Construction of Policy in Sch 1 Marine Insurance Act 1906 shall be construed in accordance with the definition of riot given by the 1986 Act.

77   [1982] 2 Lloyd's Rep 483 at p 491.

disturbances'? If this is to be the case, the 'common purpose', which is an essential ingredient for the offence of 'riot', must be in connection with a matter relating to labour and employment and not to a 'general purpose' or political issue. As will be seen, the same question may be asked of 'civil commotion'.

It is submitted that as a riot is a 'civil disturbance', it would be more appropriate if it were placed (together with civil commotion) in a separate provision of its own. Lumped with 'strikers, locked-out workmen and labour disturbances', it can only cause misunderstanding and could be interpreted (or misinterpreted as the case may be) as being associated only with 'industrial' riots.

The American and Canadian courts,[78] however, prefer the popular and ordinary meaning of 'riot' to the more technical, criminal law definition described above. Mr Staughton in *The Andreas Lemos* could see the attraction of the American approach, but felt that he could not, for an English policy of marine insurance, depart from the British understanding of the term.

'Civil commotions'

In *Levy v Assicurazioni Generali*,[79] the words 'civil commotion' appearing in what was a war risks clause of a policy in respect of a stock of merchandise stored in a warehouse, were examined. The Privy Council, which had to give a meaning to these words, cited the following passage from *Welford and Otter-Barry's Fire Insurance*[80] with approval:[81]

> 'This phrase is used to indicate a stage between a riot and civil war. It has been defined to mean an insurrection of the people *for general purposes*, though not amounting to rebellion; but it is probably not capable of any precise definition. The element of turbulence or tumult is essential; an organised conspiracy to commit criminal acts, where there is no tumult or disturbance until after the acts, does not amount to civil commotion. It is not, however, necessary to show the existence of any outside organisation at whose instigation the acts were done.'[82]

It is important to bear in mind that the term 'civil commotion' in the clause under consideration was set in a scheme which is wholly different from the current cover of the IWSC(H) and the ISC(C). The sequence of the enumerated risks was as follows: 'War, invasion, act of foreign enemy, hostilities ... riots, civil commotions, insurrection, rebellion, revolution ...'. The remark that 'civil commotion' means 'an insurrection of the people for general purposes' is, in the context of the said clause pertaining to war (and civil war) risks, correct. But whether the same definition may be attributed to cl 1.4 of the IWSC(H) and cl 1.1 of the ISC(C) is, it is submitted, questionable because 'civil commotion' is not part of the war cover, but of the cover on strikes.

---

78 See the remarks of District Judge Frankel in *Pan American World Airways Inc v The Aetna Casualty & Surety Co & Others* [1974] 1 Lloyd's Rep 207 at p 234, on appeal [1075] 1 Lloyds Rep 77; and the Canadian case of *Ford Motor Co v Prudential Assurance* (1958) 14 DLR 2d 7, Ontario Court of Appeal.

79 [1940] 3 All ER 427, PC.

80 3rd edn, p 64.

81 (1940) 3 All ER 427 at p 431, PC.

82 Emphasis added.

First, support may be drawn from the fact that, like labour disturbances, riots and civil commotions are excluded by the strikes and not the war exclusion clause. Secondly, particularly in relation to cargo, riots and civil commotions appear as insured risks under the ISC(C), and not the IWC(C). If riots and civil commotion are meant to have a 'general purpose' connotation, they should have been incorporated either in a separate clause divorced from the strikes cover of the IWSC(H) and, in the case of cargo, the ISC(C). The fact that they have been lifted out of the Strikes Exclusion Clause of the ITCH(95), IVCH(95), and all the ICC, and placed in the same provision as for a loss caused by 'strikers, locked-out workmen ... labour disturbances' could be taken to mean that they are to be read *ejusdem generis* with matters relating to labour disputes.

The Privy Council has placed 'civil commotion' as at a stage between riot and civil war, but below rebellion; this suggests that they are in the same league as civil war and the like. Furthermore, 'civil commotion' has been described as an 'insurrection of the people' and 'insurrection', it is observed, is an insured peril under the war risks clause.

In *Spinney's v Royal Insurance Co Ltd*, albeit a non-marine insurance case, Mr Justice Mustill said that he could find:[83]

'... nothing in the authorities compelling the court to hold that a civil commotion must involve a revolt against the government, although the disturbances must have a sufficient cohesion to prevent them from being the work of a mindless mob.'

This points to the fact that 'civil commotion' is a wider concept covering anti-governmental, as well as other forms of discontent. O'May, however, drew the distinction between a 'civil commotion' and an 'insurrection' as thus: 'The former is more a "domestic" disturbance whilst the latter involves action against the government with a view to supplanting it.' This statement goes some way to supporting, perhaps unwittingly, the point that 'civil commotion' should be awarded a limited meaning when it is placed alongside 'strikers, locked-out workmen, etc'. It is not unreasonable to deduce from the above discussion that 'riots' and 'civil commotions' arising from a labour or labour-related grievance, and not a political, politically-related, or general issue, are envisaged by this clause.

It is submitted that if riots and civil commotions are meant to have a wider implication, they should either be placed in a clause of their own or be left in the war risks clause.[84] Unless they are to be read *ejusdem generis* with 'labour disturbances,' there does not appear to be any good reason for keeping them in the strikes cover.

One could, of course, argue that, as the terms 'riots' and 'civil commotions' are already well-known in the insurance market to have a wide and general meaning, it does not matter where they are placed. But surely this cannot excuse or justify the present arrangement of the perils which, it is submitted, is

---

83 [1980] 1 Lloyd's Rep 406 at p 438.

84 A riot or civil commotion could, of course, develop into an insurrection, rebellion, revolution or civil war when it becomes more organised and takes the form of an attempt to overthrow the government.

unsatisfactory. To promote clarity and consistency, more thought should be given to the moving of 'riots' and 'civil commotions' to a more appropriate place.

'Any terrorist or any person acting maliciously or from a political motive'

The inclusion of loss damage liability or expense caused by 'any terrorists or any person acting from a political motive' as part of the strikes exclusion clause of the ITCH(95), the IVCH(95), and all the ICC does not pose any problem. They are now insured under a separate provision, cl 1.5 of the IWSC(H) and cl 1.2 of the ISC(C). However, in relation to hull, it is to be stressed that cl 1.5 also covers the acts of any person acting maliciously. Under the ICC (B) and (C), a loss caused by malicious acts is expressly excluded by cl 4.7 of the general exclusion clause which is worded thus:

'... deliberate damage to or deliberate destruction of the subject-matter insured or any part thereof by the wrongful act of any person or persons.'

To insure for such a loss, an assured would have to take out the Institute Malicious Damage Clause by which, in consideration for an additional premium, the exclusion for 'deliberate damage to or deliberate destruction of the subject-matter insured or any part ... is deemed to be deleted'. As there is no such exclusion in the ICC (A) (being an all risks policy) the risk of malicious damage caused by a third party is covered; consequently, there is no need to take out this special cover.

'Confiscation or expropriation'

The above are insured risks in the policy for hull, the IWSC(H), but not for cargo. Clause 1.6 of the IWSC(H) providing positive cover has to be read with cl 5.1.3 where '... confiscation or expropriation by or under the order of the government or any public or local authority of the country in which the Vessel is owned or registered' is excluded.

As no definition is given either by the Act or the Clauses to these expressions, it can perhaps be assumed that they must bear their ordinary and dictionary meanings. 'Confiscate' means to 'take or seize by authority, or appropriate to the public treasury (by way of a penalty)'. In the context of the positive cover, it has to be read to mean confiscation by the order of the government, public or local authority of a country other than the country in which the vessel is owned or registered.[85]

'Expropriation' is commonly understood to mean the taking away or the dispossession of property from its owner. It is a wide concept and, therefore, even includes 'confiscation'. It is generally accepted to embrace nationalisation and where some form of compensation is paid for the taking of the property.

---

85 See *Levin v Allnutt* (1812), 15 East 267 at p 269, a very old case, where Lord Ellenbourough CJ had given a narrow meaning to the word 'confiscation', that, it has to be 'some way beneficial to the government; though the proceeds may not strictly speaking be brought into the treasury'. Whether such a restricted meaning has to be given the term is questionable.

The detainment clause

Just as the detainment clause (discussed earlier) is applicable to capture, seizure, arrest, restraint and detainment, it is also applicable to confiscation and expropriation. After a continuous period of 12 months of loss of the free use and disposal of the vessel, the assured may claim for a constructive total loss by reason of having been deprived of the possession of the vessel without any likelihood of recovery.

The frustration clause

Clause 3.7 of the IWC(C) and cl 3.8 of the ISC(C), named as the frustration clause, state that the insurance does not cover 'any claim based upon loss of or frustration of the voyage or adventure'. As was seen, the notion of loss of or frustration of the adventure owes its existence to *The Sanday Case* where, as a consequence of restraint of princes, the voyage which was to be undertaken by a cargo of linseed was abandoned. Even though the cargo did not suffer any physical damage, the assured was allowed to recover for the loss on the basis that there was a loss of the voyage or adventure. To overcome the effects of the decision of the House, the frustration clause was introduced. It needs to be pointed out that there is no frustration clause in the IWSC(H) because the concept does not apply to a policy on hull.

'Based on'

In *The Sanday Case*, the 'loss of or frustration of the voyage or adventure' arose as a result of a restraint of princes. Restraint, however, is not the only way by which such a loss can arise: a loss of voyage could well occur by reason of any of the perils insured by the IWC(C) and the ISC(C).[86]

The construction of the frustration clause was considered in the celebrated case of *Rickards v Forestal Land, Timber and Railways Co Ltd* and two other cases,[87] sometimes referred to collectively as the 'Three Test Cases of 1941'. According to the oft-quoted explanation given by the Lord Chancellor, Viscount Simons:

'... the proper construction of the frustration clause is not "free of any claim which on the facts might be based on loss of the insured voyage", and that its proper meaning must be "free of any claim which is in fact based, because it can only be based, upon loss of the insured voyage".'

In simpler terms, this means, to cite the words of Lord Wright, that: '... it cannot be applied to a case where the assured is claiming for loss of, or damage to, the actual physical things or chattels'. He then proceeded to spell out the circumstance when the clause would apply. He said:

---

86 This explains why the current version of the frustration exclusion is couched without any qualification. The original clause, which was narrower, read as follows: 'Warranted free of any claim based upon loss of, or frustration of, the insured voyage or adventure, caused by arrests, restraints, or detainments of kings, princes or people'.

87 The other two cases are: *Robertson v Middows Ltd*; and *Kann v WW Howard Brothers & Co Ltd* [1941] 3 All ER 62, HL.

'The exception is expressly by its language limited to the loss of, or frustration of the insured voyage. Its language cannot ... be twisted to make it exclude a claim for actual loss of, or damage to, the goods themselves.'

It has to be said that if the goods themselves were to suffer physical damage, there would be no need for the assured to rely on loss of the voyage as the basis of his claim. The House took pains to explain the scope of the clause even when the issue was actually of little importance to the three cases, because there was in fact an actual total loss of the goods. Lord Wright was clear in his mind that the clause was:[88]

'... undoubtedly invented from a desire to abrogate the effect of *Sanday's case*, where only the adventure was affected by the peril, the goods being unaffected. I attach no importance to ... the words "based upon". The clause might just as well have run "for loss of".'

Unlike 'caused by', the phrase 'based upon' used in the clause is not an expression which is known to possess any causal implication. But interestingly enough, causation was the approach which Lord Justice Jenkins adopted in *Atlantic Maritime Co Inc v Gibbon*,[89] where he cited with approval the following remarks made by Lord Sumner in *Samuel v Dumas*:[90]

'Where a loss is caused by two perils operating simultaneously at the time of the loss and one is wholly excluded because the policy is warranted free of it, the question is whether it can be denied that the loss was so caused, for if not the warranty operates.'

Admittedly, it is difficult to imagine how a loss or frustration of the voyage or adventure can ever occur on its own: it can only arise as a result of an earlier event or occurrence. From this, some may argue that loss of the voyage or adventure is not a cause of loss, but the product of a cause of loss; others may consider it as a remote cause of loss. In either case, if *the* proximate cause is, for example, restraint of princes, an insured peril, the loss is recoverable. This would go against the grain of the frustration clause.

As a way out of this dilemma, Lord Justice Jenkins was prepared to regard loss of voyage as one of two proximate causes of loss; and as loss of voyage is expressly excluded, the loss is not recoverable.

As can be seen, the problem cannot always be solved by applying the rule of causation. It is submitted that, it is precisely for this very reason that the term 'based on' (and not the standard 'caused by') has been chosen for this clause. The position is best resolved by observing the words of Sir R Evershed MR, who said that:[91]

'It is applicable, on the face of it, only to cases where the claim is based on loss or frustration of a voyage or adventure, which I take to be in distinction from those cases where the vessel or the cargo is itself lost.'

---

88 [1941] 3 All ER 62 at p 85, HL.

89 (1953) 2 All ER 1086 at p 1110, CA.

90 [1924] AC 467.

91 (1953) 2 All ER 1086 at p 1099, CA.

CHAPTER 15

TOTAL LOSS

INTRODUCTION

Like the common law, the Marine Insurance Act 1906 recognises only two main types of loss: a total loss and a partial loss. A total loss may be either an actual total loss or a constructive total loss (s 56(2)). This chapter will first discuss the various types of actual total loss, and then the nature of a constructive total loss together with matters relating to the giving of a notice of abandonment and ademption of loss. Partial losses will then be discussed in the next two chapters, the first of which will study the different types of particular average loss: particular average loss of ship and goods, and the measure of indemnity therefor. This will be followed by a chapter on extraordinary expenses such as salvage, salvage charges, general average and sue and labour charges (particular charges) where each of these special claims will be dealt with separately.

As a preface to this and the next two chapters on claims for losses, it is necessary to highlight the new clause in the ITCH(95) relating to the giving of notice of claims and tenders. The new addition to cl 13.1 of the ITCH(95) is applicable to all claims whether the loss be total or partial.

Notice of claim and tenders

Whenever any accident occurs whereby loss or damage *may* result in a claim, whether for a total or a partial loss, under the insurance the assured is required to give notice to the underwriters. By cl 13 of the ITCH(95),[1] he is required to give notice to the underwriters promptly after the date on which the assured, owners or managers become or should have become aware of the loss or damage and prior to survey so that a surveyor may be appointed if the underwriters so desire. Under cl 8 of the IVCH(83)[2] the assured is only required to give notice to the underwriters prior to survey, and to the nearest Lloyd's Agent (if the vessel is abroad) so that a surveyor may be appointed if underwriters so wish.

Prompt notice

What constitutes prompt notice under the new cl 13.1 is in on each case a question of fact; in any event notice must be given as soon as it is reasonably possible after the date on which the assured, owners or managers become or *should have become* aware of the loss or damage and, definitely, before survey. Besides the owners, a mortgagee could, of course, be an 'assured' under a policy of insurance.[3] And should he have knowledge of the fact that the insured ship

---

1   Previously cl 10 of the ITCH(83).

2   And cl 10 of the ITCH(83).

3   A mortgagee could take out his own policy as an original assured of a policy. See Chapter 2.

had met with an accident, he himself would have to report to the underwriters in accordance with the terms of cl 13.1.

Whether a mere failure to report promptly in itself constitutes a breach of contract is questionable. But, of course, if the assured fails to report within the 12-month limit, then his claim becomes time-barred, in which case the underwriter is automatically discharged from liability.

Automatic discharge from liability

Clause 13.1 of the ITCH(95) requires that the assured makes a report to the underwriters within 12 months of the date when the assured (owners or managers) become aware or should have become aware of the loss or damage. The consequence for failing to report within the 12-month period is that the underwriters are *automatically* discharged from liability for any claim under the insurance in respect of any resulting claim.

The expression 'automatically discharged'[4] is borrowed from *The Good Luck*,[5] where the law on the effects of a breach of a promissory warranty was debated and settled by the House of Lords. As the concept of automatic discharge applies to a breach of a warranty, one could be misled into thinking that this clause, in stipulating the same effect for its breach, must be a promissory warranty. It is significant to note that the underwriters are discharged from liability, but only for any claim 'in respect of or arising out of *such* accident or loss or damage'.[6] In other words, the underwriters are automatically discharged from liability, but only as regards any claim arising from the particular accident of which the assured had failed to notify to the underwriters within the prescribed period.

Unlike a breach of a promissory warranty, the underwriter is not discharged from further liability as from the date of the breach. Only the claim(s) arising from the particular accident which he had failed to report is time-barred and, therefore, not recoverable. Unlike a breach of a promissory warranty, the future liability of the underwriter is clearly not brought to an end by the breach; neither is the contract of insurance itself brought to an end. The underwriters may, of course, waive the breach if they so desire, but this has, according to cl 13.1, to be confirmed in writing.

A – ACTUAL TOTAL LOSS

An actual total loss is defined by s 57 as thus:

> 'Where the subject-matter insured is destroyed, or so damaged as to cease to be a thing of the kind insured, or where the assured is irretrievably deprived thereof, there is an actual total loss.'

---

4   It is to be noted that only 'discharge' is used in cl 4, the new classification clause, and 'terminate automatically' in the new cl 5.1 of the ITCH(95).

5   [1991] 2 Lloyd's Rep 191, HL. The legal effects of a breach of a promissory warranty are discussed in depth in Chapter 7.

6   The crucial word here is 'such'.

It is necessary at the outset to mention that s 57 is applicable to any subject-matter insured, whether ship, cargo or freight. There are three parts to this definition, each of which will be analysed, and where appropriate with illustrations of loss of ship and/or of goods.

The first and the last parts of s 57 are derived from an observation made by Lord Abinger in *Roux v Salvador*,[7] where the whole basis of marine insurance was referred to in the following terms:

'The underwriter engages, that the object of the assurance shall arrive in safety at its destined termination. If, in the progress of the voyage, it becomes totally destroyed or annihilated, or if it be placed, by reason of the peril against which he insures, in such a position that it is wholly out of the power of the assured or of the underwriter to procure its arrival, he is bound by the very letter of his contract to pay the sum insured.'

It is to be noted that under s 57(2) no notice of abandonment need be given in the case of an actual total loss.[8]

WHERE THE SUBJECT-MATTER IS TOTALLY DESTROYED

A total wreck

The first part of s 57 is obviously taken from the above comments of Lord Abinger, the words 'totally destroyed or annihilated'. To what extent must a ship be damaged before she could be described as having been 'destroyed'? The first case to provide an answer to this question was *Bell v Nixon*,[9] where it was said, in reference to a wooden ship, that 'her planks and apparels had to be scattered in the sea'. In *Cambridge v Anderton*,[10] the well-known 'a congeries of planks' expression was coined by Chief Justice Abbott: 'If the subject-matter of insurance remained a ship, it was not a total loss, but if it were reduced to a mere congeries of planks, the vessel was a mere wreck ...'. Finally, in the Scottish case *Sailing Ship Blairmore Co Ltd v Macredie*,[11] Lord Watson, using strong and picturesque language, embellished upon the subject. He decided that *The Blairmore* was not a total loss because she:

'... did not become, in the strict sense of the term, *a total wreck*, seeing that she was not reduced to the condition of a mere congeries of wooden planks or of pieces of iron which could not without reconstruction be restored to the form of a ship, and that she had sunk in a depth of water which admitted of her being raised to the surface and repaired.'

The very concept of an actual total loss conjures a picture in one's mind of a ship foundering in a squall; sinking in deep waters after a collision; being consumed by fire or destroyed by the enemy – leading to a physical total loss or annihilation of the subject-matter insured. This has perhaps led Lord Halsbury

---

7   (1836) 3 Bing NC 266 at p286.

8   *Cf* s 62 on constructive total loss.

9   (1816) Holt NP 423 at p 425.

10   (1824) 2 B & C 691.

11   [1898] AC 593 at p 598, hereinafter cited as *The Blairmore*.

in *The Blairmore* to say that:[12] '... a ship was totally lost when she goes to the bottom of the sea, though modern mechanical skill may bring her up again ...'. The matter, however, is not quite as simple as was envisaged by Lord Halsbury. Fortunately, his somewhat sweeping remark was clarified in *Captain J A Cates Tug and Wharfage Co Ltd v Franklin Insurance Co*,[13] where the Privy Council warned that:

'Lord Halsbury's remark must not be taken as meaning that any ship is an actual total loss whenever she is under water, nor even when she is submerged in such circumstances as to present to salvors a problem of some difficulty.'

Thus, the mere fact that a ship has sunk even in very deep sea does not automatically mean that her owners can claim for an actual total loss. A shipowner would have to satisfy the court that in the circumstances of the case, it is either physically or commercially (in a business sense) impossible to raise the sunken vessel.[14] Proof of the former would establish an actual total loss, and of the latter, a constructive total loss.

It appears from the above authorities that to qualify as an actual total loss, the vessel has to be so severely damaged as to become a total wreck. There is, however, another approach adopted by Mr Justice Willes in *Barker v Janson*,[15] decided before the Act. He held the view that:

'If a ship is so injured that it cannot sail without repairs, and cannot be taken to a port at which the necessary repairs can be executed, there is an actual total loss, for that has ceased to be a ship which never can be used for the purpose of a ship ...'

This seems to be a more liberal and an easier requirement to fulfil. Whether the test of navigability and of the impossibility to carry out repairs should be read conjunctively is unclear. The last part of his remark, however, seems to imply that both criteria have to be fulfilled: simply being unnavigable is not enough to render the vessel an actual total loss; the vessel must also be placed in a position where it is impossible, for whatever reason, to carry out any necessary repairs. The whole statement is ambiguous to say the least. Such a situation falls more easily in line with the second limb of s 57.

Presumption of an actual total loss: missing ship

An actual total loss may be presumed where 'the ship concerned in the adventure is missing, and after the lapse of a reasonable time no news of her has been received'. What is or is not a lapse of a reasonable time is a question of fact.[16]

---

12 *Ibid.*
13 [1927] AC 698 at p 705; *per* Viscount Sumner.
14 A host of factors, eg, the place where she lies, her size, the nature of her injuries, and the available facilities for salvage work, would have to be taken into consideration.
15 (1868) LR 3 CP 303 at p 305.
16 See s 88.

As discussed earlier,[17] the common law by the case of *Green v Brown*[18] is prepared in the case of a missing ship to presume a loss by perils of the seas. This presumption, together with the presumption of a total loss allowed by s 58, should ease the plaintiff's burden of proof considerably. However, in *Houstman v Thornton*,[19] a vessel which was not heard of for nine months was presumed by the court to be a total loss, but with the caveat that should she be discovered afterwards, it will be for the benefit of the insurers.

In relation to goods, to qualify as an actual total loss under this heading, nothing short of utter and complete destruction of the goods in specie, either actual or inevitable, will suffice. In *Dyson v Rowcroft*,[20] a cargo of fruit, which was so damaged by sea-water and stunk so badly that the government prohibited its landing, was thrown overboard. The court held that there was in this case an actual total loss. However, the court noted that as there was always so much temptation in such circumstances to throw the cargo overboard, each case must be looked at with some suspicion. Thus, one should not lose sight of the fact that the necessity of having to jettison the cargo has to arise from a peril insured against.

Neither deterioration in quality nor depreciation in value will give an assured the right to terminate the adventure and recover for a total loss. For example, in *Anderson v The Royal Exchange Assurance*,[21] a vessel carrying a cargo of wheat was, to prevent her from sinking, ran on ashore. The vessel was under water for four weeks, during which time the assured rigorously made attempts to save the cargo. A greater part of the cargo was recovered, kiln-dried, and could have been sold as wheat. The assured, however, gave notice of abandonment and claimed for a total loss. The court held that, as some of the cargo had been salved, there was not, in fact, a total loss.[22]

CEASE TO BE A THING OF THE KIND INSURED

A ship which is so destroyed as to become a total wreck would not only fall within the first, but also the second part of s 57: reduced to 'pieces of iron' she would certainly 'cease to be a thing of the kind insured'. However, this category of loss is more relevant to cargo than to ship or freight. The nature of cargo is such that it lends itself more easily to the application of this principle. The authority for this rule has to be *Asfar v Blundell*,[23] where a cargo of dates, having

---

17 See Chapter 9.

18 (1743) 2 Str 1199. In *Koster v Reed* (1826) 6 B & C 19, it was said to be only a *prima facie* presumption.

19 (1816) Holt NP 242.

20 (1802) 3 B & T 474.

21 (1805) 7 East 38.

22 *Ibid*, at p 43, Lord Ellenborough pointed out that the assured '... did not however treat it as a total loss at the time [when it was submersed in water] but continued labouring on the vessel and cargo on their own account ... and succeeded in preserving part of it ... and when they did abandon it was no longer in fact a total loss'. They could not recover for a partial loss because of the free from particular (except general) average warranty.

23 [1896] 1 QB 123, CA.

been so impregnated with sewage, was held by the Court of Appeal to be a total loss for which freight was not payable on delivery. In a state of fermentation and putrefaction, they had lost 'any merchantable character as dates'. This case has highlighted the fact that to constitute an actual total loss, 'total destruction is not necessary'; a destruction of the merchantable character of the goods would suffice.[24] In each case, the test is whether 'as a matter of business, the nature of the thing has been altered'.[25]

Similarly, in *Roux v Salvador*,[26] Lord Abinger had to determine whether a cargo of hides which was so far damaged by a peril of the sea that it never could have arrived in the form of hides was a total loss. Their condition was described as follows: 'By the process of fermentation and putrefaction, which had commenced, a total destruction of them before their arrival at the port of destination, became as inevitable as if they had been cast into the sea or consumed by fire.'[27] As the hides had actually changed their form, they were sold as glue, manure, or ashes. This change in specie was sufficient to render the loss an absolute total loss.[28]

The above pair of cases have established the principle that cargo which has sustained a total destruction 'in specie', either actual or inevitable, would qualify as a total loss under this part of s 57. The expression 'in specie' in effect has the same meaning as 'so damaged as to cease to be a thing of the kind insured'.

For the purpose of contrast, the case of *Francis v Boulton*[29] may be cited. A cargo of rice which had become saturated with water was held to be only a partial loss. That the rice was capable of being conditioned, and when kiln-dried was sold as rice fetching about a third of its sound value were factors which influenced the court's decision.[30] As the rice remained as rice in specie, there was no total loss.

---

24 [1895] 2 QB 196 at p 201, *per* Mathew J, in the court of first instance. On appeal [1896] 1 QB 123, CA.

25 See also *Duthie v Hilton* (1868), LR 4 CP 138 where it was held that freight was not payable in respect of cement which had become wet and had lost its properties as cement; it had been changed into a hard substance, though all the cement was there.

26 (1836) 3 Bing NC 266 at p 281.

27 See also *Montoya & Others v The London Assurance Co* (1851) 6 Ex 451, where damage sustained by a cargo of tobacco caused by the putrefaction of hides, rendered putrid by sea water, was held recoverable as a total loss by perils of the sea.

28 In *Berger and Light Diffusers Pty Ltd v Pollock* [1973] 2 Lloyd's Rep 442, QB, steel injection moulds which had rusted so badly that they were incapable of use as moulds, with no more value than scrap metal, was held an actual total loss.

29 [1895] 1 Com Cas 217.

30 See *Glennie v The London Assurance Co* (1814) 2 M & S 371, where the court stated: 'Assuming it [cargo of rice] to have produced nine-tenths less than its value, that will not make it a total loss'; and *Boon & Cheah Steel Pipes Sdb Bhd v Asia Insurance Co Ltd* [1975] 1 Lloyd's Rep 452, Malaysia High Court, where the court expressed the view that it would only be prepared to apply the *de minimis* rule if only a single pipe or two out of the whole consignment was lost.

Partial loss

Obliteration of marks

An owner of cargo may sustain a loss because his cargo has, due to an obliteration of marks, become unidentifiable. Section 56(5) states:

> 'Where goods reach their destination in specie, but by reason of obliteration of marks, or otherwise, they are incapable of identification, the loss, if any, is partial and not total.'

In *Spence and Another v The Union Marine Insurance*,[31] cotton belonging to various owners were shipped on board the same vessel as the plaintiff's cargo of 43 bales of cotton. During the course of the voyage, some of the bales were lost, some were damaged, and on some the identification marks were so badly obliterated that they could not be identified as belonging to which of the owners. Only two of the 43 were identified and delivered to the plaintiffs. The bales have become unidentifiable not by reason of a change in specie or character, but by a loss of their identification marks. The confusion only arose because similar cargo belonging to several parties were shipped together; as there was no loss in specie, the matter was treated as a partial loss. The court dealt with the confusion in the following manner: '... when goods of different owners become by accident so mixed together as to be indistinguishable, the owners of the goods so mixed become tenants in common of the whole, in the proportion in which they have severally contributed to it'.

'IRRETRIEVABLY DEPRIVED THEREOF'

This part of s 57 takes care of the situation where the subject-matter insured is not destroyed, remains in specie, but is in the hands of a third party, whether a captor, an enemy, a purchaser or a barratrous crew. Whether the assured has or has not been 'irretrievably deprived' of the subject-matter insured is, of course, a question of fact.

In *George Cohen, Sons & Co v Standard Marine Insurance Co Ltd*,[32] an obsolete battleship which went ashore on the Dutch coast was detained by the Dutch authorities which feared that she might damage the sea defences of the area. The owners pleaded that they had suffered an actual total loss claiming that they have irretrievably lost their insured property. This plea was rejected by the court on two grounds. First, the fact that the battleship could be got off physically, even though the whole operation may be an engineering feat requiring considerable preparation and high expenditure, indicated that she was not irretrievably lost. Secondly, the order of the authorities, however influential, was not conclusive; as the possibility of appeal against the order was always available, it meant that the directive of the authorities could well be set aside by a higher body.

In *Marstrand Fishing Co Ltd v Beer, The Girl Pat*,[33] the master and crew ran off with the ship in order to use her for trading. As Mr Justice Porter could not find

---

31 (1868) LR 3 CP 427.

32 (1925) 21 Ll L Rep 30.

33 [1937] 1 All ER 158.

any evidence to suggest that the vessel was irretrievably lost to her owners, the loss to her owners was not an actual total loss.

A ship which has been captured by enemies, condemned in the Prize Court, and ultimately sold would be an actual total loss. This was the decision of *Stringer and Others v The English and Scottish Marine Insurance Co Ltd*.[34] The same decision would have been delivered in *Andersen v Marten*,[35] if it were not for the 'warranted free from capture' clause in the policy.

In relation to goods, Earl Loreburn in *The Sanday Case*[36] was prepared to hold that an assured whose goods, though they remain in specie and were effectively in the possession of the assured, has been irretrievably deprived of them because all prospect of their safe arrival on the voyage was hopelessly frustrated by the outbreak of war. Here, it has to be borne in mind that the subject-matter insured which was held to have been lost was not the goods, but the adventure. The assured was not irretrievably deprived of the goods themselves, but of the performance of the voyage.

RECOVERY FOR A PARTIAL LOSS

Section 56(4) states that, 'Where the assured brings an action for a total loss and the evidence proves only a partial loss, he may, unless the policy otherwise provides, recover for a partial loss.' A policy containing a free from particular average warranty is one which 'otherwise provides'.

In *Boon and Cheah v Asia Insurance Co Ltd*,[37] counsel for the assured had, because of the free from particular average warranty, to present a case of a total loss. It was argued that applying the maxim *de minimis no cura lex*, a loss of 98.3% of the cargo of steel pipes was sufficiently high to constitute a total loss. This contention was rejected by the Malaysian High Court which held that there was not a total loss. By reason of the warranty, the partial loss was held not recoverable under the policy.

34 (1869) LR 4 QB 676; (1870) LR 5 QB 599, CA.

35 [1908] AC 334, where a neutral ship was captured and afterwards condemned in the Prize Court. It was held that there was in fact a total loss by capture, but because of the 'free from capture' warranty, the owners could not recover on the policy.

36 [1916] 1 AC 650, HL. All the other Law Lords preferred to rest their decision on the ground that the voyage was 'reasonably abandoned' on account of its actual total loss (not of the goods but of the voyage) appearing to be unavoidable: s 60(1).

37 [1975] 1 Lloyd's Rep 452.

ACTUAL TOTAL LOSS OF FREIGHT

Payment of freight and delivery of goods

The payment of freight and delivery of goods are concurrent conditions.[38] Thus, if cargo is for whatever reason not delivered at its proper destination, freight is not payable.

A total (actual or constructive) loss of goods caused by an insured peril would naturally result in a total loss of freight. In *Denoon v The Home and Colonial Assurance Co*,[39] for example, the ship in which the cargo of rice was carried was wrecked resulting in a total loss of the rice which in turn caused a total loss of the freight of the rice. Similarly, in *Iredale and Another v China Traders Insurance Co*,[40] chartered freight was held a total loss by the peril of fire[41] when a cargo of coal which became so heated that it had, for the safety of all concerned, to be landed at a port of refuge. The abandonment of the chartered voyage resulted in an actual total loss of chartered freight.

When cargo arrives at its proper destination, even in a damaged state, or is short delivered, the agreed freight is nevertheless payable in full.[42] The charterer or consignee is, of course, entitled to claim for damages for the damaged goods or short delivery by means of a cross-action, but not as a set-off.

The common law is always prepared to presume that freight is payable only on delivery of the goods at the port of discharge. If cargo is not delivered at its agreed destination, freight is, as a general rule, not payable; and if the non-delivery of the cargo is caused by a peril insured against, the assured of freight would be able to claim for a total loss of freight.[43] This was made clear in *Rankin v Potter* by Mr Justice Brett of the House of Lords, who observed that:[44] 'There may be an actual total loss of freight under a general policy if there be ... an actual total loss of the whole cargo ...'. The word 'general' (qualifying 'policy') warns that if the policy insures freight generally (as opposed to specifically in relation to a particular cargo) earned by the ship, it may be possible for the ship to carry *other* cargo on the voyage insured and thereby earn an equal amount of, or some freight. In such a case, the assured of freight cannot by reason of the

---

38 Freight is the remuneration payable to the carrier for the conveyance of goods from the port of shipment to the destination agreed under the contract of affreightment, be it a voyage charterparty or a bill of landing.

39 (1872) LR 7 CP 341.

40 [1900] 2 QB 519, CA.

41 See *The Knight of St Michael* [1898] P 30. Fire is an insured peril under the Institute Freight Clauses.

42 Unless the freight has already been paid in advance.

43 In *Price & Another v Maritime Insurance Co Ltd* [1900] 5 Com Cas 332; [1901] 2 KB 412, CA, there would have been a total loss of freight, if it were not for the application of Italian law which allow recovery for distance freight for part of the cargo which was salved when the ship failed to arrive at its proper destination by reason of constructive total loss. The assured were, however, unable to claim for the partial loss because of the free from particular average warranty.

44 (1873) LR 6 HL 83 at 99, HL.

principle of indemnity claim for a total loss of freight, if he has earned some freight from the carriage of other cargo.

Constructive total loss of goods

As mentioned earlier, freight is payable even if the cargo is delivered in a damaged condition at its proper destination. This rule, however, does not apply where the cargo delivered is so severely damaged as to be in an unmerchantable condition. To illustrate this point, reference has to be made again to the classic case of *Asfar v Blundell*,[45] where freight was held not payable for dates which were delivered impregnated with oil and sewage and unfit for human consumption. Having lost their identity as dates, they were a constructive total loss. A constructive total loss of goods could thus engender an actual total loss of freight.

B – CONSTRUCTIVE TOTAL LOSS

INTRODUCTION

The doctrine of constructive total loss is peculiar to marine insurance.[46] The concept is defined in s 60, but before embarking upon an analysis of the terms and requirements of each of the different types of constructive total losses, it is necessary at this juncture to offer some observations as to the relationship between the subsections, and the overall scheme of the section.

Scheme of section 60

Section 60(1) introduces with a broad and general definition of a 'constructive total loss' in the following terms: 'Subject to any express provision in the policy, there is a constructive total loss where the subject-matter insured is reasonably abandoned...'.

Section 60(2) begins with the words: 'In particular, there is a constructive total loss ...' and then proceeds to set out a list of events which would cause a constructive total loss of ship and goods.

Without at this stage of going into detail as to the characteristics of a constructive total loss, it is necessary to point out certain salient features about s 60. First, it is observed that by s 60(1), a constructive total loss is dependent upon the subject-matter being 'reasonably abandoned'. No such qualification, however, appears in s 60(2). Secondly, s 60(2) offers two specific cases of a constructive total loss; the first (s 60(2)(i)) is on deprivation of possession, and the second (s 60(2)(ii) and (iii)), the cost of repairs. Are these mere examples of

---

45 [1896] 1 QB 123. See also *Duthie v Hilton* (1868) LR 4 CP 138, where freight was held not payable for the delivery of solidified cement salvaged from a vessel which had been scuttled.

46 See *Court Line Ltd v R, The Lavington Court* [1945] 2 All ER 357 at p 365, *per* Stable J; *Manchester Ship Canal Co v Horlock* [1914] 2 Ch 199 at p 208, CA, *per* Swifen Eady LJ: 'The expression "constructive total lost" has no meaning as applied to a ship, except in connection with marine insurance ...'.

the preceding subsection, or are they separate heads of claim? The phrase 'in particular' gives the impression that they are illustrations of sub-s (1). Thirdly, only ship and goods are mentioned in s 60(2), nothing is said about freight.

Section 60 is renowned for raising 'great difficulties of construction'; the fitting together of the two subsections of s 60 is by no means easy.[47] Fortunately, the matter has been resolved by the House of Lords in *Robertson v Petros M Nomikos Ltd*,[48] where Lord Wright expressed the view that: 'The two sub-ss contain two separate definitions, applicable to different conditions of circumstances'. Two years later, again in the House of Lords in *The Rickards Case*,[49] he was given yet a further opportunity to drive the point home. He confirmed that:

'... the view which this House arrived at was that the two subsections contained two separate definitions, which may be applied to different conditions of fact. Thus, an assured can base his claim on the terms of subsection (2), which give an objective criterion in each case, ship, goods or freight,[50] not only more precise than, but substantially different from that in subsection (1). Subsection (2), as compared with subsection (1), is thus additional, and not merely illustrative.'

Lord Porter, however, in *The Robertson Case*,[51] took a slightly different route to arrive at the same conclusion. He said:

But it does not follow that the first subsection lays down the general rule, whereas the second gives certain particular instances already covered by the general rule. Indeed, whatever may be the case with regard to s 60(2)(i), ss 60(2)(ii) and (iii) do not appear to be covered in terms by the definition in s 60(1). But in any case, unless there is some reason to the contrary, a definition must be held to include the whole of its wording, and if particular instances are given which include matters which are outside the more general definition, that is no reason for supposing that their application is limited by the more general words. They do not merely illustrate: they add to the terms of the definition. Section 60 does not confine constructive total loss to cases where the subject-matter of insurance has been abandoned, though in some instances there may be no constructive total loss unless abandonment has taken place.

A complete definition

The above discussion has clarified the point that the two subsections are separate, but does not answer the question as to whether s 60 contains an exhaustive definition of a constructive total loss. The matter was touched upon (by way of *obiter*) by Lord Porter in *The Robertson Case*, but came up squarely before the court in *Irvin v Hine*,[52] where counsel for the assured attempted to

---

47 Lord Wright for one in *Rickards v Forestal Land, Timber and Railways Co Ltd* [1941] 3 All ER 62 at p 79, HL, would be sympathetic to such a belief: 'That is perhaps inevitable, and is certainly excusable when it is sought in a brief section, supplemented though it is by ss 61 to 63, to embody the complicated problems of law and fact which experience has shown to arise in the case of a constructive total loss'.

48 [1939] AC 371, HL, hereinafter cited as *The Robertson Case*.

49 [1941] 3 All ER 62 at p 79, HL.

50 But s 60(2) does not mention freight.

51 [1939] AC 371 at p 392, HL.

52 [1950] 1 KB 555.

introduce a 'new' head of constructive total loss which is covered by neither s 60(1) nor 60(2).

In *Irvin v Hine*, the vessel in question grounded in a severe and prolonged storm; owing to wartime conditions, and to the licensing system then in force, it was unlikely that she would be repaired within a reasonable period of time. On this basis, the assured claimed against the insurers for a constructive total loss, alternatively, a partial loss. It was argued that the vessel was a constructive total loss because it was unlikely that the assured would be able to obtain a licence to repair her.[53] But for the evidence that her repairs would probably be deferred for an indefinite period, there was no evidence to suggest that her condition was such that an actual total loss appears to be unavoidable.[54]

Mr Justice Devlin, relying on a remark made by Lord Porter in *The Robertson Case*,[55] held that on its true construction, s 60 was a complete definition. He emphasised that the word 'defined' in the marginal note '… shows conclusively that s 60 is intended to define a constructive total loss, which is the same as saying that s 60 circumscribes completely the concept of constructive total loss'.[56]

Lord Porter, however, in *The Robertson Case*, depended on s 56 to arrive at the same result: 'That s 60 is intended to be a complete and not a partial definition appears to follow from the wording of s 56 when it says: "Any loss other than a total loss, *as hereinafter defined*, is a partial loss"'.[57]

As the assured could not bring his case within any of the heads in s 60, the vessel was held not to be a constructive total loss. Mr Justice Devlin was not at all concerned with whether or not the loss would have been a constructive total loss under common law. The fact that it was not a constructive total loss under s 60 was in itself sufficient to dispose of the plaintiff's claim for a total loss.

There is clearly no room under the Act for the introduction of any *new* form or theory of constructive total loss: in this sense, s 60 is complete and exhaustive. However, it has to be mentioned that there is another specie of constructive total loss, created by the common law, that of the loss of voyage applicable only to goods, which is not expressly acknowledged by the Act. Though not given a place in the statute book, this common law form of constructive total loss of goods was given the highest seal of approval possible by the House of Lords in *The Sanday Case*,[58] decided after the passing of the Act. '*The Sanday* principle' now stands in its own right as a type of constructive total loss peculiar only to goods.

---

53 It is to be noted that the test of 'unlikely' in s 60(2)(i) relates to the unlikelihood of recovery of possession of the subject-matter insured, and not the unlikelihood that he would be able to repair her within a reasonable time.

54 See s 60(1).

55 [1939] AC 371, HL.

56 [1950] 1 KB 555 at p 568. The marginal note to s 60 states: 'Constructive total loss defined'.

57 [1939] AC 371 at p 392, HL.

58 [1916] 1 AC 650. *The Sanday Case* has already been discussed elsewhere, see Chapter 3.

Types of constructive total loss

As each of the subsections to s 60 is held not to be a mere elaboration of the preceding subsection, but an independent head of claim, they will have to be discussed separately. Section 60, though it has only two subsections, may for the purpose of discussion be broadly divided into four main parts:

- the first part (s 60(1)) which is of general application relates to any insured subject-matter (whether ship, goods or freight) that has been 'reasonably abandoned';
- the second (s 60(2)(i)), applicable only to ship or goods, is on deprivation of the subject-matter insured;
- the third (s 60(2)(ii)) is concerned with damage to ship; and
- the fourth (s 60(2)(iii)) is on damage to goods.

REASONABLE ABANDONMENT OF SUBJECT-MATTER INSURED

There are two parts to s 60(1). To recover for a loss under this section, the assured has to show that the subject-matter insured was 'reasonably abandoned' either:

- 'on account of its actual total loss appearing to be unavoidable'; or
- 'because it could not be preserved from actual total loss without an expenditure which would exceed its value when the expenditure had been incurred.'

The word 'abandon' (and 'abandonment') appearing in ss 60–63 has, depending on the context in which it is used, different meanings in the law of marine insurance.[59] The term was subjected to thorough examination in *Court Line Ltd v R, The Lavington Court*,[60] where the Court of Appeal had to decide, though the action was not in relation to a marine policy, on a hypothetical basis, whether the vessel was 'abandoned' within the meaning of s 60(1).[61]

One would have thought that, as the requirement of reasonable abandonment is common to both parts of s 60(1), the same meaning ought to have been given to the word 'abandon' in both parts. Lord Justice Scott

---

59 Chalmers, p 98, observes that the term 'abandonment' is used in three different senses. First, an assured may where there is a constructive total loss 'abandon' the subject-matter insured to the insurer, the purpose of which is to transfer whatever rights the assured may have of the remains of the subject-matter insured to the insurer. Secondly, it is sometimes loosely used to refer to a notice of abandonment. Thirdly, it could refer to abandonment by operation of law of whatever remains of the subject-matter insured when the insurer pays for a total loss. There is, however, a fourth category, where the master and crew abandon or leave, giving up for lost, the subject-matter insured.

60 [1945] 2 All ER 357, CA.

61 The dispute was in relation to a charterparty under which there was a clause providing that: 'Should the vessel become a constructive loss such loss shall be deemed to have occurred and the hire under this contract shall cease ...'. The court had, therefore, first to determine whether the vessel was a constructive total loss as understood in the law of marine insurance.

observed that even in s 60(1) itself, the term is used in two different senses. In the light of this, it is necessary, in order to avoid confusion, that the concept of abandonment be discussed in its proper context.

Actual total loss appearing unavoidable

Reasonable abandonment of ship

Leaving the ship

According to *The Lavington Court*, an abandonment under s 60(1) takes places when the master and crew leave the ship with the intention of never returning. Such an act, said Lord Justice Scott, 'may and very often must be by the master in exercise of his authority express or implied, but usually pursuant to his general powers of agency for his owner'. An abandonment under this part of s 60(1) constitutes a physical act of leaving the ship. In similar vein, Lord Justice Scott said:[62]

'... whereas the forecast of the probability of actual total loss would, at any rate a century ago, nearly always have to be made by the master on the spot; and even in these days of easy and quick wireless communication, the decision would very often devolve on the master.'

Lord Justice Stable, however, preferred to focus his attention on the nature of the act itself. The term must be:

'... directed to the act, that is to say, the actual abandonment of the ship by the responsible person in whose charge she is. In my judgment, abandonment in the present context was complete when the master finally and irrevocably left the ship ...'

'Give up for lost'

Even though Lord Justice Du Parq did not agree with the other two Law Lords that the word 'abandoned' was capable of having two different meanings in one subsection, his understanding of the term is in effect not altogether that different. To him, the word 'abandon' refers to:[63]

'... something done by the shipowner or his agent with his authority, and I would add that the master may often be an agent of necessity. I understand "abandon" to mean "give up for lost", and when I say give up for lost I mean that the owners are renouncing all their rights in the ship except the right to recover insurance.'

To constitute abandonment under this part of s 60(1), the physical act of leaving the ship must also be accompanied with the intention of never returning. Leaving the ship temporarily would not suffice. The court held that as the master had no intention of abandoning the ship in this sense, there was no constructive total loss.[64]

---

62 [1945] 2 All ER 357 at p 363, CA.

63 *Ibid*, at p 365. 'The word "abandoned" in s 60 cannot ... be given one sense in relation to the first, and another in relation to the second limb of subsection (1)'.

64 The vessel was not 'given up for lost', as the master was mainly concerned with saving the lives of the crew and property.

Meaning of 'unavoidable'

An act of abandonment *per se*, even if made with the intention of renouncing all the owner's rights in the ship, would not satisfy s 60(1). The ship has to be abandoned by reason of 'an actual total loss appearing to be unavoidable'.[65] To illustrate this requirement of a constructive total loss, reference has to be made to the case of *Lind v Mitchell*,[66] which is directly on point. The master abandoned the vessel after she was damaged by ice and was leaking rather badly. Expecting a gale in which he thought she would be lost, he decided to abandon her; he set fire to her to prevent her from being a danger to navigation. He and the crew then abandoned her. One of the issues which concerned the Court of Appeal was whether the abandonment was 'unreasonable'. To answer this question the court had to consider whether it was made 'on account of its actual total loss appearing to be unavoidable'.

Taking into account the fact that the schooner was within only 15 miles of her home port, the direction of the wind with which the vessel could have sailed, and that she was still floating high in the water seven or eight hours after she was abandoned, the abandonment was held to be premature and, therefore, 'unreasonable'. In the light of this, her abandonment could not be justified as having been made 'on account of its actual total loss appearing to be unavoidable'.

Thus, whether the adverb 'reasonably' adds anything to the substance of the section is doubtful. The abandonment has to be made for one or the other of the reasons stated in the section.

No definition of the word 'unavoidable' is given in *Lind v Mitchell*. Mr Justice Stable, however, in *The Lavington Court*,[67] has provided us with an insight of his understanding of the term. Even though he had arrived at a different conclusion on the facts from the other two Law Lords, his interpretation of the law as regards the word 'abandon' is, nonetheless, worthy of consideration. Though he felt that 'to attempt to give a definition of the word applicable in all circumstance is likely to do more harm than good', he was clear that 'it cannot be assigned such an absolute meaning as "inevitable" in the sense of something which must in the course of nature happen'. He made it clear that the word 'unavoidable':[68]

> '... connotes a very high degree of probability, with the additional element that there is no course of action, project or plan, present at the time or place in the mind of the person concerned which offers any reasonable possibility of averting the anticipated event.'

---

65 In *Irvin v Hine* [1950] 1 KB 555 at p 569, Devlin J expressed the opinion that: 'If the delay in repairing was such that the most likely fate for the ship was that she would be left to rot so that her actual total loss would appear to be unavoidable, a claim might be maintain under s 60(1) ...'. See Park J in *Read v Bonham* (1821) 3 Brod & B 147 at p 155.

66 (1928) 45 TLR 54, CA.

67 [1945] 2 All ER 357, CA.

68 *Ibid*, at p 368.

The question of whether the test to be applied is objective or subjective was raised by the judge. However, as the facts of the case did not require an answer to be given to the question, the matter was left open. The above remarks seem to suggest that a subjective, rather than an objective test is to be employed.[69]

Reasonable abandonment of goods

As mentioned earlier, this subsection on abandonment of the subject-matter insured on account, *inter alia*, of its actual total loss appearing to be unavoidable is of general application. Clause 13, the 'constructive total loss clause' of the ICC, reiterates that: 'No claim for constructive total loss shall be recoverable hereunder unless the subject-matter insured is reasonably abandoned either on account of its actual total loss appearing to be unavoidable ...'. It does nothing more than to echo the first principle of s 60(1).

Irreparable damage

Goods may suffer physical damage which, depending on the nature and extent of the damage, may or may not be repairable. If the damage is repairable, but the cost of repairing (and forwarding the goods) is economically impracticable, the assured would plead s 60(2)(iii) to claim for a constructive total loss.[70]

However, if the damage sustained is not repairable (but leaves the goods still in specie)[71] and an actual total loss of the goods appears to be unavoidable in time to come, the assured would invoke s 60(1) to support a claim of a constructive total loss. He is not obliged to wait for an actual destruction of the goods to take place before tendering his notice of abandonment. If the damage suffered by the subject-matter insured is such that it would satisfy the criterion of 'reasonable abandonment' on account of its actual total loss appearing to be unavoidable, the assured does not have to wait for the event of an actual total loss to occur before taking action. As in the case of deprivation of possession under s 60(2)(a), this is the principle upon which the doctrine of constructive total loss is based.[72]

Loss of or frustration of the voyage or adventure

A long line of authority, culminating in the House of Lords decision in *The Sanday Case* – the leading authority on the subject – had established the principle of 'loss of voyage' applicable only in relation to insurance on goods.[73] Goods may, by a peril insured against, be prevented from arriving in safety at their port of destination. An assured, though he or his agent may be in

69 Cf s 60(2)(i) where the test is objective. In *Czarnikow Ltd v Java Sea and Fire Insurance Co Ltd* [1941] 3 All ER 256 at p 262, the court said: 'As far as the definition in subsection (1) is concerned, I should again adopt the view ... that it is the true facts which have to be considered in deciding whether the subject-matter was reasonably abandoned ...'.

70 For a discussion of s 60(2)(iii), see below.

71 If the goods are so destroyed or so damaged as to 'cease to be a thing of the kind insured', the assured would plead an actual total loss: see s 57(1) discussed above.

72 See in particular, the remarks of Lord Atkinson in *Moore v Evans* [1918] AC 185, HL.

73 For example, *Barker v Blakes* (1808) 9 East 283; *Cologan v London Assurance Co* (1816) 5 M & S 447; and *Lozano v Janson* (1859) 2 E & E 160.

possession of the goods, could, for whatever reason,[74] find it physically or practically impossible to forward them to their proper destination. A forced premature destruction, termination or frustration of the *voyage* can cause the goods to suffer a 'loss of voyage'.

Practical impossibility of forwarding the goods

Unlike insurance on ship,[75] insurance on goods for a particular voyage covers not only physical damage or loss, but also the loss of the voyage or adventure. The ancestry of this rule has been traced to the 'test' cases on war risks.[76] As the principle is well established, only two cases need be discussed, one decided before the Act and the other after the Act, to ascertain whether the law before the Act is still good law after the passing of the Act.

In *Rodocanachi v Elliot*,[77] silks were shipped at Shanghai for London, but had to be sent by rail from Marseilles, through Paris, and thence to London – a customary route for silks. When the goods arrived at Marseilles, France and Germany were at war, and though the silks had arrived at Paris, it was practically impossible to convey them to London, because Paris was then under siege. The silks existed *in specie*, were uninjured, and were effectively in the possession and control of her owners. The only problem was that they were prevented from leaving Paris, and the whole adventure was broken up, and so continued at the time when the notice of abandonment was given and up to the commencement of the action.

The court had no doubt that the loss was caused by 'restraint of princes' which was an insured peril in this case.[78] It held that the assured were entitled to abandon the goods and to recover against the insurers as for a total loss. The following is an extract of an oft-cited speech delivered by Bramwell B, which was approved in *The Sanday Case* by the House of Lords:[79]

> 'It is well established that there may be a loss of the goods by a loss of the voyage in which the goods are being transported, if it amounts, to use the words of Lord Ellenborough, "to a destruction of the contemplated adventure".'

It has to be said that the judge was keen to point out that a 'mere temporary retardation of the voyage', even if caused by an insured peril, will not give the assured a claim against the insurer.[80] Only such delay as to lead to a frustration or 'a breaking up of the whole adventure' would found a claim for loss of voyage.

---

74 Eg, goods may be detained in a blockaded port, where they are 'shut up and cannot be got out': *Rodocanachi v Elliot* (1874) LR 9 CP 518; or goods may be prevented on sanitary grounds from entering a port, as in *Miller v Law Accident Insurance Co* [1903] 1 KB 712, CA. War, capture, seizure, embargo, blockade, the operation of foreign laws, etc can all cause a loss of voyage for goods.

75 See *Doyle v Dallas* (1831), 1 M & Rob 48.

76 See O'May, p 433. This observation is correct, as all cases on the subject relate either to capture by enemies, detention, restraint or seizure by a foreign authority or state.

77 (1874) LR 9 CP 518.

78 *Ibid*, at p 522, *per* Bramwell B: 'The silks were ... as effectually prevented from coming out as if they were actually seized by the German army'.

79 *Ibid*, cited with approval by Lord Atkinson in *The Sanday Case* [1916] 1 AC 650 at p 661, HL.

80 See also s 55(2)(b) and cl 4.5 of the ICC on loss caused by delay.

The Sanday principle

The legal standing of the above principle was, in *The Sanday Case*, examined in the context of the Act. Here, a cargo of linseed oil was sent to Germany to be sold. By reason of illegality, the goods were prevented from being carried to their proper destination. The adventure of carrying the cargo to its destination became not only impracticable, but in law a serious offence. Again, as in the first case, the goods themselves were unharmed and in the actual possession of the assured.

Affirming the decisions of the trial judge and of the Court of Appeal, the House held that there was a constructive total loss of the goods: there was 'a destruction of the contemplated adventure'. Lord Atkinson said:[81]

> 'And what the assured insures against is not merely the loss sustained by injury to or destruction of the goods, but in addition the loss resulting from a failure to transport the goods to their destination, that failure being established by detention of them through one of the perils insured against, so prolonged as to amount to a destruction of the contemplated adventure.'

As regards the status of the principle in the light of the Act, the matter was succinctly explained by The Earl of Loreburn as thus:[82]

> 'In 1906 it was well settled that when goods are insured ... at and from the port of loading to the port of destination there is a loss if the adventure is frustrated by a peril insured against. It is not merely an insurance of the actual merchandise from injury, but also an insurance of its safe arrival ... I do not think the Act altered the law in the particular now under consideration.'

Reasonably abandoned

It has to be borne in mind that, as was seen, s 60 on constructive total loss is a 'complete definition'. Thus, it is now pertinent to consider which limb of the section applies to a loss of voyage. All the Law Lords were of the opinion that the first part of s 60(1) was applicable to such a loss: The Earl of Loreburn, for one, was of the view that the assured may reasonably abandon the 'subject-matter' insured because its actual total loss appeared to be unavoidable.[83] The same was expressed by Lord Atkinson as: 'the consequent loss of the market appear to be unavoidable ...'.[84] Lord Parmoor, in much more positive terms declared that: 'If the *subject-matter* in the present case includes the contemplated adventure, it was no doubt reasonably abandoned on account of its actual loss appearing to be unavoidable, and a case of constructive total loss arises'.[85]

Subject-matter insured

As far as a claim under the Act is concerned, the whole issue revolves around the words 'subject-matter' appearing in s 60(1), for which the Act has not

---

81 [1916] 1 AC 650 at p 662, HL; also discussed in Chapter 3.

82 *Ibid*, at p 656, HL.

83 He also prepared to categorise such a loss under s 57 as an actual total loss.

84 [1916] 1 AC 650 at p 663, HL.

85 *Ibid*, at p 668, HL. Emphasis added.

provided a definition. It is thus necessary to determine what the 'subject-matter' insured is in policies on goods. That it refers to the goods themselves is not in dispute, but whether it includes a loss of voyage is unclear. The problem, however, was resolved by Lord Parmoor as follows:[86]

> 'When the Act was passed the common form Lloyd policy of marine insurance on goods in transit from one port to another designated by usage that the contemplated adventure was part of the subject-matter, so that if the contemplated adventure was frustrated by a peril insured against, the insurers became liable to pay the insured the amount due under the policy. This position is not altered but preserved by subsection 4 [of s 26].'

Thus, s 60(1) could be read as follows: There is a constructive total loss where *the voyage* (to be undertaken by goods) is reasonably abandoned on account of its actual total loss appearing to be unavoidable.

The frustration clause

The frustration clause was introduced to override *The Sanday* principle. After going through several changes in wording, which need not concern us here, the current version of the clause is much simplified. Clause 3.7 and cl 3.8 of the Institute War Clauses (Cargo) and of the Institute Strikes Clauses (Cargo), respectively, read as follows:[87]

> 'In no case shall this insurance cover ... any claim based upon loss of or frustration of the voyage or adventure.'

That it refers to the *insured* voyage or adventure is implied. This clause, however, has to be read in its proper context: its scope is limited to a loss of voyage caused by war and strikes risks covered by the Institute War Clauses, and the Institute Strike Clauses, respectively.

It is noted that there is no frustration clause in any of the ICC. A loss of or frustration of the voyage or adventure caused by a marine peril, (eg, fire or peril of the seas) is not expressly excluded. To illustrate this point, reference could be made to an example raised by Arnould to the effect that the ship on which the goods are carried may be so severely damaged (by an insured marine risk) that it becomes impossible to continue with the voyage; and if the circumstance is such that it is practically impossible to procure another ship at the port of casualty or any neighbouring port to carry the goods to their proper destination, then there is a loss of voyage for which a claim for a constructive total loss could be made for the goods.[88] There is nothing in the Act, nor the Clauses, preventing recovery for a loss of voyage arising from such a form of practical impossibility caused not by war or strike, but by an insured marine peril.

---

86 *Ibid.* And as there is nothing about this common law interpretation of 'subject-matter' which is inconsistent with an express provisions of the Act, it will have the force of law: see s 91(2).

87 An earlier version was worded as: 'Warranted free of any claim based upon loss of, or frustration of, the *insured* voyage or adventure, caused by arrests, restraints or detainments of kings, princes, or peoples'. See *Atlantic Maritime Co Inc v Gibbon* [1953] 2 Lloyd's Rep 294, CA.

88 Arnould, para 1220. No case is cited for this proposition.

Expenditure which would exceed its value

The 'economic' test

Lord Justice Scott in *The Lavington Court*[89] referred to the second criterion of s 60(1) as the 'economic test'. Here, the decision, which involves the making of financial estimates, is normally made by the owner, not the master. The distinction as regards the question of abandonment was graphically drawn by Lord Justice Scott as follows:[90]

'The making of the financial estimate is, of course, merely an exercise of business judgment and discretion. The abandonment which follows after it may be expressed in a letter and not in boats as in the first alternative ...'

Compared to the abandonment described earlier, which is physically demonstrated 'on the spot' or 'on the boat'[91] by the master and crew in leaving the ship for good, an abandonment under this limb of s 60(1) is 'later in time and different in quality'.[92] Such an abandonment is made by the assured to the insurer. In as much as such a loss is grounded upon mathematical calculations, it is similar to a constructive total loss under s 60(2)(ii) and 60(2)(iii) in relation to ship and goods, respectively. As can be seen shortly, this part of s 60(1) is of particular relevance as regards the loss of voyage or adventure in relation to insurance on goods.

The 'economic test', it is noted, can also be found in cl 13 (the second part) of the ICC, which states that: 'No claim for constructive total loss shall be recoverable hereunder unless the subject-matter insured is reasonably abandoned ... because the cost of recovering, reconditioning and forwarding the subject-matter to the destination to which it is insured would exceed its value on arrival.'

Should insured goods suffer physical damage to the extent that, '... the cost of repairing the damage and forwarding the goods to their destination would exceed their value on arrival', an assured would obviously invoke s 60(2)(iii) to claim for a constructive total loss. Should he be deprived of the possession of his goods, he would rely on either (a) or (b) of s 60(2)(i), depending on the circumstances of the case, to base his claim.

Commercial impossibility of forwarding the goods

This part of s 60(1), however, is only applicable when the goods themselves suffer little or no physical damage, and the assured (or his agent) is still in possession of them.[93] Though he may be in possession of the goods, and there is no physical difficulty in sending on the goods to their destination, an assured may, for economic reasons, find it impossible to forward them to their proper

---

89 [1945] 2 All ER 357 at p 362, CA.

90 *Ibid*, at pp 362–363, CA.

91 *Ibid*.

92 *Ibid*, at p 367.

93 Eg, goods may be seized and later returned to the assured in a country other than its proper destination: such is a loss of voyage.

destination. If the cost of forwarding is so great as to be commercially prohibitive, an assured would invoke this provision to claim for a constructive total loss. This form of loss of goods, relating to a loss of voyage, is akin to that proposed by *The Sanday Case*; except that here the loss of the voyage is due to a commercial impossibility, whereas under *The Sanday* principle, it is due to a physical or practical impossibility. Further, if one were to apply the prudent uninsured shipowner criterion, a court is unlikely to expect such an expenditure to be incurred. An abandonment of a voyage, whether by reason of a physical or commercial impossibility, can hardly be described as unreasonable. It is to be recalled that to legalise the claim, the assured has to tender to the insurer a notice of abandonment. Such a safeguard has to be observed – in case the insurer may have his own special means of transporting the goods to their proper destination, and so desire to take advantage of the abandonment.

It is necessary to mention that in *The Sanday Case*,[94] Lord Wrenbury was prepared to employ the words '... and forwarding the goods to their destination ...' of s 60(2)(iii) to allow for such a loss. He has obviously read the word 'and' disjunctively to mean 'or'. In view of the opening words of the subsection, it is questionable whether such a construction is tenable.

There is no such concept as loss of voyage or adventure in a policy on ship.[95] Thus, it is difficult to see how this limb could be applied to insurance on ship. In the case of damage to ship, the assured would plead s 60(2)(ii); for deprivation of possession, he would plead either s 60(2)(i)(a) or (b).

DEPRIVATION OF POSSESSION OF SHIP OR GOODS

Section 60(2)(i), which applies to ship or goods but not freight, is divided into two parts. To invoke this section, the assured must first establish that he has been 'deprived of the possession of his ship or goods by a peril insured against' and, secondly, either that:

- it is unlikely that he can recover the ship or goods as the case may be, or
- the cost of recovering the ship or goods, as the case may be, would exceed their value when recovered.

As will be seen shortly, the cases dealing with this type of constructive total loss are generally concerned with the capture of the ship and/or goods by enemies or a belligerent state. This has led an eminent 19th century author to state in his comparative study of the laws that:[96]

'In England, the rule is more just, for there, from the moment of a capture or arrest, the owners are considered as having lost their power over the ship and cargo and are deprived of the free disposal of them; because, in the opinion of

---

94 [1916] 1 AC 650 at p 673, HL.

95 See *Doyle v Dallas* (1831) 1 M & Rob 48 at p 55; where Lord Tenterden CJ said: 'The loss of the voyage will not, in my opinion make a constructive total loss of the ship ... and as they [the insurer] indemnify only against the loss of the ship, the loss of the voyage would not injure them.'

96 Marshall, *Law of Marine Insurance* (1861, 4th edn), cited in *Polurrian SS Co Ltd v Young* [1915] 1 KB 922 at p 936, CA.

the merchant, his right of disposal being suspended or rendered uncertain, it is equivalent to a total deprivation; it is therefore unreasonable to oblige the insured to wait the event of a capture, detention or embargo.'

If judicial authority be required to confirm this proposition, it can be found in the judgment of Lord Atkinson of the House of Lords in *Moore v Evans*,[97] where the origin of the doctrine of constructive loss was traced:

'... the law of constructive total loss based upon notice of abandonment was shaped and moulded by decisions of Lord Mansfield about the middle of the eighteenth century. The doctrine had its origin in cases of capture ... *Goss v Withers* and *Hamilton v Mendes* were both cases of capture and recapture, and were apparently based upon the principle that the assured should not be obliged to wait till he had definitely ascertained whether his ship had been recaptured or not, but might upon capture proceed at once and, after notice of abandonment, recover his capital, the value of his ship, from the underwriters, provided he was not aware of her recapture when he commenced his action.'

Though the court in *Polurrian SS Co Ltd v Young*[98] was prepared to admit that s 60(1) and (2)(i)(a) relate to a constructive total loss by capture, it was not able to comment on whether the requirement embodied in the phrase 'unlikely that he can recover' originated from the cases of capture.[99]

Meaning of 'deprived of possession'

The fundamental difference between s 60(2)(i) and s 60(1) lies in the fact that in the case of the former, the assured has to be deprived of the possession of the subject-matter insured, whereas in the latter, possession has obviously to remain with the assured, his servants or agents; otherwise, no physical abandonment can take place.

An assured of ship or goods can be deprived of the possession of his insured property either by capture by enemies, a belligerent state, a barratrous crew or any third party running away with the ship. Most of the cases in this area of law, however, are in relation to deprivation as a result of capture by enemies. The capture may be by hostile or friendly means, but the assured must be deprived of the free use and disposal of his vessel.[100] To claim for a constructive total loss, it is not enough for the assured merely to show that there is actual and complete deprivation of possession of the insured property, he must also prove that its recovery is 'unlikely'.

---

97 [1918] AC 185 at p194, HL.

98 [1915] 1 KB 922; 20 Com Cas 152, CA; hereinafter referred to as *The Polurrian Case*.

99 *Ibid*, at p 937; the court said: 'Whence the statute derived the phrase "unlikely that he can recover" as expressing a necessary condition of the assured's right to recover for a constructive total loss by capture I do not know'.

100 In *The Bamburi* [1982] 1 Lloyd's Rep 312 at p 316, Staughton J held that the assured was wholly deprived of the free use and disposal of their vessel even though there were four crew members on board; there was no Iraqi presence; and neither the Iraqi nor the Iranian government had asserted any right to, interest in or claim over the vessel. Later, at p 321, after a thorough examination of case law, he concluded that 'the loss of "free use and disposal" in this case amounted to loss of possession within the meaning of the policy ...'.

Meaning of 'unlikely'

In *The Polurrian Case*,[101] the word 'unlikely' was compared to 'uncertain' which was the concept used before the passing of the Act. In substituting the test of 'unlikelihood of recovery' with 'uncertainty of recovery', the Act had modified the pre-existing law to the disadvantage of the assured. The criterion is 'not merely quite uncertain whether they would recover her within a reasonable time, but that the balance of probability was that they could not do so'.[102] As the recovery of the vessel in question was only uncertain and not unlikely, there was no constructive total loss. The court also acknowledged the fact that the test would be 'very difficult to apply with any sense of satisfaction, because it necessarily involved conjecture and speculation as to what is likely to be the outcome of a number of possible contingencies'.

Justice Stable in *The Lavington Court*[103] would place the degree of probability, 'somewhere between mere uncertainty on the one hand and inevitability on the other'. In comparison with the criterion of 'unavoidable' under s 60(1), the measure of 'unlikely' is the 'less severe' of the two.[104] That the test of 'unlikely' is more stringent than 'uncertain', but less severe than 'unavoidable' is clear.

In *Marstrand Fishing Co Ltd v Beer*,[105] the master and crew ran away with *The Girl Pat* with the intention of trading with her, and ultimately selling her. She had been seen at several places but managed to elude capture. Mr Justice Porter asked himself the question: 'Is she more likely to be lost than to be recovered?' As there was always the chance that 'her good fortune in eluding capture so far might not be repeated', his reply to the question was: 'I do not know'. Being left in complete darkness as to whether *The Girl Pat* was likely or unlikely to be recovered, he felt that he had no choice but to hold that the vessel was not a constructive total loss.[106]

In summing up, reference should be made to the illuminating words of Lord Wright of the House of Lords in *The Rickards Case*:[107]

'There is a real difference in logic between saying that a future happening is uncertain and saying that it is unlikely. In the former, the balance is even. No one can say one way or the other. In the latter, there is some balance against the event. It is true that there is nothing in the Act to show what degree of unlikelihood is required. If, on the test of uncertainty, the scales are level, any degree of unlikelihood would seem to shift the balance, however slightly. It is not required that the scale should spring up and kick the beam.'

---

101 (1915) 1 KB 922, CA.

102 *Ibid*, at p 937

103 [1945] 2 All ER 357 at p 369.

104 See *Polurrian SS Co Ltd v Young* (1915) 1 KB 922, at p 937, CA.

105 [1937] 1 All ER 158

106 In contrast, in *George Cohen, Sons & Co v Standard Marine Insurance Co Ltd* (1925) 21 Ll L Rep 30 at p 34, the facts of which have been referred to earlier, the vessel was held a constructive total loss because there was a 'distinct unlikelihood ... that under any circumstances, or on any terms which the shipowners as commercial men were likely to be able to offer, the courts would ever have allowed the operation to have been attempted'.

107 [1941] 3 All ER 62 at p 81, HL.

Clause 13 of the ICC (A), (B) and (C) is silent as regards deprivation of possession of goods. Thus the above general legal principles relating to s 60(2)(i) apply. On the subject of deprivation of possession of goods, reference should be made to *Stringer v English and Scottish Marine Insurance Co Ltd*,[108] decided before the Act, where the ship and cargo were seized, condemned, and ultimately (about 18 months after capture) sold by the Prize Court. The assured initially elected to treat the loss as a partial loss and concerted efforts were made to recover the cargo. More than a year later, when it became clear to the assured, by reason of a change of circumstances, that they were unlikely to recover their cargo because of the impending sale by the Prize Court, they immediately gave notice of abandonment. When the sale took place and the proceeds paid into court, they again tendered a fresh notice of abandonment.

The Court of Appeal held that there was a total loss. As the cargo all the time existed *in specie*, the total loss can today be described as a constructive total loss, though the word 'constructive' was not used in the case. The assured were deprived of the possession of the goods, and the sale had rendered it not just 'unlikely', but impossible of recovery.

Whether a recovery is or is not unlikely raises several questions which have to be considered:

- Is the judgment to be based on an objective or subjective assessment of the facts of the case?
- When must the judgment be exercised?
- For what length of time must the period of recovery be unlikely? and
- From when is the period of unlikelihood of recovery to be measured?

The first question was in *Marstrand Fishing Co Ltd v Beer*[109] framed as thus: 'Was the recovery unlikely on the true facts as then existing and not upon the facts as known to the assured?' Citing *The Polurrian Case*[110] as authority, Mr Justice Porter held that 'the person to whom it must appear that the vessel is unlikely to be recovered is not the individual concerned, but is the reasonable man'.[111] Of course, in giving notice of abandonment, he may act on a reasonable guess. The test has to be objective, for to hold otherwise would be to hold that, 'the insurance had been effected, not against loss, but against bad news'.

On the second question, s 60(2)(i) has not specified a time limit which the assured is allowed to take to arrive at a decision as to whether recovery is or is not unlikely. In the absence of an express provision, he is given a reasonable period of time to make an assessment of the situation. This is said to be implicit in the subsection.[112] What is or is not a reasonable period of time is, of course, a

---

108 (1869) LR 4 QB 677; (1870) LR 5 QB 599, CA.

109 [1937] 1 All ER 158; see also *Czanrnikow Ltd v Java Sea and Fire Insurance Co Ltd* [1941] 3 All ER 256, where the principles laid down in *The Polurrian* and *The Marstrand* Cases were applied.

110 [1915] 1 KB 1922.

111 The same test, he said, is to be given to s 60(1).

112 See *The Polurrian Case* [1915] 1 KB 922 at p 937, *Irvin v Hine* [1950] 1 KB 555 at p 569; and *The Bamburi* [1982] 1 Lloyd's Rep 312 at p 314.

question of fact.[113] In any event, the assured is given a period of grace to make inquiries by s 62(3) which states that:

> '... notice of abandonment must be given with reasonable diligence after the receipt of reliable information of the loss, but where the information is of a doubtful character the assured is entitled to a reasonable time to make inquiry.'

The third and fourth questions may be conveniently discussed together. It was argued in *Irvin v Hine*,[114] that, as the subsection is silent on the matter, it was open to construction as to whether the deprivation of possession has to be perpetual or not. Mr Justice Devlin expressed the view that provided that there was no inconsistency with any express provision, this lacuna could be filled by the common law. Referring to the case of deprivation of possession, for example, by capture, he was of the opinion that '... the prospect of indefinite delay negatives the likelihood of return within a reasonable time'. But, an assured is not obliged to wait indefinitely with the hope of recovering his ship. If he can demonstrate that it is unlikely that he would recover possession of his ship within a reasonable period of time, he is entitled to give notice of abandonment and claim for a constructive total loss. It is noted that the Court of Appeal in *The Polurrian Case*[115] had also, without hesitation applied the 'reasonable time' test.

The test of 'reasonable time', however, may be applied only if there is no express provision in the policy stating otherwise, such as the Detainment Clause of the Institute War and Strikes Clauses (Time).

The detainment clause

By the Detainment Clause, cl 3 of the Institute War and Strikes Clauses, Hulls, (Time), and for (Voyage), an assured who has lost 'the free use and disposal of the vessel for a continuous period of 12 months' shall be deemed, for the purpose of ascertaining whether the Vessel is a constructive total loss, to have been 'deprived of the possession of the Vessel without any likelihood of recovery'. [116] As in the case of the Act, the clause has failed to specify the date when the 12-month period (or in the case of the common law, the 'reasonable time') is to commence. It could be 12 months from the date of the 'capture seizure arrest restraint detainment confiscation or expropriation' or 12 months from the date of the giving of the notice of abandonment. In *The Bamburi*,[117] it was construed as follows: '... a reasonable time to be 12 months from the notice of abandonment, without taking into account any period of detainment before the notice.' The reason being that the vessel must be a constructive total loss on that date for the notice to be valid.

The rule stated in *The Bamburi*[118] was in relation to the Institute Detainment Clause. Under common law, however, the possibilities for the date for the

---

113 See s 88.

114 [1950] 1 KB 555 at p 567.

115 See also *Marstrand Fishing Co Ltd v Beer* [1937] 1 All ER 158 at p 164.

116 See *The Bamburi* [1982] 1 Lloyd's Rep 312.

117 [1982] 1 Lloyd's Rep 312 at p 321.

118 *Ibid*.

commencement of the 'reasonable time' period are: the date of the casualty, the date of the notice of abandonment, or the date of the issue of the writ. The law, however, is unclear on the subject: *The Polurrian Case* seems to suggest that the crucial date is the date of the issue of the writ, or the notional issue of the writ, that is to say, the date which the underwriter has agreed to treat the matter as if the writ had been issued. On the other hand, Mr Justice Devlin, in *Irvin v Hine*, was of the opinion that the reasonable time is to be judged prospectively from the time of the casualty, it is then that recovery must be unlikely within a reasonable time.

Cost of recovery

It is to be observed that s 60(2)(i)(b) refers to the cost of 'recovering' the ship or goods; whilst s 60(2)(ii) and (iii), to the cost of 'repairing' the damage to ship and goods respectively. Clause 13 of the ICC amplifies s 60(2)(i)(b) by specifying that not only 'the cost of recovering', but also of 'reconditioning and forwarding the subject-matter to the destination' may be considered. If the total cost for recovering, reconditioning and forwarding exceeds its value on arrival, the assured may claim for a constructive total loss of the goods. The law in this regard is the same before and after the Act.

In *Farnworth v Hyde*,[119] decided before the Act, the court held that the cost of drying, landing, warehousing and reshipping the goods may be taken into account for the purpose of deciding whether there was a constructive total loss of the goods. The court also made it clear that the assured may not take into account 'the freight originally contracted to be paid; that being a charge to which the goods are liable when delivered, whether the perils of the sea affect them or not.'[120]

In *Vacuum Oil Co v Union Insurance Soc of Canton*,[121] the decision of the trial judge was overturned when the Court of Appeal, in taking into account the expense of obtaining new tins for the petroleum and of shipping them, arrived at a different finding of fact: as the oil would not have been worth the expense of reconditioning and sending on, the assured were held to have established a case of a constructive total loss.

---

119 (1866) LR 2 CP 204, applying the rule laid down in *Rosetto v Gurney* (1851) 11 CP 176, that if the cost of transhipping could only be effected at a higher than the original rate of freight, only the cost of the difference of transit could be taken into account.

120 In *Stringer v English and Scottish Marine Insurance Co* (1869), LR 4 QB 677 at p 691; (1870) LR 5 QB 599, CA; the assured could have recovered possession of their goods if they were prepared to pay the Prize Court about 150-180% more than the value of the goods. Though the rule as framed by s 60(2)(i)(b) was not then available, the court applied the 'prudent uninsured owner' criterion to support their decision that the assured were not in default in not preventing the sale of the cargo. The seizure, which ultimately led to the enforced sale, was held to have occasioned the total loss of the vessel and cargo.

121 (1926) 25 Ll L Rep 546, CA.

DAMAGE TO SHIP

Unlike a loss under s 60(2)(i), a constructive total loss under this heading entails the assured having possession and control over his property. For the section to apply, the damage sustained by the ship has to be repairable. The issue here is primarily concerned with a comparison of figures between the cost of repairs and the value of the ship when repaired. Section 60(2)(ii) states:

'In particular, there is a constructive total loss –

(ii) In the case of damage to a ship, where she is so damaged by a peril insured against, that the cost of repairing the damage would exceed the value of the ship when repaired.'

The above principle was recognised as early as 1836 by Chief Justice Tindal in *Roux v Salvador*.[122] In 1850, however, in *Moss v Smith*,[123] Mr Justice Maule was able to describe with clarity the nature of this form of a constructive total loss, even though the concept was then still somewhat undeveloped. Though the expression 'constructive total loss' was not used, nonetheless, the concept he had then envisaged is the same as current law:

'... it may be physically possible to repair the ship, but at an enormous cost; and there also the loss would be total; for, in matters of business, a thing is said to be impossible when it is not practicable; and a thing is impracticable when it can only be done at an excessive or unreasonable cost ... So, if a ship sustains such extensive damage, that it would not be reasonably practicable to repair her – seeing that the expense of repairs would be such that no man of common sense would incur the outlay – the ship is said to be totally lost.'

As will be seen shortly, this is by far the most complex of all statutory provisions on constructive total loss. It has generated a host of problems, some of which a solution has yet to be found.

The foundation of the rule is essentially premised on commercial or economic considerations, whereas an actual total loss is effectively a case of physical impossibility, a constructive total loss is a business impossibility.

The basis of the section is dependent upon a comparison between the cost of repairs and the value of the ship when repaired: these are basically the two main features of the section which require examination. As the law in relation to the latter is no longer in dispute it would be more convenient to dispose of it first, before proceeding to discuss the other part of the section which is more contrived and troublesome.

The value of the ship when repaired

The first question which immediately springs to mind is: which of the following values is the section referring to – the real market value of the ship when repaired or her insured value?

In an unvalued policy, it was never been doubted that the real value of the ship when repaired is the value to be taken for comparison: a prudent owner,

---

122 (1836) 3 Bing NC 266.
123 (1850) 9 CB 94 at p 103.

uninsured, would have taken the market value of the ship as the figure for determining whether he ought to carry out the repairs on his ship.[124]

In relation to a valued policy, the matter is governed by s 27(4) which states that: 'Unless the policy otherwise provides, the value fixed by the policy is not conclusive for the purpose of determining whether there has been a constructive total loss.'

Before the passing of the Act, the courts were at one stage uncertain as to the value which was to be taken into account.[125] In 1847, the matter was finally settled by the House of Lords in *Irving v Manning*,[126] which held that the real market value of the ship when repaired was the figure to be used for the purpose of comparison. The House said that the inquiry was in each case '... what a prudent uninsured owner would have done in the state in which the vessel was placed by the perils insured against'. The matter was considered as if there was no policy at all. Lord Campbell felt greatly relieved that this question which had 'agitated Westminster Hall for the last 30 years is at last solemnly decided'. Unless the policy otherwise provides, this would still be the general rule.

In practice, however, the Institute Hulls Clauses have taken advantage of the words 'unless the policy otherwise provides' to set aside the rule embodied in s 27(4). Clause 19.1 of the ITCH(95) and cl 17.1 of the IVCH(95) state that: 'In ascertaining whether the vessel is a constructive total loss, the insured value shall be taken as the repaired value ...'.[127]

An assured could also, if he so desires, specify in the policy that where the cost of repairs exceeds a certain percentage of the insured value, the vessel may be deemed to be a constructive total loss. This was the case in *Sailing Ship Holt Hill Co v United Kingdom Marine Association*,[128] where a special clause provided that: 'No vessel insured ... shall be deemed to be a constructive total loss unless the cost of repairing the damage ... shall amount to 80% of the value in the ordinary hull ... policy for £12,500.'

Mr Justice Rowlatt held that the parties had not provided that in *all* cases where the cost of repairs amounted to 80% of £12,500 there was a constructive total loss. He said that if they had intended to substitute the agreed figure for the repaired value, it would have used 'the direct and plain language of the well-known Institute Clause' which was 'ready to hand as a precedent'. The

---

124 In *Irving v Manning* (1847) 1 HL Cas 287 at p 304, HL, though the problem at hand was in relation to a valued policy, nevertheless, Patteson J pointed out that: 'If this had not been the case of a valued policy ... the course has been in all cases in modern times to consider the loss as total where a prudent owner, uninsured, would not have repaired'.

125 See *Allen v Sugrue* (1828) 8 B & C 561, the matter was left to the jury to decide. In *Young v Turing* (1841), 2 Man & Gr 593, the judge directed the jury that they ought not to have taken into account the value in the policy, but to apply the prudent uninsured owner test to arrive at its decision.

126 (1847) 1 HL Cas 287.

127 See *North Atlantic SS Co Ltd v Burr* (1904) 9 Com Cas 164; 20 TLR 260, a case decided before the Act, where the policy contained a clause that the 'insured value to be taken as the repaired value in ascertaining whether the vessel is a constructive total loss'.

128 [1919] 2 KB 789 at p 793.

purpose of the clause was to eliminate claims for a constructive total loss unless the estimated cost of repairs was equal to 80% of the declared value. This could be described as a hurdle (perhaps, the first of two) which the assured has to satisfy before he could claim for a constructive total loss. Allowing for the goodwill of underwriters, Mr Justice Rowlatt's parting words are as follows:

'I do not know whether underwriters usually pay when the condition provided for in the clause is satisfied without agitating the question of the actual repaired value, but I cannot read the clause as compelling them to do so.'

Freight earning capacity of the ship

If the market value of the vessel is to be used for the purpose of determining whether a ship is or is not a constructive total loss, a 'prudent uninsured owner' would be expected to include any pending freight in his calculation.[129]

Clause 19.1 of the ITCH(95) has simplified matters inasmuch as it has specified a single figure, namely, the insured value of the ship which is to be taken for comparison. On a strict interpretation, however, it means that, unless the freight-earning capacity of the ship has already been incorporated in the insured value of the ship, it cannot later be added to the insured value for the purpose of ascertaining whether the ship is or is not a constructive total loss. Arnould holds the view that, as any pending freight will in normal cases already have been allowed for, this should not pose much of a problem in practice. Provided that the sum is not counted twice, there seems to be a willingness to apply the principle of the 'prudent uninsured owner'.[130]

The cost of repairing the damage

What may or may not be included in 'the cost of repairing the damage' is of critical importance to the question as to whether there is a constructive total loss of a ship. Section 60(2)(ii) itself goes some way to answering this question, but is silent on a number of other issues which have since been raised and considered by the courts.

Value of the wreck

The question as to whether an assured may add the value of the wreck, and thereby inflate the cost of repairs, was examined in cases before and after the passing of the Act. In view of the somewhat erratic practice which existed before the passing of the Act, it would be sensible in this study to follow the course which Mr Justice Bray had taken in *Hall v Hayman*[131] by going straight to the words of the section in order to ascertain its real and natural meaning.[132]

---

129 See *Macbeth & Co v Maritime Insurance Co Ltd* [1908] AC 144, HL.

130 Arnould, para 1214.

131 [1912] 2 KB 5; 17 Com Cas 81.

132 Bray J took heed of the advice given by Lord Herschell in *Bank of England v Vagliano Brothers* [1891] AC 107 at pp 144 and 145, that one should be 'uninfluenced by any considerations derived from the previous state of the law and not to start with inquiring how the law previously stood ...'.

Relying on both subsections (1) and (2)(ii) of s 60, he placed emphasis on the word 'expenditure' and the phrase 'the cost of repairing the damage' appearing in the respective sub-ss. The value of the wreck can neither be described as an 'expenditure' of money to be incurred by her owner, nor 'the cost of repairing the damage'. Boldly, he swept aside all previous inconsistent rulings, including that emanating from the House of Lords in *Macbeth & Co v Maritime Insurance Co*,[133] which had declared that the assured was entitled to add the break-up value of the ship to the estimated costs of repairs.[134] In summing up, he said:[135]

> 'The rule therefore of the common law, that the value of the wreck ought to be added to the estimated cost of repairs in determining whether the ship can be treated as a constructive total loss, is, in my opinion, inconsistent with the express provision of s 60 and can no longer be treated as the law.'

However, as a first instance judgment, *Hall v Hyman* does not stand on the firmest of foundation. In the light of the somewhat changeable course which the law has so far taken, the Institute Hulls Clauses have done well to have set the problem at rest by inserting cl 19.1 of the ITCH(95) which states that '... nothing in respect of the damaged or break-up value of the vessel or wreck shall be taken into account'. This is endorsement of the rule laid down in *Hall v Hyman*.

A shipowner who wishes to include the value of the wreck in the account may, of course, do so by inserting a stipulation to that effect in the policy. Such a course is allowed by the opening words 'unless the policy otherwise provides' of s 60.

Cost of repairs

Nature of repair

The standard to which the ship may be repaired is a matter which Arnould[136] has described as now clearly settled by *Reid v Darby*.[137] Here, the vessel was found to be navigable, but she was not capable of being navigated home with her then cargo on board. Is such a vessel a constructive total loss? It was held that there could not be a constructive total loss because a policy on ship is only against the loss of the ship, not of the voyage. That she may be made good physically – as she was before the casualty or at the time when the valuation was agreed – appears to be accepted as the general rule, which was applied in *Doyle v Dallas*.[138]

The basis of the rule is probably sound for, unlike insurance of cargo, there is no equivalent to the principle of law laid down in *The Sanday Case*,[139] which

---

133 [1908] AC 144. It is to be noted that this case, though it was decided after the Act came into force, was not based on the Act, because the loss had occurred before the passing of the Act. See also *The Wild Rose SS Co v Jupe & Others* (1903) 19 TLR 289.

134 *Macbeth & Co v Maritime Insurance Co* [1908] AC 144, HL, overruled the decision of the Court of Appeal in *Angel v Merchants' Marine Insurance Co* [1903] 1 KB 811.

135 [1912] 2 KB 5 at p 14.

136 Arnould, para 1206.

137 (1808) 10 East 143.

138 (1831) 1 Mood & Ro 48.

139 [1916] 1 AC 650, HL, see Chapter 3.

is only applicable to cargo, in insurance on ship. As such, only repairs for damage which affects the physical condition of the ship (sailing either in ballast or with any kind of cargo), not loss of the adventure, may be taken into consideration. But having said that, it has to be pointed out that these cases were decided almost two centuries ago, and there is no recent direct authority on the subject.

Should temporary repairs be necessary to enable the vessel to proceed to sea from the place of the casualty or from the port of refuge, the assured is entitled to claim for both the estimated costs of the temporary and complete repairs from the insurers. As regards deduction of new for old, cl 14 of the ITCH(95) and cl 12 of the IVCH(95) provide that claims are payable 'without deduction new for old'.

Estimating the cost of repairs

In estimating the cost of repairs, s 60(2)(ii) has, as mentioned earlier, offered some guidance as to the items which may and may not be taken into account for the purpose of determining whether a ship is a constructive total loss. It states that:

> 'In estimating the cost of repairs, no deduction is to be made in respect of general average contributions to those repairs payable by other interests, but account is to be taken of the expense of future salvage operations and of any future general average contributions to which the ship would be liable if repaired.'

It is to be noted that three elements are covered by the above provision:

(1) general average contributions payable by other interests;

(2) expense of future salvage operations to which the ship would be liable if repaired; and

(3) future general average contributions to which the ship would be liable if repaired.

As both (2) and (3) above relate to the liability of the ship, they can be conveniently discussed together. There is, however, another category of payment which is not covered by the subsection, namely, expense of future salvage operations *payable by other interests*. Whether such an expense, which could well be a component of the 'general average contribution ... payable by the other interests', is to be deducted from the cost of repairs is a controversial matter which will dominate a substantial part of this discussion.

General average contributions payable by other interests

First, the very notion of general average connotes that other interests are involved. A general average situation can only occur when the whole adventure, ship and goods, is exposed to a common danger. Thus, there can be no question of general average contribution when a ship sails in ballast; when only one interest is at stake or at risk, general average contribution cannot possibly arise. Interests which have benefited from a general average act (expenditure or sacrifice) would naturally have to make a contribution towards the general average loss incurred. This is referred to in the subsection as 'general average contributions ... payable by other interests'. This sum would include all expenses which would necessarily have to be incurred to extricate the whole adventure from a position of danger.

The subsection has conferred an advantage upon the assured, inasmuch as he is permitted to add the general average contributions payable by other interests to the cost of repairs. He is able, thereby, to increase the total figure which is to be used for the purpose of comparison with the value of the vessel when repaired. Such additions would obviously enlarge the aggregate cost of repairs, making it easier for the assured to claim for a constructive total loss.

One would have thought that, as the sum is payable by third parties, it ought to be deducted from the cost of repairs. Arnould endeavours to provide an explanation for the rule by rationalising along the following lines:[140]

> 'The final incidents of such expenses should no more be taken into consideration in the case suggested than in a case where they are recoverable from a wrongdoer. But it could not be contended that a vessel which has been damaged by a collision is any the less a constructive total loss, because the cost of repairing her is recoverable by way of damages from the owners of another ship, by the negligent navigation of which the collision was occasioned.'

Against this, one is tempted to argue that an uninsured prudent owner, when considering the real cost (to him) to have the ship raised (if necessary) and repaired, would probably take into the account the amount which he will recover from the other interests.

Though it may probably be too late in the day to query the rationale for the rule, it is not too late to examine the wording of the provision which, on first reading, seems to suggest that an assured may add the whole of the general average contributions payable by other interests to the cost of repairs. But when read in the light of the ruling in *Kemp v Halliday*,[141] the only direct authority on the subject, albeit a pre-statute case, the position is far from clear.

Before taking any further step to examine the scope of the provision, it may be prudent here to take heed of the advice handed down by the Law Lords in *Bank of England v Vagliano Brothers*,[142] to the effect that the words of a codifying statute must in the first instance be construed according to their ordinary and natural meaning, without regard to the state of the law previously established by cases. Thus *Kemp v Halliday* is left for discussion at a later stage.

Expense of future salvage operations payable by other interests

In the first place, it is noted that the subsection, using general terms, declares that 'no deduction is to be made in respect of general average contributions to those repairs payable by other interests'. This raises the question whether the expense of future salvage operations payable by other interests may be added to the cost of repairs. The provision is capable of admitting to two interpretations.

A literal construction of the subsection should allow the whole sum of the general average contributions 'payable by other interests' to be added to the

---

140 Arnould, para 1200.
141 (1866) LR 1 QB 520; 6 B & S 723.
142 [1891] AC 107.

cost of repairs. The words 'cost of repairs' are wide and neutral enough to include all expenses which would necessarily have to be incurred to raise the ship and her cargo in order to place the whole adventure in a position of safety. Arnould has observed that: '... on one view of the construction of the subsection the words "cost of repairs" are intended to cover all those expenses, including salvage operations, which would have to be incurred before the ship was restored to a navigable condition'.[143]

Furthermore, it has to be said that as no exception is made in the subsection as regards such an expense, it would not be unreasonable to assume that the whole sum of the general average contribution payable by the other interests, including *expense of salvage operations*, is to be added to the cost of repairs.

If the raising of the ship is necessary for the safety of both ship and goods, the expense therefor would be regarded as for general average. As an integral part of the process of lifting the whole adventure from a position of danger, the cargo interests which have benefited from the operation are expected to make a contribution towards it.[144] Such an interpretation would not only be in line with the wording of the subsection, but would also promote consistency in the law. It would, however, oppose the rule laid down in *Kemp v Halliday*, decided before the passing of the Act.

On the other hand, it could also with equal force be argued that, as the expense of future salvage payable by other interests is not expressly stipulated in the subsection as an item which may be added to the cost of repairs, it should be deducted. Arnould, attracted to this line of reasoning, states that[145] ' ... although s 60 of the Act expressly states that no deduction need be made in respect of general average contributions to the cost of repairs, it makes no such concession with regard to the expense of salvage operations. The implication is that general average contributions to expenses of the latter class must be deducted'.[146]

Support for this interpretation can also be derived from the next part of the subsection, which is concerned with items that may be added to the cost of repairs: It specifies that account is to be taken of the 'expense of future salvage operation and of future general average contributions to which the *ship* would be liable if repaired'. Again, by implication, it is possible to contend that, as the expense of future salvage operations payable by other interests is not expressly included in this list as an element which the shipowner may add to the cost of repairs, it has to be excluded from the cost of repairs. Such a construction would be in line with the ruling in *Kemp v Halliday*, which will now be considered.

The rule in Kemp v Halliday

The facts of the case are as follows. The vessel laden with cargo suffered severe damage in a storm and had to put into a port of refuge for repair. Whilst she

---

143 See Arnould, para 1202. Thus, the 'cost of repairs' is taken in the wider sense to include the cost of raising or salving the vessel in order that she may be repaired.

144 The position would, of course, be different if the expense of salvage operations is incurred to raise only the ship.

145 Arnould, para 1201.

146 But is the expense of salvage not an integral element of a general average contribution?

was undergoing repairs, she sank at her moorings in a violent squall with some cargo still on board. Surveyors had formed the judgment that the ship, submerged in deep water with heavy cargo on board, was in imminent danger of destruction, and that the most convenient mode of saving the ship or cargo, or both, was by raising the ship together with the cargo. It was estimated that it would cost more to raise and repair than she would be worth when repaired. Relying on this advice, the plaintiffs accordingly gave notice of abandonment and claimed that the vessel was a constructive total loss. Three days later, a surveyor, acting solely on his own initiative, commenced salvage operations, and eventually succeeded in raising the ship with all the cargo on board.

The question for the court was whether the amount of general average (in the nature of expense for salvage operations) which would be contributed by the cargo must be taken into account in determining whether or not the ship was a constructive total loss. The outcome of the case was critically dependent upon whether this item was to be taken into account in estimating the cost of repairs. If the expense for salvage was not allowed in the calculation, it would reduce the total cost of repair, and accordingly the loss would not qualify as a constructive total loss.

In the Court of Queen's Bench, Mr Justice Blackburn held that there was neither an actual nor a constructive total loss. As regards the latter, he was of the opinion that the contribution of the cargo to the general average must be taken into account, thus reducing the cost of raising the ship. Mr Justice Shee was of the contrary opinion, but withdrew his judgment. Judgment was thus awarded in favour of the defendant.

In delivering the judgment of the court in the special case, Chief Justice Erle said:[147]

> 'But we hold that the plaintiff, in considering whether the submersion of his ship, containing cargo ... was a constructive total loss, was bound to take into his estimate the fact that cargo would be saved by the operation which raised the ship, and would contribute to the expense thereof ...'

The decision of the court was based on two main grounds. First, if need be, it was prepared to invoke the good old common law – the prudent uninsured owner test – to arrive at its decision. Secondly, the more important of the two, it was greatly influenced, and rightly so, by the fact that the shipowner would have a lien on the cargo to secure the payment of that general average.[148] The court said:[149]

> '... the plaintiff, in calculating the cost of raising, was bound to take into his estimate the contribution which would become due to him from the cargo secured to him by a lien thereon; and if so, the special case provides that the defendant should succeed.'

---

147 (1866) LR 1 QB 520 at p 527.

148 Under current practice, a shipowner would, for the release of the cargo (the lien), exact an average bond from its owner.

149 *Ibid.*

But the same can be said for all the components of a general average contribution.[150] If this is the basis for the rule, one can then ask why has the Act expressly allowed 'general average contributions ... payable by other interests' to be added to the cost of repairs? Should the expense of salvage operations be treated differently?

Kemp v Halliday was decided in 1866. Thus parliament cannot claim that it was unaware of this 40 year old principle of law when it passed the Marine Insurance Act in 1906. Whether parliament had intended to overrule *Kemp v Halliday* when it enacted s 60(2)(ii) (or more accurately its first limb) is unclear. The question which has now to be examined is whether it is permissible to use *Kemp v Halliday* to interpret the statutory law on the subject. Such a recourse would not, of course, be allowed if the wording of the section is in itself unambiguous. Section 91(2) declares: 'The rules of the Common Law, including the law merchant, save in so far as they are inconsistent with the express provisions of this Act, shall continue to apply to contracts of marine insurance'. Indeed, this is all very well, but unless the meaning of the express provision of the Act is known, it is not possible to say whether a section is or is not inconsistent with the rules of the common law.

As was seen, the wording of the subsection itself is capable of admitting to two conflicting meanings. On the one hand, based on a strict interpretation of its wording, it would appear that the whole of the general average contribution (including expenses for salvage operation) payable should be added to the repair costs. On the other, based primarily on the rule in *Kemp v Halliday* and a strained construction of the subsection, expenses for salvage payable by other interests ought to be deducted from the cost of repairs. Neither approach appears to be satisfactory – the reason being that in the case of the former, it is hard to see the rationale for the rule; in the latter it opposes the tenor of the section.

It is difficult to see the sense for giving a different treatment to a general average contribution towards salvage expenses. As the subsection has not expressly stated that it should be deducted from the repair bill, the general rule (of inclusion) should apply. Viewed in this light, one could say that s 60(2)(ii) has overruled *Kemp v Halliday*. Surely, we should safely be able to assume that parliament must have had the rule of *Kemp v Halliday* in mind when it drafted the Act. If it had wanted to preserve the *Kemp v Halliday* principle, it could have easily created an exception to the rule.

The language used in this part of the subsection is intolerably imprecise. That the underlying principle of the matter was not fully considered is obvious. Summing up, the scales are, as Arnould has found, '... so nicely balanced that it scarcely seems possible to prefer one view or the other'. In reality, it is not the rule in *Kemp v Halliday* which is difficult to accept, but the general rule laid

---

150 Expenditure incurred by a shipowner for the common safety of the adventure may, *inter alia*, include any of the following items: expenses for lightening a ship; expenses at port of refuge; wages and maintenance of crew and other expenses bearing up for and in a port of refuge; cost for temporary repairs; and salvage whether incurred under contract or otherwise. See the York-Antwerp Rules, 1994 (see Appendix 24), for a complete list of items allowable as general average.

down in s 60(2)(ii). To have to rely on innuendoes in order to ascertain the meaning of a provision is clearly not the best approach to adopt in order to ascertain the meaning of a section.

This whole area of law on a rather important issue is in need of clarification: a clear ruling on the subject is urgently required. In order to arrive at any meaningful understanding, the underlying basis of the matter has to be fully and carefully examined.

'Expense of future salvage operations and of future general average contributions to which the ship would be liable if repaired'

This is another provision which could be phrased in clearer terms. The word 'but' is misleading and can cause confusion.[151] It does not really add anything to the rest of the sentence which could well stand on its own. The phrase 'account is to be taken' means that the two items listed, namely, the expense of future salvage operations and of any future general average contributions to which the ship would be liable if repaired, may be added to the cost of repairs. As such expenses have necessarily to be incurred because of a peril insured against, the assured should be allowed to include them in the repair costs.

Meaning of 'future'

The adjective 'future' is used for both the expense of salvage operations and of general average contributions. As it is not defined, it is also capable of generating problems. However, it connotes a prospective event, or an event of time to come; it has to be 'counted' or 'measured' from a particular event or date. The section does not specify with reference to what time or event the salvage operations are 'future'. The time of the 'future' could commence from the date of the casualty or the date of the giving of the notice of abandonment. Arnould has correctly stated the law as:[152]

> 'If notice of abandonment is rightly given the loss dates back to the casualty, and the test for ascertaining whether or not there is a constructive total loss ought presumably to be applied, actually or notionally, at the same date.'

'Salvage operations'

First, it is observed that the term used is not 'salvage charges' but 'salvage operations'. This alone should be adequate to discount pure maritime salvage from the scope of the subsection. Support for this contention can also be found in the word 'expense': pure maritime salvage is never referred as an 'expense' but as an 'award'. According to Arnould, a pure salvage award, whether derived from maritime law or under LOF does not cause any serious difficulty.[153] The reason being that: 'Since liability attaches to each party only for that part of the total cost that is referable to his own interest, and can therefore be no question of contribution.'[154]

---

151 On first reading, it could give the impression that 'no deduction is to be made in respect of general average contribution ...', but deduction is to be made to future salvage operations.
152 See Arnould, para 1203.
153 See Appendix 25.
154 Arnould, at para 1201

General average contributions

This part of the section has to be read with s 66(4) which allows an assured the right to recover from the insurer the proportion of the general average loss (expenditure and sacrifice) which falls upon him.[155]

DAMAGE TO GOODS

Sections 60(1) and 60(2)(i)

To recapitulate, there are essentially four types of constructive total losses of goods, three of which have already been discussed, and the last is to be examined here. As was seen, a claim for a constructive total loss of goods may be made when:

- the goods are 'reasonably abandoned' on account of their actual total loss appearing to be 'unavoidable': s 60(1) and cl 13 of the ICC;

- the goods are 'reasonably abandoned' because 'it could not be preserved from actual total loss without an expenditure which would exceed its value when the expenditure had been incurred': s 60(1) and cl 13 of the ICC; and

- the assured has been deprived of the possession of his goods, and (a) it is unlikely that he can recover them, or (b) the cost of recovering them would exceed their value when recovered: s 60(2)(i)(a) or (b) and cl 13 of the ICC.

The first and second involve a loss of voyage or adventure by reason of a practical and commercial impossibility, respectively. And in the third case, whether the goods are or are not damaged is inconsequential.

Section 60(2)(iii) is in fact an exemplification of the general concept of a constructive total loss defined in the second limb of s 60(1).[156] It has to be noted that, as the opening words suggest, this subsection to s 60 is applicable only if the goods are physically damaged, and the damage is repairable. Under this head of claim, unlike a case falling within s 60(2)(i), the assured does not have to be deprived of the possession of his goods.

Cost of repairing the damage

As far as s 60(2)(i) is concerned, whether the goods, of which the assured has been deprived of possession, are or are not themselves physically damaged is really quite irrelevant. By this section, the assured is not claiming that the cost of repairing the damage (if any), but of 'recovering' the goods, is uneconomical.[157]

---

155 For a fuller discussion of general average loss, see Chapter 17.

156 Lord Wright in *The Rickards Case* [1941] 3 All ER 62 at p 79, HL, said that 'Subsection (2), as compared with subsection (1), is thus additional, and not merely illustrative'. The choice of the words 'not merely' could be interpreted to mean that s 60(2) does more than just simply illustrate the general terms of s 60(1).

157 The word 'recovery' here is used in the sense of a recovery from a third party who is in possession of the goods: *Stringer v English and Scottish Marine Insurance Co* (1869), LR 4 QB 677; (1870) LR 5 QB 599, CA.

But should the goods be also damaged, he would also be able to invoke s 60(2)(iii) (and cl 13 of the ICC) in support of his claim for a constructive total loss.

Section 60(2)(iii) allows the assured in the case of damage to goods to take into account not only the cost of repairing the damage, but also the cost of forwarding the goods to their destination for the purpose of determining whether they are a constructive total loss. As s 60(2)(iii) does not envisage a loss of possession of the goods, it should not come as a surprise that the cost of 'recovery' is not included.

Clause 13 of the ICC, as was seen earlier, declares a most comprehensive rule on a constructive total loss for goods. The second part of the clause has brought the concepts of the second part of s 60(1), s 60(2)(i)(b), and s 60(2)(iii)[158] all under one umbrella. In this format, it would appear that should the cost of either recovering, reconditioning, or forwarding the goods, (to its insured destination) exceed their value on arrival, there is a constructive total loss. It is to be noted that, unlike the Institute Hulls Clauses,[159] it is the value of the goods on arrival, not their insured value, which is to be taken for the purpose of comparison.

The cost of 'forwarding' the goods

The main controversy as regards this section relates to the word 'forwarding', which also appears in cl 13 of the ICC. Whether the assured may add the whole or only the additional cost of forwarding the goods to their proper destination was considered in a pre-statute case, *Farnworth v Hyde*.[160] The law before the Act was that only the additional freight (if any) payable may be included in the calculation. Whether s 60(2)(iii) has altered the legal position is unclear. It could be argued that if parliament, which we can only assume was well aware of the existence of this rule when it drafted the section, had intended to depart from the common law rule of *Farnworth v Hyde*, it would have made a point of using clearer terms.[161]

Any loss of the original bill of lading freight sustained by the assured (which if paid in advance) would be recoverable under his freight policy. As such, it could be argued that a prudent uninsured owner would probably not take this into account in his calculation. The extra freight payable, which he has not insured under his freight policy, ought therefore to be added to the cost. Clause 13 does not in any way help to resolve this problem.

---

158 If 'reconditioning' appearing in cl 13 is taken to have the same meaning as 'repairing' in s 60(2)(iii). As opposed to 'repairing', the word 'reconditioning' is also capable of a lesser meaning of just rendering the goods in a state (like temporary repairs made to a ship) in order for that they may safely undertake the journey to their proper destination.

159 See cl 19.1 of the ITCH(95) and cl 17.1 of the IVCH(95).

160 (1866) LR 2 CP 204, which applied the rule in *Rosetto v Gurney* (1851) 11 CP 176. For a detailed analysis of the pros and cons of the rule in *Farnworth v Hyde*; see Arnould at paras. 1224–1230.

161 Parliament has yet again left another matter in doubt: the problem here is identical to that encountered in s 60(2)(ii) which, when read with *Kemp v Halliday* (1866) LR 1 QB 520; 6 B & S 723, has left the law with much uncertainty.

EFFECT OF CONSTRUCTIVE TOTAL LOSS

Abandonment of the subject-matter insured

Sections 61, 62 and 63 spell out what may be described as the procedural aspects of the law relating to constructive total loss. They lay down the steps which an assured has to take to 'validate' his claim for a constructive total loss. Section 61 should be read with s 62(1): the former relates to abandonment of the subject-matter insured, whilst the latter to the notice of abandonment which the assured has to give to the insurer when he elects to treat the loss as if it were 'an actual total loss'. Section 62(1) provides that:

> 'Subject to the provisions of this section, where the assured elects to abandon the subject-matter to the insurer he must give notice of abandonment. If he fails to do so the loss can only be treated as a partial loss.'

The opening words of s 61 are significant: only 'Where there is a constructive total loss' may the assured 'abandon' the subject-matter insured to the insurer. But once he has decided to 'abandon' the subject-matter insured, he has to manifest his intention by giving the insurer a notice of abandonment.

Meaning of 'abandon'

The word 'abandon' is used here in a sense quite different from that in s 57 discussed earlier.[162] As expressly stated in s 61, the abandonment is to be made by the assured 'to the insurer'. The meaning of the word 'abandon', the purpose of a notice of abandonment, and various other aspects of the doctrine of abandonment were all given a thorough examination by the House of Lords in *Rankin v Potter*.[163] Later, a few more words on the subject were added by the Court of Appeal in *Kaltenbach v Mackenzie*.[164]

Mr Baron Martin in *Rankin v Potter*[165] expressed the opinion that '... there is not a word in the English language used in a more highly artificial and technical sense than the word "abandon"'. He was conscious of the fact that the words 'abandonment' and 'notice of abandonment', though frequently confounded together in expression, are distinct and separate concepts.[166] As regards the former, he said:[167]

> '... in reference to a constructive total loss, it is defined to be a cession or transfer of the ship from the owner to the underwriter, and of all his property and

---

162 See above for a discussion of the meaning of 'abandon' appearing in s 60(1).

163 (1873) LR 6 HL 83.

164 (1878) 3 CPD 467; 4 Asp MLA 39, CA. Reference will be made only to the first citation as it contains a fuller report of the case, hereinafter referred to as *The Kaltenbach Case*.

165 (1873) LR 6 HL 83. A panel of judges – Mr Baron Martin, Mr Baron Bramwell, Blackburn J, Mellor J, Keating J and Brett J – was summoned to advise the House, presided by Lord Chelmsford, Lord Colonsay and Lord Hatherley.

166 In similar vein, Blackburn J, *ibid*, at p 118, remarked: 'This cession or abandonment is a very different thing from a notice of abandonment, though the ambiguous word, "abandonment", often leads to confounding the two'.

167 *Ibid* at p 144.

interest in it, with all the claims that may arise from its ownership, and all the profits that may arise from it ...'

When an assured 'abandons' the subject-matter insured, he is effectively relinquishing all his rights in the property to the insurer.

The basis for this requirement of abandonment is explained by Mr Justice Brett in *Rankin v Potter* in the following terms:[168]

'The end to be obtained by abandonment would seem to be the preservation of the cardinal principle of marine insurance, the principle of indemnity, and to that end to prevent the assured from having at the same time payment in full of the sum insured, and the thing insured, a thing of value, in his hands.'

Notice of abandonment

Once an assured has decided to claim for a constructive total loss – giving up his interest in the subject-matter insured or the remains of it – he has to notify the insurer of his intention to denounce his rights in the property. The requirement to give a notice of abandonment is peculiar to marine insurance; Lord Justice Brett said that he was not aware of its existence in any contract of indemnity, except in the case of contracts of marine insurance.[169] But having said that, there is really nothing mysterious about abandonment or the giving of a notice of abandonment, the purpose of which was described by Lord Porter in *Rankin v Potter*[170] as follows:

'In cases of marine insurance, the regular mercantile mode of letting the underwriters know that the assured mean to come upon them for a complete indemnity, is by giving notice of abandonment, which is a very different thing from the abandonment or cession itself. This notice when given is conclusive ... the consequence of which is that everything is ceded to ... the underwriters.'

In *The Kaltenbach Case*,[171] Lord Justice Cotton offered two reasons for the requirement of a notice of abandonment. The first is that an assured, on giving the notice, 'cannot go back from his decision'; and the second, the insurers on receipt of the notice may then 'do the best they can and make the most they can'[172] as regards the claim and, in particular, the subject-matter insured or what remains of it.

A further explanation can be found in the following passage of the judgment of Lord Justice Brett who, relying on practical grounds, remarked:[173]

'Now, a loss may occur in any part of the world, and losses frequently occur in places where the underwriter has no power to get notice of the loss except from the assured, and there must be great danger that the owner of the ship or goods might take his own time to consider what to do, and to wait and find out

---

168 *Ibid*, at p 101.
169 (1878) 3 CPD 467 at p 471, CA; 4 Asp MLC 39, CA.
170 (1873) LR 6 HL 83 at p 119.
171 (1878) 3 CPD 467 at 471, CA.
172 4 Asp MLC 39, at p 42, CA.
173 (1878) 3 CPD 467 at p 472, CA.

whether the markets were likely to rise or fall before he arrived at any decision, and this is the reason why in all cases it is made a part of the contract that, when there is a claim for constructive total loss, notice of abandonment must be given.'

He thought that the notice of abandonment was 'introduced by the unanimous consent of shipowners and underwriters, and has therefore become part of their contract'. It has become a condition precedent to the validity of a claim for a constructive total loss.[174]

A condition precedent

In the course of the development of the law of the doctrine of abandonment, there was at one stage a degree of confusion as regards the function of a notice of abandonment. Not surprisingly, this was partly brought about by the use of the words 'condition precedent'. The point of debate was framed in *Roura & Forgas v Townend*[175] as, 'whether the giving of such notice is an integral element of a constructive total loss or is rather a condition precedent to a claim by the owner of ship and goods based upon such a loss'. As will be seen, the operative word here is 'claim'.

In *The Robertson Case*, Lord Wright took time in the House of Lords to clarify the confusion in the following way:[176]

'... notice of abandonment is not an essential ingredient of a constructive total loss. The Appellant's argument confuses two different concepts, because it confuses constructive total loss with the *right to claim* for a constructive total loss. The right to claim ... depends on due notice of abandonment under s 62 of the Act. The distinction is explicitly stated in s 61 ... The section makes it clear that the right to abandon only arises when there is a constructive total loss *in fact*. That is the necessary precondition to a right to abandon.'

As Lord Porter's summary of this legal issue is concise and illuminating it may be useful, for a deeper understanding of the point, to quote a passage from his judgment:[177]

'... abandonment may be a condition or consequence of recovery and not a condition precedent to the existence of a total loss whether actual or constructive. A constructive total loss may exist, but if the assured wishes to take advantage of it he must give notice of abandonment, at any rate in a case where there would be any possibility of benefit to the insurer.'

A notice of abandonment is not an essential ingredient of a constructive total loss, but is an essential prerequisite to claim for a constructive total loss. It has to be said that a notice of abandonment cannot convert what is otherwise not a constructive total loss into a constructive total loss. It must be borne in mind that the subject-matter insured must first be a constructive total loss to justify the giving of a notice of abandonment. In other words, a constructive total loss must exist before a notice of abandonment can be given.

---

174 See also *Vacuum Oil Co v Union Insurance Society of Canton* (1926) 25 Ll L Rep 546 at p 553, CA, for further discussion of the objectives of a notice of abandonment; see below.

175 [1919] 1 KB 189.

176 [1939] AC 371 at p 381, HL. Emphasis added.

177 *Ibid*, at p 393, HL.

An 'idle ceremony'

There are exceptions to the general rule requiring the giving of a notice of abandonment. Should it constitute an 'idle ceremony' or a pointless exercise, both statute and case law are prepared to dispense with the requirement. There are essentially three circumstances where the giving of a notice of abandonment would be an 'idle ceremony'. The first, expressed in general terms in s 62(7) occurs when 'no possibility of benefit to the insurer' could arise even if notice were given to him. The second, specifically declared by common law, is in relation to freight: this is now probably subsumed under s 62(7); and the third, governed by s 62(9) relates to re-insurance.

No possibility of benefit to the insurer

Section 62(7) which is of general application states that:

'Notice of abandonment is unnecessary where at the time when the assured receives information of the loss there would be no possibility of benefit to the insurer if notice were given to him.'

The origin of this exception to the general rule can be traced to the much celebrated case of *Rankin v Potter*,[178] where the term 'idle ceremony' was used by most of the judges. Leaving the niceties of the other issues in the case for discussion elsewhere, it is suffice here to say that the House, adopting the opinions of the majority of the judges, held that in so far as freight was concerned, no notice of abandonment need be given. Some of the judges were of the view that, as there was an actual total loss of freight, the assured was not required to give notice of abandonment. Others, without giving a direct answer to the question as regards constructive total loss of freight, took the safe route by supporting their decision with the explanation that the giving of a notice of abandonment was in any event, in the circumstances of the case, excused because there was in reality nothing to abandon. Thus, there was no necessity for the assured to give notice of abandonment of the chartered freight to the underwriters.[179]

In contrast, *The Kaltenbach Case* was able, by reason of the facts of the case, to provide a more direct account of the law relating to the requirement of a notice of abandonment. As the subject-matter was in relation to a constructive total loss of a ship (and not freight) it lent itself more easily for the court to provide a more 'honest' statement of the law in this regard. The facts of the case have to be reiterated, as they are particularly relevant for the purpose of illustrating the principle of law established therein. Briefly, the plaintiff's vessel was insured for a voyage with the defendants. On 22 January, she struck upon a bank and was damaged. She was surveyed on 24 and was recommended that she should be sold. On 7 February, the owners made up their minds to sell her and wrote to the captain to that effect. On 11 she was condemned, and on 23 she was sold. On 11 March, the plaintiffs claimed for a total loss against the insurers.

178 (1873) LR 6 HL 83. Though the case is primarily concerned with the question as to whether a notice of abandonment is required as regards a total loss of freight, it is also well known as the authority which is concerned with the sensitive issue of whether there is such a concept as a constructive total loss of freight.

179 *Ibid*, at p 157.

The question as to whether the sale was or was not justifiable need not concern us here, for the court was prepared to accept the fact that the ship was (before the sale) in such a condition that the assured was entitled to abandon her and claim for a constructive total loss. On this basis, the court was then able to proceed to determine whether the assured was excused from giving notice of abandonment. The plaintiffs argued that, as it was impossible for them to communicate to the insurers in time to enable them to take any advantage of the situation, or to give any orders in reference to the vessel, it was not necessary for them to give a notice of abandonment; and even if the defendants were to receive a notice of abandonment, they could not have obtained any benefit from it.

Lord Justice Brett, after having closely examined the sequence of events, concluded that the plaintiffs ought either on 7 February, by the next post, or next telegraph to have sent forward the notice to the insurers. None of the judges was able to find an excuse to absolve the assured from the necessity of having to give notice of abandonment; notifying the insurer of the circumstances was in the circumstances of the case not an idle ceremony. The rationale for the decision can be found in a remark made by Lord Justice Theisger:[180]

'One can see that if at any moment an assured, who is entitled to treat a loss as a constructive total loss, may at the same time absolve himself from the necessity of giving notice of abandonment by selling the vessel, which although a prudent course, is not a necessary course, it would lead to the greatest danger of fraud upon the underwriters, and at all event to very considerable inconvenience in reference to policies of marine insurance.'

For a post-statute authority on the subject, reference should be made to *Vacuum Oil Co v Union Insurance Soc of Canton*,[181] where Lord Justice Bankes in the Court of Appeal gave an insight into his conception of the statutory term 'no possibility of benefit.' He said:

'What it means ... is that when the circumstances are such that the underwriter, if the goods had been abandoned and he had had the absolute control over them, could have exercised that control and done what he thought best under the circumstances.'

In simple terms, the criterion is: were the insurers in a position to make something out of the property?[182] More recently in *The Litsen Pride*,[183] salvage of a vessel sunk in a war zone was impracticable, and so abandonment could not have benefited the insurers. Mr Justice Hirst said:[184]

'I hold that there was no possibility of benefit to the underwriters if notice had been given, since any notion of salvage was completely impracticable by reason of the place where, and the war-time circumstances in which, this vessel was sunk.'

---

180 (1878) 3 CPD 467 at p 486, CA.

181 (1926) 25 Ll L Rep 546 at p 549, CA.

182 *Per* Sargant LJ, *ibid*.

183 [1985] 1 Lloyd's Rep 437 QBD.

184 *Ibid*, at p 478.

Sale of the subject-matter insured

A master of a ship may be, by reason of necessity in an emergency, entitled to sell either the ship and/or the goods. Though he may not have express authority from the owners to sell, nonetheless, his act, if it arises from necessity, would bind the owners. Thus, a constructive loss could be accompanied by the sale of the subject matter-insured.

With the advancement in communication, the problems relating to a sale by the master are unlikely to arise. Thus, it is unnecessary to analyse the extensive comments made on this aspect of the law in *Farnworth v Hyde*,[185] *Rankin v Potter*[186] and *The Kaltenbach Case*.[187] Perhaps, all that is required to be mentioned here is the principle of law delivered by Lord Justice Brett, in *The Kaltenbach Case*, which reads as follows:[188]

> 'A sale cannot make a total loss; notice of abandonment cannot enable the assured to recover for a total loss unless the sale was justifiable by the circumstances, and the circumstances were such as to justify a person in claiming for a total loss. The constructive total loss, in other words, must exist before either the sale or the notice of abandonment; the circumstances must be such as to justify it.'

Briefly, this means that the ship or goods must be in a condition 'to justify what was done afterwards, otherwise the fact of sale or the fact of giving notice of abandonment had no effect whatever.'[189]

Reasonable time

Section 62(3) provides:

> 'Notice of abandonment must be given with reasonable diligence after the receipt of reliable information of the loss, but where the information is of a doubtful character the assured is entitled to a reasonable time to make inquiry.'

An assured is not expected, on receipt of information of the loss of his ship, to react immediately to give notice of abandonment. He is allowed by law a reasonable period of time to determine the exact nature of the loss, and to decide on the course of action which he should take.

Lord Justice Brett in *The Kaltenbach Case*,[190] who had devoted some time to consider this issue, said: '... the assured must have a reasonable time to ascertain the nature of the loss with which he is made acquainted ... he must have certain and accurate information as to the nature of the damage.' Such is a question of fact.[191] Lord Wright in *Rickards v Forestal Land Co*[192] has, however, placed a limit on the time allowed for reflection. An assured would not be allowed '... to await events to see how things turn out or to decide what may best suit his interests'.

---

185 (1866) LR 2 CP 204; 18 CB (NS) 835; 34 LL (CP) 207.
186 (1873) LR 6 HL 83, HL.
187 (1878) 3 CPD 467, CA.
188 *Ibid*, at p 476.
189 *Ibid*, at p 475.
190 *Ibid*, at p 472, CA.
191 See s 88.
192 [1942] AC 50 at p 79, HL.

Form of notice of abandonment

Section 62(2) states that a notice of abandonment:

> '... may be given in writing or by word of mouth or partly in writing and partly by word of mouth and may be given in any terms which indicate the intention of the assured to abandon his interest in the subject matter insured unconditionally to the insurer.'

In *Parmeter v Todhunter*,[193] it was held that 'an implied parol abandonment is too uncertain, and cannot be supported'. In this case, the insurers were simply given directions as to how the ship and cargo were to be disposed of. As this alone did not manifest an intention to abandon the subject-matter insured, it was held not to constitute a proper notice of abandonment.

Acceptance of notice of abandonment

There is no duty imposed on the insurer either to accept or reject a notice of abandonment, though in practice they are very rarely accepted. He may choose to remain silent the effect of which does not constitute acceptance of the notice. This is clarified by s 62(5). The acceptance of an abandonment may be either express or implied. If the behaviour of the insurer is such that it can only be construed as being consistent with their having accepted the abandonment, then they will be held to have impliedly accepted the abandonment by their conduct.[194] But, of course, any measure taken by the assured or the underwriters with the object of saving, protecting or recovering the subject-matter insured shall not, by cl 11.3 of the ITCH(95) and cl 9.3 of the IVCH(95), be considered as a waiver or acceptance of the abandonment or otherwise prejudice the rights of either party.

The assured may at any time withdraw his notice of abandonment, but the underwriters, once they have accepted the notice, cannot withdraw their acceptance: they are bound by their acceptance[195] unless it was accepted under a mistake of fact.[196] A notice of abandonment acts merely as 'an offer' which remains executory unless and until it is accepted. As pointed out by Mr Justice Atkinson in *Pesquerias y Secaderos de Espana SA v Beer*,[197] 'until it is accepted the assured has the right to look for intervening events which may restore in whole or in part his former situation, and may limit his claim accordingly if it suits him better to claim as for a partial loss ...'. This right of withdrawal preserves the right of the assured to treat a constructive total loss as a partial loss.[198]

---

193 (1808) 1 Camp 540.

194 *Hudson v Harrison* (1821) 3 Brod & Bing 9. Cf *Provincial Insurance Co of Canada v Leduc* (1874) LR 6 PC 224; and *Captain J A Cates Tug & Wharfage Co Ltd v Franklin Insurance Co* (1927) 137 LT 709, PC. Merely requesting that the assured should do the best they can with the damaged property was held in *Thellusson v Flethcer* (1793) 1 Esp NP 72, not to amount to an acceptance.

195 See *Smith v Robertson* (1814) 2 Dow 474.

196 *Norwich Union Fire Insurance Soc v Price* [1934] AC 455 at p 467.

197 (1946) 79 Ll L Rep 417, at p 433, KB, reversed on the facts on appeal, (1947) 80 Ll L Rep 318, CA.

198 Section 61.

Ademption of loss

Whenever there is a constructive total loss, the sequence of events following from the casualty would generally begin with the assured electing to abandon the subject-matter insured to the insurer; this would be followed by the giving of a notice of abandonment, then the issuing of a writ, the trial, and, finally, the delivery of the court's verdict. During this period of time, there is every likelihood that events (beyond the control of the parties) may change: property may be restored – a captured ship could be released – and a constructive total loss may by reason of a change in circumstances become only a partial loss. This raises a question of considerable importance: what point in time is to be taken for determining when there is a constructive total loss?

For certainty in the law, a cut-off point has to be set from which any event occurring thereafter would be considered as inconsequential and of no avail to either of the parties to the contract. An event or time has to be determined from which moment the rights of the parties are regarded as fixed and unaffected by anything which may happen between that date and the verdict of the trial.

In *Ruys v Royal Exchange Assurance Corpn*,[199] Mr Justice Collin who, after having conducted a most careful and meticulous research on the subject, arrived at the following conclusion:

> 'But the object of litigation being to settle disputes, it is obvious that some date must be fixed upon when the respective rights of the parties may be finally ascertained, and the line of the writ may be regarded as a line of convenience which has been settled by uniform practice for at least seventy years ...'

The assured in this case, upon the capture of the vessel, immediately gave notice of abandonment and, shortly afterwards commenced an action on the policy. By the time of the trial, the war being at an end, the ship was returned to her owners. Applying the above rule, Mr Justice Collins held that the return of the ship after the commencement of the action did not disentitle the owners of the right to recover as for a constructive total loss.

In the House of Lords in *The Blairmore*,[200] the facts of which could be more relevantly discussed elsewhere to illustrate another related issue, Lord Herschell framed the English principle of law as follows:

> 'I take it, then, that the general rule applicable is, according to the law of this country, that if in the interval between the notice of abandonment and the time when legal proceedings are commenced there has been a change of circumstances reducing the loss from a total to a partial one, or, in other words, if at the time of action brought the circumstances are such that a notice of abandonment would not be justifiable, the assured can only recover for a partial loss.'

In summing up, reference should be made to the succinct and informative remarks made in the Court of Appeal in *The Polurrian Case*:[201]

199 [1897] 2 QB 135 at p 142.
200 [1898] AC 593 at p 610, HL.
201 (1915) 1 KB 922 at p 929 CA.

'Now it is indisputable that, according to the law of England, in deciding upon the validity of claims of this nature between the assured and the insurer, the matters must be considered as they stood on the date of the commencement of the action. That is the governing date. If there then existed a right to maintain a claim for a constructive total loss by capture, that right would not be affected by a subsequent recovery or restoration of the insured vessel.'

For a more recent confirmation of this rule by a higher authority, reference should be made to *The Rickards Case*[202] where Lord Wright of the House of Lords expressed his approval of the historical account given of the law by Mr Justice Collins in *Ruys v Royal Exchange Assurance Corpn.*[203]

The above principle is sometimes, in the law of marine insurance, referred to as the theory of 'ademption of loss'. Basically, restoration of the subject-matter insured before (but not after) the commencement of an action could preclude a claim. The Act is silent on this point, but the authorities decided after the passing of the Act have, without qualification, confirmed the validity of the rule.

In practice, there is in effect no problem, as the date of the giving of the notice of abandonment is almost invariably taken as the date of the issue of the writ. The current position is vividly described by the trial judge, Mr Justice Pickford, in *The Polurrian Case*[204] as follows:

'... the underwriters are asked in case they refuse to accept the abandonment to put the assured in the same position as if a writ had been issued. In nine cases out of ten, and probably a much larger proportion, the underwriters agree to do so, and, if they did not, the consequence is that the assured issues his writ immediately, and therefore the two dates in ordinary English insurance practice correspond.'

More recently, in *The Bamburi*,[205] the usual practice of agreeing to place the assured in the same position as if a writ had been issue was again confirmed.

The waiver clause

The above discussion on a change of circumstances relates to events beyond the control of the parties. But should either party interfere with the subject-matter insured after the loss, cl 11.3 of the ITCH(95) and cl 9.3 of the IVCH(95) would apply. It provides that:

'Measures taken by the assured or the underwriters with the object of saving, protecting or recovering the subject-matter insured shall not be considered as a waiver or acceptance of abandonment or otherwise prejudice the rights of either party.'

---

202 [1941] 3 All ER 62 at p 80, *per* Lord Wright: 'By the English common law, the date of giving notice of abandonment was not treated as the decisive date, which was taken up to be the date of issuing the writ in the action.'

203 (1897) 2 QB 135.

204 (1913) 19 Com Cas 143 at p 153; on appeal (1915) 1 KB 922.

205 [1982] 1 Lloyd's Rep 312. See also *Panamanian Oriental SS Corpn v Wright* [1970] 2 Lloyd's Rep 365, QB, where the insurer had agreed to place the assured in the same position as if a writ had been issued.

Just as an assured would not be allowed to take advantage of any benefit which he had derived from interfering with the subject-matter insured, likewise, an insurer would not be allowed to convert what was in effect a total (actual or constructive) loss into a partial loss, by raising the ship,[206] without the consent of the shipowner.

---

206 See *The Blairmore Case* [1898] AC 593, HL.

CHAPTER 16

PARTICULAR AVERAGE LOSS

MEANING OF 'PARTICULAR AVERAGE LOSS'

Section 64(1) declares that: 'A particular average loss is a *partial loss* of the subject-matter insured, caused by a peril insured against, and which is not a general average loss'. The term 'partial loss' is generic[1] and should not be loosely used to refer to a 'particular average loss'. Thus, if one wishes to be precise or pedantic, the terms should not, strictly speaking, be used interchangeably as if they are synonymous. The Act, though it has taken care to distinguish between the different types of partial losses,[2] is nevertheless itself guilty of using the terms indiscriminately.

General average losses, salvage charges, and particular charges (sue and labour charges) are all examples of a partial loss. However, general average and particular charges have been expressly excluded from the umbrella of a 'particular average loss' by ss 64(1) and 64(2) respectively. The former states that a particular average loss is a partial loss which is not a general average loss. And s 64(2) states that 'Particular charges are not included in particular average'. Thus, it is fair to say that with the exception of general average and particular charges, all partial losses (including salvage charges) are particular average losses. On an even higher level, one could go further and deduce that all losses, except a total loss, a general average loss and a particular charge, are particular average losses.

It would appear from the above sections that the expression 'particular average loss' was coined simply to distinguish it from general average and particular charges, both of which are extraordinary expenses incurred for the preservation of the maritime property from loss at sea. Thus, it is necessary to distinguish these special types of losses from a particular average loss; and to facilitate a proper understanding of this chapter, a very brief comparison of a particular average loss with these special types of losses will first have to be undertaken.

Particular average loss and general average loss

The main difference between a particular average loss and a general average loss was described in simple but clear language in *Hingston v Wendt* as follows:[3]

'In insurance law, the phrase "general average" is commonly used to express what is chargeable on all, ship, cargo, and freight, and "particular average", to express a charge against some one thing.'

---

1   This is also made obvious by the main heading of the Act which reads as: 'Partial Losses (*including* Salvage and General Average and Particular Charges)'.

2   See, eg, ss 64(2), 65(2), 76(2) and 78(2). It is interesting to note that under its rules relating to the measure of indemnity, the Act has carelessly used the term 'partial loss' in ss 69–71 when, in effect, they can hardly be relevant to a general average loss where the measure of indemnity is specifically laid down in s 73(1). See also s 77(2), discussed below.

3   (1864) 1 QBD 367 at p 371.

Though both must be caused by an insured peril,[4] the fundamental distinction between them lies in the fact that in the case of a particular average loss, there is no question of contribution because the loss lies where it falls – entirely upon the person who has actually suffered the loss. A general average loss (expenditure or sacrifice), however, is a loss voluntarily incurred for the common safety of the adventure. As such, any interested party who has derived benefit from the general average act is legally obliged to make a (rateable) contribution to the party(ies)[5] who has/have suffered the loss.

The operative words are 'particular' and 'general'. In the case of a particular average loss, the liability is 'particular' to the interest which has sustained the loss; whilst in a general average loss, it is 'general' in the sense that all the interested parties must make a contribution to the loss.

Particular average loss and particular charges

The first part of s 64(2) defines 'particular charges' as:

'Expenses incurred by or on behalf of the assured for the safety or preservation of the subject-matter insured, other than general average and salvage charges, are called particular charges.'

That a 'particular charge' is distinct from a 'particular average loss' is made clear in the last sentence of s 64(2).

The key word is 'charges' which are expenses incurred for the preservation of the subject-matter insured. Such charges (or expenses) may be incurred only after an insured peril has caused some damage to the subject-matter insured. The word 'loss' (in the term 'particular average loss'), on the other hand, connotes damage directly sustained by the subject-matter insured caused by a peril insured against.

It is generally accepted that particular charges are recoverable from the insurer by way of the sue and labour clause,[6] even though there is nothing in the Act (not even in s 78 containing the law on sue and labour) which expressly declares that expenses incurred for suing and labouring are recoverable as 'particular charges'. But as the expense to sue and labour is by definition (s 78(4)) one incurred to 'avert or minimise' a loss, it also falls within the scope of the words 'expenses incurred ... for the safety or preservation of the subject-matter insured ...' appearing in s 64(2). Sue and labour charges are thus deemed to be 'particular charges'. But whether there are, besides sue and labour, any other types of particular charges is unclear. The term 'particular charges' is indeed elusive.[7]

---

4   See ss 64(1) and 66(6).

5   See s 66(3).

6   Discussed in Chapter 17.

7   Arnould, at para 1132, states that 'It is not specified anywhere in the Act whether an expense which falls within the definition of "particular charges" may be recovered as a partial loss otherwise that under the suing and labour clause'.

Section 78(1), which confirms that sue and labour charges are recoverable '… notwithstanding that the insurer may have paid for a total loss or that the subject-matter may have been warranted free from particular average, either wholly or under a certain percentage …' gives another hint (besides s 76(2)) that a particular charge is not the same thing as a particular average loss.[8]

Particular average loss and salvage charges

Salvage charges are, however, particular average losses. Though salvage charges are very much like general average and particular charges in the sense that they are also extraordinary expenses incurred to save maritime property from loss at sea, they are also distinct and exist as a separate type of loss. This is clarified by ss 64(2) and 65(2).

Types of partial loss

The term 'partial loss' is simply a handy and general expression used to embrace any loss which is not a total loss. The expression 'particular average loss' covers all types of partial loss, except a general average loss and a particular charge. For the purposes of clarity and discussion, it is necessary to divide partial losses into two classes:

- A loss which arises when the subject-matter insured sustains direct *physical* damage caused by a peril insured against: this type of loss may be described as a true particular average loss; and

- A loss engendered by *extraordinary expenses* incurred, after the casualty had arisen, for rescue operations undertaken to prevent further losses from taking place. General average losses (expenditure or sacrifice), particular charges (and sue and labour charges) and salvage charges[9] are all partial losses, but of an extraordinary nature in the sense that they represent expenses specially incurred for the preservation of the insured subject-matter and/or maritime property, as the case may be, from loss at sea. The nature, incidence, and method of payment of these extraordinary expenses will be discussed in the next chapter.

This chapter will only concentrate on the first type of partial loss where physical damage is sustained by the subject-matter insured. It will cover all the various forms of particular average losses (except salvage charges) on ship, goods and freight.

PARTICULAR AVERAGE LOSS OF SHIP

The divide between certain types of constructive total loss and a particular average loss of a ship may not initially appear to be clear-cut. This is because in

---

8 The engagement to sue and labour is 'supplementary' to the contract of insurance: see s 78(1) and cl 11.6 of the ITCH(95) and cl 9.6 of the IVCH(83).

9 General average and particular charges are not particular average losses.

both cases the damage sustained by the ship is repairable.[10] The extent of the damage[11] and the cost of repairs will, however, determine whether a loss is a constructive total loss or a particular average loss. Should the cost of repairs exceed the value of the ship when repaired,[12] the law would be prepared to regard her as a constructive total loss, but only if her owner chooses to make a claim on that basis.[13] But should the cost of repairs be not commercially prohibitive, the loss to her owners will be for particular average, and the total sum which they are entitled to recover under the policy is known as the 'measure of indemnity'[14] Before embarking upon an analysis of this subject, it is necessary to say a few words about the deductible clause.

The deductible clause

The deductible clause (cl 12.1 of the ITCH(95))[15] is a simplified version of the Common Memorandum under the old SG policy,[16] the purpose of which was to exclude small claims and certain inevitable losses in relation to goods of a perishable and wasteful nature. Instead of being worded as under the common memorandum as 'free from average warranty' (with exceptions), which was indeed a clumsy and contrived formula, the deductible clause of the ITCH(95) states that:

> 'No claim arising from a peril insured against shall be payable ... unless the aggregate of all such claims arising out of each separate accident or occurrence ... exceeds *the deductible amount agreed* in which case this sum shall be deducted.'

The deductible clause is applicable to all claims for a partial loss arising from a peril insured against. To remove all doubts, cl 8 (3/4ths collision liability), cl 10 (general average and salvage), and cl 11 (duty of assured – sue and labour) of the ITCH(95) are specifically included as being governed by the deductible clause.[17]

It also clarifies that it does 'not apply to a claim for total or constructive total loss of the vessel, or in the event of such a claim, to any associated claim under

---

10 The purpose of the opening words of s 69 – 'Where a ship is damaged, but is not totally lost ...' is to eliminate an actual and a constructive total loss from the scope of the section.

11 If a ship is destroyed or so damaged as to become a total wreck, her owners will be entitled to claim for an actual total loss. If the damage sustained by the ship is irreparable, rendering her to 'cease to be a thing of the kind insured', she would be classified as an actual total loss.

12 See s 60(2)(ii), or the insured value as is the case under cl 19 of the ITCH(95) and cl 17 of the IVCH(95).

13 See s 61. *Pitman v Universal Marine Insurance Co* (1882) 9 QBD 192; *The Medina Princess* [1965] 1 Lloyd's Rep 361; and *Peele v Merchants Insurance Co* (1822) 3 Mason R 27 at p 64, where Story J observed that: 'The insured is in no case bound to abandon. He may in all cases elect to repair the damage at the expense of the underwriter ...'. On the law of constructive total loss, see Chapter 15.

14 See s 67.

15 Corresponding cl 10 of the IVCH(95). Note that under the old cl 12.1 of the ITCH(83), the deductible amount had to be inserted in the space provided. The practice under the new cl 12.1 is to state the deductible in the schedule attached to the policy.

16 In relation to ship, the Memorandum stated: '... this ship warranted free from average, under three pounds per cent, unless general, or the ship be stranded'.

17 Corresponding cll 6, 8 and 10 of the IVCH(95).

clause 1 arising from the same accident or occurrence'. The expense of 'sighting the bottom after stranding, if reasonably incurred specially for that purpose ... and even if no damage be found' is also excluded from the scope of the clause.

The deductible clause has also settled beyond doubt the question of whether the amount was an excess or a franchise. Under the common memorandum, it was construed as a franchise by which the insurer is liable for the full amount of the loss incurred. The deductible clause, however, has by the use of the words 'this sum shall be deducted' made it clear that it is an excess clause meaning that the assured has to bear the loss up to the amount stated in the clause.

Measure of indemnity

Section 69 stipulates three sets of rules for computing the measure of indemnity for a particular average loss in relation to:

- A ship which has been wholly repaired;
- A ship which has been only partially repaired; and
- A ship which has not been repaired, and has not been sold in her damaged state during the risk.

There is, however, a fourth category of loss which is overlooked by the Act, namely, where a ship has not been repaired and has been sold in her damaged state during the risk. For convenience and to avoid repetition, the statutory provisions are divided into two main parts, namely, repaired damage and unrepaired damage, for the purpose of the ensuing discussion. The fourth class of loss will be examined separately.

Repaired damage

An owner may chose to repair either the *whole* or only part of the damage sustained by his ship. Should he elect to repair the whole of the damage, the measure of indemnity for such a particular average loss is spelt out in s 69(1) which states that:

> 'Where the ship has been repaired, the assured is entitled to the reasonable cost of the repairs, less the customary deductions, but not exceeding the sum insured in respect of any one casualty.'

Should he decide to repair only *part* of the damage sustained by the ship, the measure of indemnity as regards *that* part which has been repaired is contained in the first limb of s 69(2) which reads as follows:

> 'Where the ship has been only partially repaired, the assured is entitled to the reasonable cost of such repairs, computed as above ...'

This clarifies that the legal principles to be applied for that part of the damage which had been repaired is the same as in the case where the ship had been wholly repaired. As the measure of indemnity for both s 69(1) and the first part of s 69(2) is the same, they will be examined together.

It is noted that the above subsections do not specify a time factor as to when the repairs have to be made.[18] As the Act is silent on the subject, it can be assumed that her owner is at liberty to have her repaired at any time after the accident, during, and even after the termination of the risk. But once she has been repaired, whether wholly or partially, during the risk the following rules will apply to the repaired damage.

'Reasonable cost of the repairs'

That an assured is entitled to the 'reasonable cost of the repairs' is clear. The only issue which is likely to arise in such a case is, what may and may not be included in the cost of repairs. Fortunately, the matter is now reasonably well-settled by case law and the Institute Hulls Clauses.

Expenses of docking

Pilotage, towage, and dock dues, are all recoverable from the insurer, if the ship must be docked for repairs. It would appear from *Ruabon SS Co v London Assurance*[19] that an assured may take advantage of the fact that the ship is docked, to have her surveyed and to effect necessary improvements. Provided that he does not lengthen her stay at the dock or cause any increase in docks dues, the cost will have to be borne by the insurer.[20]

Bottom treatment

With exceptions, cl 15 of the ITCH(95) states the general rule as: 'In no case shall a claim be allowed in respect of scraping gritblasting and/or other surface preparation or painting of the Vessel's bottom ...'.[21]

Wages and maintenance

The general rule in cl 16 of the ITCH(95) is that: 'No claim shall be allowed ... for wages and maintenance of the master, officers and crew ...'.[22]

Surveyor's fees

Agenoria SS Co Ltd v Merchants Marine Insurance Co Ltd[23] and *Helmville Ltd v Yorkshire Insurance Co Ltd, The Medina Princess*[24] have allowed reasonable fees for classification and other surveyors fees to be included in the cost of repairs.

---

18 In the case of a ship which has not been repaired and has not sold, a time is expressly specified in s 69(3) by the words 'during the risk'.

19 [1900] AC 6, HL.

20 *Cf Marine Insurance Co v The China Transpacific SS Co, The Vancouver* (1886) 11 App Cas 573, HL, where the House of Lords was prepared to apportion the dock charges, to repairs for particular average damage, and to scraping and painting. Arnould, para 1124, states that *The Vancouver* would probably not be followed.

21 Clause 13 of the IVCH(95).

22 Clause 14 of the IVCH(95).

23 (1903) 8 Com Cas 212.

24 [1965] 1 Lloyd's Rep 361 QBD (Com Ct).

Consequential damage

On the subject of consequential damage, the case which immediately springs to mind is *Field v Burr*,[25] where the cost of removing a putrid cargo in order to enable repairs to be carried out was held not recoverable as particular average. The court canvassed the possibility of a cargo, for example of cement which had adhered to the hull and had to be removed because it was not only causing damage to the ship, but was also preventing repair works on the ship from being carried out. In such a situation, it is said that the cost of removing and cleaning the solidified cargo may properly be regarded as part of the cost of repairs to the hull. But whether the cost of removal or disposal of the cargo may be included in the repair bill is questionable.

'Less customary deductions'

This rule contemplates the 'one-third new for old' rule which was commonly applied to wooden ships. As a rough guide, one-third used to be subtracted from the cost of repairs to take into account the benefit which the owner had perceived to have derived from the new materials replacing the old.[26] This somewhat arbitrary rule of thumb can no longer be applied because of cl 14 of the ITCH(95) which declares that 'Claims [are] payable without deduction new for old'.[27] Such a departure from the general rule is permissible because of the words 'subject to any provision in the policy' appearing in s 69.

'Not exceeding the sum insured'

There is nothing in the Act or the policy which prevents an assured from claiming the total sum insured as indemnity for a particular average loss. He is entitled to utilise the whole sum, for one casualty, for a particular average loss. This is spelt out in s 69(1).[28]

Unrepaired damage

The law on the measure of indemnity for unrepaired particular average damage is contained in s 69(2) (the second part) and s 69(3). The former declares that the assured is entitled:

> '... also to be indemnified for the reasonable depreciation, if any, arising from the unrepaired damage, provided that the aggregate amount shall not exceed the cost of repairing the whole damage, computed as above.'

An assured is, of course, entitled to be indemnified for that *part* of the damage which is unrepaired. The purpose of this part of the subsection is to compensate him for any 'reasonable depreciation' arising from the unrepaired damage.

The maximum amount which an assured is allowed to recover for the repaired and the unrepaired damage must not exceed the cost of repairing the whole damage. This is a reasonable and sensible rule, for he should not be

---

25 [1899] 1 QB 571.

26 See r D7 of the Rules of Practice of the Association of Average Adjusters.

27 The same rule appears in cl 12 of the IVCH(95).

28 See *Goole & Hull Steam Towing Co v Ocean Marine Insurance Co Ltd* (1929) 29 Ll L Rep 242.

allowed to benefit by not repairing the whole of the damage sustained by the ship.

The 'reasonable depreciation' rule also applies where no repair at all has been made to the damage. Section 69(3) provides that:

'Where the ship has not been repaired, and has not been sold in her damaged state during the risk, the assured is entitled to be indemnified for the reasonable depreciation arising from the unrepaired damage, but not exceeding the reasonable cost of repairing such damage computed as above.'

'Reasonable depreciation'

A comparison of the above statutory provisions will reveal that the legal principles for adjustment applicable to that part of the damage which has not been repaired is the same as in the case where the whole of the damage has not been repaired. The 'reasonable depreciation' rule can be found in both s 69(2) (the second part) and s 69(3). The Institute Hulls Clauses have, however, not surprisingly, incorporated both circumstances under one provision – cl 18 of the ITCH(95) – named as the 'unrepaired damage' clause, which reads as follows:

'The measure of indemnity in respect of claims for unrepaired damage shall be the reasonable depreciation in the market value of the Vessel at the time this insurance terminates arising from such unrepaired damage, but not exceeding the reasonable cost of repairs'.

It echoes parts of ss 69(2) and 69(3), but the legal principles laid down therein are by no means identical.

Neither the Act nor the Clauses have defined how 'reasonable depreciation' is to be calculated and quantified in monetary terms. As can be seen shortly, this is indeed a very difficult task. Under English law, there are essentially four cases which have dealt with the subject of 'reasonable depreciation'. The first was *Pitman v Universal Marine Insurance Co.*[29] As it is largely concerned with the fourth situation mentioned earlier, where the ship has not been repaired and has been sold during the risk, it is best that it be left for discussion separately at a later stage.

Irvin v Hine,[30] was the first authority to interpret s 69(3). The vessel sustained a particular average damage when she stranded, and as her owners (the plaintiffs) were unable to make out a case of a constructive total loss, they had to rely on their alternative claim for a partial loss. As the ship was neither repaired nor sold, they pleaded s 69(3) in support their claim for indemnity for the unrepaired damage. The figures which the Court of Appeal had to consider were:

Agreed or insured value:	£9,000
Cost of repairs:	£4,620
Sound or undamaged value:	£2,000[31]
Damaged value:	£ 685

---

29   (1882) 9 QBD 192, henceforth referred to as *The Pitman Case*.

30   [1950] 1 KB 555.

31   £3,000 was the court's estimate.

Altogether, three proposals, two of which were offered by the insurers, were tendered to the court for consideration:

- The assured argued that they were entitled to be indemnified the sum of £8,315, which was arrived at by subtracting the damaged value of £685 from the insured value of £9,000 [£9,000 – £685 = £8,315].

- The insurers contended that the court should simply subtract the damaged value of £685 from the undamaged value of £2,000, leaving the sum of £1,315 [£2,000 – £685 = £1,315].

- Alternatively, the insurers suggested that 'reasonable depreciation' was to be calculated as a percentage, which was then to be applied to the insured value. To ascertain the extent or rate of reasonable depreciation, a comparison was to be made between her true undamaged value of £2,000 and her true damaged value of £685. On this basis, she had depreciated in value by approximately two-thirds. The formula was:

$$\frac{£2,000 - £685 \times £9,000}{£2,000} = £5,917.50$$

This sum was, of course, subject to the overriding maximum of the cost of repairs.

The second of the above methods was swiftly rejected by Mr Justice Devlin, who found it totally unacceptable on the ground that it infringed the principle contained in s 27(3) that: 'the value fixed by the policy is, as between the insurer and the assured, conclusive of the insurance value of the subject intended to be insured, whether the loss be total or partial.'

As regards the first and third methods of calculation, he was not prepared to commit himself as to which one was to be applied. Fortunately for Mr Justice Devlin, it was unnecessary for him in the circumstances of the case to express his preference for one or the other, because they both produced a sum well in excess of the reasonable cost of repairs. The plaintiffs were accordingly awarded the sum of £4,620 (reasonable cost of repairs) as compensation for the unrepaired particular average loss. The proper ceiling has to be the 'reasonable cost of repairs': for any larger sum would place the assured in a more advantageous position than if he were to repair the damage.

At about the time when *Irvin v Hine* was being heard, the same problem was encountered by the court in a non-marine case,[32] *Elcock and Another v Thomson*,[33] where the court had effectively applied the third method of calculation described above. Mr Justice Morris, referring to s 69(3) of the Marine Insurance Act for guidance, observed that: 'Indemnification for reasonable depreciation must ... take into account any agreed valuation. Such agreed valuation is the *corpus* out of which depreciation takes place and by reference to which the depreciation must be measured.'[34]

---

32 The principle of the law of reasonable depreciation should be the same whether the policy be marine or non-marine, both being contracts of indemnity.

33 [1949] 2 All ER 381. It is interesting to note that Morris J found support also in s 71(3) which applies to goods.

34 *Ibid*, at p 386.

In 1965, the issue arose again in *The Medina Princess*,[35] where the vessel was insured for an agreed value of £350,000. Her sound value was £65,000, and her damaged value was nil. In terms of percentage, her rate of depreciation was 100%. Once again, no solution to the problem was given: for, as in *Irvine v Hine*, both the first and the third methods of calculation produced a sum greater than the reasonable cost of repairs. Mr Justice Morris was content to let matters rest by saying that: 'Its solution must wait until the occasion for its decision arises.'

In the ultimate analysis, it is fair to say that the English authorities are all in agreement that the insured value has a role to play in the calculation of reasonable depreciation. What exactly this role is, is unclear.[36] The choice has been narrowed down to either the first or the third method of calculation.

The unrepaired damage clause

Clause 18.1 of the ITCH(95)[37] has introduced the 'market value' of the vessel (at the termination of the risk) for the calculation of 'reasonable depreciation'. There is nothing in the clause to suggest that the 'insured value', or a percentage of it, is to be applied in the equation. The method proposed in cl 18.1 is, in effect, not dissimilar to the second method of assessment described above;[38] instead of the sound or undamaged value, the 'market value' is to be used. It has to be pointed out that the sound or undamaged value may or may not coincide with the 'market value' which, as its name suggests, would take market forces into account.

There are two ceilings imposed by cl 18. First, in relation to the question of 'reasonable depreciation', the highest figure that may be taken is the 'reasonable cost of repairs'. Secondly, the uppermost limit of the 'insured value' spelled out in cl 18.3 relates to the overall *liability* of the insurer for the unrepaired damage.[39] The phrase 'at the time this insurance terminates' (qualifying the insured value) creates the impression that the insured value could vary or fluctuate during the course of the policy. This, however, is not the case for, as a rule, the original insured value is rarely altered. One author suggests that the phrase relating to time has been inserted in order to take into account cl 1.3[40] which provides that 'the original insured value may be reduced if the ship sails to be broken up'.[41] If anything, cl 1.3 is an exception to the general rule.[42]

---

35 [1965] 1 Lloyd's Rep 361.

36 It would appear that in the United States in the case of *Compania Maritima Astra SA v Archdale, The Armar* [1954] 2 Lloyd's Rep 95, the Supreme Court had interpreted *Irvin v Hine* as having approved the third as the correct method for calculating 'reasonable depreciation'.

37 Corresponding cl 16.1 of the IVCH(95).

38 Which it is to be recalled was disapproved in *Irvin v Hine* [1950] 1 KB 505, because it did not taken into account the insured value of the ship.

39 Emphasis added. Clause 18.3: 'The underwriters shall not be liable in respect of repaired damage for more than the insured value at the time the insurance terminates.'

40 Now cl 1.5 of the ITCH(95).

41 See O'May, p 448.

42 It is to be noted that there is no equivalent to cl 1.5 in the IVCH(95).

The final sum which an insurer can be made liable for an unrepaired damage is, assuming that the vessel is fully insured,[43] the agreed or insured value. Thus, if the reasonable depreciation, however computed, is more than the cost of reasonable repairs, the latter applies. And should the reasonable cost of repairs be higher than the insured value, then the insured value has to prevail. Howbeit, it is also important to remember that the assured can never recover, whether the loss be partial or total, more than the sum insured.[44] It is worthwhile recalling the words of Jessel MR in *The Pitman Case*:[45]

'... as a general rule in no case can the insured become richer by reason of these perils, or in other words ... the insured ought not to be entitled to receive from the insurer a larger sum for a single partial loss than if the ship was wholly lost.'

'During the risk'

In *The Medina Princess*,[46] Mr Justice Roskill said that the point in time at which the measure of indemnity for an unrepaired damage is to be ascertained and quantified can to be found in the words 'during the risk'. Right up until the time the policy expires, an assured may repair the damage. This necessarily means that an adjustment cannot be undertaken until the expiry of the policy when the matter is clinched or finalised.[47] Mr Justice Roskill's interpretation of the section is as follows:

'But if "during the risk" which I construe as meaning "during the peril between the casualty and the expiry of the policy whether by effluxion of time or otherwise" she is neither repaired nor sold, then subsection (3) comes into operation. Until the moment when the risk expires, the ship might be repaired or indeed might be sold.'

Whilst the policy remains in force, there is always the chance of a change in circumstance: the damage might be partially or wholly repaired; the ship might not be repaired and not sold during the risk; or she might be sold in her unrepaired state during the risk.

Where the ship has not been repaired and has been sold during the risk

The Act is silent as to how this contingency is to be resolved. It is somewhat surprising, not to mention the least regrettable, that parliament had deemed it fit to ignore the subject when the problems associated therewith, which were all brought into the open by *The Pitman Case* in 1882, were staring at them in the face when s 69 was enacted. In the said case, the ship was sold in her damaged state during the risk for £3,897. Her sound value was taken at £4,000, and the cost of repairing her assessed at about £5,300.

---

43 The measure of indemnity is always based on the hypothesis that the subject-matter insured is to be regarded as fully insured. See s 67(1).

44 See s 81.

45 (1882) 9 QBD 192 at p 204.

46 [1965] 1 Lloyd's Rep 361, QBD (Com Ct).

47 What an assured does with his ship after the termination of the risk is his own business, and no concern to the insurers. See *Knight v Faith* (1850) 19 LJ QB 509 at p 518, on the question of a sale (by the master) after the expiration of the policy; Lord Campbell CJ commented that: '... there is no such loss known in insurance law as a sale by the master, unless it be barratrous ...'.

'Fixes his loss'

First, it has to be pointed out that there is nothing in the Act nor the Institute Hulls Clauses prohibiting an assured from selling the ship during the risk. However, certain consequences flow from such a sale.[48] In relation to a claim for particular average, the effect of a sale was summed up by Lord Justice Cotton in *The Pitman Case* as follows:[49]

> 'Where, as in the present case, there is not a constructive total loss, he is not against the insurers entitled to sell so as to bind them by the loss resulting therefrom; but when he elects to take this course ... he, as against himself, *fixes* his loss, that is, he cannot, as against the underwriters, say that the depreciation of the vessel exceeds that which is ascertained by the result of the sale.'

What this means is that an assured is bound by the consequences of the sale. He 'cannot possibly increase his actual loss by saying that he would have lost more if the ship had not sold for so much as she in fact realised'.[50] The price for which the ship was sold for will affect the measure of indemnity for the particular average loss. It will 'fix' the amount recoverable, and the assured is bound by any gain or loss resulting from the sale.

Measure of depreciation

In *The Pitman Case*, all the judges agreed that where an owner has not repaired the vessel, '... he is entitled to have made good to him the depreciation at the end of the risk in the value of his vessel, so far as this is caused by the peril insured against'.[51] That the principle of reasonable depreciation applied to unrepaired damage even before the Act was not in dispute. The controversy centred around the measure that was to be used to ascertain the extent of the deterioration. The assured argued that the estimated cost of repairs was the measure of indemnity; whilst the insurer naturally went for the lesser sum – the difference between the sound value and the damaged value, namely, the sale price. The court, therefore, had to decide which was the correct method to employ to ascertain the depreciation in the value of the ship.

Lord Justice Cotton commenced his judgment by comparing the legal position of a ship which has been repaired to one which has not been repaired:[52]

> 'As a general rule where there is a partial loss in consequence of injury to a vessel by reason of perils insured against, the insured is entitled to recover the sum properly expended in executing the necessary repairs, or, if the work has not been done, the estimated expense of the necessary repairs ...'

Not only did he stress that: 'As a general rule the estimated cost of the repairs is the measure of deterioration ...', but he also made it perfectly clear that this is not the 'only', but 'a' method of estimating the deterioration of the vessel. In the present case, he felt that if he were to apply the general rule, and allow recovery to be based on the estimated cost of repairs, the assured would

---

48 See, eg, cl 5.2 of the ITCH(95). No corresponding clause in the IVCH(95).

49 (1882) 9 QBD 192 at p 218.

50 *Ibid*, at p 202, *per* Lindley J.

51 *Ibid*, at p 216, *per* Cotton LJ.

52 *Ibid*, at p 215.

in the end be able to recover more than the loss which he had actually sustained. Such a method of calculation would be contrary to the cardinal principle of insurance law that a contract of insurance is a contract of indemnity. With this in mind, he accordingly concluded that the amount of deterioration is to be fixed by subtracting the proceeds of the sale from the value of the ship when uninjured.

Having said that, it is observed that the majority of the court agreed that the decision of the judge in the court below, Mr Justice Lindley, was 'substantially right'.[53] Mr Justice Lindley had held that the proportion of loss sustained by the assured – by reason of the depreciation – was to be calculated by subtracting her damaged value, being what she sold for, from the sound value of the ship. This proportion must then be applied to the declared or insured value. He had effectively applied the principles of the third method described above. In the circumstances of the case, it was unnecessary for him to ascertain the damaged value of the ship, which was taken as the nett proceeds of the sale.

The next question which arises is: is there is a ceiling to the amount recoverable? The answer can perhaps be found in the following statement made by Lord Justice Cotton, often cited by writers as laying down the formula to be applied in such a case:[54]

'Probably the most accurate way of stating the measure of what, under such circumstances, he is to recover is that it will be the estimated cost of repairs, less the usual deduction, not exceeding the depreciation in value of the vessel as ascertained by the sale.'

Arnould[55] construes the decisions of both the lower court and of the Court of Appeal as limiting the assured to the depreciation or the estimated cost of repairs 'whichever should be the less'.[56] 'That', he said, 'certainly, is the effect of s 69(3) of the Marine Insurance Act 1906 in cases where the ship is not sold.' It would appear that the result is the same whether the cost of repairs or the depreciation in value is named as the ceiling. As only two figures are involved, the lesser of the two is the measure of indemnity.

The sale of the ship will alter the complexion of the case in so far as the sale price is to be taken as the damaged value. As was seen, depreciation in value may be measured in one of two ways. According to *The Pitman Case*, the general rule, under the common law, is to use the estimated cost of repairs as the measure of indemnity. However, in certain circumstances, a court may be minded not to apply the general rule, and may prefer to subtract the nett proceeds of the sale from the undamaged value, and then apply this figure to the insured value.

However, it has to be said that the dissenting judgment delivered by Lord Justice Brett is equally persuasive. He held that the assured was entitled to the cost of repairs, and any loss or gain resulting from the sale was outside the

---

53 *Ibid*, at p 205, *per* Jessel MR.

54 *Ibid*, at pp 218– 219.

55 Arnould, para 1131.

56 In the present case, the lesser sum is the depreciation in value as ascertained by the sale.

contract of insurance and, therefore, irrelevant as between the assured and the insurer in the adjustment of a partial loss of the ship. A straightforward application of the estimated cost of repairs as the measure of indemnity has its appeal.

At the end of the day, it could be said that parliament had probably left the matter open with the intention of leaving the courts with the discretion to choose the method of calculation which would produce the most equitable result. The lesson, if any is to be learnt from *The Pitman Case*, is that the principle of indemnity should always be borne in mind in any adjustment of loss. In each case, whether the general rule or the exception to the rule is to be employed depends largely on the circumstances of the case: the principle of indemnity has to be the guiding star.

Successive losses

A ship could well encounter a number of accidents, and thereby sustain several particular average losses during the currency of a single policy. Provided that the limit declared in the deductible clause (cl 12) of the ITCH(95)[57] is complied with for each separate accident, s 77(1) allows an assured the right to be indemnified for each of the successive partial losses.

Claims for several accidents are, by cl 12.2, to be treated as being due to one accident if they are sustained by reason of heavy weather during a single passage between two successive ports. There is no definition given for 'heavy weather'; the clause merely states that the expression 'shall be deemed to include contact with floating ice'. 'Heavy weather' has presumably to fall within the definition of 'perils of the seas'.[58] It is pertinent to note that cl 12.2 is limited in scope and is not concerned with, for instance, successive losses caused by fire, theft or barratry, occurring in a single passage between two successive ports.

An assured is, by s 77(1), to be indemnified for each and every accident 'even though the total amount of such losses may exceed the sum insured'. He may thus claim the whole of the sum insured (insured value)[59] for each separate accident.[60] He is not, however, permitted to add up all the separate partial losses sustained during the currency of the policy in order to make up a constructive total loss. This is expressly prohibited by the constructive total loss clause, cl 19.2 of the ITCH(95), which states that: '... only the cost relating to a single accident or sequence of damage arising from the same accident shall be taken into account' for the purpose of determining whether there is a constructive total loss.[61]

---

57 Corresponding cl 10 of the IVCH(95).

58 See Chapter 9.

59 Note, however, the Institute Dual Valuation Clause (see Appendix 15) where there is an insured value for a total loss, and one for 'other than total loss'.

60 This is consistent with the fact that he may treat a constructive total loss as a partial loss: s 61.

61 Because of cl 19.2 of the ITCH(95), the possibility raised by Roskill J in *The Medina Princess* [1965] 1 Lloyd's Rep 361 at pp 514–515, of adding up several partial losses in order to make a claim a constructive total loss cannot now arise.

The doctrine of merger

Section 77(2) is the statutory version of the doctrine of merger which was first enunciated in *Livie v Janson*[62] and later affirmed by the House of Lords in *British and Foreign Insurance Co Ltd v Wilson Shipping Co Ltd*,[63] Section 77(2) states:

> 'Where under the same policy, a partial loss, which has not been repaired or otherwise made good, is followed by a total loss, the assured can only recover in respect of the total loss ...'

The same principle is reiterated in cl 18.2 of the ITCH(95).[64]

It is to be noted that the section is applicable only if the damage is unrepaired, and that both the partial loss and the subsequent total loss occur under the same policy.

Unrepaired damage

First, as noted earlier, any expense actually incurred to repair a particular average damage is always recoverable.[65] This right stems from the fundamental principle of insurance law, the doctrine of indemnity. As can be seen in *Le Cheminant v Pearson*,[66] the cost of repairs actually expended is recoverable under the policy, even though the assured may also have been indemnified for the total loss. Any repair cost expended is recoverable either as a loss caused by the insured peril, or as a sue and labour charge for which the liability of the insurer therefor is expressly preserved by the proviso to the section.[67]

In *Livie v Janson* and *The Wilson Case*, the vessel sustained a particular average loss (caused by a peril of the seas), which was then followed by a total loss (caused by an uninsured risk) during the currency of the policy. Viscount Finlay in *The Wilson Case* said that:[68]

> 'If the damage resulting from the sea perils had been repaired the amount disbursed for that purpose would have been recoverable on the policy in spite of the subsequent loss. But if the repairs have *not* been executed the liability cannot accrue until the termination of the risk under the policy, and if, before that happens, there is a total loss, the partial loss is "swallowed up" in the total.'

---

62 (1810) 12 East 648.

63 [1921] 1 AC188, HL, hereinafter referred to as *The Wilson Case*.

64 'In no case shall the underwriters be liable for unrepaired damage in the event of a subsequent total loss (whether or not covered under this insurance) sustained during the period covered by this insurance or any extension thereof.' Corresponding cl 16.2 of the IVCH(95). It is noted that s 77(2) uses the term 'partial loss' when in fact it refers to a particular average loss. This is an example of the danger, which has been described earlier, of using these terms as if they are synonymous. A general average loss, salvage and a particular charge are partial losses, but they are clearly not envisaged by the subsection because they are not losses which are repairable as such. The direct and simple expression 'unrepaired damage' used in cl 18.2 of the ITCH(95) is thus preferred. Unrepaired damage, 'made good' (that is, indemnified) by the insurer before a total loss would not be affected by the doctrine of merger laid down in s 77(2).

65 See s 69.

66 (1812) 4 Taunt 367.

67 The proviso states: 'Provided that nothing in this section shall affect the liability of the insurer under the suing and labouring clause.'

68 [1921] 1 AC 188 at p 202, HL.

In *Livie v Janson*,[69] Lord Ellenborough explained that the unrepaired partial loss, having been absorbed by the total loss, was not recoverable because it had become a matter of indifference to the owners. In similar terms, Lord Campbell in *Knight v Faith*[70] expressed the view that the assured were 'not in any degree prejudiced by the partial loss ... [he] being in the same situation as if the partial loss had never occurred'.

It is on these bases that unrepaired partial losses which have been absorbed by a total loss are not recoverable. This is regardless of whether the total loss is or is not indemnifiable under the policy. Clause 18.2, however, has made this point patently clear by stating that an insurer is not liable for the unrepaired damage in the event of a subsequent total loss 'whether or not covered under this insurance'. Needless to say, in so far as the liability of the insurer for the total loss is concerned, it is dependent upon whether it is caused by a peril insured against. This means that if the subsequent total loss is caused by an uninsured peril, neither the unrepaired damage nor the later total loss is recoverable.

In *Woodside v Globe Marine Insurance Co*,[71] the vessel, by perils of the sea, was driven ashore and sustained such damage that the cost of repairing her would have been greater than her value when repaired.[72] Thirty-six hours after the stranding, she was totally destroyed by fire. Both parties agreed to argue the case on the assumption that the vessel was, as a result of the stranding, a constructive total loss. The plaintiffs claimed for a total loss of the ship by fire, to which the insurers denied liability on the ground that the ship was already a constructive total loss at the time of the fire. The insurers had endeavoured to apply the doctrine of merger in reverse, to the effect that the damage by fire had merged with the previous (constructive) total loss by stranding, a peril of the seas.

Mr Justice Mathew held that the loss by stranding would only become a total loss if the assured gave timely notice of abandonment, and as none was given the loss would be for particular average. The doctrine of merger does not apply in the reverse: a later actual total loss is not absorbed by an earlier constructive total loss. Provided that the claim for the (earlier) constructive total loss has not been accepted, there can be no question of the assured being allowed to recover twice over. The judge observed that:[73] 'A particular average loss, however serious, could not impair the right of the assured to recover for a subsequent total loss ...'.

'Where under the same policy'

First, it is to be observed that the opening words of s 77(2) – 'Where under the same policy ...' – are significant. The same point is made in cl 18.2 of the ITCH(95) by the phrase 'sustained during the period covered by this insurance

---

69 (1810) 12 East 648.

70 (1805) 15 QB 649.

71 [1896] 1 QB 105.

72 On this basis, the assured could have by tendering a notice of abandonment claimed for a constructive total loss: see s 60(ii).

73 [1896] 1 QB 105 at p 107.

or any extension thereof'. On this requirement, it is necessary to refer to *Lidgett v Secretan*,[74] where the vessel sustained a particular average damage which was only partially repaired when, after the expiration of the first policy, she was totally destroyed by fire which broke out during the currency of the second policy. As two policies were involved, there was no question of the merger of the losses. The cost incurred to repair part of the damage was naturally recoverable. As regards that part of the damage which was not repaired, the court made an allowance for the diminution in the value of the vessel.[75] The insurers were held liable under the first policy for both the repaired and unrepaired damage. The fact that they were also the insurers for the second policy did not exempt them from liability for the total loss. For all intents and purposes, the claims were treated as if the insurers of the two policies were different persons.

The death blow theory

A ship may well sustain a particular average damage during the currency of one policy only to become a total loss, by reason of the damage sustained during a later policy. In such a situation, she is described to have sustained her 'death blow' during the first policy and for which damage the insurers for that policy is liable. Such an event occurred in *Knight v Faith*,[76] where the vessel in question stranded during the currency of the policy. Eight days after the policy had expired, the extent of the damage was ascertained. The severity of the damage rendered it impossible for her to be repaired or to be taken to any port where she could be repaired. For the benefit of all concerned, the master and part-owner sold her for a meagre sum.

Clearly, there was not an actual total loss.[77] And if there was a constructive total loss, the insurers were not liable for the assured had failed to tender notice of abandonment. So at best, the assured could only claim for a particular average loss. The circumstances was described as thus: 'But here the insurers have not paid, and they deny their liability to pay a total loss; and they are not at liberty to allege that the partial loss is merged in a total loss, from which they are exempt'.

As the doctrine of merger did not apply, the judge held the insurers liable on the basis of a partial loss – which was calculated on the same principle as if she had actually been repaired and proceeded on her voyage or had foundered at sea without having been repaired soon after the policy expired.

It has to be pointed out that, in truth, there was in this case only one accident which had caused the loss of the vessel. And as that was the casualty which inflicted her the death blow, the loss can only be said to have arisen under that policy. The doctrine of merger obviously cannot apply when the death blow theory operates. The former relates to two separate accidents or causes of loss,

---

74 (1871) LR 6 CP 616.

75 See s 69(2).

76 (1850) 19 LJ QB 509; 15 QB 649.

77 *Ibid* at p 518, *per* Lord Campbell CJ: '... there is no such loss known in insurance law as a sale by the master, unless it be barratrous ...'.

whereas the latter, to only one accident (occurring during the currency of the policy), and the damage which she has sustained therefrom manifested itself as a total loss only after the expiration of the policy.

It is necessary to distinguish *Lockyer v Offley*[78] from the above situation. In this case, the act of barratry was committed during the currency of one policy, and the seizure by the custom authorities for the barratrous act took place after the expiration of the policy. First, even though the seizure was as a result of barratry, nonetheless, it was regarded as a separate accident. Secondly, seizure, not barratry, was held to be the proximate cause of loss. In causative terms, it could be argued that the chain of causation was broken by the seizure. The law of causation has clearly played a critical role in this case. It was not possible to apply the doctrine of merger in the circumstances of this case.

PARTICULAR AVERAGE LOSS OF GOODS

Unlike a partial loss of ship and of freight,[79] there is no minimum limit, such as an excess or franchise, which a partial loss of goods has to be attain before a claim would be entertained. There is no warranty, either wholly or under a certain percentage, free from particular average. But presumably, the courts would, if necessary, invoke the *de minimis* rule in order to dismiss petty and small claims. The parties are, of course, free to insert a special clause into the contract of insurance if they so wish to restrict the liability of the insurer for a total loss only.

Goods are capable of sustaining any of the following types of particular average loss:

(1) there may be a total loss of part of the goods;

(2) the whole of the goods may be partially damaged;

(3) part of the goods may be partially damaged; or

(4) goods may become incapable of identification because of obliteration of marks.

As the same principles of law apply to (2) and (3) above, they will be discussed together under the heading 'Damage to the whole or part of the goods'.

Total loss of part of the goods

It is not always easy to discern whether a loss is a total loss of part or a partial loss of the whole of the goods. Whether a total loss of part of goods is to be considered as a partial loss or a total loss depends largely upon the terms of the policy: unless the goods are separately insured, identified and packed separately,[80] the loss will not as a general rule be treated as a total loss of part. It

---

78 (1786) 1 TR 252, See also *The Ikarian Reefer* [1993] 2 Lloyd's Rep 68; [1995] 1 Lloyd's Rep 455, CA, where the plaintiffs claimed for a total loss by fire and/or perils of the sea. The advantages for resting a claim by fire, as opposed to a peril of the seas, are discussed in Chapter 9.

79 There is the deductible clause in the case of ship and the franchise clause for freight; see cl 12 of the Institute Time Clause Freight.

80 Eg, 100 bags of rice insured under one policy for £5,000, valued at £50 per bag.

is pertinent to note that this relates to goods of the same specie insured under a single valuation, and not goods of different species insured under a single valuation, which is governed by s 72.[81]

If a loss is not apportionable, it will be regarded as a particular average loss and will not be recoverable if the policy contains a free from particular average warranty. Such a warranty, however, will not prevent recovery for 'salvage charges', 'particular charges' and expenses properly incurred under the suing and labouring clause.[82] The distinction between a total loss of part, and a partial loss of the whole is of importance only if the policy contains such a warranty. This can be seen in s 76(1) which states that:

'Where the subject-matter insured is warranted free from particular average, the assured cannot recover for loss of part ... unless the contract contained in the policy be apportionable; but, if the contract be apportionable, the assured may recover for a total loss of any apportionable part.'

The effect of the above section is to allow an assured the right to be indemnified for a total loss of any apportionable part of the subject-matter insured, in spite of the fact that the policy contains a warranty free from particular average the purpose of which is to restrict recovery under the policy only for total losses. Provided that the contract is apportionable, s 76(2) will treat such a partial loss as if it were a total loss, albeit of a part.[83] But if the contract be not apportionable, then the loss is partial, and would not be recoverable by reason of the warranty. As the warranty is now rarely found in cargo policies, the above problem is in practice unlikely to arise. In the absence of the warranty, such partial losses would be recoverable in accordance with s 71(3) described below.

The measure of indemnity for a total loss of a part is governed by s 71(1) and 71(2). Subsection (1) applies to a valued policy and sub-s (2) to an unvalued policy. The measure of indemnity for a valued policy is '... such proportion of the sum fixed by the policy as the insurable value of the part lost bears to the insurable value of the whole ...'. In simple terms, the liability of the insurer is the insured value of the part lost. In an unvalued policy, the method of computation is the insurable value of the part lost, ascertained in accordance with s 16(3).

Damage to the whole or part of the goods

Section 71(3), which applies to a particular average loss of goods, is founded upon the cases of *Lewis v Rucker*[84] and *Johnson v Sheddon*.[85] It states that:

'Where the whole or any part of the goods or merchandise insured has been delivered damaged at its destination, the measure of indemnity is such proportion of the sum fixed by the policy, in the case of a valued policy, or of the insurable value in the case of an unvalued policy, as the difference between the

---

81   Eg, 200 tins of sardines and 100 bags of nuts valued at £2,000.

82   See s 76(2).

83   See *Duff v Mackenzie* (1857) 26 LJCP 313; 3 CB (NS) 16.

84   (1761) 2 Burr 1167.

85   (1802) 2 East 581.

gross sound and damaged values at the place of arrival bears to the gross sound value.'

Percentage of depreciation

As in the case of a ship which is damaged,[86] the measure of indemnity for (part or whole of) goods which are partially damaged is based also upon the principle of depreciation. The measure of indemnity prescribed above, which applies only if the goods arrive 'at its destination', is not difficult to calculate.[87] First, whether the policy be valued or unvalued, the extent of depreciation in value has to be ascertained. This is achieved by comparing the gross sound value with the gross damaged value of the goods. The meaning of the term 'gross value' can be found in s 71(4).

The words 'at the place of arrival' limit the time and place at which the gross sound and the damaged values of the goods are to be ascertained. As the law on the subject is now well settled, it is unnecessary to enter into any in depth discussion of the cases. The problem which arose in the above pair of cases relates to the question as to whether fluctuations in the market value of the goods ought to be taken into account when considering the value of the goods. Suffice it is to say that the guiding principle expressed by Lord Mansfield in *Lewis v Rucker*[88] should be borne in mind. He said that the insurer '... only engages so far as the prime cost or value in the policy, that the thing shall come safe; he has no concern with any profit or loss which may rise to the merchant from the goods; he had no concern with any subsequent value'.

Regardless of a fall or rise in the market, it is the 'arrival' value which is relevant. In *Whiting v New Zealand Insurance Co*,[89] Mr Justice Roche referring to s 71(3) observed that: '... the difference between the gross sound and the damaged values of the goods in question ... means at the place and time of arrival.'

Insured value and insurable value

Once the percentage of the diminution in value is determined, it is then applied to the insured value in a valued policy, and to the insurable value in an unvalued policy. As there is no express valuation of the goods in the case of the latter, reference has to be made to s 16(3) or (4) for the insurable value of the goods. The gross sound value of the goods is the aggregate of 'the prime cost of the property insured, plus the expenses of and incidental to shipping and the charges of insurance upon the whole'. In *Usher v Noble*,[90] Lord Ellenborough CJ noted that in an unvalued policy, '... the invoice price at the loading port, including premiums of insurance and commission, is, for all purpose of either

---

86   See s 69(2) and (3).

87   There is, it is noted, no provision relating to goods which are delivered damaged at a place short of its proper destination.

88   (1761) 2 Burr 1167.

89   (1932) 44 Ll LRep 179 at p 180.

90   (1810) 12 East 639.

total or average loss, the usual standard of calculation resorted to for the purpose of ascertaining this [insurable] value'.

Goods incapable of identification

Goods may reach their destination *in specie*, but by reason of obliteration of marks, or otherwise, become incapable of identification. Section 56(5) declares that such a loss is partial, not total. As was seen, *Spence v Union Marine Insurance*[91] has clarified that where marks are so obliterated as to render identification to any particular consignee impossible, the owners become tenants in common of the damaged goods.

PARTICULAR AVERAGE LOSS OF FREIGHT

In *Rankin v Potter*,[92] Mr Justice Brett took time to express his views on the subject of particular average loss of freight even though the facts of the case did not call for its consideration. A partial loss of freight under a general policy, he said, may arise if there was:

- a general average loss caused by a peril insured against giving rise to a general average contribution;
- a total loss of part of a cargo;
- a total loss of the cargo and the ship earns some freight in respect of other goods carried on the voyage insured; or
- a total loss of the ship and the cargo is sent on in a substituted ship.

General average loss and salvage charges

The first situation should also include salvage charges, as both general average contributions and salvage charges are recoverable under s 73 and cl 10.1 of the ITCH(95).[93]

Total loss of part of the cargo

As a general rule, full freight is payable for goods even if they arrive in damaged condition or are short delivered at its proper destination. But if freight is, according to the terms of the contract of carriage, payable for the quantity delivered, then there would be a loss, say, for example, 40% of the freight if only 60% of the goods is delivered at its destination. Presumably, this is what Mr Justice Brett had in mind for his second illustration. Such is a total loss of part of the freight for which an insurer of freight would be liable if the loss of the cargo be caused by a peril insured against. In *Price and Another v Maritime Insurance Co Ltd*,[94] the assured were allowed by Italian law, which applied to the contract, to recover for a loss of freight even though the ship which did not arrive at the

---

91 (1868) LR 3 CP 427.
92 (1873) LR 6 HL 83 at p 99, HL.
93 Corresponding cl 8 of the IVCH(95).
94 [1900] 5 Com Cas 332; [1901] 2 KB 412, CA.

port of destination because she became a constructive total loss during the voyage. 'Distance' freight was, under Italian law, payable for the part of the cargo that was salved. If it were not for the free from particular average warranty, the assured would have been able to claim for a partial loss of freight.

A policy could provide cover for a percentage of the loss of freight even for goods which are delivered in a damaged condition. In *Griffiths and Others v Bramley-Moore and Others*,[95] for example, the policy provided that: 'If any portion of the cargo be delivered sea-damaged the freight on such sea-damaged portion to be two-thirds of the above rate' and 'To cover only the one-third loss of freight in consequence of sea-damage as per charterparty'. By virtue of these clauses, the assured was able to recover the one-third loss of freight on the sea-damaged portion of the cargo which was deducted by the charterers from the total amount of freight.

Freight at risk

It is to be remembered that only freight which is at risk is covered by the policy. Thus if cargo upon which freight is to be derived is not actually on board, then there cannot be a loss of freight.[96]

Advance freight

Freight paid in advance is not at the risk of the carrier. As he cannot be called upon to refund any or part of it whether the voyage be successful or not, the risk lies obviously lies with the person who had paid the advance freight.[97]

Pro rata freight

Pro rata freight, or freight proportionate to the part of the voyage completed, is generally not payable when goods are delivered short of its proper destination. However, the parties to the contract of carriage could expressly or impliedly agree that *pro rata* freight be payable. Should an insured peril prevent the carriage of the goods to its proper destination, a particular average loss of freight would result for which the carrier could claim from his insurer.

Substituted cargo

Under a general policy, freight may be earned if the assured is able to procure a different cargo for the voyage, and if a lesser sum is earned for the carriage of a substituted cargo, he would obviously suffer a partial loss of freight. In the words of Mr Justice Brett:[98]

'An actual total loss of the whole *cargo* will occasion an actual total loss of freight, unless such loss should so happen as to leave the ship capable, as to time, place and condition, of earning an equal or some freight by carrying other cargo on the voyage insured.'

---

95   (1878) 4 QB 70.

96   Note the words 'at the risk of the assured' in s 16(2).

97   See s 12 for meaning of advance freight.

98   *Rankin v Potter* (1873) LR 6 HL 83. Emphasis added.

Goods carried in substituted ship

In the fourth situation, freight is payable for the delivery of the cargo which is carried to its proper destination in a substituted ship. An assured, who has incurred additional costs for the hire of a substituted ship, is likely to suffer a particular average loss of freight. Mr Justice Brett explained the position as follows:[99]

> 'An actual total loss of *ship* will occasion an actual total loss of freight, unless when the ship is lost, cargo is on board, and the whole or a part of such cargo is saved, and might be sent on in a substituted ship so as to earn freight.'

Suing and labouring

The expense for procuring a substituted ship is recoverable, if the freight policy does not contain a free from particular average warranty. However, having said that, it is important to recall that, when a substituted ship is procured to carry the cargo to its proper destination the assured is, in effect, suing and labouring: he is endeavouring to prevent a total loss of freight. In such circumstances, reference has to be made to *Kidston v Empire Insurance*,[100] where the court held that a free from particular average warranty would not prevent a claim for suing and labouring. This principle of law is now embodied in ss 76(2) and 78(1).[101] However, it would helpful to quote the relevant part of the judgment of the court on this matter:[102]

> '... the warranty against particular average, does no more than limit the insurance to total loss of the freight by the peril insured against, without reference to extraordinary labour or expense which may be incurred by the assured in preserving the freight from loss, or rather from never becoming due, by reason of the operation of perils insured against; and that the latter expenses are specially provided for by the suing and labouring clause, and may be recovered thereunder.'

It is to be noted that such an expense is not recoverable, if the policy contains a free from particular average warranty, and does not have a suing and labouring clause. It is interesting to note that there is no suing and labouring clause in the Institute Freight Clauses. Such a loss, therefore, would be recoverable simply as a particular average loss.

Measure of indemnity

The Franchise

First, it is to be noted that, as in the case of policy on ship, there is an express limit (of loss) which has to be complied with before the assured would be allowed to claim for a partial loss of freight. As was seen earlier, the 'deductible' under the Institute Hulls Clauses is an excess clause: under the Institute Freight

---

99 *Ibid*. Emphasis added.

100 (1866) LR 1 CP 535.

101 On the subject of sue and labour, see Chapter 17.

102 (1866) LR 1 CP 535 at pp 546–547.

Clauses, however, it is a 'franchise'. Clause 12 of the Institute Freight (Time) Clauses states that:[103]

> 'This insurance does not cover partial loss, other than general average loss, under 3% unless caused by fire, sinking, stranding or collision with another vessel. Each craft and/or lighter to be deemed a separate insurance if required by the Assured.'

Certain aspects of the clause resembles the old Common Memorandum. As it is a franchise, the whole of the loss including the 3% is recoverable.

Gross freight

The measure of indemnity for a particular average loss of freight is governed by s 70 read with s 16(2) and cl 14.1 of the Institute Freight (Time) Clauses which states: 'The amount recoverable under this insurance for any claim for loss of freight shall not exceed the *gross freight* actually lost.'

The measure of indemnity is 'such proportion of the sum fixed by the policy' in a valued policy, and of the insurable value in an unvalued policy. Section 16(2) states that 'the insurable value is the gross amount of the freight at the risk of the assured, plus the charges of insurance'.

What may and may not be included in the gross freight was considered in *United States Shipping v Empress Assurance Corpn*:[104] commission upon getting a premium was held recoverable, but not commission paid in obtaining the sub-charterparty.

---

103 Corresponding cl 9 of the Institute Freight (Voyage) Clause.

104 [1907] 1 KB 259; [1908] 1 KB 115, CA. See also *Palmer v Blackburn* (1822) 1 Bing 61; 7 Moore 339.

CHAPTER 17

SALVAGE, GENERAL AVERAGE, AND SUE AND LABOUR

INTRODUCTION

Salvage or salvage charges, general average losses, and sue and labour charges are all partial losses which are incurred during rescue operations where either the subject-matter insured and/or other property, as the case may be, are at risk from loss by a peril insured against. The nature of the service performed, the rights of parties against each other, and the incidence of the loss depend on the circumstances of the case. Salvage charges, for example, where properly incurred may, according to the circumstances under which they were incurred, be recovered as a particular charge or as a general average loss. Each of these losses is distinct, but it is not always easy to distinguish one from the other.

Before proceeding to examine the characteristics of each of these losses, it is necessary, first, to determine whether they are affected by particular average warranties.

Particular average warranties

It is to be noted that salvage charges, though they are in fact particular average losses, are, nevertheless, recoverable, even if the subject-matter insured is 'warranted free from particular average, either wholly or under a certain percentage'.[1] This concession is made clear in s 76(2).[2] As general average and particular charges are not particular average losses,[3] they are not, strictly speaking, affected by a particular average warranty. As such, there is no real need for the Act to clarify or confirm that they are recoverable even in a policy containing a particular average warranty. In relation to general average, this is clarified by s 76(1) which states that 'a loss incurred by a general average sacrifice' is not affected by a particular average warranty.[4] And in the case of particular charges (and 'other expenses properly incurred pursuant to the

---

1   It has frequently been said that in marine insurance, particular average warranties are clauses excepting the insurer from liability for 'partial losses': see s 76(1) where it is stated that this means that 'the assured cannot recover for a loss of part'; and r 13 of the Rules for Construction in reference to the expression 'average unless general' states that it means a 'partial loss of the subject-matter insured other than a general average loss, and does not include "particular charges"'. To be precise, the term 'particular average' in the warranty excepts the insurer from liability only for 'particular average' losses. This means that general average losses and particular charges, as they are not particular average losses, are not affected by the exception: see s 64(1) and (2). This reinforces the point made above regarding the use of terms 'partial loss' and 'particular average loss': see Chapter 16.

2   Note the use of the word 'nevertheless' in s 76(2).

3   Section 64.

4   The use of the word 'sacrifice', not 'loss', is liable to cause confusion, suggesting that only a general average sacrifice, and not a general expenditure, is recoverable. Cf s 76(3) where 'general average loss' is used.

provisions of the sue and labour clause in order to avert a loss insured against') ss 76(2) and 78(1) confirm that they are recoverable.

A – SALVAGE CHARGES

INTRODUCTION

The law of salvage, like general average, originated and developed independently of marine insurance. Though it cannot claim a lineage as old as that for general average, nevertheless its ancestry still precedes that of marine insurance. The origin of salvage and general average was in *Aitchison v Lohre*[5] traced by Lord Blackburn as follows:

'... the liability of the articles saved to contribute proportionally with the rest to general average and salvage, in no way depends on the policy of insurance. It is a consequence of the perils of the sea, first imposed, as regards general average, by the Rhodian Law many centuries before insurance was known at all, and, as regards salvage, by the maritime law, not so early, but at least long before any policies of insurance in the present form were thought of.'

There is no statutory definition of 'salvage'. Under common law, the word 'salvage' is used in two senses: it could refer either to the 'reward' earned by salvors or the 'service' they render.[6] In the law of marine insurance, the former is described as a 'salvage charge'. Though the focus of this chapter is on the insurance aspects of salvage, nevertheless, it is necessary for a proper understanding of the subject briefly to mention the essential ingredients of salvage.

First, the right to salvage arises only if maritime property, namely, ship, apparel, cargo or wreckage is salved. Secondly, the service has to be voluntarily rendered, meaning that the salvor must not be under a pre-existing duty to come to the aid of the vessel in distress. Thirdly, the maritime property or lives must be rescued from danger. This means that the salvage operation has to be successful before the salvors would be entitled to an award. Unless all these requirements are met, there can be no salvage award under the common law.[7]

The whole basis of salvage was summed up by Chief Justice Eyre in *Nicholson v Chapman*[8] as follows:

'Principles of public policy dictate to civilised and commercial countries not only the propriety but even the absolute necessity of establishing a liberal recompense for the encouragement of those who engaged in so dangerous a service ... Such are the grounds upon which salvage stands.'

In the context of marine insurance, the problem lies not so much as in determining what constitutes salvage, but in distinguishing salvage from two

---

5   (1879) 4 App Cas 755 at p 760.

6   See s 60(2)(ii) where the term 'salvage operations' is used.

7   For a complete study of the law of salvage, reference should be made to classic works such as W R Kennedy, *Law of Salvage* (1985, 5th edn); and Brice, *Maritime Law of Salvage* (1993).

8   (1793) 2 H Bl 254.

other kindred forms of extraordinary losses, namely, general average and sue and labour. Section 65(2), first, sets out to define 'salvage charges' and then proceeds to distinguish it from other contractual forms of salvage services, which could be mistaken for maritime salvage, rendered by way of general average or sue and labour.

Section 65(1) declares that '... salvage charges incurred in preventing a loss by perils insured against may be recovered as a loss by those perils'. That salvage charges are recoverable under the ITCH(95) and the IVCH(95) is made clear by cl 10.1 and cl 8, respectively. These clauses simply state: 'This insurance covers the vessel's proportion of salvage, salvage charges ... reduced in respect of any under-insurance ...'. A similar provision can be found in cl 2 of the ICC (A), (B) and (C).

DEFINITION OF 'SALVAGE CHARGES'

Section 65(1) defines 'salvage charges' to mean 'the charges recoverable under maritime law by a salvor independently of contract'. The purpose of this statement is not only to restrict salvage charges to those 'recoverable under maritime law', but also to distinguish it from salvage performed pursuant to contractual arrangement. These words point to the fact that only salvage 'awards' or salvage strictly so called, as understood in 'maritime law', are recoverable as salvage charges. It could be said that the words 'independently of contract' are superfluous, for the very essence of maritime salvage is that the salvors must act voluntarily, and not under contractual compulsion. They were, presumably, inserted for emphasis.

For a picturesque account of what maritime salvage entails, reference should be made to the remarks of Lord Hatherley in *Aitchison v Lohre*:[9]

'But ... where the salvage seems to have been an ordinary sort of salvage, namely, a ship perceiving another at a distance and in a state of distress comes to the rescue *no bargain being made*. We were expressly told in the case that no bargain was made as to any remuneration which should be given, but it was rescued upon the simple and common principle for salvage.'

Life salvage

Prior to 1846, a claim for salvage of life could not be maintained under the maritime law or the common law of England. Salvage was never awarded for the saving of life alone, and the reason for this being that it is of no benefit whatever to the owner of either ship or cargo.

In 1846, life salvage was created by the Merchant Shipping Act, and this later raised the question as to whether such a loss imposed upon the shipowner by statute could be claimed for under the ordinary form of a Lloyd's policy. This issue first came before the court in *Nourse v Liverpool Sailing Ship Owners' Mutual Protection and Indemnity Association*,[10] where the Court of Appeal had to

---

9   (1879) 4 App Cas 755 at p 768. Emphasis added.

10 [1896] 2 QB 16.

determine whether the standard form Lloyd's policy covered a life salvage which the plaintiff had become liable to pay under the statute.

Lord Esher MR was adamant that '... there could be no question of recovering in respect of such salvage under a Lloyd's policy'. For fear of turning an ordinary Lloyd's policy on ship into an insurance on the master and crew, Lord Justice Rigby held that the plaintiffs' claim was not recoverable. It was thought that as life salvage only came into existence in 1846, it could not have been in the contemplation of those who framed the ordinary form of Lloyd's policy which had existed much earlier.

However, the argument today should be based along the line that s 65(2) envisages only awards 'recoverable under maritime law' – and as a pure life salvage is a creation of statute, it does not fit within the traditional understanding of the term.

An enhanced award for saving of life

The Admiralty Court has never been averse to the making of an enhanced salvage award if lives were *also* saved in the process of the salving of property. To take into account the saving of the lives of the persons on board the ship when she was in peril, an increased amount may be awarded as salvage.[11] The whole of the enhanced award has always been regarded as maritime salvage. But whether the whole sum is recoverable as salvage charges under a Lloyd's policy is another separate matter.

This question was considered in *The Bosworth (No 3)*[12] which held that the award was recoverable under the terms of a standard marine policy. Mr Justice McNair, who felt somewhat uneasy in having to force the language of s 65(1), said:

'It needs possibly a little stretching of the language to say that a salvage award in so far as it reflects an element of life salvage gives rise to a charge incurred in preventing a loss by peril insured against.'

However, he found comfort in the fact that 'by the practice of the Admiralty Court an award made in these circumstance is treated as being, and is in fact, an award for service rendered to the ship and cargo'. As such, an enhanced award is 'recoverable under maritime law' as maritime salvage, it follows that it would also be recoverable, by reason of s 65(2), under a standard policy of insurance.

An enhanced award for preventing or minimising damage to the environment

Amidst the exclusions in cl 10, cl 10.6 of the ITCH(95) has made a special effort to clarify that any salvage reward which has taken art 13(1)(b) of the International Convention on Salvage 1989 into consideration is covered by the insurance. Clause 10.6 has made it clear that the exclusions stated in cl 10.5 shall

---

11 See art 13(1)(e) of the International Convention on Salvage, 1989. The relevant articles of this Convention can be found in the LOF 1995: see Appendix 25.

12 *Grand Union Shipping Ltd v London SS Owners' Mutual Insurance Assocn Ltd* [1962] 1 Lloyd's Rep 483 at p 490, QBD.

not affect a claim for salvage in respect of a reward where the skill and efforts of the salvors in preventing or minimising damage to the environment have been taken into account. Though a salvage reward may have been enhanced by reason of art 13(1)(b), it is still recoverable under the insurance as salvage or salvage charges. Unlike the exclusions spelt out in cl 10.5 of the ITCH(95), such an award, though enhanced is still for salvage services rendered.

Meaning of 'independently of contract'

The above words are somewhat ambiguous, especially when read in modern day context. It is now almost the invariable practice amongst professional salvors to use the Lloyd's Open Form (LOF) 1995, 'no cure, no pay' agreement.[13] It has been argued that because of this, such a form of salvage is not independent of contract and, accordingly, cannot be recovered as a 'salvage charge'.[14] There is, however, another point of view, held by Arnould, Carver and Lowndes, which is not so concerned with the fact that a contract has been entered into but more realistically, with its terms.

LOF agreement

The LOF agreement does not stipulate the amount payable for the service rendered;[15] as such, it has preserved one of the most basic of the attributes of maritime salvage. The 'no cure, no pay' basis of the agreement indelibly stamps it with the hallmark of maritime salvage. As no fixed amount is stated in the LOF agreement, the salvor has to submit to maritime law for his remuneration. In this sense, the payment is 'recoverable under maritime law' and not by contract. Though the liability to pay salvage may be under contract, the nature and quantification of the claim are not recoverable by way of contract. Provided that the salvor's remuneration is not pre-determined, but has to be assessed subsequently (whether by arbitration or court of law) according to the rules of maritime law, the fact that an agreement has been entered into is quite immaterial.

If one wishes to be pedantic, one has to acknowledge the fact that there is a contractual element even in the case of a maritime salvage or salvage properly so called: the fact that the salved vessel has (whether expressly or impliedly) accepted the service offered by the salvor is, in itself, sufficient to create a contract. Thus, provided that the fundamental characteristics or elements of a salvage proper remain intact, namely, that a salvage award is payable only upon a successful completion of the operation, and in accordance with the principles of maritime law, the fact that an LOF agreement has been entered into should not change the character of the service rendered.

---

13 See Appendix 25.

14 See Templeman, p 371: '... if the services were rendered under the terms of Lloyd's Standard Form of Salvage agreement, the amount awarded thereunder would not come within the definition of 'salvage charges' in s 65(2) of the Marine Insurance Act, as the parties to that agreement are clearly in a contractual relationship'.

15 See cl 1(c) of the LOF 1995.

The question as to whether salvage paid by an assured pursuant to an LOF agreement is recoverable under a policy of insurance as a 'salvage charge' has never been directly considered in the law of marine insurance. The case which comes closest to the subject is *The Raisby*[16] which, though not an insurance case, is nevertheless relevant to the present discussion. Here, the master of *The Raisby* had, when she was in distress, entered into a contract with the master of *The Gironde* which had agreed to tow *The Raisby* to the nearest port for repairs. It was also agreed that 'the matter of compensation to be left to arbitrators at home'. The contract is similar to an LOF agreement. Paying very little regard to the agreement, the judge said that it:[17]

> '... in no way alters the position of the matter from what it would have been if the captain of the *Raisby* had simply accepted the services of the *Gironde*, in which case it has not been contended that a claim could have been maintained against the ship or its owners for salvage of the cargo. The only agreement contained in the document is that "the matter of compensation"... is to be left to arbitrators at home. This, however, was valueless as an agreement.'

The court had no doubt that this was salvage proper and not general average. In spite of the contract entered into by the parties, the service rendered was treated as maritime, and not as contractual salvage.

Salvage and general average

The similarities between salvage and general average need not concern us here, for what is significant in relation to marine insurance are the features which differentiate them, and this can be found in the last limb of s 65(2). As this section is also crucial for the purpose of comparing salvage with sue and labour, the relevant part of the subsection will be cited here in full. Section 65(2) states that 'salvage charges':

> '... do not include the expenses of services in the nature of salvage rendered by the assured or his agents, or any person employed for hire by them, for the purpose of averting a peril insured against. Such expenses, where properly incurred, may be recovered as particular charges or as a general average loss, according to the circumstances under which they were incurred.'

The objective of s 65(2) is to stress the fact that a general average loss (and particular charges), even if it takes the form of salvage, is not an expense incurred 'independently of contract': it is, therefore, not recoverable as a 'salvage charge'. The fundamental difference between salvage and general average is that in the case of the former, the salvage service is performed by a person who intervenes voluntarily, whereas in the latter, it is performed by a person who is specially hired or employed by the shipowner, on a *quantum meruit* basis, to save the whole adventure from a common danger. The service may be in the nature of salvage, but the circumstances under which it is rendered and the method of payment are quite different from salvage proper.

---

16 (1885) 10 PD 114. In *The Kryiaki* [1993] 1 Lloyd's Rep 137, the matter was not argued, as it was settled by the insurers: the salvage under an LOF agreement, payable only if the vessel is successfully towed to port.

17 *Ibid*, at p 117.

This special quality of salvage was referred to by the Lord Chancellor in *Aitchison v Lohre* as follows:[18]

> 'Now salvage expenses are not assessed upon the *quantum meruit* principle; they are assessed upon the general principle of maritime law, which gives to the persons who bring in the ship a sum quite out of proportion to the actual expense incurred and the actual service rendered, the largeness of the sum being based upon this consideration – that if the effort to save the ship (however laborious in itself, and dangerous in its circumstances) had not been successful, nothing whatever would have been paid.'

Another distinguishing feature between salvage and general average came to light in *The Raisby*,[19] the facts of which have already been referred to. It is necessary to add that the plaintiffs (salvors) had successfully brought an action against *The Raisby* for the salvage of the ship and freight, but failed in their claim against the cargo owners. They then brought this action against the owners of *The Raisby* personally to recover from them remuneration for the salvage of the cargo, or damages for not obtaining a proper average bond. The plaintiffs contended that the defendants were liable in the first instance to pay salvage in respect of freight and cargo, and to recover a proportion of it back from the cargo owners. By this argument, they were in effect proposing that the loss was recoverable as general average.

The nature of, and the liability to pay, salvage were in this case called into question. As the service was considered by the court as maritime, and not contractual, salvage, it held that 'no primary liability rests on the ship or its owners to pay for the salvage of the cargo'. The liability of the interests which had benefited from the salvage was described as follows:

> 'As the liability both as to the parties responsible and as to the amount is left at large to be determined in due course of law ... the plaintiffs must seek their remedy for salvage of cargo, as distinct from ship, from those who have had the benefit of that salvage.'

This remark has clarified that the liability for salvage is not joint, but several. Unlike general average, each interest is individually or severally liable to the salvor for the value of the salvage services rendered. Each party whose property has been salved is liable to settle *directly* with the salvors for their own individual share of any award. There is not, as in the case of general average, a common purse, from which funds could be drawn by the salvors.[20]

Salvage remuneration: The York-Antwerp Rules

The distinction between salvage and general average, though subtle, is nowadays, for all commercial and practical purposes, not of great importance, as is the distinction between salvage and sue and labour. Even though both the Act and the common law have drawn a clear line between salvage and general

---

18 (1879) 4 App Cas 755 at pp 766–767.

19 (1885) 10 PD 114; 5 Asp MLC 473.

20 In contrast, *Anderson, Tritton & Co v Ocean SS Co* (1884) 10 App Cas 107 has held that where the owners of a salved vessel had entered into a binding agreement with the salvors to pay, and had paid a particular sum for salvage of ship and cargo, they might recover such portion of it from the owners of cargo as general average.

average, they are now in practice treated in the same way. This can be seen in the Institute Clauses: cl 10 of the ITCH(95),[21] cl 8 of the IVCH(95), and cl 2 (general average clause) of all the ICC apply to both general average and salvage.

Moreover, r VI of the York-Antwerp Rules 1994, in declaring that 'expenditure incurred by the parties to the adventure in the nature of salvage, whether under contract or otherwise, shall be allowed in general average', has also brought salvage under the same umbrella as general average. However, it is observed that the said rule has chosen a more neutral term, 'salvage remuneration', to describe the loss. This, together with the words 'under contract or otherwise', is meant to clarify that both contractual and maritime salvage are, provided that they are 'carried out for the purpose of preserving from the peril the property involved in the common maritime adventure', to be allowed as general average. By reason of this practice, the difference between salvage and general average has paled into insignificance.

It has to be borne in mind that the York-Antwerp Rules 1994 are applicable only if the 'contract of affreightment so provides that the adjustment be according to the York-Antwerp Rules'.[22] In the unlikely event that the contract of affreightment does not so provide, then the above-mentioned differences between salvage and general average would become important. Moreover, it is to be remembered that only the 'adjustment' of the loss is governed by the York-Antwerp Rules. Thus, an assured has still to identify the nature of his loss as one falling within the terms of his policy.

Salvage and sue and labour

The distinction between salvage and sue and labour is of critical importance. This is clearly illustrated in *Aitchison v Lohre*,[23] the principles of which are now embodied in s 65(2). In a policy containing a sue and labour clause, the ship was insured with the defendant for £1,200, being valued at £2,600. During the voyage, she encountered very severe weather and was in grave danger of sinking when she was rescued by a steamer. The salvors were afterwards awarded £800 for salvage by the Admiralty Court. The owners did not abandon the vessel, but chose to have her repaired. That the insurers were under the policy liable to pay the assured the sum of up to £1,200 for the repairs was never in dispute. The controversy was whether the assured was also entitled to recover from the insurer the £800 which they had paid to the salvors. Naturally, as sue and labour is recoverable in *addition* to the sum insured, it is not surprising that counsel for the assured argued that the amount was recoverable, if not as general average, as a sue and labour charge.

The actual decision of the House is contained in the following remark made by Lock Blackburn:[24]

---

21 Previously, cl 11 of the ITCH(83).

22 Clause 10.2 of the ITCH(95) and cl 8.2 of the IVCH(95).

23 (1879) 4 App Cas 755.

24 *Ibid*, at p 765.

'The amount of such salvage occasioned by a peril has always been recovered, without dispute, under an averment that there was a loss by that peril ... and I have not been able to find any case in which it was recovered under a count for suing and labouring.'

Indeed, it was a golden opportunity for the House to elicit the fundamental differences between salvage and sue and labour. A distinguishing feature which the House had pointed out was in relation to the capacity in which the salvors were employed: as the salvors in this case were not labouring as agents of the assured, but were acting as salvors in the maritime law, the award was held not recoverable as sue and labour. The criterion is stated by the said Law Lord as follows:[25]

'It is all one whether the labour is by the assured or their agents themselves, or by persons whom they have hired for the purpose, but the object was to encourage exertion on the part of the assured; not to provide an additional remedy for the recovery, by the assured, of indemnity for a loss which was, by the maritime law, a consequence of the peril.'

Another distinguishing mark was noted by The Lord Chancellor:[26]

'... if any expenses were to be recoverable under the suing and labouring clause, they must be expenses assessed upon the *quantum meruit* principle ... If the payment were to be assessed and made under the suing and labouring clause it would be payment for services rendered, *whether the service had succeeded* in bringing the ship into port or not.'

The rule in *Aitchson v Lohre* was applied to a different set of circumstances in *Dixon v Whitworth*.[27] In this instance, the plaintiff (the assured) having paid the sum of £2,000 awarded to the salvors, sought to recover the same from his own insurers with whom he had taken up a policy containing a sue and labour clause, but against a total loss *only*. As the sum paid by the plaintiff for salvage was a partial loss, it was held not recoverable. Were it sue and labour, the loss would have been recoverable, notwithstanding that the fact that the policy was for a total loss only.[28] This decision has reinforced the rule that a salvage charge may be recovered only as a loss by a peril insured against, and not as an additional or supplementary payment.[29]

A PERIL INSURED AGAINST

Like general average and sue and labour, a salvage charge is, according to s 65(2), recoverable only if it is 'incurred in preventing a loss by perils insured against'. This point is also stressed by cl 10.4 of the ITCH(95) and cl 8.4 of the IVCH(95).[30] The Court of Appeal decision in *Ballantyne v Mackinnon*[31] clearly

---

25   *Ibid.*

26   *Ibid*, at p 766. Emphasis added.

27   (1880) 4 Asp MLC 327 CA; 43 LT 365.

28   See s 78(1).

29   Section 78(1) states that sue and labour is 'supplementary to the contract of insurance ...'.

30   Clause 2 of the ICC (A), (B) and (C).

31   (1896) 2 QB 455, CA.

illustrates the need to satisfy this requirement.[32] The plaintiffs (the assured) were ordered by the Admiralty Court to pay the owner of a trawler a sum of money for salvage services performed by a trawler in towing the plaintiffs' vessel to safety when she ran short of coal during a voyage. The plaintiffs then brought this action against their insurers to recover the salvage they had incurred. As the unseaworthiness of the ship, and not an insured peril, had engendered the need for the salvage aid, the plaintiffs failed in their claim. It was also held that the defendants were not precluded, by the judgment of the Admiralty Court, from setting up the defence that the loss did not arise from any of the perils insured against.

Another aspect of s 65(1), which complements the above requirement, is the rule that salvage charges may be 'recovered as a loss by those perils' meaning the perils insured against which brought about the need for salvage aid. This rule was described by Lord Blackburn in *Aitchison v Lohre* as thus: 'The amount of such salvage occasioned by a peril has always been recovered without dispute, under an averment that there was a loss by that peril'.[33]

EXCLUSIONS

The ITCH (95) has, through its new cl 10.5, clarified that, though the insurance covers 'the vessels proportion of salvage, salvage charges and/or general average', no claim is allowed for or in respect of:

- special compensation payable to a salvor under art 14 of the International Convention on Salvage 1989,[34] and

- expenses or liabilities incurred in respect of damage (actual or threatened) to the environment, or due to the escape or release (actual or threatened) of pollutants substances from the vessel.

The reason for these exclusions is that they relate to environmental risks which are not insured perils under a standard policy of insurance.

As was seen, an enhanced award made under art 13(1)(b) is not affected by the above exclusions. Clause 10.6 of the ITCH(95) has specifically noted that any salvage remuneration which, by reason of Article 13(1)(b) of the International Convention on Salvage 1989, has taken into account 'the skill and efforts of the salvors in preventing or minimising damage to the environment' is not affected by the above exclusions. Clause 10.6 clarifies that the whole of the salvage reward is recoverable, even though one of the criteria used in fixing the reward may relate to an environmental issue.

---

32 *Pyman SS Co v Lords Commissioners of the Admiralty* [1919] 1 KB 49, CA, is another authority which vividly illustrates the point that the salvage has to be incurred in preventing a loss by a peril insured against. Though the litigation was not in relation to marine insurance, the points raised are, nevertheless, indirectly relevant. If the same issue were to arise in a dispute in marine insurance, the court would probably have to determine the proportion of the salvage charge which is occasioned by the consequence of hostilities or warlike operations, and that, by marine risks.

33 (1879) 4 App Cas 755 at p 765.

34 See Appendix 25.

It is to be noted that by cl 8.4.5 of the ITCH(95), any sum which the assured shall pay for or in respect of salvage remuneration made under Article 13(1)(b), as in the case cl 10.6, is not excluded in a claim made under the 3/4ths collision liability clause. Such an enhanced award is specifically excluded from the exclusions clause to the 3/4ths collision liability clause.[35]

Special compensation

Article 14 (and art 13(1)(b)) is concerned with rewarding and compensating a salvor for steps taken by him to prevent or minimise damage to the environment. A salvor who has failed to earn an award under art 13 'shall be entitled' to a special compensation from the owner of the vessel under art 14.[36] By art 14,[37] he is entitled to special compensation from the owner of the vessel of an amount 'equivalent to his expenses' as defined by art 14(1). Further, by art 14(2), if the salvor by his salvage operations has 'prevented or minimised damage to the environment', the special compensation 'payable by the owner to the salvor, may be increased up to a maximum of 30% of the expenses incurred by the salvor. Such special compensation payable by the owner to the salvor is not, by reason of cl 10.5 of the ITCH(95), recoverable by the assured from his insurer as salvage, salvage charges, general average or sue and labour.[38]

Expenses or liabilities incurred by the assured

Clause 10.5.2 of the ITCH(95), which excludes claims for 'expenses or liabilities incurred in respect of damage to the environment, or the threat to such damage, or as a consequence of the escape of pollutants substances from the vessel, or the threat of such escape or release', is, strictly speaking, a separate provision which may or may not be connected with the subject of salvage.[39] The said expenses or liabilities could, but need not necessarily arise as a result of a salvage operation. The expenses or liabilities are not payable to the salvors as a salvage award or as a special compensation. As in the case of the special compensation, such expenses or liabilities are neither recoverable from the insurer as salvage, salvage charges, general average nor as sue and labour.[40]

---

35 Discussed in Chapter 13.

36 A special compensation under art 14 may be made to a salvor where no award is made under art 13 (because the salvage services were unsuccessful) or as a supplement to an art 13 award in certain circumstances.

37 'Expenses' is defined in art 14(3) to mean 'out-of-pocket expenses reasonably incurred by the salvor ... and a fair rate for equipment ... actually and reasonably used in the salvage operation ...'. See *Semco Salvage & Marine Pte Ltd v Lancer Navigation Co Ltd, The Nagasaki Spirit* [1995] 2 Lloyd's Rep 44, QBD, for a discussion of the meaning of 'fair rate' and arts 13 and 14 of the said Convention.

38 See new cl 11.2 of the ITCH(95).

39 Neither the word 'salvage' nor 'salvor' appear in cl 10.5.2 of the ITCH(95).

40 A shipowner may take out the Institute General Average – Pollution Expenditure Clause to cover such expenses and liabilities.

B – GENERAL AVERAGE

INTRODUCTION

The law of general average exists as an independent branch of the law of maritime distinct from carriage of goods by sea and marine insurance. In *The Brigella*, Lord Gorell Barnes said that:[41]

'... the obligation to contribute in general average exists between the parties to the adventure whether they are insured or not. The circumstances of a party being insured can have no influence upon the adjustment of general average, the rules of which ... are entirely independent of insurance.'

In *Simonds v White*,[42] it was pointed out that the origin of the principle of general average is of 'very ancient date' and the obligation to contribute depends 'not so much upon the terms of any particular instrument as upon a general rule of maritime law.' The fact that it 'had existed for ages before the practice of insurance was known'[43] explains why it does not depend on insurance (or any other branch of law) for sustenance or for its existence.[44]

In relation to marine insurance, the legal position was summarised by Mr Justice Bailhache in *Brandeis Goldschmidt and Co v Economic Insurance Co Ltd* as follows:[45] 'The liability in general average before 1906 arose at common law, and since the Act of 1906 by statute. It did not arise under the policy, but the policy might contain express provisions modifying or excluding it.'

There is a vast body of case law on the subject with litigation pertaining not just to basic principles of the law of general average, but also to its application in relation to contracts of affreightment and marine insurance. This chapter will, as far as it is possible so to do, focus on only the legal problems relating to general average when applied to marine insurance[46] and, as and when necessary, the general principles of the law of general average will only be briefly mentioned.[47]

---

41 (1893) P 189 at p 195.

42 (1824) 2 B & C 805 at p 811.

43 *Price v Noble* (1811) 4 Taunt 123 at p 126.

44 Lord Blackburn in *Anderson, Tritton, and Co v Ocean SS Co* (1884) 5 Asp MLC 401 at p 403, HL, said: 'No more contribution is exigible from the owner of a parcel of goods that are insured than from the owner of a parcel that is not insured'.

45 (1922) 38 TLR 609 at p 610.

46 Obviously, scientific and mathematical adjustments and calculations as to how general average is to be apportioned is outside the scope of this work.

47 It is not possible in this work to engage in any in-depth study of general legal principles, or the rules relating to adjustment, of general average. For a complete study of the subject, reference should be made to classic works on the subject such as R Lowndes and G R Rudolf, *The Law of General Average and the York-Antwerp Rules* (1990, 11th edn). *Burton v English* (1883) 12 QBD 218, CA, contains a good account of the basis and origin of the law of general average.

DEFINITIONS OF A 'GENERAL AVERAGE ACT'

In marine insurance, the law of general average is regulated by the Act, the Institute Clauses and, the York-Antwerp Rules 1994[48] as envisaged by all the Institute Clauses for Hulls,[49] and Cargo,[50] if the contract of affreightment so provides. Even though the obligation to contribute does not really arise from contract, but from 'the old Rhodian laws' which have 'become incorporated into the law of England as the law of the ocean',[51] nevertheless, the law is tolerant enough to allow for the obligation to be 'limited, qualified or even excluded by the special terms of a contract'.[52]

As the Act has its own definition of general average, it would be more appropriate to begin this study with the statutory, rather than the common law definition of the term. A 'general average act' is defined by s 66(2) as follows:

'There is a general average act where any extraordinary sacrifice or expenditure is voluntarily and reasonably made or incurred in time of peril for the purpose of preserving the property imperilled in the common adventure.'

Mr Justice Roche in *Green Star Shipping Co v The London Assurance, The Andree*[53] was correct when he said that: 'Subsections (1) to (3) define or formulate the rules of general average as between the parties to the contract of affreightment. The rest of the subsections deal with the rights of the assured or liabilities of insurers'.

The principles underlying the statutory definition are derived from cases,[54] the most notable of which is *Birkley v Presgrave*.[55] It would appear that no work on the subject of general average can be complete without citation of the well-accepted definition enunciated therein by Mr Justice Lawrence:

'All loss which arises in consequence of extraordinary sacrifice made, or expenses incurred for the preservation of the ship and cargo, comes within general average, and must be borne proportionally by all who are interested.'

Another comprehensive and illustrative definition was delivered by Lord Blackburn of the House of Lords in *Kemp v Halliday*:[56]

---

48 The 1994 Rules have replaced the 1974 Rules (as amended 1990). To bring cl 10.3 of the ITCH(95) up to date, 'York-Antwerp Rules 1994' has been substituted for 'York-Antwerp Rules 1974': see Appendix 24.

49 Clause 10.2 of the ITCH(95) (previously cl 11.2 of the ITCH(83)) and cl 9.2 of the IVCH(95) state: '... but where the contract of affreightment so provides the adjustment shall be according to the York-Antwerp Rules'. But if the contract of affreightment does not so provide, 'the law and practice obtaining at the place where the adventure ends' would apply.

50 Clause 2 of the ICC (A), (B) and (C).

51 *Per* Brett MR *Burton v English* (1883) 12 QBD 218 at p 223.

52 *Per* Abbott CJ in *Simonds v White* (1824) 2 B & C 805 at p 811.

53 [1933] 1 KB 378 at p 387.

54 Eg *Hallett v Wigram* (1850) 9 CB 580; *Burton v English* (1883) 12 QBD 218; *Atwood v Sellar & Co* (1880) 5 QBD 286; and *Svendsen v Wallace Brothers* (1885) 10 App Cas 404.

55 (1801) 1 East 220 at p 228.

56 (1865) 6 B & S 723 at pp 746–747.

'In order to give rise to a charge as general average, it is essential that there should be a voluntary sacrifice to preserve more subjects than one exposed to a common jeopardy as if, instead of money being expended for the purpose, money's worth were thrown away. It is immaterial whether the shipowner sacrifices a cable or an anchor to get the ship off a shoal, or pays the worth of it to hire those extra services which get her off.'

It has to be pointed out that these definitions are supplemented by the York-Antwerp Rules 1994 which has its own definition of a 'general average act'. Rule A states: 'There is a general average act, when, and only when, any extraordinary sacrifice or expenditure is intentionally and reasonably made or incurred for the common safety for the purpose of preserving from peril the property involved in a common maritime adventure.'

However defined, the single common golden thread is the 'for the sake of all'[57] principle, the cardinal rule of the law of general average, proposed by Lord Denning MR in *Australian Shipping Commission v Green and Others*,[58] in which he said that 'general average arises when the master of a vessel gives something for the sake of all (*quod pro omnibus datum est*).' He then proceeded to simplify matters in the following way: 'It arises when a ship, laden with cargo, is in peril on the sea, such peril indeed that the whole adventure, both ship and cargo, is in danger of being lost'.

The word 'general' has been defined in *Harris v Scaramanga*[59] to mean that the loss is to be 'generally distributed, or the contribution to be generally made by all. In this sense, it is distinguished from a 'particular' average loss.

That there are two aspects to general average is also clear. Section 66(1) states that: 'It includes a general average expenditure as well as a general average sacrifice.' As this distinction is of importance, especially in relation to s 66(4) and the Institute Hulls Clauses,[60] it is necessary to say something about it. The two classic examples of a general average sacrifice are the cutting away of a mast[61] and the throwing overboard of cargo in order that the whole venture may be saved from a common peril. [62] But when a ship has, as a result of an insured peril, to be towed into a port of refuge for the safety of the whole venture, the cost for this service and for other necessary collateral operations,

---

57 In *Power v Whitmore* (1815) 4 M & S 141 at p 149, Lord Ellenborough CJ said that 'general average must lay its foundation in a sacrifice of part for the sake of the rest ...' *Cf* whereas the 'stitch in time' applies to sue and labour, the notion of the 'for the sake of all' applies to general average.

58 [1971] 1 All ER 353 at p 355, CA.

59 (1872) LR 7 CP 481 at p 496.

60 The relevant part of s 66(4) states: ' ... in the case of a general average sacrifice he may recover from the insurer in respect of the whole loss without having enforced his right of contribution from other parties liable to contribute'. The same principle is applied in cl 10.1 of the ITCH(95) and cl 8.1 of the IVCH(95).

61 In *Plummer v Wildman* (1815) 3 M & S 482, the master was compelled to cut away his rigging in order to preserve the ship; *Austin Friars SS Co Ltd v Spillers & Bakers Ltd* [1915] 3 KB 586; *Whitecross Wire Co Ltd v Savill* (1882) 8 QBD 653, CA; and *The Bona* [1895] P 125, CA.

62 Eg *Dickenson v Jardine* (1868) LR 3 CP 639; *Gregson v Gilbert* (1783) Doug KB 232; *Entwistle v Ellis* (1857) 2 H & N 549; *Stewart v West India & Pacific SS Co* (1873) LR 8 QB 362, Ex Ch; *Robinson v Price* (1877) 2 QBD 295, CA; and *The Gratitudine* (1801) 3 Ch Rob 240.

such as for unloading, landing, warehousing and re-shipping the cargo, are general average expenditures.[63]

General average contribution

The whole foundation of general average is contribution: the owner of the interest which has been saved has to make a contribution to the party who has sacrificed his property or expended money to save the whole venture. The liability of the interested parties to make a contribution is declared in s 66(3):

> 'Where there is a general average loss, the party on whom it falls is entitled, subject to the conditions imposed by maritime law, to a rateable contribution from the other parties interested, and such contribution is called a general average contribution.'

The liability of the insurer is embodied in ss 66 (4) and (5): an assured who 'has paid, or is liable to pay, a general average contribution in respect of the subject insured ... may recover therefor from the insurer'. The insurer is also liable to reimburse the assured who has himself expended money or sacrificed the subject-matter insured to save the whole adventure from a common peril.

Certain requirements have to satisfied before a loss can be classified as to be by way of general average. Four of its main features are expressly stated in s 66(2). First, the sacrifice or expenditure has to be 'extraordinary'; secondly, it has to be 'voluntarily and reasonably' made; thirdly, it has to be incurred in time of 'peril'; and finally, the sacrifice or expenditure has to be incurred for the purpose of preserving the property 'imperilled in the common adventure'. To understand fully these attributes, references to cases have to be made.

Extraordinary sacrifice or expenditure

A sacrifice or expenditure has to be extraordinary before it would be classed as general average. Surprisingly, it has not always been easy to discern the ordinary from the extraordinary; and this is evident from the number of suits which have been brought before the courts for adjudication as to whether a particular expense incurred was or was not extraordinary. As to be expected, most of the actions seem to revolve around cases relating to contracts of affreightment. For example, in *Wilson v Bank of Victoria*,[64] due to a collision with an iceberg, a sailing vessel sustained so much damage to her masts that she had to resort to the use her steam power in order to continue with her voyage. The dispute between the parties, the shipowner and the shippers, concerned the cost incurred for the purchase of extra coal consumed, for which the shippers were called upon to make a contribution. The court held that the fact that the engine was used to a much greater extent than would generally occur on such a voyage, and so caused the disbursement for coals to be extraordinarily heavy,

---

63   See *Job v Langton* (1856) 6 E & B 779; and *Svendsen v Wallace Brothers* (1885) 10 App Cas 404, HL.

64   (1867) LR 2 QB 203. See also *The Bona* [1895] P 125 where extra costs incurred for coal used in order to accelerate the speed of a vessel was held not be a general average act.

did not render it an extraordinary disbursement.[65] A factor which greatly influenced the court's decision is that the shipowners were, by the contract of affreightment on such a ship, bound to give the services of the auxiliary screw and to make all the necessary disbursement for fuel. As such an expenditure was expected of them, there was nothing extraordinary about it, for when they were incurred, the owners were merely carrying out their obligation under the contract of carriage.

In *Hingston v Wendt*,[66] the owner of a ship which, having gone ashore with cargo on board, had, for the benefit of all concerned, to expend money to discharge the cargo in order to bring it to a place of safety. Mr Justice Blackburn held that as the expenditure was incurred for the purpose of saving the whole venture, ship as well as cargo, it constituted general average. He was clear that the 'expenditure was not incurred on behalf of the master as agent of the shipowner, performing his contract to carry on the cargo to its destination and earn freight, but was an extraordinary expenditure for the purpose of saving the property at risk'. As such, the owners of each part of the property saved were required to contribute rateably.

A clearer illustration can be found in a more recent case, *Societe Nouvelle D'Armement v Spillers & Bakers Ltd*,[67] where for fear of being attacked by enemies during the war, the master hired a tug to tow the vessel to port. One of the issues which the court had to decide was whether the cost for the hiring of the tug qualified as an 'extraordinary' expenditure. Relying on an earlier authority,[68] the court expressed the opinion that: 'General average expenditure must be incurred to avoid extraordinary and abnormal peril as distinguished from the ordinary and normal perils of the sea ...'. And as 'the risk of being attacked or destroyed by the King's enemies was not an extraordinary and abnormal peril' in the circumstances of the case, the loss was not recoverable as general average.[69]

Using much simpler language, Lord Blackburn in *Kemp v Halliday* summarised the legal position as follows:[70]

> 'It is quite true that so long as the expenditure by the shipowner is merely such as he would incur in the fulfilment of his ordinary duty as shipowner, it cannot be general average.'

---

65 See also *Harrison v Bank of Australasia* (1872) LR 7 Ex 39; 1 Asp MLC 198, where it was held that there was no right to general average contribution in respect of costs incurred to purchase further supplies of coals to pump the vessel; the burning of spars and ship's stores was held an extraordinary sacrifice.

66 (1876) 1 QBD 367 at p 370.

67 [1917] 1 KB 865.

68 *Taylor v Curtis* (1816) 6 Taunt 608 at p 624, where in similar circumstances, the losses were held to fall 'where the fortune of war cast them'.

69 [1917] 1 KB 865 at p 872.

70 (1866) 6 B & S 723 at pp 746–747. See also *Anderson, Tritton & Co v Ocean SS Co* [1884] 15 Asp MLC 401.

Voluntarily and reasonably made

According to s 66(2), to constitute a general average loss, the sacrifice or expenditure has to be 'voluntarily and reasonably' made in time of peril. In r A of the York-Antwerp Rules 1994, the terms 'intentionally and reasonably' are used. There is very little English authority on the subject. However, *Athel Line v Liverpool and London War Risks Association Ltd*[71] has given an insight into the meaning of the word 'intentionally'. In this case, an expenditure was incurred for the purchase of fuel and stores consumed during the course of a voyage, when a vessel sailing in convoy was ordered by the naval officer in charge to return to the port from which she had sailed. As the expenditure was incurred as a result of 'the blind and unreasoning obedience of a subordinate to the lawful orders of a superior authority', it was held not recoverable as general average.[72]

Properly charged

The fact that an expenditure or sacrifice has been 'reasonably' made in order to save the adventure from a common peril does not necessarily mean that the whole of the loss is automatically allowable as general average. The sum which is 'properly' chargeable to general average for which a contribution may be claimed has to be ascertained.

In *Anderson, Tritton & Co v Ocean Steamship Co*,[73] the House of Lords pointed out that the mere fact that an expenditure may have been 'reasonably' made does not necessarily mean that the 'whole' of such sum is chargeable as general average against the other interested parties. It was stressed that there is neither reason nor authority for saying that 'the whole amount which the owners of the ship choose to pay is, as a matter of law, to be charged to general average'.

Peril or danger

Joseph Watson & Son Ltd v Firemen's Fund Insurance Co of San Francisco[74] is, of course, the classic authority on this aspect of the law relating to general average. It held that to constitute a general average act, a peril must in fact exist and any situation which 'looks as if there was a peril' was not good enough. In this case, cargo was damaged when the master caused steam to be turned into the hold of the ship in order to extinguish a supposed fire. The court had no doubt whatsoever that general average 'does not touch losses incurred in a mistaken attempt to avoid a peril in fact non-existent'.

This does not, however, mean that the peril has to be 'immediate' before the master can take action. In *Vlassopoulos v British and Foreign Marine Insurance Co, The Makis*, the matter was taken further by Mr Justice Roche when he explained that:[75]

---

71 [1944] 1 KB 87.

72 See also *Papayanni & Jeromia v Grampian SS Co Ltd* (1896) 1 Com Cas 448 which, though not an insurance case, is relevant for the purpose of illustrating the meaning of the word 'voluntary'.

73 (1884) 10 App Cas 107.

74 [1922] 2 KB 355.

75 [1929] 1 KB 187 at p 199.

'It is not necessary that the ship should be actually in the grip, or even nearly in the grip, of the disaster that may raise from a danger. It would be a very bad thing if shipmasters had to wait until that state of things arose in order to justify them do an act which would be a general average act.'

The judge drew attention to the fact that both the Act and the York-Antwerp Rules use the word 'peril', not 'immediate peril', and 'peril' means the same thing as 'danger'. He concluded that 'the peril must be real and not imaginary, that it must be substantial and not merely slight or negatory. In short, it must be a real danger'.

In very similar terms, Mr Justice Sankey in *Societe Nouvelle D'Armement v Spillers & Bakers Ltd*[76] pointed out that even though the word 'peril' is not qualified, it has always been understood to mean that it has to be 'imminent', and that implies that 'it must be substantial and threatening and something more than the ordinary perils of the seas ...'.

Common adventure

The requirement that the sacrifice or expenditure has to be incurred for the purpose of preserving the property 'imperilled in the *common* adventure' is an important one, for it distinguishes general average from sue and labour. If only one interest is at risk, the loss is not general average and any extraordinary expenditure incurred to avert or minimise the loss would fall within the realm of sue and labour. It is to be noted that this feature is stressed throughout the York-Antwerp Rules. The word 'common' is used in relation to safety, the maritime adventure and appears in almost all the rules. That the sacrifice or expenditure has to be incurred for the joint or common benefit of ship, cargo and freight[77] is a well-established principle under common law.[78] In *Oppenhein v Fry*,[79] Mr Justice Blackburn observed that 'any expenditure incurred entirely and exclusively for saving the whole subject of insurance should for the purpose of adjusting the loss on this policy, be treated as general average ...'.

Ballast voyages not under charter

A sacrifice or expenditure incurred to prevent a loss during a voyage in which no cargo was carried on board at the time of loss can hardly be described as having been incurred for common benefit: there being no common adventure, such a loss would not be recoverable by way of general average. If it were not for cl 10.3 of the ITCH(95) and cl 8.3 of the IVCH(95), such a loss would not be recovered by way of general averages, there being no common adventure. The essential parts of the said clause state:

---

76 [1917] 1 KB 865 at p 871.

77 See *Carisbrook SS Co Ltd v London & Provincial Marine & General Insurance Co Ltd* [1902] 2 KB 681.

78 See *Kemp v Halliday* (1866) 6 B & S 723.

79 (1864) 3 B & S 873 at p 884. Perhaps, a better choice of words would be 'the whole adventure' rather than 'the whole subject of insurance'.

'When the vessel sails in ballast, not under charter, the provisions of the York-Antwerp Rules, 1994 ... shall be applicable, and the voyage for this purpose shall be deemed to continue from the port or place of departure until the arrival of the Vessel at the first port or place thereafter ...'

The purpose of this clause is to deem a ballast voyage, not under charter, as if she were proceeding under a contract of affreightment containing the York-Antwerp Rules, 1994: an artificial voyage has been created for the benefit of the assured.

Ballast voyages under charter

To illustrate the case of a ballast voyage made whilst the ship is under charter, *Carisbrook SS Co Ltd v London and Provincial Marine and General Insurance Co Ltd*[80] has to be discussed. In this case, a sacrifice of ship's materials was made during a voyage when the ship was in ballast. The court held this to be a general average loss to which chartered freight was made to contribute, even though cargo was not board the vessel at the time of loss. It has to be emphasised that the circumstances of the case were rather special in the sense that the voyage charterparty was for one indivisible out-and-home voyage under which the ship was to fetch a cargo and bring it home. Thus, though the loss was sustained during the outward voyage, when no cargo was on board, the homeward freight was held liable to contribute to a general average sacrifice. In each case, the terms of the charterparty would have to be closely examined.[81]

Avoidance of a peril insured against

Another very important feature of general average relevant only to marine insurance is contained in s 66(6) which states that: 'In the absence of express stipulation, the insurer is not liable for any general average loss or contribution where the loss was not incurred for the purpose of avoiding, or in connection with the avoidance of, a peril insured against'. The same principle is enunciated in simpler terms in cl 10.4 of the ITCH(95) as follows: 'No claim under this Clause 10 shall in any case be allowed where the loss was not incurred to avoid or in connection with the avoidance of a peril insured against.' Thus, for example, in a policy subject to a war exclusion clause, the assured would not be able to recover for any loss incurred arising from a war peril.

The Institute Cargo Clauses

In this regard, it is observed that the ICC are more generous in its application of general average: cl 2 states that general average 'incurred to avoid or in connection with the avoidance of loss from *any cause* except those excluded in Clauses 4, 5, 6 and 7 or elsewhere in this insurance' is recoverable. This means that provided that the event does not fall within any of the exceptions listed, the loss would be recoverable, even though it may not have arisen from a peril

---

80 [1902] 2 KB 681.

81 The outcome of the case would have been different if the loss was sustained during a preliminary voyage, which was not part of the charterparty.

insured against. In so far as general average is concerned, the ICC(B) and (C) are treated as if they are for 'all risks'.[82]

Success

The element of success is implicit in the doctrine of general average (and also of salvage); and yet neither the Act, the Institute Clauses nor the York-Antwerp Rules 1994 has made provision for this. Interestingly enough, though there is no authority on the subject, there seems to be an understanding that if the act (whether a sacrifice or expenditure) completely fails and nothing is saved, there can be no contribution, for 'there is nothing left to contribute'[83] and, consequently, the loss has to fall where it lies.

In the case where there is some measure of success, such as when only cargo has been saved, the legal position is less clear, as there are two schools of thought on the subject,[84] but the great masters such as Arnould, Carver and Lowndes seem to favour the view that, if some of the property be saved, there must be contribution. In such a circumstance, there is, in a manner of speech, a 'fund' or a 'value' upon which average adjustment could be made, and it is expected of a party whose property has been saved to make a contribution.

Clause 11.5 of the ITCH(95)

By virtue of cl 11.2, cl 11.5 of the ITCH(95)[85] is made to apply to general average (and salvage charges) even though the clause is entitled 'duty of the assured (sue and labour)'.[86] The effect of the cl 11.5 is to allow an assured, when a claim for a total loss of the vessel is admitted, the right to recover expenses incurred for 'saving or attempting to save the vessel and other property', even though 'there are no proceeds, or the expenses exceed the proceeds'. The words 'and other property' seem to suggest that it applies to general average, and not sue and labour which arises when only one interest is at risk. Though the word 'proceeds' could be given a wide interpretation to include both 'the vessel and other property' (cargo?), in the context that the policy relates only to hull, it would not be unreasonable to assume that it applies only to the proceeds of the 'vessel' and not of 'the other property', which is not part of the ship.[87]

The objective of cl 11.5 is to allow an assured the right of recovery, even though the expenditure incurred for common good is abortive, and no real benefit has been derived by the vessel from the general average act. In the absence of this clause, the assured would not be in a position to recover any of

---

82 The opening words of s 66(6) – 'In the absence of express stipulation' – allow exceptions to be made to the general rule.

83 This is Arnould's view, see para 919.

84 For a survey of the rules employed in different countries, see Arnould at para 977.

85 Clause 11.5 of the ITCH(95) has been updated to incorporate the exclusion of special compensations and expenses referred to in cl 10.5. This update need not concern us here and will be discussed below.

86 See cl 19.2 read with cl 9.5 of the IVCH(95).

87 See Arnould at paras 919 and 978; O'May, pp 340 and 351. It is noted that there is no equivalent to cl 11.5 in any of the ICC. Clause 11.5 of the ITCH(95) is not happily worded.

the expenses so incurred as general average because the act has proved to be unsuccessful: there is no value upon which a contribution could be apportioned.

The extent of the *insurer's liability* is also spelt out in cl 11.5. It is limited to 'a *pro rata* share of such proportion of the expenses or of the expenses in excess of the proceeds as the case may be, as may reasonably be regarded as having been incurred in respect of the vessel ...'. In this calculation, the proportion of under-insurance has to be taken into account.[88]

Another rather thorny problem which has to be addressed is if the ship and/or cargo are damaged or destroyed in a separate and unrelated accident arising after they have been saved from a common peril by an earlier general average act. Should an interest which had derived benefit from an earlier general average act be made liable to contribute to the general average loss when the property no longer exists *in specie* or, is of no value 'at the termination of the adventure'?[89]

It is fair to say that no contribution is expected of a party whose property fails to survive the voyage in any shape or form: there is simply nothing left to contribute. But if some value could be placed on the remains of the property, then it would not be so unreasonable to extract contribution from that 'fund'. Arnould, applying the principle that 'without such previous sacrifice nothing would have been saved at all',[90] would be amenable to hold that 'the wreck must make good that which was previously sacrificed'. The legal position is unclear, as there is no authority on the subject.

Owned by the same assured

Contribution being the essence of general average, it was at one time thought that there could never be a general average contribution unless the various interests in the maritime adventure were owned by different parties.[91] This myth was dispelled by *Montgomery & Co v Indemity Mutual Marine Insurance Co Ltd* when the Court of Appeal expressed its opinion on the matter as follows:[92]

'The object of this maritime law seems to be to give the master of the ship absolute freedom to make whatever sacrifice he thinks best to avert the perils of the sea, without any regard whatsoever to the ownership of the property sacrificed ... such a sacrifice is a general average act, quite independently of unity or diversity of ownership.'

The above principle is adopted by s 66(7): regardless of the ownership of the interests concerned, the liability of the insurer is to be determined 'as if those

---

88 See s 73(1) and *Balmoral SS Co Ltd v Marten* (1902) AC 511 upon which s 73(1) is based. If the subject-matter is not insured for its full contributory value, the indemnity payable by the insurer must be reduced in proportion to the under insurance.

89 See r 17 York-Antwerp Rules 1994.

90 Arnould, para 978.

91 See *The Brigella* [1893] P 187, overruled by *Montgomery v Indemnity Mutual Marine Insurance Co* [1902] 1 KB 734.

92 [1902] 1 KB 734 at p 740.

subjects were owned by different persons'.[93] Of course, the word 'subjects' has to be read to mean 'interests'.

LIABILITY OF THE INSURER

Distinction between sacrifice and expenditure

The distinction between a general average sacrifice and a general average expenditure is of considerable importance in so far as the procedure for a claim under the policy is concerned. This is made clear in s 66(4) and cl 10.1 of the ITCH(95).[94] To illustrate this distinction in relation to an assured's right to be reimbursed, it would be more convenient to discuss the principles as regards a general average sacrifice first.

General average sacrifice

The relevant part of s 66(4) on general average *sacrifice* lays down the rule that an assured 'may recover from the insurer in respect of the whole loss without having enforced his right of contribution from the other parties liable to contribute'.[95] This principle of full and direct recovery is derived from *Dickenson v Jardine*[96] where an owner of goods, which had been sacrificed in a time of danger for the benefit of all the interests concerned, was allowed recovery for the full insured value of the goods even though he was in a position, by reason of the loss being for general average, to recover from the other interests which had benefited from the sacrifice. In the words of Mr Justice Willes, the procedure is as follows:[97]

> 'If the assured proceeds against the underwriters in the first instance, the latter cannot avail themselves by way of plea of the fact that the assured has a distinct right against some other person. They must pay the amount claimed in the first instance, and will then be entitled to use the name of the assured, and proceed against the other parties who are liable ...'

By s 66(4), an assured is able to recover directly from his insurer the full amount of the loss.[98] Naturally, he cannot retain the proceeds of both, so as to be repaid the value of his loss twice over.

---

93   See *Carisbrook SS Co Ltd v London & Provincial Marine & General Insurance Co Ltd* [1902] 2 KB 681; and *Oppenhein and Others v Fry* (1864) 3 B & S 873 at p 884, *per* Blackburn J: '... where a voluntary sacrifice is made for the benefit of the whole adventure, it is general average; whether the ship and cargo and freight belong to one only or to different adventurers, or whether they are partially interested ...'.

94   Clause 8.1 of the IVCH(95).

95   The same principle is reiterated in cl 10.1 of the ITCH(95) as: '... the assured may recover in respect of the whole loss without first enforcing their right of contribution from other parties.'

96   (1868) LR 3 CP 639.

97   *Ibid*, at p 644.

98   He would, of course, have to give credit for contributions related to any other interests vested in him which has benefited from the sacrifice: see s 66(7).

General average expenditure

The above rule as regards general average sacrifice does not apply to a general average expenditure. The reason for making of this distinction, according to Arnould, is that expenditures 'do not involve the loss or destruction of any part of any particular interest, so as to make the underwriters on that interest directly liable in respect of the whole thereof'.[99]

As regards general average expenditure, the material part of s 66(4) states that an assured 'may recover from the insurer in respect of the whole proportion of the loss which falls upon him'. *The Mary Thomas*[100] is said to be responsible for the formulation of this rule; the decision of the court was based on the ground that the English courts would not allow a shipowner to go behind a foreign adjustment and recover from their own hull underwriters what they had failed to recover from the cargo owners their share of contribution.

'The proportion of the loss'

Indeed, the above words are important for they define the amount which an assured may recover from his insurer. After expending a sum of money in order to save the whole adventure from a common peril, a shipowner could well find himself out of pocket, should he fail to recover from the cargo owners their share of the general average contribution. In such a circumstance he would, of course, like to look to his own insurer for indemnity for the loss which he had sustained. Without a doubt, he would be able to claim, by virtue of s 66(5), his *own* share of the contribution. But whether he would always be in a position to recover from his own insurer any outstanding amount of the expenses which he had incurred for the sake of all concerned is another matter.

Green Star Shipping Co Ltd v The London Assurance and Others, The Andree[101] has dealt with one aspect of this problem. The relevant facts may be summarised as follows. The Andree was insured for a voyage during the course of which a fire and, later, a collision took place in respect of which two sets of general average expenses were incurred. After making the necessary deductions for the plaintiffs' own share of contribution (on the salved value of the ship) and the cargo owners' proportion (on the salved value of the cargo), the plaintiffs found themselves still out of pocket. The issue the court had to consider was whether this amount, which remained unsatisfied, was recoverable from the plaintiffs' own hull insurer. It has to be said that the deficit arose because the value of the salved cargo was greatly reduced by the collision.

Mr Justice Roche, relying heavily on the wording of s 66(4), held the insurer responsible for this loss. His reasoning was stated as follows:

'...if a shipowner, being the assured under a policy in the present form, incurs expenditure for general average and the cargo's contribution falls short of what is hoped or expected by reason of the diminution or extinction of its value before the adventure terminates, then I think that loss falls into the category of the

---

99   Arnould, para 1003.
100   (1894) P 108.
101   [1933] 1 KB 378.

proportion of the loss which falls upon the assured, the shipowner, and is within the meaning of those words in the Marine Insurance Act, section 66(4).'

The shipowner was able to recover the whole amount of his expenses, including the amount which he would have been able to recover from the cargo owners had the value of the cargo not been reduced between the date of the expenditure and the 'termination of the adventure'. The phrase 'the proportion of the loss which falls upon him' is by no means free from ambiguity. However, it does not mean that an assured is entitled to be indemnified only for his share of contribution in respect of the ship. These words were interpreted as being wide enough to enable him to recover *any* outstanding amount which he was not able to recover from the cargo interests.

As the net result appears to be the same as that in the case of a sacrifice, one could be tempted to argue that there is hardly any difference between them. The difference lies in the fact that as regards a sacrifice the assured may proceed directly against his own insurer without first having to make any attempt to seek recovery from the other contributory interests. Whereas in the case of an expenditure, the assured would have to exhaust his right of claim against the other interested parties first, before he could proceed against his own insurer. The difference was noted in *Brandeis Goldschmidt and Co v Economic Insurance Co Ltd* by Mr Justice Bailhache as thus:[102]

'A general sacrifice was different from general average expenditure, and if there had been a sacrifice here, the underwriters would have been immediately liable ... But this was a claim for general average expenditure, and ... could only be enforced when there had been an adjustment.'

By reason of the diminution or extinction of the value of the cargo before the termination of the adventure, the shipowner was in this case unable to recover the cargo's share of general average contribution. Where there are no proceeds or the expenses exceed the proceeds, the general rule is that a general average claim cannot be levied.[103] Whether the rule laid down in *Green Star Shipping Co Ltd v The London Assurance and Others, The Andree*[104] is to be restricted to the facts of the case is unclear. But there does not appear to be any reason why it cannot be applied to other situations, such as when an assured who, for some other reason or other (for example, bankruptcy) is unable to recover contribution from any of the other interested parties. As worded, s 66(4) is wide enough to allow an assured to recover 'the proportion of the loss which falls upon him'. If parliament had intended to limit the extent of his claim only to his share of general average contribution in respect of the subject insured, it could have easily said so. It could have stipulated that he may recover only in respect of the 'vessel's' proportion of general average, as in the case of cl 10.1 of the ITCH(95) and cl 8.1 of the IVCH(95). But as worded, s 66(4) refers to the proportion of loss which falls upon 'him', meaning the 'assured'. Provided that he has made all reasonable attempts to enforce his right of contribution from the other parties liable to contribute, an assured should be able to look to his own

---

102 (1922) 38 TLR 609 at p 610.
103 *Cf* cl 11.5 of the ITCH(95) and cl 9.5 of the IVCH(95).
104 [1933] 1 KB 378.

insurer for indemnity for 'the *whole* proportion of the loss which falls upon him'.

AVERAGE ADJUSTMENT

It is observed that as early as 1824, it was already recognised that shipowners have the freedom to stipulate the law and practice that is to govern the adjustment of general average. In *Simonds v White*,[105] the esteemed Chief Justice Abbott noted that the obligation to contribute may be 'limited, qualified or even excluded by the special terms of a contract, as between the parties to the contract'. This necessarily means that in relation to marine insurance, the adjustment of general average is in each case to be determined by the terms of the policy.

Before any claim for reimbursement for general average could be made by an assured against his insurer, the assured is required to obtain an adjustment.[106] The rules relating to adjustment are contained in cl 10.2 of the ITCH(95). There are two distinct parts to this clause, and general average may be adjusted according to either:

- the law and practice obtaining 'at the place where the adventure ends', as if the contract of affreightment contained no special terms upon the subject, or

- the York-Antwerp Rules, if the contract of affreightment so provides.

Only two possibilities are envisaged by this provision. Thus, an insurer is not bound by an adjustment which does not fall within either one of the above alternatives. For example, an adjustment obtained from a place, other than 'the place where the adventure ends' would not be acceptable. The second alternative should not pose any problem, as the York-Antwerp Rules are a well-known and established regime.

Foreign adjustment

Under common law, it was generally accepted that 'the place at which the average shall be adjusted is the place of the ship's destination or delivery of her cargo'. Even though different words are used in cl 10.2 of the ITCH(95),[107] the effect is the same as under common law, for an adventure could end either at the port of final destination named in the contract of carriage or, prematurely, at an intermediate port where the cargo, whether by necessity or consent, had to be discharged. As worded, it is wide enough to embrace both situations. Due to a common peril, an adventure could suddenly terminate in a country not within

---

105 (1824) 2 B & C 805 at p 811. See also *Brandeis Goldschmidt & Co v Economic Insurance Co Ltd* (1922) 38 TLR 609 at p 610.

106 See *Brandeis Goldschmidt & Co v Economic Insurance Co Ltd, ibid.* A cargo owner has, therefore, first to obtain an adjustment from the shipowner before he proceeds against his insurer. The initial responsibility to take the necessary steps to secure an adjustment and payment of the general average lies with the shipowner: see *Crooks v Allan* (1879) 5 QBD 36. The shipowner is not, however, according to *Wavertree Sailing Ship Co Ltd v Love and Another* [1897] AC 373, bound to employ an average stater to make out his average statement. He may do this himself. But the usual practice is to appoint a professional average adjuster to do the job.

107 Clause 8.2 of the IVCH(95).

the contemplation of the parties. Thus, by this clause an adjustment could be made according to a foreign system of law, the principles of which might well be contrary to British law and practice. The adjustment so made is called a foreign adjustment. That raises the question as to how far insurers are bound by a general average adjustment issued abroad.

In *Simonds v White*,[108] the plaintiffs, the owners of certain goods carried on board the defendant's ship, were compelled under Russian law to pay the defendants a sum of money as general average contribution, before they were allowed delivery of their cargo. As a large part of this sum would not have been charged to them as general average according to English law, the plaintiffs brought this action to recover the excess paid. The court held that, whether the terms of adjustment be beneficial or disadvantageous, the parties, were bound by it.[109]

It has, of course, to be noted that the dispute between the parties was in relation to a contract of affreightment. Whether an insurer would also by cl 10.2 be conclusively bound by a foreign adjustment made at 'the place where the adventure ends' is another matter. There is no case law on cl 10.2 and, therefore, one should be excused for referring to common law for guidance.

It is interesting to note that in *Simonds v White*,[110] the plaintiffs, in support of their cases, cited *Power v Whitemore*,[111] a marine insurance case, as authority for the proposition that a foreign adjustment was not conclusive. Naturally, counsel on the other side argued that *Power v Whitemore* was irrelevant, as the dispute in question was in relation to a contract of carriage. But as *Power v Whitemore* is an insurance case, it is necessary to examine it here.

In *Power v Whitemore*, the assured was compelled under a foreign adjustment made in Lisbon to pay contribution for a loss which under English law does not belong to general average. The issue was whether this foreign adjustment was binding upon the insurer. Lord Ellenborough held that it was not binding, but the true basis of his judgment is, regrettably, not easy to fathom. It would appear that had the plaintiffs tendered sufficient proof to show that the adjustment was made in accordance with the laws and usages of Lisbon, the adjustment would have been upheld.

Understandably, in view of the ambiguous language found in Lord Ellenborough's judgment, the case was sometimes cited as authority for laying down the principle that a foreign adjustment is not conclusive. This, however, is clearly not an accurate account of the legal position: the plaintiffs had failed in their action not because a foreign adjustment is not binding, but because of the want of proof.

---

108 (1824) 2 B & C 811.

109 *Ibid*, at p 813, in the words of Abbot CJ: '... by assenting to general average, he must be understood to assent also to its adjustment ... according to the usage and law of the place at which the adjustment is to be made.'

110 (1824) 2 B & C 805.

111 (1815) 4 M & S 141.

The legal position was eventually clarified in the celebrated case of *Harris v Scramanga*, where Mr Justice Brett, in a forthright and succinct speech, observed that:[112]

> 'Now I think that it is clearly established that, upon such a policy [referring to an "ordinary English policy", one without a special foreign adjustment clause], English underwriters are bound by the foreign adjustment as an adjustment, if made according to the law of the country in which it was made. They are bound although contributions are apportioned between the different interests in a manner different from the English mode, or though matters are brought into or omitted from general average which would not be so treated in England.'

However unpalatable a foreign adjustment may be, the parties are, as a general rule, bound by it.[113] There is, however, an exception to this rule.

Exception to the general rule

In *Harris v Scaramanga*,[114] Mr Justice Brett warned that 'if the general average loss be not incurred, or the general average contribution be not made, in order to avert the loss by a peril insured against', the adjustment is not be binding. This necessarily means that a loss incurred to save the adventure from a peril which is not insured against, or which is expressly excluded by the policy, is not recoverable. Needless to say, this is the case whether the loss be general or particular. This is fair enough: it has to borne in mind that only a 'general average loss' requires adjustment and, by s 66(6), a loss can only be claimed as general average loss if it is incurred for the purpose of 'avoiding, or in connection with the avoidance of, a peril insured against'.[115] As the insurer had taken pains to exclude certain losses, it would seem only fair that, as between him and the assured, the exception clause has to be respected. If this matter be overlooked, the whole foundation of the law of marine insurance could be at risk. It is submitted that the whole subject has to be thoroughly re-examined in the context of cl 10.2 of the ITCH(95).[116]

Foreign adjustment clause

Right up to the earlier part of the 20th century, foreign adjustment clauses, by which insurers agreed to pay general average, 'as *per* foreign statement, if so made up' or, 'according to foreign statement',[117] were commonly used. As they have now fallen into disuse – having been replaced by cl 10.2 – it is unnecessary

---

112 (1872) LR 7 CP 481 at p 496.

113 Later, this principle was followed in *Mavro v Ocean Marine Insurance Co* (1874) LR 7 CP 481.

114 *Ibid*, at p 496.

115 See also *Power v Whitemore* (1815) 4 M & S 141.

116 See Arnould, para 999, does not feel comfortable at all with the present uncertain state of the law in this regard.

117 See *Harris v Scaramanga* (1872) LR 7 CP 481; *Mavro v The Ocean Marine Insurance Co* (1874) LR 9 CP 595; *The Brigella* (1893) P 189; *The Mary Thomas* (1893) P 108, CA; *Hick v The Governor & Co of The London Assurance* (1895) 1 Com Cas 244; and *De Hart v Compania Anonima de Seguros, The Aurora* [1903] 2 KB 503, which appears to be the last reported case on the subject of foreign adjustment clause.

to raise the problems which these clauses had generated. However, for the purpose of comparing a foreign adjustment clause with cl 10.2, it is necessary to refer to certain remarks made by Mr Justice Roche in *Green Star Shipping Co v The London Assurance*[118] regarding an older version of a clause which differs slightly, but not materially, from cl 10.2. A group of authorities, comprising of *Harris v Scaramanga*,[119] *De Hart v Compania Anoninma de Seguros, The Aurora*[120] and *The Mary Thomas*[121] have conclusively ruled that foreign adjustments were binding. And according to Mr Justice Roche, the foreign adjustments were only binding because the 'contracts provided that general average was payable according to (or *per*) foreign statements'. And as these words do not appear in cl 10.2, he contended that it should not be treated in the same way. The pertinent part of his judgment read follows:[122]

> 'Here there is no such stipulation [foreign adjustment clause] but merely cl 9 [now cl 10.2 of the ITCH(95)] of the Institute Clauses, and it seems clear from the language of Romer LJ in *De Hart's case* that had the Institute Clauses stood alone the foreign adjustments would not have been held to be binding. In my judgment there is nothing in the present case making the New York adjusters' view or statement binding upon the parties ...'

The judge, it would appear, was advocating that an adjustment made under cl 10.2 is open to review.

As can be seen from the above remarks, Mr Justice Roche drew support from the observations made by Mr Justice Romer in *The De Hart Case*,[123] where the policy contained two clauses: a foreign adjustment clause – worded as 'General average according to foreign statement if so made up' – and a corresponding clause in the Institute Time Clauses, but without the words 'if so made up'. Lord Justice Romer was of the opinion that, even though the parties have in effect agreed to be bound by the foreign statement, if so made up, nonetheless it is open to challenge on two grounds. First, to bind the parties, 'the statement so made up must have been made up in good faith':[124] nothing more need be said about this. Secondly, he said that:[125]

> '... if the statement were made according to the law of the port which recognised the special terms of the contract of affreightment, I doubt if the parties to the policy of insurance in a case like the present be bound by the statement if the contract of affreightment imported terms as to general average of a special and unusual character, which could not reasonably have been contemplated by the parties to the policy of insurance.'

Insurers were clearly not prepared to pay general average in accordance with provisions that might appear in the contract of affreightment. As the case

---

118 [1933] 1 KB 378.
119 (1872) LR 7 CP 481.
120 [1903] 2 KB 503.
121 (1893) P 108, CA.
122 [1933] 1 KB 378 at p 389.
123 [1903] 2 KB 503.
124 *See Harris v Scaramanga* (1872) LR 7 CP 481 at p 495, where Brett J pointed out that until the contrary is proved, a foreign adjustment is deemed to have been made in good faith.
125 [1903] 2 KB 503 at p 509.

has demonstrated, an insurer could well be placed in a disadvantageous position by an express clause in a charterparty.[126] This warning issued by Lord Justice Romer had caused the insertion of the phrase 'as if the contract of affreightment contained no special terms upon the subject' to be made in cl 10.2. One gap in the law has thus been plugged.

C – SUE AND LABOUR

INTRODUCTION

The subject of sue and labour is governed by both the Act and the Institute Clauses. Each of the Institute Clauses for hulls and cargo has its own provision on sue and labour.[127] In the ITCH(95), and cl 9.2 of the IVCH(95), it is named as the 'duty of assured (sue and labour)' clause, whilst in all the ICC, as the 'minimising losses' clause. They amplify the terms of the Act, restating in modern language the principles of the old SG policy.

That sue and labour is an extraordinary expense and a type of 'particular charges'[128] distinct from other forms of partial losses, such as general average and salvage charges (which are also extraordinary expenses), have been repeatedly stressed not only by the Act but also by the Clauses.[129] Besides general average and salvage charges, legal costs incurred to institute or defend a collision action[130] are also expressly excluded from sue and labour by the Institute Hulls Clauses.[131] The distinction between the different types of partial losses can be more conveniently discussed elsewhere.[132]

---

126 The Court of Appeal, which affirmed the decision of Kennedy J decided that the insurers were bound by the foreign statement.

127 As such, unless the clause has been struck off, the conflict between the decision of the Australian case, *Emperor Goldmining Co v Switzerland General Insurance Co* [1964] 1 Lloyd's Rep 348, which decided that there was a right of recovery even in the absence of a sue and labour clause; and the opposing view held by Neill J at first instance in *Integrated Contained Service Inc v British Traders Insurance Co* [1981] 2 Lloyd's Rep 460, does not arise. The preponderant British view appears to be the latter: see Arnould, para 914, and Ivamy, p 451. The fact that a party may by agreement delete the sue and labour clause appearing in a standard policy goes some way to support the view that recovery for sue and labour expenses is only possible, if there is a clause in the policy authorising reimbursement for such expenses: see *Western Assurance Co of Toronto v Poole* [1903] 1KB 376, where the letters 'No s/c' ('No salvage charges') meaning in the language of re-insurers that sue and labour charges are not covered by the policy.

128 See s 64(2) and Arnould, para 1132.

129 See ss 64(2), 65(2), 76(2) and 78(2); and cl 11.2 of the ITCH(95) (previously cl 13 of the ITCH(83)) and cl 9.2 of the IVCH(95).

130 See *Xenos v Fox* (1868) LR 3 CP 630; 4 CP 665; and cl 8.3 of the ITCH(95) and cl 6.3 of the IVCH(83).

131 See cll 11.2 of the ITCH(95) and cl 9.2 of the IVCH(95). Note that under the new cl 11.2 of the ITCH(95), 'special compensation and expenses as referred to in clause 10.5' are also not recoverable under cl 11 as sue and labour. Clause 10.5 of the ITCH(95) also refers to special compensation payable to a salvor.

132 See Chapter 16.

For a proper understanding of the subject, it may be helpful to initiate this study with a brief comment on the rationale for the principle of sue and labour. In *Aitchison v Lohre*, Lord Blackburn said:[133]

> 'And the object of this is to encourage and induce the assured to exert themselves, and therefore the insurers bind themselves to pay in proportion any expense incurred, whenever such expense is reasonably incurred for the preservation of the thing from loss, in consequence of the efforts of the assured or their agents.'

Reference should also be made to a passage made by McArthur, whose remarks, though on an ancient version of the clause, are nonetheless informative and succinct:[134]

> 'This clause was inserted in the policy to counteract an apprehension likely to suggest itself to the assured, that any interference on the part of himself or his agents to avert an impending danger or rescue damaged property from total destruction might invalidate or otherwise operate to the prejudice of the insurance. The underwriters, on grounds of interest as well as principle, guarantee that this shall not be the case, and authorise the assured, in case of need, to make every exertion, either in person or by deputy, to avert or alleviate misfortune.'

Any such apprehension or reservation is now specially taken care of by the waiver clause, which ensures that any steps taken or effort made to sue and labour will not prejudice the rights of either party.[135]

ASSURED AND THEIR SERVANTS OR AGENTS

Section 78(4) states: 'It is the duty of the assured and his agents, in all cases, to take such measures as may be reasonable for the purpose of averting or minimising a loss.' All the Institute Clauses, however, have added the words 'their servants' to the clause.[136] This means that a duty to sue and labour is now imposed not only on the assured and their agents but also upon the master and crew.

In *The Gold Sky*,[137]Mr Justice Mocatta had to interpret the scope of the words 'the assured and his agents'. It is suffice to mention here that he was of the view that the master and crew were not included within the term 'agents' in s 78(4), unless they were specially instructed by the assured to sue and labour.[138] But now that the 'servants' of the assured are expressly included in the clause, it would be extremely difficult to support this interpretation of the clause.[139]

---

133 (1879) 4 App Cas 755 at p 765. In similar terms, Lord Hatherley (at p 768) said: '... the suing and labouring clause was inserted by the underwriters for the purpose of securing the benefit of any pains that the shipowner might be inclined to take in preserving, for their benefit, as much as he possibly could preserve'.

134 *The Policy of Marine Insurance* (1875, 2nd edn), p 57.

135 See cl 11.3 of the ITCH(95) and cl 9.3 of the IVCH(95), and cl 17 of the ICC.

136 Under the old SG policy, the wording was 'the assured, their factors, servants and assigns'.

137 [1972] 2 Lloyd's Rep 187.

138 It has to be said that the endeavour of the trial judge was to reconcile the apparent conflict between ss 55(2)(a) and 78(4) of the Act.

139 See O'May, p 328.

That the person who has incurred the expense for suing and labouring has to fall within the description of one of the classes listed is well illustrated in *Uzielli v Boston Marine Insurance Co.*[140] The party ('A') who had incurred the expenses of floating of the ship was not the plaintiff, but a re-insurer with whom the plaintiff had taken out a policy. As 'A' was neither a factor, servant, nor an assign of the plaintiff, who was himself a re-insurer, but an assured in a policy of reinsurance upon a reinsurance with the defendants, he was unable to seek reimbursement for the suing and labouring expenses incurred. A strict interpretation was adopted by the Court of Appeal. Likewise, in *Aitchison v Lohre*[141] the House of Lords ruled that salvors, when acting on the maritime law, were not labouring as agents of the assured.

An insurer who has taken upon himself the initiative to sue and labour would not be able to claim (or counterclaim) for such expenses incurred from the assured. The reason for this being, said Mr Justice Kennedy in *Crouan v Stanier*[142] that '... the underwriters did what the assured might have done himself, and the cost of which, if he had done it, he would have been entitled to recover from the underwriters ...'.[143]

It has to be pointed out that the word 'assured' (not shipowner) used in s 78(4) would include a mortgagee who has taken up a policy of his own (as opposed to an assignment) to protect his interest. As such, unless the policy otherwise provides, it would seem that he also has a duty to sue and labour.

TO AVERT OR MINIMISE A LOSS

The whole concept of sue and labour is based on the 'stitch in time' approach.[144] The word 'minimise'[145] implies that some damage (caused by an insured peril) has already been sustained by the subject-matter insured. In such a situation, the assured, their servants or agents would have to take action to prevent the partial loss from turning into a total loss.[146] The word 'avert', however, means to prevent (or ward off) a loss from happening, thus an assured does not have to wait for damage to occur to take action.

But in either event, the subject-matter has to be in danger of loss (of a type which is covered by the policy). There has to be an anticipation of a 'loss or misfortune'. These words, which appeared in the SG policy, have been adopted by cl 11.1 of the ITCH(95) and cl 9.1 of the IVCH(95). A casualty or accident

---

140 (1884) 15 QBD 11, CA. For criticisms of this decision, see *British Dominions General Insurance Co v Duder* [1915] 2 KB 394, and *Western Assurance Co of Toronto v Poole* [1903] 1 KB 376.

141 (1879) 4 App Cas 755.

142 [1904] 1 KB 87 at 91.

143 See also *Buchanan v London & Provincial Marine Insurance Co* (1895) 65 LJ QB 92.

144 *Per* Lord Justice Dillion's in *Integrated Container Service Inc v British Traders Insurance Co Ltd* [1984] 1 Lloyd's Rep 154 at p163, CA.

145 It is observed that s 78(4) uses the terms 'averting or minimising', whereas s 78(3), 'averting or diminishing'. Whether anything could be made of this is doubtful. Unless a different meaning is intended, it would be better for consistency if the same term was used for both subsections.

146 A failure so to do might disentitle them of the right to claim for the loss.

must have arisen whereby the insured property is exposed to damage or loss by a peril insured against.

If illustrations are needed to show what sue and labour entails, the facts of *The Pomerian*[147] and *Kidston v The Empire Marine Insurance Co*[148] are particularly suitable. In both cases the expenses incurred were held recoverable. In the former, the policy was on live cattle for 'all risks of shipping and until safely landed'. During the course of the voyage, the plaintiffs had to pay for extra fodder supplied to the cattle whilst the vessel in which they were shipped was detained in a port of refuge for necessary repairs. In the second case, goods wetted in a storm which, if not dried out when the damage was slight, would decay and become even more damaged. *Irvin v Hine*,[149] however, affords a good contrast to the above cases. The plaintiff, who had refused to have a survey in dry dock, was held not to have been in breach of any duty laid down on him by s 78(4). Such a survey, said the judge, 'would not avert or minimise the loss but would merely ascertain its extent'.

The Institute Cargo Clauses contain an additional provision connected with carriage: by cl 16.2 the assured, their servants and agents have to ensure that 'all rights against carriers, bailees or other third parties are properly preserved and exercised'.

LOSS COVERED BY THE POLICY

Section 78(3) declares in negative terms that 'expenses incurred for the purpose of averting or diminishing any loss not covered by the policy are not recoverable under the suing and labouring clause'. The same principle is reiterated in the Clauses, but couched in more positive language. Clause 11.1 of the ITCH(95) states that measures need only be taken to avert or minimise a loss which 'would be recoverable under this insurance', and cl 16 of the Cargo Clauses, 'in respect of loss recoverable hereunder'.

There are clearly two aspects to this rule. First, the effort made must be to avert or minimise a loss caused by a peril insured against. Secondly, and less obvious, the type or nature of loss (whether total or partial) has to be one covered by the policy.

Loss caused by insured peril

Naturally, any expense incurred to avert or minimise a loss caused by inherent vice or nature of the subject-matter insured, which is not a peril insured against, would not be recoverable. The authority for this is *Berk v Style*,[150] where the cost for rebagging a cargo of kieselguhr, packed in paper bags, which broke and

---

147 [1895] P 349.
148 (1866) LR 1 CP 535; 2 CP 357 (Ex Ch), hereinafter referred to as *The Kidston Case*.
149 [1950] 1 KB 555.
150 [1956] 1 QB 180.

burst during the voyage, was held not recoverable. Any costs expended to avert or minimise a loss occasioned by delay would suffer the same fate.[151]

In an 'all risks' policy, however, the scope to sue and labour is naturally greater. This is demonstrated in *Integrated Container Service Inc v British Traders Insurance Co Ltd*,[152] where extraordinary costs were incurred by the assured in order to retrieve his containers, the subject-matter insured, which he had leased to a third party who later became a bankrupt. As the containers were abandoned – scattered at various places over the Far East – they were at risk of theft, misuse, enforcement of a lien, and of loss or damage from some cause or another. The insurers' defence was that the risk of a lawful sale of the containers by a person who has, under local law, a power of sale to recover unpaid port, harbour dues or warehouse charges was not a risk covered by the policy. This contention was roundly rejected by Lord Justice Dillion who could see no reason why, as the policy was for 'all risks', the risk of lawful sale by a third party should be excluded. He went so far to say that:[153] 'The plaintiffs effectively lose their containers whether the sale is lawful under a lien – port regulations or a process of judicial execution – or unlawful'. The 'all risks' policy saved the day.

Type of loss

Unless the policy otherwise provides, both partial and total losses are insured in a standard form policy. An insurance against a total loss only can be achieved by the insertion of the 'warranted free from particular average' clause. Whether such a clause can affect the right of the assured to recover expenses for sue and labour has to be considered.

'Warranted free from particular average'

In marine insurance, the term 'particular average' is often loosely used to refer to a partial loss. Its nature is clarified by s 64(1) as follows: 'A particular average loss is a partial loss of the subject-matter insured, caused by a peril insured against, and which is not a general average loss'. In marine insurance, the expression 'warranted free from ...' denotes an exception of liability. Though the word 'warranted' is used, it is not a promissory warranty in the sense of a contractual term which has to be strictly complied with.[154] Read together, it means that (with the exception of general average) the insurer is not liable for a partial loss, or more accurately a particular average loss.

A degree of confusion is evident in this area of law. First, it was at one time thought that any expenses incurred for suing and labouring, regardless of whether the action taken was to mitigate a partial or total loss, is excluded if a

---

151 See s 55(2)(b); *Weissburg v Lamb* (1950) 84 Ll L Rep 509; and *Meyer v Ralli* (1876) CPD 358.

152 [1984] 1 Lloyd's Rep 154, CA.

153 *Ibid*, at p 162

154 For a discussion on warranties, see Chapter 7.

policy contains a 'free from particular average' warranty.[155] Secondly, it has been argued that in a policy containing a 'warranted free from particular average' clause, suing and labouring expenses is recoverable only if the effort expended was to avert or minimise a 'total' loss; any costs incurred to avert or minimise a 'partial' loss would not be recoverable by reason of the fact that the loss is not one 'covered by the policy'. As the answer to both these questions revolves around the same cases, namely, *The Great Indian Peninsular Railway Co v Saunders*,[156] *Booth v Gair*,[157] *The Kidston Case*,[158] and *Wilson Brothers Bobbin Co Ltd v Green*[159] it is best that they be discussed together. In each of these cases, the expenses fell within what may be described as the 'travel'[160] part of the old clause where, by reason of a peril insured against, insured cargo left stranded at a foreign port had to be transported (to 'travel') to its proper destination.

With the exception of the fact that in one case the subject-matter insured was iron rails and in the other, bacon, the events occurring in the first pair cases are remarkably similar. In both cases, the policy contained a sue and labour clause and a 'free from particular average' warranty. As a result of exceptional weather, the insured cargo had to be landed, warehoused and reshipped to its proper destination. In each case, the extra costs (freight and ancillary expenses) incurred by the assured were the subject of the claim. The plaintiffs claimed that as the loss incurred was for suing and labouring, they were entitled to be reimbursed by the insurer. In both actions, the loss was held not recoverable. As the same judge, Chief Justice Erle, presided in both cases, it is not surprising that their outcome was also the same.

Both *The Great Indian Peninsular Railway Co v Saunders*[161] and *Booth v Gair*,[162] it is noticed, have been cited as authority for laying down the proposition that the presence of a 'free from particular average' warranty in a policy would render the sue and labour clause otiose. Curiously enough, Mr Justice Bray in *Wilson Brothers Bobbin Co Ltd v Green*[163] took the view that the former was 'decided upon the ground that the loss was a particular average loss, and the policy contained a warranty that it was 'free from particular average'.[164] This remark gives the impression that because a sue and labour expense is a type of partial loss, the assured is prevented from recovery by the warranty. He felt that

155 In *The Kidston Case* (1866) LR 1 CP 535; 2 CP 357 (Ex Ch), this issue was framed with admirable clarity by Willes J, who delivered the judgment of the court as follows: 'And this depends upon whether the expression "particular average" ... includes expenses which fall within the suing and labouring clause, so that in effect the suing and labouring clause is expunged by the warranty'.

156 (1862) 2 B & S 266. See also *Meyer v Ralli* (1876) CPD 358.

157 (1863) 33 LJCP 99.

158 (1866) LR 1 CP 535.

159 [1917] 1 KB 860.

160 Read as: '... to sue, labour, and travel for ...'.

161 (1862) 2 B & S 266.

162 (1863) 33 LJCP 99.

163 [1917] 1 KB 860.

164 Similarly, in *Booth v Gair* (1863) 33 LJCP 99, counsel for the plaintiffs, citing *The Great Indian Peninsular Railway Co v Saunders* (1862) 2 B & S 266 as authority argued that the warranty exempted the underwriters from liability.

as the policy which he had to consider did not contain the warranty, he was able to distinguish them, and, accordingly, decide in favour of the assured.[165] If this is the only ground on which Mr Justice Bray had based his decision it would clearly, for more than one reason, be insupportable.

First, even if one were to assume that the basis of the decision of *The Great Indian Peninsular Railway Co v Saunders*[166] (and *Booth v Gair*[167]) was as described by Mr Justice Bray, it is no longer good law.[168] It cannot now stand in the light of the later decision of *The Kidston Case*,[169] where, in an endeavour to reconcile the warranty and the sue and labour clause, Mr Justice Willes held that the former 'does no more than limit the insurance to total loss of the freight by the perils insured against, without reference to extraordinary labour or expense which may be incurred by the assured in preserving the freight from loss ...'. The principle enunciated therein is now encapsulated in ss 76(2) and 78(1):[170] notwithstanding the warranty, expenses for suing and labouring are now clearly recoverable.

Secondly, with due respect, it is contended that Mr Justice Bray's interpretation of the judgment of *The Great Indian Peninsular Railway Co v Saunders* does not bear scrutiny. Closer examination will reveal that the said case was decided in favour of the insurer, not on the ground that the warranty excluded the operation of the sue and labour clause, but that the insured property was never at risk or in danger of loss when the expenses were incurred.[171] Whether this ground is itself sustainable is another matter which will be considered shortly.[172] But for the present, it is suffice to mention that Chief Justice Erle had in fact refused to consider the question whether sue and labour expenses fell within the scope of 'particular average', as he was of the view that the expense in question had 'nothing to do with the labour and travel clause'.[173] In *Booth v Gair*,[174] he expressed himself more clearly when he said that

---

165 He concluded that as there was no warranty in the policy, there was nothing to exclude the operation of the sue and labour clause.

166 (1862) 2 B & S 266.

167 (1863) 33 LJCP 99.

168 Arnould, at para 909 (in a footnote), wondered whether this point was appreciated in *Wilson Bros Bobbin Co Ltd v Green* [1917] 1 KB 860, which it is noted was decided after the passing of the Act.

169 (1886) LR 1 CP 535.

170 Section 76(2) states: 'Where the subject-matter insured is warranted free from particular average ... the insurer is nevertheless liable for ... expenses properly incurred pursuant to the provisions of the suing and labouring clause ...'. Section 78(1): '... the assured may recover from the insurer any expenses properly incurred ... notwithstanding that the ... subject-matter may have been warranted free from particular average ...'.

171 This was the interpretation given to the case and *Booth v Gair* (1863) 33 LJCP 99 by Willes J in *Kidston v Empire Insurance Co* (1866) LR 1 CP 535; and by Gorell Barnes J, in *The Pomerian* [1895] P 349 at p 353, even though he felt some unease about the finding of fact in *Booth v Gair*. Thus, Arnould's remarks, at para 909 in fn 20, that: 'The explanation of these decisions is that in neither case were the goods, at the time when the expenditure was incurred, in danger of any loss, total or partial, from an insured peril' is correct.

172 See below.

173 *Ibid*, at p 274, he said: 'But all this is beside the question now before us, as these expenses have nothing to do with the labour and travel.'

174 (1863) 33 LJCP 99 at p 101.

there was 'no peril creating a risk of a total loss from which the underwriter was saved by the expenses in question'.

The real principle of law handed down by both *The Great Indian Peninsular Railway Co v Saunders*[175] and *Booth v Gair*[176] is that in relation to sue and labour, the warranty is relevant only for the purpose of defining the type of loss which the assured has to avert or minimise. As the warranty renders the insurance for liability for a total loss only, it follows that only expenses incurred to prevent the risk of a total (not partial) loss would be covered. 'The question,' said the Chief Justice, 'is, were these expenses incurred to prevent a total loss?'

Cargo insurance

Risk of loss of the adventure

The decision in both the above cases was based on the finding that, as the cargo was safely landed *in specie* and in the hands of the assured, they were no longer physically in danger of an impending loss. In *Wilson Brothers Bobbin Co Ltd v Green*,[177] counsel for the plaintiffs raised an interesting argument which regrettably was not given deeper and more serious consideration by the court. It was argued that *The Great Indian Peninsular Railway Co v Saunders*[178] was wrongly decided because it ignored the principle laid down in *The Sanday Case*[179] that what is insured is not only cargo, but also the venture. Mr Justice Bray had very little to say about *The Sanday Case*[180] except that nothing new was proposed in the case, and that, 'it was the law long before the passing of the Marine Insurance Act 1906 that what was insured in a policy of this kind on goods was their safe arrival at the port of destination.'[181] This can hardly be a helpful reply.

It is submitted that there is merit and substance in the argument raised by counsel. The principle, whether new or old at the time, should have been considered, if not applied, in the two cases. It cannot be denied that the venture would almost certainly be at risk of loss, if the cargo was left behind and not forwarded to its proper destination.

It is worthwhile remembering that a policy on cargo is not just to insure for its physical well-being, but also for its safe arrival at the proper destination. In this regard, an analogy can perhaps be drawn from a policy on freight. The nature of freight is such that it is itself physically incapable of being at risk, but the cargo to which the freight is 'attached' or dependent upon could be at risk. As such, if the cargo is not conveyed to its proper destination the freight would be lost.

---

175 (1862) 2 B & S 266.
176 (1863) 33 LJCP 99.
177 [1917] 1 KB 860.
178 (1862) 2 B & S 266.
179 [1916] 2 KB 156, HL.
180 *Ibid*.
181 [1917] 1 KB 860 at p 865.

In *The Kidston Case*,[182] the policy was for chartered freight. During the course of the voyage, the ship encountered severe weather and was so badly damaged as not to be worth repairing. The cargo of guano, having been safely landed and warehoused, was later forwarded to its proper destination, for which the plaintiffs had to pay freight, landing, warehousing and reloading charges. When the cargo finally arrived at its proper destination, the plaintiffs (the assured) were paid the chartered freight. They brought this action to recover from the freight-insurers the expenses of transhipment and forwarding. As they did not suffer any loss (partial or total) of freight, the claim was preferred as a 'particular charge'. Mr Justice Willes held that the loss was recoverable as sue and labour because:

> '... they represented so much labour beyond and besides the ordinary labour of the voyage, rendered necessary for the salvation of the subject-matter of insurance, by reason of a damage and loss within the scope of the policy, the immediate effect of which was that the subject-matter insured would also be lost, or rather would never come into existence, unless such labour was bestowed.'

Like an assured of any other insurable property, an assured of freight is also under a duty to take reasonable steps to avert or minimise a loss. In fact, if it is possible and reasonable so to do, he has no option but to tranship and forward the cargo to its proper destination in order that freight be earned. He can then charge the insurer with the expenses he had incurred. It cannot be denied that the actions taken by the plaintiffs did prevent a loss of adventure of the cargo which in turn prevented a loss of freight. Viewed in this light, the decision of the first pair of cases is surely open to question.

Effect of transhipment

The liability of the insurer is in such a case specifically preserved by s 59 and cl 12 (the forwarding charges clause) of all the ICC. Furthermore, the transit clause (cl 8) of all the ICC provides that the insurance shall remain in force during 'forced discharge, reshipment or transhipment ...'.

REASONABLE MEASURES

Section 78(4) states that the measures taken by the assured for the purpose of suing and labouring must be 'reasonable'. This means that he would have to take into account all the circumstances of the case when assessing not only whether he ought to take any action, but also the course of action, if any is to be taken, for the purpose of averting or minimising a loss.[183] In *The ICS*,[184] it was queried whether the test of probability was to be applied.[185] This issue was

---

182 (1866) LR 1 CP 535.

183 See *Meyer v Ralli* (1876) CPD 358, where charges incurred in order to warehouse a cargo of rye for more than a year was not recoverable.

184 [1984] 1 Lloyd's Rep 154 at p 158, CA.

185 This notion was taken from a remark made by Brett LJ, in *Lohre v Aitchison* (1878) 3 QBD 558 at p 566, where he said that: 'If by perils insured against the subject-matter is brought into such danger that without unusual or extraordinary labour or expense a loss will *very probably* fall on the underwriters ...' [emphasis added].

swiftly dismissed by Lord Justice Eveleigh who was clear that: 'It should not be possible for insurers to be able to contend that, upon an ultimate investigation and analysis of the facts, a loss, while possible or even probable, was not very probable.'[186] The criterion, he said, was to be found in the wording of s 78(4) which imposed:

> '... a duty to act in circumstances where a reasonable man intent upon preserving his property, as opposed to claiming upon insurers, would act. Whether or not the assured can recover should depend upon the reasonableness of his assessment of the situation and the action taken by him.'

In *Stringer and Others v The English and Scottish Marine Insurance Co Ltd*,[187] the plaintiffs could have prevented the sale of their cargo ordered by the Prize Court by depositing the full value of the goods. The court was of the view that it can seldom be reasonable to require an assured to adopt such a course of action, especially in a foreign court and country Thus, it was held that their refusal to make the payment did not constitute a breach of their duty to sue and labour.

ADDITIONAL COVERAGE

That sue and labour expenses are recoverable 'in addition' to any claims recoverable under the policy is clarified not only by the Institute Clauses, but also by s 78(1), which stresses that the engagement to sue and labour is 'supplementary to the contract of insurance' and that 'notwithstanding that the insurer may have paid for a total loss, or that the subject-matter may have been warranted free from particular average, either wholly or under a certain percentage.'[188] The same holds true even if no loss whatsoever is sustained by the subject-matter insured. This is demonstrated in *The Kidston Case*[189] where, even though full freight was earned, as the cargo was forwarded to its proper destination in another vessel, the costs incurred to land, warehouse and forward the cargo was held recoverable under the suing and labouring clause.

There is, however, under the Institute Hulls Clauses an express limit as to the amount which may be recovered as sue and labour. The ceiling prescribed by cl 11.6 of the ITCH(95) and cl 9.6 of the IVCH(95) is that, 'in no circumstances' should it 'exceed the amount insured under this insurance in respect of the vessel'. Even without a fixed limit, it would indeed be difficult to argue that an expense in excess of the insured value of the vessel is 'reasonably incurred'. In the event of a total loss, the maximum amount which an insurer can be made liable, taking into account sue and labour charges, is twice the insured value of the vessel. But having said this, it has to be noted that the liability of the insurer has to be apportioned according to the normal rule of marine insurance: the

---

186 [1984] 1 Lloyd's Rep 154 at p 158, CA.

187 (1869) LR 4 QB 691; (1870) LR 5 QB 599, CA.

188 See s 78(1) and *Dixon v Whitworth* (1879) 40 LT (NS) 365; 4 Asp MLC 327 (CA): *per* Lindley LJ: 'It is now clearly established that this clause is a distinct and independent agreement which, although occurring in and forming part of the policy, may entitle the assured to recover more than the amount underwritten'.

189 (1866) LR 1 CP 535.

share he has to bear is proportionate to the amount which he has underwritten to the whole value of the property or interest insured.[190]

As no fixed limit is set by the ICC, the test of reasonableness must apply. In *Lee and Another v The Southern Insurance Co*,[191] a cargo of palm oil was landed at an intermediate port when the ship in which it was carried stranded. The assured could have re-shipped the cargo to its proper destination in another ship for £70, but instead chose rail as the means of transport at three times the cost. The court held that, as the reasonable course to adopt was to have them re-shipped in another vessel, the proper measure of liability of the underwriters was £70. Similarly, in *Wilson Brothers Bobbin v Green*,[192] the assured was only allowed recovery for a lower freight rate, the amount they would have paid if the cargo was reshipped earlier.

BREACH OF DUTY TO SUE AND LABOUR

It is indeed unfortunate that neither the Act nor the Clauses has spelt out the legal consequences for a breach of the duty to sue and labour. There are two aspects to this problem which require separate attention. The position where the assured is himself guilty of negligence will first be examined, followed with a discussion of the case where the master or crew has failed to take action to avert or minimise a loss.

Negligence of the assured

An assured may be guilty of negligence (or even wilful misconduct depending on the facts of the case) should he instruct his servants or agents not to sue and labour, or prevent them from so doing, when the circumstances clearly warrant that such action be taken. Whether an assured may recover for the loss in such a case largely depends upon what the court regards as the proximate cause of loss. If a judge were to find negligence or the wilful misconduct of the assured as the proximate cause the loss would not be recoverable, as neither causes of loss is insured against.[193]

To illustrate this point, reference should be made to the facts of two rather ancient cases, namely, *Currie and Co v The Bombay Native Insurance Co*[194] and *Tanner v Bernett*,[195] which are particularly relevant for this purpose. In the former, the cargo policy was for a total loss only. The ship in which the cargo was carried was wrecked and the master (who was an uninsured part-owner but was left in control of everything by the assured) was advised by various

---

190 See cl 11.5 of the ITCH(95) and cl 9.5 of the IVCH(95). Note the addition of the exclusion of special compensation and expenses referred to in cl 10.5 of the ITCH(95).

191 (1870) LR 5 CP 397.

192 [1917] 1 KB 860.

193 If a loss would have happened in any event, regardless of whether suing and labouring measures were or were not taken by the assured, then, any negligence committed by the assured in not taking action is unlikely to be held as the proximate cause of loss.

194 (1869) 6 Moo PC (NS) 302.

195 (1825) Ry & M 182.

surveyors to take steps to save the cargo. He refused to take heed of this advice and consequently the wreck of the vessel and her cargo were auctioned. The assured brought an action to recover for a total loss of the cargo but failed in his claim because he was unable to prove a loss by an insured peril.

After taking note of the fact that the captain, acting for the assured, had chosen not to make the slightest attempt to save the cargo, whose exertions might have saved a portion of it, the court asked: '... how can the assured recover from the underwriters a loss which was made total by their own negligence?' The crux of the decision lies in the following statement delivered by the court:[196]

'This omission of the captain to take any steps towards saving the cargo, at a time when it was probable that his endeavours would be successful, in their Lordships' judgment, precludes the assured from claiming for a total loss of the cargo into whatever condition it might have been brought afterwards.'

The decision could be interpreted in two ways. First, it could be said that, as the servants of the assured had blatantly and without cause refused to take preventive measures to save the cargo, the assured had committed a breach of their duty to sue and labour, and this in itself was sufficient to disentitle them of the right of recovery. In effect, the breach of duty to sue and labour was used by the insurer as a defence to resist the plaintiff's claim. Secondly, though not said in so many words, it could also rest on the ground of causation: the careless behaviour of the master had not only converted what would otherwise have been only a partial loss into a total loss, but had also rendered negligence as the proximate cause of loss. And as neither the negligence of the assured nor that of the master or crew operating as the proximate cause of loss was a peril insured against under the policy, the loss was not recoverable.

Similarly in *Tanner v Bennett*,[197] the master of the ship should have had her repaired after she had received damage by striking on a rock. However, because of the negligence of the master and the resident agents of the owners, she was not repaired and had to be sold as fire-wood. From the somewhat brief and vague report, it would appear that, due to the negligence of these persons, the assured was not allowed to claim under the policy for a total loss. They were, however, offered indemnity for a partial loss by the court; but as they were unable to show its extent, they were awarded only nominal damages.

In both cases, it is to be noted that crew negligence was not an insured peril. Such cases would now have to be considered in the light of s 55(2)(a) and cl 6.2.2 of the ITCH(95) and cl 4.2.2 of the IVCH(95). The question is: would a failure by the master to take such measures as may be reasonable to avert or minimise a loss militate against his owner's claim against his insurers? Whether an insurer has the right to sue for damages, counterclaim, or raise the breach of

196 (1869) 6 Moo PC (NS) 302 at p 317.
197 (1825) Ry & M 182.

the duty to sue and labour as a (complete or partial) defence[198] to a plaintiff's claim is unclear.[199] The best account of the legal position can be found in *The ICS*, where Lord Justice Eveleigh said that:[200]

'While it is not possible to state with certainty all the adverse consequences which will be suffered by an assured who fails to perform his duty under the sue and labour clause, there is no doubt that he incurs a risk of his claim for loss or damage being rejected in whole or in part if it can be show that he failed to act when he should have done.'

As the legal position is uncertain it would be advisable for an insurer to plead the breach of the duty to sue and labour in the alternative, as a defence or counterclaim.[201]

It is necessary here to be reminded of the doctrine of utmost good faith, which underlines every contract of insurance. An assured who unashamedly without good cause refuses to sue and labour when the circumstances of the case cries out for preventive measures to be taken can hardly be described as having acted in good faith. If the utmost good faith be not observed, an insurer may avoid the contract.[202] Furthermore, his conduct, though passive, is no better than that of conniving to scuttle the ship. A court could well be persuaded to hold that such an act constitutes wilful misconduct. By s 55(2)(a), an insurer is not liable for any loss 'attributable' to the wilful misconduct of the assured.

Negligence of the crew

The inter-relationship between all these provisions is indeed complex. The inconsistency, it would appear, lies in the fact that on the one hand, s 78(4) and cl 11.1 of the ITCH(95) and cl 9.1 of the IVCH(95) have imposed a duty to sue and labour on the assured, their servants and agents, and on the other, s 55(2)(a) and cl 6.2.2 of the ITCH(95) and cl 4.2.2 of the IVCH(95) have provided coverage for a loss which 'would not have happened but for the misconduct or negligence of the master or crew' and for a loss (proximately) 'caused by negligence of master

---

198 In *Currie v Bombay Native Insurance Co* (1869) LR 3 PC 72, if proper measures for preventive action were taken, the partial loss would not have become a total loss. The insurer's plea of negligence was held a complete defence to the plaintiff's claim: as they could not be made liable for a partial loss by reason of the 'free from particular average' warranty, there can be no question of a set-off. See also *Meyer v Ralli* (1876) 1 CPD 358. *Cf Tanner v Bennett* (1825) Ry & M 182 where, on similar facts, the insurers were held liable for a partial loss: the court was able to make this order because there was no 'free from particular average' warranty in this case. The same defence proved to be only partially effective.

199 Arnould, at para 770 in fn 96, states that 'there can be very few cases where it matters whether the insurer's right is one of defence or of counterclaim'. In *The Gold Sky* [1972] 2 Lloyd's Rep 187 at p 221, Mocatta J, by way of *obiter*, expressed the view that a breach of s 78(4) gives a right to set-off or counterclaim. In the final analysis, it would operate as a complete defence: for if the plaintiff is liable to pay to the defendant damages, it would most probably be the amount which they would have to indemnify the plaintiffs for the damage or loss sustained by the subject-matter insured.

200 (1984) 1 Lloyd's Rep 154 at p 157, CA.

201 As was done in *The Gold Sky* [1972] 2 Lloyd's Rep 187.

202 Section 17. For a discussion on good faith, see Chapter 6.

officers crew or pilots' respectively. Are they reconcilable?[203] Various suggestions have been put forward to resolve this anomaly.

First, in *The Gaunt Case*,[204] the relationship between cl 6.2.3 of the ITCH(83) (now cl 6.2.2 of the ITCH(95)) and s 78(4) was raised by counsel, but was dismissed without much discussion. The insurers had pleaded that they were not liable by reason of s 78(4), because the assured had neglected to take precautions to protect the goods from the wet. Needless to say, this line of reasoning, if upheld by the court, would negate the scope of not only cl 6.2.3 of the ITCH(83), but also s 55(2)(a). Lord Sumner was the only judge who was prepared to express his thoughts on the subject. He said:

> '[s 78(4)] cannot possibly be read as meaning that if the agents of the assured are not reasonably careful throughout the transit he cannot recover for anything to which their want of care contribute.'

In *Lind v Mitchell*,[205] even though s 78(4) was not pleaded as a ground of defence, Lord Justice Scrutton nevertheless felt that he had to comment on the unreasonable conduct of the master. After expressing his approval for the above remarks, he added that:

> 'There has been negligence of the master, not negligence of the assured. There has been negligence of the master which has resulted in the *continuing action of a previously existing peril* of the sea. Now, in my view, that is covered, if it were necessary to cover it, by cl 8 of the Institute Time Clauses[206]... Now if it were true – and I do not think it is – that under the existing law but for that clause you would treat the direct cause of the loss as being the premature abandonment and not the entry of sea water from a *previously existing peril*, in my view that clause requires the underwriters to pay where the negligence of the master has caused the loss of the ship.'

These remarks may initially appear to be somewhat obscure, but there are clearly two sides to it. First, Lord Justice Scrutton was of the view that even though the master had acted negligently and unreasonably in abandoning the ship prematurely the proximate cause of the loss was, nonetheless, contrary to the then popular opinion, still a peril of the seas and, as such, was recoverable. In this sense, it was unnecessary to invoke the negligence clause. Secondly, if perils of the seas was not the proximate cause of loss, there was cl 8 (now cl 6.2.2 of the ITCH(95)) to rely on in order to render the insurer liable for the loss. Fortunately for the assured, he was covered on both counts. This necessarily means that, so long as the 'previously existing peril' continues to operate at the time of loss, the loss is recoverable in spite of the fact that the assured may have acted negligently in his response to the casualty. But how s 78(4) fits within this scheme of things, the judge, regrettably, did not explain.

---

203 In *The Gold Sky* [1972] 2 Lloyd's Rep 187 at p 218, the problem was framed as follows: 'It is extremely difficult to give effect to s 78(4) if "the assured and his agents" is to include the master or other members of the crew, without negativing much of the cover given by s 55(2)(a) ...'.

204 [1972] 2 Lloyd's Rep 187.

205 (1928) 45 TLR 54 at p 57, CA. Emphasis added.

206 Clause 6.2.3 of the ITCH(83) and now cl 6.2.2 of the ITCH(95).

In *The Gold Sky*,[207] counsel for the insurers argued that the master's refusal to accept salvage assistance from a tug standing nearby constituted a breach of duty to sue and labour. It was contended that s 78(4) imposed a general duty to take care throughout the risk. Such a construction of s 78(4) is clearly repugnant to s 55(2)(a). Mr Justice Mocatta found himself in difficulty when he took it upon himself (as it was unnecessary for him to do, having reached a decision on another ground) to answer the question as to how s 78(4) was to be reconciled with s 55(2)(a).

He found it 'difficult to believe that it [s 78(4)] was intended to cut down the effect of s 55(2)(a)'. One cannot help but feel that he had somehow forced his own hand into taking the stand which he did by holding that the word 'agents' did not include the master or crew. In actual fact, his true feelings and sentiments on the subject are contained in the following passage:[208]

> 'If a loss is recoverable by a shipowner owing to his master having unreasonably and negligently set a risky course whereby the ship has suffered a gash in her plating from a rock which should have been given a wide berth, why should the shipowner be unable to recover in respect of subsequent loss, whether total or partial, due to subsequent unreasonable and negligent conduct by the master such as, for example, continuing to his destination relying on the pumps coupled, perhaps with welding and the tightness of bulkheads, rather than putting into a nearby port of refuge for repairs?'

From this and an earlier remark he had made to the effect that it would be 'irrational' to nullify s 55(2)(a), all of which are *obiter*, it is clear that he felt strongly about the s 55(2)(a) and would go as far as he could to uphold its cover.[209]

Negligence before and after a casualty

Sections 78(4) and 55(2)(a)

Another way to resolve the conflict, proposed by Arnould, is to distinguish between negligence committed before and after a casualty. If effect is to be given to both ss 55(2)(a) and 78(4), it may be necessary to draw this line. He states: 'Another possible view is that s 55(2)(a) in the relevant part is concerned only with conduct before a casualty, and therefore does not conflict with s 78(4) which is concerned with conduct in response to a casualty'.[210] The purpose for making this distinction is to give each section its own respective sphere of coverage. This necessarily means that the moment a casualty arises, s 78(4) begins to operate and would prevail over s 55(2)(a): the assured would only be able to rely on s 55(2)(a) for negligence committed before a casualty arises, but

---

207 [1972] 2 Lloyd's Rep 187.

208 *Ibid*, at p 221.

209 As discussed earlier, it is now difficult to sustain this interpretation in the light of the current wording of cl 11.1 Moreover, unease is felt in several quarters as regards this ruling, as it has always been known both in the context of marine insurance and in contract of affreightment that a master has the duty to take proper measures after a casualty: see Arnould, para 770 and O'May, p 328.

210 In para 770 fn 85, Arnould criticised Scrutton LJ for having overlooked this distinction.

not after. Can the same divide be applied to the conflict between s 78(4) and the negligence cover of cl 6.2.2 of the ITCH(95) and cl 4.2.2 of the IVCH(95)?

Section 78(4) and the negligence cover (clause 6.2.2)

Surprisingly, Arnould states that this problem can be 'more easily resolved'. The problem, he said, would disappear 'if one applies the principle that the duty to sue and labour only arises when a casualty occurs'. He proceeded to say that: 'If negligent conduct takes place in response to a marine casualty, the underwriter is unable to rely on s 78(4) in answer to a claim for loss caused by such conduct, when it constitutes an insured peril.' But the point is, it is an insured peril regardless of when the negligent conduct took place. There is nothing in the wording of cl 6.2.2 to restrict its application one way or the other. Negligent conduct, whether it be committed in response to a marine casualty or not, is an insured peril under cl 6.2.2. Arnould, though not quite so explicit, is in effect advocating that the negligence cover of cl 6.2.2 prevails over s 78(4).

Neither s 55(2)(a) nor cl 6.2.2, however, contemplates a before and after casualty divide. In all fairness, it has to be said that Arnould notes that there is no solution which is 'wholly free from difficulty', and that 's 55(2)(a) does not admit of such a construction'.[211] The terms of both provisions are wide and general enough to cover all forms of negligence committed before and after the commencement of a casualty by master or crew.

Proximate cause of loss

Another method which has been canvassed to circumvent this conflict is to apply the rule of causation. Of all the suggestions, Arnould finds this the most 'satisfactory', but again warns that it is also not free from objection.[212] As crew negligence is now an insured peril, there should not be any problems in so far as the assured is concerned: if a negligent response to a casualty is held the proximate cause of loss, the assured is covered by cl 6.2.2; and if it is held as a remote cause of loss, s 55(2)(a) would render it inconsequential. In either case the assured is protected. In fact, the legal position as described by Lord Justice Scrutton in *Lind v Mitchell*[213] is not far from the truth. He demonstrated in his speech, cited earlier, that the assured has nothing to lose. Thus, whether the 'previously existing peril' or the subsequent act of neglect is the proximate cause of loss, the assured is covered. The only obstacle placed in the way of the assured is the due diligence proviso to the negligence cover. In the case of cl 4.2 of the IVCH(95), the assured would be denied the right of recovery if the loss or damage had resulted from the want of due diligence on his part, as the 'assured' or of the 'owners or managers'. The ITCH(95), however, has extended 'due diligence' to include also, 'superintendents or any of their onshore management.'[214]

---

211 See Arnould, para 770.
212 Arnould, para 770, footnote 96.
213 (1928) 45 TLR 54, CA.
214 The due diligence proviso is discussed in Chapter 12.

If the proximate cause of loss is not an insured peril, there is also no problem, as then the negligent response of the master or crew to the casualty is irrelevant, for there is no duty to avert or minimise a loss which is not covered by the policy.

Returning to the subject of the proviso, there is, however, another problem which has to be mentioned. As discussed earlier, it is not unknown for an assured, especially a shipowner, to act as master or crew of his ship.[215] But unlike the issue relating to negligent navigation where the nature of the assured's conduct – whether acting in the capacity as owner or master – can be more easily identified, it is not possible here to draw such a distinction. Even though he (the assured) may, whilst acting as master or crew, be protected by the negligence cover of cl 6.2.2, he would, as the 'assured' have difficulty in satisfying the terms of proviso.

These 'extremely interesting and difficult matter of law arising under s 78(4)'[216] have to be addressed. That there is no simple solution is obvious. But now that all the issues have been aired, it is up to the insurance market, if it wishes to resolve the conflict, to decide which course of action to take. The insertion of a clause, similar to a paramount clause, declaring the provision which is to prevail would be helpful. The matter would one day have to go to court to be resolved.

---

215 See Chapter 9.
216 *Per* Mocatta J in *The Gold Sky* [1972] 2 Lloyd's Rep 187 at p 217.

APPENDIX 1

MARINE INSURANCE ACT 1906
[6 Edw 7 Ch 41]

ARRANGEMENT OF SECTIONS

Marine Insurance

Section

1	Marine insurance defined
2	Mixed sea and land risks
3	Marine adventure and maritime perils defined

Insurable Interest

4	Avoidance of wagering or gaming contracts
5	Insurable interest defined
6	When interest must attach
7	Defeasible or contingent interest
8	Partial interest
9	Re-insurance
10	Bottomry
11	Master's and seamen's wages
12	Advance freight
13	Charges of insurance
14	Quantum of interest
15	Assignment of interest

Insurable Value

16	Measure of insurable value

Disclosure and Representations

17	Insurance is *uberrimae fidei*
18	Disclosure by assured
19	Disclosure by agent effecting insurance
20	Representations pending negotiation of contract
21	When contract is deemed to be concluded

THE POLICY

DOUBLE INSURANCE

WARRANTIES, &C

THE VOYAGE

CHAPTER 41

An Act to codify the Law relating to Marine Insurance

[21 December 1906]

BE it enacted by the King's most Excellent Majesty, by and with the advice and consent of the Lords Spiritual and Temporal, and Commons, in this present Parliament assembled, and by the authority of the same, as follows:

MARINE INSURANCE

1. Marine insurance defined

A contract of marine insurance is a contract whereby the insurer undertakes to indemnify the assured, in manner and to the extent thereby agreed, against marine losses, that is to say, the losses incident to marine adventure.

2. Mixed sea and land risks

(1) A contract of marine insurance may, by its express terms, or by usage of trade, be extended so as to protect the assured against losses on inland waters or on any land risk which may be incidental to any sea voyage.

(2) Where a ship in course of building, or the launch of a ship, or any adventure analogous to a marine adventure, is covered by a policy in the form of a marine policy, the provisions of this Act, in so far as applicable, shall apply thereto; but, except as by this section provided, nothing in this Act shall alter or affect any rule of law applicable to any contract of insurance other than a contract of marine insurance as by this Act defined.

3. Marine adventure and maritime perils defined

(1) Subject to the provisions of this Act, every lawful marine adventure may be the subject of a contract of marine insurance.

(2) In particular there is a marine adventure where—

(a) Any ship goods or other moveables are exposed to maritime perils. Such property is in this Act referred to as 'insurable property';

(b) The earning or acquisition of any freight, passage money, commission, profit, or other pecuniary benefit, or the security for any advances, loan, or disbursements, is endangered by the exposure of insurable property to maritime perils;

(c) Any liability to a third party may be incurred by the owner of, or other person interested in or responsible for, insurable property, by reason of maritime perils.

'Maritime perils' means the perils consequent on, or incidental to, the navigation of the sea, that is to say, perils of the seas, fire, war perils, pirates, rovers, thieves, captures, seizures, restraints, and detainments of princes and peoples, jettisons, barratry, and any other perils, either of the like kind or which may be designated by the policy.

INSURABLE INTEREST

4. Avoidance of wagering or gaming contracts

(1) Every contract of marine insurance by way of gaming or wagering is void.

(2) A contract of marine insurance is deemed to be a gaming or wagering contract—

(a) Where the assured has not an insurable interest as defined by this Act and the contract is entered into with no expectation of acquiring such an interest; or

(b) Where the policy is made 'interest or no interest', or 'without further proof of interest than the policy itself', or 'without benefit of salvage to the insurer', or subject to any other like term:

Provided that, where there is no possibility of salvage, a policy may be effected without benefit of salvage to the insurer.

5. Insurable interest defined

(1) Subject to the provisions of this Act, every person has an insurable interest who is interested in a marine adventure.

(2) In particular a person is interested in a marine adventure where he stands in any legal or equitable relation to the adventure or to any insurable property at risk therein, in consequence of which he may benefit by the safety or due arrival of insurable property, or may be prejudiced by its loss, or damage thereto, or by the detention thereof, or may incur liability in respect thereof.

6. When interest must attach

(1) The assured must be interested in the subject-matter insured at the time of the loss though he need not be interested when the insurance is effected:

Provided that where the subject-matter is insured 'lost or not lost', the assured may recover although he may not have acquired his interest until after the loss, unless at the time of effecting the contract of insurance the assured was aware of the loss, and the insurer was not.

(2) Where the assured has no interest at the time of the loss, he cannot acquire interest by any act or election after he is aware of the loss.

7. Defeasible or contingent interest

(1) A defeasible interest is insurable, as also is a contingent interest.

(2) In particular, where the buyer of goods has insured them, he has an insurable interest, notwithstanding that he might, at his election, have rejected the goods, or have treated them as at the seller's risk, by reason of the latter's delay in making delivery or otherwise.

8. Partial interest

A partial interest of any nature is insurable.

9. Re-insurance

(1) The insurer under a contract of marine insurance has an insurable interest in his risk, and may re-insure in respect of it.

(2) Unless the policy otherwise provides, the original assured has no right or interest in respect of such re-insurance.

10. Bottomry

The lender of money on bottomry or *respondentia* has an insurable interest in respect of the loan.

11. Master's and seamen's wages

The master or any member of the crew of a ship has an insurable interest in respect of his wages.

12. Advance freight

In the case of advance freight, the person advancing the freight has an insurable interest, in so far as such freight is not repayable in case of loss.

13. Charges of insurance

The assured has an insurable interest in the charges of any insurance which he may effect.

14. Quantum of interest

(1) Where the subject-matter insured is mortgaged, the mortgagor has an insurable interest in the full value thereof, and the mortgagee has an insurable interest in respect of any sum due or to become due under the mortgage.

(2) A mortgagee, consignee, or other person having an interest in the subject-matter insured may insure on behalf and for the benefit of other persons interested as well as for his own benefit.

(3) The owner of insurable property has an insurable interest in respect of the full value thereof, notwithstanding that some third person may have agreed, or be liable, to indemnify him in case of loss.

15. Assignment of interest

Where the assured assigns or otherwise parts with his interest in the subject matter insured, he does not thereby transfer to the assignee his rights under the contract of insurance, unless there be an express or implied agreement with the assignee to that effect.

But the provisions of this section do not affect a transmission of interest by operation of law.

INSURABLE VALUE

16. Measure of insurable value

Subject to any express provision or valuation in the policy, the insurable value of the subject-matter insured must be ascertained as follows:—

(1) In insurance on ship, the insurable value is the value, at the commencement of the risk, of the ship, including her outfit, provisions and stores for the officers and crew, money advanced for seamen's wages, and other disbursements (if any) incurred to make the ship fit for the voyage or adventure contemplated by the policy, plus the charges of insurance upon the whole:

The insurable value, in the case of a steamship, includes also the machinery, boilers, and coals and engine stores if owned by the assured, and, in the case of a ship engaged in a special trade, the ordinary fittings requisite for that trade:

(2) In insurance on freight, whether paid in advance or otherwise, the insurable value is the gross amount of the freight at the risk of the assured, plus the charges of insurance:

(3) In insurance on goods or merchandise, the insurable value is the prime cost of the property insured, plus the expenses of and incidental to shipping and the charges of insurance upon the whole:

(4) In insurance on any other subject-matter, the insurable value is the amount at the risk of the assured when the policy attaches, plus the charges of insurance.

DISCLOSURE AND REPRESENTATIONS

17. Insurance is *uberrimae fidei*

A contract of marine insurance is a contract based upon the utmost good faith and, if the utmost good faith be not observed by either party, the contract may be avoided by the other party.

18. Disclosure by assured

(1) Subject to the provisions of this section, the assured must disclose to the insurer, before the contract is concluded, every material circumstance which is known to the assured, and the assured is deemed to know every circumstance which, in the ordinary course of business, ought to be known by him. If the assured fails to make such disclosure, the insurer may avoid the contract.

(2) Every circumstance is material which would influence the judgment of a prudent insurer in fixing the premium, or determining whether he will take the risk.

(3) In the absence of inquiry the following circumstances need not be disclosed, namely: –

(a) Any circumstance which diminishes the risk;

(b) Any circumstance which is known or presumed to be known to the insurer. The insurer is presumed to know matters of common notoriety or knowledge, and matters which an insurer in the ordinary course of his business, as such, ought to know;

(c) Any circumstance as to which information is waived by the insurer;

(d) Any circumstance which it is superfluous to disclose by reason of any express or implied warranty.

(4) Whether any particular circumstance, which is not disclosed, be material or not is, in each case, a question of fact.

(5) The term 'circumstance' includes any communication made to, or information received by, the assured.

19. Disclosure by agent effecting insurance

Subject to the provisions of the preceding section as to circumstances which need not be disclosed, where an insurance is effected for the assured by an agent, the agent must disclose to the insurer—

(a) Every material circumstance which is known to himself, and an agent to insure is deemed to know every circumstance which in the ordinary course of business ought to be known by, or to have been communicated to, him; and

(b) Every material circumstance which the assured is bound to disclose, unless it come to his knowledge too late to communicate it to the agent.

20. Representations pending negotiation of contract

(1) Every material representation made by the assured or his agent to the insurer during the negotiations for the contract, and before the contract is concluded, must be true. If it be untrue the insurer may avoid the contract.

(2) A representation is material which would influence the judgment of a prudent insurer in fixing the premium, or determining whether he will take the risk.

(3) A representation may be either a representation as to a matter of fact, or as to a matter of expectation or belief.

(4) A representation as to matter of fact is true, if it be substantially correct, that is to say, if the difference between what is represented and what is actually correct would not be considered material by a prudent insurer.

(5) A representation as to a matter of expectation or belief is true if it be made in good faith.

(6) A representation may be withdrawn or corrected before the contract is concluded.

(7) Whether a particular representation be material or not is, in each case, a question of fact.

21. When contract is deemed to be concluded

A contract of marine insurance is deemed to be concluded when the proposal of the assured is accepted by the insurer, whether the policy be then issued or not; and, for the purpose of showing when the proposal was accepted, reference may be made to the slip or covering note or other customary memorandum of the contract, although it be unstamped.

THE POLICY

22. Contract must be embodied in policy

Subject to the provisions of any statute, a contract of marine insurance is inadmissible in evidence unless it is embodied in a marine policy in accordance with this Act. The policy may be executed and issued either at the time when the contract is concluded, or afterwards.

23. What policy must specify

A marine policy must specify—

(1) The name of the assured, or of some person who effects the insurance on his behalf;

(2) The subject-matter insured and the risk insured again;

(3) The voyage, or period of time, or both, as the case may be, covered by the insurance;

(4) The sum or sums insured;

(5) The name or names of the insurers.

24. Signature of insurer

(1) A marine policy must be signed by or on behalf of the insurer, provided that in the case of a corporation the corporate seal may be sufficient, but nothing in this section shall be construed as requiring the subscription of a corporation to be under seal.

(2) Where a policy is subscribed by or on behalf of two or more insurers, each subscription, unless the contrary be expressed, constitutes a distinct contract with the assured.

25. Voyage and time policies

(1) Where the contract is to insure the subject-matter 'at and from', or from one place to another or others, the policy is called a 'voyage policy', and where the contract is to insure the subject-matter for a definite period of time the policy is called a 'time policy'. A contract for both voyage and time may be included in the same policy.

(2) Subject to the provisions of section eleven of the Finance Act, 1901, a time policy which is made for any time exceeding twelve months is invalid.

26. Designation of subject-matter

(1) The subject-matter insured must be designated in a marine policy with reasonable certainty.

(2) The nature and extent of the interest of the assured in the subject-matter insured need not be specified in the policy.

(3) Where the policy designates the subject-matter insured in general terms, it shall be construed to apply to the interest intended by the assured to be covered.

(4) In the application of this section regard shall be had to any usage regulating the designation of the subject-matter insured.

27. Valued policy

(1) A policy may be either valued or unvalued.

(2) A valued policy is a policy which specifies the agreed value of the subject-matter insured.

(3) Subject to the provisions of this Act, and in the absence of fraud, the value fixed by the policy is, as between the insurer and assured, conclusive of the insurable value of the subject intended to be insured, whether the loss be total or partial.

(4) Unless the policy otherwise provides, the value fixed by the policy is not conclusive for the purpose of determining whether there has been a constructive total loss.

28. Unvalued policy

An unvalued policy is a policy which does not specify the value of the subject-matter insured, but, subject to the limit of the sum insured, leaves the insurable value to be subsequently ascertained, in the manner herein-before specified.

29. Floating policy by ship or ships

(1) A floating policy is a policy which describes the insurance in general terms, and leaves the name of the ship or ships and other particulars to be defined by subsequent declaration.

(2) The subsequent declaration or declarations may be made by indorsement on the policy, or in other customary manner.

(3) Unless the policy otherwise provides, the declarations must be made in the order of dispatch or shipment. They must, in the case of goods, comprise all consignments within the terms of the policy, and the value of the goods or other property must be honestly stated, but an omission or erroneous declaration may be rectified even after loss or arrival, provided the omission or declaration was made in good faith.

(4) Unless the policy otherwise provides, where a declaration of value is not made until after notice of loss or arrival, the policy must be treated as an unvalued policy as regards the subject-matter of that declaration.

30. Construction of terms in policy

(1) A policy may be in the form in the First Schedule to this Act.

(2) Subject to the provisions of this Act, and unless the context of the policy otherwise requires, the terms and expressions mentioned in the First Schedule to this Act shall be construed as having the scope and meaning in that schedule assigned to them.

31. Premium to be arranged

(1) Where an insurance is effected at a premium to be arranged, and no arrangement is made, a reasonable premium is payable.

(2) Where an insurance is effected on the terms that an additional premium is to be arranged in a given event, and that event happens but no arrangement is made, then a reasonable additional premium is payable.

32. Double insurance

(1) Where two or more policies are effected by or on behalf of the assured on the same adventure and interest or any part thereof, and the sums insured exceed the indemnity allowed by this Act, the assured is said to be over-insured by double insurance.

(2) Where the assured is over-insured by double insurance—

(a) The assured, unless the policy otherwise provides, may claim payment from the insurers in such order as he may think fit, provided that he is not entitled to receive any sum in excess of the indemnity allowed by this Act;

(b) Where the policy under which the assured claims is a valued policy the assured must give credit as against the valuation for any sum received by him under any other policy without regard to the actual value of the subject-matter insured

(c) Where the policy under which the assured claims is an unvalued policy he must give credit, as against the full insurable value, for any sum received by him under any other policy

(d) Where the assured receives any sum in excess of the indemnity allowed by this Act, he is deemed to hold such sum in trust for the insurers, according to their right of contribution among themselves.

WARRANTIES, &C

33. Nature of warranty

(1) A warranty, in the following sections relating to warranties, means a promissory warranty, that is to say, a warranty by which the assured undertakes that some particular thing shall or shall not be done, or that some condition shall be fulfilled, or whereby he affirms or negatives the existence of a particular state of facts.

(2) A warranty may be express or implied.

(3) A warranty, as above defined, is a condition which must be exactly complied with, whether it be material to the risk or not. If it be not so complied with, then, subject to any express provision in the policy, the insurer is discharged from liability as from the date of the breach of warranty, but without prejudice to any liability incurred by him before that date.

34. When breach of warranty excused

(1) Non-compliance with a warranty is excused when, by reason of a change of circumstances, the warranty ceases to be applicable to the circumstances of the contract, or when compliance with the warranty is rendered unlawful by any subsequent law.

(2) Where a warranty is broken, the assured cannot avail himself of the defence that the breach has been remedied, and the warranty complied with, before loss.

(3) A breach of warranty may be waived by the insurer.

35. Express warranties

(1) An express warranty may be in any form of words from which the intention to warrant is to be inferred.

(2) An express warranty must be included in, or written upon, the policy, or must be contained in some document incorporated by reference into the policy.

(3) An express warranty does not exclude an implied warranty, unless it be inconsistent therewith.

36. Warranty of neutrality

(1) Where insurable property, whether ship or goods, is expressly warranted neutral, there is an implied condition that the property shall have a neutral character at the commencement of the risk, and that, so far as the assured can control the matter, its neutral character shall be preserved during the risk.

(2) Where a ship is expressly warranted 'neutral' there is also an implied condition that, so far as the assured can control the matter, she shall be properly documented, that is to say, that she shall carry the necessary papers to establish her neutrality, and that she shall not falsify or suppress her papers, or use simulated papers. If any loss occurs through breach of this condition, the insurer may avoid the contract.

37. No implied warranty of nationality

There is no implied warranty as to the nationality of a ship, or that her nationality shall not be changed during the risk.

38. Warranty of good safety

Where the subject-matter insured is warranted 'well' or 'in good safety' on a particular day, it is sufficient if it be safe at any time during that day.

39. Warranty of seaworthiness of ship

(1) In a voyage policy there is an implied warranty that at the commencement of the voyage the ship shall be seaworthy for the purpose of the particular adventure insured.

(2) Where the policy attaches while the ship is in port, there is also an implied warranty that she shall, at the commencement of the risk, be reasonably fit to encounter the ordinary perils of the port.

(3) Where the policy relates to a voyage which is performed in different stages, during which the ship requires different kinds of or further preparation or equipment, there is an implied warranty that at the commencement of each stage the ship is seaworthy in respect of such preparation or equipment for the purposes of that stage.

(4) A ship is deemed to be seaworthy when she is reasonably fit in all respects to encounter the ordinary perils of the seas of the adventure insured.

(5) In a time policy there is no implied warranty that the ship shall be seaworthy at any stage of the adventure, but where, with the privity of the

assured, the ship is sent to sea in an unseaworthy state, the insurer is not liable
for any loss attributable to unseaworthiness.

40. No implied warranty that goods are seaworthy

(1) In a policy on goods or other moveables there is no implied warranty that
the goods or moveables are seaworthy.

(2) In a voyage policy on goods or other moveables there is an implied
warranty that at the commencement of the voyage the ship is not only
seaworthy as a ship, but also that she is reasonably fit to carry the goods or
other moveables to the destination contemplated by the policy.

41. Warranty of legality

There is an implied warranty that the adventure insured is a lawful one, and
that, so far as the assured can control the matter, the adventure shall be carried
out in a lawful manner.

THE VOYAGE

42. Implied condition as to commencement of risk

(1) Where the subject-matter is insured by a voyage policy 'at and from' or
'from' a particular place, it is not necessary that the ship should be at that place
when the contract is concluded, but there is an implied condition that the
adventure shall be commenced within a reasonable time, and that if the
adventure be not so commenced the insurer may avoid the contract.

(2) The implied condition may be negatived by showing that the delay was
caused by circumstances known to the insurer before the contract was
concluded or by showing that he waived the condition.

43. Alteration of port of departure

Where the place of departure is specified by the policy, and the ship instead of
sailing from that place sails from any other place, the risk does not attach.

44. Sailing for different destination

Where the destination is specified in the policy, and the ship, instead of sailing
for that destination, sails for any other destination, the risk does not attach.

45. Change of voyage

(1) Where, after the commencement of the risk, the destination of the ship is
voluntarily changed from the destination contemplated by the policy, there is
said to be a change of voyage.

(2) Unless the policy otherwise provides, where there is a change of voyage,
the insurer is discharged from liability as from the time of change, that is to say,
as from the time when the determination to change it is manifested; and it is
immaterial that the ship may not in fact have left the course of voyage
contemplated by the policy when the loss occurs.

46. Deviation

(1) Where a ship, without lawful excuse, deviates from the voyage contemplated by the policy, the insurer is discharged from liability as from the time of deviation, and it is immaterial that the ship may have regained her route before any loss occurs.

(2) There is a deviation from the voyage contemplated by the policy—

(a) Where the course of the voyage is specifically designated by the policy, and that course is departed from; or

(b) Where the course of the voyage is not specifically designated by the policy, but the usual and customary course is departed from.

(3) The intention to deviate is immaterial; there must be a deviation in fact to discharge the insurer from his liability under the contract.

47. Several ports of discharge

(1) Where several ports of discharge are specified by the policy, the ship may proceed to all or any of them, but, in the absence of any usage or sufficient cause to the contrary, she must proceed to them, or such of them as she goes to, in the order designated by the policy. If she does not there is a deviation.

(2) Where the policy is to 'ports of discharge', within a given area, which are not named, the ship must, in the absence of any usage or sufficient cause to the contrary, proceed to them, or such of them as she goes to, in their geographical order. If she does not there is a deviation.

48. Delay in voyage

In the case of a voyage policy, the adventure insured must be prosecuted throughout its course with reasonable dispatch, and, if without lawful excuse it is not so prosecuted, the insurer is discharged from liability as from the time when the delay became unreasonable.

49. Excuses for deviation or delay

(1) Deviation or delay in prosecuting the voyage contemplated by the policy is excused—

(a) Where authorised by any special term in the policy; or

(b) Where caused by circumstances beyond the control of the master and his employer; or

(c) Where reasonably necessary in order to comply with an express or implied warranty; or

(d) Where reasonably necessary for the safety of the ship or subject-matter insured, or

(e) For the purpose of saving human life, or aiding a ship in distress where human life may be in danger; or

(f) Where reasonably necessary for the purpose of obtaining medical or surgical aid for any person on board the ship; or

(g) Where caused by the barratrous conduct of the master or crew, if barratry be one of the perils insured against.

(2) When the cause excusing the deviation or delay ceases to operate, the ship must resume her course, and prosecute her voyage, with reasonable dispatch.

50. When and how policy is assignable

(1) A marine policy is assignable unless it contains terms expressly prohibiting assignment. It may be assigned either before or after loss.

(2) Where a marine policy has been assigned so as to pass the beneficial interest in such policy, the assignee of the policy is entitled to sue thereon in his own name; and the defendant is entitled to make any defence arising out of the contract which he would have been entitled to make if the action had been brought in the name of the person by or on behalf of whom the policy was effected.

(3) A marine policy may be assigned by indorsement thereon or in other customary manner.

51. Assured who has no interest cannot assign

Where the assured has parted with or lost his interest in the subject-matter insured, and has not, before or at the time of so doing, expressly or impliedly agreed to assign the policy, any subsequent assignment of the policy is inoperative:

Provided that nothing in this section affects the assignment of a policy after loss.

52. When premium payable

Unless otherwise agreed, the duty of the assured or his agent to pay the premium, and the duty of the insurer to issue the policy to the assured or his agent, are concurrent conditions, and the insurer is not bound to issue the policy until payment or tender of the premium.

53. Policy effected through broker

(1) Unless otherwise agreed, where a marine policy is effected on behalf of the assured by a broker, the broker is directly responsible to the insurer for the premium, and the insurer is directly responsible to the assured for the amount which may be payable in respect of losses, or in respect of returnable premium.

(2) Unless otherwise agreed, the broker has, as against the assured, a lien upon the policy for the amount of the premium and his charges in respect of effecting the policy, and, where he has dealt with the person who employs him as a principal, he has also a lien on the policy in respect of any balance on any insurance account which may be due to him from such person, unless when the debt was incurred he had reason to believe that such person was only an agent.

54. Effect of receipt on policy

Where a marine policy effected on behalf of the assured by a broker acknowledges the receipt of the premium, such acknowledgment is, in the absence of fraud, conclusive as between the insurer and the assured, but not as between the insurer and broker.

LOSS AND ABANDONMENT

55. Included and excluded losses

(1) Subject to the provisions of this Act, and unless the policy otherwise provides, the insurer is liable for any loss proximately caused by a peril insured against, but, subject as aforesaid, he is not liable for any loss which is not proximately caused by a peril insured against.

(2) In particular,—

(a) The insurer is not liable for any loss attributable to the wilful misconduct of the assured, but, unless the policy otherwise provides he is liable for any loss proximately caused by a peril insured against even though the loss would not have happened but for the misconduct or negligence of the master or crew;

(b) Unless the policy otherwise provides, the insurer on ship or goods is not liable for any loss proximately caused by delay, although the delay be caused by a peril insured against;

(c) Unless the policy otherwise provides, the insurer is not liable for ordinary wear and tear, ordinary leakage and breakage, inherent vice or nature of the subject-matter insured, or for any loss proximately caused by rats or vermin, or for any injury to machinery not proximately caused by maritime perils.

56. Partial and total loss

(1) A loss may be either total or partial. Any loss other than a total loss, as hereinafter defined, is a partial loss.

(2) A total loss may be either an actual total loss, or a constructive total loss.

(3) Unless a different intention appears from the terms of the policy, an insurance against total loss includes a constructive, as well as an actual, total loss.

(4) Where the assured brings an action for a total loss and the evidence proves only a partial loss, he may, unless the policy otherwise provides, recover for a partial loss.

(5) Where goods reach their destination in specie, but by reason of obliteration of marks, or otherwise, they are incapable of identification the loss, if any, is partial, and not total.

57. Actual total loss

(1) Where the subject-matter insured is destroyed, or so damaged as to cease to be a thing of the kind insured, or where the assured is irretrievably deprived thereof, there is an actual total loss.

(2) In the case of an actual total loss no notice of abandonment need be given.

58. Missing ship

Where the ship concerned in the adventure is missing, and after the lapse of a reasonable time no news of her has been received, an actual total loss may be presumed.

59. Effect of transhipment, etc

Where, by a peril insured against, the voyage is interrupted at an intermediate port or place, under such circumstances as, apart from any special stipulation in the contract of affreightment, to justify the master in landing and re-shipping the goods or other moveables, or in transhipping them, and sending them on to their destination, the liability of the insurer continues, notwithstanding the landing or transhipment.

60. Constructive total loss defined

(1) Subject to any express provision in the policy, there is a constructive total loss where the subject-matter insured is reasonably abandoned on account of its actual total loss appearing to be unavoidable, or because it could not be preserved from actual total loss without an expenditure which would exceed its value when the expenditure had been incurred.

(2) In particular, there is a constructive total loss—

(i) Where the assured is deprived of the possession of his ship or goods by a peril insured against, and (a) it is unlikely that he can recover the ship or goods, as the case may be, or (b) the cost of recovering the ship or goods, as the case may be, would exceed their value when recovered; or

(ii) In the case of damage to a ship, where she is so damaged by a peril insured against that the cost of repairing the damage would exceed the value of the ship when repaired.

In estimating the cost of repairs, no deduction is to be made in respect of general average contributions to those repairs payable by other interests, but account is to be taken of the expense of future salvage operations and of any future general average contributions to which the ship would be liable if repaired; or

(iii)In the case of damage to goods, where the cost of repairing the damage and forwarding the goods to their destination would exceed their value on arrival.

61. Effect of constructive total loss

Where there is a constructive total loss the assured may either treat the loss as a partial loss, or abandon the subject-matter insured to the insurer and treat the loss as if it were an actual total loss.

62. Notice of abandonment

(1) Subject to the provisions of this section, where the assured elects to abandon the subject-matter insured to the insurer, he must give notice of abandonment. If he fails to do so the loss can only be treated as a partial loss.

(2) Notice of abandonment may be given in writing, or by word of mouth, or partly in writing and partly by word of mouth, and may be given in terms which indicate the intention of the assured to abandon his insured interest in the subject-matter insured unconditionally to the insurer.

(3) Notice of abandonment must be given with reasonable diligence after the receipt of reliable information of the loss, but where the information is of a doubtful character the assured is entitled to a reasonable time to make inquiry.

(4) Where notice of abandonment is properly given, the rights of the assured are not prejudiced by the fact that the insurer refuses to accept the abandonment.

(5) The acceptance of an abandonment may be either express or implied from the conduct of the insurer. The mere silence of the insurer after notice is not an acceptance.

(6) Where a notice of abandonment is accepted the abandonment is irrevocable. The acceptance of the notice conclusively admits liability for the loss and the sufficiency of the notice.

(7) Notice of abandonment is unnecessary where, at the time when the assured receives information of the loss, there would be no possibility of benefit to the insurer if notice were given to him.

(8) Notice of abandonment may be waived by the insurer.

(9) Where an insurer has re-insured his risk, no notice of abandonment need be given by him.

63. Effect of abandonment

(1) Where there is a valid abandonment the insurer is entitled to take over the interest of the assured in whatever may remain of the subject-matter insured, and all proprietary rights incidental thereto.

(2) Upon the abandonment of a ship, the insurer thereof is entitled to any freight in course of being earned, and which is earned by her subsequent to the casualty causing the loss, less the expenses of earning it incurred after the casualty, and, where the ship is carrying the owner's goods, the insurer is entitled to a reasonable remuneration for the carriage of them subsequent to the casualty causing the loss.

PARTIAL LOSSES (INCLUDING SALVAGE AND GENERAL AVERAGE AND PARTICULAR CHARGES)

64. Particular average loss

(1) A particular average loss is a partial loss of the subject-matter insured, caused by a peril insured against, and which is not a general average loss.

(2) Expenses incurred by or on behalf of the assured for the safety or preservation of the subject-matter insured, other than general average and salvage charges, are called particular charges. Particular charges are not included in particular average.

65. Salvage charges

(1) Subject to any express provision in the policy, salvage charges incurred in preventing a loss by perils insured against may be recovered as a loss by those perils.

(2) 'Salvage charges' means the charges recoverable under maritime law by a salvor independently of contract. They do not include the expenses of services in the nature of salvage rendered by the assured or his agents, or any person employed for hire by them, for the purpose of averting a peril insured against. Such expenses, where properly incurred, may be recovered as particular charges or as a general average loss, according to the circumstances under which they were incurred.

66. General average loss

(1) A general average loss is a loss caused by or directly consequential on a general average act It includes a general average expenditure as well as a general average sacrifice.

(2) There is a general average act where any extraordinary sacrifice or expenditure is voluntarily and reasonably made or incurred in time of peril for the purpose of preserving the property imperilled in the common adventure.

(3) Where there is a general average loss, the party on whom it falls is entitled, subject to the conditions imposed by maritime law, to a rateable contribution from the other parties interested, and such contribution is called a general average contribution.

(4) Subject to any express provision in the policy, where the assured has incurred a general average expenditure, he may recover from the insurer in respect of the proportion of the loss which falls upon him; and, in the case of a general average sacrifice, he may recover from the insurer in respect of the whole loss without having enforced his right of contribution from the other parties liable to contribute.

(5) Subject to any express provision in the policy, where the assured has paid, or is liable to pay, a general average contribution in respect of the subject insured, he may recover therefor from the insurer.

(6) In the absence of express stipulation, the insurer is not liable for any general average loss or contribution where the loss was not incurred for the purpose of avoiding, or in connexion with the avoidance of, a peril insured against.

(7) Where ship, freight, and cargo, or any two of those interests, are owned by the same assured, the liability of the insurer in respect of general average losses or contributions is to be determined as if those subjects were owned by different persons.

MEASURE OF INDEMNITY

67. Extent of liability of insurer for loss

(1) The sum which the assured can recover in respect of a loss on a policy by which he is insured, in the case of an unvalued policy to the full extent of the

insurable value, or, in the case of a valued policy to the full extent of the value fixed by the policy, is called the measure of indemnity.

(2) Where there is a loss recoverable under the policy, the insurer, or each insurer if there be more than one, is liable for such proportion of the measure of indemnity as the amount of his subscription bears to the value fixed by the policy in the case of a valued policy, or to the insurable value in the case of an unvalued policy.

68. Total loss

Subject to the provisions of this Act and to any express provision in the policy where there is a total loss of the subject-matter insured,—

(1) If the policy be a valued policy, the measure of indemnity is the sum fixed by the policy.

(2) If the policy be an unvalued policy, the measure of indemnity is the insurable value of the subject-matter insured.

69. Partial loss of ship

Where a ship is damaged, but is not totally lost, the measure of indemnity subject to any express provision in the policy, is as follows:—

(1) Where the ship has been repaired, the assured is entitled to the reasonable cost of the repairs, less the customary deductions, but not exceeding the sum insured in respect of any one casualty;

(2) Where the ship has been only partially repaired, the assured is entitled to the reasonable cost of such repairs, computed as above, and also to be indemnified for the reasonable depreciation, if any, arising from the unrepaired damage, provided that the aggregate amount shall not exceed the cost of repairing the whole damage, computed as above;

(3) Where the ship has not been repaired, and has not been sold in her damaged state during the risk, the assured is entitled to be indemnified for the reasonable depreciation arising from the unrepaired damage, but not exceeding the reasonable cost of repairing such damage, computed as above.

70. Partial loss of freight

Subject to any express provision in the policy, where there is a partial loss of freight, the measure of indemnity is such proportion of the sum fixed by the policy in the case of a valued policy, or of the insurable value in the case of an unvalued policy, as the proportion of freight lost by the assured bears to the whole freight at the risk of the assured under the policy.

71. Partial loss of goods, merchandise, etc

Where there is a partial loss of goods, merchandise, or other moveables, the measure of indemnity, subject to any express provision in the policy, is as follows —

(1) Where part of the goods, merchandise or other moveables insured by a valued policy is totally lost, the measure of indemnity is such proportion of the sum fixed by the policy as the insurable value of the part lost bears to the insurable value of the whole, ascertained as in the case of an unvalued policy;

(2) Where part of the goods, merchandise, or other moveables insured by an unvalued policy is totally lost, the measure of indemnity is the insurable value of the part lost, ascertained as in case of total loss;

(3) Where the whole or any part of the goods or merchandise insured has been delivered damaged at its destination, the measure of indemnity is such proportion of the sum fixed by the policy in the case of a valued policy, or of the insurable value in the case of an unvalued policy, as the difference between the gross sound and damaged values at the place of arrival bears to the gross sound value;

(4) 'Gross value' means the wholesale price or, if there be no such price the estimated value, with, in either case, freight, landing charges, and duty paid beforehand; provided that, in the case of goods or merchandise customarily sold in bond, the bonded price is deemed to be the gross value. 'Gross proceeds' means the actual price obtained at a sale where all charges on sale are paid by the sellers.

72. Apportionment of valuation

(1) Where different species of property are insured under a single valuation, the valuation must be apportioned over the different species in proportion to their respective insurable values, as in the case of an unvalued policy. The insured value of any part of a species is such proportion of the total insured value of the same as the insurable value of the part bears to the insurable value of the whole ascertained in both cases as provided by this Act.

(2) Where a valuation has to be apportioned, and particulars of the prime cost of each separate species, quality, or description of goods cannot be ascertained, the division of the valuation may be made over the net arrived sound values of the different species, qualities, or descriptions of goods.

73. General average contributions and salvage charges

(1) Subject to any express provision in the policy, where the assured has paid, or is liable for, any general average contribution, the measure of indemnity is the full amount of such contribution, if the subject-matter liable to contribution is insured for its full contributory value; but, if such subject-matter be not insured for its full contributory value, or if only part of it be insured, the indemnity payable by the insurer must be reduced in proportion to the under insurance, and where there has been a particular average loss which constitutes a deduction from the contributory value, and for which the insurer is liable, that amount must be deducted from the insured value in order to ascertain what the insurer is liable to contribute.

(2) Where the insurer is liable for salvage charges the extent of his liability must be determined on the like principle.

74. Liabilities to third parties

Where the assured has effected an insurance in express terms against any liability to a third party, the measure of indemnity, subject to any express provision in the policy, is the amount paid or payable by him to such third party in respect of such liability.

75. General provisions as to measure of indemnity

(1) Where there has been a loss in respect of any subject-matter not expressly provided for in the foregoing provisions of this Act, the measure of indemnity shall be ascertained, as nearly as may be, in accordance with those provisions, in so far as applicable to the particular case.

(2) Nothing in the provisions of this Act relating to the measure of indemnity shall affect the rules relating to double insurance, or prohibit the insurer from disproving interest wholly or in part, or from showing that at the time of the loss the whole or any part of the subject-matter insured was not at risk under the policy.

76. Particular average warranties

(1) Where the subject-matter insured is warranted free from particular average, the assured cannot recover for a loss of part, other than a loss incurred by a general average sacrifice unless the contract contained in the policy be apportionable; but, if the contract be apportionable, the assured may recover for a total loss of any apportionable part.

(2) Where the subject-matter insured is warranted free from particular average, either wholly or under a certain percentage, the insurer is nevertheless liable for salvage charges, and for particular charges and other expenses properly incurred pursuant to the provisions of the suing and labouring clause in order to avert a loss insured against.

(3) Unless the policy otherwise provides, where the subject-matter insured is warranted free from particular average under a specified percentage, a general average loss cannot be added to a particular average loss to make up the specified percentage.

(4) For the purpose of ascertaining whether the specified percentage has been reached, regard shall be had only to the actual loss suffered by the subject matter insured. Particular charges and the expenses of and incidental to ascertaining and proving the loss must be excluded.

77. Successive losses

(1) Unless the policy otherwise provides, and subject to the provisions of this Act, the insurer is liable for successive losses, even though the total amount of such losses may exceed the sum insured.

(2) Where, under the same policy, a partial loss, which has not been repaired or otherwise made good, is followed by a total loss, the assured can only recover in respect of the total loss:

Provided that nothing in this section shall affect the liability of the insurer under the suing and labouring clause.

78. Suing and labouring clause

(1) Where the policy contains a suing and labouring clause, the engagement thereby entered into is deemed to be supplementary to the contract of insurance, and the assured may recover from the insurer any expenses properly incurred pursuant to the clause, notwithstanding that the insurer may have

paid for a total loss, or that the subject-matter may have been warranted free from particular average, either wholly or under a certain percentage.

(2) General average losses and contributions and salvage charges, as defined by this Act, are not recoverable under the suing and labouring clause.

(3) Expenses incurred for the purpose of averting or diminishing any loss not covered by the policy are not recoverable under the suing and labouring clause.

(4) It is the duty of the assured and his agents, in all cases, to take such measures as may be reasonable for the purpose of averting or minimising a loss.

79. Right of subrogation

(1) Where the insurer pays for a total loss, either of the whole, or in the case of goods of any apportionable part, of the subject-matter insured, he thereupon becomes entitled to take over the interest of the assured in whatever may remain of the subject-matter so paid for, and he is thereby subrogated to all the rights and remedies of the assured in and in respect of that subject-matter as from the time of the casualty causing the loss.

(2) Subject to the foregoing provisions, where the insurer pays for a partial loss, he acquires no title to the subject-matter insured, or such part of it as may remain, but he is thereupon subrogated to all rights and remedies of the assured in and in respect of the subject-matter insured as from the time of the casualty causing the loss, in so far as the assured has been indemnified, according to this Act, by such payment for the loss.

80. Right of contribution

(1) Where the assured is over-insured by double insurance, each insurer is bound, as between himself and the other insurers, to contribute rateably to the loss in proportion to the amount for which he is liable under his contract.

(2) If any insurer pays more than his proportion of the loss, he is entitled to maintain an action for contribution against the other insurers, and is entitled to the like remedies as a surety who has paid more than his proportion of the debt.

81. Effect of under insurance

Where the assured is insured for an amount less than the insurable value or, in the case of a valued policy, for an amount less than the policy valuation, he is deemed to be his own insurer in respect of the uninsured balance.

82. Enforcement of return

Where the premium or a proportionate part thereof is, by this Act, declared to be returnable,—

(a) If already paid, it may be recovered by the assured from the insurer; and

(b) If unpaid, it may be retained by the assured or his agent.

83. Return by agreement

Where the policy contains a stipulation for the return of the premium, or a proportionate part thereof, on the happening of a certain event, and that event happens, the premium, or, as the case may be, the proportionate part thereof, is thereupon returnable to the assured.

84. Return for failure of consideration

(1) Where the consideration for the payment of the premium totally fails, and there has been no fraud or illegality on the part of the assured or his agents, the premium is thereupon returnable to the assured.

(2) Where the consideration for the payment of the premium is apportionable and there is a total failure of any apportionable part of the consideration, a proportionate part of the premium is, under the like conditions, thereupon returnable to the assured.

(3) In particular—

(a) Where the policy is void, or is avoided by the insurer as from the commencement of the risk, the premium is returnable, provided that there has been no fraud or illegality on the part of the assured; but if the risk is not apportionable, and has once attached, the premium is not returnable;

(b) Where the subject-matter insured, or part thereof, has never been imperilled, the premium, or, as the case may be, a proportionate part thereof, is returnable:

Provided that where the subject-matter has been insured 'lost or not lost' and has arrived in safety at the time when the contract is concluded, the premium is not returnable unless, at such time, the insurer knew of the safe arrival.

(c) Where the assured has no insurable interest throughout the currency of the risk, the premium is returnable, provided that this rule does not apply to a policy effected by way of gaming or wagering;

(d) Where the assured has a defeasible interest which is terminated during the currency of the risk, the premium is not returnable;

(e) Where the assured has over-insured under an unvalued policy, a proportionate part of the premium is returnable

(f) Subject to the foregoing provisions, where the assured has overinsured by double insurance, a proportionate part of the several premiums is returnable:

Provided that, if the policies are effected at different times, and any earlier policy has at any time borne the entire risk, or if a claim has been paid on the policy in respect of the full sum insured thereby, no premium is returnable in respect of that policy, and when the double insurance is effected knowingly by the assured no premium is returnable.

MUTUAL INSURANCE

85. Modification of Act in case of mutual insurance

(1) Where two or more persons mutually agree to insure each other against marine losses there is said to be a mutual insurance.

(2) The provisions of this Act relating to the premium do not apply to mutual insurance, but a guarantee, or such other arrangement as may be agreed upon, may be substituted for the premium.

(3) The provisions of this Act, in so far as they may be modified by the agreement of the parties, may in the case of mutual insurance be modified by the terms of the policies issued by the association, or by the rules and regulations of the association.

(4) Subject to the exceptions mentioned in this section, the provisions of this Act apply to a mutual insurance.

SUPPLEMENTAL

86. Ratification by assured

Where a contract of marine insurance is in good faith effected by one person on behalf of another, the person on whose behalf it is effected may ratify the contract even after he is aware of a loss.

87. Implied obligations varied by agreement or usage

(1) Where any right, duty, or liability would arise under a contract of marine insurance by implication of law, it may be negatived or varied by express agreement, or by usage, if the usage be such as to bind both parties to the contract.

(2) The provisions of this section extend to any right, duty, or liability declared by this Act which may be lawfully modified by agreement.

88. Reasonable time, etc, a question of fact

Where by this Act any reference is made to reasonable time, reasonable premium, or reasonable diligence, the question what is reasonable is a question of fact.

89. Slip as evidence

Where there is a duly stamped policy, reference may be made, as heretofore, to the slip or covering note, in any legal proceeding.

90. Interpretation of terms

In this Act, unless the context or subject-matter otherwise requires,—

'Action' includes counter-claim and set off;

'Freight' includes the profit derivable by a shipowner from the employment of his ship to carry his own goods or moveables, as well as freight payable by a third party, but does not include passage money;

'Moveables' means any moveable tangible property, other than the ship, and includes money, valuable securities, and other documents;

'Policy' means a marine policy.

91. Savings

(1) Nothing in this Act, or in any repeal effected thereby, shall affect—

(a) The provisions of the Stamp Act 1891, or any enactment for the time being in force relating to the revenue;

(b) The provisions of the Companies Act 1862, or any enactment amending or substituted for the same;

(c) The provisions of any statute not expressly repealed by this Act.

(2) The rules of the common law including the law merchant, save in so far as they are inconsistent with the express provisions of this Act, shall continue to apply to contracts of marine insurance.

92. Repeals

The enactments mentioned in the Second Schedule to this Act are hereby repealed to the extent specified in that schedule.

93. Commencement

This Act shall come into operation on the first day of January one thousand nine hundred and seven.

94. Short title

This Act may be cited as the Marine Insurance Act 1906.

SCHEDULES

FIRST SCHEDULE

Section 30

FORM OF POLICY

Lloyd's S.G. policy

Be it known that   as well in   own name as for and in the name and names of all and every other person or persons to whom the same doth, may, or shall appertain, in part or in all doth make assurance and cause
and them, and every of them, to be insured lost or not lost, at and from

Upon any kind of goods and merchandises, and also upon the body, tackle, apparel, ordnance, munition, artillery, boat, and other furniture, of and in the good ship or vessel called the
whereof is master under God, for this present voyage,
or whosoever else shall go for master in the said ship, or by whatsoever other name or names the said ship, or the master thereof, is or shall be named or called; beginning the adventure upon the said goods and merchandises from the loading thereof aboard the said ship.

upon the said ship, &c.

and so shall continue and endure, during her abode there, upon the said ship, &c. And further, until the said ship, with all her ordnance, tackle, apparel, &c, and goods and merchandises whatsoever shall be arrived at

upon the said ship, &c, until she hath moored at, anchor twenty-four hours in good safety; and upon the goods and merchandises, until the same be there discharged and safely landed. And it shall be lawful for the said ship, &c, in this voyage, to proceed and sail to and touch and stay at any ports or places whatsoever

with prejudice to this insurance. The said ship, &c, goods and merchandises, &c, for so much as concerns the assured by agreement between the assured and assurers in this policy, are and shall be valued at

Touching the adventures and perils which we the assurers are contented to bear and do take upon us in this voyage: they are of the seas, men of war, fire, enemies, pirates, rovers, thieves, jettisons, letters of mart and countermart, surprisals, takings at sea, arrests, restraints, and detainments of all kings, princes, and people, of what nation, condition, or quality soever, barratry of the master and mariners, and of all other perils, losses, and misfortunes, that have or shall come to the hurt, detriment, or damage of the said goods and merchandises, and ship, &c, or any part thereof. And in the case of any loss or misfortune it shall be lawful to the assured, their factors, servants and assigns, to sue, labour, and travel for, in and about the defence, safeguards, and recovery of the said goods and merchandises, and ship, &c, or any part thereof, without prejudice to this insurance; to the charges whereof we, the assurers, will contribute each one according to the rate and quantity of his sum herein assured. And it is especially declared and agreed that no acts of the insurer or insured in recovering, saving, or preserving the property insured shall be considered as a waiver, or acceptance of abandonment. And it is agreed by us, the insurers, that this writing or policy of assurance shall be of as much force and effect as the surest writing or policy of assurance heretofore made in Lombard Street, or in the Royal Exchange, or elsewhere in London. And so we, the assurers, are contented, and do hereby promise and bind ourselves, each one for his own part, our heirs, executors, and goods to the assured, their executors, administrators, and assigns, for the true performance of the premises, confessing ourselves paid the consideration due unto us for this assurance by the assured, at and after the rate of

IN WITNESS whereof we, the assurers, have subscribed our names and sums assured in London.

NB–Corn, fish, salt, fruit, flour and seed are warranted free from average, unless general, or the ship be stranded – sugar, tobacco, hemp, flax, hides and skins are warranted free from average, under five pounds per cent, and all other goods, also the ship and freight, are warranted free from average, under three pounds per cent, unless general, or the ship be stranded.

RULES FOR CONSTRUCTION OF POLICY

The following are the rules referred to by this Act for the construction of a policy in the above or other like form, where the context does not otherwise require—

1. Lost or not lost

Where the subject-matter is insured 'lost or not lost', and the loss has occurred before the contract is concluded, the risk attaches unless, at such time the assured was aware of the loss, and the insurer was not.

2. From

Where the subject-matter is insured 'from' a particular place, the risk does not attach until the ship starts on the voyage insured.

3. At and from [Ship]

(a) Where a ship is insured 'at and from' a particular place, and she is at that place in good safety when the contract is concluded, the risk attaches immediately.

(b) If she be not at that place when the contract is concluded, the risk attaches as soon as she arrives there in good safety, and, unless the policy otherwise provides, it is immaterial that she is covered by another policy for a specified time after arrival.

(c) Where chartered freight is insured 'at and from' a particular place, and the ship is at that place in good safety when the contract is concluded the risk attaches immediately. If she be not there when the contract is concluded, the risk attaches as soon as she arrives there in good safety.

(d) Where freight, other than chartered freight, is payable without special conditions and is insured 'at and from' a particular place, the risk attaches pro rata as the goods or merchandise are shipped, provided that if there be cargo in readiness which belongs to the shipowner, or which some other person has contracted with him to ship, the risk attaches as soon as the ship is ready to receive such cargo.

4. From the loading thereof

Where goods or other moveables are insured 'from the loading thereof,' the risk does not attach until such goods or moveables are actually on board, and the insurer is not liable for them while in transit from the shore to ship.

5. Safely landed

Where the risk on goods or other moveables continues until they are 'safely landed,' they must be landed in the customary manner and within a reasonable time after arrival at the port of discharge, and if they are not so landed the risk ceases.

6. Touch and stay

In the absence of any further license or usage, the liberty to touch and stay 'at any port or place whatsoever' does not authorise the ship to depart from the course of her voyage from the port of departure to the port of destination.

7. Perils of the seas

The term 'perils of the seas' refers only to fortuitous accidents or casualties of the seas. It does not include the ordinary action of the winds and waves.

8. Pirates

The term 'pirates' includes passengers who mutiny and rioters who attack the ship from the shore.

9. Thieves

The term 'thieves' does not cover clandestine theft or a theft committed by any one of the ship's company, whether crew or passengers.

10. Restraint of princes

The term 'arrests, etc, of kings, princes, and people' refers to political or executive acts, and does not include a loss caused by riot or by ordinary judicial process.

11. Barratry

The term 'barratry' includes every wrongful act wilfully committed by the master or crew to the prejudice of the owner, or, as the case may be, the charterer.

12. All other perils

The term 'all other perils' includes only perils similar in kind to the perils specifically mentioned in the policy.

13. Average unless general

The term 'average unless general' means a partial loss of the subject-matter insured other than a general average loss, and does not include 'particular charges'.

14. Stranded

Where the ship has stranded, the insurer is liable for the excepted losses, although the loss is not attributable to the stranding, provided that when the stranding takes place the risk has attached and, if the policy be on goods, that the damaged goods are on board.

15.

The term 'ship' includes the hull, materials and outfit, stores and provisions for the officers and crew, and, in the case of vessels engaged in a special trade, the ordinary fittings requisite for the trade, and also, in the case of a steamship, the machinery, boilers and coals and engine stores, if owned by the assured.

16. Freight

The term 'freight' includes the profit derivable by a shipowner from the employment of his ship to carry his own goods or moveables, as well as freight payable by a third party, but does not include passage money.

17. Goods

The term 'goods' means goods in the nature of merchandise, and does not include personal effects or provisions and stores for use on board.

In the absence of any usage to the contrary, deck cargo and living animals must be insured specifically, and not under the general denomination of goods.

SECOND SCHEDULE

Section 92

ENACTMENTS REPEALED

Session and Chapter	Title or Short Title	Extent of Repeal
19 Geo 2 c 37.	An Act to regulate insurance on ships belonging to the subjects of Great Britain, and on merchandizes or effects laden thereon.	The whole Act.
28 Geo 3.c 56.	An Act to repeal an Act made in the twenty-fifth year of the reign of his present Majesty, intituled 'An Act for regulating Insurances on Ships, and on goods, merchandizes, or effects,' and for substituting other provisions for the like purpose in lieu thereof.	The whole Act so far as it relates to marine insurance.
31 & 32 Vict c 86.	The Policies of Marine Assurance Act, 1868.	The whole Act.

APPENDIX 2

MARINE INSURANCE (GAMBLING POLICIES) ACT 1909

An Act to prohibit gambling on loss by maritime perils [20th October, 1909]

BE it enacted by the King's most Excellent Majesty, by and with the advice and consent of the Lords Spiritual and Temporal, and Commons, in this present Parliament assembled, and by the authority of the same, as follows—

1. Prohibition of gambling on loss by maritime perils

(1) If–

(a) any person effects a contract of marine insurance without having any bona fide interest, direct or indirect, either in the safe arrival of the ship in relation to which the contract is made or in the safety or preservation of the subject-matter insured, or a bona fide expectation of acquiring such an interest; or

(b) any person in the employment of the owner of a ship, not being a part owner of the ship, effects a contract of marine insurance in relation to the ship, and the contract is made 'interest or no interest', or 'without further proof of interest than the policy itself', or 'without benefit of salvage to the insurer,' or subject to any other like term,

the contract shall be deemed to be a contract by way of gambling on loss by maritime perils, and the person effecting it shall be guilty of an offence, and shall be liable, on summary conviction, to imprisonment, with or without hard labour, for a term not exceeding six months or to a fine not exceeding [level 3 on the standard scale], and in either case to forfeit to the Crown any money he may receive under the contract.

(2) Any broker or other person through whom, and any insurer with whom, any such contract is effected shall be guilty of an offence and liable on summary conviction to the like penalties if he acted knowing that the contract was by way of gambling on loss by maritime perils within the meaning of this Act.

(3) Proceedings under this Act shall not be instituted without the consent in England of the Attorney-General, in Scotland of the Lord Advocate, and in Ireland of the Attorney-General for Ireland.

(4) Proceedings shall not be instituted under this Act against a person (other than a person in the employment of the owner of the ship in relation to which the contract was made) alleged to have effected a contract by way of gambling on loss by maritime perils until an opportunity has been afforded him of showing that the contract was not such a contract as aforesaid, and any information given by that person for that purpose shall not be admissible in evidence against him in any prosecution under this Act.

(5) If proceedings under this Act are taken against any person (other than a person in the employment of the owner of the ship in relation to which the contract was made) for effecting such a contract, and the contract was made 'interest or no interest,' or 'without further proof of interest than the policy itself,' or 'without benefit of salvage to the insurer,' or subject to any other like term, the contract shall be deemed to be a contract by way of gambling on loss by maritime perils unless the contrary is proved.

(6) For the purpose of giving jurisdiction under this Act, every offence shall be deemed to have been committed either in the place in which the same actually was committed or in any place in which the offender may be.

(7) Any person aggrieved by an order or decision of a court of summary jurisdiction under this Act, may appeal to [the Crown Court].

(8) For the purposes of this Act the expression 'owner' includes charterer.

(9) Subsection (7) of this section shall not apply to Scotland.

2. Short title

This Act may be cited as the Marine Insurance (Gambling Policies) Act, 1909, and the Marine Insurance Act, 1906, and this Act may be cited together as the Marine Insurance Acts, 1906 and 1909.

NOTES

Subs (1): words omitted repealed by virtue of the Criminal Justice Act 1948, s 1(2); words in square brackets substituted by virtue of the Criminal Justice Act 1982, ss 37, 38, 46.

Subs (7): amended by the Courts Act 1971, s 56, Sched 9, Part 1.

APPENDIX 3

THIRD PARTIES (RIGHTS AGAINST INSURERS) ACT 1930

An Act to confer on third parties rights against insurers of third-party risks in the event of the insured becoming insolvent, and in certain other events [10th July 1930]

1. Rights of third parties against insurers on bankruptcy etc of the insured

(1) Where under any contract of insurance a person (hereinafter referred to as the insured) is insured against liabilities to third parties which he may incur, then—

(a) in the event of the insured becoming bankrupt or making a composition or arrangement with his creditors; or

(b) in the case of the insured being a company, in the event of a winding-up order being made, or a resolution for a voluntary winding-up being passed, with respect to the company, or of a receiver or manager of the company's business or undertaking being duly appointed, or of possession being taken, by or on behalf of the holders of any debentures secured by a floating charge, of any property comprised in or subject to the charge;

if, either before or after that event, any such liability as aforesaid is incurred by the insured, his rights against the insurer under the contract in respect of the liability shall, notwithstanding anything in any Act or rule of law to the contrary, be transferred to and vest in the third party to whom the liability was so incurred.

(2) Where an order is made under section one hundred and thirty of the Bankruptcy Act, 1914, for the administration of the estate of a deceased debtor according to the law of bankruptcy, then, if any debt provable in bankruptcy is owing by the deceased in respect of a liability against which he was insured under a contract of insurance as being a liability to a third party, the deceased debtor's rights against the insurer under the contract in respect of that liability shall, notwithstanding anything in the said Act, be transferred to and vest in the person to whom the debt is owing.

(3) In so far as any contract of insurance made after the commencement of this Act in respect of any liability of the insured to third parties purports, whether directly or indirectly, to avoid the contract or to alter the rights of the parties thereunder upon the happening to the insured of any of these events specified in paragraph (a) or paragraph (b) of subsection (1) of this section or upon the making of an order under section one hundred and thirty of the Bankruptcy Act, 1914, in respect of his estate, the contract shall be of no effect.

(4) Upon a transfer under subsection (1) or subsection (2) of this section, the insurer shall, subject to the provisions of section three of this Act, be under the

same liability to the third party as he would have been under to the insured, but—

(a) if the liability of the insurer to the insured exceeds the liability of the insured to the third party, nothing in this Act shall affect the rights of the insured against the insurer in respect of the excess, and

(b) if the liability of the insurer to the insured is less than the liability of the insured to the third party, nothing in this Act shall affect the rights of the third party, against the insured in respect of the balance.

(5) For the purposes of this Act, the expression 'liabilities to third parties, ' in relation to a person insured under any contract of insurance, shall not include any liability of that person in the capacity of insurer under some other contract of insurance.

(6) This Act shall not apply—

(a) where a company is wound up voluntarily merely for the purposes of reconstruction or of amalgamation with another company; or

(b) to any case to which subsections (1) and (2) of section seven of the Workmen's Compensation Act, 1925, applies.

2. Duty to give necessary information to third parties

(1) In the event of any person becoming bankrupt or making a composition or arrangement with his creditors, or in the event of an order being made under section one hundred and thirty of the Bankruptcy Act, 1914, in respect of the estate of any person, or in the event of a winding-up order being made, or a resolution for a voluntary winding-up being passed, with respect to any company or of a receiver or manager of the company's business or undertaking being duly appointed or of possession being taken by or on behalf of the holders of any debentures secured by a floating charge of any property comprised in or subject to the charge it shall be the duty of the bankrupt, debtor, personal representative of the deceased debtor or company, and, as the case may be, of the trustee in bankruptcy, trustee, liquidator, receiver, or manager, or person in possession of the property to give at the request of any person claiming that the bankrupt, debtor, deceased debtor, or company is under a liability to him such information as may reasonably be required by him for the purpose of ascertaining whether any rights have been transferred to and vested in him by this Act and for the purpose of enforcing such rights, if any, and any contract of insurance, in so far as it purports, whether directly or indirectly, to avoid the contract or to alter the rights of the parties thereunder upon the giving of any such information in the events aforesaid or otherwise to prohibit or prevent the giving thereof in the said events shall be of no effect.

(2) If the information given to any person in pursuance of subsection (1) of this section discloses reasonable ground for supposing that there have or may have been transferred to him under this Act rights against any particular insurer, that insurer shall be subject to the same duty as is imposed by the said subsection on the persons therein mentioned.

(3) The duty to give information imposed by this section shall include a duty to allow all contracts of insurance, receipts for premiums, and other relevant documents in the possession or power of the person on whom the duty is so imposed to be inspected and copies thereof to be taken.

3. Settlement between insurers and insured persons

Where the insured has become bankrupt or where in the case of the insured being a company, a winding-up order has been made or a resolution for a voluntary winding-up has been passed, with respect to the company, no agreement made between the insurer and the insured after liability has been incurred to a third party and after the commencement of the bankruptcy or winding up, as the case may be, nor any waiver, assignment, or other disposition made by, or payment made to the insured after the commencement aforesaid shall be effective to defeat or affect the rights transferred to the third party under this Act, but those rights shall be the same as if no such agreement, waiver, assignment, disposition or payment had been made.

4. Application to Scotland

In the application of this Act to Scotland—

(a) the expression 'company' includes a limited partnership;

(b) any reference to an order under section one hundred and thirty of the Bankruptcy Act, 1914, for the administration of the estate of a deceased debtor according to the law of bankruptcy, shall be deemed to include a reference to an award of sequestration of the estate of a deceased debtor, and a reference to an appointment of a judicial factor, under section one hundred and sixty-three of the Bankruptcy (Scotland) Act, 1913, on the insolvent estate of a deceased person.

5. Short title

This Act may be cited as the Third Parties (Rights Against Insurers) Act, 1930.

In all communications please quote
the following reference

Lloyd's
Marine
Policy

The Assured is requested to **read this Policy** and, if it is incorrect, return it immediately for alteration to:

FOR CARGO INSURANCES ONLY

In the event of loss or damage which may result in a claim under this Insurance immediate notice must be given to the Lloyd's Agent at the port or place where the loss or damage is discovered in order that he may examine the goods and issue a survey report

Lloyd's Marine Policy

We, The Underwriters, hereby agree, in consideration of the payment to us by or on behalf of the Assured of the premium specified in the Schedule, to insure against loss damage liability or expense in the proportions and manner hereinafter provided. Each Underwriting Member of a Syndicate whose definitive number and proportion is set out in the following Table shall be liable only for his own share of his respective Syndicate's proportion.

This insurance shall be subject to the exclusive jurisdiction of the English Courts, except as may be expressly provided herein to the contrary.

In Witness whereof the General Manager of Lloyd's Policy Signing Office has subscribed his Name on behalf of each of Us .

LLOYD'S POLICY SIGNING OFFICE
General Manager

MAR 91

<u>SCHEDULE</u>

POLICY NUMBER

NAME OF ASSURED

VESSEL

VOYAGE OR PERIOD OF INSURANCE

SUBJECT-MATTER INSURED

AGREED VALUE
(if any)

AMOUNT INSURED HEREUNDER

PREMIUM

CLAUSES. ENDORSEMENTS. SPECIAL CONDITIONS AND WARRANTIES

THE ATTACHED CLAUSES AND ENDORSEMENTS FORM PART OF THIS POLICY

Definitive numbers of the Syndicates and proportions

The List of Underwriting Members of Lloyd's mentioned in the above Table shows their respective Syndicates and Shares therein, and is deemed to be incorporated in and to form part of this Policy. It is available for inspection at Lloyd's Policy Signing Office by the Assured or his or their representatives and a true copy of the material parts of it certified by the General Manager of Lloyd's Policy Signing Office will be furnished to the Assured on application.

APPENDIX 5

In all communications please quote
the following reference

The Institute of London Underwriters

Companies Marine Policy

This Policy is subscribed by Insurance
Companies
Members of The Institute of London
Underwriters
49, Leadenhall Street,
London, EC3A 2BE

THE INSTITUTE OF LONDON UNDERWRITERS

COMPANIES' MARINE POLICY

WE, THE COMPANIES, hereby agree, in consideration of the payment to us by or on behalf of the Assured of the premium specified in the Schedule, to insure against loss damage liability or expense in the proportions and manner hereinafter provided. Each Company shall be liable only for its own respective proportion.

This insurance shall be subject to the exclusive jurisdiction of the English Courts, except as may be expressly provided herein to the contrary.

IN WITNESS whereof the General Manager and Secretary of The Institute of London Underwriters has subscribed his name on behalf of each Company.

....
General Manager and Secretary
The Institute of London Underwriters

This Policy is not valid unless it bears the embossment of the Policy Department of The Institute of London Underwriters.

MAR 91

SCHEDULE

POLICY NUMBER

NAME OF ASSURED

VESSEL

VOYAGE OR PERIOD OF INSURANCE

SUBJECT-MATTER INSURED

AGREED VALUE
(if any)

AMOUNT INSURED HEREUNDER

PREMIUM

CLAUSES, ENDORSEMENTS, SPECIAL CONDITIONS AND WARRANTIES

THE ATTACHED CLAUSES AND ENDORSEMENTS FORM PART OF THIS POLICY

COMPANIES' PROPORTIONS

For use by the Policy Department

of

The Institute of London Underwriters

1/10/83

INSTITUTE TIME CLAUSES
HULLS

This insurance is subject to English law and practice

1   NAVIGATION

1.1   The Vessel is covered subject to the provisions of this insurance at all times and has leave to sail or navigate with or without pilots, to go on trial trips and to assist and tow vessels or craft in distress, but it is warranted that the Vessel shall not be towed, except as is customary or to the first safe port or place when in need of assistance, or undertake towage or salvage services under a contract previously arranged by the Assured and/or Owners and/or Managers and/or Charterers. This Clause 1.1 shall not exclude customary towage in connection with loading and discharging.

1.2   In the event of the Vessel being employed in trading operations which entail cargo loading or discharging at sea from or into another vessel (not being a harbour or inshore craft) no claim shall be recoverable under this insurance for loss of or damage to the Vessel or liability to any other vessel arising from such loading or discharging operations, including whilst approaching, lying alongside and leaving, unless previous notice that the Vessel is to be employed in such operations has been given to the Underwriters and any amended terms of cover and any additional premium required by them have been agreed.

1.3   In the event of the Vessel sailing (with or without cargo) with an intention of being (a) broken up, or (b) sold for breaking up, any claim for loss of or damage to the Vessel occurring subsequent to such sailing shall be limited to the market value of the Vessel as scrap at the time when the loss or damage is sustained, unless previous notice has been given to the Underwriters and any amendments to the terms of cover, insured value and premium required by them have been agreed. Nothing in this Clause 1.3 shall affect claims under Clauses 8 and/or 11.

2   CONTINUATION

Should the Vessel at the expiration of this insurance be at sea or in distress or at a port of refuge or of call, she shall, provided previous notice be given to the Underwriters, be held covered at a pro rata monthly premium to her port of destination.

3 BREACH OF WARRANTY

Held covered in case of any breach of warranty as to cargo, trade, locality, towage salvage services or date of sailing, provided notice be given to the Underwriters immediately after receipt of advices and any amended terms of cover and any additional premium required by them be agreed.

4 TERMINATION

This Clause 4 shall prevail notwithstanding any provision whether written typed or printed in this insurance inconsistent therewith.

4.1 Unless the Underwriters agree to the contrary in writing, this insurance shall terminate automatically at the time of change of the Classification Society of the Vessel, or change, suspension, discontinuance, withdrawal or expiry of her Class therein, provided that if the Vessel is at sea such automatic termination shall be deferred until arrival at her next port. However where such change, suspension, discontinuance or withdrawal of her Class has resulted from loss or damage covered by Clause 6 of this insurance or which would be covered by an insurance of the Vessel subject to current Institute War and Strikes Clauses Hulls – Time such automatic termination shall only operate should the Vessel sail from her next port without the prior approval of the Classification Society,

4.2 Any change, voluntary or otherwise, in the ownership or flag, transfer to new management or charter on a bareboat basis, or requisition for title or use of the Vessel, provided that, if the Vessel has cargo on board and has already sailed from her loading port or is at sea in ballast, such automatic termination shall if required be deferred, whilst the Vessel continues her planned voyage, until arrival at final port of discharge if with cargo or at port of destination if in ballast. However, in the event of requisition for title or use without the prior execution of a written agreement by the Assured, such automatic termination shall occur fifteen days after such requisition whether the Vessel is at sea or in port.

A pro rata daily net return of premium shall be made.

5 ASSIGNMENT

No assignment of or interest in this insurance or in any moneys which may be or become payable thereunder is to be binding on or recognised by the Underwriters unless a dated notice of such assignment or interest signed by the Assured, and by the assignor in the case of subsequent assignment, is endorsed on the Policy and the Policy with such endorsement is produced before payment of any claim or return of premium thereunder.

6 PERILS

6.1 This insurance covers loss of or damage to the subject-matter insured caused by

6.1.1   perils of the seas rivers lakes or other navigable waters

6.1.2   fire, explosion

6.1.3   violent theft by persons from outside the Vessel

6.1.4   jettison

6.1.5   piracy

6.1.6   breakdown of or accident to nuclear installations or reactors

6.1.7   contact with aircraft or similar objects, or objects falling therefrom, land conveyance, dock or harbour equipment or installation

6.1.8   earthquake volcanic eruption or lightning.

6.2   This insurance covers loss of or damage to the subject-matter insured caused by

6.2.1   accidents in loading discharging or shifting cargo or fuel

6.2.2   bursting of boilers breakage of shafts or any latent defect in the machinery or hull

6.2.3   negligence of Master Officers Crew or Pilots

6.2.4   negligence of repairers or charterers provided such repairers or charterers are not an Assured hereunder

6.2.5   barratry of Master Officers or Crew,

       provided such loss or damage has not resulted from want of due diligence by the Assured, Owners or Managers.

6.3   Master Officers Crew or Pilots not to be considered Owners within the meaning of this Clause 6 should they hold shares in the Vessel.

7 POLLUTION HAZARD

This insurance covers loss of or damage to the Vessel caused by any governmental authority acting under the powers vested in it to prevent or mitigate a pollution hazard, or threat thereof, resulting directly from damage to the Vessel for which the Underwriters are liable under this insurance, provided such act of governmental authority has not resulted from want of due diligence by the Assured, the Owners, or Managers of the Vessel or any of them to prevent or mitigate such hazard or threat. Master, Officers, Crew or Pilots not to be considered Owners within the meaning of this Clause 7 should they hold shares in the Vessel.

8 3/4ths COLLISION LIABILITY

8.1   The Underwriters agree to indemnify the Assured for three-fourths of any sum or sums paid by the Assured to any other person or persons by reason of the Assured becoming legally liable by way of damages for

8.1. 1 loss of or damage to any other vessel or property on any other vessel

8.1.2   delay to or loss of use of any such other vessel or property thereon

8.1.3   general average of, salvage of, or salvage under contract of, any such other vessel or property thereon, where such payment by the Assured is in consequence of the Vessel hereby insured coming into collision with any other vessel

8.2   The indemnity provided by this Clause 8 shall be in addition to the indemnity provided by the other terms and conditions of this insurance and shall be subject to the following provisions:

8.2.1   Where the insured Vessel is in collision with another vessel and both vessels are to blame then, unless the liability of one or both vessels becomes limited by law, the indemnity under this Clause 8 shall be calculated on the principle of cross-liabilities as if the respective Owners had been compelled to pay to each other such proportion of each other's damages as may have been properly allowed in ascertaining the balance or sum payable by or to the Assured in consequence of the collision.

8.2.2   In no case shall the Underwriters' total liability under Clauses 8.1 and 8.2 exceed their proportionate part of three-fourths of the insured value of the Vessel hereby insured in respect of any one collision.

8.3   The Underwriters will also pay three-fourths of the legal costs incurred by the Assured or which the Assured may be compelled to pay in contesting liability or taking proceedings to limit liability, with the prior written consent of the Underwriters.

EXCLUSIONS

8.4   Provided always that this Clause 8 shall in no case extend to any sum which the Assured shall pay for or in respect of

8.4.1   removal or disposal of obstructions, wrecks, cargoes or any other thing whatsoever

8.4.2   any real or personal property or thing whatsoever except other vessels or property on other vessels

8.4.3   the cargo or other property on, or the engagements of, the insured Vessel

8.4.4   loss of life, personal injury or illness

8.4.5   pollution or contamination of any real or personal property or thing whatsoever (except other vessels with which the insured Vessel is in collision or property on such other vessels).

9   SISTERSHIP

Should the Vessel hereby insured come into collision with or receive salvage services from another vessel belonging wholly or in part to the same Owners or under the same management, the Assured shall have the same rights under this insurance as they would have were the other vessel entirely the property of Owners not interested in the Vessel hereby insured; but in such cases the liability for the collision or the amount payable for the services rendered shall be referred to a sole arbitrator to be agreed upon between the Underwriters and the Assured.

10 NOTICE OF CLAIM AND TENDERS

10.1   In the event of accident whereby loss or damage may result in a claim under this insurance, notice shall be given to the Underwriters prior to survey and also, if the Vessel is abroad, to the nearest Lloyd's Agent so that a surveyor may be appointed to represent the Underwriters should they so desire.

10.2   The Underwriters shall be entitled to decide the port to which the Vessel shall proceed for docking or repair (the actual additional expense of the voyage arising from compliance with the Underwriters' requirements being refunded to the Assured) and shall have a right of veto concerning a place of repair or a repairing firm.

10.3   The Underwriters may also take tenders or may require further tenders to be taken for the repair of the Vessel. Where such a tender has been taken and a tender is accepted with the approval of the Underwriters, an allowance shall be made at the rate of 30% per annum on the insured value for time lost between the despatch of the invitations to tender required by Underwriters and the acceptance of a tender to the extent that such time is lost solely as the result of tenders having been taken and provided that the tender is accepted without delay after receipt of the Underwriters' approval.

Due credit shall be given against the allowance as above for any amounts recovered in respect of fuel and stores and wages and maintenance of the Master Officers and Crew or any member thereof, including amounts allowed in general average, and for any amounts recovered from third parties in respect of damages for detention and/or loss of profit and/or running expenses, for the period covered by the tender allowance or any part thereof.

Where a part of the cost of the repair of damage other than a fixed deductible is not recoverable from the Underwriters the allowance shall be reduced by a similar proportion

10.4   In the event of failure to comply with the conditions of this Clause 10 a deduction of 15% shall be made from the amount of the ascertained claim.

11 GENERAL AVERAGE AND SALVAGE

11.1   This insurance covers the Vessel's proportion of salvage, salvage charges and/or general average, reduced in respect of any under-insurance, but in case of general average sacrifice of the Vessel the Assured may recover in respect of the whole loss without first enforcing their right of contribution from other parties.

11.2   Adjustment to be according to the law and practice obtaining at the place where the adventure ends, as if the contract of affreightment contained no special terms upon the subject; but where the contract of affreightment so provides the adjustment shall be according to the York-Antwerp Rules.

11.3 When the Vessel sails in ballast, not under charter, the provisions of the York-Antwerp Rules, 1974 (excluding Rules XX and XXI) shall be applicable, and the voyage for this purpose shall be deemed to continue from the port or place of departure until the arrival of the Vessel at the first port or place thereafter other than a port or place of refuge or a port or place of call for bunkering only. If at any such intermediate port or place there is an abandonment of the adventure originally contemplated the voyage shall thereupon be deemed to be terminated.

11.4 No claim under this Clause 11 shall in any case be allowed where the loss was not incurred to avoid or in connection with the avoidance of a peril insured against.

12 DEDUCTIBLE

12.1 No claim arising from a peril insured against shall be payable under this insurance unless the aggregate of all such claims arising out of each separate accident or occurrence (including claims under Clauses 8, 11 and 13) exceeds .... in which case this sum shall be deducted. Nevertheless the expense of sighting the bottom after stranding, if reasonably incurred specially for that purpose, shall be paid even if no damage be found. This Clause 12.1 shall not apply to a claim for total or constructive total loss of the Vessel or, in the event of such a claim, to any associated claim under Clause 13 arising from the same accident or occurrence.

12.2 Claims for damage by heavy weather occurring during a single sea passage between two successive ports shall be treated as being due to one accident. In the case of such heavy weather extending over a period not wholly covered by this insurance the deductible to be applied to the claim recoverable hereunder shall be the proportion of the above deductible that the number of days of such heavy weather falling within the period of this insurance bears to the number of days of heavy weather during the single sea passage.

The expression 'heavy weather' in this Clause 12.2 shall be deemed to include contact with floating ice.

12.3 Excluding any interest comprised therein, recoveries against any claim which is subject to the above deductible shall be credited to the Underwriters in full to the extent of the sum by which the aggregate of the claim unreduced by any recoveries exceeds the above deductible.

12.4 Interest comprised in recoveries shall be apportioned between the Assured and the Underwriters, taking into account the sums paid by the Underwriters and the dates when such payments were made, notwithstanding that by the addition of interest the Underwriters may receive a larger sum than they have paid.

13 DUTY OF ASSURED (SUE AND LABOUR)

13.1   In case of any loss or misfortune it is the duty of the Assured and their servants and agents to take such measures as may be reasonable for the purpose of averting or minimising a loss which would be recoverable under this insurance.

13.2   Subject to the provisions below and to Clause 12 the Underwriters will contribute to charges properly and reasonably incurred by the Assured their servants or agents for such measures. General average, salvage charges (except as provided for in Clause 13.5) and collision defence or attack costs are not recoverable under this Clause 13.

13.3   Measures taken by the Assured or the Underwriters with the object of saving, protecting or recovering the subject-matter insured shall not be considered as a waiver or acceptance of abandonment or otherwise prejudice the rights of either party.

13.4   When expenses are incurred pursuant to this Clause 13 the liability under this insurance shall not exceed the proportion of such expenses that the amount insured hereunder bears to the value of the Vessel as stated herein, or to the sound value of the Vessel at the time of the occurrence giving rise to the expenditure if the sound value exceeds that value. Where the Underwriters have admitted a claim for total loss and property insured by this insurance is saved, the foregoing provisions shall not apply unless the expenses of suing and labouring exceed the value of such property saved and then shall apply only to the amount of the expenses which is in excess of such value.

13.5   When a claim for total loss of the Vessel is admitted under this insurance and expenses have been reasonably incurred in saving or attempting to save the Vessel and other property and there are no proceeds, or the expenses exceed the proceeds, then this insurance shall bear its pro rata share of such proportion of the expenses, or of the expenses in excess of the proceeds, as the case may be, as may reasonably be regarded as having been incurred in respect of the Vessel; but if the Vessel be insured for less than its sound value at the time of the occurrence giving rise to the expenditure, the amount recoverable under this clause shall be reduced in proportion to the under-insurance.

13.6   The sum recoverable under this Clause 13 shall be in addition to the loss otherwise recoverable under this insurance but shall in no circumstances exceed the amount insured under this insurance in respect of the Vessel.

14 NEW FOR OLD

Claims payable without deduction new for old.

15 BOTTOM TREATMENT

In no case shall a claim be allowed in respect of scraping gritblasting and/or other surface preparation or painting of the Vessel's bottom except that

15.1 gritblasting and/or other surface preparation of new bottom plates ashore and supplying and applying any 'shop' primer thereto,

15.2 gritblasting and/or other surface preparation of:

the butts or area of plating immediately adjacent to any renewed or refitted plating damaged during the course of welding and/or repairs,

areas of plating damaged during the course of fairing, either in place or ashore,

15.3 supplying and applying the first coat of primer/anti-corrosive to those particular areas mentioned in 15.1 and 15.2 above,

shall be allowed as part of the reasonable cost of repairs in respect of bottom plating damaged by an insured peril.

16 WAGES AND MAINTENANCE

No claim shall be allowed, other than in general average, for wages and maintenance of the Master, Officers and Crew, or any member thereof, except when incurred solely for the necessary removal of the Vessel from one port to another for the repair of damage covered by the Underwriters, or for trial trips for such repairs, and then only for such wages and maintenance as are incurred whilst the Vessel is under way.

17 AGENCY COMMISSION

In no case shall any sum be allowed under this insurance either by way of remuneration of the Assured for time and trouble taken to obtain and supply information or documents or in respect of the commission or charges of any manager, agent, managing or agency company or the like, appointed by or on behalf of the Assured to perform such services.

18 UNREPAIRED DAMAGE

18.1 The measure of indemnity in respect of claims for unrepaired damage shall be the reasonable depreciation in the market value of the Vessel at the time this insurance terminates arising from such unrepaired damage, but not exceeding the reasonable cost of repairs.

18.2 In no case shall the Underwriters be liable for unrepaired damage in the event of a subsequent total loss (whether or not covered under this insurance) sustained during the period covered by this insurance or any extension thereof.

18.3 The Underwriters shall not be liable in respect of unrepaired damage for more than the insured value at the time this insurance terminates.

19 CONSTRUCTIVE TOTAL LOSS

19.1 In ascertaining whether the Vessel is a constructive total loss, the insured value shall be taken as the repaired value and nothing in respect of the damaged or break-up value of the Vessel or wreck shall be taken into account.

19.2 No claim for constructive total loss based upon the cost of recovery and/or repair of the Vessel shall be recoverable hereunder unless such cost would exceed the insured value. In making this determination, only the cost relating to a single accident or sequence of damages arising from the same accident shall be taken into account.

20 FREIGHT WAIVER

In the event of total or constructive total loss no claim to be made by the Underwriters for freight whether notice of abandonment has been given or not.

21 DISBURSEMENTS WARRANTY

21.1   Additional insurances as follows are permitted:

21.1.1 *Disbursements, Managers' Commissions, Profits or Excess or Increased Value of Hull and Machinery.* A sum not exceeding 25% of the value stated herein.

21.1.2 *Freight, Chartered Freight or Anticipated Freight, insured for time.* A sum not exceeding 25% of the value as stated herein less any sum insured, however described, under 21.1.1.

21.1.3 *Freight or Hire, under contracts for voyage.* A sum not exceeding the gross freight or hire for the current cargo passage and next succeeding cargo passage (such insurance to include, if required, a preliminary and an intermediate ballast passage) plus the charges of insurance. In the case of a voyage charter where payment is made on a time basis, the sum permitted for insurance shall be calculated on the estimated duration of the voyage, subject to the limitation of two cargo passages as laid down herein. Any sum insured under 21.1.2 to be taken into account and only the excess thereof may be insured, which excess shall be reduced as the freight or hire is advanced or earned by the gross amount so advanced or earned.

21.1.4 *Anticipated Freight if the Vessel sails in ballast and not under Charter.* A sum not exceeding the anticipated gross freight on next cargo passage, such sum to be reasonably estimated on the basis of the current rate of freight at time of insurance plus the charges of insurance. Any sum insured under 21.1.2 to be taken into account and only the excess thereof may be insured.

21.1.5 *Time Charter Hire or Charter Hire for Series of Voyages.* A sum not exceeding 50% of the gross hire which is to be earned under the charter in a period not exceeding 18 months. Any sum insured under 21.1.2 to be taken into account and only the excess thereof may be insured, which excess shall be reduced as the hire is advanced or earned under the charter by 50% of the gross amount so advanced or earned but the sum insured need not be reduced while the total of the sums insured under 21.1.2 and 21.1.5 does not exceed 50% of the gross hire still to be earned under the charter. An insurance under this Section may begin on the signing of the charter.

21.1.6 *Premiums.* A sum not exceeding the actual premiums of all interests insured for a period not exceeding 12 months (excluding premiums insured under the foregoing sections but including, if required, the premium or estimated calls on any Club or War etc Risk insurance) reducing pro rata monthly.

21.1.7 *Returns of Premium.* A sum not exceeding the actual returns which are allowable under any insurance but which would not be recoverable thereunder in the event of a total loss of the Vessel whether by insured perils or otherwise.

21.1.8 *Insurance irrespective of amount against.* Any risks excluded by Clauses 23, 24, 25 and 26 below.

21.2 Warranted that no insurance on any interests enumerated in the foregoing 21.1.1 to 21.1.7 in excess of the amounts permitted therein and no other insurance which includes total loss of the Vessel P.P.I., F.I.A., or subject to any other like term, is or shall be effected to operate during the currency of this insurance by or for account of the Assured, Owners, Managers or Mortgagees. Provided always that a breach of this warranty shall not afford the Underwriters any defence to a claim by a Mortgagee who has accepted this insurance without knowledge of such breach.

22 RETURNS FOR LAY-UP AND CANCELLATION

22.1 To return as follows:

22.1.1 Pro rata monthly net for each uncommenced month if this insurance be cancelled by agreement.

22.1.2 For each period of 30 consecutive days the Vessel may be laid up in a port or in a lay-up area provided such port or lay-up area is approved by the Underwriters (with special liberties as hereinafter allowed)

> (a) .... per cent net not under repair
>
> (b) .... per cent net under repair.

If the Vessel is under repair during part only of a period for which a return is claimable, the return shall be calculated pro rata to the number of days under (a) and (b) respectively.

22.2 PROVIDED ALWAYS THAT

22.2.1 a total loss of the Vessel, whether by insured perils or otherwise, has not occurred during the period covered by this insurance or any extension thereof

22.2.2 in no case shall a return be allowed when the Vessel is lying in exposed or unprotected waters, or in a port or lay-up area not approved by the Underwriters but, provided the Underwriters agree that such non-approved lay-up area is deemed to be within the vicinity of the approved port or lay-up area, days during which the Vessel is laid up in such non-approved lay-up area may be added to days in the approved port or lay-up area to calculate a period of 30 consecutive days and a return shall be allowed for the proportion of such period during which the Vessel is actually laid up in the approved port or lay-up area

22.2.3 loading or discharging operations or the presence of cargo on board shall not debar returns but no return shall be allowed for any period during which the Vessel is being used for the storage of cargo or for lightering purposes

22.2.4 in the event of any amendment of the annual rate, the above rates of return shall be adjusted accordingly

22.2.5 in the event of any return recoverable under this Clause 22 being based on 30 consecutive days which fall on successive insurances effected for the same Assured, this insurance shall only be liable for an amount calculated at pro rata of the period rates 22.1.2(a) and/or (b) above for the number of days which come within the period of this insurance and to which a return is actually applicable. Such overlapping period shall run, at the option of the Assured, either from the first day on which the Vessel is laid up or the first day of a period of 30 consecutive days as provided under 22.1.2(a) or (b), or 22.2.2 above.

The following clauses shall be paramount and shall override anything contained in this insurance inconsistent therewith.

23 WAR EXCLUSION

In no case shall this insurance cover loss damage liability or expense caused by

23.1 war civil war revolution rebellion insurrection, or civil strife arising therefrom, or any hostile act by or against a belligerent power

23.2 capture seizure arrest restraint or detainment (barratry and piracy excepted), and the consequences thereof or any attempt thereat

23.3 derelict mines torpedoes bombs or other derelict weapons of war.

24 STRIKES EXCLUSION

In no case shall this insurance cover loss damage liability or expense caused by

24.1 strikers, locked-out workmen, or persons taking part in labour disturbances, riots or civil commotions

24.2 any terrorist or any person acting from a political motive.

25 MALICIOUS ACTS EXCLUSION

In no case shall this insurance cover loss damage liability or expense arising from

25.1 the detonation of an explosive

25.2 any weapon of war

and caused by any person acting maliciously or from a political motive.

26 NUCLEAR EXCLUSION

In no case shall this insurance cover loss damage liability or expense arising from any weapon of war employing atomic or nuclear fission and/or fusion or other like reaction or radioactive force or matter.

APPENDIX 7

1/11/95

(FOR USE ONLY WITH THE CURRENT MAR POLICY FORM)

INSTITUTE TIME CLAUSES
HULLS

This insurance is subject to English law and practice

1 NAVIGATION

1.1   The Vessel is covered subject to the provisions of this insurance at all times and has leave to sail or navigate with or without pilots, to go on trial trips and to assist and tow vessels or craft in distress, but it is warranted that the Vessel shall not be towed, except as is customary or to the first safe port or place when in need of assistance, or undertake towage or salvage services under a contract previously arranged by the Assured and/or Owners and/or Managers and/or Charterers. This Clause 1.1 shall not exclude customary towage in connection with loading and discharging.

1.2   This insurance shall not be prejudiced by reason of the Assured entering into any contract with pilots or for customary towage which limits or exempts the liability of the pilots and/or tugs and/or towboats and/or their owners when the Assured or their agents accept or are compelled to accept such contracts in accordance with established local law or practice.

1.3   The practice of engaging helicopters for the transportation of personnel, supplies and equipment to and/or from the Vessel shall not prejudice this insurance.

1.4   In the event of the Vessel being employed in trading operations which entail cargo loading or discharging at sea from or into another vessel (not being a harbour or inshore craft) no claim shall be recoverable under this insurance for loss of or damage to the Vessel or liability to any other vessel arising from such loading or discharging operations, including whilst approaching, lying alongside and leaving, unless previous notice that the Vessel is to be employed in such operations has been given to the Underwriters and any amended terms of cover and any additional premium required by them have been agreed.

1.5   In the event of the Vessel sailing (with or without cargo) with an intention of being (a) broken up, or (b) sold for breaking up, any claim for loss of or damage to the Vessel occurring subsequent to such sailing shall be limited to the market value of the Vessel as scrap at the time when the loss or damage is sustained unless previous notice has been given to the Underwriters and any amendments to the terms of cover, insured value and premium required by them have been agreed. Nothing in this Clause 1.5 shall affect claims under Clauses 8 and/or 10.

2   CONTINUATION

Should the Vessel at the expiration of this insurance be at sea and in distress or missing, she shall, provided notice be given to the Underwriters prior to the expiration of this insurance, be held covered until arrival at the next port in good safety, or if in port and in distress until the Vessel is made safe, at a pro rata monthly premium.

3   BREACH OF WARRANTY

Held covered in case of any breach of warranty as to cargo, trade, locality, towage, salvage services or date of sailing provided notice be given to the Underwriters immediately after receipt of advices and any amended terms of cover and any additional premium required by them be agreed.

4   CLASSIFICATION

4.1   It is the duty of the Assured, Owners and Managers at the inception of and throughout the period of this insurance to ensure that

4.1.1   the Vessel is classed with a Classification Society agreed by the Underwriters and that her class within that Society is maintained,

4.1.2   any recommendations requirements or restrictions imposed by the Vessel's Classification Society which relate to the Vessel's seaworthiness or to her maintenance in a seaworthy condition are complied with by the dates required by that Society.

4.2   In the event of any breach of the duties set out in Clause 4.1 above, unless the Underwriters agree to the contrary in writing, they will be discharged from liability under this insurance as from the date of the breach provided that if the Vessel is at sea at such date the Underwriters' discharge from liability is deferred until arrival at her next port.

4.3   Any incident condition or damage in respect of which the Vessel's Classification Society might make recommendations as to repairs or other action to be taken by the Assured, Owners or Managers must be promptly reported to the Classification Society.

4.4   Should the Underwriters wish to approach the Classification Society directly for information and/or documents, the Assured will provide the necessary authorization.

5   TERMINATION

This Clause 5 shall prevail notwithstanding any provision whether written typed or printed in this insurance inconsistent therewith.

Unless the Underwriters agree to the contrary in writing, this insurance shall terminate automatically at the time of

5.1 change of the Classification Society of the Vessel, or change, suspension, discontinuance, withdrawal or expiry of her Class therein, or any of the Classification Society's periodic surveys becoming overdue unless an extension of time for such survey be agreed by the Classification Society, provided that if the Vessel is at sea such automatic termination shall be deferred until arrival at her next port. However where such change, suspension, discontinuance or withdrawal of her Class or where a periodic survey becoming overdue has resulted from loss or damage covered by Clause 6 of this insurance or which would be covered by an insurance of the Vessel subject to current Institute War and Strikes Clauses Hulls – Time such automatic termination shall only operate should the Vessel sail from her next port without the prior approval of the Classification Society or in the case of a periodic survey becoming overdue without the Classification Society having agreed an extension of time for such survey,

5.2 any change, voluntary or otherwise, in the ownership or flag, transfer to new management, or charter on a bareboat basis or requisition for title or use of the Vessel, provided that, if the Vessel has cargo on board and has already sailed from her loading port or is at sea in ballast, such automatic termination shall if required be deferred, whilst the Vessel continues her planned voyage, until arrival at final port of discharge if with cargo or at port of destination if in ballast. However, in the event of requisition for title or use without the prior execution of a written agreement by the Assured, such automatic termination shall occur fifteen days after such requisition whether the Vessel is at sea or in port.

A pro rata daily net return of premium shall be made provided that a total loss of the Vessel, whether by insured perils or otherwise, has not occurred during the period covered by this insurance or any extension thereof.

6 PERILS

6.1 This insurance covers loss of or damage to the subject-matter insured caused by

6.1.1 perils of the seas rivers lakes or other navigable waters

6.1.2 fire, explosion

6.1.3 violent theft by persons from outside the Vessel

6.1.4 jettison

6.1.5 piracy

6.1.6 contact with land conveyance, dock or harbour equipment or installation

6.1.7 earthquake volcanic eruption or lightning

6.1.8 accidents in loading discharging or shifting cargo or fuel.

6.2 This insurance covers loss of or damage to the subject-matter insured caused by

6.2.1 bursting of boilers breakage of shafts or any latent defect in the machinery or hull

6.2.2 negligence of Master Officers Crew or Pilots

6.2.3 negligence of repairers or charterers provided such repairers or charterers are not an Assured hereunder

6.2.4 barratry of Master Officers or Crew

6.2.5 contact with aircraft, helicopters or similar objects, or objects falling therefrom

provided that such loss or damage has not resulted from want of due diligence by the Assured, Owners, Managers or Superintendents or any of their onshore management.

6.3 Masters Officers Crew or Pilots not to be considered Owners within the meaning of this Clause 6 should they hold shares in the Vessel.

7 POLLUTION HAZARD

This insurance covers loss of or damage to the Vessel caused by any governmental authority acting under the powers vested in it to prevent or mitigate a pollution hazard or damage to the environment, or threat thereof, resulting directly from damage to the Vessel for which the Underwriters are liable under this insurance, provided that such act of governmental authority has not resulted from want of due diligence by the Assured, Owners or Managers to prevent or mitigate such hazard or damage, or threat thereof. Master Officers Crew or Pilots not to be considered Owners within the meaning of this Clause 7 should they hold shares in the Vessel.

8 3/4ths COLLISION LIABILITY

8.1 The Underwriters agree to indemnify the Assured for three-fourths of any sum or sums paid by the Assured to any other person or persons by reason of the Assured becoming legally liable by way of damages for

8.1.1 loss of or damage to any other vessel or property on any other vessel

8.1.2 delay to or loss of use of any such other vessel or property thereon

8.1.3 general average of, salvage of, or salvage under contract of, any such other vessel or property thereon,

where such payment by the Assured is in consequence of the Vessel hereby insured coming into collision with any other vessel.

8.2 The indemnity provided by this Clause 8 shall be in addition to the indemnity provided by the other terms and conditions of this insurance and shall be subject to the following provisions:

8.2.1 where the insured Vessel is in collision with another vessel and both vessels are to blame then, unless the liability of one or both vessels becomes limited by law, the indemnity under this Clause 8 shall be calculated on the principle of cross-liabilities as if the respective Owners had been compelled to pay to each other such proportion of each other's damages as may have been properly allowed in ascertaining the balance or sum payable by or to the Assured in consequence of the collision,

8.2.2   in no case shall the Underwriters' total liability under Clauses 8.1 and 8.2 exceed their proportionate part of three-fourths of the insured value of the Vessel hereby insured in respect of any one collision.

8,3   The Underwriters will also pay three-fourths of the legal costs incurred by the Assured or which the Assured may be compelled to pay in contesting liability or taking proceedings to limit liability, with the prior written consent of the Underwriters.

EXCLUSIONS

8.4   Provided always that this Clause 8 shall in no case extend to any sum which the Assured shall pay for or in respect of

8.4.1   removal or disposal of obstructions, wrecks, cargoes or any other thing whatsoever

8.4.2   any real or personal property or thing whatsoever except other vessels or property on other vessels

8.4.3   the cargo or other property on, or the engagements of, the insured Vessel

8.4.4   loss of life, personal injury or illness

8.4.5   pollution or contamination, or threat thereof, of any real or personal property or thing whatsoever (except other vessels with which the insured Vessel is in collision or property on such other vessels) or damage to the environment, or threat thereof, save that this exclusion shall not extend to any sum which the Assured shall pay for or in respect of salvage remuneration in which the skill and efforts of the salvors in preventing or minimising damage to the environment as is referred to in Article 13 paragraph 1(b) of the International Convention on Salvage, 1989 have been taken into account.

9 SISTERSHIP

Should the Vessel hereby insured come into collision with or receive salvage services from another vessel belonging wholly or in part to the same Owners or under the same management, the Assured shall have the same rights under this insurance as they would have were the other vessel entirely the property of Owners not interested in the Vessel hereby insured: but in such cases the liability for the collision or the amount payable for the services rendered shall be referred to a sole arbitrator to be agreed upon between the Underwriters and the Assured.

10 GENERAL AVERAGE AND SALVAGE

10.1   This insurance covers the Vessel's proportion of salvage, salvage charges and/or general average, reduced in respect of any under-insurance. but in case of general average sacrifice of the Vessel the Assured may recover in respect of the whole loss without first enforcing their right of contribution from other parties.

10.2   Adjustment to be according to the law and practice obtaining at the place where the adventure ends, as if the contract of affreightment contained no special terms upon the subject; but where the contract of affreightment so provides the adjustment shall be according to the York-Antwerp Rules.

10.3   When the Vessel sails in ballast, not under charter, the provisions of the York-Antwerp Rules 1994 (excluding Rules XI(d), XX and XXI) shall be applicable, and the voyage for this purpose shall be deemed to continue from the port or place of departure until the arrival of the Vessel at the first port or place thereafter other than a port or place of refuge or a port or place of call for bunkering only. If at any such intermediate port or place there is an abandonment of the adventure originally contemplated the voyage shall thereupon be deemed to be terminated.

10.4   No claim under this Clause 10 shall in any case be allowed where the loss was not incurred to avoid or in connection with the avoidance of a peril insured against.

10.5   No claim under this Clause 10 shall in any case be allowed for or in respect of

10.5.1 special compensation payable to a salvor under Article 14 of the International Convention on Salvage, 1989 or under any other provision in any statute, rule, law or contract which is similar in substance

10.5.2 expenses or liabilities incurred in respect of damage to the environment, or the threat of such damage, or as a consequence of the escape or release of pollutant substances from the Vessel, or the threat of such escape or release.

10.6   Clause 10.5 shall not however exclude any sum which the Assured shall pay to salvors for or in respect of salvage remuneration in which the skill and efforts of the salvors in preventing or minimising damage to the environment as is referred to in Article 13 paragraph 1(b) of the International Convention on Salvage, 1989 have been taken into account.

11 DUTY OF ASSURED (SUE AND LABOUR)

11.1   In case of any loss or misfortune it is the duty of the Assured and their servants and agents to take such measures as may be reasonable for the purpose of averting or minimising a loss which would be recoverable under this insurance.

11.2   Subject to the provisions below and to Clause 12 the Underwriters will contribute to charges properly and reasonably incurred by the Assured their servants or agents for such measures. General average, salvage charges (except as provided for in Clause 11.5), special compensation and expenses as referred to in Clause 10.5 and collision defence or attack costs are not recoverable under this Clause 11.

11.3   Measures taken by the Assured or the Underwriters with the object of saving, protecting or recovering the subject-matter insured shall not be considered as a waiver or acceptance of abandonment or otherwise prejudice the rights of either party.

11.4   When expenses are incurred pursuant to this Clause 11 the liability under this insurance shall not exceed the proportion of such expenses that the amount insured hereunder bears to the value of the Vessel as stated herein or to the sound value of the Vessel at the time of the occurrence giving rise to the expenditure if the sound value exceeds that value. Where the Underwriters have admitted a claim for total loss and property insured by this insurance is saved, the foregoing provisions shall not apply unless the expenses of suing and labouring exceed the value of such property saved and then shall apply only to the amount of the expenses which is in excess of such value.

11.5   When a claim for total loss of the Vessel is admitted under this insurance and expenses have been reasonably incurred in saving or attempting to save the Vessel and other property and there are no proceeds, or the expenses exceed the proceeds, then this insurance shall bear its pro rata share of such proportion of the expenses, or of the expenses in excess of the proceeds, as the case may be, as may reasonably be regarded as having been incurred in respect of the Vessel, excluding all special compensation and expenses as referred to in Clause 10.5; but if the Vessel be insured for less than its sound value at the time of the occurrence giving rise to the expenditure, the amount recoverable under this clause shall be reduced in proportion to the under-insurance.

11.6   The sum recoverable under this Clause 11 shall be in addition to the loss otherwise recoverable under this insurance but shall in no circumstances exceed the amount insured under this insurance in respect of the Vessel.

12 DEDUCTIBLE

12.1   No claim arising from a peril insured against shall be payable under this insurance unless the aggregate of all such claims arising out of each separate accident or occurrence (including claims under Clauses 8, 10 and 11) exceeds the deductible amount agreed in which case this sum shall be deducted. Nevertheless the expense of sighting the bottom after stranding, if reasonably incurred specially for that purpose, shall be paid even if no damage be found. This Clause 12.1 shall not apply to a claim for total or constructive total loss of the Vessel or, in the event of such a claim, to any associated claim under Clause 11 arising from the same accident or occurrence.

12.2   Claims for damage by heavy weather occurring during a single sea passage between two successive ports shall be treated as being due to one accident. In the case of such heavy weather extending over a period not wholly covered by this insurance the deductible to be applied to the claim recoverable hereunder shall be the proportion of the above deductible that the number of days of such heavy weather falling within the period of this insurance bears to the number of days of heavy weather during the single sea passage. The expression 'heavy weather' in this Clause 12.2 shall be deemed to include contact with floating ice.

12.3   Excluding any interest comprised therein. recoveries against any claim which is subject to the above deductible shall be credited to the Underwriters in full to the extent of the sum by which the aggregate of the claim unreduced by any recoveries exceeds the above deductible.

12.4   Interest comprised in recoveries shall be apportioned between the Assured and the Underwriters, taking into account the sums paid by the Underwriters and the dates when such payments were made, notwithstanding that by the addition of interest the Underwriters may receive a larger sum than they have paid.

13 NOTICE OF CLAIM AND TENDERS

13.1   In the event of accident whereby loss or damage may result in a claim under this insurance, notice must be given to the Underwriters promptly after the date on which the Assured, Owners or Managers become or should have become aware of the loss or damage and prior to survey so that a surveyor may be appointed if the Underwriters so desire. If notice is not given to the Underwriters within twelve months of that date unless the Underwriters agree to the contrary in writing, the Underwriters will be automatically discharged from liability for any claim under this insurance in respect of or arising out of such accident or the loss or damage.

13.2   The Underwriters shall be entitled to decide the port to which the Vessel shall proceed for docking or repair (the actual additional expense of the voyage arising from compliance with the Underwriters' requirements being refunded to the Assured) and shall have a right of veto concerning a place of repair or a repairing firm.

13.3   The Underwriters may also take tenders or may require further tenders to be taken for the repair of the Vessel, Where such a tender has been taken and a tender is accepted with the approval of the Underwriters, an allowance shall be made at the rate of 30% per annum on the insured value for time lost between the despatch of the invitations to tender required by the Underwriters and the acceptance of a tender to the extent that such time is lost solely as the result of tenders having been taken and provided that the tender is accepted without delay after receipt of the Underwriters' approval. Due credit shall be given against the allowance as above for any amounts recovered in respect of fuel and stores and wages and maintenance of the Master Officers and Crew or any member thereof, including amounts allowed in general average, and for any amounts recovered from third parties in respect of damages for detention and/or loss of profit and/or running expenses, for the period covered by the tender allowance or any part thereof. Where a part of the cost of the repair of damage other than a fixed deductible is not recoverable from the Underwriters the allowance shall be reduced by a similar proportion.

13.4 In the event of failure by the Assured to comply with the conditions of Clauses 13.2 and/or 13.3 a deduction of 15% shall be made from the amount of the ascertained claim.

14 NEW FOR OLD

Claims payable without deduction new for old.

15 BOTTOM TREATMENT

In no case shall a claim be allowed in respect of scraping gritblasting and/or other surface preparation or painting of the Vessel's bottom except that

15.1 gritblasting and/or other surface preparation of new bottom plates ashore and supplying and applying any 'shop' primer thereto,

15.2 gritblasting and/or other surface preparation of: the butts or area of plating immediately adjacent to any renewed or refitted plating damaged during the course of welding and/or repairs, areas of plating damaged during the course of fairing, either in place or ashore,

15.3 supplying and applying the first coat of primer/anti-corrosive to those particular areas mentioned in 15.1 and 15.2 above,

shall be allowed as part of the reasonable cost of repairs in respect of bottom plating damaged by an insured peril.

16 WAGES AND MAINTENANCE

No claim shall be allowed, other than in general average, for wages and maintenance of the Master Officers and Crew or any member thereof, except when incurred solely for the necessary removal of the Vessel from one port to another for the repair of damage covered by the Underwriters, or for trial trips for such repairs, and then only for such wages and maintenance as are incurred whilst the Vessel is under way.

17 AGENCY COMMISSION

In no case shall any sum be allowed under this insurance either by way of remuneration of the Assured for time and trouble taken to obtain and supply information or documents or in respect of the commission or charges of any manager, agent, managing or agency company or the like, appointed by or on behalf of the Assured to perform such services.

18 UNREPAIRED DAMAGE

18.1 The measure of indemnity in respect of claims for unrepaired damage shall be the reasonable depreciation in the market value of the Vessel at the time this insurance terminates arising from such unrepaired damage, but not exceeding the reasonable cost of repairs.

18.2 In no case shall the Underwriters be liable for unrepaired damage in the event of a subsequent total loss (whether or not covered under this insurance) sustained during the period covered by this insurance or any extension thereof.

18.3   The Underwriters shall not be liable in respect of unrepaired damage for more than the insured value at the time this insurance terminates.

19 CONSTRUCTIVE TOTAL LOSS

19.1   In ascertaining whether the Vessel is a constructive total loss, the insured value shall be taken as the repaired value and nothing in respect of the damaged or break-up value of the Vessel or wreck shall be taken into account.

19.2   No claim for constructive total loss based upon the cost of recovery and/or repair of the Vessel shall be recoverable hereunder unless such cost would exceed the insured value. In making this determination, only the cost relating to a single accident or sequence of damages arising from the same accident shall be taken into account.

20 FREIGHT WAIVER

In the event of total or constructive total loss no claim to be made by the Underwriters for freight whether notice of abandonment has been given or not.

21 ASSIGNMENT

No assignment of or interest in this insurance or in any moneys which may be or become payable thereunder is to be binding on or recognised by the Underwriters unless a dated notice of such assignment or interest signed by the Assured, and by the assignor in the case of subsequent assignment, is endorsed on the Policy and the Policy with such endorsement is produced before payment of any claim or return of premium thereunder.

22 DISBURSEMENTS WARRANTY

22.1   Additional insurances as follows are permitted:

22.1.1   *Disbursements, Managers' Commissions, Profits or Excess or Increased Value of Hull and Machinery.* A sum not exceeding 25% of the value stated herein.

22.1.2   *Freight, Chartered Freight or Anticipated Freight, insured for time.* A sum not exceeding 25% of the value as stated herein less any sum insured, however described, under 22.1.1.

22.1.3   *Freight or Hire, under contracts for voyage.* A sum not exceeding the gross freight or hire for the current cargo passage and next succeeding cargo passage (such insurance to include, if required, a preliminary and an intermediate ballast passage) plus the charges of insurance. In the case of a voyage charter where payment is made on a time basis, the sum permitted for insurance shall be calculated on the estimated duration of the voyage, subject to the limitation of two cargo passages as laid down herein. Any sum insured under 22.1.2 to be taken into account and only the excess thereof may be insured, which excess shall be reduced as the freight or hire is advanced or earned by the gross amount so advanced or earned.

22.1.4 *Anticipated Freight if the Vessel sails in ballast and not under Charter.* A sum not exceeding the anticipated gross freight on next cargo passage, such sum to be reasonably estimated on the basis of the current rate of freight at time of insurance plus the charges of insurance. Any sum insured under 22.1.2 to be taken into account and only the excess thereof may be insured.

22.1.5 *Time Charter Hire or Charter Hire for Series of Voyages.* A sum not exceeding 50% of the gross hire which is to be earned under the charter in a period not exceeding 18 months. Any sum insured under 22.1.2 to be taken into account and only the excess thereof may be insured, which excess shall be reduced as the hire is advanced or earned under the charter by 50% of the gross amount so advanced or earned but the sum insured need not be reduced while the total of the sums insured under 22.1.2 and 22.1.5 does not exceed 50% of the gross hire still to be earned under the charter. An insurance under this Section may begin on the signing of the charter.

22.1.6 *Premiums.* A sum not exceeding the actual premiums of all interests insured for a period not exceeding 12 months (excluding premiums insured under the foregoing sections but including, if required, the premium or estimated calls on any Club or War etc. Risk insurance) reducing pro rata monthly.

22.1.7 *Returns of Premium.* A sum not exceeding the actual returns which arc allowable under any insurance but which would not be recoverable thereunder in the event of a total loss of the Vessel whether by insured perils or otherwise.

22.1.8 *Insurance irrespective of amount against:* Any risks excluded by Clauses 24, 25, 26 and 27 below.

22.2 Warranted that no insurance on any interests enumerated in the foregoing 22.1.1 to 22.1.7 in excess of the amounts permitted therein and no other insurance which includes total loss of the Vessel P.P.I., F.I.A. or subject to any other like term, is or shall be effected to operate during the currency of this insurance by or for account of the Assured, Owners, Managers or Mortgagees. Provided always that a breach of this warranty shall not afford the Underwriters any defence to a claim by a Mortgagee who has accepted this insurance without knowledge of such breach.

23 RETURNS FOR LAY-UP AND CANCELLATION

23.1 To return as follows:

23.1.1 pro rata monthly net for each uncommenced month if this insurance be cancelled by agreement,

23.1.2 for each period of 30 consecutive days the Vessel may be laid up in a port or in a lay-up area provided such port or lay-up area is approved by the Underwriters

    (a) .... per cent net not under repair

    (b) .... per cent net under repair.

23.1.3 The Vessel shall not be considered to be under repair when work is undertaken in respect of ordinary wear and tear of the Vessel and/or following recommendations in the Vessel's Classification Society survey, but any repairs following loss of or damage to the Vessel or involving structural alterations, whether covered by this insurance or otherwise shall be considered as under repair.

23.1.4 If the Vessel is under repair during part only of a period for which a return is claimable, the return shall be calculated pro rata to the number of days under 23.1.2 (a) and (b) respectively.

23.2   PROVIDED ALWAYS THAT

23.2.1 a total loss of the Vessel, whether by insured perils or otherwise, has not occurred during the period covered by this insurance or any extension thereof

23.2.2 in no case shall a return be allowed when the Vessel is lying in exposed or unprotected waters, or in a port or lay-up area not approved by the Underwriters

23.2.3 loading or discharging operations or the presence of cargo on board shall not debar returns but no return shall be allowed for any period during which the Vessel is being used for the storage of cargo or for lightering purposes

23.2.4 in the event of any amendment of the annual rate, the above rates of return shall be adjusted accordingly.

23.2.5 in the event of any return recoverable under this Clause 23 being based on 30 consecutive days which fall on successive insurances effected for the same Assured, this insurance shall only be liable for an amount calculated at pro rata of the period rates 23.1.2(a) and/or (b) above for the number of days which come within the period of this insurance and to which a return is actually applicable. Such overlapping period shall run, at the option of the Assured, either from the first day on which the Vessel is laid up or the first day of a period of 30 consecutive days as provided under 23.1.2(a) or (b) above.

The following clauses shall be paramount and shall override anything contained in this insurance inconsistent therewith.

24 WAR EXCLUSION

In no case shall this insurance cover loss damage liability or expense caused by

24.1   war civil war revolution rebellion insurrection, or civil strife arising therefrom, or any hostile act by or against a belligerent power

24.2   capture seizure arrest restraint or detainment (barratry and piracy excepted), and the consequences thereof or any attempt thereat

24.3   derelict mines torpedoes bombs or other derelict weapons of war.

25 STRIKES EXCLUSION

In no case shall this insurance cover loss damage liability or expense caused by

25.1   strikers, locked-out workmen, or persons taking part in labour disturbances, riots or civil commotions

25.2   any terrorist or any person acting from a political motive.

26 MALICIOUS ACTS EXCLUSION

In no case shall this insurance cover loss damage liability or expense arising from

26.1   the detonation of an explosive

26.2   any weapon of war

and caused by any person acting maliciously or from a political motive.

27 RADIOACTIVE CONTAMINATION EXCLUSION CLAUSE

In no case shall this insurance cover loss damage liability or expense directly or indirectly caused by or contributed to by or arising from

27.1   ionising radiations from or contamination by radioactivity from any nuclear fuel or from any nuclear waste or from the combustion of nuclear fuel

27.2   the radioactive, toxic, explosive or other hazardous or contaminating properties of any nuclear installation, reactor or other nuclear assembly or nuclear component thereof

27.3   any weapon of war employing atomic or nuclear fission and/or fusion or other like reaction or radioactive force or matter.

APPENDIX 8

INSTITUTE TIME CLAUSES
HULLS

RESTRICTED PERILS

This insurance is subject to English law and practice

1 NAVIGATION

1.1 The Vessel is covered subject to the provisions of this insurance at all times and has leave to sail or navigate with or without pilots, to go on trial trips and to assist and tow vessels or craft in distress. but it is warranted that the Vessel shall not be towed, except as is customary or to the first safe port or place when in need of assistance, or undertake towage or salvage services under a contract previously arranged by the Assured and/or Owners and/or Managers and/or Charterers. This Clause 1.1 shall not exclude customary towage in connection with loading and discharging.

1.2 This insurance shall not be prejudiced by reason of the Assured entering into any contract with pilots or for customary towage which limits or exempts the liability of the pilots and/or tugs and/or towboats and/or their owners when the Assured or their agents accept or are compelled to accept such contracts in accordance with established local law or practice.

1.3 The practice of engaging helicopters for the transportation of personnel, supplies and equipment to and/or from the Vessel shall not prejudice this insurance.

1.4 In the event of the Vessel being employed in trading operations which entail cargo loading or discharging at sea from or into another vessel (not being a harbour or inshore craft) no claim shall be recoverable under this insurance for loss of or damage to the Vessel or liability to any other vessel arising from such loading or discharging operations, including whilst approaching, lying alongside and leaving, unless previous notice that the Vessel is to be employed in such operations has been given to the Underwriters and any amended terms of cover and any additional premium required by them have been agreed.

1.5 In the event of the Vessel sailing (with or without cargo) with an intention of being (a) broken up, or (b) sold for breaking up, any claim for loss of or damage to the Vessel occurring subsequent to such sailing shall be limited to the market value of the Vessel as scrap at the time when the loss or damage is sustained, unless previous notice has been given to the Underwriters and any amendments to the terms of cover, insured value and premium required by them have been agreed. Nothing in this Clause 1.5 shall affect claims under Clauses 8 and/or 10.

2 CONTINUATION

Should the Vessel at the expiration of this insurance be at sea and in distress or missing, she shall, provided notice be given to the Underwriters prior to the expiration of this insurance, be held covered until arrival at the next port in good safety, or if in port and in distress until the Vessel is made safe, at a pro rata monthly premium.

3 BREACH OF WARRANTY

Held covered in case of any breach of warranty as to cargo, trade, locality, towage, salvage services or date of sailing, provided notice be given to the Underwriters immediately after receipt of advices and any amended terms of cover and any additional premium required by them be agreed.

4 CLASSIFICATION

4.1   It is the duty of the Assured, Owners and Managers at the inception of and throughout the period of this insurance to ensure that

4.1.1   the Vessel is classed with a Classification Society agreed by the Underwriters and that her class within that Society is maintained.

4.1.2   any recommendations requirements or restrictions imposed by the Vessel's Classification Society which relate to the Vessel's seaworthiness or to her maintenance in a seaworthy condition are complied with by the dates required by that Society.

4.2   In the event of any breach of the duties set out in Clause 4.1 above, unless the Underwriters agree to the contrary in writing, they will be discharged from liability under this insurance as from the date of the breach provided that if the Vessel is at sea at such date the Underwriters' discharge from liability is deferred until arrival at her next port.

4.3   Any incident condition or damage in respect of which the Vessel's Classification Society might make recommendations as to repairs or other action to be taken by the Assured Owners or Managers must be promptly reported to the Classification Society.

4.4   Should the Underwriters wish to approach the Classification Society directly for information and/or documents, the Assured will provide the necessary authorisation

5 TERMINATION

This Clause 5 shall prevail notwithstanding any provision whether written typed or printed in this insurance inconsistent therewith.

Unless the Underwriters agree to the contrary in writing, this insurance shall terminate automatically at the time of

5.1 change of the Classification Society of the Vessel, or change, suspension, discontinuance, withdrawal or expiry of her Class therein, or any of the Classification Society's periodic surveys becoming overdue unless an extension of time for such survey be agreed by the Classification Society, provided that if the Vessel is at sea such automatic termination shall be deferred until arrival at her next port. However where such change, suspension, discontinuance or withdrawal of her Class or where a periodic survey becoming overdue has resulted from loss or damage covered by Clause 6 of this insurance or which would be covered by an insurance of the Vessel subject to current Institute War and Strikes Clauses Hulls – Time such automatic termination shall only operate should the Vessel sail from her next port without the prior approval of the Classification Society or in the case of a periodic survey becoming overdue without the Classification Society having agreed an extension of time for such survey,

5,2 any change, voluntary or otherwise, in the ownership or flag, transfer to new management, or charter on a bareboat basis, or requisition for title or use of the Vessel. provided that, if the Vessel has cargo on board and has already sailed from her loading port or is at sea in ballast, such automatic termination shall if required be deferred. whilst the Vessel continues her planned voyage, until arrival at final port of discharge if with cargo or at port of destination if in ballast. However, in the event of requisition for title or use without the prior execution of a written agreement by the Assured, such automatic termination shall occur fifteen days after such requisition whether the Vessel is at sea or in port. A pro rata daily net return of premium shall be made provided that a total loss of the Vessel, whether by insured perils or otherwise, has not occurred during the period covered by this insurance or any extension thereof.

6 PERILS

6.1 This insurance covers loss of or damage to the subject-matter insured caused by

6.1.1 perils of the seas rivers lakes or other navigable waters

6.1.2 fire, explosion

6.1.3 violent theft by persons from outside the Vessel

6.1.4 jettison

6.1.5 piracy

6.1.6 contact with land conveyance, dock or harbour equipment or installation

6.1.7 earthquake volcanic eruption or lightning

6.1.8 accidents in loading discharging or shifting cargo or fuel.

6.2 This insurance covers loss of or damage to the subject-matter insured caused by

6.2.1   any latent defect in the machinery or hull

6.2.2   negligence of Pilots provided such Pilots are not a Master, Officer or Member of the Crew of the Vessel

6.2.3   negligence of repairers or charterers provided such repairers or charterers are not an Assured hereunder

6.2.4   contact with aircraft. helicopters or similar objects, or objects falling therefrom provided that such loss or damage has not resulted from want of due diligence by the Assured, Owners, Managers or Superintendents or any of their onshore management.

6.3   Masters Officers Crew or Pilots not to be considered Owners within the meaning of this Clause 6 should they hold shares in the Vessel.

7   POLLUTION HAZARD

This insurance covers loss of or damage to the Vessel caused by any governmental authority acting under the powers vested in it to prevent or mitigate a pollution hazard or damage to the environment or threat thereof resulting directly from damage to the Vessel for which the Underwriters are liable under this insurance provided that such act of governmental authority has not resulted from want of due diligence by the Assured, Owners or Managers to prevent or mitigate such hazard or damage, or threat thereof. Master Officers Crew or Pilots not to be considered Owners within the meaning of this Clause 7 should they hold shares in the Vessel.

8   3/4ths COLLISION LIABILITY

8.1   The Underwriters agree to indemnify the Assured for three-fourths of any sum or sums paid by the Assured to any other person or persons by reason of the Assured becoming legally liable by way of damages for

8.1.1   loss of or damage to any other vessel or property on any other vessel

8.1.2   delay to or loss of use of any such other vessel or property thereon

8.1.3   general average of, salvage of, or salvage under contract of, any such other vessel or property thereon, where such payment by the Assured is in consequence of the Vessel hereby insured coming into collision with any other vessel.

8.2   The indemnity provided by this Clause 8 shall be in addition to the indemnity provided by the other terms and conditions of this insurance and shall be subject to the following provisions:

8.2.1   where the insured Vessel is in collision with another vessel and both vessels are to blame then, unless the liability of one or both vessels becomes limited by law, the indemnity under this Clause 8 shall be calculated on the principle of cross-liabilities as if the respective Owners had been compelled to pay to each other such proportion of each other's damages as may have been properly allowed in ascertaining the balance or sum payable by or to the Assured in consequence of the collision,

8.2.2 in no case shall the Underwriters' total liability under Clauses 8.1 and 8.2 exceed their proportionate part of three-fourths of the insured value of the Vessel hereby insured in respect of any one collision,

8.3 The Underwriters will also pay three-fourths of the legal costs incurred by the Assured or which the Assured may be compelled to pay in contesting liability or taking proceedings to limit liability, with the prior written consent of the Underwriters.

EXCLUSIONS

8.4 Provided always that this Clause 8 shall in no case extend to any sum which the Assured shall pay for or in respect of

8.4.1 removal or disposal of obstructions. wrecks, cargoes or any other thing whatsoever

8.4.2 any real or personal property or thing whatsoever except other vessels or property on other vessels

8.4.3 the cargo or other property on, or the engagements of, the insured Vessel

8.4.4 loss of life, personal injury or illness

8.4.5 pollution or contamination. or threat thereof. of any real or personal property or thing whatsoever (except other vessels with which the insured Vessel is in collision or property on such other vessels) or damage to the environment, or threat thereof, save that this exclusion shall not extend to any sum which the Assured shall pay for or in respect of salvage remuneration in which the skill and efforts of the salvors in preventing or minimising damage to the environment as is referred to in Article 13 paragraph 1(b) of the International Convention on Salvage, 1989 have been taken into account.

9 SISTERSHIP

Should the Vessel hereby insured come into collision with or receive salvage services from another vessel belonging wholly or in part to the same Owners or under the same management, the Assured shall have the same rights under this insurance as they would have were the other vessel entirely the property of Owners not interested in the Vessel hereby insured; but in such cases the liability for the collision or the amount payable for the services rendered shall be referred to a sole arbitrator to be agreed upon between the Underwriters and the Assured.

10 GENERAL AVERAGE AND SALVAGE

10.1 This insurance covers the Vessel's proportion of salvage, salvage charges and/or general average, reduced in respect of any under-insurance. but in case of general average sacrifice of the Vessel the Assured may recover in respect of the whole loss without first enforcing their right of contribution from other parties.

10.2 Adjustment to be according to the law and practice obtaining at the place where the adventure ends, as if the contract of affreightment contained no special terms upon the subject; but where the contract of affreightment so provides the adjustment shall be according to the York-Antwerp Rules.

10.3 When the Vessel sails in ballast, not under charter. the provisions of the York-Antwerp Rules, 1994 (excluding Rules XI(d), XX and XXI) shall be applicable, and the voyage for this purpose shall be deemed to continue from the port or place of departure until the arrival of the Vessel at the first port or place thereafter other than a port or place of refuge or a port or place of call for bunkering only. If at any such intermediate port or place there is an abandonment of the adventure originally contemplated the voyage shall thereupon be deemed to be terminated.

10.4 No claim under this Clause 10 shall in any case be allowed where the loss was not incurred to avoid or in connection with the avoidance of a peril insured against.

10.5 No claim under this Clause 10 shall in any case be allowed for or in respect of

10.5.1 special compensation payable to a salvor under Article 14 of the International Convention on Salvage, 1989 or under any other provision in any statute, rule, law or contract which is similar in substance

10.5.2 expenses or liabilities incurred in respect of damage to the environment, or the threat of such damage, or as a consequence of the escape or release of pollutant substances from the Vessel, or the threat of such escape or release.

10.6 Clause 10.5 shall not however exclude any sum which the Assured shall pay to salvors for or in respect of salvage remuneration in which the skill and efforts of the salvors in preventing or minimising damage to the environment as is referred to in Article 13 paragraph 1(b) of the International Convention on Salvage, 1989 have been taken into account.

11 DUTY OF ASSURED (SUE AND LABOUR)

11.1 In case of any loss or misfortune it is the duty of the Assured and their servants and agents to take such measures as may be reasonable for the purpose of averting or minimising a loss which would be recoverable under this insurance.

11.2 Subject to the provisions below and to Clause 12 the Underwriters will contribute to charges properly and reasonably incurred by the Assured their servants or agents for such measures. General average, salvage charges (except as provided for in Clause 11.5), special compensation and expenses as referred to in Clause 10.5 and collision defence or attack costs are not recoverable under this Clause 11.

11.3 Measures taken by the Assured or the Underwriters with the object of saving, protecting or recovering the subject-matter insured shall not be considered as a waiver or acceptance of abandonment or otherwise prejudice the rights of either party.

11.4　　When expenses are incurred pursuant to this Clause 11 the liability under this insurance shall not exceed the proportion of such expenses that the amount insured hereunder bears to the value of the Vessel as stated herein, or to the sound value of the Vessel at the time of the occurrence giving rise to the expenditure if the sound value exceeds that value. Where the Underwriters have admitted a claim for total loss and property insured by this insurance is saved, the foregoing provisions shall not apply unless the expenses of suing and labouring exceed the value of such property saved and then shall apply only to the amount of the expenses which is in excess of such value.

11.5　　When a claim for total loss of the Vessel is admitted under this insurance and expenses have been reasonably incurred in saving or attempting to save the Vessel and other property and there are no proceeds, or the expenses exceed the proceeds, then this insurance shall bear its pro rata share of such proportion of the expenses, or of the expenses in excess of the proceeds, as the case may be, as may reasonably be regarded as having been incurred in respect of the Vessel, excluding all special compensation and expenses as referred to in Clause 10.5; but if the Vessel be insured for less than its sound value at the time of the occurrence giving rise to the expenditure, the amount recoverable under this clause, shall be reduced in proportion to the under-insurance.

11.6　　The sum recoverable under this Clause 11 shall be in addition to the loss otherwise recoverable under this insurance but shall in no circumstances exceed the amount insured under this insurance in respect of the Vessel.

12 DEDUCTIBLE

12.1　　No claim arising from a peril insured against shall be payable under this insurance unless the aggregate of all such claims arising out of each separate accident or occurrence (including claims under Clauses 8, 10 and 11) exceeds the deductible amount agreed in which case this sum shall be deducted. Nevertheless the expense of sighting the bottom after stranding, if reasonably incurred specially for that purpose, shall be paid even if no damage be found. This Clause 12.1 shall not apply to a claim for total or constructive total loss of the Vessel or, in the event of such a claim, to any associated claim under Clause 11 arising from the same accident or occurrence.

12.2　　Claims for damage by heavy weather occurring during a single sea passage between two successive ports shall be treated as being due to one accident. In the case of such heavy weather extending over a period not wholly covered by this insurance the deductible to be applied to the claim recoverable hereunder shall be the proportion of the above deductible that the number of days of such heavy weather falling within the period of this insurance bears to the number of days of heavy weather during the single sea passage. The expression heavy weather in this Clause 12.2 shall be deemed to include contact with floating ice.

12.3 Excluding any interest comprised therein, recoveries against any claim which is subject to the above deductible shall be credited to the Underwriters in full to the extent of the sum by which the aggregate of the claim unreduced by any recoveries exceeds the above deductible.

12.4 Interest comprised in recoveries shall be apportioned between the Assured and the Underwriters, taking into account the sums paid by the Underwriters and the dates when such payments were made, notwithstanding that by the addition of interest the Underwriters may receive a larger sum than they have paid.

13 NOTICE OF CLAIM AND TENDERS

13.1 In the event of accident whereby loss or damage may result in a claim under this insurance, notice must be given to the Underwriters promptly after the date on which the Assured, Owners or Managers become or should have become aware of the loss or damage and prior to survey so that a surveyor may be appointed if the Underwriters so desire. If notice is not given to the Underwriters within twelve months of that date unless Underwriters agree to the contrary in writing, the Underwriters will be automatically discharged from liability for any claim under this insurance in respect of or arising out of such accident or the loss or damage.

13.2 The Underwriters shall be entitled to decide the port to which the Vessel shall proceed for docking or repair (the actual additional expense of the voyage arising from compliance with the Underwriters' requirements being refunded to the Assured) and shall have a right of veto concerning a place of repair or a repairing firm.

13.3 The Underwriters may also take tenders or may require further tenders to be taken for the repair of the Vessel. Where such a tender has been taken and a tender is accepted with the approval of the Underwriters, an allowance shall be made at the rate of 30% per annum on the insured value for time lost between the despatch of the invitations to tender required by the Underwriters and the acceptance of a tender to the extent that such time is lost solely as the result of tenders having been taken and provided that the tender is accepted without delay after receipt of the Underwriters' approval.

Due credit shall be given against the allowance as above for any amounts recovered in respect of fuel and stores and wages and maintenance of the Master Officers and Crew or any member thereof, including amounts allowed in general average, and for any amounts recovered from third parties in respect of damages for detention and/or loss of profit and/or running expenses, for the period covered by the tender allowance or any part thereof.

Where a part of the cost of the repair of damage other than a fixed deductible is not recoverable from the Underwriters the allowance shall be reduced by a similar proportion.

13.4   In the event of failure by the Assured to comply with the conditions of Clauses 13.2 and/or 13.3 a deduction of 15% shall be made from the amount of the ascertained claim.

14 NEW FOR OLD

Claims payable without deduction new for old.

15 BOTTOM TREATMENT

In no case shall a claim be allowed in respect of scraping gritblasting and/or other surface preparation or painting of the Vessel's bottom except that

15.1   gritblasting and/or other surface preparation of new bottom plates ashore and supplying and applying any 'shop ' primer thereto.

15.2   gritblasting and/or other surface preparation of:

the butts or area of plating immediately adjacent to any renewed or refitted plating damaged during the course of welding and/or repairs,

areas of plating damaged during the course of fairing, either in place or ashore,

15.3   supplying and applying the first coat or primer/anti-corrosive to those particular areas mentioned in 15.1 and 15.2 above,

shall be allowed as part of the reasonable cost of repairs in respect of bottom plating damaged by an insured peril.

16 WAGES AND MAINTENANCE

No claim shall be allowed, other than in general average, for wages and maintenance of the Master Officers and Crew or any member thereof, except when incurred solely for the necessary removal of the Vessel from one port to another for the repair of damage covered by the Underwriters, or for trial trips for such repairs, and then only for such wages and maintenance as are incurred whilst the Vessel is under way.

17 AGENCY COMMISSION

In no case shall any sum be allowed under this insurance either by way of remuneration of the Assured for time and trouble taken to obtain and supply information or documents or in respect of the commission or charges of any manager, agent, managing or agency company or the like, appointed by or on behalf of the Assured to perform such services.

18 UNREPAIRED DAMAGE

18.1   The measure of indemnity in respect of claims for unrepaired damage shall be the reasonable depreciation in the market value of the Vessel at the time this insurance terminates arising from such unrepaired damage, but not exceeding the reasonable cost of repairs.

18.2   In no case shall the Underwriters be liable for unrepaired damage in the event of a subsequent total loss (whether or not covered under this insurance) sustained during the period covered by this insurance or any extension thereof.

18.3 The Underwriters shall not he liable in respect of unrepaired damage for more than the insured value at the time this insurance terminate.

19 CONSTRUCTIVE TOTAL LOSS

19.1 In ascertaining whether the Vessel is a constructive total loss, the insured value shall be taken as the repaired value and nothing in respect of the damaged or break-up value of the Vessel or wreck shall be taken into account.

19.2 No claim for constructive total loss based upon the cost of recovery and/or repair of the Vessel shall be recoverable hereunder unless such cost would exceed the insured value. In making this determination only the cost relating to a single accident or sequence of damages arising from the same accident shall be taken into account.

20 FREIGHT WAIVER

In the event of total or constructive total loss no claim to be made by the Underwriters for freight whether notice of abandonment has been given or not.

21 ASSIGNMENT

No assignment of or interest in this insurance or in any moneys which may be or become payable thereunder is to be binding on or recognised by the Underwriters unless a dated notice of such assignment or interest signed by the Assured, and by the assignor in the case of subsequent assignment, is endorsed on the Policy and the Policy with such endorsement is produced before payment of any claim or return of premium thereunder.

22 DISBURSEMENTS WARRANTY

22 1 Additional insurances as follows are permitted:

22.1.1 *Disbursements, Managers' Commissions, Profits or Excess or Increased Value of Hull and Machinery.* A sum not exceeding 25% of the value stated herein.

22.1.2 *Freight, Chartered Freight or Anticipated Freight, insured for time.* A sum not exceeding 25% of the value as stated herein less any sum insured, however described, under 22.1.1.

22.1.3 *Freight or Hire, under contracts for voyage.* A sum not exceeding the gross freight or hire for the current cargo passage and next succeeding cargo passage (such insurance to include, if required, a preliminary and an intermediate ballast passage) plus the charges of insurance. In the case of a voyage charter where payment is made on a time basis, the sum permitted for insurance shall be calculated on the estimated duration of the voyage, subject to the limitation of two cargo passages as laid down herein. Any sum insured under 22.1.2 to be taken into account and only the excess thereof may be insured, which excess shall be reduced as the freight or hire is advanced or earned by the gross amount so advanced or earned.

22.1.4 *Anticipated Freight if the Vessel sails in ballast and not under Charter.* A sum not exceeding the anticipated gross freight on next cargo passage, such sum to be reasonably estimated on the basis of the current rate of freight at time of insurance plus the charges of insurance. Any sum insured under 22.1.2 to be taken into account and only the excess thereof may be insured.

22.1.5 *Time Charter Hire or Charter Hire for Series of Voyages.* A sum not exceeding 50% of the gross hire which is to be earned under the charter in a period not exceeding 18 months. Any sum insured under 22.1.2 to be taken into account and only the excess thereof may be insured, which excess shall be reduced as the hire is advanced or earned under the charter by 50% of the gross amount so advanced or earned but the sum insured need not be reduced while the total of the sums insured under 22.1.2 and 22.1.5 does not exceed 50% of the gross hire still to be earned under the charter. An insurance under this Section may begin on the signing of the charter.

22.1.6 *Premiums.* A sum not exceeding the actual premiums of all interests insured for a period not exceeding 12 months (excluding premiums insured under the foregoing sections but including, if required, the premium or estimated calls on any Club or War etc Risk insurance) reducing pro rata monthly.

22.1.7 *Returns of Premium.* A sum not exceeding the actual returns which are allowable under any insurance but which would not be recoverable thereunder in the event of a total loss of the Vessel whether by insured perils or otherwise.

22.1.7 *Insurance irrespective of amount against:*

Any risks excluded by Clauses 24, 25, 26 and 27 below.

22.2 Warranted that no insurance on any interests enumerated in the foregoing 22.1.1 to 22.1.7 in excess of the amounts permitted therein and no other insurance which includes total loss of the Vessel P.P.I., F.I.A. or subject to any other like term, is or shall be effected to operate during the currency of this insurance by or for account of the Assured, Owners, Managers or Mortgagees. Provided always that a breach of this warranty shall not afford the Underwriters any defence to a claim by a Mortgagee who has accepted this insurance without knowledge of such breach.

23 RETURNS FOR LAY-UP AND CANCELLATION

23.1 To return as follows:

23.1.1 pro rata monthly net for each uncommenced month if this insurance be cancelled by agreement.

23.1.2 for each period of 30 consecutive days the Vessel may be laid up in a port or in a lay-up area provided such port or lay-up area is approved by the Underwriters

(a) .... per cent net not under repair

(b) .... per cent net under repair.

23.1.3 The Vessel shall not be considered to be under repair when work is undertaken in respect of ordinary wear and tear of the Vessel and/or following recommendations in the Vessel's Classification Society survey but any repairs following loss of or damage to the Vessel or involving structural alterations whether covered by this insurance or otherwise shall be considered as under repair.

23.1.4 If the Vessel is under repair during part only of a period for which a return is claimable, the return shall be calculated pro rata to the number of days under 23.1.2 (a) and (b) respectively.

23.2 PROVIDED ALWAYS THAT

23.2.1 a total loss of the Vessel, whether by insured perils or otherwise, has not occurred during the period covered by this insurance or any extension thereof

23.2.2 in no case shall a return be allowed when the Vessel is lying in exposed or unprotected waters or in a port or lay-up area not approved by the Underwriters

23.2.3 loading or discharging operations or the presence of cargo on board shall not debar returns but no return shall be allowed for any period during which the Vessel is being used for the storage of cargo or for lightering purposes

23.2.4 in the event of any amendment of the annual rate, the above rates of return shall be adjusted accordingly

23.2.5 in the event of any return recoverable under this Clause 23 being based on 30 consecutive days which fall on successive insurances effected for the same Assured this insurance shall only be liable for an amount calculated at pro rata of the period rates 23.1.2(a) and/or (b) above for the number of days which come within the period of this insurance and to which a return is actually applicable. Such overlapping period shall run, at the option of the Assured, either from the first day on which the Vessel is laid up or the first day of a period of 30 consecutive days as provided under 23.1.2(a) or (b) above.

The following clauses shall be paramount and shall override anything contained in this insurance inconsistent therewith.

24 WAR EXCLUSION

In no case shall this insurance cover loss damage liability or expense caused by

24.1 war civil war revolution rebellion insurrection or civil strife arising therefrom or any hostile act by or against a belligerent power

24.2 capture seizure arrest restraint or detainment (piracy excepted) and the consequences thereof or any attempt thereat

24.3 derelict mines torpedoes bombs or other derelict weapons of war.

25 STRIKES EXCLUSION

In no case shall this insurance cover loss damage liability or expense caused by

25.1   strikers, locked-out workmen, or persons taking part in labour disturbances, riots or civil commotions

25.2   any terrorist or any person acting from a political motive.

26 MALICIOUS ACTS EXCLUSION

In no case shall this insurance cover loss damage liability or expense arising from

26.1   the detonation of an explosive

26.2   any weapon of war and caused by any person acting maliciously or from a political motive.

27 RADIOACTIVE CONTAMINATION EXCLUSION CLAUSE

In no case shall this insurance cover loss damage liability or expense directly or indirectly caused by or contributed to by or arising from

27.1   ionising radiations from or contamination by radioactivity from any nuclear fuel or from any nuclear waste or from the combustion of nuclear fuel

27.2   the radioactive, toxic, explosive or other hazardous or contaminating properties of any nuclear installation, reactor or other nuclear assembly or nuclear component thereof

27.3   any weapon of war employing atomic or nuclear fission and/or fusion or other like reaction or radioactive force or matter.

APPENDIX 9

1/11/95

(FOR USE ONLY WITH THE CURRENT MAR POLICY FORM)

INSTITUTE VOYAGE CLAUSES
HULLS

This insurance is subject to English law and practice

1 NAVIGATION

1.1   The Vessel is covered subject to the provisions of this insurance at all times and has leave to sail or navigate with or without pilots, to go on trial trips and to assist and tow vessels or craft in distress, but it is warranted that the Vessel shall not be towed, except as is customary or to the first safe port or place when in need of assistance, or undertake towage or salvage services under a contract previously arranged by the Assured and/or Owners and/or Managers and/or Charterers. This Clause 1.1 shall not exclude customary towage in connection with loading and discharging.

1.2   This insurance shall not be prejudiced by reason of the Assured entering into any contract with pilots or for customary towage which limits or exempts the liability of the pilots and/or tugs and/or towboats and/or their owners when the Assured or their agents accept or are compelled to accept such contracts in accordance with established local law or practice.

1.3   The practice of engaging helicopters for the transportation of personnel, supplies and equipment to and/or from the Vessel shall not prejudice this insurance.

1.4   In the event of the Vessel being employed in trading operations which entail cargo loading or discharging at sea from or into another vessel (not being a harbour or inshore craft) no claim shall be recoverable under this insurance for loss of or damage to the Vessel or liability to any other vessel arising from such loading or discharging operations, including whilst approaching, lying alongside and leaving, unless previous notice that the Vessel is to be employed in such operations has been given to the Underwriters and any amended terms of cover and any additional premium required by them have been agreed.

2 CHANGE OF VOYAGE

Held covered in case of deviation or change of voyage or any breach of warranty as to towage or salvage services, provided notice be given to the

Underwriters immediately after receipt of advices and any amended terms of cover and any additional premium required by them be agreed.

3 CLASSIFICATION

3.1   It is the duty of the Assured, Owners and Managers at the inception of and throughout the period of this insurance to ensure that

3.1.1   the Vessel is classed with a Classification Society agreed by the Underwriters and that her class within that Society is maintained,

3.1.2   any recommendations requirements or restrictions imposed by the Vessel's Classification Society which relate to the Vessel's seaworthiness or to her maintenance in a seaworthy condition are complied with by the dates required by that Society.

3.2   In the event of any breach of the duties set out in Clause 3.1 above, unless the Underwriters agree to the contrary in writing, they will be discharged from liability under this insurance as from the date of the breach provided that if the Vessel is at sea at such date the Underwriters' discharge from liability is deferred until arrival at her next port.

3.3   Any incident condition or damage in respect of which the Vessel's Classification Society might make recommendations as to repairs or other action to be taken by the Assured, Owners and Managers must be promptly reported to the Classification Society.

3.4   Should the Underwriters wish to approach the Classification Society directly for information and/or documents, the Assured will provide the necessary authorization.

4 PERILS

4.1   This insurance covers loss of or damage to the subject-matter insured caused by

4.1.I   perils of the seas rivers lakes or other navigable waters

4.1.2   fire, explosion

4.1.3   violent theft by persons from outside the Vessel

4.1.4   jettison

4.1.5   piracy

4.1.6   contact with land conveyance, dock or harbour equipment or installation

4.1.7   earthquake volcanic eruption or lightning

4.1.8   accidents in loading discharging or shifting cargo or fuel.

4.2   This insurance covers loss of or damage to the subject-matter insured caused by

4.2.1   bursting of boilers breakage of shafts or any latent defect in the machinery or hull

4.2.2   negligence of Master Officers Crew or Pilots

4.2.3 negligence of repairers or charterers provided such repairers or charterers are not an Assured hereunder

4.2.4 barratry of Master Officers or Crew

4.2.5 contact with aircraft, helicopters or similar objects, or objects falling therefrom

provided such loss or damage has not resulted from want of due diligence by the Assured, Owners, Managers or Superintendents or any of their onshore management.

4.3 Master Officers Crew or Pilots not to be considered Owners within the meaning of this Clause 4 should they hold shares in the Vessel.

5 POLLUTION HAZARD

This insurance covers loss of or damage to the Vessel caused by any governmental authority acting under the powers vested in it to prevent or mitigate a pollution hazard or damage to the environment, or threat thereof, resulting directly from damage to the Vessel for which the Underwriters are liable under this insurance, provided that such act of governmental authority has not resulted from want of due diligence by the Assured, Owners or Managers to prevent or mitigate such hazard or damage, or threat thereof. Master Officers Crew or Pilots not to be considered Owners within the meaning of this Clause 5 should they hold shares in the Vessel.

6 3/4ths COLLISION LIABILITY

6.1 The Underwriters agree to indemnify the Assured for three-fourths of any sum or sums paid by the Assured to any other person or persons by reason of the Assured becoming legally liable by way of damages for

6.1.1 loss of or damage to any other vessel or property on any other vessel

6.1.2 delay to or loss of use of any such other vessel or property thereon

6.1.3 general average of, salvage of, or salvage under contract of, any such other vessel or property thereon, where such payment by the Assured is in consequence of the Vessel hereby insured coming into collision with any other vessel.

6.2 The indemnity provided by this Clause 6 shall be in addition to the indemnity provided by the other terms and conditions of this insurance and shall be subject to the following provisions:

6.2.1 where the insured Vessel is in collision with another vessel and both vessels are to blame then, unless the liability of one or both vessels becomes limited by law, the indemnity under this Clause 6 shall be calculated on the principle of cross-liabilities as if the respective Owners had been compelled to pay to each other such proportion of each other's damages as may have been properly allowed in ascertaining the balance or sum payable by or to the Assured in consequence of the collision,

6.2.2 in no case shall the Underwriters' total liability under Clauses 6.1 and 6.2 exceed their proportionate part of three-fourths of the insured value of the Vessel hereby insured in respect of any one collision.

6.3 The Underwriters will also pay three-fourths of the legal costs incurred by the Assured or which the Assured may be compelled to pay in contesting liability or taking proceedings to limit liability, with the prior written consent of the Underwriters.

EXCLUSIONS

6.4 Provided always that this Clause 6 shall in no case extend to any sum which the Assured shall pay for or in respect of

6.4.1 removal or disposal of obstructions, wrecks, cargoes or any other thing whatsoever

6.4.2 any real or personal property or thing whatsoever except other vessels or property on other vessels

6.4.3 the cargo or other property on, or the engagements of, the insured Vessel

6.4.4 loss of life, personal injury or illness

6.4.5 pollution or contamination, or threat thereof, of any real or personal property or thing whatsoever (except other vessels with which the insured Vessel is in collision or property on such other vessels) or damage to the environment, or threat thereof, save that this exclusion shall not extend to any sum which the Assured shall pay for or in respect of salvage remuneration in which the skill and efforts of the salvors in preventing or minimising damage to the environment as is referred to in Article 13 paragraph 1(b) of the International Convention on Salvage, 1989 have been taken into account.

7 SISTERSHIP

Should the Vessel hereby insured come into collision with or receive salvage services from another vessel belonging wholly or in part to the same Owners or under the same management, the Assured shall have the same rights under this insurance as they would have were the other vessel entirely the property of Owners not interested in the Vessel hereby insured, but in such cases the liability for the collision or the amount payable for the services rendered shall be referred to a sole arbitrator to be agreed upon between the Underwriters and the Assured.

8 GENERAL AVERAGE AND SALVAGE

8.1 This insurance covers the Vessel's proportion of salvage, salvage charges and/or general average, reduced in respect of any under-insurance, but in case of general average sacrifice of the Vessel the Assured may recover in respect of the whole loss without first enforcing their right of contribution from other parties.

8.2 Adjustment to be according to the law and practice obtaining at the place where the adventure ends, as if the contract of affreightment contained no special terms upon the subject; but where the contract of affreightment so provides the adjustment shall be according to the York-Antwerp Rules.

8.3   When the Vessel sails in ballast, not under charter the provisions of the York-Antwerp Rules, 1994 (excluding Rules XI(d), XX and XXI) shall be applicable, and the voyage for this purpose shall be deemed to continue from the port or place of departure until the arrival of the Vessel at the first port or place thereafter other than a port or place of refuge or a port or place of call for bunkering only. If at any such intermediate port or place there is an abandonment of the adventure originally contemplated the voyage shall thereupon be deemed to be terminated.

8.4   No claim under this Clause 8 shall in any case be allowed where the loss was not incurred to avoid or in connection with the avoidance of a peril insured against.

8.5   No claim under this Clause 8 shall in any case be allowed for or in respect of

8.5.1   special compensation payable to a salvor under Article 14 of the International Convention on Salvage, 1989 or under any other provision in any statute, rule, law or contract which is similar in substance

8.5.2   expenses or liabilities incurred in respect of damage to the environment, or the threat of such damage, or as a consequence of the escape or release of pollutant substances from the Vessel, or the threat of such escape or release.

8.6   Clause 8.5 shall not however exclude any sum which the Assured shall pay to salvors for or in respect of salvage remuneration in which the skill and efforts of the salvors in preventing or minimising damage to the environment as is referred to in Article 13 paragraph 1(b) of the International Convention on Salvage, 1989 have been taken into account.

9 DUTY OF ASSURED (SUE AND LABOUR)

9.1   In case of any loss or misfortune it is the duty of the Assured and their servants and agents to take such measures as may be reasonable for the purpose of averting or minimising a loss which would be recoverable under this insurance.

9.2   Subject to the provisions below and to Clause 10 the Underwriters will contribute to charges properly and reasonably incurred by the Assured their servants or agents for such measures. General average, salvage charges (except as provided for in Clause 9.5), special compensation and expenses as referred to in Clause 8.5, and collision defence or attack costs are not recoverable under this Clause 9.

9.3   Measures taken by the Assured or the Underwriters with the object of saving, protecting or recovering the subject-matter insured shall not be considered as a waiver or acceptance of abandonment or otherwise prejudice the rights of either party.

9.4   When expenses are incurred pursuant to this Clause 9 the liability under this insurance shall not exceed the proportion of such expenses that the amount insured hereunder bears to the value of the Vessel as stated herein, or to the sound value of the Vessel at the time of the occurrence giving rise to the expenditure if the sound value exceeds that value. Where the Underwriters have admitted a claim for total loss and property insured by this insurance is saved, the foregoing provisions shall not apply unless the expenses of suing and labouring exceed the value of such property saved and then shall apply only to the amount of the expenses which is in excess of such value.

9.5 When a claim for total loss of the Vessel is admitted under this insurance and expenses have been reasonably incurred in saving or attempting to save the Vessel and other property and there are no proceeds, or the expenses exceed the proceeds, then this insurance shall bear its pro rata share of such proportion of the expenses, or of the expenses in excess of the proceeds, as the case may be, as may reasonably be regarded as having been incurred in respect of the Vessel, excluding all special compensation and expenses as referred to in Clause 8.5; but if the Vessel be insured for less than its sound value at the time of the occurrence giving rise to the expenditure, the amount recoverable under this clause shall be reduced in proportion to the under-insurance.

9.6 The sum recoverable under this Clause 9 shall be in addition to the loss otherwise recoverable under this insurance but shall in no circumstances exceed the amount insured under this insurance in respect of the Vessel.

10 DEDUCTIBLE

10.1 No claim arising from a peril insured against shall be payable under this insurance unless the aggregate of all such claims arising out of each separate accident or occurrence (including claims under Clauses 6, 8 and 9) exceeds the deductible amount agreed in which case this sum shall be deducted. Nevertheless the expense of sighting the bottom after stranding, if reasonably incurred specially for that purpose shall be paid even if no damage be found. This Clause 10.1 shall not apply to a claim for total or constructive total loss of the Vessel or, in the event of such a claim, to any associated claim under Clause 9 arising from the same accident or occurrence.

10.2 Claims for damage by heavy weather occurring during a single sea passage between two successive ports shall be treated as being due to one accident. In the case of such heavy weather extending over a period not wholly covered by this insurance the deductible to be applied to the claim recoverable hereunder shall be the proportion of the above deductible that the number of days of such heavy weather falling within the period of this insurance bears to the number of days of heavy weather during the single sea passage. The expression 'heavy weather' in this Clause 10.2 shall be deemed to include contact with floating ice.

10.3   Excluding any interest comprised therein, recoveries against any claim which is subject to the above deductible shall be credited to the Underwriters in full to the extent of the sum by which the aggregate of the claim unreduced by any recoveries exceeds the above deductible.

10.4   Interest comprised in recoveries shall be apportioned between the Assured and the Underwriters, taking into account the sums paid by the Underwriters and the dates when such payments were made, notwithstanding that by the addition of interest the Underwriters may receive a larger sum than they have paid.

11 NOTICE OF CLAIM AND TENDERS

11. I   In the event of accident whereby loss or damage may result in a claim under this insurance, notice must be given to the Underwriters promptly after the date on which the Assured, Owners or Managers become or should have become aware of the loss or damage and prior to survey and so that a surveyor may be appointed if the Underwriters so desire.

       If notice is not given to the Underwriters within twelve months of that date, unless the Underwriters agree to the contrary in writing, the Underwriters will be automatically discharged from liability for any claim under this insurance in respect of or arising out of such accident or the loss or damage.

11.2   The Underwriters shall be entitled to decide the port to which the Vessel shall proceed for docking or repair (the actual additional expense of the voyage arising from compliance with the Underwriters' requirements being refunded to the Assured) and shall have a right of veto concerning a place of repair or a repairing firm.

11.3   The Underwriters may also take tenders or may require further tenders to be taken for the repair of the Vessel. Where such a tender has been taken and a tender is accepted with the approval of the Underwriters, an allowance shall be made at the rate of 30% per annum on the insured value for time lost between the despatch of the invitations to tender required by the Underwriters and the acceptance of a tender to the extent that such time is lost solely as the result of tenders having been taken and provided that the tender is accepted without delay after receipt of the Underwriters' approval.

       Due credit shall be given against the allowance as above for any amounts recovered in respect of fuel and stores and wages and maintenance of the Master Officers and Crew or any member thereof, including amounts allowed in general average, and for any amounts recovered from third parties in respect of damages for detention and/or loss of profit and/or running expenses, for the period covered by the tender allowance or any part thereof.

       Where a part of the cost of the repair of damage other than a fixed deductible is not recoverable from the Underwriters the allowance shall be reduced by a similar proportion.

11.4 In the event of failure by the Assured to comply with the conditions of Clauses 11.2 and/or 11.3 a deduction of 15% shall be made from the amount of the ascertained claim.

12 NEW FOR OLD

Claims payable without deduction new for old.

13 BOTTOM TREATMENT

In no case shall a claim be allowed in respect of scraping gritblasting and/or other surface preparation or painting of the Vessel's bottom except that

13.1 gritblasting and/or other surface preparation of new bottom plates ashore and supplying and applying any 'shop' primer thereto,

13.2 gritblasting and/or other surface preparation of:

the butts or area of plating immediately adjacent to any renewed or refitted plating damaged during the course of welding and/or repairs,

areas of plating damaged during the course of fairing, either in place or ashore,

13.3 supplying and applying the first coat of primer/anti-corrosive to those particular areas mentioned in 13.1 and 13.2 above,

shall be allowed as part of the reasonable cost of repairs in respect of bottom plating damaged by an insured peril.

14 WAGES AND MAINTENANCE

No claim shall be allowed, other than in general average, for wages and maintenance of the Master Officers and Crew or any member thereof, except when incurred solely for the necessary removal of the Vessel from one port to another for the repair of damage covered by the Underwriters, or for trial trips for such repairs, and then only for such wages and maintenance as are incurred whilst the Vessel is under way.

15 AGENCY COMMISSION

In no case shall any sum be allowed under this insurance either by way of remuneration of the Assured for time and trouble taken to obtain and supply information or documents or in respect of the commission or charges of any manager, agent, managing or agency company or the like, appointed by or on behalf of the Assured to perform such services.

16 UNREPAIRED DAMAGE

16.1 The measure of indemnity in respect of claims for unrepaired damage shall be the reasonable depreciation in the market value of the Vessel at the time this insurance terminates arising from such unrepaired damage, but not exceeding the reasonable cost of repairs.

16.2 In no case shall the Underwriters be liable for unrepaired damage in the event of a subsequent total loss (whether or not covered under this insurance) sustained during the period covered by this insurance or any extension thereof.

16.3 The Underwriters shall not be liable in respect of unrepaired damage for more than the insured value at the time this insurance terminates.

17 CONSTRUCTIVE TOTAL LOSS

17.1 In ascertaining whether the Vessel is a constructive total loss, the insured value shall be taken as the repaired value and nothing in respect of the damaged or break-up value of the Vessel or wreck shall be taken into account.

17.2 No claim for constructive total loss based upon the cost of recovery and/or repair of the Vessel shall be recoverable hereunder unless such cost would exceed the insured value. In making this determination only the cost relating to a single accident or sequence of damages arising from the same accident shall be taken into account.

18 FREIGHT WAIVER

In the event of total or constructive total loss no claim to be made by the Underwriters for freight whether notice of abandonment has been given or not.

19 ASSIGNMENT

No assignment of or interest in this insurance or in any moneys which may be or become payable thereunder is to be binding on or recognised by the Underwriters unless a dated notice of such assignment or interest signed by the Assured, and by the assignor in the case of subsequent assignment, is endorsed on the Policy and the Policy with such endorsement is produced before payment of any claim or return of premium thereunder.

20 DISBURSEMENTS WARRANTY

20.1 Additional insurances as follows are permitted:

20.1.1 *Disbursements, Managers' Commissions, Profits or Excess or Increased Value of Hull and Machinery.* A sum not exceeding 25% of the value stated herein.

20.1.2 *Freight, Chartered Freight or Anticipated Freight, insured for time.* A sum not exceeding 25% of the value as stated herein less any sum insured, however described, under 20.1.1.

20.1.3 *Freight or Hire, under contracts for voyage.* A sum not exceeding the gross freight or hire for the current cargo passage and next succeeding cargo passage (such insurance to include, if required, preliminary and an intermediate ballast passage) plus the charges of insurance. In the case of a voyage charter where payment is made on a time basis, the sum permitted for insurance shall be calculated on the estimated duration of the voyage, subject to the limitation of two cargo passages as laid down herein. Any sum insured under 20.1.2 to be taken into account and only the excess thereof may be insured, which excess shall be reduced as the freight or hire is advanced or earned by the gross amount so advanced or earned.

20.1.4 *Anticipated Freight if the Vessel sails in ballast and not under Charter.* A sum not exceeding the anticipated gross freight on next cargo passage, such sum to be reasonably estimated on the basis of the current rate of freight at time of insurance plus the charges of insurance. Any sum insured under 20.1.2 to be taken into account and only the excess thereof may be insured.

20.1.5 *Time Charter Hire or Charter Hire for Series of Voyages.* A sum not exceeding 50% of the gross hire which is to be earned under the charter in a period not exceeding 18 months. Any sum insured under 20.1.2 to be taken into account and only the excess thereof may be insured, which excess shall be reduced as the hire is advanced or earned under the charter by 50% of the gross amount so advanced or earned but the sum insured need not be reduced while the total of the sums insured under 20.1.2 and 20.1.5 does not exceed 50% of the gross hire still to be earned under the charter. An insurance under this Section may begin on the signing of the charter.

20.1.6 *Premiums.* A sum not exceeding the actual premiums of all interests insured for a period not exceeding 12 months (excluding premiums insured under the foregoing sections but including, if required, the premium or estimated calls on any Club or War etc. Risk insurance) reducing pro rata monthly.

20.1.7 *Returns of Premium.* A sum not exceeding the actual returns which are allowable under any insurance but which would not be recoverable thereunder in the event of a total loss of the Vessel whether by insured perils or otherwise.

20.1.8 *Insurance irrespective of amount against*: Any risks excluded by Clauses 21, 22, 23 and 24 below.

20.2 Warranted that no insurance on any interests enumerated in the foregoing 20.1.1 to 20.1.7 in excess of the amounts permitted therein and no other insurance which includes total loss of the Vessel P.P.I., F.I.A., or subject to any other like term, is or shall be effected to operate during the currency of this insurance by or for account of the Assured, Owners, Managers or Mortgagees. Provided always that a breach of this warranty shall not afford the Underwriters any defence to a claim by a Mortgagee who has accepted this insurance without knowledge of such breach.

The following clauses shall be paramount and shall override anything contained in this insurance inconsistent therewith.

21 WAR EXCLUSION

In no case shall this insurance cover loss damage liability or expense caused by

21.1 war civil war revolution rebellion insurrection, or civil strife arising therefrom, or any hostile act by or against a belligerent power

21.2 capture seizure arrest restraint or detainment (barratry and piracy excepted), and the consequences thereof or any attempt thereat

21.3 derelict mines torpedoes bombs or other derelict weapons of war.

22 STRIKES EXCLUSION

In no case shall this insurance cover loss damage liability or expense caused by

22.1   strikers, locked-out workmen, or persons taking part in labour disturbances, riots or civil commotions

22.2   any terrorist or any person acting from a political motive.

23 MALICIOUS ACTS EXCLUSION

In no case shall this insurance cover loss damage liability or expense arising from

23.1   the detonation of an explosive

23.2   any weapon of war and caused by any person acting maliciously or from a political motive.

24 RADIOACTIVE CONTAMINATION EXCLUSION CLAUSE

In no case shall this insurance cover loss damage liability or expense directly or indirectly caused by or contributed to by or arising from

24.1   ionising radiations from or contamination by radioactivity from any nuclear fuel or from any nuclear waste or from the combustion of nuclear fuel

24.2   the radioactive, toxic, explosive or other hazardous or contaminating properties of any nuclear installation, reactor or other nuclear assembly or nuclear component thereof

24.3   any weapon of war employing atomic or nuclear fission and/or fusion or other like reaction or radioactive force or matter.

1/1/82

INSTITUTE CARGO CLAUSES (A)

RISKS COVERED

1   This insurance covers all risks of loss of or damage to the subject-matter insured except as provided in Clauses 4, 5, 6 and 7 below.

2   This insurance covers general average and salvage charges, adjusted or determined according to the contract of affreightment and/or the governing law and practice, incurred to avoid or in connection with the avoidance of loss from any cause except those excluded in Clauses 4, 5, 6 and 7 or elsewhere in this insurance.

3   This insurance is extended to indemnify the Assured against such proportion of liability under the contract of affreightment 'Both to Blame Collision' Clause as is in respect of a loss recoverable hereunder. In the event of any claim by shipowners under the said Clause the Assured agree to notify the Underwriters who shall have the right, at their own cost and expense, to defend the Assured against such claim.

EXCLUSIONS

4   In no case shall this insurance cover

4.1   loss damage or expense attributable to wilful misconduct of the Assured

4.2   ordinary leakage, ordinary loss in weight or volume, or ordinary wear and tear of the subject-matter insured

4.3   loss damage or expense caused by insufficiency or unsuitability of packing or preparation of the subject-matter insured (for the purpose of this Clause 4.3 'packing' shall be deemed to include stowage in a container or liftvan but only when such stowage is carried out prior to attachment of this insurance or by the Assured or their servants)

4.4   loss damage or expense caused by inherent vice or nature of the subject-matter insured

4.5   loss damage or expense proximately caused by delay, even though the delay be caused by a risk insured against (except expenses payable under Clause 2 above)

4.6   loss damage or expense arising from insolvency or financial default of the owners managers charterers or operators of the vessel

4.7   loss damage or expense arising from the use of any weapon of war employing atomic or nuclear fission and/or fusion or other like reaction or radioactive force or matter.

5 5.1 In no case shall this insurance cover loss damage or expense arising from

unseaworthiness of vessel or craft,

unfitness of vessel craft conveyance container or liftvan for the safe carriage of the subject-matter insured,

where the Assured or their servants are privy to such unseaworthiness or unfitness, at the time the subject-matter insured is loaded therein.

5.2 The Underwriters waive any breach of the implied warranties of seaworthiness of the ship and fitness of the ship to carry the subject-matter insured to destination, unless the Assured or their servants are privy to such unseaworthiness or unfitness.

6 In no case shall this insurance cover loss damage or expense caused by

6.1 war civil war revolution rebellion insurrection, or civil strife arising therefrom, or any hostile act by or against a belligerent power

6.2 capture seizure arrest restraint or detainment (piracy excepted), and the consequences thereof or any attempt thereat

6.3 derelict mines torpedoes bombs or other derelict weapons of war.

7 In no case shall this insurance cover loss damage or expense

7.1 caused by strikers, locked-out workmen, or persons taking part in labour disturbances, riots or civil commotions

7.2 resulting from strikes, lock-outs, labour disturbances, riots or civil commotions

7.3 caused by any terrorist or any person acting from a political motive.

DURATION

8 8.1 This insurance attaches from the time the goods leave the warehouse or place of storage at the place named herein for the commencement of the transit, continues during the ordinary course of transit and terminates either

8.1.1 on delivery to the Consignees' or other final warehouse or place of storage at the destination named herein,

8.1.2 on delivery to any other warehouse or place of storage, whether prior to or at the destination named herein, which the Assured elect to use either

8.1.2.1 for storage other than in the ordinary course of transit or

8.1.2.2 for allocation or distribution,

or

8.1.3 on the expiry of 60 days after completion of discharge overside of the goods hereby insured from the oversea vessel at the final port of discharge,

whichever shall first occur.

8.2   If, after discharge overside from the oversea vessel at the final port of discharge, but prior to termination of this insurance, the goods are to be forwarded to a destination other than that to which they are insured hereunder, this insurance, whilst remaining subject to termination as provided for above, shall not extend beyond the commencement of transit to such other destination.

8.3   This insurance shall remain in force (subject to termination as provided for above and to the provisions of Clause 9 below) during delay beyond the control of the Assured, any deviation, forced discharge, reshipment or transhipment and during any variation of the adventure arising from the exercise of a liberty granted to shipowners or charterers under the contract of affreightment.

9   If owing to circumstances beyond the control of the Assured either the contract of carriage is terminated at a port or place other than the destination named therein or the transit is otherwise terminated before delivery of the goods as provided for in Clause 8 above, then this insurance shall also terminate unless prompt notice is given to the Underwriters and continuation of cover is requested when the insurance shall remain in force, subject to an additional premium if required by the Underwriters, either

9.1   until the goods are sold and delivered at such port or place, or, unless otherwise specially agreed, until the expiry of 60 days after arrival of the goods hereby insured at such port or place, whichever shall first occur, or

9.2   if the goods are forwarded within the said period of 60 days (or any agreed extension thereof) to the destination named herein or to any other destination, until terminated in accordance with the provisions of Clause 8 above.

10 Where, after attachment of this insurance, the destination is changed by the Assured, held covered at a premium and on conditions to be arranged subject to prompt notice being given to the Underwriters.

CLAIMS

11 11.1   In order to recover under this insurance the Assured must have an insurable interest in the subject-matter insured at the time of the loss.

11.2   Subject to 11.1 above, the Assured shall be entitled to recover for insured loss occurring during the period covered by this insurance, notwithstanding that the loss occurred before the contract of insurance was concluded, unless the Assured were aware of the loss and the Underwriters were not.

12 Where, as a result of the operation of a risk covered by this insurance, the insured transit is terminated at a port or place other than that to which the subject-matter is covered under this insurance, the Underwriters will reimburse the Assured for any extra charges properly and reasonably incurred in unloading storing and forwarding the subject-matter to the destination to which it is insured hereunder.

This Clause 12, which does not apply to general average or salvage charges, shall be subject to the exclusions contained in Clauses 4, 5, 6 and 7 above, and shall not include charges arising from the fault negligence insolvency or financial default of the Assured or their servants.

13 No claim for Constructive Total Loss shall be recoverable hereunder unless the subject-matter insured is reasonably abandoned either on account of its actual total loss appearing to be unavoidable or because the cost of recovering, reconditioning and forwarding the subject-matter to the destination to which it is insured would exceed its value on arrival.

14 14.1 If any Increased Value insurance is effected by the Assured on the cargo insured herein the agreed value of the cargo shall be deemed to be increased to the total amount insured under this insurance and all Increased Value insurances covering the loss, and liability under this insurance shall be in such proportion as the sum insured herein bears to such total amount insured.

In the event of claim the Assured shall provide the Underwriters with evidence of the amounts insured under all other insurances.

14.2 **Where this insurance is on Increased Value the following clause shall apply:**

The agreed value of the cargo shall be deemed to be equal to the total amount insured under the primary insurance and all Increased Value insurances covering the loss and effected on the cargo by the Assured, and liability under this insurance shall be in such proportion as the sum insured herein bears to such total amount insured.

In the event of claim the Assured shall provide the Underwriters with evidence of the amounts insured under all other insurances.

BENEFIT OF INSURANCE

15 This insurance shall not inure to the benefit of the carrier or other bailee.

MINIMISING LOSSES

16 It is the duty of the Assured and their servants and agents in respect of loss recoverable hereunder

16.1 to take such measures as may be reasonable for the purpose of averting or minimising such loss, and

16.2 to ensure that all rights against carriers, bailees or other third parties are properly preserved and exercised

and the Underwriters will, in addition to any loss recoverable hereunder, reimburse the Assured for any charges properly and reasonably incurred in pursuance of these duties.

17 Measures taken by the Assured or the Underwriters with the object of saving, protecting or recovering the subject-matter insured shall not be considered as a waiver or acceptance of abandonment or otherwise prejudice the rights of either party.

AVOIDANCE OF DELAY

18 It is a condition of this insurance that the Assured shall act with reasonable despatch in all circumstances within their control.

LAW AND PRACTICE

19 This insurance is subject to English law and practice.

NOTE— *It is necessary for the Assured when they become aware of an event which is 'held covered' under this insurance to give prompt notice to the Underwriters and the right to such cover is dependent upon compliance with this obligation.*

APPENDIX 11

1/1/82

INSTITUTE CARGO CLAUSES (B)

RISKS COVERED

1   This insurance covers, except as provided in Clauses 4, 5, 6 and 7 below,

   1.1   loss of or damage to the subject-matter insured reasonably attributable to

   1.1.1   fire or explosion

   1.1.2   vessel or craft being stranded grounded sunk or capsized

   1.1.3   overturning or derailment of land conveyance

   1.1.4   collision or contact of vessel craft or conveyance with any external object other than water

   1.1.5   discharge of cargo at a port of distress

   1.1.6   earthquake volcanic eruption or lightning,

   1.2   loss of or damage to the subject-matter insured caused by

   1.2.1   general average sacrifice

   1.2.2   jettison or washing overboard

   1.2.3   entry of sea lake or river water into vessel craft hold conveyance container liftvan or place of storage,

   1.3   total loss of any package lost overboard or dropped whilst loading on to, or unloading from, vessel or craft.

2   This insurance covers general average and salvage charges, adjusted or determined according to the contract of affreightment and/or the governing law and practice, incurred to avoid or in connection with the avoidance of loss from any cause except those excluded in Clauses 4, 5, 6 and 7 or elsewhere in this insurance

3   This insurance is extended to indemnify the Assured against such proportion of liability under the contract of affreightment 'Both to Blame Collision' Clause as is in respect of a loss recoverable hereunder. In the event of any claim by shipowners under the said Clause the Assured agree to notify the Underwriters who shall have the right, at their own cost and expense, to defend the Assured against such claim.

EXCLUSIONS

4   In no case shall this insurance cover

   4.1   loss damage or expense attributable to wilful misconduct of the Assured

   4.2   ordinary leakage, ordinary loss in weight or volume, or ordinary wear and tear of the subject-matter insured

4.3   loss damage or expense caused by insufficiency or unsuitability of packing or preparation of the subject-matter insured (for the purpose of this Clause 4.3 'packing' shall be deemed to include stowage in a container or liftvan but only when such stowage is carried out prior to attachment of this insurance or by the Assured or their servants)

4.4   loss damage or expense caused by inherent vice or nature of the subject-matter insured

4.5   loss damage or expense proximately caused by delay, even though the delay be caused by a risk insured against (except expenses payable under Clause 2 above)

4.6   loss damage or expense arising from insolvency or financial default of the owners managers charterers or operators of the vessel

4.7   deliberate damage to or deliberate destruction of the subject-matter insured or any part thereof by the wrongful act of any person or persons

4.8   loss damage or expense arising from the use of any weapon of war employing atomic or nuclear fission and/or fusion or other like reaction or radioactive force or matter.

5   5.1   In no case shall this insurance cover loss damage or expense arising from unseaworthiness of vessel or craft, unfitness of vessel craft conveyance container or liftvan for the safe carriage of the subject-matter insured, where the Assured or their servants are privy to such unseaworthiness or unfitness, at the time the subject-matter insured is loaded therein.

5.2   The Underwriters waive any breach of the implied warranties of seaworthiness of the ship and fitness of the ship to carry the subject-matter insured to destination, unless the Assured or their servants are privy to such unseaworthiness or unfitness.

6   In no case shall this insurance cover loss damage or expense caused by

6.1   war civil war revolution rebellion insurrection, or civil strife arising therefrom, or any hostile act by or against a belligerent power

6.2   capture seizure arrest restraint or detainment, and the consequences thereof or any attempt thereat

6.3   derelict mines torpedoes bombs or other derelict weapons of war.

7   In no case shall this insurance cover loss damage or expense

7.1   caused by strikers, locked-out workmen, or persons taking part in labour disturbances, riots or civil commotions

7.2   resulting from strikes, lock-outs, labour disturbances, riots or civil commotions

7.3   caused by any terrorist or any person acting from a political motive.

DURATION

8   8.1   This insurance attaches from the time the goods leave the warehouse or place of storage at the place named herein for the commencement

of the transit, continues during the ordinary course of transit and terminates either

8.1.1 on delivery to the Consignees' or other final warehouse or place of storage at the destination named herein,

8.1.2 on delivery to any other warehouse or place of storage, whether prior to or at the destination named herein, which the Assured elect to use either

8.1.2.1 for storage other than in the ordinary course of transit or

8.1.2.2 for allocation or distribution,

or

8.1.3 on the expiry of 60 days after completion of discharge overside of the goods hereby insured from the oversea vessel at the final port of discharge, whichever shall first occur.

8.2 If, after discharge overside from the oversea vessel at the final port of discharge, but prior to termination of this insurance, the goods are to be forwarded to a destination other than that to which they are insured hereunder, this insurance, whilst remaining subject to termination as provided for above, shall not extend beyond the commencement of transit to such other destination.

8.3 This insurance shall remain in force (subject to termination as provided for above and to the provisions of Clause 9 below) during delay beyond the control of the Assured, any deviation, forced discharge, reshipment or transhipment and during any variation of the adventure arising from the exercise of a liberty granted to shipowners or charterers under the contract of affreightment.

9 If owing to circumstances beyond the control of the Assured either the contract of carriage is terminated at a port or place other than the destination named therein or the transit is otherwise terminated before delivery of the goods as provided for in Clause 8 above, then this insurance shall also terminate unless prompt notice is given to the Underwriters and continuation of cover is requested when the insurance shall remain in force, subject to an additional premium if required by the Underwriters, either

9.1 until the goods are sold and delivered at such port or place, or, unless otherwise specially agreed, until the expiry of 60 days after arrival of the goods hereby insured at such port or place, whichever shall first occur,

or

9.2 if the goods are forwarded within the said period of 60 days (or any agreed extension thereof) to the destination named herein or to any other destination, until terminated in accordance with the provisions of Clause 8 above.

10 Where, after attachment of this insurance, the destination is changed by the Assured, held covered at a premium and on conditions to be arranged subject to prompt notice being given to the Underwriters.

CLAIMS

11 11.1 In order to recover under this insurance the Assured must have an insurable interest in the subject-matter insured at the time of the loss.

11.2 Subject to 11.1 above, the Assured shall be entitled to recover for insured loss occurring during the period covered by this insurance, notwithstanding that the loss occurred before the contract of insurance was concluded, unless the Assured were aware of the loss and the Underwriters were not.

12 Where, as a result of the operation of a risk covered by this insurance, the insured transit is terminated at a port or place other than that to which the subject-matter is covered under this insurance, the Underwriters will reimburse the Assured for any extra charges properly and reasonably incurred in unloading storing and forwarding the subject-matter to the destination to which it is insured hereunder.

This Clause 12, which does not apply to general average or salvage charges, shall be subject to the exclusions contained in Clauses 4, 5, 6 and 7 above, and shall not include charges arising from the fault negligence insolvency or financial default of the Assured or their servants.

13 No claim for Constructive Total Loss shall be recoverable hereunder unless the subject-matter insured is reasonably abandoned either on account of its actual total loss appearing to be unavoidable or because the cost of recovering, reconditioning and forwarding the subject-matter to the destination to which it is insured would exceed its value on arrival.

14 14.1 If any Increased Value insurance is effected by the Assured on the cargo insured herein the agreed value of the cargo shall be deemed to be increased to the total amount insured under this insurance and all Increased Value insurances covering the loss, and liability under this insurance shall be in such proportion as the sum insured herein bears to such total amount insured.

In the event of claim the Assured shall provide the Underwriters with evidence of the amounts insured under all other insurances.

14.2 Where this insurance is on Increased Value the following clause shall apply:

The agreed value of the cargo shall be deemed to be equal to the total amount insured under the primary insurance and all Increased Value insurances covering the loss and effected on the cargo by the Assured, and liability under this insurance shall be in such proportion as the sum insured herein bears to such total amount insured.

In the event of claim the Assured shall provide the Underwriters with evidence of the amounts insured under all other insurances.

BENEFIT OF INSURANCE

15 This insurance shall not inure to the benefit of the carrier or other bailee.

MINIMISING LOSSES

16 It is the duty of the Assured and their servants and agents in respect of loss recoverable hereunder

16.1   to take such measures as may be reasonable for the purpose of averting or minimising such loss, and

16.2   to ensure that all rights against carriers, bailees or other third parties are properly preserved and exercised and the Underwriters will, in addition to any loss recoverable hereunder, reimburse the Assured for any charges properly and reasonably incurred in pursuance of these duties.

17 Measures taken by the Assured or the Underwriters with the object of saving, protecting or recovering the subject-matter insured shall not be considered as a waiver or acceptance of abandonment or otherwise prejudice the rights of either party.

AVOIDANCE OF DELAY

18 It is a condition of this insurance that the Assured shall act with reasonable despatch in all circumstances within their control.

LAW AND PRACTICE

19 This insurance is subject to English law and practice.

NOTE— *It is necessary for the Assured when they become aware of an event which is 'held covered' under this insurance to give prompt notice to the Underwriters and the right to such cover is dependent upon compliance with this obligation.*

1/1/82

INSTITUTE CARGO CLAUSES (C)

RISKS COVERED

1 This insurance covers, except as provided in Clauses 4, 5, 6 and 7 below,

1.1   loss of or damage to the subject-matter insured reasonably attributable to

1.1.1   fire or explosion

1.1.2   vessel or craft being stranded grounded sunk or capsized

1.1.3   overturning or derailment of land conveyance

1.1.4   collision or contact of vessel craft or conveyance with any external object other than water

1.1.5   discharge of cargo at a port of distress,

1.2   loss of or damage to the subject-matter insured caused by

1.2.1   general average sacrifice

1.2.2   jettison.

2 This insurance covers general average and salvage charges, adjusted or determined according to the contract of affreightment and/or the governing law and practice, incurred to avoid or in connection with the avoidance of loss from any cause except those excluded in Clauses 4, 5, 6 and 7 or elsewhere in this insurance.

3 This insurance is extended to indemnify the Assured against such proportion of liability under the contract of affreightment 'Both to Blame Collision' Clause as is in respect of a loss recoverable hereunder. In the event of any claim by shipowners under the said Clause the Assured agree to notify the Underwriters who shall have the right, at their own cost and expense, to defend the Assured against such claim.

EXCLUSIONS

4 In no case shall this insurance cover

4.1   loss damage or expense attributable to wilful misconduct of the Assured

4.2   ordinary leakage, ordinary loss in weight or volume, or ordinary wear and tear of the subject-matter insured

4.3   loss damage or expense caused by insufficiency or unsuitability of packing or preparation of the subject-matter insured (for the purpose of this Clause 4.3 'packing' shall be deemed to include stowage in a container or liftvan but only when such stowage is carried out prior to attachment of this insurance or by the Assured or their servants)

4.4   loss damage or expense caused by inherent vice or nature of the subject-matter insured

4.5   loss damage or expense proximately caused by delay, even though the delay be caused by a risk insured against (except expenses payable under Clause 2 above)

4.6   loss damage or expense arising from insolvency or financial default of the owners managers charterers or operators of the vessel

4.7   deliberate damage to or deliberate destruction of the subject-matter insured or any part thereof by the wrongful act of any person or persons

4.8   loss damage or expense arising from the use of any weapon of war employing atomic or nuclear fission and/or fusion or other like reaction or radioactive force or matter.

5   5.1   In no case shall this insurance cover loss damage or expense arising from unseaworthiness of vessel or craft, unfitness of vessel craft conveyance container or liftvan for the safe carriage of the subject-matter insured,

where the Assured or their servants are privy to such unseaworthiness or unfitness, at the time the subject-matter insured is loaded therein.

5.2   The Underwriters waive any breach of the implied warranties of seaworthiness of the ship and fitness of the ship to carry the subject-matter insured to destination, unless the Assured or their servants are privy to such unseaworthiness or unfitness.

6   In no case shall this insurance cover loss damage or expense caused by

6.1   war civil war revolution rebellion insurrection, or civil strife arising therefrom, or any hostile act by or against a belligerent power

6.2   capture seizure arrest restraint or detainment, and the consequences thereof or any attempt thereat

6.3   derelict mines torpedoes bombs or other derelict weapons of war.

7   In no case shall this insurance cover loss damage or expense

7.1   caused by strikers, locked-out workmen, or persons taking part in labour disturbances, riots or civil commotions

7.2   resulting from strikes, lock-outs, labour disturbances, riots or civil commotions

7.3   caused by any terrorist or any person acting from a political motive.

DURATION

8   8.1   This insurance attaches from the time the goods leave the warehouse or place of storage at the place named herein for the commencement of the transit, continues during the ordinary course of transit and terminates either

8.1.1   on delivery to the Consignees' or other final warehouse or place of storage at the destination named herein,

8.1.2   on delivery to any other warehouse or place of storage, whether prior to or at the destination named herein, which the Assured elect to use either

8.1.2.1 for storage other than in the ordinary course of transit or

8.1.2.2 for allocation or distribution,

 or

8.1.3   on the expiry of 60 days after completion of discharge overside of the goods hereby insured from the oversea vessel at the final port of discharge, whichever shall first occur.

8.2   If, after discharge overside from the oversea vessel at the final port of discharge, but prior to termination of this insurance, the goods are to be forwarded to a destination other than that to which they are insured hereunder, this insurance, whilst remaining subject to termination as provided for above, shall not extend beyond the commencement of transit to such other destination.

8.3   This insurance shall remain in force (subject to termination as provided for above and to the provisions of Clause 9 below) during delay beyond the control of the Assured, any deviation forced discharge, reshipment or transhipment and during any variation of the adventure arising from the exercise of a liberty granted to shipowners or charterers under the contract of affreightment.

9   If owing to circumstances beyond the control of the Assured either the contract of carriage is terminated at a port or place other than the destination named therein or the transit is otherwise terminated before delivery of the goods as provided for in Clause 8 above, then this insurance shall also terminate unless prompt notice is given to the Underwriters and continuation of cover is requested when the insurance shall remain in force, subject to an additional premium if required by the Underwriters, either

9.1   until the goods are sold and delivered at such port or place, or, unless otherwise specially agreed, until the expiry of 60 days after arrival of the goods hereby insured at such port or place, whichever shall first occur, or

9.2   if the goods are forwarded within the said period of 60 days (or any agreed extension thereof) to the

 destination named herein or to any other destination, until terminated in accordance with the provisions of Clause 8 above.

10 Where, after attachment of this insurance, the destination is changed by the Assured, held covered at a premium and on conditions to be arranged subject to prompt notice being given to the Underwriters.

CLAIMS

11 11.1   In order to recover under this insurance the Assured must have an insurable interest in the subject-matter insured at the time of the loss.

 11.2   Subject to 11.1 above, the Assured shall be entitled to recover for insured loss occurring during the period covered by this insurance, notwithstanding that the loss occurred before the contract of insurance was concluded, unless the Assured were aware of the loss and the Underwriters were not.

12 Where, as a result of the operation of a risk covered by this insurance, the insured transit is terminated at a port or place other than that to which the subject-matter is covered under this insurance, the Underwriters will reimburse the Assured for any extra charges properly and reasonably incurred in unloading storing and forwarding the subject-matter to the destination to which it is insured hereunder.

This Clause 12, which does not apply to general average or salvage charges, shall be subject to the exclusions contained in Clauses 4, 5, 6 and 7 above, and shall not include charges arising from the fault negligence insolvency or financial default of the Assured or their servants.

13 No claim for Constructive Total Loss shall be recoverable hereunder unless the subject-matter insured is reasonably abandoned either on account of its actual total loss appearing to be unavoidable or because the cost of recovering, reconditioning and forwarding the subject-matter to the destination to which it is insured would exceed its value on arrival.

14 14.1   If any Increased Value insurance is effected by the Assured on the cargo insured herein the agreed value of the cargo shall be deemed to be increased to the total amount insured under this insurance and all Increased Value insurances covering the loss, and liability under this insurance shall be in such proportion as the sum insured herein bears to such total amount insured.

            In the event of claim the Assured shall provide the Underwriters with evidence of the amounts insured under all other insurances.

   14.2   Where this insurance is on Increased Value the following clause shall apply:

            The agreed value of the cargo shall be deemed to be equal to the total amount insured under the primary insurance and all Increased Value insurances covering the loss and effected on the cargo by the Assured, and liability under this insurance shall be in such proportion as the sum insured herein bears to such total amount insured.

            In the event of claim the Assured shall provide the Underwriters with evidence of the amounts insured under all other insurances.

BENEFIT OF INSURANCE

15 This insurance shall not inure to the benefit of the carrier or other bailee.

MINIMISING LOSSES

16 It is the duty of the Assured and their servants and agents in respect of loss recoverable hereunder

   16.1   to take such measures as may be reasonable for the purpose of averting or minimising such loss,

            and

16.2   to ensure that all rights against carriers, bailees or other third parties are properly preserved and exercised

and the Underwriters will, in addition to any loss recoverable hereunder, reimburse the Assured for any charges properly and reasonably incurred in pursuance of these duties.

17 Measures taken by the Assured or the Underwriters with the object of saving, protecting or recovering the subject-matter insured shall not be considered as a waiver or acceptance of abandonment or otherwise prejudice the rights of either party.

AVOIDANCE OF DELAY

18 It is a condition of this insurance that the Assured shall act with reasonable despatch in all circumstances within their control.

LAW AND PRACTICE

19 This insurance is subject to English law and practice.

NOTE— *It is necessary for the Assured when they become aware of an event which is 'held covered' under this insurance to give prompt notice to the Underwriters and the right to such cover is dependent upon compliance with this obligation.*

APPENDIX 13

1/11/95
(FOR USE ONLY WITH THE CURRENT MAR POLICY FORM)

INSTITUTE TIME CLAUSES
FREIGHT

This insurance is subject to English law and practice

1 NAVIGATION

1.1 The Vessel has leave to dock and undock, to go into graving dock, to sail or navigate with or without pilots, to go on trial trips and to assist and tow vessels or craft in distress, but it is warranted that the Vessel shall not be towed, except as is customary or to the first safe port or place when in need of assistance, or undertake towage or salvage services under a contract previously arranged by the Assured and/or Owners and/or Managers and/or Charterers. This Clause 1 shall not exclude customary towage in connection with loading and discharging.

1.2 This insurance shall not be prejudiced by reason of the Assured entering into any contract with pilots or for customary towage which limits or exempts the liability of the pilots and/or tugs and/or towboats and/or their owners when the Assured or their agents accept or are compelled to accept such contracts in accordance with established local law or practice.

1.3 The practice of engaging helicopters for the transportation of personnel, supplies and equipment to and/or from the Vessel shall not prejudice this insurance.

2 CRAFT RISK

Including risk of craft and/or lighter to and from the Vessel.

3 CONTINUATION

Should the Vessel at the expiration of this insurance be at sea and in distress or missing, the subject-matter insured shall, provided notice be given to the Underwriters prior to the expiration of this insurance, be held covered until arrival of the Vessel at the next port in good safety, or if in port and in distress until the Vessel is made safe, at a pro rata monthly premium.

4 BREACH OF WARRANTY

Held covered in case of any breach of warranty as to cargo, trade, locality, towage, salvage services or date of sailing, provided notice be given to the Underwriters immediately after receipt of advices and any amended terms of cover and any additional premium required by them be agreed.

5 CLASSIFICATION

5.1   It is the duty of the Assured, Owners and Managers at the inception of and throughout the period of this insurance to ensure that

5.1.1   the Vessel is classed with a Classification Society agreed by the Underwriters and that her class within that Society is maintained,

5.1.2   any recommendations requirements or restrictions imposed by the Vessel's Classification Society which relate to the Vessel's seaworthiness or to her maintenance in a seaworthy condition are complied with by the dates required by that Society.

5.2   In the event of any breach of the duties set out in Clause 5.1 above, unless the Underwriters agree to the contrary in writing, they will be discharged from liability under this insurance as from the date of the breach, provided that if the Vessel is at sea at such date the Underwriters' discharge from liability is deferred until arrival at her next port.

5.3   Any incident condition or damage in respect of which the Vessel's Classification Society might make recommendations as to repairs or other action to be taken by the Assured, Owners or Managers must be promptly reported to the Classification Society.

5.4   Should the Underwriters wish to approach the Classification Society directly for information and/or documents, the Assured will provide the necessary authorization.

6 TERMINATION

This Clause 6 shall prevail notwithstanding any provision whether written typed or printed in this insurance inconsistent therewith.

Unless the Underwriters agree to the contrary in writing, this insurance shall terminate automatically at the time of

6.1   change of the Classification Society of the Vessel, or change, suspension, discontinuance, withdrawal or expiry of her Class therein, or any of the Classification Society's periodic surveys becoming overdue unless an extension of time for such survey be agreed by the Classification Society, provided that if the Vessel is at sea such automatic termination shall be deferred until arrival at her next port. However where such change, suspension discontinuance or withdrawal of her Class or where a periodic survey becoming overdue has resulted from loss or damage covered by Clause 7 of this insurance or which would be covered by an insurance of the Vessel subject to current Institute Time Clauses Hulls or Institute War and Strikes Clauses Hulls–Time such automatic termination shall only operate should the Vessel sail from her next port without the prior approval of the Classification Society or in the case of a periodic survey becoming overdue without the Classification Society having agreed an extension of time for such survey,

6.2   any change, voluntary or otherwise, in the ownership or flag transfer to new management, or charter on a bareboat basis, or requisition for title or use of the Vessel, provided that, if the Vessel has cargo on board and has already sailed from her loading port or is at sea in ballast, such automatic termination shall if required be deferred, whilst the Vessel continues her planned voyage, until arrival at final port of discharge if with cargo or at port of destination if in ballast. However, in the event of requisition for title or use without the prior execution of a written agreement by the Assured, such automatic termination shall occur fifteen days after such requisition whether the Vessel is at sea or in port.

A pro rata daily net return of premium shall be made provided that a total loss of the Vessel, whether by insured perils or otherwise, has not occurred during the period covered by this insurance or any extension thereof.

7 PERILS

7.1 This insurance covers loss of the subject-matter insured caused by

7.1.1 perils of the seas rivers lakes or other navigable waters

7.1.2 fire, explosion

7.1.3 violent theft by persons from outside the Vessel

7.1.4 jettison

7.1.5 piracy

7.1.6 contact with land conveyance, dock or harbour equipment or installation

7.1.7 earthquake volcanic eruption or lightning

7.1.8 accidents in loading discharging or shifting cargo or fuel.

7.2 This insurance covers loss of the subject-matter insured caused by

7.2.1 bursting of boilers breakage of shafts or any latent defect in the machinery or hull

7.2.2 negligence of Master Officers Crew or Pilots

7.2.3 negligence of repairers or charterers provided such repairers or charterers are not an Assured hereunder

7.2.4 barratry of Master Officers or Crew

7.2.5 contact with aircraft, helicopters or similar objects or objects falling therefrom

provided that such loss has not resulted from want of due diligence by the Assured, Owners. Managers or Superintendents or any of their onshore management.

7.3 Masters Officers Crew or Pilots not to be considered Owners within the meaning of this Clause 7 should they hold shares in the Vessel.

8 POLLUTION HAZARD

This insurance covers loss of the subject matter insured caused by any governmental authority acting under the powers vested in it to prevent or mitigate a pollution hazard or damage to the environment, or threat thereof, resulting directly from a peril covered by this insurance, provided that such act of governmental authority has not resulted from want of due diligence by the Assured, Owners or Managers to prevent or mitigate such hazard or damage, or threat thereof. Masters Officers Crew or Pilots not to be considered Owners within the meaning of this Clause 8 should they hold shares in the Vessel.

9   FREIGHT COLLISION

9.1   It is further agreed that if the Vessel shall come into collision with any other vessel and the Assured shall in consequence thereof become liable to pay and shall pay by way of damages to any other person or persons any sum or sums in respect of the amount of freight taken into account in calculating the measure of the liability of the Assured for

9.1.1   loss of or damage to any other vessel or property on any other vessel

9.].2   delay to or loss of use of any such other vessel or property thereon

9.1.3   general average of, salvage of, or salvage under contract of, any such other vessel or property thereon, the Underwriters will pay the Assured such proportion of three-fourths of such sum or sums so paid applying to freight as their respective subscriptions hereto bear to the total amount insured on freight, or to the gross freight earned on the voyage during which the collision occurred if this be greater.

9.2   Provided always that:

9.2.1   liability of the Underwriters in respect of any one such collision shall not exceed their proportionate part of three-fourths of the total amount insured hereon on freight, and in cases in which, with the prior consent in writing of the Underwriters, the liability of the vessel has been contested or proceedings have been taken to limit liability, they will also pay a like proportion of three-fourths of the costs, appertaining proportionately to the freight portion of damages. which the Assured shall thereby incur or be compelled to pay:

9.2.2   no claim shall attach to this insurance:

9.2.2.1 which attaches to any other insurances covering collision liabilities

9.2.2.2 which is or would be, recoverable in the terms of the Institute 3/4ths Collision Liability Clause if the Vessel were insured in the terms of such Institute 3/4ths Collision Liability Clause for a value not less than the equivalent in pounds sterling, at the time of commencement of this insurance, of the Vessel's limit of liability calculated in accordance with Article 6.1(b) of the 1976 Limitation Convention,

9.2.3   this Clause 9 shall in no case extend or be deemed to extend to any sum which the Assured may become liable to pay or shall pay for or in respect of

9.2.3.1 removal or disposal, under statutory powers or otherwise, of obstructions, wrecks, cargoes or any other thing whatsoever

9.2.3.2 any real or personal property or thing whatsoever except other vessels or property on other vessels

9.2.3.3 pollution or contamination, or threat thereof, of any real or personal property or thing whatsoever (except other vessels with which the insured Vessel is in collision or property on such other vessels) or damage to the environment, or threat thereof, save that this exclusion shall not extend to any sum which the Assured shall pay for or in respect of salvage remuneration in which the skill and efforts of the salvors in preventing or minimising damage to the environment as is referred to in Article 13 paragraph 1(b) of the International Convention on Salvage, 1989 have been taken into account

9.2.3.4 the cargo or other property on or the engagements of the Vessel

9.2.3.5 loss of life, personal injury or illness.

10 SISTERSHIP

Should the Vessel named herein come into collision with or receive salvage services from another vessel belonging wholly or in part to the same Owners, or under the same management, the Assured shall have the same rights under this insurance as they would have were the other vessel entirely the property of Owners not interested in the Vessel named herein; but in such cases the liability for the collision or the amount payable for the services rendered shall be referred to a sole arbitrator to be agreed upon between the Underwriters and the Assured.

11 GENERAL AVERAGE AND SALVAGE 143

11.1   This insurance covers the proportion of general average, salvage and/or salvage charges attaching to freight at risk of the Assured, reduced in respect of any under-insurance.

11.2   Adjustment to be according to the law and practice obtaining at the place where the adventure ends, as if the contract of affreightment contained no special terms upon the subject; but where the contract of affreightment so provides the adjustment shall be according to the York-Antwerp Rules.

11.3   No claim under this Clause 11 shall in any case be allowed where the loss was not incurred to avoid or in connection with the avoidance of a peril insured against.

11.4   No claim under this Clause 11 shall in any case be allowed for or in respect of

11.4.1 special compensation payable to a salvor under Article 14 of the International Convention on Salvage, 1989 or under any other provision in any statute, rule, law or contract which is similar in substance

11.4.2 expenses or liabilities incurred in respect of damage to the environment, or the threat of such damage, or as a consequence of the escape or release of pollutant substances from the Vessel, or the threat of such escape or release.

11.5   Clause 11.4 shall not however exclude any sum which the Assured shall pay to salvors for or in respect of salvage remuneration in which the skill and efforts of the salvors in preventing or minimising damage to the environment as is referred to in Article 13 paragraph 1(b) of the International Convention on Salvage, 1989 have been taken into account.

12 FRANCHISE

This insurance does not cover partial loss, other than general average loss, under 3% unless caused by fire, sinking, stranding or collision with another vessel. Each craft and/or lighter to be deemed a separate insurance if required by the Assured.

13 ASSIGNMENT

No assignment of or interest in this insurance or in any moneys which may be or become payable thereunder is to be binding on or recognised by the Underwriters unless a dated notice of such assignment or interest signed by the Assured, and by the assignor in the case of subsequent assignment, is endorsed on the Policy and the Policy with such endorsement is produced before payment of any claim or return of premium thereunder.

14 MEASURE OF INDEMNITY

14.1 The amount recoverable under this insurance for any claim for loss of freight shall not exceed the gross freight actually lost.

14.2 Where insurances on freight other than this insurance are current at the time of the loss, all such insurances shall be taken into consideration in calculating the liability under this insurance and the amount recoverable hereunder shall not exceed the rateable proportion of the gross freight lost, notwithstanding any valuation in this or any other insurance.

14.3 In calculating the liability under Clause 11 all insurances on freight shall likewise be taken into consideration.

14.4 Nothing in this Clause 14 shall apply to any claim arising under Clause 16.

15 LOSS OF TIME

This insurance does not cover any claims consequent on loss of time whether arising from a peril of the sea or otherwise.

16 TOTAL LOSS

16.1 In the event of the total loss (actual or constructive) of the Vessel named herein the amount insured shall be paid in full, whether the Vessel be fully or partly loaded or in ballast, chartered or unchartered.

16.2 In ascertaining whether the Vessel is a constructive total loss, the insured value in the insurances on hull and machinery shall be taken as the repaired value and nothing in respect of the damaged or break-up value of the Vessel or wreck shall be taken into account.

16.3 Should the Vessel be a constructive total loss but the claim on the insurances on hull and machinery be settled as a claim for partial loss, no payment shall be due under this Clause 16.

17 RETURNS FOR LAY-UP AND CANCELLATION

17.1 To return as follows:

17.1.1 pro rata monthly net for each uncommenced month if this insurance be cancelled by agreement,

17.1.2 for each period of 30 consecutive days the Vessel may be laid up in a port or in a lay-up area provided such port or lay-up area is approved by the Underwriters

(a) .... per cent net not under repair

(b) .... per cent net under repair.

17.1.3 The Vessel shall not be considered to be under repair when work is undertaken in respect of ordinary wear and tear of the Vessel and/or following recommendations in the Vessel's Classification Society survey, but any repairs following loss of or damage to the Vessel or involving structural alterations. whether covered by this insurance or otherwise shall be considered as under repair.

17.1.4 If the Vessel is under repair during part only of a period for which a return is claimable, the return shall be calculated pro rata to the number of days under 17.1.2(a) and (b) respectively.

17.2 PROVIDED ALWAYS THAT

17.2.1 a total loss of the Vessel, whether by insured perils or otherwise, has not occurred during the period covered by this insurance or any extension thereof

17.2.2 in no case shall a return be allowed when the Vessel is lying in exposed or unprotected waters, or in a port or lay-up area not approved by the Underwriters

17.2.3 loading or discharging operations or the presence of cargo on board shall not debar returns but no return shall be allowed for any period during which the Vessel is being used for the storage of cargo or for lightering purposes

17.2.4 in the event of any amendment of the annual rate, the above rates of return shall be adjusted accordingly

17.2.5 in the event of any return recoverable under this Clause 17 being based on 30 consecutive days which fall on successive insurances effected for the same Assured, this insurance shall only be liable for an amount calculated at pro rata of the period rates 17.1.2(a) and/or (b) above for the number of days which come within the period of this insurance and to which a return is actually applicable. Such overlapping period shall run, at the option of the Assured, either from the first day on which the Vessel is laid up or the first day of a period of 30 consecutive days as provided under 17.1.2(a) or (b) above.

The following clauses shall be paramount and shall override anything contained in this insurance inconsistent therewith.

18 WAR EXCLUSION

In no case shall this insurance cover loss damage liability or expense caused by

18.1   war civil war revolution rebellion insurrection, or civil strife arising therefrom, or any hostile act by or against a belligerent power

18.2   capture seizure arrest restraint or detainment (barratry and piracy excepted), and the consequences thereof or any attempt thereat

18.3   derelict mines torpedoes bombs or other derelict weapons of war.

19 STRIKES EXCLUSION

In no case shall this insurance cover loss damage liability or expense caused by

19.1   strikers, locked-out workmen, or persons taking part in labour disturbances, riots or civil commotions

19.2   any terrorist or any person acting from a political motive.

20 MALICIOUS ACTS EXCLUSION

In no case shall this insurance cover loss damage liability or expense arising from

20.1 the detonation of an explosive

20.2 any weapon of war

and caused by any person acting maliciously or from a political motive.

21 RADIOACTIVE CONTAMINATION EXCLUSION CLAUSE

In no case shall this insurance cover loss damage liability or expense directly or indirectly caused by or contributed to by or arising from

21.1   ionising radiation from or contamination by radioactivity from any nuclear fuel or from any nuclear waste or from the combustion of nuclear fuel

21.2   the radioactive, toxic, explosive or other hazardous or contaminating properties of any nuclear installation, reactor or other nuclear assembly or nuclear component thereof

21.3   any weapon of war employing atomic or nuclear fission and/or fusion or other like reaction or radioactive force or matter.

APPENDIX 14

1/11/95

(FOR USE ONLY WITH THE CURRENT MAR POLICY FORM)

INSTITUTE VOYAGE CLAUSES
FREIGHT

This insurance is subject to English law and practice

1 NAVIGATION

1.1 The Vessel has leave to dock and undock, to go into graving dock, to sail or navigate with or without pilots, to go on trial trips and to assist and tow vessels or craft in distress, but it is warranted that the Vessel shall not be towed, except as is customary or to the first safe port or place when in need of assistance, or undertake towage or salvage services under a contract previously arranged by the Assured and/or Owners and/or Managers and/or Charterers. This Clause 1 shall not exclude customary towage in connection with loading and discharging.

1.2 This insurance shall not be prejudiced by reason of the Assured entering into any contract with pilots or for customary towage which limits or exempts the liability of the pilots and/or tugs and/or towboats and/or their owners when the Assured or their agents accept or are compelled to accept such contracts in accordance with established local law or practice.

1.3 The practice of engaging helicopters for the transportation of personnel, supplies and equipment to and/or from the Vessel shall not prejudice this insurance.

2 CRAFT RISK

Including risk of craft and/or lighter to and from the Vessel.

3 CHANGE OF VOYAGE

Held covered in case of deviation or change of voyage or any breach of warranty as to towage or salvage services, provided notice be given to the Underwriters immediately after receipt of advices and any amended terms of cover and any additional premium required by them be agreed.

4 PERILS

4.1 This insurance covers loss of the subject-matter insured caused by

4.1.1 perils of the seas rivers lakes or other navigable waters

4.1.2 fire, explosion

4.1.3 violent theft by persons from outside the Vessel

4.1.4   jettison

4.1.5   piracy

4.1.6   contact with land conveyance, dock or harbour equipment or installation

4.1.7   earthquake volcanic eruption or lightning

4.1.8   accidents in loading discharging or shifting cargo or fuel.

4.2   This insurance covers loss of the subject-matter insured caused by

4.2.1   bursting of boilers breakage of shafts or any latent defect in the machinery or hull

4.2.2   negligence of Master Officers Crew or Pilots

4.2.3   negligence of repairers or charterers provided such repairers or charterers are not an Assured hereunder

4.2.4   barratry of Master Officers or Crew

4.2.5   contact with aircraft, helicopters or similar objects, or objects falling therefrom

provided that such loss has not resulted from want of due diligence by the Assured, Owners, Managers or Superintendents or any of their onshore management.

4.3   Masters Officers Crew or Pilots not to be considered Owners within the meaning of this Clause should they hold shares in the Vessel.

5   POLLUTION HAZARD

This insurance covers loss of the subject matter insured caused by any governmental authority acting under the powers vested in it to prevent or mitigate a pollution hazard or damage to the environment, or threat thereof, resulting directly from a peril covered by this insurance, provided that such act of governmental authority has not resulted from want of due diligence by the Assured, Owners and Managers to prevent or mitigate such hazard or damage, or threat thereof. Masters Officers Crew or Pilots not to be considered Owners within the meaning of this Clause 5 should they hold shares in the Vessel.

6   FREIGHT COLLISION

6.1   It is further agreed that if the Vessel shall come into collision with any other vessel and the Assured shall in consequence thereof become liable to pay and shall pay by way of damages to any other person or persons any sum or sums in respect of the amount of freight taken into account in calculating the measure of the liability of the Assured for

6.1.1   loss of or damage to any other vessel or property on any other vessel

6.1.2   delay to or loss of use of any such other vessel or property thereon

6.1.3   general average of, salvage of or salvage under contract of, any such other vessel or property thereon, the Underwriters will pay the Assured such proportion of three-fourths of such sum or sums so paid applying to freight as their respective subscriptions hereto bear to the total amount insured on freight, or to the gross freight earned on the voyage during which the collision occurred if this be greater.

6.2   Provided always that:

6.2.1   liability of the Underwriters in respect of any one such collision shall not exceed their proportionate part of three-fourths of the total amount insured hereon on freight, and in cases in which, with the prior consent in writing of the Underwriters, the liability of the Vessel has been contested or proceedings have been taken to limit liability, they will also pay a like proportion of three-fourths of the costs, appertaining proportionately to the freight portion of damages, which the Assured shall thereby incur or be compelled to pay;

6.2.2   no claim shall attach to this insurance:

6.2.2.1 which attaches to any other insurances covering collision liabilities

6.2.2.2 which is, or would be, recoverable in the terms of the Institute 3/4ths Collision Liability Clause if the Vessel were insured in the terms of such Institute 3/4ths Collision Liability Clause for a value not less than the equivalent in pounds sterling, at the time of commencement of this insurance, of the Vessel's limit of liability calculated in accordance with Article 6.1(b) of the 1976 Limitation Convention,

6.2.3   this Clause 6 shall in no case extend or be deemed to extend to any sum which the Assured may become liable to pay or shall pay for in respect of:

6.2.3.1 removal or disposal, under statutory powers or otherwise, of obstructions, wrecks, cargoes or any other thing whatsoever

6.2.3.2 any real or personal property or thing whatsoever except other vessels or property on other vessels

6.2.3.3 pollution or contamination, or threat thereof, of any real or personal property or thing

whatsoever (except other vessels with which the insured Vessel is in collision or property on such other vessels) or damage to the environment, or threat thereof, save that this exclusion shall not extend to any sum which the Assured shall pay for or in respect of salvage remuneration in which the skill and efforts of the salvors in preventing or minimising damage to the environment as is referred to in Article 13 paragraph 1(b) of the International Convention on Salvage, 1989 have been taken into account

6.2.3.4 the cargo or other property on or the engagements of the Vessel

6.2.3.5 loss of life, personal injury or illness.

7   SISTERSHIP

Should the Vessel named herein come into collision with or receive salvage services from another vessel belonging wholly or in part to the same Owners or under the same management, the Assured shall have the same rights under this insurance as they would have were the other vessel entirely the property of Owners not interested in the Vessel named herein; but in such cases the liability for the collision or the amount payable for the services rendered shall be referred to a sole arbitrator to be agreed upon between the Underwriters and the Assured.

8 GENERAL AVERAGE AND SALVAGE

8.1 This insurance covers the proportion of general average, salvage and/or salvage charges attaching to freight at risk of the Assured, reduced in respect of any under-insurance.

8.2 Adjustment to be according to the law and practice obtaining at the place where the adventure ends. as if the contract of affreightment contains no special terms upon the subject, but where the contract so provides the adjustment shall be according to the York-Antwerp Rules.

8.3 No claim under this Clause 8 shall in any case be allowed where the loss was not incurred to avoid or in connection with the avoidance of a peril insured against.

8.4 No claim under this Clause 8 shall be in any case allowed for or in respect of

8.4.1 special compensation payable to a salvor under Article 14 of the International Convention on Salvage, 1989 or under any other provision in any statute, rule, law or contract which is similar in substance;

8.4.2 expenses or liabilities incurred in respect of damage to the environment, or the threat of such damage, or as a consequence of the escape or release of pollutant substances from the Vessel, or the threat of such escape or release.

8.5 Clause 8.4 shall not however exclude any sum which the Assured shall pay to salvors for or in respect of salvage remuneration in which the skill and efforts of the salvors in preventing or minimising damage to the environment as is referred to in Article 13 paragraph 1(b) of the International Convention on Salvage, 1989 have been taken into account.

9 FRANCHISE

This insurance does not cover partial loss, other than general average loss, under 3% unless caused by fire, sinking, stranding or collision with another vessel. Each craft and/or lighter to be deemed a separate insurance if required by the Assured.

10 MEASURE OF INDEMNITY

10.1 The amount recoverable under this insurance for any claim for loss of freight shall not exceed the gross freight actually lost.

10.2 Where insurances on freight other than this insurance are current at the time of the loss, all such insurances shall be taken into consideration in calculating the liability under this insurance and the amount recoverable hereunder shall not exceed the rateable proportion of the gross freight lost, notwithstanding any valuation in this or any other insurance. In calculating the liability under Clause 8 all insurances on freight shall likewise be taken into consideration.

10.4 Nothing in this Clause 10 shall apply to any claim arising under Clause 12.

11 LOSS OF TIME

This insurance does not cover any claim consequent on loss of time whether arising from a peril of the sea or otherwise.

12 TOTAL LOSS

12.1 In the event of the total loss (actual or constructive) of the Vessel named herein the amount insured shall be paid in full, whether the Vessel be fully or partly loaded or in ballast, chartered or unchartered.

12.2 In ascertaining whether the Vessel is a constructive total loss, the insured value in the insurances on hull and machinery shall be taken as the repaired value and nothing in respect of the damaged or break-up value of the Vessel or wreck shall be taken into account.

12.3 Should the Vessel be a constructive total loss but the claim on the insurances on hull and machinery be settled as a claim for partial loss, no payment shall be due under this Clause 12.

13 ASSIGNMENT

No assignment of or interest in this insurance or in any moneys which may be or become payable thereunder is to be binding on or recognised by the Underwriters unless a dated notice of such assignment or interest signed by the Assured, and by the assignor in the case of subsequent assignment, is endorsed on the Policy and the Policy with such endorsement is produced before payment of any claim or return of premium thereunder.

The following clauses shall be paramount and shall override anything contained in this insurance inconsistent therewith.

14 WAR EXCLUSION

In no case shall this insurance cover loss damage liability or expense caused by

14.1 war civil war revolution rebellion insurrection, or civil strife arising therefrom, or any hostile act by or against a belligerent power

14.2 capture seizure arrest restraint or detainment (barratry and piracy excepted), and the consequences thereof or any attempt thereat

14.3 derelict mines torpedoes bombs or other derelict weapons of war.

15 STRIKES EXCLUSION

In no case shall this insurance cover loss damage liability or expense caused by

15.1 strikers, locked-out workmen, or persons taking part in labour disturbances, riots or civil commotions

15.2 any terrorist or any person acting from a political motive.

16 MALICIOUS ACTS EXCLUSION

In no case shall this insurance cover loss damage liability or expense arising from

16.1   the detonation of an explosive

16.2   any weapon of war and caused by any person acting maliciously or from a political motive.

17 RADIOACTIVE CONTAMINATION EXCLUSION CLAUSE

In no case shall this insurance cover loss damage liability or expense directly or indirectly caused by or contributed to by or arising from

17.1   ionising radiations from or contamination by radioactivity from any nuclear fuel or from any nuclear waste or from the combustion of nuclear fuel

17.2   the radioactive, toxic, explosive or other hazardous or contaminating properties of any nuclear installation, reactor or other nuclear assembly or nuclear component thereof

17.3   any weapon of war employing atomic or nuclear fission and/or fusion or other like reaction or radioactive force or matter.

APPENDIX 15

1/5/61

INSTITUTE DUAL VALUATION CLAUSE

(a) Insured value for purposes of Total Loss (Actual

or Constructive). . . . .£...............................

(b) Insured value for purposes other than Total

Loss . . . .£...............................

In the event of a claim for Actual or Constructive Total Loss (a) shall be taken to be the insured value and payment by the Underwriters of their proportions of that amount shall be for all purposes payment of a Total Loss.

In ascertaining whether the vessel is a Constructive Total Loss (a) shall be taken as the repaired value and nothing in respect of the damaged or break-up value of the vessel or wreck shall be taken into account.

No claim for Constructive Total Loss based upon the cost of recovery and/or repair of the Vessel shall be recoverable hereunder unless such cost would exceed the insured value as in (a).

In no case shall Underwriters' liability in respect of a claim for unrepaired damage exceed the insured value as in (a).

Additional insurances allowed under the Disbursements Clause to be calculated on the amount of the insured value as in (a).

APPENDIX 16

1/11/95

(FOR USE ONLY WITH THE CURRENT MAR POLICY FORM)

INSTITUTE ADDITIONAL PERILS CLAUSES – HULLS

(For use only with the Institute Time Clauses – Hulls 1/11/95)

1 In consideration of an additional premium this insurance is extended to cover

   1.1   the cost of repairing or replacing

   1.1.1 any boiler which bursts or shaft which breaks

   1.1.2 any defective part which has caused loss of or damage to the Vessel covered by Clause 6.2.1 of the Institute Time Clauses – Hulls 1/11/95.

   1.2   loss of or damage to the Vessel caused by any accident or by negligence, incompetence or error of judgment of any person whatsoever.

2 Except as provided in 1.1.1 and 1.1.2, nothing in these Additional Perils Clauses shall allow any claim for the cost of repairing or replacing any part found to be defective as a result of a fault or error in design or construction and which has not caused loss of or damage to the Vessel.

3 The cover provided in Clause 1 is subject to all other terms, conditions and exclusions contained in this insurance and subject to the proviso that the loss or damage has not resulted from want of due diligence by the Assured, Owners or Managers, Masters Officers Crew or Pilots not to be considered Owners within the meaning of this Clause should they hold shares in the Vessel.

APPENDIX 17

1/7/76

INSTITUTE WARRANTIES

1. Warranted no:
    (a)   Atlantic Coast of North America, its rivers or adjacent islands,
        (i)   north of 52° 10' N Lat and west of 50° W Long;
        (ii) south of 52° 10' N Lat in the area bounded by lines drawn between Battle Harbour/Pistolet Bay; Cape Ray/Cape North; Port Hawkesbury/Port Mulgrave and Baie Comeau/Matane between 21st December and 30th April both days inclusive.
        (iii) west of Baie Comeau/Matane (but not west of Montreal) between 1st December and 30th April both days inclusive.
    (b)   Great Lakes or St Lawrence Seaway west of Montreal.
    (c)   Greenland Waters.
    (d)   Pacific Coast of North America its rivers or adjacent islands north of 54° 30' N Lat, or west of 130° 50' W Long

2. Warranted no Baltic Sea or adjacent waters east of 15° E Long:
    (a)   North of a line between Mo (63° 24' N Lat) and Vasa (63° 06' N Lat) between 10th December and 25th May bdi.
    (b)   East of a line between Viipuri (Vyborg) (28° 47' E Long) and Narva (28° 12' E Long) between 15th December and 15th May bdi.
    (c)   North of a line between Stockholm (59° 20' N Lat) and Tallinn (59° 24' N Lat) between 8th January and 5th May bdi.
    (d)   East of 22° E Long, and south of 59° N Lat between 28th December and 5th May bdi.

3. Warranted not North of 70° N Lat other than voyages direct to or from any port or place in Norway or Kola Bay.

4. Warranted no Bering Sea, no East Asian waters north of 46° N Lat and not to enter or sail from any port or place in Siberia except Nakhodka and/or Vladivostock.

5. Warranted not to proceed to Kerguelen and/or Croset Islands or south of 50° S Lat, except to ports and/or places in Patagonia and/or Chile and/or Falkland Islands, but liberty is given to enter waters south of 50° S Lat, if en route to or from ports and/or places not excluded by this warranty.

6. Warranted not to sail with Indian Coal as cargo:
    (a)   between 1st March and 30th June, bdi.
    (b)   between 1st July and 30th September, bdi, except to ports in Asia, not West of Aden or East of or beyond Singapore.

APPENDIX 18

1/8/82

INSTITUTE MALICIOUS DAMAGE CLAUSE

In consideration of an additional premium, it is hereby agreed that the exclusion 'deliberate damage to or deliberate destruction of the subject-matter insured or any part thereof by the wrongful act of any person or persons' is deemed to be deleted and further that this insurance covers loss of or damage to the subject-matter insured caused by malicious acts vandalism or sabotage, subject always to the other exclusions contained in this insurance.

APPENDIX 19

1/12/82

INSTITUTE THEFT, PILFERAGE AND NON-DELIVERY CLAUSE

(For use only with Institute Clauses)

In consideration of an additional premium, it is hereby agreed that this insurance covers loss of or damage to the subject-matter insured caused by theft or pilferage, or by non-delivery of an entire package, subject always to the exclusions contained in this insurance.

APPENDIX 20

1/11/95

(FOR USE ONLY WITH THE CURRENT MAR POLICY FORM)

INSTITUTE WAR AND STRIKES CLAUSES

HULLS–TIME

This insurance is subject to English law and practice

1 PERILS

Subject always to the exclusions hereinafter referred to, this insurance covers loss of or damage to the Vessel caused by

1.1 war civil war revolution rebellion insurrection, or civil strife arising therefrom, or any hostile act by or against a belligerent power

1.2 capture seizure arrest restraint or detainment. and the consequences thereof or any attempt thereat

1.3 derelict mines torpedoes bombs or other derelict weapons of war

1.4 strikers, locked-out workmen, or persons taking part in labour disturbances, riots or civil commotions

1.5 any terrorist or any person acting maliciously or from a political motive

1.6 confiscation or expropriation.

2 INCORPORATION

The Institute Time Clauses–Hulls 1/11/95 (including 3/4ths Collision Liability Clause amended to 4/4ths) except Clauses 1.4, 2, 3, 4, 5, 6, 12, 22,1.8, 23, 24, 25, 26 and 27 are deemed to be incorporated in this insurance in so far as they do not conflict with the provisions of these clauses.

Held covered in case of breach of warranty as to towage or salvage services provided notice be given to the Underwriters immediately after receipt of advices and any additional premium required by them be agreed.

3 DETAINMENT

In the event that the Vessel shall have been the subject of capture seizure arrest restraint detainment confiscation or expropriation, and the Assured shall thereby have lost the free use and disposal of the Vessel for a continuous period of 12 months then for the purpose of ascertaining whether the Vessel is a constructive total loss the Assured shall be deemed to have been deprived of the possession of the Vessel without any likelihood of recovery.

4 NOTICE OF CLAIM AND TENDERS

In the event of accident whereby loss or damage may result in a claim under this insurance, notice must be given to the Underwriters promptly after the date on which the Assured, Owners or Managers become or should have become aware of the loss or damage and prior to survey so that a surveyor may be appointed if the Underwriters so desire. If notice is not given to Underwriters within twelve months of that date unless the Underwriters agree to the contrary in writing, the Underwriters will be automatically discharged from liability for any claim under this insurance in respect of or arising out of such accident or the loss or damage.

5 EXCLUSIONS

This insurance excludes

5.1   loss damage liability or expense arising from

5.1.1   the outbreak of war (whether there be a declaration of war or not) between any of the following countries:

United Kingdom, United States of America, France, the Russian Federation, the People's Republic of China

5.1.2   requisition, either for title or use, or pre-emption

5.1.3   capture seizure arrest restraint detainment confiscation or expropriation by or under the order of the government or any public or local authority of the country in which the Vessel is owned or registered

5.1.4   arrest restraint detainment confiscation or expropriation under quarantine regulations or by reason of infringement of any customs or trading regulations

5.1.5   the operation of ordinary judicial process, failure to provide security or to pay any fine or penalty or any financial cause

5.1.6   piracy (but this exclusion shall not affect cover under Clause 1.4),

5.2   loss damage liability or expense directly or indirectly caused by or contributed to by or arising from

5.2.1   ionising radiations from or contamination by radioactivity from any nuclear fuel or from any nuclear waste or from the combustion of nuclear fuel

5.2.2   the radioactive, toxic, explosive or other hazardous or contaminating properties of any nuclear installation, reactor or other nuclear assembly or nuclear component thereof

5.2.3   any weapon of war employing atomic or nuclear fission and/or fusion or other like reaction or radioactive force or matter.

5.3   loss damage liability or expense covered by the Institute Time Clauses–Hulls 1/11/95 (including 3/4ths Collision Liability Clause amended to 4/4ths) or which would be recoverable thereunder but for Clause 12 thereof,

5.4 any claim for any sum recoverable under any other insurance on the Vessel or which would be recoverable under such insurance but for the existence of this insurance,

5.5 any claim for expenses arising from delay except such expenses as would be recoverable in principle in English law and practice under the York-Antwerp Rules 1994.

6 TERMINATION

6.1 This insurance may be cancelled by either the Underwriters or the Assured giving 7 days notice (such cancellation becoming effective on the expiry of 7 days from midnight of the day on which notice of cancellation is issued by or to the Underwriters). The Underwriters agree however to reinstate this insurance subject to agreement between the Underwriters and the Assured prior to the expiry of such notice of cancellation as to new rate of premium and/or conditions and/or warranties.

6.2 Whether or not such notice of cancellation has been given this insurance shall TERMINATE AUTOMATICALLY

6.2.1 upon the outbreak of war (whether there be a declaration of war or not) between any of the following countries:

United Kingdom, United States of America, France, the Russian Federation, the People's Republic of China

6.2.2 in the event of the Vessel being requisitioned, either for title or use.

6.3 In the event either of cancellation by notice or of automatic termination of this insurance by reason of the operation of this Clause 6, or of the sale of the Vessel, pro rata net return of premium shall be payable to the Assured.

This insurance shall not become effective if, subsequent to its acceptance by the Underwriters and prior to the intended time of its attachment, there has occurred any event which would have automatically terminated this insurance under the provisions of Clause 6 above.

1/1/82

INSTITUTE WAR CLAUSES (CARGO)

RISKS COVERED

1   This insurance covers, except as provided in Clauses 3 and 4 below, loss of or damage to the subject-matter insured caused by

   1.1   war civil war revolution rebellion insurrection, or civil strife arising therefrom, or any hostile act by or against a belligerent power

   1.2   capture seizure arrest restraint or detainment, arising from risks covered under 1.1 above, and the consequences thereof or any attempt thereat

   1.3   derelict mines torpedoes bombs or other derelict weapons of war.

2   This insurance covers general average and salvage charges, adjusted or determined according to the contract of affreightment and/or the governing law and practice, incurred to avoid or in connection with the avoidance of loss from a risk covered under these clauses.

EXCLUSIONS

3   In no case shall this insurance cover

   3.1   loss damage or expense attributable to wilful misconduct of the Assured

   3 2   ordinary leakage, ordinary loss in weight or volume, or ordinary wear and tear of the subject-matter insured

   3.3   loss damage or expense caused by insufficiency or unsuitability of packing or preparation of the subject-matter insured (for the purpose of this Clause 3.3 'packing' shall be deemed to include stowage in a container or liftvan but only when such stowage is carried out prior to attachment of this insurance or by the Assured or their servants)

   3.4   loss damage or expense caused by inherent vice or nature of the subject-matter insured

   3.5   loss damage or expense proximately caused by delay, even though the delay be caused by a risk insured against (except expenses payable under Clause 2 above)

   3.6   loss damage or expense arising from insolvency or financial default of the owners managers charterers or operators of the vessel

   3.7   any claim based upon loss of or frustration of the voyage or adventure

   3.8   loss damage or expense arising from any hostile use of any weapon of war employing atomic or nuclear fission and/or fusion or other like reaction or radioactive force or matter.

4   4.1   In no case shall this insurance cover loss damage or expense arising from

unseaworthiness of vessel or craft,

unfitness of vessel craft conveyance container or liftvan for the safe carriage of the subject-matter insured,

where the Assured or their servants are privy to such unseaworthiness or unfitness, at the time the subject-matter insured is loaded therein.

4.2   The Underwriters waive any breach of the implied warranties of seaworthiness of the ship and fitness of the ship to carry the subject-matter insured to destination, unless the Assured or their servants are privy to such unseaworthiness or unfitness.

DURATION

5   5.1   This insurance

5.1.1   attaches only as the subject-matter insured and as to any part as that part is loaded on an oversea vessel

and

5.1.2   terminates, subject to 5.2 and 5.3 below, either as the subject-matter insured and as to any part as that part is discharged from an oversea vessel at the final port or place of discharge,

or

on expiry of 15 days counting from midnight of the day of arrival of the vessel at the final port or place of discharge,

whichever shall first occur;

nevertheless,

subject to prompt notice to the Underwriters and to an additional premium, such insurance

5.1.3   reattaches when, without having discharged the subject-matter insured at the final port or place of discharge, the vessel sails therefrom,

and

5.1.4   terminates subject to 5.2 and 5.3 below, either as the subject-matter insured and as to any part as that part is thereafter discharged from the vessel at the final (or substituted) port or place of discharge,

or

on expiry of 15 days counting from midnight of the day of re-arrival of the vessel at the final port or place of discharge or arrival of the vessel at a substituted port or place of discharge, whichever shall first occur.

5.2   If during the insured voyage the oversea vessel arrives at an intermediate port or place to discharge the subject-matter insured for on-carriage by oversea vessel or by aircraft, or the goods are discharged from the vessel at a port or place of refuge, then, subject to 5.3 below and to an additional premium if required, this insurance continues until the expiry of 15 days counting from midnight of the day of arrival of the vessel at such port or place, but thereafter reattaches as the subject-matter insured and as to any part as that part is loaded on an on-carrying oversea vessel or aircraft. During the period of 15 days the insurance remains in force after discharge only whilst the subject-matter insured and as to any part as that part is at such port or place. If the goods are on-carried within the said period of 15 days or if the insurance reattaches as provided in this Clause 5.2

5.2.1   where the on-carriage is by oversea vessel this insurance continues subject to the terms of these clauses,

or

5.2.2   where the on-carriage is by aircraft, the current Institute War Clauses (Air Cargo) (excluding sendings by Post) shall be deemed to form part of this insurance and shall apply to the on-carriage by air.

5.3   If the voyage in the contract of carriage is terminated at a port or place other than the destination agreed therein, such port or place shall be deemed the final port of discharge and such insurance terminates in accordance with 5.1.2. If the subject-matter insured is subsequently reshipped to the original or any other destination, then provided notice is given to the Underwriters before the commencement of such further transit and subject to an additional premium, such insurance reattaches

5.3.1   in the case of the subject-matter insured having been discharged, as the subject-matter insured and as to any part as that part is loaded on the on-carrying vessel for the voyage;

5.3.2   in the case of the subject-matter not having been discharged, when the vessel sails from such deemed final port of discharge; thereafter such insurance terminates in accordance with 5.1.4.

5.4   The insurance against the risks of mines and derelict torpedoes, floating or submerged, is extended whilst the subject-matter insured or any part thereof is on craft whilst in transit to or from the oversea vessel, but in no case beyond the expiry of 60 days after discharge from the oversea vessel unless otherwise specially agreed by the Underwriters.

5.5   *Subject to prompt notice to Underwriters, and to an additional premium if required*, this insurance shall remain in force within the provisions of these Clauses during any deviation, or any variation of the adventure arising from the exercise of a liberty granted to shipowners or charterers under the contract of affreightment

(For the purpose of Clause 5

'arrival' shall be deemed to mean that the vessel is anchored, moored or otherwise secured at a berth or place within the Harbour Authority area. If such a berth or place is not available, arrival is deemed to have occurred when the vessel first anchors, moors or otherwise secures either at or off the intended port or place of discharge 'oversea vessel' shall be deemed to mean a vessel carrying the subject-matter from one port or place to another where such voyage involves a sea passage by that vessel)

6 Where, after attachment of this insurance, the destination is changed by the Assured, *held covered at a premium and on conditions to be arranged subject to prompt notice being given to the Underwriters.*

7 **Anything contained in this contract which is inconsistent with Clauses 3.7, 3.8 or 5 shall, to the extent of such inconsistency, be null and void.**

CLAIMS

8 8.1 In order to recover under this insurance the Assured must have an insurable interest in the Insurable subject-matter insured at the time of the loss.

 8.2 Subject to 8.1 above, the Assured shall be entitled to recover for insured loss occurring during the period covered by this insurance, notwithstanding that the loss occurred before the contract of insurance was concluded, unless the Assured were aware of the loss and the Underwriters were not.

9 9.1 If any Increased Value insurance is effected by the Assured on the cargo insured herein the Increased agreed value of the cargo shall be deemed to be increased to the total amount insured under this Value insurance and all insurances covering the loss, and liability under this insurance shall be in such proportion as the sum insured herein bears to such total amount insured.

 In the event of claim the Assured shall provide the Underwriters with evidence. of the amounts insured under all other insurances.

 9.2 **Where this insurance is on Increased Value the following clause shall apply:**

 The agreed value of the cargo shall be deemed to be equal to the total amount insured under the primary insurance and all Increased Value insurances covering the loss and effected on the cargo by the Assured, and liability under this insurance shall be in such proportion as the sum insured herein bears to such total amount insured.

 In the event of claim the Assured shall provide the Underwriters with evidence of the amounts insured under all other insurances.

BENEFIT OF INSURANCE

10 This insurance shall not inure to the benefit of the carrier or other bailee.

MINIMISING LOSSES

11 It is the duty of the Assured and their servants and agents in respect of loss recoverable hereunder

 11.1 to take such measures as may be reasonable for the purpose of averting or minimising such loss,

 and

11.2   to ensure that all rights against carriers, bailees or other third parties are properly preserved and exercised

and the Underwriters will, in addition to any loss recoverable hereunder, reimburse the Assured for any charges properly and reasonably incurred in pursuance of these duties.

12 Measures taken by the Assured or the Underwriters with the object of saving, protecting or recovering the subject-matter insured shall not be considered as a waiver or acceptance of abandonment or otherwise prejudice the rights of either party.

AVOIDANCE OF DELAY

13 It is a condition of this insurance that the Assured shall act with reasonable despatch in all circumstances within their control.

LAW AND PRACTICE

14 This insurance is subject to English law and practice.

NOTE— *It is necessary for the Assured when they become aware of an event which is 'held covered' under this insurance (o give prompt notice to the Underwriters and the right to such cover is dependent upon compliance with this obligation.*

1/1/82

INSTITUTE STRIKES CLAUSES (CARGO)

RISKS COVERED

1   This insurance covers, except as provided in Clauses 3 and 4 below, loss of or damage to the subject-matter insured caused by

   1.1   strikers, locked-out workmen, or persons taking part in labour disturbances, riots or civil commotions

   1.2   any terrorist or any person acting from a political motive.

2   This insurance covers general average and salvage charges, adjusted or determined according to the contract of affreightment and/or the governing law and practice, incurred to avoid or in connection with the avoidance of loss from a risk covered under these clauses.

EXCLUSIONS

3   In no case shall this insurance cover

   3.1   loss damage or expense attributable to wilful misconduct of the Assured

   3.2   ordinary leakage, ordinary loss in weight or volume, or ordinary wear and tear of the subject-matter insured

   3.3   loss damage or expense caused by insufficiency or unsuitability of packing or preparation of the subject-matter insured (for the purpose of this Clause 3.3 'packing' shall be deemed to include stowage in a container or liftvan but only when such stowage is carried out prior to attachment of this insurance or by the Assured or their servants)

   3.4   loss damage or expense caused by inherent vice or nature of the subject-matter insured

   3.5   loss damage or expense proximately caused by delay, even though the delay be caused by a risk insured against (except expenses payable under Clause 2 above)

   3.6   loss damage or expense arising from insolvency or financial default of the owners managers charterers or operators of the vessel

   3.7   loss damage or expense arising from the absence shortage or withholding of labour of any description whatsoever resulting from any strike, lockout, labour disturbance, riot or civil commotion

   3.8   any claim based upon loss of or frustration of the voyage or adventure

   3.9   loss damage or expense arising from the use of any weapon of war employing atomic or nuclear fission and/or fusion or other like reaction or radioactive force or matter

3.10   loss damage or expense caused by war civil war revolution rebellion insurrection, or civil strife arising therefrom, or any hostile act by or against a belligerent power.

4   4.1   In no case shall this insurance cover loss damage or expense arising from

unseaworthiness of vessel or craft,

unfitness of vessel craft conveyance container or liftvan for the safe carriage of the subject-matter insured,

where the Assured or their servants are privy to such unseaworthiness or unfitness, at the time the subject-matter insured is loaded therein.

4.2   The Underwriters waive any breach of the implied warranties of seaworthiness of the ship and fitness of the ship to carry the subject-matter insured to destination, unless the Assured or their servants are privy to such unseaworthiness or unfitness.

DURATION

5   5.1   This insurance attaches from the time the goods leave the warehouse or place of storage at the place named herein for the commencement of the transit, continues during the ordinary course of transit and terminates either

5.1.1   on delivery to the Consignees' or other final warehouse or place of storage at the destination named herein,

5.1.2   on delivery to any other warehouse or place of storage, whether prior to or at the destination named herein, which the Assured elect to use either

5.1.2.1   for storage other than in the ordinary course of transit or

5.1.2.2   for allocation or distribution,

or

5.1.3   on the expiry of 60 days after completion of discharge overside of the goods hereby insured from the oversea vessel at the final port of discharge,

whichever shall first occur.

5.2   If, after discharge overside from the oversea vessel at the final port of discharge, but prior to termination of this insurance, the goods are to be forwarded to a destination other than that to which they are insured hereunder, this insurance, whilst remaining subject to termination as provided for above, shall not extend beyond the commencement of transit to such other destination.

5.3   This insurance shall remain in force (subject to termination as provided for above and to the provisions of Clause 6 below) during delay beyond the control of the Assured, any deviation forced discharge, reshipment or transhipment and during any variation of the adventure arising from the exercise of a liberty granted to shipowners or charterers under the contract of affreightment.

6   If owing to circumstances beyond the control of the Assured either the contract of carriage is terminated at a port or place other than the destination named therein or the transit is otherwise terminated before delivery of the goods as provided for in Clause 5 above, then this insurance shall also terminate unless prompt notice is given to the Underwriters and continuation of cover is requested when the insurance shall remain in force, subject to an additional premium if required by the Underwriters, either

6.1   until the goods are sold and delivered at such port or place, or, unless otherwise specially agreed, until the expiry of 60 days after arrival of the goods hereby insured at such port or place, whichever shall first occur,

or

6.2   if the goods are forwarded within the said period of 60 days (or any agreed extension thereof) to the destination named herein or to any other destination, until terminated in accordance with the provisions of Clause 5 above.

7   Where, after attachment of this insurance, the destination is changed by the Assured, *held covered at a premium and on conditions to be arranged subject to prompt notice being given to the Underwriters.*

CLAIMS

8   8.1   In order to recover under this insurance the Assured must have an insurable interest in the subject-matter insured at the time of the loss.

8.2   Subject to 8.1 above, the Assured shall be entitled to recover for insured loss occurring during the period covered by this insurance, notwithstanding that the loss occurred before the contract of insurance was concluded, unless the Assured were aware of the loss and the Underwriters were not.

9   9.1   If any Increased Value insurance is effected by the Assured on the cargo insured herein the agreed value of the cargo shall be deemed to be increased to the total amount insured under this insurance and all Increased Value insurances covering the loss, and liability under this insurance shall be in such proportion as the sum insured herein bears to such total amount insured.

In the event of claim the Assured shall provide the Underwriters with evidence of the amounts insured under all other insurances.

9.2   **Where this insurance is on Increased Value the following clause shall apply:**

The agreed value of the cargo shall be deemed to be equal to the total amount insured under the primary insurance and all Increased Value insurances covering the loss and effected on the cargo by the Assured, and liability under this insurance shall be in such proportion as the sum insured herein bears to such total amount insured.

In the event of claim the Assured shall provide the Underwriters with evidence of the amounts insured under all other insurances.

BENEFIT OF INSURANCE

10 This insurance shall not inure to the benefit of the carrier or other bailee.

MINIMISING LOSSES

11 It is the duty of the Assured and their servants and agents in respect of loss recoverable hereunder

11.1 to take such measures as may be reasonable for the purpose of averting or minimising such loss,

and

11.2 to ensure that all rights against carriers, bailees or other third parties are properly preserved and exercised

and the Underwriters will, in addition to any loss recoverable hereunder, reimburse the Assured for any charges properly and reasonably incurred in pursuance of these duties.

12 Measures taken by the Assured or the Underwriters with the object of saving, protecting or recovering the subject-matter insured shall not be considered as a waiver or acceptance of abandonment or otherwise prejudice the rights of either party.

AVOIDANCE OF DELAY

13 It is a condition of this insurance that the Assured shall act with reasonable despatch in all circumstances within their control.

LAW AND PRACTICE

14 This insurance is subject to English law and practice.

NOTE— *It is necessary for the Assured when they become aware of an event which is 'held covered' under this insurance to give prompt notice to the Underwriters and the right to such cover is dependent upon compliance with this obligation.*

APPENDIX 23

30/5/86

INSTITUTE MORTGAGEES INTEREST CLAUSES

HULLS

This contract is subject to English law and practice

1   SUBJECT-MATTER INSURED

1.1   This contract commences on .... and is to insure, subject to the conditions stated herein, the interest of .... as first mortgagees, in vessels to be declared for periods not in excess of 12 months each declaration.

1.2   This contract does not cover the interest of any other party and is not assignable or otherwise transferable.

2   DECLARATIONS

Subject to the provisions of Clause 3 it is a condition of this contract that the Assured must declare, without exception and the Underwriters must accept, all interest by way of first mortgage in any vessel or vessels, giving provisional notice of the name(s) of the vessel(s) and their owner(s) and the amount(s) of the loan(s).

3   SUM INSURED

This contract is for an open amount not to exceed .... in respect of any one vessel unless specially agreed. In the event of loss after provisional but before final declaration the basis of valuation shall be the amount of the loan not exceeding the sound market value of the vessel at the time of the granting of the loan.

4   WARRANTIES

It is warranted in respect of each vessel that:

4.1   Hull and Machinery Policies on terms equivalent to Institute Time Clauses Hulls or American Institute Hull Clauses and where applicable Increased Value Policies equivalent to Institute Time Clauses–Hulls Disbursements and Increased Value (Total Loss Only including Excess Liabilities) or American Institute Increased Value and Excess Liabilities Clauses, also War Risks Policies equivalent to Institute War and Strikes Clauses Hulls–Time and full Protection and Indemnity Risks (hereafter referred to as 'the Owners' Policies and Club Entries') have been taken out and shall be maintained throughout the currency of this contract.

4.2   the Owners' Policies and Club Entries, warranted in 4.1 above shall be taken out and maintained in respect of each vessel at all times for an insured value and limit of liability not less than the amount insured hereunder or the amount of the outstanding loan.

4.3   each of the Owners' Policies and Club Entries is endorsed to the extent of the Assured's interest.

5   CHANCE OF OWNERSHIP OR CONTROL

This insurance will terminate automatically at the time of any change of ownership, management or control, of which the Assured hereunder has knowledge or privity, unless the Assured gives prompt notice of such change in writing to the Underwriters hereon and agrees to pay an additional premium, if required.

6   INDEMNITY

6.1   This contract is to indemnify the Assured for loss resulting from loss of or damage to or liability of each vessel which is prima facie covered by the Owners' Policies or Club Entries but in respect of which there is subsequent non-payment (or reduced payment which is approved in advance by the Underwriters hereon):

6.1.1   by reason of any act or omission of any one or more of the Owners, Operators, Charterers or Managers of the vessel or their servants or agents including breach or alleged breach of warranty or condition whether expressed or implied or non-disclosure or alleged non-disclosure of any fact or circumstances of any kind whatsoever.

6.1.2   by virtue of any alleged deliberate, negligent or accidental act or omission or any knowledge or privity of any one or more of the Owners, Operators, Charterers or Managers of the vessel or their servants or agents, including the deliberate or negligent casting away or damaging of the vessel or the vessel being unseaworthy.

6.2   The cover provided under Clause 6.1 above shall only apply while any such act, omission, non-disclosure breach of warranty or conditions, knowledge or privity occurs or exists without the privity of the Assured.

6.3   The indemnity payable hereunder shall be an amount equal to whichever shall be the least of

6.3.1   the unrecoverable claim or part thereof under Owners' Policies and/or Club Entries

6.3.2   the outstanding indebtedness under the declared loan at the time for payment under Clause 8 hereof

6.3.3   the sum insured,

provided that if the subject-matter insured is not fully insured hereunder by reason of Clause 3 or otherwise, the indemnity shall be reduced in proportion to the under-insurance.

7 EXCLUSIONS

7.1 Excluding the Assured's legal costs and expenses incurred in relation to any claim under Hull Policies and/or Club Entries.

7.2 In no case shall this insurance cover loss damage liability or expense arising from:

7.2.1 the relevant Owners' Policies or Club Entries having been lawfully terminated by the Underwriters thereof due to non-payment of premium or call

7.2.2 insolvency or financial default of any of the Underwriters of the Owners' Policies or Club Entries

7.2.3 inability of any party to transmit funds

7.2.4 any fluctuation in exchange rates

7.2.5 the operation of any franchise deductible or provision for self-insurance.

8 TIME FOR PAYMENT

8.1 There shall be deemed to be a non-payment by the Underwriters of the Owners' Policies and/or Club Entries

8.1.1 when a final court judgment is delivered in favour of those Underwriters, or

8.1.2 at such earlier time as the Assured can demonstrate to the satisfaction of the Underwriters hereon that there is no reasonable prospect of the owners and/or Assured succeeding in the claim against the Underwriters of the Owners' Policies and/or Club Entries. In the event of disagreement between the Assured and the Underwriters hereon this issue shall be referred to a sole arbitrator to be agreed upon between the Underwriters hereon and the Assured.

8.2 Thereafter the Assured shall formally present their claim hereunder and any amount recoverable hereunder shall be payable within three calendar months of the date on which the Assured shall have presented their properly documented claim to the Underwriters of this contract.

9 SUBROGATION

9.1 Upon payment to the Assured of a claim hereunder the Underwriters shall be subrogated to all the rights and remedies of the Assured in respect of such payment.

9.2 It is a condition of this contract that any payment(s) by the Underwriters shall not be applied by the Assured in or towards discharge or satisfaction of the outstanding indebtedness.

10 DUTY OF ASSURED (SUE & LABOUR)

10.1 It is a condition of this insurance that the Assured shall give notice in writing to the Underwriters hereon of any circumstances which may give rise to a claim under this contract and shall thereafter keep the Underwriters fully informed of all developments.

10.2   It is the duty of the Assured and their servants and agents to take such measures as may be reasonable for the purpose of averting or minimising a loss which would be recoverable under this contract.

10.3   Except as provided in Clause 7.1 the Underwriters will reimburse charges properly and reasonably incurred by the Assured their servants or agents for such measures provided that if the subject-matter insured is not fully insured by reason of Clause 3 or otherwise, the indemnity shall be reduced in proportion to the under-insurance.

10.4   Measures taken by the Assured or the Underwriters with the object of averting or minimising a loss which would be recoverable under this contract shall not be considered as a waiver or acceptance of a claim or otherwise prejudice the rights of either party.

10.5   The sum recoverable under this Clause 10 shall be in addition to the loss otherwise recoverable under this contract.

11 CANCELLATION

This contract may be cancelled by either the Underwriters or the Assured giving thirty days notice in writing. Notice to commence from midnight of the day when it is issued but such cancellation shall not apply to any risks which have attached in accordance with the cover granted hereunder before the cancellation becomes effective.

12 AUTOMATIC TERMINATION AND NOTICE OF CANCELLATION–WAR AND STRIKES RISKS

Cover hereunder in respect of the risks which are covered by the Institute War and Strikes Clauses Hulls–Time 1/10/83 shall terminate

12.1   automatically upon the occurrence of any of the events mentioned in Clauses 5.2.1 and 5.2.2 of the Termination Clause in the Institute War and Strikes Clauses Hulls–Time 1/10/83.

12.2   in respect of any vessel

12.2.1 automatically in the event of the vessel being requisitioned either for title or use

12.2.2 7 days after the Underwriters of Owners' War Risks Insurances or any of them have given notice of cancellation, or

12.2.3 7 days after the Underwriters hereon have given notice of cancellation in respect of the said risks.

12.3   Cancellation in accordance with Clauses 12.2.2 or 12.2.3 shall become effective on the expiry of 7 days from midnight of the day on which the notice of cancellation is given. The Underwriters agree however to reinstate this insurance subject to agreement between the Underwriters and the Assured prior to the expiry of such notice of cancellation as to new rate of premium and/or conditions and/or warranties.

YORK-ANTWERP RULES 1994

Rule of Interpretation

In the adjustment of general average the following Rules shall apply to the exclusion of any Law and Practice inconsistent therewith.

Except as provided by the Rule Paramount and the numbered Rules, general average shall be adjusted according to the lettered Rules.

Rule Paramount

In no case shall there be any allowance for sacrifice or expenditure unless reasonably made or incurred.

Rule A

There is a general average act when, and only when, any extraordinary sacrifice or expenditure is intentionally and reasonably made or incurred for the common safety for the purpose of preserving from peril the property involved in a common maritime adventure.

General average sacrifices and expenditures shall be borne by the different contributing interests on the basis hereinafter provided.

Rule B

There is a common maritime adventure when one or more vessels are towing or pushing another vessel or vessels, provided that they are all involved in commercial activities and not in a salvage operation.

When measures are taken to preserve the vessels and their cargoes, if any, from a common peril, these Rules shall apply.

A vessel is not in common peril with another vessel or vessels if by simply disconnecting from the other vessel or vessels she is in safety; but if the disconnection is itself a general average act the common maritime adventure continues.

Rule C

Only such losses, damages or expenses which are the direct consequence of the general average act shall be allowed as general average.

In no case shall there be any allowance in general average for losses, damages or expenses incurred in respect of damage to the environment or in consequence of the escape or release of pollutant substances from the property involved in the common maritime adventure.

Demurrage, loss of market, and any loss or damage sustained or expense incurred by reason of delay, whether on the voyage or subsequently, and any indirect loss whatsoever, shall not be admitted as general average.

Rule D

Rights to contribution in general average shall not be affected, though the event which gave rise to the sacrifice or expenditure may have been due to the fault of one of the parties to the adventure; but this shall not prejudice any remedies or defences which may be open against or to that party in respect of such fault.

Rule E

The onus of proof is upon the party claiming in general average to show that the loss or expense claimed is properly allowable as general average.

All parties claiming in general average shall give notice in writing to the average adjuster of the loss or expense in respect of which they claim contribution within 12 months of the date of the termination of the common maritime adventure.

Failing such notification, or if within 12 months of a request for the same any of the parties shall fail to supply evidence in support of a notified claim, or particulars of value in respect of a contributory interest, the average adjuster shall be at liberty to estimate the extent of the allowance or the contributory value on the basis of the information available to him, which estimate may be challenged only on the ground that it is manifestly incorrect.

Rule F

Any additional expense incurred in place of another expense which would have been allowable as general average shall be deemed to be general average and so allowed without regard to the saving, if any, to other interests, but only up to the amount of the general average expense avoided.

Rule G

General average shall be adjusted as regards both loss and contribution upon the basis of values at the time and place when and where the adventure ends.

This rule shall not affect the determination of the place at which the average statement is to be made up.

When a ship is at any port or place in circumstances which would give rise to an allowance in general average under the provisions of Rules X and XI, and the cargo or part thereof is forwarded to destination by other means, rights and liabilities in general average shall, subject to cargo interests being notified if practicable, remain as nearly as possible the same as they would have been in the absence of such forwarding, as if the adventure had continued in the original ship for so long as justifiable under the contract of affreightment and the applicable law.

The proportion attaching to cargo of the allowances made in general average by reason of applying the third paragraph of this Rule shall not exceed the cost which would have been borne by the owners of cargo if the cargo had been forwarded at their expense.

Rule I – Jettison of Cargo

No jettison of cargo shall be made good as general average, unless such cargo is carried in accordance with the recognised custom of the trade.

Rule II – Loss or Damage by Sacrifices for the Common Safety

Loss of or damage to the property involved in the common maritime adventure by or in consequence of a sacrifice made for the common safety, and by water which goes down a ship's hatches opened or other opening made for the purpose of making a jettison for the common safety, shall be made good as general average.

Rule III – Extinguishing Fire on Shipboard

Damage done to a ship and cargo, or either of them, by water or otherwise, including damage by beaching or scuttling a burning ship, in extinguishing a fire on board the ship, shall be made good as general average; except that no compensation shall be made for damage by smoke however caused or by heat of the fire.

Rule IV – Cutting away Wreck

Loss or damage sustained by cutting away wreck or parts of the ship which have previously carried away or are effectively lost by accident shall not be made good as general average.

Rule V – Voluntary Stranding

When a ship is intentionally run on shore for the common safety, whether or not she might have been driven on shore, the consequent loss or damage to the property involved in the common maritime adventure shall be allowed in general average.

Rule VI – Salvage Remuneration

(a) Expenditure incurred by the parties to the adventure in the nature of salvage, whether under contract or otherwise, shall be allowed in general average provided that the salvage operations were carried out for the purpose of preserving from peril the property involved in the common maritime adventure.

Expenditure allowed in general average shall include any salvage remuneration in which the skill and efforts of the salvors in preventing or minimising damage to the environment such as is referred to in Article 13 paragraph 1(b) of the International Convention on Salvage, 1989 have been taken into account.

(b) Special compensation payable to a salvor by the shipowner under Article 14 of the said Convention to the extent specified in paragraph 4 of that Article or under any other provision similar in substance shall not be allowed in general average.

Rule VII – Damage to Machinery and Boilers

Damage caused to any machinery and boilers of a ship which is ashore and in a position of peril, in endeavouring to refloat, shall be allowed in general average when shown to have arisen from an actual intention to float the ship for the common safety at the risk of such damage; but where a ship is afloat no loss or damage caused by working the propelling machinery and boilers shall in any circumstances be made good as general average.

Rule VIII – Expenses lightening a Ship when Ashore, and Consequent Damage

When a ship is ashore and cargo and ship's fuel and stores or any of them are discharged as a general average act, the extra cost of lightening, lighter hire and reshipping (if incurred), and any loss or damage to the property involved in the common maritime adventure in consequence thereof, shall be admitted as general average.

Rule IX – Cargo, Ship's Materials and Stores used for Fuel

Cargo, ship's materials and stores, or any of them, necessarily used for fuel for the common safety at a time of peril shall be admitted as general average, but when such an allowance is made for the cost of ship's materials and stores the general average shall be credited with the estimated cost of the fuel which would otherwise have been consumed in prosecuting the intended voyage.

Rule X – Expenses at Port of Refuge etc

(a) When a ship shall have entered a port or place of refuge or shall have returned to her port or place of loading in consequence of accident, sacrifice or other extraordinary circumstances which render that necessary for the common safety, the expenses of entering such port or place shall be admitted as general average; and when she shall have sailed thence with her original cargo, or a part of it, the corresponding expenses of leaving such port or place consequent upon such entry or return shall likewise be admitted as general average.

When a ship is at any port or place of refuge and is necessarily removed to another port or place because repairs cannot be carried out in the first port or place, the provisions of this Rule shall be applied to the second port or place as if it were a port or place of refuge and the cost of such removal including temporary repairs and towage shall be admitted as general average. The provisions of Rule XI shall be applied to the prolongation of the voyage occasioned by such removal.

(b) The cost of handling on board or discharging cargo, fuel or stores whether at a port or place of loading, call or refuge, shall be admitted as general average, when the handling or discharge was necessary for the common safety or to enable damage to the ship caused by sacrifice or accident to be repaired, if the repairs were necessary for the safe prosecution of the voyage, except in cases where the damage to the ship is discovered at a port or place of loading or call without any accident or other extraordinary circumstances connected with such damage having taken place during the voyage.

The cost of handling on board or discharging cargo, fuel or stores shall not be admissible as general average when incurred solely for the purpose of restowage due to shifting during the voyage, unless such restowage is necessary for the common safety.

(c) Whenever the cost of handling or discharging cargo, fuel or stores is admissible as general average, the costs of storage, including insurance if reasonably incurred, reloading and stowing of such cargo, fuel or stores shall likewise be admitted as general average. The provisions of Rule XI shall be applied to the extra period of detention occasioned by such reloading or restowing.

But when the ship is condemned or does not proceed on her original voyage, storage expenses shall be admitted as general average only up to the date of the ship's condemnation or of the abandonment of the voyage or up to the date of completion of discharge of cargo if the condemnation or abandonment takes place before that date.

Rule XI – Wages and Maintenance of Crew and other expenses bearing up for and in a port of refuge etc

(a) Wages and maintenance of master, officers and crew reasonably incurred and fuel and stores consumed during the prolongation of the voyage occasioned by a ship entering a port or place of refuge or returning to her port or place of loading shall be admitted as general average when the expenses of entering such port or place are allowable in general average in accordance with Rule X(a).

(b) When a ship shall have entered or been detained in any port or place in consequence of accident, sacrifice or other extraordinary circumstances which render that necessary for the common safety, or to enable damage to the ship caused by sacrifice or accident to be repaired, if the repairs were necessary for the safe prosecution of the voyage, the wages and maintenance of the master, officers and crew reasonably incurred during the extra period of detention in such port or place until the ship shall or should have been made ready to proceed upon her voyage, shall be admitted in general average

Fuel and stores consumed during the period of detention shall be admitted as general average, except such fuel and stores as are consumed in effecting repairs not allowable in general average.

Port charges incurred during the extra period of detention shall likewise be admitted as general average except such charges as are incurred solely by reason of repairs not allowable in general average.

Provided that when damage to the ship is discovered at a port or place of loading or call without any accident or other extraordinary circumstance connected with such damage having taken place during the voyage, then the wages and maintenance of master, officers and crew and fuel and stores consumed and port charges incurred during the extra detention for repairs to damages so discovered shall not be admissible as general average, even if the repairs are necessary for the safe prosecution of the voyage.

When the ship is condemned or does not proceed on her original voyage, the wages and maintenance of the master, officers and crew and fuel and stores consumed shall and port charges be admitted as general average only up to the date of the ship's condemnation or of the abandonment of the voyage or up to the date of completion of discharge of cargo if the condemnation or abandonment takes place before that date.

(c) For the purpose of this and the other Rules wages shall include all payments made to or for the benefit of the master, officers and crew, whether such payments be imposed by law upon the shipowners or be made under the terms of articles of employment

(d) The cost of measures undertaken to prevent or minimise damage to the environment shall be allowed in general average when incurred in any or all of the following circumstances:

    (i)   as part of an operation performed for the common safety which, had it been undertaken by a party outside the common maritime adventure, would have entitled such party to a salvage reward;

    (ii)   as a condition of entry into or departure from any port or place in the circumstances prescribed in Rule X(a);

    (iii)   as a condition of remaining at any port or place in the circumstances prescribed in Rule X(a), provided that when there is an actual escape or release of pollutant substances the cost of any additional measures required on that account to prevent or minimise pollution or environmental damage shall not be allowed as general average;

    (iv)   necessarily in connection with the discharging, storing or reloading of cargo whenever the cost of those operations is admissible as general average.

Rule XII – Damage to Cargo in Discharging, etc.

Damage to or loss of cargo, fuel or stores sustained in consequence of their handling. discharging, storing, reloading and stowing shall be made good as general average, when and only when the cost of those measures respectively is admitted as general average.

Rule XIII – Deduction from Cost of Repairs

Repairs to be allowed in general average shall not be subject to deductions in respect of 'new for old' where o!~ material or parts are replaced by new unless the ship is over fifteen years old in which case there shall be a deduction of one third. The deductions shall be regulated by the age of the ship from the 31st December of the year of completion of construction to the date of the general average act, except for insulation, life and similar boats, communications and navigational apparatus and equipment, machinery and boilers for which the deductions shall be regulated by the age of the particular parts to which they apply.

The deductions shall be made only from the cost of the new material or parts when finished and ready to be installed in the ship.

No deduction shall be made in respect of provisions, stores, anchors and chain cables.

Drydock and slipway dues and costs of shifting the ship shall be allowed in full

The costs of cleaning, painting or coating of bottom shall not be allowed in general average unless the bottom has been painted or coated within the twelve months preceding the date of the general average act in which case one-half of such costs shall be allowed.

Rule XIV – Temporary Repairs

Where temporary repairs are effected to a ship at a port of loading, call or refuge, for the common safety, or of damage caused by general average sacrifice, the cost of such repairs shall be admitted as general average.

Where temporary repairs of accidental damage are effected in order to enable the adventure to be completed, the cost of such repairs shall be admitted as general average without regard to the saving, if any, to other interests, but only up to the saving in expense which would have been incurred and allowed in general average if such repairs had not been effected there.

No deductions 'new for old' shall be made from the cost of temporary repairs allowable as general average.

Rule XV – Loss of Freight

Loss of freight arising from damage to or loss of cargo shall be made good as general average, either when caused by a general average act, or when the damage to or loss of cargo is so made good.

Deduction shall be made from the amount of gross freight lost, of the charges which the owner thereof would have incurred to earn such freight, but has, in consequence of the sacrifice, not incurred.

Rule XVI – Amount to be made good for Cargo Lost or Damaged by Sacrifice

The amount to be made good as general average for damage to or loss of cargo sacrificed shall be the loss which has been sustained thereby based on the value at the time of discharge, ascertained from the commercial invoice rendered to the receiver or if there is no such invoice from the shipped value The value at the time of discharge shall include the cost of insurance and freight except insofar as such freight is at the risk of interests other than the cargo.

When cargo so damaged is sold and the amount of the damage has not been otherwise agreed, the loss to be made good in general average shall be the difference between the net proceeds of sale and the net sound value as computed in the first paragraph of this Rule.

Rule XVII – Contributory Values

The contribution to a general average shall be made upon the actual net values of the property at the termination of the adventure except that the value of cargo shall be the value at the time of discharge, ascertained from the commercial invoice rendered to the receiver or if there is no such invoice from the shipped value. The value of the cargo shall include the cost of insurance and freight unless and insofar as such freight is at the risk of interests other than the cargo, deducting therefrom any loss or damage suffered by the cargo prior to or at the time of discharge. The value of the ship shall be assessed without taking into account the beneficial or detrimental effect of any demise or time charterparty to which the ship may be committed.

To these values shall be added the amount made good as general average for property sacrificed, if not already included, deduction being made from the freight and passage money at risk of such charges and crew's wages as would not have been incurred in earning the freight had the ship and cargo been totally lost at the date of the general average; deduction being also made from the value of the property of all extra charges incurred in respect thereof subsequently to the general average act, except such charges as are allowed in general average or fall upon the ship by virtue of an award for special compensation under Article 14 of the International Convention on Salvage, 1989 or under any other provision similar in substance.

In the circumstances envisaged in the third paragraph of Rule G, the cargo and other property shall contribute on the basis of its value upon delivery at original destination unless sold or otherwise disposed of short of that destination, and the ship shall contribute upon its actual net value at the time of completion of discharge of cargo.

Where cargo is sold short of destination, however, it shall contribute upon the actual net proceeds of sale, with the addition of any amount made good as general average.

Mails, passengers' luggage, personal effects and accompanied private motor vehicles shall not contribute in general average.

Rule XVIII – Damage to Ship

The amount to be allowed as general average for damage or loss to the ship, her machinery and/or gear caused by a general average act shall be as follows:

(a) When repaired or replaced,

The actual reasonable cost of repairing or replacing such damage or loss, subject to deductions in accordance with Rule XIII;

(b) When not repaired or replaced,

The reasonable depreciation arising from such damage or loss, but not exceeding the estimated cost of repairs. But where the ship is an actual total loss or when the cost of repairs of the damage would exceed the value of the ship when repaired, the amount to be allowed as general average shall be the difference between the estimated sound value of the ship after deducting therefrom the estimated cost of repairing damage which is not general average and the value of the ship in her damaged state which may be measured by the net proceeds of sale, if any.

Rule XIX – Undeclared or Wrongfully Declared Cargo

Damage or loss caused to goods loaded without the knowledge of the shipowner or his agent or to goods wilfully misdescribed at time of shipment shall not be allowed as general average, but such goods shall remain liable to contribute, if saved.

Damage or loss caused to goods which have been wrongfully declared on shipment at a value which is lower than their real value shall be contributed for at the declared value, but such goods shall contribute upon their actual value.

Rule XX – Provision of Funds

A commission of 2 per cent on general average disbursements, other than the wages and maintenance of master, officers and crew and fuel and stores not replaced during the voyage, shall be allowed in general average.

The capital loss sustained by the owners of goods sold for the purpose of raising funds to defray general average disbursements shall be allowed in general average.

The cost of insuring general average disbursements shall also be admitted in general average.

Rule XXI – Interest on Losses made good in General Average

Interest shall be allowed on expenditure, sacrifices and allowances in general average at the rate of 7 per cent per annum, until three months after the date of issue of the general average adjustment, due allowance being made for any payment on account by the contributory interests or from the general average deposit fund.

Rule XXII – Treatment of Cash Deposits

Where cash deposits have been collected in respect of cargo's liability for general average, salvage or special charges, such deposits shall be paid without any delay into a special account in the joint names of a representative nominated on behalf of the shipowner and a representative nominated on behalf of the depositors in a bank to be approved by both. The sum so deposited, together with accrued interest, if any, shall be held as security for payment to the parties entitled thereto of the general average, salvage or special charges payable by cargo in respect to which the deposits have been collected, Payments on account or refunds of deposits may be made if certified to in writing by the average adjuster. Such deposits and payments or refunds shall be without prejudice to the ultimate liability of the parties.

LOF 1995

LLOYD'S

STANDARD FORM OF

SALVAGE AGREEMENT

(APPROVED AND PUBLISHED BY THE COUNCIL OF LLOYD'S)

NO CURE – NO PAY

On board the...

Dated..................................

IT IS HEREBY AGREED between Captain...
for and on behalf of the Owners of the '..'
her cargo freight bunkers stores and any other property thereon (hereinafter
collectively called 'the Owners') and...for
and on behalf of ....
(hereinafter called 'the Contractor') that:

1. (a)   The Contractor shall use his best endeavours:

   (i) to salve the '..' and/or her cargo
   freight bunkers stores and any other property thereon and take them
   to .... or to such other place as
   may hereafter be agreed either place to be deemed a place of safety or
   if no such place is named or agreed to a place of safety and

   (ii) while performing the salvage services to prevent or minimize
   damage to the environment.

   (b)   Subject to the statutory provisions relating to special compensation
   the services shall be rendered and accepted as salvage services upon
   the principle of 'no cure – no pay'.

   (c)   The Contractor's remuneration shall be fixed by Arbitration in
   London in the manner hereinafter prescribed and any other
   difference arising out of this Agreement or the operations thereunder
   shall be referred to Arbitration in the same way.

   (d)   In the event of the services referred to in this Agreement or any part
   of such services having been already rendered at the date of this
   Agreement by the Contractor to the said vessel and/or her cargo

freight bunkers stores and any other property thereon the provisions of this Agreement shall apply to such services.

(e) The security to be provided to the Council of Lloyd's (hereinafter called 'the Council') the Salved Value(s) the Award and/or any Interim Award(s) and/or any Award on Appeal shall be in .... currency.

(f) If Clause 1(e) is not completed then the security to be provided and the Salved Value(s) the Award and/or Interim Award(s) and/or Award on Appeal shall be in Pounds Sterling.

(g) This Agreement and Arbitration thereunder shall except as otherwise expressly provided be governed by the law of England, including the English law of salvage.

PROVISIONS AS TO THE SERVICES

2. *Definitions*: In this Agreement any reference to 'Convention' is a reference to the International Convention on Salvage 1989 as incorporated in the Merchant Shipping (Salvage and Pollution) Act 1994 (and any amendment thereto). The terms 'Contractor' and 'services'/'salvage services' in this Agreement shall have the same meanings as the terms 'salvor(s)' and 'salvage operation(s)' in the Convention.

3. *Owners Cooperation*: The Owners their Servants and Agents shall co-operate fully with the Contractor in and about the salvage including obtaining entry to the place named or the place of safety as defined in Clause 1. The Contractor may make reasonable use of the vessel's machinery gear equipment anchors chains stores and other appurtenances during and for the purpose of the salvage services free of expense but shall not unnecessarily damage abandon or sacrifice the same or any property the subject of this Agreement.

4. *Vessel Owners Right to Terminate*: When there is no longer any reasonable prospect of a useful result leading to a salvage reward in accordance with Convention Article 13 the owners of the vessel shall be entitled to terminate the services of the Contractor by giving reasonable notice to the Contractor in writing.

PROVISIONS AS TO SECURITY

5. (a) The Contractor shall immediately after the termination of the services or sooner notify the Council and where practicable the Owners of the amount for which he demands salvage security (inclusive of costs expenses and interest) from each of the respective Owners.

(b) Where a claim is made or may be made for special compensation, the owners of the vessel shall on the demand of the Contractor whenever made provide security for the Contractor's claim for special compensation provided always that such demand is made within two years of the date of termination of the services.

(c) The amount of any such security shall be reasonable in the light of the knowledge available to the Contractor at the time when the demand is made. Unless otherwise agreed such security shall be provided (i) to the Council (ii) in a form approved by the Council and (iii) by persons firms or corporations either acceptable to the Contractor or resident in the United Kingdom and acceptable to the Council. The Council shall not be responsible for the sufficiency (whether in amount or otherwise) of any security which shall be provided nor the default or insolvency of any person firm or corporation providing the same.

(d) The owners of the vessel their Servants and Agents shall use their best endeavours to ensure that the cargo owners provide their proportion of salvage security before the cargo is released.

6. (a) Until security has been provided as aforesaid the Contractor shall have a maritime lien on the property salved for his remuneration.

(b) The property salved shall not without the consent in writing of the Contractor (which shall not be unreasonably withheld) be removed from the place to which it has been taken by the Contractor under Clause l(a). Where such consent is given by the Contractor on condition that the Contractor is provided with temporary security pending completion of the voyage the Contractor's maritime lien on the property salved shall remain in force to the extent necessary to enable the Contractor to compel the provision of security in accordance with Clause 5(c).

(c) The Contractor shall not arrest or detain the property salved unless:

> (i) security is not provided within 14 days (exclusive of Saturdays and Sundays or other days observed as general holidays at Lloyd's) after the date of the termination of the services or

> (ii) he has reason to believe that the removal of the property salved is contemplated contrary to Clause 6(b) or

> (iii) any attempt is made to remove the property salved contrary to Clause 6(b).

(d) The Arbitrator appointed under Clause 7 or the Appeal Arbitrator(s) appointed under Clause 13(d) shall have power in their absolute discretion to include in the amount awarded to the Contractor the whole or part of any expenses reasonably incurred by the Contractor in:

> (i) ascertaining demanding and obtaining the amount of security reasonably required in accordance with Clause 5.

> (ii) enforcing and/or protecting by insurance or otherwise or taking reasonable steps to enforce and/or protect his lien.

PROVISIONS AS TO ARBITRATION

7. (a) Whether security has been provided or not the Council shall appoint an Arbitrator upon receipt of a written request made by letter telex facsimile or in any other permanent form provided that any party requesting such appointment shall if required by the Council undertake to pay the reasonable fees and expenses of the Council and/or any Arbitrator or Appeal Arbitrator(s).

(b) Where an Arbitrator has been appointed and the parties do not proceed to arbitration the Council may recover any fees costs and/or expenses which are outstanding.

8. The Contractor's remuneration and/or special compensation shall be fixed by the Arbitrator appointed under Clause 7. Such remuneration shall not be diminished by reason of the exception to the principle of 'no cure – no pay' in the form of special compensation.

REPRESENTATION

9. Any party to this Agreement who wishes to be heard or to adduce evidence shall nominate a person in the United Kingdom to represent him failing which the Arbitrator or Appeal Arbitrator(s) may proceed as if such party had renounced his right to be heard or adduce evidence.

CONDUCT OF THE ARBITRATION

10. (a) The Arbitrator shall have power to:

(i) admit such oral or documentary evidence or information as he may think fit

(ii) conduct the Arbitration in such manner in all respects as he may think fit subject to such procedural rules as the Council may approve

(iii) order the Contractor in his absolute discretion to pay the whole or part of the expense of providing excessive security or security which has been unreasonably demanded under Clause 5(b) and to deduct such sum from the remuneration and/or special compensation

(iv) make Interim Award(s) including payment(s) on account on such terms as may be fair and just

(v) make such orders as to costs fees and expenses including those of the Council charged under Clauses 10(b) and 14(b) as may be fair and just.

(b) The Arbitrator and the Council may charge reasonable fees and expenses for their services whether the Arbitration proceeds to a hearing or not and all such fees and expenses shall be treated as part of the costs of the Arbitration.

(c) Any Award shall (subject to Appeal as provided in this Agreement) be final and binding on all the parties concerned whether they were represented at the Arbitration or not.

INTEREST & RATES OF EXCHANGE

11. *Interest*: Interest at rates per annum to be fixed by the Arbitrator shall (subject to Appeal as provided in this Agreement) be payable on any sum awarded taking into account any sums already paid:

(i) from the date of termination of the services unless the Arbitrator shall in his absolute discretion otherwise decide until the date of publication by the Council of the Award and/or Interim Award(s) and

(ii) from the expiration of 21 days (exclusive of Saturdays and Sundays or other days observed as general holidays at Lloyd's) after the date of publication by the Council of the Award and/or Interim Award(s) until the date payment is received by the Contractor or the Council both dates inclusive.

For the purpose of sub-clause (ii) the expression 'sum awarded' shall include the fees and expenses referred to in Clause 10(b).

12. *Currency Correction*: In considering what sums of money have been expended by the Contractor in rendering the services and/or in fixing the amount of the Award and/or Interim Award(s) and/or Award on Appeal the Arbitrator or Appeal Arbitrator(s) shall to such an extent and in so far as it may be fair and just in all the circumstances give effect to the consequences of any change or changes in the relevant rates of exchange which may have occurred between the date of termination of the services and the date on which the Award and/or Interim Award(s) and/or Award on Appeal is made.

PROVISIONS AS TO APPEAL

13. (a) Notice of Appeal if any shall be given to the Council within 14 days (exclusive of Saturdays and Sundays or other days observed as general holidays at Lloyd's) after the date of the publication by the Council of the Award and/or Interim Award(s).

(b) Notice of Cross-Appeal if any shall be given to the Council within 14 days (exclusive of Saturdays and Sundays or other days observed as general holidays at Lloyd's) after notification by the Council to the parties of any Notice of Appeal. Such notification if sent by post shall be deemed received on the working day following the day of posting.

(c) Notice of Appeal or Cross-Appeal shall be given to the Council by letter telex facsimile or in any other permanent form.

(d) Upon receipt of Notice of Appeal the Council shall refer the Appeal to the hearing and determination of the Appeal Arbitrator(s) selected by it.

(e) If any Notice of Appeal or Cross-Appeal is withdrawn the Appeal hearing shall nevertheless proceed in respect of such Notice of Appeal or Cross-Appeal as may remain.

(f) Any Award on Appeal shall be final and binding on all the parties to that Appeal Arbitration whether they were represented either at the Arbitration or at the Appeal Arbitration or not.

CONDUCT OF THE APPEAL

14. (a) The Appeal Arbitrator(s) in addition to the powers of the Arbitrator under Clauses 10(a) and 11 shall have power to:

(i) admit the evidence which was before the Arbitrator together with the Arbitrator's notes and reasons for his Award and/or Interim Award(s) and any transcript of evidence and such additional evidence as he or they may think fit.

(ii) confirm increase or reduce the sum awarded by the Arbitrator and to make such order as to the payment of interest on such sum as he or they may think fit.

(iii) confirm revoke or vary any order and/or Declaratory Award made by the Arbitrator.

(iv) award interest on any fees and expenses charged under paragraph (b) of this clause from the expiration of 21 days (exclusive of Saturdays and Sundays or other days observed as general holidays at Lloyd's) after the date of publication by the Council of the Award on Appeal and/or Interim Award(s) on Appeal until the date payment is received by the Council both dates inclusive.

(b) The Appeal Arbitrator(s) and the Council may charge reasonable fees and expenses for their services in connection with the Appeal Arbitration whether it proceeds to a hearing or not and all such fees and expenses shall be treated as part of the costs of the Appeal Arbitration.

PROVISIONS AS TO PAYMENT

15. (a) In case of Arbitration if no Notice of Appeal be received by the Council in accordance with Clause 13(a) the Council shall call upon the party or parties concerned to pay the amount awarded and in the event of non-payment shall subject to the Contractor first providing to the Council a satisfactory Undertaking to pay all the costs thereof realize or enforce the security and pay therefrom to the Contractor (whose receipt shall be a good discharge to it) the amount awarded to him together with interest if any. The Contractor shall reimburse the parties concerned to such extent as the Award is less than any sums paid on account or in respect of Interim Award(s).

(b) If Notice of Appeal be received by the Council in accordance with Clause 13 it shall as soon as the Award on Appeal has been published by it call upon the party or parties concerned to pay the amount awarded and in the event of non-payment shall subject to the Contractor first providing to the Council a satisfactory Undertaking to pay all the costs thereof realize or enforce the security and pay therefrom to the Contractor (whose receipt shall be a good discharge to it) the amount awarded to him together with interest if any. The Contractor shall reimburse the parties concerned to such extent as the Award on Appeal is less than any sums paid on account or in respect of the Award or Interim Award(s).

(c) If any sum shall become payable to the Contractor as remuneration for his services and/or interest and/or costs as the result of an agreement made between the Contractor and the Owners or any of them the Council in the event of non-payment shall subject to the Contractor first providing to the Council a satisfactory Undertaking to pay all the costs thereof realize or enforce the security and pay therefrom to the Contractor (whose receipt shall be a good discharge to it) the said sum.

(d) If the Award and/or Interim Award(s) and/or Award on Appeal provides or provide that the costs of the Arbitration and/or of the Appeal Arbitration or any part of such costs shall be borne by the Contractor such costs may be deducted from the amount awarded or agreed before payment is made to the Contractor unless satisfactory security is provided by the Contractor for the payment of such costs.

(e) Without prejudice to the provisions of Clause 5(c) the liability of the Council shall be limited in any event to the amount of security provided to it.

GENERAL PROVISIONS

16. *Scope of Authority*: The Master or other person signing this Agreement on behalf of the property to be salved enters into this Agreement as agent for the vessel her cargo freight bunkers stores and any other property thereon and the respective Owners thereof and binds each (but not the one for the other or himself personally) to the due performance thereof.

17. *Notices*: Any Award notice authority order or other document signed by the Chairman of Lloyd's or any person authorised by the Council for the purpose shall be deemed to have been duly made or given by the Council and shall have the same force and effect in all respects as if it had been signed by every member of the Council.

18. *Sub-Contractor(s)*: The Contractor may claim salvage and enforce any Award or agreement made between the Contractor and the Owners against security provided under Clause 5 or otherwise if any on behalf of any Sub-Contractors his or their Servants or Agents including Masters and members of the crews of vessels employed by him or by any Sub-Contractors in the services provided that he first provides a reasonably satisfactory indemnity to the Owners against all claims by or liabilities to the said persons.

19. *Inducements prohibited*: No person signing this Agreement or any party on whose behalf it is signed shall at any time or in any manner whatsoever offer provide make give or promise to provide demand or take any form of inducement for entering into this Agreement.

For and on behalf of the Contractor	For and on behalf of the Owners of property to be salved
....	....
(To be signed by the Contractor personally or by the Master of the salving vessel or other person whose name is inserted in line 4 of this Agreement)	(To be signed by the Master or other person whose name is inserted in line 4 of this Agreement)

INTERNATIONAL CONVENTION ON SALVAGE 1989

The following provisions of the Convention are set out below for information only.

Article 1

Definitions

(a) *Salvage operation* means any act or activity undertaken to assist a vessel or any other property in danger in navigable waters or in any other waters whatsoever

(b) *Vessel* means any ship or craft, or any structure capable of navigation

(c) *Property* means any property not permanently and intentionally attached to the shoreline and includes freight at risk

(d) *Damage to the environment* means substantial physical damage to human health or to marine life or resources in coastal or inland waters or areas adjacent thereto, caused by pollution, contamination, fire, explosion or similar major incidents

(e) *Payment* means any reward, remuneration or compensation due under this Convention

Article 6

Salvage Contracts

1. This Convention shall apply to any salvage operations save to the extent that a contract otherwise provides expressly or by implication

2. The master shall have the authority to conclude contracts for salvage operations on behalf of the owner of the vessel. The master or the owner of the vessel shall have the authority to conclude such contracts on behalf of the owner of the property on board the vessel

Article 8

Duties of the Salvor and of the Owner and Master

1. The salvor shall owe a duty to the owner of the vessel or other property in danger:

    (a)   to carry out the salvage operations with due care;

    (b)   in performing the duty specified in subparagraph (a), to exercise due care to prevent or minimize damage to the environment;

    (c)   whenever circumstances reasonably require, to seek assistance from other salvors; and

    (d)   to accept the intervention of other salvors when reasonably requested to do so by the owner or master of the vessel or other property in danger; provided however that the amount of his reward shall not be prejudiced should it be found that such a request was unreasonable

2. The owner and master of the vessel or the owner of other property in danger shall owe a duty to the salvor:

    (a)   to co-operate fully with him during the course of the salvage operations;

    (b)   in so doing, to exercise due care to prevent or minimize damage to the environment; and

    (c)   when the vessel or other property has been brought to a place of safety, to accept redelivery when reasonably requested by the salvor to do so

Article 13

Criteria for fixing the reward

1. The reward shall be fixed with a view to encouraging salvage operations, taking into account the following criteria without regard to the order in which they are presented below:

(a)   the salved value of the vessel and other property;

(b)   the skill and efforts of the salvors in preventing or minimizing damage to the environment;

(c)   the measure of success obtained by the salvor;

(d)   the nature and degree of the danger;

(e)   the skill and efforts of the salvors in salving the vessel, other property and life;

(f)   the time used and expenses and losses incurred by the salvors;

(g)   the risk of liability and other risks run by the salvors or their equipment;

(h)   the promptness of the services rendered;

(i)   the availability and use of vessels or other equipment intended for salvage operations;

(j)   the state of readiness and efficiency of the salvor's equipment and the value thereof

2.   Payment of a reward fixed according to paragraph 1 shall be made by all of the vessel and other property interests in proportion to their respective salved values

3.   The rewards, exclusive of any interest and recoverable legal costs that may be payable thereon, shall not exceed the salved value of the vessel and other property

Article 14

Special Compensation

1.   If the salvor has carried out salvage operations in respect of a vessel which by itself or its cargo threatened damage to the environment and has failed to earn a reward under Article 13 at least equivalent to the special compensation assessable in accordance with this Article, he shall be entitled to special compensation from the owner of that vessel equivalent to his expenses as herein defined

2.   If, in the circumstances set out in paragraph 1, the salvor by his salvage operations has prevented or minimized damage to the environment, the special compensation payable by the owner to the salvor under paragraph I may be increased up to a maximum of 30% of the expenses incurred by the salvor. However, the Tribunal, if it deems it fair and just to do so and bearing in mind the relevant criteria set out in Article 13, paragraph 1, may increase such special compensation further, but in no event shall the total increase be more than 100% of the expenses incurred by the salvor

3.   Salvor's expenses for the purpose of paragraphs 1 and 2 means the out-of-pocket expenses reasonably incurred by the salvor in the salvage operation and a fair rate for equipment and personnel actually and reasonably used in the salvage operation, taking into consideration the criteria set out in Article 13, paragraph 1(h), (i) and (j)

4. The total special compensation under this Article shall be paid only if and to the extent that such compensation is greater than any reward recoverable by the salvor under Article 13

5. If the salvor has been negligent and has thereby failed to prevent or minimize damage to the environment, he may be deprived of the whole or part of any special compensation due under this Article

6. Nothing in this Article shall affect any right of recourse on the part of the owner of the vessel.

INDEX

C

H

I

Law of Marine Insurance